THE NEW BALKANS: DISINTEGRATION AND RECONSTRUCTION

Co–edited by
George A. Kourvetaris, Northern Illinois University
Victor Roudometof, Miami University, Ohio
Kleomenis Koutsoukis, Panteion University, Athens
Andrew G. Kourvetaris, Columbia University

EAST EUROPEAN MONOGRAPHS, BOULDER
DISTRIBUTED BY COLUMBIA UNIVERSITY PRESS, NEW YORK

2002

EAST EUROPEAN MONOGRAPHS, NO. DC

ISBN 0-88033-498-3
Library of Congress Control Number 2002108617

Printed in the United States of America

PROLOGUE

The editors of this volume selected the papers for inclusion on the basis of the contributors' expertise and scholarship. In 1996, the *Journal of Political and Military Sociology* published a special issue on the Balkans, which provided the basis for the present volume. Prior to the publication of the special issue, George Kourvetaris organized a special session on the disintegration of Yugoslavia for the 1993 annual meetings of the American Sociological Association, held at Miami, Florida. George Kourvetaris and Victor Roudometof met for the first time on that occasion.

Victor Roudometof was working on his dissertation on the origins of ethnic conflict in the Balkans at the time. The dissertation was completed in 1996 and Victor Roudometof spent the 1996-1997 academic year as the Mary Seeger O'Boyle Post-doctoral Fellow of the Program in Hellenic Studies at Princeton University. There he revised the dissertation and took the first steps toward turning the dissertation into a book. Eventually, the book was published in 2001 under the title *Nationalism, Globalization & Orthodoxy: The Social Origins of Ethnic Conflict in the Balkans* (Westport, CT: Greenwood).

In the meantime, George and Victor established a working relationship, which was renewed when both of them attended the 1998 annual meetings of the American Sociological Association at Chicago, IL. The Balkans continued to be on the news and the bombing of Serbia and Kosovo by NATO and the US in the Spring of 1999 compelled George Kourvetaris to consider publishing the original special issue of the journal as a book.

At the same time, working in his capacity as the Modern Greek Studies Association's liaison to the American Sociological Association, Victor Roudometof organized a special panel on "Southeastern Europe at the Dawn of the 21st Century" for the 2000 annual meetings of the American Sociological Association, held at Washington, DC. After the 2000 meetings, George asked Victor to work together and co-edit this volume. Victor graciously accepted and promised to ask the participants of the special session to revise their papers to be included in the volume.

George Kourvetaris also asked Kleomenis Koutsoukis, Professor of Political Science at Panteion University, Director of the Hellenic Centre for Political Research (Athens, Greece), and the co-editor of the 1996 special issue on the Balkans, to come aboard and try to secure additional articles that would cover those countries and topics not addressed in the special issue. Kleomenis agreed and was able to solicit additional contributions for this project. Andrew

Kourvetaris, son of George Kourvetaris, was working toward his Ph.D. in Sociology at Columbia University at the time. He was also interested in participating in the project and accepted an invitation to become a co-editor of the volume. Despite the high workload of his graduate work, Andrew also co-authored the revised version of George Kourvetaris' original 1996 essay on the causes of Yugoslav disintegration.

In the aftermath of the 1999 bombing of Serbia and Kosovo by NATO, as well as the 2000 civil strife between Albanians and Macedonians in the former Yugoslav Republic of Macedonia (FYROM), it became clear to all of us that a new reader on the Balkans can make a meaningful contribution to the growing scholarly literature on the subject. Moreover, as this brief overview of this project's history illustrates, this volume is the product of research and scholarship pursued jointly or independently for several years. In the 1990s, the Balkans have become the focus not only of US foreign policy but also of NATO and the European Union (EU) as well. To capture these international currents, George Kourvetaris solicited two additional articles by Edward Tiryakian and Raju George Thomas. These contributions have added an additional dimension in the analysis and have broadened the volume's scope. Overall, the present volume is a constellation of 16 scholarly contributions and a selective bibliography of literature on the new post-1989 Balkans. The individual contributions shed additional light to the region's complexity and the rich tapestry of regional concerns that have come to the forefront of public policy debates in the 1990s. The collective effort of an illustrious roster of young emerging scholars and some senior ones, alongside the support and enthusiasm of the publisher, has resulted in a final product of exceptional quality.

TABLE OF CONTENTS

PROLOGUE iii

TABLE OF CONTENTS v

ACKNOWLEDGEMENTS ix

INTRODUCTION 1

ABSTRACTS 17

PART I
HISTORICAL LEGACY AND ISSUES OF ETHNIC CONFLICT

1. THE NATURE OF ETHNONATIONALISM AND SUBNATIONALISM: THE CASE OF YUGOSLAVIA 29
George A. Kourvetaris, Northern Illinois University,
Andrew G. Kourvetaris, Columbia University, USA

2. NATIONAL MINORITIES, NATION-STATES, AND EXTERNAL NATIONAL HOMELANDS IN SOUTHEASTERN EUROPE 55
Victor Roudometof, Miami University, Oxford Ohio, USA

3. PARDON? A CONFLICT FOR A NAME? FYROM'S DISPUTE WITH GREECE REVISITED 85
Demetrius Andreas Floudas, Anglia Polytechnic University, England

4. THE BOSNIAN WAR, 1992-1995: STRATEGIC ANALYSIS . . 129
Harry Papasotiriou, Panteion University, Greece

5. CROATIA–SERBIA: ISSUES OF CONTENTION 145
Kleomenis Koutsoukis, Panteion University, Athens and
Pantelis Sklias, Democritus University of Thrace, Greece

6. **CROATIA'S NATIONAL INTEGRATION: PASSING FROM THE 19th TO THE 21st CENTURY** 171
Dimitrios Koukourdinos, London School of Economics and Political Science, England

7. **THE IDEA OF SELF-DETERMINATION: LESSONS FROM THE FORMER YUGOSLAVIA** 193
George Raju G. G. Thomas, Allis Chalmers Professor of International Affairs, Marquette University, USA

8. **THIRD PARTY INVOLVEMENT IN ETHNIC CONFLICT: THE CASE OF THE KOSOVO WAR** 207
Edward A. Tiryakian, Duke University, USA

PART II
ECONOMIC DEVELOPMENT AND CIVIL SOCIETY

9. **SOUTHEAST EUROPE IN TRANSITION** 231
Eleftherios N. Botsas, Oakland University, USA

10. **SOUTHEASTERN EUROPE: PROSPECTS FOR INCREASED ECONOMIC INTEGRATION** 253
Bob Donnorummo, Center for Russian and East European Studies, University of Pittsburgh, USA

11. **THE DEVELOPMENT OF CIVIL SOCIETY IN SOUTHEASTERN EUROPE** 273
Tina Mavrikos-Adamou, American College of Thessaloniki, Greece

12. **"WE BELONG TO THE WEST?" REPRESENTATIONS OF EASTERN AND WESTERN EUROPE IN THE GREEK PRESS AND THE POSITIONING OF THE "WE"** 293
Anna Triandafyllidou, Marie Curie Fellow, Institute of Psychology, Italian National Research Council, Italy

PART III
GEOPOLITICS AND SECURITY POLICIES

13. THE BALKANS AND A TRANSFORMING NATO 319
S. Victor Papacosma, Lemnitzer Center, Kent State University, USA

14. INSTITUTIONALIZED RESTRAINT AS POLICY: THE EUROPEAN UNION AND THE DISINTEGRATION OF YUGOSLAVIA 351
Kostas A. Lavdas, University of Crete, Greece

15. THE EMERGENCE OF A NEW OTTOMAN MODEL: A NEW FOREIGN POLICY IN TURKEY 379
Stephanos Constantinides, Université du Québec, à Montréal, Canada

16. AN ASSESSMENT OF AMERICAN STRATEGY IN THE SOUTH BALKANS SINCE THE DISSOLUTION OF YUGOSLAVIA 401
Alexandros K. Kyrou, Salem State College, USA

A SELECTIVE ANNOTATED BIBLIOGRAPHY 439
By the contributors

PROFILES ON THE CONTRIBUTORS 463

ACKNOWLEDGEMENTS

The co-editors would like to express their appreciation to Karen Blaser, Director of Manuscript Services of the College of Liberal Arts and Sciences of Northern Illinois University, for her professional attention, diligence, and hard work on the entire project. Also thanks must be extended to Alice Hall, faculty secretary for the Sociology Department of Northern Illinois University, for her logistical support and assistance in communicating both e-mail and regular messages to the contributors and co-editors of the volume. Also, we would like to thank Terry Danner, Copy Center Operator. Last but not least, the co-editors would like to thank their publisher the East European and social Science Monographs and Professor Stephen Fischer-Galati for consenting in publishing this collective scholarly endeavor as a reader titled THE NEW BALKANS: FROM DISINTEGRATION TO RECONSTRUCTION

INTRODUCTION THE NEW, BALKANS: FROM DISINTEGRATION TO RECONSTRUCTION

By

George A. Kourvetaris, Victor Roudometof,
Kleomenis Koutsoukis & Andrew G. Kourvetaris

For a long time Southeast Europe, commonly known as the Balkans, has been a region torn by intervention, antagonism of Great Powers and turmoil among the peoples of the region. Indeed, in the past the Balkans have become the apple of discord among the Great powers—Russia, England, Germany, France and later on, the USSR and the United States. The prolonged decline of the Ottoman Empire—the "sick man of Europe"—in the nineteenth century provided the backdrop for persistent warfare, ranging from the recurrent Russo-Turkish wars to the wars and the insurrections of the Balkan peoples themselves (for details, see Jelavich 1991; Djordjevic and Fischer-Galati 1981).

By the early twentieth century, the eventual collapse of the Ottoman Empire did not bring an end to the infamous "Eastern Question" (Anderson 1966). On the contrary, the Balkans have been the theater of conflicts and wars throughout most of the 20th century. The historical record includes the two Balkan Wars in 1912 and 1913, World War I (1914-1918), the Greco-Turkish War of 1919-1923, World War II (1940-1945), the Cold War (1945-1989), the demise of the former Yugoslavia (1989-1990); and finally, the resurgence of ethnonationalism and conflicts among Yugoslavia's successor nation-states in the 1990s, culminating in the NATO (mostly U.S. and Britain) led bombing of Kosovo and Serbia in the Spring of 1999, and more recently, the 2000 civil strife between Albanians and Macedonians in the former Yugoslav Republic of Macedonia (FYROM).

The legacy of ethnic conflict is also present in the long-standing disputes between Greece, Bulgaria and the Former Yugoslav Republic of Macedonia (FYROM). The declaration of FYROM's independence in 1991 set off a cultural, political, and diplomatic conflict between Athens and Skopje. The affair was settled in part through the 1995 Interim Accord between the two parties, however, the Greeks refuse to this day to recognize the new state as "Macedonia." For the Greek public and government, this name is part of the Greek historical legacy and can not be appropriated by the Macedonian Slavs without infringing upon the Greek cultural space (for discussions, see

Roudometof 1996; Danforth 1995). The Bulgarian nation-state has adopted a less vocal stance, however, up until 1999, it refused to recognize that the Macedonians are a nation, and that the Macedonian language is a language distinct from Bulgarian. In addition to these issues, both Greece and Bulgaria have persistently refuted the claims of the Macedonian human rights movement that there are sizeable Macedonian national minorities in the two states. A complete treatment of the Macedonian issue obviously falls outside the scope of this volume (for discussions, see Shea 1997; Poulton 2000; Roudometof 2000; Cowan 2000; Mackridge and Yiannakakis 1997).

In this introduction, we set forward some of the key concerns and issues that have been raised in the voluminous literature addressing the peculiarities of the Balkans. (For further analyses and discussion see Coufoudakis, et al. 1999). First, we address the geopolitical dimension of the Balkan tinderbox. Second, we address the troublesome issue of the "transition" of the region from a trouble spot in the international scene toward inclusion and eventual incorporation into the European Union. One of the most important issues pertaining the transition of the Balkans from communism to democracy is the extent to which these societies are capable of developing a civil society that would strengthen the public sphere and allow for democratization of social life to occur. This, of course, is not a new issue in the domain of the social sciences (Almond and Verba 1963 1989; for the Balkans in particular, see Dawisha and Parrott 1997; Bianchini & Schoepflin 1998). Although this issue has obvious connections to the Balkans' geopolitical dimension, it is important to highlight the critical significance of economic development and regional cooperation. With these broader issues in mind, then, we will try to place the individual chapters' arguments in the broader context of the scholarly debate on these matters.

From a geopolitical and strategic perspective, the Balkan Peninsula is conventionally depicted as the bridge between East and West, North and South. To use the classic remark by the Yugoslav statesman Vodislav Marinkovic the Balkans are above all a "geographic expression." This gives this Southeast Region of Europe its geopolitical physiognomy, its strategic importance, and character. It is worth pointing out that, despite the region's apparent strategic importance in the 19th and 20th century Great Power rivalry; accurate geographical and ethnographic knowledge about the region eluded Western European observers. In fact, over the last two centuries, the consolidation of the very term "Balkan" in Western discourse was closely related to its saturation with political, cultural and ideological overtone (Skopetea 1992: 17-92). The term itself lacks precision and does not represent a concrete geographical territory. In Wester European historiography it surfaced in 1808 when the German geographer Johan August Zeune first employed the word

Balkanhalbinsel (Balkan Peninsula). In 1831 Major George Thomas Keppel published a book entitled *Narrative of a Journey across the Balkans*; but it was only after the middle of the nineteenth century that the term gained currency (Stoianovich 1994:1; Carter 1977:7). By the early twentieth century the terms "Balkan" and Balkanization" had achieved their pejorative connotation. Consequently, they were further connected back to the original geographical territory (for a discussion, see Todorova 1997). Throughout most of the 20th century the Balkans were entangled in regional conflicts; they were involved in both world wars, and the last half of the 20th century were under Communism until its demise in 1989.

In the 1980s and 1990s, journalistic and public policy analyses and interpretations have revived these particularly dark images (Kaplan 1992; Kennan 1993). In perhaps the most extreme of all cases, the Balkans are considered as a region lying outside the boundaries of "Western Civilization" (Huntington 1996). It is important to highlight the degree to which such interpretations stand in sharp contrast to the hopes and aspirations of the overwhelming majority of the Balkan peoples—who, in most cases, aspire to have their states join the European Union, and become accepted into a common European commonwealth, whereby escaping the reality of poverty and the spectrum of falling wages and standard of living into Third World levels.

However, according to the logic propagated by Huntington, Kaplan and others, the cultural boundaries of "Europe" are restricted to the more developed, Catholic and Protestant northern part of Eastern Europe (see, for example, Gemerek 1996; Delanty 1995: 48-58). This notion has provided the backdrop for an entire debate on the meaning, boundaries, and political significance of Central Europe (Schopflin and Wood 1989; Gaubard 1991). In the late 1980s, this intellectual debate led to the gradual formation of the clumsy term "East Central Europe," defined as the former communist Catholic and Protestant countries (Poland, Czechoslovakia, Hungary, Slovenia). The ultimate goal of this cultural and political designation was the inclusion of these countries into the enlarged EU and NATO.

As an offshoot of this political and cultural marker, the poorer countries of Southeastern Europe have been excluded from fast track EU membership. This ideological exclusion of the Balkans from a community of shared values and norms provides the context for emotional detachment from the passions involved or what Mestrovic (1996) calls "post-emotionalism." For Mestrovic post-emotionalism is responsible for the weak Western response to the Balkan conflicts of the 1990s.

Historically, the Balkans were the demarcating line between the Western and Eastern (Byzantine) components of the Roman Empire. During the Ottoman period, they also served as the "frontier" separating Western Christianity from the world of Islam. In more modern times, the Balkans served as the dividing line separating Eastern Orthodox (Byzantine) Christianity and Europe into two antagonistic camps.

At the height of the entanglement of Great Powers during World War I, the Balkans were considered "the power keg of Europe." This awkward metaphor still persists in contemporary discussion of regional geopolitics (see Larrabee 1994). However in reality, the Balkans were not the primary causal factor for the Greater Power rivalry that turned the region into a Pandora's Box for Europe in 1914. In sharp contrast to reality, Western commentators are extremely prone in attribution the greater geopolitical issues that have propelled Greater Power intervention to the "nature of the Balkans peoples" (see Glenny 2000 for a critique). Indeed, the geopolitical importance of the region compelled the military intervention of outside powers both in the past and more recent times. In the name of stability and world peace the Great powers have ignored the problems and grievances of the people in the region. Over the years the so-called "protecting powers" have taken a cavalier attitude and expediency adopting the old formula of divide and rule.

It was here that the beginnings of the Cold War between (Communist East) and (Capitalist West) commenced. The Truman Doctrine in 1947 was the official involvement of the United States in the region after the defeat of the Nazis in 1945. The stated purpose of the Truman Doctrine was the decision of the United States to stop the spread of Communism in Greece and Turkey. This led to the formation of NATO in 1949. Yugoslavia under Tito was also under the hegemony of the former Soviet Union before its neutrality. The Cold War between East and West already began in the Balkans and expanded later in the rest of Eastern and Western Europe. With the exception of Greece and Turkey the rest of the Balkans (which originally included the countries of Romania, Bulgaria, Albania, and former Yugoslavia and the successor states of Croatia, Slovenia, Bosnia-Herzegovina, the former Republic of Macedonia (FYROM)) were under the Eastern Communist camp. (For more details of Post-World War II Greek society and Politics, see Kourvetaris 1999; on Turkey, see Karpat 1973.)

It must be stressed here that, despite the region's apparent heterogeneity, the Balkans do share a historical past and, for several centuries, they also used to share a common cultural tradition. Throughout the last two millennia, the region served as the power-base for the Eastern Roman Empire and later on, the Ottoman Empire. The long periods of domination brought to the region by these

two empires meant that considerable cultural intermingling took place. Cultural syncretism in region, took the form of numerous cultural and societal expression such as food practices or family and kinship relations. It must also be noted that while the West held its Renaissance, Reformation, and Industrial Revolution, Southeastern Europe was under the long Ottoman Turkish (Islamic) rule and domination for over 500 years (1453-1912-1913) which slowed down the progress of the region.

It was only in the last two centuries that this variety of peoples and cultures underwent dramatic changes. Specifically, the import of the Western idea of the nation-state challenged the entire Ottoman system of social organization in the 19th century. Throughout the 19th century, the Balkan peoples struggled to develop alternative models of governance. Intellectuals and politicians pursued various forms of federalism, while the Ottoman bureaucracy and many among the Ottoman Orthodox Christians attempted to construct a model of secular citizenship applicable for all the peoples of the European part of the Ottoman Empire (for a review, see Roudometof 2001: 75-95).

With the Balkan Wars (1912-1913) a different vision succeeded in providing the road map for the social reorganization of the peninsula. It was the state-sponsored cultural nationalism of the Balkan nation-states that provided the foundational model for the construction of national societies in the region (for a discussion, see Roudometof 1998). The consolidation and territorial expansion of independent nation states in the region signaled the abandonment of the earlier alternative to the nation-state model. With this turn of events, the Balkan nation-states proceeded to nationalize their population, thereby setting off a whole series of competing claims and counterclaims about the territorial division of the peninsula, national minorities and their rights, and related issues (Roudometof 2002).

The result was bitter inter-ethnic and national rivalry, a rivalry that, to varying degrees, has persisted to this very day in the regional politics of individual nation-states. The Balkan nation-states' conflicts and wars included some of the most massive and violent cases of ethnic cleansing during the 20th century (Vardy & Tooley 2002). The list of victims includes practically all of the peoples currently inhabiting the region (Albanians, Bosnian Muslims, Macedonians, Bulgarians, Greeks, Turks, Serbs, and Croats). The state-sponsored policy of ethnic cleansing has had important repercussions for the human geography of the region.

Among the most notable, massive consequences of this policy are: the uprooting of Anatolian Greeks from their ancestral homes in Asia Minor and their resettlement within the boundaries of the modern Greek nation-state; the Armenian Genocide and subsequent cultural homogenization of the Turkish

Republic; the deportation of the Balkan Jews and their subsequent extermination by the Nazis during World War II and their eventual numerical decline in most countries in the region; the violence and mass extermination of Muslims, Serbs, and others during the Fascist Ustasa regime in World War II; the forced deportations of Albanians from Kosovo and Macedonia to Turkey during the inter-war period; the periodic and recurrent violence against the Turkish and Muslim minority in Bulgaria; the Turkish pogrom and destruction of the Greek community in Constantinople in 1955 (see Speros Vryonis 2001) and finally, the most well publicized cases of ethnic cleansing in Cyprus, Bosnia, Croatia, and Kosovo.

The title of our volume *The New Balkans: Disintegration and Reconstruction* serves as a benchmark indicating a new era for the countries and the peoples of this turbulent region. Following the collapse of socialism both in the former Soviet Union and former Yugoslavia, the Balkans were caught again in an imbroglio reminiscent of the World War I. However, there are important differences between the contemporary situation and the past, and uncritical comparisons between the two are unwarranted. The nature of contemporary international relations is markedly different from the Great Power rivalry of the early 20th century or that of the 19th century.

The post-World War II era has been an era of novel increases in international communication and interaction. Global economic restructuring has led to a reorganization of labor within large corporations—with extensive headquarters located in advanced industrial countries while the actual plans are relocated in the global periphery (see Sassen 1996: 6-20; Lash and Urry 1994). This reorganization has led to the growing need for transnational legal regimes to foster common sets of global rules as a means of ensuring the standardization of legal codes on a global basis (Held 1995). The global circulation of goods has been accompanied by the growing movement of peoples across borders. Although estimates vary, there are close to 120 million immigrants worldwide. Indeed, the challenges posed by the new post-1945 immigration from the less developed nations to more advanced ones are closely connected with the shift toward the global accountability of the state (Sassen 1996: 59-100).

The nation-state is gradually reconceptualized as an agent responsible for the human rights of every person within its territory (Jacobson 1996), and this provides a terrain for minority and immigrant groups to participate within the state's political body. Such participation is possible even when the immigrants do not have formal membership to the state (Soyal 1994). Protection of minorities becomes a topic of global significance, for a significant percentage of conflicts involves issues of minority rights (Gurr 1993). This strategy grew

out of the desire of World War II victors to avoid the repetition of the post-World War I disastrous situation.

The growing realization that international standards had to be applied in a uniform manner if they were to be respected world wide provided the impetus for a whole series of international treaties, culminating with the Helsinki accords of the 1970s (Musgrave 1997). The dramatic increase in international organizations has been well-documented (McGrew et. al. 1992; McNeely 1995). Organizations such as Amnesty International, Doctors Without Borders, or Helsinki Watch have been active in the Balkans over the last decade, thereby publicizing the plight of the civilians and suppression of the people's rights. These organizations have offered a variety of constituencies the opportunity to bypass the state and appeal directly to an international audience. The marked trend for uniform international patterns is an important new constraint on state action and a de facto limitation of state sovereignty.

All these trends influence the Balkans in important ways. The post-1989 Balkans have become, somewhat unwittingly, test cases for the application and global institutionalization of the still emerging, post-communist legal, moral, ethical, and geopolitical rules of conduct. This shift in international practices is quite consequential for the local geopolitics. For the long period of the Cold War and also during the inter-war period (1918-1939), the Balkan nation-states operated on the basis of regional geopolitics and—by and large—in accordance to international rules of conduct. In fact, it is rarely observed that the Lausanne Treaty (1923)—a treaty that officially sanctioned state-sponsored ethnic cleansing of Greeks and Turks—was not an international aberration. On the contrary, it was accepted and endorsed by the international community at the time. This stands in sharp contrast to the international attitude toward similar policies of "ethnic cleansing" implemented during the wars of the Yugoslav successor states in the 1990s or, more recently, during the 1999 Kosovo Crisis.

The Balkans have also been greatly affected by the accelerating gap between developed and underdeveloped countries and the growing inequality gap between underdeveloped countries and the advanced industrialized societies of Western Europe and North America. Although by the late 1970s the Balkan nation-states were no longer agricultural societies, their urban sector failed to become competitive in the world market. Indeed, their external debt grew in leaps and bounds in the post-1950 period (Stoianovich 1994: 212-15, 223-25; Wallden 1996). Additionally, the Balkans were negatively impacted by the "information revolution" of the post-1960 period. The information revolution fosters the rise of a "network society" (Castells 1996), where the human interaction and association are reshaped by information technology. In the post-industrial "network societies" of Western Europe and North American information

becomes absorbed into the fabric of diverse social, economic, and cultural activities. For most of the 20th century, the Balkan nation-states have failed to increase their levels of mass consumption and have remained within the lowest consumption levels among European countries (Therborn 1995: 144). As a result of this failure, mass media and culture industries have had a limited effect within individual Balkan societies. Hence, the Balkan nation-states lack of engagement in the global circuits of mass consumption increases their socio-cultural and economic distance from the advanced industrialized societies of Western Europe and North America.

While Greece and Yugoslavia, for example, enjoyed brief periods of spectacular growth in the 1960s and 1970s respectively, their economies declined significantly in the 1980s. The gradual consolidation of international trading blocs (EU, US, South Asia) further marginalized the region. Soaring unemployment rates and the proliferation of underground economy characterized the Balkan countries throughout the 1980s (Bookman 1994: 75-87). The statism of the local economies has further contributed to economic failure. In the 1980s, the Yugoslav experience was indicative of this trend. The local managerial elites of the republics found themselves caught in a situation of decreasing economic performance. Their inability to arrive at compromise solutions was the outcome of their desire to protect the locally based clientele of largely inefficient state enterprises (Rusinow 1985: 131-65; Woodward 1995: 47-81).

During the 1990s things became worse due to various regional conflicts among the successor nation-states. The post-1989 period initiated a new cycle of decline as the wars, economic sanctions, and the problem of transition to a capitalist economic system contributed to a significant decline in socioeconomic indicators (Danopoulos and Ianeva 1999). The reversal of these conditions will be undoubtedly gradual. The necessity of a Marshall-style plan for the region has been pointed out repeatedly by recent commentaries, as well as the fact that Serbia can not be excluded from such a plan. The post-1989 proliferation of small states in the region is likely to increase the need for regional cooperation (for a discussion, see Giannaris 1996). The consolidation of a new economic zone in the region is a task largely incomplete, mainly because cooperation among the countries remains troublesome. Their national rivalries are among the key factors preventing greater regional cooperation (Larrabee 1994). The same reason keeps foreign investment away. Therefore, while economic decline potentially fosters ethnic tension, economic development requires regional stability.

Finally, it is necessary to point out that the failures of economic development have been compounded by similar failures in the international community's attempts to establish political stability in the region. For example,

the treaties of Sevres (1920), Lausanne (1923), Loukarmo (1925) (Belgrade), San Stefano (1878), and Berlin (1878) failed to provide for a permanent political solution to the political problems of inter-Balkan relations. This was despite the apparent attempt of Great Powers to bring about regional stability. In this respect, the current efforts by the European Union and the United States to impose stable political regimes in Bosnia and Kosovo are reminiscent of similar attempts of the pre-World War II era. It may be useful to remind the reader that, in 19th century Balkans, the treaties of San Stefano and Berlin did not provide for an end to Bulgarian nationalism but, on the contrary, they served as reference point to Bulgaria's obsession with the conquest of Ottoman Macedonia. This "idee fixe," as Todorova (1995) calls it, provided the context for the inter-state relations among the Balkan nation-states from the 1870s until the end of World War II. In this respect, one finds interesting similarities between the current fervor of Albanian nationalists and that of Bulgarian nationalists during the pre-world War II period. It is rather ironic that, following the collapse of communism in the region, these problems of ethnonationalsim have resurfaced in the region. On the surface, the evens of the past and the present seem to confirm the cyclical view of history. Many believe that the resurgence of nationalism in the Balkans was the result of the failure of local authoritarian regimes to deal effectively with the "national question." The regimes of Marshall Tito in the former Yugoslavia and that of Emver Hotza in Albania entailed the imposition of communism on the Balkans in a fashion that did not allow the local societies to address issues of ethnic, cultural, and religious difference. Consequently, these issues resurfaced once these regimes collapsed. Indeed, this time we are witnessing the emergence of perhaps more violent forms of ethnonationalism. While Western Europe and the Americas are moving toward political and economic integration, the disintegration of Yugoslavia led to a series of bloody wars in the Balkans.

This volume, the *New Balkans: Disintegration and Reconstruction* is a scholarly effort that examines in depth the socio-historical, cultural, political, economic, sociological, diplomatic, geopolitical, and security parameters of this complex and turbulent region. The co-editors believe that an analysis by a galaxy of area specialists of the Balkans will shed a new light and help us understand the roots of the conflicts. The contributors as well as the co-editors think that an analysis of the various dimensions & challenges facing the region will contribute to a better understanding of the vicissitudes of Southeastern Europe.

For purposes of organization and clarification the volume is divided into three parts—Part I Historical Legacy and Issues of Ethnic Conflict, Part II

Economic Development and Civil Society, and Part III Geopolitics and Security Policies. Each part addresses a separate set of issues. Part I includes eight chapters.

Chapter 1. "The nature of ethnonationalism and subnationalism: The case of Yugoslavia" by George and Andrew Kourvetaris explores the conceptual and contextual underpinnings of ethnonationalism and subnationalism. Various types of these phenomena are discussed in a number of developed and developing countries with emphasis on the disintegration of Yugoslavia.

Chapter 2. "National Minorities, Nation-States and External Homelands in Southeastern Europe"; by Victor Roudometof looks at the causes of the Balkan ethnic conflicts and, in particular, the role played by real or potential minorities in providing an essential ingredient of their ethnic conflicts. He argues that the consolidation of national minorities in the region is a major factor contributing to increase ethnic tensions in the 1990s.

Chapter 3. "Pardon? A Conflict for a Name? FYROM'S Dispute with Greece Revisited" An analysis of Greece's dispute with FYROM" by Demetrius Andreas Floudas explores the conflict between Greece and the Former Republic of Macedonia (FYROM) over the issue of the name "Macedonia."

Chapter 4. "The Bosnian War 1992-1995: Strategic Analysis by Harry Papasotiriou looks at the conflicting political objectives and strategies pursued by the three combatants: Bosnia's Serbs, Croats, and Muslims.

Chapter 5. "Croatia-Serbia: Issues of Contention" by Kleomenis Koutsoukis and Pantelis Sklias considers a number of issues between Croatia and Serbia. Among the most important issues the authors examine are the issue of legitimacy of the independence of Croatia, the issue of territorial disputes, and the issue of refugees.

Chapter 6. "Croatia's Integration: Passing from the 19th to 21st Century" by Dimitrios Koukourdinos analyzes Croatia's process of national integration and statehood following the disintegration of Yugoslavia.

Chapter 7. "The Idea of Self-Determination: Lessons from the Former Yugoslavia" by George Raju G.G. Thomas focuses on the opposing claims of territorial integrity of state and the right of national self-determination for ethnic minorities within a state.

Chapter 8. "Third Party Involvement in Ethnic Conflict: The Case of the Kosovo War" by Edward A. Tiryakian introduces a new element by looking at the role of third parties in severe ethnic conflicts.

Part II Economic Development and Civil Society consists of four chapters.

Chapter 9. "Southeast Europe in Transition" by Eleftherios N. Botsas examines the economic transition of the countries of Southeastern Europe from central planning during the communist regimes to that of market capitalist economic system.

Chapter 10. "Southeastern Europe: Prospects for Increased Economic Integration" by Bob Donnorummo examines three important developments have increased chances for enhanced economic integration in Southeastern Europe. These developments are seen as necessary for sustained economic growth in the region. The three developments are (1) the expansion of the European Union (EU) to countries in the area beyond Greece, (2) the revolutions of 1989 which began the transformation to democracy and market economies, and (3) continuing technological advances which make connections to the global economy imperative for sustainable growth for all countries.

Chapter 11. "The Development of Civil Society in Southeastern Europe" by Tina Mavrikos-Adamou explores the consolidation of democracy and the legitimization of social, legal, and economic institutions for a viable civil society.

Chapter 12. "We Belong to the West?" Representations of Eastern and Western Europe in the Greek Press and the positioning of the "We" by Anna Triandafyllidou deals with the issue of whether the Balkans can be considered "western" societies or not. In her chapter, Triandafyllidou explores the cultural—political dimensions of collective identification. She rhetorically poses her research question via a political slogan("We belong to the West?") that provided the backdrop of an entire political debate between conservatives and socialists in Greece during the 1970s and early 1980s. Her aim is to show the contextual nature of Greece's identity by looking at the issues covered in the Greek press, and the ways in which the popular press is addressing European problems and local issues—ranging from the Macedonian issue to Greece's geopolitical rivalry with Turkey or to the various problems associated with the project of European Union.

Part III Geopolitics and Security Policies includes the remaining four chapters.
Chapter 13 "The Balkans and A Transforming NATO" by S. Victor Papacosma makes an effort to re-define NATO's strategic mission and belated role in Kosovo as a peace keeping military organization.
Chapter 14 "Institutionalized Restraint as Policy: The European Union and the Disintegration of Yugoslavia" by Kostas A. Lavdas examines European Union's policy toward the Yugoslav conflict.

Chapter 15 "The Emergence of a New Ottoman Model: A New Foreign Policy in Turkey" by Stephanos Constantinides, focuses on the changing role of Turkey's foreign policy by suggesting a new Ottoman model which according to the author is inseparable from re-Islamization in Turkey.
Chapter 16 "An Assessment of American Strategy in the South Balkans Since the Dissolution of Yugoslavia" by Alexandros K. Kyrou examines the role of the United States and its long-term implications in the Balkans.

All in all, the 16 contributors make an effort to address, in depth, a number of issues concerning the Balkans. The end product of such an analysis helps us understand the complexities of the region and assist both the people of the area and those outside to come to a better understanding and appreciation of the diversity and multiculturalism of the region. For a greater focus of each chapter the co-editors found necessary to ask the authors to submit an abstract for their chapter, which follows this introduction.

REFERENCES

Almond, Gabriel A. and Sidney Verba (eds.). 1963. *The civic culture: political attitudes and democracy in five nations*. Princeton, N.J.; Princeton University Press.

Almond, Gabriel A. and Sidney Verba eds.). 1989. *The civic culture revisited.* Newbury Park, Calif. : Sage Publications.

Anderson, Matthew Smith. 1966. *The Eastern Question: a study in international relations*. New York, St. Martin's Press.

Bianchini, Stefano and George Schoepflin (eds.). 1998. *State building in the Balkans: dilemmas on the eve of the 21st century*. London: Longo Editore Publ.

Bookman, Milica Zarkovic. 1994. *Economic Decline and Nationalism in the Balkans*. New York: St. Martin's Press.

Carter, F. W. 1977. "Introduction to the Balkan Scene," pp. 1-24 in F. W. Carter (ed.), *An Historical Geography of the Balkans*. New York: Academic Press.

Castells, Manuel. 1996. *The Rise of the Network Society: Vol. I of the Information Age*. London: Basil Blackwell.

Coufoudakis, Van, Harry Psomiades and Andre Gerolymatos (eds.). 1999. *Greece and the New Balkans: Challenges and Opportunities*. New York: Pella Publishing Co., Inc.

Cowan, Jane (ed.). 2000. *Macedonia: The Politics of Identity and Difference*. London: Pluto.

Danforth, Loring. 1995. *The Macedonian Conflict*. Princeton, NJ: Princeton University Press.

Danopoulos, Constantine and Emilia Ianeva. 1999. "Poverty in the Balkans and the Issue of Reconstruction: Bulgaria and Yugoslavia Compared," *Journal of Southern Europe* and the Balkans (1) 2: 185-99.

Dawisha, Karen, and Bruce Parrott (eds.). 1997. *Politics, power, and the struggle for democracy in Southeast Europe*. Cambridge: Cambridge University Press.

Delanty, Gerard. 1995. *Inventing Europe: Idea, Identity, Reality*. New York: St. Martin's Press.

Djordjevic, Dimitrije and Stephen Fischer-Galati. 1981. *The Balkan revolutionary tradition*. New York: Columbia University Press.

Gaubard, Stephen R. (ed.). 1991. *Eastern Europe . . . Central Europe . . . Europe*. Boulder, Co: Westview.

Gemerek, Bronislaw. 1996. *The Idea of Europe*. Cambridge: Polity.

Giannaris, Nicholas V. 1996. *Geopolitical and Economic Changes in the Balkan Countries*. Westport, Co: Greenwood.

Glenny, Misha. 2000. *The Balkans: Nationalism, war, and the Great Powers. 1804-1999* New York: Viking.

Gurr, Ted R. 1993. *Minorities at Risk: A Global View of Ethnopolitical Conflict*. Washington DC: US Institute of Peace Press.

Held, David 1995. *Democracy and the Global Order: From the Modem State to Cosmopolitan Governance*. Cambridge, UK: Polity Press.

Huntington, Samuel P. 1996. *The Clash of Civilizations and the Remaking of World Order*. New York: Simon and Schuster.

Jacobson, David. 1996. *Rights Across Borders: Immigration and the Decline of Citizenship*. Baltimore: Johns Hopkins University Press.

Jelavich, Barbara. 1991. *Russia's Balkan Entanglements 1806-1914*. Cambridge: Cambridge University Press.

Kaplan, R. 1992. *Balkan Ghosts: A Journey Through History*. New York: St. Martin's Press.

Karpat, Kemal H. 1973. *Social Change and Politics in Turkey. A Structural-Historical Analysis*. Leiden: Brill.

Kennan, G. F. 1993. "Introduction," in *The Other Balkan Wars: A 1913 Carnegie Endowment Inquiry*. Washington: Carnegie Endowment for International Peace.

Kourvetaris, George. 1999. *Studies on Modern Greek Society and Politics*. Boulder, Colorado: East European Monographs.

Larrabee, Stephen S. (ed.). 1994. *The Volatile Powder Keg. Balkan Security After the* Cold War. Washington DC: American University Press.

Lash, Scott and John Urry. 1994. *Economies of Signs and Space*. London: Sage.

Mackridge, Peter and Eleni Yiannakakis (eds.). 1997. *Ourselves and Others: The Development of a Greek Macedonian Identity since 1913*. Oxford: Berg.

McGrew, A., Lewis, P. et. al. 1992. *Global Politics: Globalization and the Nation-State*. Cambridge: Polity.

McNeely, Connie L. 1995. *Constructing the Nation-State*. Westport: Greenwood.

Mestrovic, Stjepan (ed.). 1996. *Genocide After Emotion: The Postemotional Balkan War*. London: Routledge.

Musgrave, Thomas D. 1997. *Self-Determination and National Minorities*. Oxford: Clarendon Press.

Poulton, Hugh. 2000. *Who are the Macedonians?* Bloomington. IN: Indiana University Press.

Roudometof, Victor. 1996. "Nationalism and Identity Politics in the Balkans: Greece and the Macedonian Question," *Journal of Modern Greek Studies* (14) 2: 253-301.

_________. 1998. "Invented Traditions, Symbolic Boundaries and National Identity in Southeastern Europe: Greece and Serbia in Comparative-Historical Perspective, 1830-1880," *East European Quarterly* (32) 4: 429-71.

_________. (ed.). 2000. *The Macedonian Question: Culture. Historiography, Politics*. Boulder, Colo.: East European Monographs.

_________. 2001. *Nationalism. Globalization & Orthodoxy: The Social Origins of Ethnic Conflict in the Balkans*. Westport, CT: Greenwood.

_________. 2002. "Ethnic Heterogeneity, Cultural Homogenization, and State Policy in the Inter-war Balkans," in Steven B. Vardy and Hunt Tooley (eds.), *Ethnic Cleansing in Twentieth-Century Europe*. Boulder, Co.: East European Monographs, forthcoming.

Rusinow, Dennison. 1985. "Nationalities Policy and the 'National Question'," pp. 131-65 in Pedro Ramet (ed.), *Yugoslavia in the 1980s*. Boulder, Co: Westview.

Sassen, Saskia. 1996. *Losing Control? Sovereignty in An Age of Globalization.* New York: Columbia University Press.

Schopflin George and Nancy Wood (eds.). 1989. *In Search of Central Europe.* Cambridge: Polity.

Shea, John. 1997. *Macedonia and Greece.* Jefferson, North Carolina and London: McFariand and Co.

Skopetea, Elli. 1992. *The Twilight of the East. Images from the Fall of the Ottoman Empire.* Athens: Athens: Gnosi (in Greek).

Soysal, Y. N. 1994. *Limits of Citizenship: Migrants and Post-national Membership in Europe.* Chicago, IL: University of Chicago Press.

Sloianovich, Traian. 1994. *The Balkan Worlds: The First and Last Europe.* New York: M. E. Sharpe.

Therbon, Goran. 1995. *European Modernity and Beyond: The Trajectory of European Societies 1945-2000.* London: Sage.

Todorova, M. 1995. "The Course and Discourses of Bulgarian Nationalism" pp. 55-102 in P. Sugar (ed.), *Eastern European Nationalism in the 20th Century.* Washington DC: American University Press.

__________. 1997. *Imagining the Balkans.* Oxford; Oxford University Press.

Vardy, Steven B. and Hunt Tooley (eds.). 2002. *Ethnic Cleansing in Twentieth-Century Europe.* Boulder, Co.: East European Monographs, forthcoming.

Vryonis, Speros, Jr. 2001 "Krystallnacht in Constantinople: in *Greek America* vol. 7, issue 1. Pp. 48-51.

Wallden, S. 1996. "The Balkans in the International Division of Labor," pp. 79-150 in *The European Community and the Balkans.* Athens: Sakkoula [in Greek].

Woodward, S. 1995. *Balkan Tragedy. Chaos and Dissolution After tile Cold War.* Washington DC: Brookings Institution.

ABSTRACTS

CHAPTER 1. The Nature of Ethnonationalism and Subnationalism: The Case of Yugoslavia George A. Kourvetaris, Northern Illinois University, Andrew G. Kourvetaris, Columbia University, USA

Using published material, the concepts of ethonationalism and subnationalism are explored and clarified. *First*, the conceptual clarification and perspectives of both concepts are discussed. *Second*, both the causes and determinants of early and late forms of ethnonationalism and subnationalism are briefly examined. *Third*, an analysis of various types of ethnonationalist movements in various countries including religious, ethnic, linguistic, cultural, and class are examined. Finally, an in-depth discussion of ethnic subnationalism in former Yugoslavia is attempted in view of the demise of former Soviet Union and disintegration of former Yugoslavia federal states.

CHAPTER 2. National Minorities, Nation-states, and External National Homelands in Southeastern Europe Victor Roudometof, Miami University, Oxford Ohio, USA

The consolidation of national minorities in Southeastern Europe has been the major factor for increasing ethnic tensions and violence in the region in the post-1989 period. Historically, nation-building efforts in the Balkans emphasized ethnoreligious components (nationhood) over impersonal, universalistic criteria (citizenship) and this has contributed to the tendency of ethnic minorities to seek an "exit" rather than a "voice" within the states' political body. The close geographical proximity of ethnic minorities with their external national homelands and (in some cases) their high birth rates have intensified this structural strain. Political mobilization along nationalist lines prevailed during the 1990s and this led to the collapse of the second Yugoslavia and the wars in Croatia, Bosnia-Herzegovina, and Kosovo. The neighboring Balkan states (Bulgaria, Albania, and the Republic of Macedonia) have been able to manage ethnic tensions (and irredentism) more successfully. However, as the 1999 Kosovo Crisis illustrated, the thread of further ethnic unrest in the region remains present.

CHAPTER 3. "Pardon? A Conflict for a Name? FYROM'S Dispute with Greece Revisited" Demetrius Andreas Floudas, Anglia Polytechnic University, England

This article attempts an exposé of the dispute between Greece and the Former Yugoslav Republic of Macedonia over the issue of the name of the latter, from its beginnings in 1991 up until the 1995 interim accord signed between the two countries. It also contains an evaluation of the Greek foreign policy during that period.

The work is to a large extent based on the author's personal research in Greek government archives and other unpublished sources, as well as on interviews with leading Greek politicians and diplomats who were immediately involved in the issue.

It traces the origins of the controversy and portrays the current dispute as the latest stage in evolution of the Macedonian Question of the past. The diplomatic strategies of the two countries involved are examined for the 1991-1995 period. In addition, the content and significance of the contentious issues of this debate are put under scrutiny. Finally, the factors which contributed to the diplomatic exacerbation of the issue (causing a failure of both parties to secure a resolution to the dispute that they would consider as 'positive') are analysed and the general repercussions for the Balkans' geopolitical *status quo* are outlined.

CHAPTER 4. The Bosnian War, 1992-1995: Strategic Analysis Harry Papasotiriou, Panteion University, Greece

The chapter provides a strategic analysis of the Bosnian War. It analyzes first the conflicting political objectives of the adversaries, and second the strategies that they pursued against each other. It is argued that the strategy of the Bosnian Serbs achieved its most important operational objectives on the ground in the first twelve months of the war, but its strategically unnecessary and indeed counterproductive brutality delegitimized the Serbian cause, resulting in an escalating international involvement that changed the balance of power in Bosnia and brought about the compromise of Dayton accords. It is further argued that the Dayton agreements have frustrated the political objectives of Bosnia's Serbs and Croats, who together constitute the majority of Bosnia's population, so that the current status quo is unstable and directly dependent on the operation of an indefinite international military protectorate.

CHAPTER 5. Croatia–Serbia: Issues of Contention Kleomenis Koutsoukis, Panteion University, Athens and Pantelis Sklias, Thrace University, Greece

Considering contention issues as being an integral part and one of the main characteristics of political life in the Balkans, this article examines such issues between Serbia and Croatia. We take the separatism demands of Croatia as being a typical type of destabilizing event for the integrity of a state. In the case of Croatia, such demands have caused atrocities which compared to the ones caused during the Second World War. Ethnolinguistic disagreements, unilateral declarations of autonomy, interposition or exception to the administration of law, and rejection or assertions of allegiance or rights and responsibilities of citizenship have been formulating the political activity and behavior of the Croats. Independence has not brought the issues of contention among the Croats and the Serbs to an end. On the contrary, there are three main issues which still remain valid: First is the issue of the legitimacy of the independence of Croatia, an issue of limited (due to the fact of the independence) relevance. The second issue is the one of the territorial disputes of Eastern Slovenia and the Pravlaka Peninsula. Third is the return of the refugees and the respects of their rights. This is an issue which is going to last for a long time. Finally, in the article we mention the use of Internet as a means of propaganda in order to demonstrate that contention may take different forms besides the traditional ones. However, the issues still remain the same.

CHAPTER 6. Croatia's National Integration: Passing from the 19th to the 21st Century Dimitrios Koukourdinos, London School of Economics and Political Science, England

Croatia's independence in the 1990s has been so far the last stage in a process of statehood affirmation that started back in the 19th century. Then Croatian national integration acted as a pendulum between wider plans for South Slavic unity and more strict ideas for a typical nation-state. During the 20th century, external conditions brought Croatians twice to a supranational Yugoslav integration and once to a nation-state, sponsored by the occupying forces during WWII. As a part of 2nd Yugoslavia, Croatia acquired the first attributes of a state. With the disintegration of Yugoslavia and its constituting idea, Yugoslavism, nation-state building remained the only game in town. President Tudjman based his political program on past ideas of Croatian statehood that brought Croatians in conflict with the Serb minority. The war that took place

during four years on its soil had as a result the affirmation of Croatia's sovereignty, through a process of power centralization where democracy was "a collateral damage."

CHAPTER 7. The Idea of Self-determination: Lessons from the Former Yugoslavia George Raju G. G. Thomas, Allis Chalmers Professor of International Affairs, Marquette University, USA

This chapter examines opposing claims based on the principle of the sovereignty and territorial integrity of states, and the principle of the right of national self-determination for ethnic minorities within a state who wish to secede from it. Granting self-determination in one case could produce a domino effect among other ethnic minorities causing the entire state to unravel amidst widespread bloodshed and refugee flows, e.g. Chechnya in Russia, Kashmir in India, East Timor in Indonesia. Moreover, the self-determination principle is not an extension of the democratic principle. While democracy operates on majority rule, self-determination promotes minority demands. In the Yugoslav case, the West provided the right of self-determination and secession to Slovenes, Croats, Bosnian Muslims and Kosovo Albanians, but not to Serbs in the newly created states of Croatia and Bosnia, and the de facto virtually independent Kosovo province.

CHAPTER 8. Third Party Involvement in Ethnic Conflict: The Case of the Kosovo War Edward A. Tiryakian, Duke University, USA

War as a phenomenon of modernity has received modest sociological attention, yet it has played a central role in constructing national identities and the periodization of history. How war relates to ethnic conflict when states as third parties intervene in severe ethnic conflict offers an important new dimension of research both to the sociology of war and to the comparative study of ethnic conflict. The 1999 war in Kosovo offers materials for such an analysis since Western democratic states, led by the United States and NATO, launched a war against a Balkan state that had an internal ethnic conflict.

To invoke a sociological perspective on what was in effect the "Fourth Balkan War" of the 20th Century, this paper adapts to the Kosovo situation a structural-functional analysis derived from Merton's well-known paradigm. While humanitarian assistance was an important manifest function of the

intervention, one effective in mobilizing support for the aerial warfare of continuous bombardment, there are also latent functions to be considered, as well as unintended consequences, short term and long term, of this war.

A final consideration pertains to broaden the issue of responsibility in ethnic conflict, even in this instance of democratic states intervening to mitigate ethnic conflict. The modernity of "virtual warfare" heightens the responsibility of mass media, television in particular.

CHAPTER 9. Southeast Europe in Transition Eleftherios N. Botsas, Oakland University, USA

The chapter deals with the countries of Southeastern Europe that are in transition from central planning to market economic system. Although all transitional countries faced severe problems of adjustment, the problems became more acute the less industrialized a country was at the end of World War II. Those countries that were relatively poor in the beginning of the postwar period fell further behind after the collapse of central planning. The adjustment process varied from shock therapy applied by Poland to no therapy a la Albania. However, the more rigorous the introduction of reforms the faster the adjustment was. Inflow of foreign capital and technological change became critical in the process of catching up.

Since all these countries aspire to be part of the European Union, the speed and success of adjustment becomes critical in determining the time horizon of European integration as well as the cost of adjustment for both the center and the periphery of the European Union. This chapter makes no forecasts for the Balkan economies.

CHAPTER 10. Southeastern Europe: Prospects for Increased Economic Integration by Bob Donnorummo, Center for Russian and East European Studies, University of Pittsburgh, USA

Over the last two decades three important developments have increased chances for enhanced economic integration in Southeastern Europe, which is also seen as necessary for sustained economic growth in the region. The three developments are (1) the expansion of the European Union (EU) to countries in the area beyond Greece, (2) the revolutions of 1989 which began the transformation to democracy and market economies, and (3) continuing

technological advances which make connections to the global economy imperative for sustainable growth for all countries. The obstacles to increased economic integration are significant and are both economic and political. The positive impact of the October 2000 elections in Yugoslavia and improvement in Greek-Turkish relations, are countered by the political instability in Kosovo and Macedonia. The economic obstacles are also significant and include the fact that most of these countries are poor and have a relatively high percentage of their GDP dependent on agriculture. This reduced the amount of goods and services for inter-regional trade. Yet this chapter takes the view that given the three developments noted above, increased economic integration is possible and that this provides the best base for both political stability and economic growth.

CHAPTER 11. The Development of Civil Society in Southeastern Europe
Tina Mavrikos-Adamou, American College of Thessaloniki, Greece

The focus of this contribution will be to explore the possibilities of a civil society forming in the countries of southeastern Europe. The countries of southeastern Europe under examination will be limited to Albania, Bulgaria, FYROM (Former Yugoslavian Republic of Macedonia), the remnants of Yugoslavia, and Greece. If democracy and a sense of legitimacy are to be maintained in the Balkans, these societies must carve out their own version of a civil society to support and strengthen their fragile political systems. The question remains as to what shape and form civil society can take in these countries based upon what already exists, and what can be done to further encourage and enhance civic formation in these societies.

CHAPTER 12. "We Belong to the West?" Representations of Eastern and Western Europe in the Greek Press and the Positioning of the "We" Anna Triandafyllidou, Marie Curie Fellow, Institute of Psychology, Italian National Research Council, Italy

The reorganization of geopolitical alliances in Europe and the Balkans and the drive towards a fuller integration into the EU have had important implications not only for Greek policies but also for the representation of the Greek nation as part of a "united" Europe and the new international order. The aim of this chapter is to explore the contextual nature of identity and study the implications of the new international context for images of Greece and Greeks presented in

the Greek press. The study concentrates on representations of the EU, fellow EU partners, CEEC countries, minorities and immigrant communities developed in the Greek press discourse over the past 20 years. Attention is paid to the ways in which these are related to conception(s) of the ingroup, i.e. the Greek nation. The chapter highlights aspects of Greek identity that have been increasingly emphasized (e.g. the belief in common genealogical descent), elements that have been downplayed (e.g. the Greek tradition of emigration), and new features that are emerging (e.g. its "Europeanness"). The material analyzed has been collected from two major daily newspapers in four selected years: 1983, 1989, 1993 and 1999. Texts have been analyzed both quantitatively and qualitatively (discourse analysis).

CHAPTER 13. The Balkans and a Transforming NATO S. Victor Papacosma, Lemnitzer Center, Kent State University, USA

NATO, the premier military-political alliance, found itself challenged by the onset of the uncertain strategic environment upon the Cold War's sudden termination. Concurrent with the efforts to redefine itself and its mission, NATO, after initial hesitation, joined other international organizations in seeking to bring an end to the fighting in the former Yugoslavia. NATO's belated involvement in Bosnia proved decisive, set the stage for the uneasy peace that followed, and contributed to its new, albeit controversial, strategic mission. Declining conditions in Kosovo offered another unprecedented security challenge for the transforming NATO, which involved itself in a second Balkan conflict with decision making and policies that were at times fallible and quite controversial.

CHAPTER 14. Institutionalized Restraint as Policy: The European Union and the Disintegration of Yugoslavia Kostas A. Lavdas, University of Crete, Greece

This chapter address the European Union's involvement in and policy response to the Yugoslav conflict. Applying the concept of negative integration to the area of European foreign and security policy, the author argues that the European Union's profile in this particular area should be examined in terms of policy being structured and reproduced on the basis of institutionalized restraint. Against the background of intense European rivalries in the historical Balkans,

the Yugoslav conflict presented the emerging European defence and security capacities with a particularly demanding test. A number of conditions allowed national foreign policies to take precedence over the pursuit of coherent EU policies. At the same time, and despite the lack of positive integration in the policy area, the attainment of a degree of negative integration has restricted further re-nationalization of foreign and security policy. In the future, the role in preventing and regulating conflict in its periphery will depend (a) on the institutionalization of mechanisms which will prevent or restricting the re-nationalization of European foreign policies, and (b) on the outcomes of internal EU debates about the relations between deepening and widening. The EU's role will depend on its medium and long-term capacity to expand the perimeter of its institutionalized governance structures without significantly diluting their content

CHAPTER 15. The Emergence of a New Ottoman Model: A new Foreign Policy in Turkey Stephanos Constantinides, Université du Québec, à Montréal, Canada

This chapter focuses on Turkey's foreign policy and suggests that contrary to Atatürk's heritage, contemporary Turkey is returning to what we call neo-Ottomanism. That is to say an expansionist foreign policy based on the Imperial Ottoman tradition coupled with the Islamic tradition.

This paper suggests that after the failure of the military interventions in 1960 and 1980 to limit Islamic influence and support the eroded Kemalist ideology of secularism, the Kemalist establishment went ahead with a working compromise with Islam. This arrangement confirms that re-Islamization was an inextricable reality of Turkish society and opened the door to a profound re-Ottomanization of Turkish foreign policy. In fact, re-Islamization in Turkey is inseparable from re-Ottomanization. However, Turkish Islamism has nothing to do with the Iranian, the Algerian or Afgan version. Indeed what makes Turkish Islamism more moderate and acceptable to the West is the Ottoman tradition. It seems that the military in Ankara cautioned this compromise with the political Islam which gives it the possibility to dominate the country's political life and particularly to control its foreign policy. As far as this expansionist policy enables Turkey to play a hegemonic role in the region, the army's powerful political role will be reinforced. From the West's point of view, this imperial neo-Ottoman policy is compatible with Turkey's European ambition as long as Europe is not prepared to accept this country as a full member of the Union. Nevertheless, the neo-

Ottoman model will operate at the expense of Turkey's democratization and respect of human rights.

CHAPTER 16. An Assessment of American Strategy in the South Balkans Since the Dissolution of Yugoslavia Alexandros K. Kyrou, Salem State College, USA

This contribution will evaluate the recast strategic ambitions underlying American interventionism in the Balkans and the attendant prospects for success or failure of these policies. Consideration of previously unexamined evidence of American state penetration and the establishment of a Great Power sphere of influence following the collapse of Yugoslavia distinguish this inquiry from previous work by other researchers. The primary claim of this article, based on an analysis of Washington's policy goals and their structural deficiencies and internal contradictions, is that American activism in Southeastern Europe, in general, and the South Balkans, in particular, has and continues to undermine regional stability. An evaluation of the long-term implications of this American initiative for interstate rivalry and conflict in the Balkans will conclude the study.

PART I

HISTORICAL LEGACY AND ISSUES OF ETHNIC CONFLICT

CHAPTER 1
THE NATURE ETHNONATIONALISM AND SUBNATIONALISM: THE CASE OF YUGOSLAVIA*

George A. Kourvetaris
Northern Illinois University
Andrew G. Kourvetaris
Columbia University

The disintegration of former Yugoslavia and the recognition of Croatia and Slovenia, first by Germany in 1991 and later by other countries, created a crisis of ethnic violence reminiscent of World War I and the Balkan imbroglio during the late nineteenth and early twentieth centuries. Historically, nationalism[1] and ethnonationalism in particular, was the most powerful force in the 19th Century. In the early 1990s, Yugoslavia's experiment in building a multinational state, through theroutes of modernization, political participation, demographic considerations, and majority vs. minority intergroup relations, proved insufficient to override the centrifugal forces of rising ethnonationalism and subnationalism in former Yugoslavia (Seculik et al. 1994:83-97).

The ethnic conflicts in Bosina Herzegovina, Kosovo, and the former Republic of Macedonia (FYROM)[2] is evidence that the old animosities among nations and religions in former Yugoslavia were merely dormant during the half century of communist authoritarian rule. It is ironic that while a number of western European countries are converging toward political and economic integration, i.e., the European Union, former Yugoslavia and the republics of the former Soviet Union are unraveling toward ethnic antagonism, subnationalism, and divergence of political and economic forces.

---

*Paper presented at the Second International Hellenic-American Conference on the theme of "Nationalism and Sexuality: Crises of Identity," Thessaloniki, Greece, May 17-22, 1995. I would like to thank the Sociology Department, The Graduate School, and the College of Liberal Arts and Sciences for providing in part some financial support for attending the conference. Also, I would like to express my thanks to my colleagues, Van Coufoudakis and Victor Roudemetof, for making useful suggestions for improvement of the manuscript and my son, Andrew, for his thorough copyediting. The present chapter is an updated version from the special issue on the Balkans published in the *Journal of Political and Military Sociology* Vol. 25, No. 2 (winter 1996): 163-187. However, any omissions or shortcomings are mine alone.

The resurgence of ethnic conflicts in the successor states in former Yugoslavia, as well as the former republics of the Soviet Union has provoked a renewed debate and interest in the nature and the dynamics of ethnicity in contemporary societies and states. The post-Cold War ethnic resurgence can be seen as a continuation of a trend that began in the 1960s. According to Gurr (1994:347-77), the most current ethnopolitical conflict is the contention for state power among communal groups, or what he terms "peoples against states" in a changing world system. Former Yugoslavia and the former Soviet Union are classic examples of subnationalism in which almost all-former nationalities of both states pursued self-determination and secessionist movements for the creation of independent nation states.

Briefly, the present analysis will focus on the following: *first*, the concepts and theories of ethnonationalism and subnationalism will be briefly examined; *second*, the resurgence of ethnonationalism, subnationalism, and disintegration of former Yugoslavia will be discussed; and *finally*, the implications of the disintegration of Yugoslavia in Southeastern Europe will be assessed.

CONCEPTUAL CLARIFICATION AND PERSPECTIVES

Ethnic conflict at both the national and international levels became at the center of politics and power relations within and between states especially following the demise of communism in former Soviet Union and former Yugoslavia in 1989 and 1990. Connor (1991) defines ethnonationalism as subnationalism, movements for autonomy or independence organized along linguistic, ethnic, religious, or cultural lines. Ethnonationalism can be seen as a form of ethnic mobilization for political and economic advantages. When groups engage in violent collective action against the state, they either calculate the costs and benefits of such conflict behavior or they are motivated by a sense of deprivation. Much of Charles Tilly's (1978) and Ted Robert Gurr's (1970,) (1993b) scholarly work on violent political conflict has focused on such collective action. Gurr's work (1993a 1993b) represents the first step toward a systematic comparative analysis of ethnic conflict. His work provides an opportunity to bridge the gap that exists between civil conflict studies and ethnic studies.

At the international level, ethnic conflict and mobilization can arise as a result of social and political change; or it may result from an identity crisis in the process of historical and political transformation of nations or from an external cause. The demise of communism in former Yugoslavia and the Soviet Union brought about a series of new subnationalist, secessionist, and

ethnopolitcal movements in these former socialist states. However, outside the Soviet and Yugoslav successor states, no serious secessionist movements occurred since 1989.

Gurr (1994:354-55) differentiates between three analytically distinct orientations toward state power and communal groups in ethnopolitcal disputes and issues of conflict: *ethnonationalism*, *indigenous rights*, *and contention of power*. Ethnonationalism is the central issue that motivates regionally concentrated peoples to "exit" or pursue independent statehood or extensive regional autonomy. For example, in his study *Minorities at Risk* (1993a) of 233 politicized communal groups, Gurr found that 81 pursued ethnonational objectives.

By *indigenous rights* Gurr refers to the preoccupation of conquered descendants of original inhabitants of a country for "autonomy" as a means of the protection of their lands, resources, and culture from the inroads of state builders and developers. Some indigenous people go beyond autonomy seeking independent statehood. Gurr's study (1993a) found that 83 of 233 groups studied were indigenous peoples.

Contention for power is also a principal issue in conflict among communal contenders. The resurgence of ethnonationalism of former Yugoslavia is a case in point of distinct ethnic cultures and national groups locked in rivalries about the distribution or access to state power. According to Gurr, (1994:355) ethnonationalism was the most important issue (characterizing 31 conflicts); contention of power was second most common (18 conflicts); and indigenous rights were salient in 16 conflicts. Gurr (1994:355) found that in the 50 ethnopolitcal conflicts that occurred between 1993-94, 54 percent began before 1987 and 46 percent after 1987.

During the Cold War (1945-1989/90) many interethnic conflicts erupted in violence, particularly in the former European colonies of Asia and Africa. Some of these conflicts were supported by the East-West competition for economic and geopolitical advantages in the global arena. The present ethnic conflicts of the former Yugoslavia and the Soviet Union have their roots in the ethnic rivalries, which, had been dormant during the Cold War period. These rivalries can usually be traced through the history of the region, as well as through more current sources of economic, political, and ideological conflict. However, despite the resurgence of ethnic conflicts, it must be noted that most of the former Soviet republics remain free of interethnic conflicts.

It is interesting to note that during the nineteenth century two contradictory principles emerged: nationalism and liberalism. The former encouraged "uniformity," while the latter supported "diversity." The French statesman de

Tocqueville observed that a liberal society and polity nourishes diversity, which can potentially undermine social cohesion and stability. Indeed, it was the same potential problem that the founding fathers of the United States faced. At present, most nation states are held together by shared ethnic identity. While the United States promotes unity within ethnic diversity and multiculturalism, the U.S. Constitution is not based on ethnicity, race, or religion but on citizenship and the *modus operandi* of federalism.

At a different level of analysis, one can identify three basic forces that seem to generate ethnic conflict: *retribalization* of the world, *ethnic heterogeneity*, and *ethnic diaspora*. The end of the Cold War has strengthened rather than weakened the forces of ethnonationalism and ethnic fragmentation. This ethnonationalism is reflected in the membership of the United Nations, reaching almost two hundred nation states by 1993. Despite the ethnic identity as a basis of nation building, only a handful of nations are culturally and ethnically homogenous. Not only are most nations ethnically heterogeneous, but the processes and causes of ethnic *diaspora* of particular ethnic groups are different. Jalali and Lipset (1992-93:586) argue that only sixteen percent of all Jews live in Israel, Arabs are found in thirty-seven states and Kurds in six states. Forty percent of all Albanians live outside Albania, and twenty-three percent of Hungarians live outside of Hungary. Finally, the issue of ethnic conflict is more likely to increase in the years ahead especially in ethnically mixed populations. The former New York Senator Daniel Patrick Moynihan, who was also a former Harvard professor and has written on race relations, predicted that in the next fifty years another fifty states would be riddled with ethnic conflict. In addition, Binder and Crossette (1993) listed forty-eight trouble spots in the world in which the major players were tribes or ethnic groups. As of 1993, the United Nations has peacekeeping forces in thirteen countries to prevent domestic insurrection and civil strife.[3]

ETHNONATIONALISM AND SUBNATIONALISM: CAUSES AND DETERMINANTS

Many thought that the end of the Cold War and the global market economy would move the world beyond nationalism and the provincial confines of ethnic identities. In the words of Michagel Ignatieff (1993:5), however, the "repressed has returned, and its name is nationalism," or ethnonationalism. Samarasinghe (1909:9) and Nagel (1993:103-12) argue that the nation state has been challenged from two sides: from above, or the supranational level, and from below, or the ethnic nationalist level. The supranational level deals with the

external threat or intervention of one country against another. This type of irredentism will not preoccupy us here. From below, at the subnational level, ethnonationalism has challenged the existence of a number of existing national states. In this case within a multi-ethnic nation state, ethnic groups mobilize to establish their own separate state or autonomy on the basis of shared "ethnic consciousness" and "ethnic subculture." Ethnic mobilization is predicated on a number of issues including primordial ethnic ties, shared religion, language, nationality, race, or a combination of these. Many ethnic movements challenge the existing political arrangement of multi-ethnic and multi-religious nations and borders. Horowitz (1985) believes the bulk of literature on ethnonationalism focuses on certain unique socio-historical, economic, political, ideological, and cultural developments that led to the emergence and re-emergence of ethnonationalism, especially since the Second World War. The origin of ethnonationalism has a long history but emerged primarily in Western Europe after the French Revolution (1789).

The special status of minority groups, vis-à-vis the majority within a nation state, has been articulated by Hirschman's (1970) and Roudometof (1996) by using the notion of choice between "exit" or "voice-participation." The minority group can either "exit" or secede from the state, or it may cooperate within the existing state structure. Hirschman believes in the importance of "loyalty" as a determinant between exit and voice participation. In other words, if the minority group is loyal to the state, it may decide to opt for participation. On the other hand, if loyalty is low, the minority may decide to "exit" the state or pursue autonomy or secession (i.e., the secession of Eritrea from Ethiopia during the 1980s is an example of a minority that decides to exit the state and establish an independent nation state). However, loyalty is difficult to establish when common bonds between minority and majority groups are absent. In this case, if ethnonationalism prevails, the unity of the nation state is at stake.

The resurgence of ethnonationalism has also been facilitated by a number of factors and recent developments, the most salient of which will be briefly discussed here. These include a) *democratization*, b) *concern for human* rights, c) *self-determination* (for ethnic minorities), d) *modernization* and *development*, and e) *the emergence of regional powers*. The trend toward democratization in recent years has contributed to the re-emergence of ethnonationalism. Democratization demands freedom of ethnic minorities from authoritarian regimes within various nation states so that they may express themselves both politically and economically. Thus, it can be argued that the demise of communism in former Yugoslavia and the former Soviet Union, and the process

of democratization in these republics, has contributed to re-emergence of ethnic strife in the former socialist states.

The violation of the human rights of subnational ethnic minorities by ethnic majorities also fosters separatist ethnic movements for statehood and autonomy. For example, the Kurds, one of the largest Middle Eastern ethnic groups, have struggled for years for establishing their own separate state in Turkey and Iraq. Yet their basic human rights have been denied by the ethnic Turkish and Iraqi majorities. It is interesting to note that during the Persian Gulf War in 1991, the Kurds in Iraq were treated sympathetically by both the United States and other western European countries. They were looked upon as victims of aggression by Iraq but not by Turkey. In 1995, however, Turkish troops actually invaded Iraqi territory pursuing Kurdish insurgents and decimated the Kurdish population there. Thousands of Kurdish villages were destroyed. The U.S. media barely reported the attack, except to quickly point to the Kurds en masses as an egregious "terrorist" group. Turkey, as a member of NATO and a client state of the United States, has a human rights record against the ethnic Kurds. Human rights violations by Turkey have been documented by most international human rights groups, such as Helsinki Watch.

Along with democratization an element for human rights, self-determination is an important determinant of ethnonationalism. Self-determination, which was reaffirmed after World War I by the League of Nations and later by the United Nations, means that every nationality or ethnic group has the right to pursue its own destiny and independence. However, while originally self-determination was intended to assist the independence of oppressed and subjugated people within a multi-ethnic state, it has lost its original democratic meaning. Instead, it has increasingly become a political and ideological weapon for power advantages of one ethnic group over another, commonly known as *ethnocracy*. An ethnocracy is quite different than a democracy. Democracy is based on the principle of political equality among individuals irrespective of their ethnic, religious, or racial status; *ethnocracy* is the antagonism and power struggle of one ethnic group against another to maximize economic and political advantages. According to Premdas et al. (1990), most of the secessionist movements in different parts of the world justify themselves on the basis of the self-determination principle. One can argue that the absence of a strong tradition of democratic rights and citizenship in the Balkans, and the failure of the Yugoslav experiment of a federal state serving diverse nationalities peacefully, has led to the re-emergence of ethnonationalism and sub-nationalism in former Yugoslavia. Obviously, the international community does not uniformly accept the principal of self-

determination. In some instances, it is supported by great powers while in others it is not.

Another factor that fosters ethnonationalism is modernization. Modernization theorists argue that communication and increased intergroup contact reinforce, rather than weaken, solidarity among various ethnic groups around the world. One of the more popular models of this resulting ethnic mobilization is the economic competition thesis. Olzak (1983), Nagel (1993) and Jalali and Lipset (1992-93:596) argue persuasively that modernization tends to increase levels of competition for jobs and housing among ethnic groups. This increased ethnic competition exacerbates ethnic conflicts and social movements based on ethnic boundaries. The literature on the economic basis of ethnonationalism also lends support to the economic competition thesis of ethnic mobilization.

Ethnonationalism has become part of the political landscape, not only in countries of the Third World, but also in many western European industrialized countries (e.g., Germany following unification of the two Germanies in 1990). To understand the causes of interethnic conflict and polarization among various multi-ethnic and multi-racial societies, we must consider not only the "nationalist-subnationalist dialectic," but also the role of the supranational forces, such as historical colonialism, multinationalism, modern militarism, and arm sales.

Usually ethnonationalist movements become secessionist movements, if they develop certain characteristics. Premdas (1990:14-16) has identified five major factors contributing to these movements: a) *An organized struggle*; any ethnic group within a multi-ethnic nation state, whose members share primordial ethnic ties, can organize, mobilize, and struggle for territorial autonomy and independence; b) *Territorial self government*; an ethnic group participating in a secessionist movement seeks a territorial base that it call its "homeland," such as the Kosovars in Kosovo, Serbia; c) *Primordial and secondary factors*; primordial ties are "mythical claims" of ethnic identity and "ethnic consciousness" which may lack historical objectivity and authenticity. Secondary claims may include feelings of discrimination or oppression of the minorities by the dominant groups who pursue territorial self-government. These two factors are believed to facilitate ethnic identification with a secessionist movement; d) *The principle of self-determination* is another contributing factor to secessionist movements. Under this notion every nation has a God-given, natural right to pursue its own destiny through self-rule and independence. This principle can be traced to World War I and the League of Nations, the antecedent of the United Nations. Finally, e) *International recognition*; recognition by other nations is essential for the legitimacy of the secessionist movement and self-

government by an ethnic group. The break-up of the former Yugoslavia in the Balkans into new nation-states, such as Croatia, Slovenia, Bosnia-Herzegovina, and so on, are examples of secessionist (subnationalist) movements. Following a successful secessionist movement, the new emerging nation state must be internationally recognized by other nation states in order to achieve legitimacy.

In general, secessionist movements are ethnonationalist movements found in many developed and undeveloped countries. While most secessionist movements are ethnic, religious, and racial in nature, (or a combination of all three), not all secessionist movements are ethnically motivated. However, since World War II, most secessionist movements have been ethnonationalist in nature.

TYPES OF ETHNONATIONALIST MOVEMENTS

One can identify many types of ethnonationalist movements. Nagel (1993:103-11) identified two major types of ethnonationalism: a) historical ethnonationalism or anti-colonialism and b) ethnic subnationalism or secessionist movements. The first wave of ethnonationalism, also known as de-colonization, can be traced to various indigenous ethnic movements in many Asian and African countries after World War II pursuing independent secessionist movements against the western European colonial powers. For example, many "artificial" states were carved up by colonial powers in Africa without regard to ethnic demography, so that most of the borders of the emerging nations were arbitrary colonial boundaries first. These ethnic secessionist movements were designated by the colonial powers as Indian nationalism, Ghanaian nationalism, Nigerian nationalism, and so on. As we mentioned before, Gurr views ethnic subnationalist movements as "peoples against states." According to him, "all but five of the twenty-three wars fought in 1994 were based on communal rivalries and ethnic challenges to states." (Gurr 1994:350).

It must be noted that for the last half century, ethnonationalism was kept in check by both forms of rival political ideologies and economic systems, that is, communism and capitalism. Communism, as a global ideology, discourages ethnonationalism. Instead, it stresses class-consciousness and transnational proletarian rule. Needless to say, the end of the Cold War has changed all that. At present we see more and more communist states engaged in market capitalism (China, Cuba). Capitalism, on the other hand, while allowing ethnic diversity, especially in terms of religion, discourages ethnonationalism, especially if it endangers the capitalist's own economic and geopolitical interests. In fact, most peoples of Africa, Asia, and other regions of the world had to struggle against the capitalist-colonialist powers for their independence. The old

formula of 'divide and conquer' was practiced by the colonial powers. Dividing a country usually took the form of fracturing people into various ethnic, religious, racial, cultural, or regional groups. Through this ethnic fragmentation, the colonial powers ruled entire continents with a few hundred administrators and a few thousand military personnel. Furthermore, the idea of ethnonationalism and the creation of nation states is predicated on the notion that one has to match the territory and boundaries with a distinct ethnic group. Not long after national independence of many new nation-states from the colonial powers, new waves of subnationalist movements from within the new nation-states emerged. These secessionist subnationalist movements proliferated during the 1960s and 1970s. However, with the exception of former Yugoslavia and former Soviet Union, few such movements are taking place presently.

Subnationalist ethnic movements have sometimes been more violent than the first wave of ethnonationalism that strove against the colonial powers for national independence and statehood. However, not all ethnonationalisms lead to ethnic conflict and ethnic subnationalist secessionist movements. In Europe, we find a number of ethnic subnationalist movements in northern Spain among the Basques, where the issues are ethnic and linguistic in nature. In Northern Ireland the main issue is religion between Roman Catholics and Protestants. In Belgium, the two basic ethnic groups the Flemish (related to the Germanic language or Flanders) and the Wallons (related to the French) coexist peacefully in a constitutional monarchy-type government. Even in England there is a movement by Scots to become independent of England. The majority of subnationalist movements, however, are occurring in the developing world. A separatist movement in Sri Lanka by the Tamils has been going on for years. According to Samarasinghe (1990:49), about 74 percent of Sri Lanks's population (total 16.9 million in 1989) are Sinhalese, 18 percent Tamils, 7 percent Muslims, and 1 percent belonging to the other small minority groups. The secessionist ethnic movement has been initiated by the Tamils, although the Indian or Plantation Tamils are against secession. The geographic division between the Sinhalese and the Tamils has been reinforced by religious and linguistic cleavages. Ninety-four percent of the Sinhalese are Buddhists and eighty-five percent of the Tamils are Hindus. A similar secessionist movement is found in the Philippines where the minority Muslim Moros want to be independent from the dominant Roman Catholic Filipinos.

Similar secessionist subnationalist movements are found in some parts of Africa. For example, the southern Sudanese have rebelled against the northern Sudanese (there, the cleavage involves both religion and class).

During the 1960s and early 1970s, there was the Biafran secessionist movement against the central government of Nigeria. The Ibos, a different

ethnic group, spearheaded the Biafran secessionist movement. Who thought of themselves as more educated and progressive, and wanted to establish a separate nation from that of Nigeria. In Ethiopia Arab Islamic counties assisted the Eritreans, with a large Muslim population, in their secessionist movement against Ethiopia. which is mostly comprised of Coptic Christians. In the late 1980s the Eritreans succeeded in establishing a separate country of Eritrea. More recently in Rwanda the issue there is also ethnic conflict between the minority Tutsie and majority Hutu.

In the Middle East, the Kurds have tried for years to establish a separate state in Turkey. In Cyprus, the Turkish Cypriot minority declared themselves and independent pseudo-state in 1983 following the Turkish invasion of Cyprus in 1974. They seek independence from the Greek Cypriot majority. In Israel, the conflict there has been between two different religious and ethnic groups, the Jews and the Palestinians. Both groups claim the same land as their own. While the majority of Palestinians are Arab Muslims and some Christian, the Israelis are Jewish in religion and culture. Likewise, in Canada there is a division between Francophones and Anglophones, or along French and English linguistic, cultural, and religious lines. In order to further understand the issue of ethnonationalism as it applies to the Balkans, we will analyze the ethnic conflict among various national groups in former Yugoslavia with some reference to the former Soviet Union.

ETHNIC SUBNATIONALISM IN FORMER YUGOSLAVIA

The resurgence of ethnonationalism in the former Soviet republics and former Yugoslavia is one of the most severe expressions of ethnic subnationalism (Vujacic and Zaslavsky 1991:121; Sekulic et al. 1994). In the former Soviet Union, Marxism and ethnonationalism were seen as ideologically incompatible. Both the Bolsheviks, including Lenin himself and Marxists in general, understood the political potential of ethnonationalism in the former Soviet Union and elsewhere. Nevertheless, the national policy of the Soviets was predicated on the assumption of the transitory nature of nationalism (Vujacic and Zaslavsky 1991:121). Prior to the Bolshevik Revolution of 1917, the Bolsheviks did not spell out a clear nationality policy and rights of various nationalities to attain self-determination. National policy, however, became one of the major components of their political strategy. This strategy failed to bring about equality among the various nationalities and to foster a shared socialist political agenda of economic modernization both in former Yugoslavia and former Soviet Union. The end of the Cold war and the failure of economic and political modernization did not succeed in stopping the resurgence of ethnic subnationalism.

The successful manipulation of various ethnic minorities helped the Bolshevik's victory in the (1917-1921) civil war (Vujacic and Zaslavsky 1991:121). This manipulation, or Soviet-style federalism, was influenced by Stalin's definition of the concept of "nation," which linked language, culture, ethnicity, territory, and political administration. Soviet Russia was the first modern state to accept the nationality principle as the basis of its federal structure (Vujacic and Zaslavsky 1991:122). In this way, the Soviet federal system was seen as a collection of sovereign nation-states, controlled by a strong center. The purpose of the Soviet federalism was to accommodate the various nationalities within an all-Soviet framework, giving each Soviet republic a role in the centralized communist party, state administration, cadre selection, and central planning. All Soviet Union republics had similar bureaucratic and educational structures. This "structural isomorphism" appealed to ethnic middle classes. Despite this "structural isomorphism," however, preferential treatment of nationalities was a Soviet policy of ethnic stratification rather than the exception. A Soviet quota system favored indigenous populations and those ethnic groups who had developed a Russian sense of nationhood. Indeed, the Russians, as a distinct ethnic group, could be regarded as the Anglo-Saxons of the former Soviet Union. Similar to the Anglo-Saxons (Protestants) in the United States, the Russians are the largest ethnoreligious (Russian Orthodox) ethnic group in the former Soviet republics.

Yugoslavia, like its Soviet counterpart, was also a multi-ethnic and multi-religious society and federal state. As Russians were dominant in the former Soviet Union, the Serbs were and still are the dominant ethnic group in former Yugoslavia. The partisans' success in Yugoslavia during World War II appealed to many ethnic minorities who were promised national self-determination after the war. Indeed, the communists promised to put an end to prewar "greater Serbian hegemony." Centralism and the state were to be recognized on a federal basis along the Soviet model. Thus, the 1946 Yugoslav constitution, based on the 1936 Stalinist institutionalization of federalism, divided the country into six republics, one autonomous province (Vojvodina, the northern autonomous province of Serbia) and one autonomous region (Kosovo). Both of these autonomous subunits were located within the largest republic of Serbia and were designed to contain centralist Serbian aspirations. It must be stressed, however, that both the Serbian Academy of Sciences and 200 Belgrade prominent intellectuals were against the partition of Serbia proper into three parts under the 1974 constitution (Roudometof 1996). At least one republic, Bosnia-Herzegovina, was created as a compromise between Serbs and Croats (the two largest ethnic groups), because it did not have a clear titular nationality. Yugoslavia republics were thus designed as "homelands" for indigenous

nationalities residing within them. According to the 1981 Yugoslav census, Yugoslavia had a population of 22,427,000 of which 36.3 percent were Serbs and 19.8 percent Croats. Muslims were the third largest group with 8.9 percent, and the rest of the Yugoslavian population was an assortment of 18 or so different nationalities (Petrovic 1987:30-31).

The Yugoslav state was established during World War I on December 1, 1918, following the unification of the Kingdom of Serbia and Montenegro with the South Slavic lands of the former Austro-Hungarian monarchy (Sekelj 1993:XV). Indeed, the entire Balkan system of states emerged out of the Balkan wars of 1912, 1913, and the ensuing World War I (1914-1918). This led to the issue of national minorities and the factors of interstate relationships. In reality, no state, including Rumania, Bulgaria, Albania, Serbia (Yugoslavia) and Greece, was in a position to incorporate all of its potential nationals within its territory. The emergence of the first Yugoslavia in the post World War I as a multi-national and multi-religious federal state was an effort to manage the coexistence of Croats, Slovenes, and Serbs along with a number of other small groups (Djilas 1991). The Serbian dynasty and the Serbian dominance in the army were the two the two major reasons for the Serbian dominance in the state apparatus. In 1938, out of 165 generals, 161 were Serbs, two were Croats, and two were Slovenians. Since its inception as a federated state, Yugoslavia has been a multinational and multi-religious country (Roman Catholic, Serbian Orthodox, and Islamic faith) with ethnic nationalities and regional differences like those found among Balkan groups.[4] Historically, all Balkan states have pursued the route of ethnonationalism in their nation-building process (Stavrianos 1958). Indeed, the Balkan states in their national histories, public institutions, and their national literature emphasize nationhood and ethnicity rather than citizenship as the most important elements of the nation state. Under these structural conditions, the minority group finds itself in institutional separation from the majority in the fields of education, religion and language. In many instances, it is seen as a threat to the very stability of state boundaries.

The communists came to power in the winter 1945-46 and proclaimed a federation[5] in Yugoslavia as a solution to the prewar ethnic fragmentation. Tito's charismatic and authoritarian personality managed to suppress the nationalist feeling and create an authoritarian communist federation. However, it was a federation of ethnic and religious groups rather than a political democracy built on the basis of a unified identification as Yugoslavian citizens. For example, Tito's irredentist policy against Greece during Greece's Civil War (1946-1949-) artificially created the so called Macedonian nationality in the post War World II era. While the Macedonian nationalist movement existed for a long time, Tito built on this concept and gave it new dimensions during and

after the Greek Civil War (1946-1949). However, Macedonia is the northern region of Greece which is a historically, ethnically, and culturally homogenous Greek territory.

In Yugoslavia, while the ethnic and religious federal unit maintained their separate distinct identities, they failed to develop a common universalistic core Yugoslavian identity that could transcend these ethnic and religious particularities. Using survey data from 1985 and 1989, just prior to Yugoslavia's eruption into ethnic hostilities, Seculic et al., (1994:83) found that those with urban backgrounds, the young, those of mixed parentage, communist members, and those from minority nationalities were more likely to espouse a common Yugoslav identity.

This identity, however, was not strong enough to stop the rising tides of ethnonationalism. Federalism failed to function under the communist socialist system in either the former Yugoslav or former Soviet Union. This can be partially explained because both former Socialist systems lacked the principles of liberal political and economic democracy. Instead of a common political national identity, based on citizenship and a common constitution and by overlooking this populations' ethnic, religious, and linguistic diversity and animosity, former Yugoslavia and Soviet Union set the state for ethnic tribalism and militant ethnonationalism.

The breakdown of former Yugoslavia has many causes; economic, political, ethnic rivalries, and cultural. We can not go into detail here. The demise of the former Soviet Union and the collapse of Soviet dominated eastern European regimes brought about the "ethnic revival" of the early 1990s and provided the context that led to the disintegration of Yugoslavia and to the bloodshed in Croatia, Bosnia-Herzegovina, and Kosovo. The threat of ethnic conflict and consolidation continues to exist in many other regions in the Balkans. In a short period of time, four of the six Yugoslav federal units demanded complete national independence and sovereignty: Slovenia, Croatia, the former Yugoslav Republic of Macedonia[6] (FYROM), and Bosnia-Herzegovina. The other two, Serbia and Montenegro, formed a federation and retained the name of former Yugoslavia. In addition, the largest ethnic minority, the Albanians[7] (about 1 million in 1991), are concentrated in Kosovo, an autonomous province in Serbian territory. Kosovo also seeks independence, which Serbia opposes. After the Albanians, the second largest national minorities are the ethnic Hungarians (426,000) who live primarily in Vojvodina, a northern autonomous province of Serbia. There are also about 200,000 Roma (gypsies) and more than twenty other minorities with less than 100,000 members. The only federal unit with a population that coincides with a state is Slovenia (1,871,000) inhabitants of whom 90 percent are Slovenians). Serbs make up 60 percent of the inhabitants

of Serbia (9,313,000), and 32 percent of the inhabitants of Bosnia-Herzegovina. Croats make up 75 percent of the population of Croatia (4,600,100) and 18.4 percent of the population of Bosnia and Herzegovina (4,124,000). Muslims comprise 39.5 percent of the population of Bosnia-Herzegovina, while Montenegrins are 68 percent of the population of Montenegro, with Muslims (12.5 percent) as the largest minority. The former Yugoslav Republic of Macedonia (FYROM) is inhabited by 67 percent Skopjeans, Orthodox Christian Slavs (1,912,000) and 20 percent Muslim Albanians, Gypsies, and other ethnic groups, (Yugoslav Census 1981). Hayden (1993: 654-73) argues that the constitutional reforms undertaken by Slovenia, Croatia, FYROM, and Bosnia-Herzegovina are to a large extent responsible for aggravating ethnonationalist tensions in former Yugoslavia. To these constitutional reforms we must add the role of Serbian nationalists who were skillfully manipulated by Milosevic, the former president of Serbia (who was handed to The Hague International Court), in order to provide a way out of the failure of communist elites struggling with the country's deteriorating economic conditions and the legitimization crisis of Yugoslav communism in general (Rusinow 1968; Ramet 1992; Roudometof 1996).

The present disintegration of Yugoslavia appears to be the result of certain weaknesses it had shared with the Soviet Union: a) the failure of modernization and restructuring of the economy, b) the problem of redistribution of social and political power, c) the rise of ethnonationalism, and d) the failure of nationality policies in socialist type societies (Sekelj 1993; Vujacik and Zaslavskey 1991; Seculic, Massey, and Hodson 1994). Economically, prior to World War II, the Kingdom of Yugoslavia was an agrarian society with over 80 percent of the population being rural. The state provided 10 percent of available jobs 20 percent of investments, and 25 percent of industrial production (Sekelj 1993:2). The very foundation of the crisis in Yugoslavia can be traced back to 1945-46 with the Sovietization of Yugoslav society (Sekelj 1993:2). Yugoslavia was the first European country to establish a dictatorship of the proletariat along the Soviet-Stalinist model. Furthermore, due to its anti-fascist struggle during the war and the achievements by the communist party of Yugoslavia, there was no overt Soviet intervention in the internal affairs of Yugoslavia, although it was attempted but failed. This, of course, was true with the other eastern European countries of Bulgaria, Hungary, Rumania, Czechoslovakia, where the Soviet doctrine gave Russia "the right" to intervene. Initially, the communist party elite of Yugoslavia established an equalitarian society and enjoyed broad popular support. However, during 1948-1950, the Yugoslav leadership, through its party-state organ, forced collectivization and nationalization of the economy. The

last remnants of bourgeois society were eliminated, and a Stalinist order was established in Yugoslavia (Sekelj 1993:3).

The structural crisis of Yugoslavia was above all a crisis of modernization and economic developments. The political regime failed to formulate a coherent economic strategy of development and modernization. Others have sought the roots of the crisis in the administrative regulation of the economy and the practice of informal politics. Kosta Mihailovic (1986) considered the state of Yugoslav economy in the 1980s as the direct outcome of political developments. Until 1965, politics were preoccupied with industrialization and rapid growth, and after 1965 the concern was mainly with distribution and consumption problems instead of democratization (Mihailovic 1986).

From a different level of analytic Meštrović *et al* (1993) seek to understand the independent role of culture and "social character" as independent explanatory factors in the dissolution of communism in the Balkans. Meštrović and his colleagues argue that is the cultural "habits of the heart" which characterize the Balkans, and not ethnonationalism and "rational choice" alone. By "habits of the heart" Meštrović and his colleagues mean the local habits, customs, traditions, values, including folk literature and history of the people in the region. Culture, Meštrović believes, help us explain both the demise of communism and present conflict in post-communist Balkan lands. Meštrović thinks that in order for the capitalists economic and democratic structures to succeed in the Balkans, one must understand the local culture of the people rather than Western ideologies, or in Meštrović words "the balancing of the indulgent, emotional, dependent femaleness of the Eastern European cultures with the maleness of Protestantism, with its traits of self-reliance, individual responsibility, and order" (Meštrović 1993). Meštrović has been criticized for omitting Islamic cultures, which also produce "virulent" ethnonationalism. In addition, Meštrović thesis of culture as an independent explanatory variable lacks systematic measurement and methodology. It fails to explain the relationship of individual behavior and the larger social cultural phenomena.

By the end of the 1980s, Yugoslavia was undergoing not only an economic crisis but also a deep political crisis. A number of Yugoslav sociologists of Marxist orientation, especially those associated with the Marxist journal *Praxis*, had prophesized Yugoslavia's imminent deep social and political crisis as early as 1971. By the end of the 1980s, most Yugoslav social scientists reduced the main source of structural crisis to a political one. Miric (1984:118), for example, was the first to openly insist that the crisis in Yugoslavia was more political than economic in nature. The Slovenian sociologist Pavel Gantar also believed that the major source of the crisis was political (Selkelj 1993:157)—and

that the party-dominated system was undergoing a legitimization crisis. Gantar's views were shared by other social scientists including former officials of the communist party. The views advocated by the sociologist Zagorka Golubovic best depict this political crisis, and her views were shared by those associated with the Marxist journal *Praxis*. She wrote:

> Yugoslav society is in crisis because it has never gone beyond the decisive line of social change to uproot the state structure of power and lead to the gradual establishment of self-management relations both at the base and the social structure as a whole. The half-way changes which had never actually challenged the domination of political power and the state as its instrument, resulted in the preservation of etatistic relations as the prevailing form of power, which thwarted and further socially marginalized self-management, with simultaneous deepening of social disintegration and disfunctioning of social system through quasi self-management relations (Sekelj 1993:157).

Others traced the causes of the present crisis to the unresolved contradictions of the political system, which failed to go beyond etatistic (state) tendencies and the party monopoly because of its oligarchic patronage politics. The communist party of Yugoslavia failed to adjust to modern industrial society and professionalization. In addition, there seemed to be an absence of political pluralism and civil political consciousness on the part of the citizens of Yugoslavia.

Yugoslavism and socialism gave way to both ethnonationalism and ethnic mobilization. The anti-Yugoslav demonstration of ethnic Albanians in Kosovo in 1968, 1980, 1981 and the waves of political ethnic agitation in Slovenia and Croatia, reflected more than casual grievances. These disturbances were the manifestation of deep-rooted historical ethnic cleavages which socialism and Yugoslavism, over the years, failed to heal. Indeed, the constitution of 1974 recognized neither the concept of Yugoslav citizenship nor the Yugoslav political community. The only recognized entities in Yugoslavia were the separate ethnic nationalities that occupied different territories. An ethnic Albanian living in Kosovo developed a distinct ethnic identity but had no psychological and historical ties with Yugoslavia as a federal state. Ethnic Albanians living in Yugoslavia were not integrated into the Yugoslav society.

In a sense, ethnic mobilization and primordial ethnonationalisms replaced collectivism in post communist Yugoslavia and in the former Soviet Union as well. Thus Serbs, Croats, Slovenians, and Bosnians became strangers and enemies in their own country. During the summer and fall of 1990 the Yugoslav

Social Science Institute reported that 61 percent of a representative sample of 11,737 persons all over Yugoslavia were against the creation of independent national states. However, by 1993 only 5 percent of the population identified themselves as Yugoslavians (Sekelj 1993:277). This fact alone revealed how shallow and volatile Yugoslavism and socialism as forms of collective identity were. The failed common identity and citizenship in Yugoslavia is also shown in Table One below in 1961, 1971, and 1981 statistical surveys in former Yugoslavia.

TABLE 1. PERCENTAGES OF ADULT POPULATION OF YUGOSLAVIA IDENTIFYING THEMSELVES AS YUGOSLAVS IN YUGOSLAVIA AND WITHIN EACH REPUBLIC AND PROVIDENCE: 1961, 1971 AND 1981

	Percentage Identifying as Yugoslav			Predominant Nationality in 1981
	1961	**1971**	**1981**	
Geographic Area				
All of Yugoslavia	1.7	1.3	5.4	36.3% Serbian
Republic and Provinces				
Croatia	.4	1.9	8.2	75.1% Croatian
Serbia	.2	1.4	8.2	85.4% Serbian
Bosnia/Herzegovina	8.4	1.2	7.9	39.5% Moslem
Kosovo	.5	.1	.1	77.4% Albanian
Skopje	.1	.2	.7	67.0% Skopjean
Montenegro	.3	2.1	5.3	68.3% Montenegro
Slovenia	.2	.4	1.4	90.5% Slovenian
Vojvodina	.2	2.4	8.2	54.3% Serbian

Sources: From Sekulic et al.; adapted and reprinted by permission from the *American Sociological Review* 1994 (Feb.):85

Despite the diverse ethnic composition of a federation, for a multinational liberal federal state to function, it must be based on the same liberal principles as nation states. These principles include economic integration with a unified market along the model of the European Union, protection of individual and collective human rights, common defense and foreign policy, and a balance of power between federalism and constituent federal units. The multinational state and its constitution should not be based on nationality, religion, race, or a combination of these, but on political and legal principles of citizenship. The absence of a representative democracy, and the resurgence of ethnocracies in its place, made civil war in the former Yugoslavia inevitable. The Yugoslav crisis had its structural failure in the communist nationality policy and the collapse of state communism in general. The linkage between territory, language, administration,

and ethnicity, and the overlap between regional, economic, and ethnic interests resulted in ethnic mobilization and ethnic subnationalism for political and economic advantages (Vujacic and Zaslavsky 1991:137). It must also be pointed out that the type of federalism found in the United States cannot be replicated in Europe (Kourvetaris and Kourvetaris 1996). Europe is made up of distinct national states and geographical entities with different histories, languages, and cultures.

Finally, interethnic conflicts and historical cleavages led to ethnic homogenization in the republics of Yugoslavia by means of ethnic cleansing and transfers. According to Vujacic and Zaslavsky (1991:138), Yugoslavia exemplified the inherent difficulties associated with the simultaneous pursuit of marketization and democratization of multinational Soviet-type societies. These two processes, in this type of society, are somewhat incompatible. While marketization exacerbates tensions between more and less developed regions, democratization leads the way to self-determination for nationalist parties pursuing separatist goals. In such a state of affairs the superimposition of economic, ethnic, and political conflicts favors the disintegration of the state. Linz (1978) described the potential threats to democracy under conditions of ethnic polarization. In practical terms Yugoslavia, as a unitary federal state, no longer exists. State socialism and authoritarian rule, whether politically from the left or the right, have not been viable alternatives to liberal democracy and market capitalism.

Are ethnonationalism and ethnic subnationalism always undesirable? One can argue that both negative and positive consequences seem to surface from such concepts. Kriesberg (1992:43) listed three negative aspects of ethnonationalism: parochialism, oppression, and violence. Parochialism refers to members of the same ethnic or racial group of collectivity who look primarily at the interests of its own collectivity. This inward or intra-ethnic concern quite often hampers large scale cooperation in society. Oppression is cruel treatment of one group by another, taking such forms as slavery, imperialism, institutional racism, discrimination, exploitation, and domination. Finally, the most brutal consequence of ethnonationalism is physical violence of one group against another, which includes genocide, pogroms, and massacres. Rwanda and Bosnia are two recent examples where oppression and violence occur jointly (not to mention Turkey and Nazi Germany which conducted the Armenian and Jewish genocides, respectively). The virtues of one group or in-group, and the perceived vices of the out-group, seem to justify for some the dehumanization, oppression, and violence of the out-group by the more dominant in-group (e.g., Whites vs. Blacks in South Africa prior to the dismantling of apartheid).

Although the negative aspects of ethnic identity are the most salient, positive aspects do exist. Ethnic identity gives the individual a sense of belonging to a larger entity. In a real sense, we are all members of various groups on the basis of attributes such as ethnicity, religion, race, gender, and class. These social differentiations in themselves are not necessarily problematic. Problems and conflicts arise when one collectivity dominates and oppresses another collectivity because of its differences also known as ethnocentrism—the notion that the values of one group are better than those of another group.

SUMMARY AND CONCLUSION

Initially, the concepts and perspectives of ethnonationalism and subnationalism were discussed. It was shown that ethnonationalism and subnationalism are movements of peoples to "exit," or pursue independent statehood or regional autonomy within a multiethnic and multi-religious state. This movement or revolt of peoples against the unitary nature of the state is reinforced by indigenous rights and contention of power. While ethnic diversity and multiculturalism are compatible with democracy and pluralism, ethnonationalism and subnationalism lead to ethnic mobilization and *ethnocracy* for political and economic advantages of one ethnic group against another.

Second, the determinants and causes of ethnonationalism and subnationalism were examined. It was noted that the nation state has been challenged from both supranationalism (above) and ethnonationalism (below). In this analysis only ethnonationalism was our main concern. Five major determinants of ethnonationalism and subnationalism were discussed: democratization, human rights, self-determination, modernization/development, and the emergence of regional powers. It was found that before ethnonationalist movements become transformed to secessionist movements, they must develop five major characteristics: an organized struggle, territorial self-government, primordial and secondary factors, self-determination, and international recognition.

Finally, ethnic subnationalism was examined in detail in former Yugoslavia. Both political and economic structural elements along with the failure of Yugoslav federalism were discussed. The end of the Cold War could not stop the centrifugal forces of subnationalism. Indeed, the end of communism brought back the re-emergence of nationalism. Thus, the disintegration of former Yugoslavia was inevitable. Along with the analysis of disintegration of former Yugoslavia, both the positive and negative aspects of ethnonationalism and subnationalism were briefly discussed. In short, it was concluded that as long as nationality, religion, race, and other such ascriptive characteristics, or a

combination of these, are the basis of a federal state—and if the state is based on unshared citizenship, political and economic democracy—there is always the danger that the unitary nature of the state may dissolve and lead to the re-emergence of nationalism.

ENDNOTES

[1] The literature on the topic of nationalism is extensive mostly written by historians and political scientists. With the exception of Max Weber, Mauss, Michels, and Znaniecki, the classical sociologists were not interested in the political sociology of nationalism. Indeed, nationalism was a fairly marginal concern during the classical period of the discipline. Only recently it has been a renewed interest in the systematic analysis of nationalism and its related concepts of ethnicity, nationality, ethnonationalism, subnationalism, ethnic mobilization, ethnocracy and the like. For more in depth analysis see Anderson (1991), Breuilly (1993a and 1993b), Connor (1994), Denitch (1994), Gellner (1983), Hobsbawm (1990), Kellas (1991), Smith (1986, 1991, 1992, 1996a, 1996b, 1998) Tilly (1975, 1990), and Schnee (2001).

[2] An ethnic subnationalist movement has recently emerged in FYROM especially around that region adjacent to Kosovo and Albania where Muslim minorities live. This armed subnationalist movement is supported by the neighboring Albania, Kosovo, and other Muslim minorities in the Balkans and the greater Middle East. The insurgents stated purpose is to create a greater nation of Albania by incorporating the Albanians of FYROM into Albania.

[3] The United Nations operates primarily as a peacekeeping broker between warring factions. Its mandate is to maintain the peace and not take sides. Different nations contribute soldiers to the UN-peacekeeping force. These soldiers are known as "peace soldiers" (see, for examples, Charles Moskos, 1976). United Nations troops are stationed on the borders between Israel and its Arab neighbors, on the frontiers dividing India and Pakistan, and between Iraq and Kuwait. United Nations observers are found inside Cyprus, along the dividing zone between Greek Cypriots and Turkish Cypriots, Lebanon, Angola, El Salvador, the western Sahara, in Yugoslavia (Bosnia-Herzegovina), Cambodia, Somalia, and Mozambique.

[4] Prior to the breakup of Yugoslavia, the Balkans, which means mountain included Greece, Yugoslavia, Rumania, Albania, Bulgaria, and only a small part of European Turkey. Now, of course, the Balkan region will encompass all the independent nation states of former Yugoslavia including Croatia, Slovenia, FYROM, and Yugoslavia (Serbia and Montenegro).

[5] Federation (federalism) is a mechanism of organizing constituent units into a state power. There is a central (federal) government and regional governments each independent within its own territory or sphere of influence. The United States has a federal system of government. The territory of a federal state is divided into units: canton, provinces, or republics. Former Yugoslavia and former Soviet republics were examples of federal states. There is a balance of power in this type of system between the central federal government and the regional (state) governments. Related to federalism is the idea of confederation. Confederation is simply two or more separate states within the same territory or country with a weak government.

[6] Greece objects vehemently to the use of the name Macedonia by former Yugoslav republic of Macedonia (FYROM). Historically there is only one Greek Macedonia, which is the northern province of Greece. According to the late British historian Woodhouse (1992), Tito invented the former Yugoslavian republic of Macedonia (prior to 1945 this region was known as Skopje) as a "bridgehead for the penetration and annexation of Greece's northern province, which is the real Macedonia with its capital of Salonika." After 1945, Tito openly talked of greater Macedonia that would include his small artificial province but also the major Greek province that he calls: Aegean Macedonia." Indeed, Tito supported the Greek communist movement during the bitter Greek Civil War of 1946-1949 (Woodhouse 1992). At present while Greece accepts the independence of the former republic of Yugoslavia, it still objects to the use of the name of Macedonia and the use of symbols such as the star of Verginia in its flag. In addition Greece objects to paragraph 49 in their constitution which has expansionist designs against northern province of Greece that bears historically the same name for 4,000 years of Greek history. For Greece, Macedonia is a region not a nationality. In later 1995, Greece lifted the embargo of the harbor of Thessaloniki against (FYROM) and recognized that country. In return FYROM agreed to change the star of Verginia from its flag and delete the irredentist sentences against Greece in its constitution.

[7] Albania and Greece have a long history of disputes over northern Eperus, which once was part of Greece and now is under Albania. There is a large

ethnic Greek population in Albania. Albania was the most Stalinist and backward country in Europe. For a number of years, Albania was allied with the Chinese communists after breaking off from Russia. Then it broke off from the Chinese and became the most isolated communist country in the Balkans. During World War II fascist Italy used Albania as a springboard to attack and invade Greece. Greece repelled and defeated fascist Italy and retook northern Eperus. Later however, the German Nazis assisted the Italians and together they invaded and occupied Greece for four years, from 1941-1944.

REFERENCES

Anderson, Benedict. 1991. *Imagined Communities*. New York: Verso Press.

Binder, David and Barbara Crossette. 1993. "As Ethnic Wars Multiply, U.S. Strives for a Policy." *New York Times*. (Feb. 7).

Breuilly, John. 1993a. *Nationalism and the State*. Chicago, IL: University of Chicago Press.

__________. 1993b. "Nationalism and the State." *Nationality, Patriotism, and Nationalism*, edited by Roger Michener. St. Paul, MN: Paragon House.

Connor, Walker. 1991. What is a Nation? *Ethnic and Racial Studies*. Vol. 13 (January): 92-103

__________. 1994. *Ethnonationalism: the Quest for Understanding*. Princeton NJ: Princeton University Press.

Djilas, Aleksa. 1991. *The Contested Country: Yugoslav Unity and Communist Revolution 1919-1953*. Cambridge, MA: Harvard University Press

Gurr, Ted Robert. 1970. *Why Men Rebel*. Princeton: Princeton University Press.

__________. 1993a. *Minorities at Risk: A Global View of Ethnopolitical Conflict*. Washington, DC: United States Institute of Peace Press.

__________. 1993b. "Why minorities Rebel: A Global Analysis of Communal Mobilization and Conflict Since 1945." *International Political Science R.* 14:161-201

__________. 1994. "Peoples Against States: Ethnopolitical Conflict and the Changing World System" in *International Studies Quarterly* Vol. 38: (347-377).

Hayden, Robert M. 1993. "The Partition of Bosnia and Herzegovina." RFE/RL Research Report. 2(22) May 28: 1-14.

Hirschman, Albert O. 1970. *Exit, Voice, and Loyalty*. Cambridge: Harvard University Press.

Horowitz, Donald. 1985. *Ethnic Groups in Conflict*. Berkeley: University of California Press.

Ignatief, Michael. 1993. *Blood and Belonging*. New York: Farvar, Straus and Giroux.

Jalali, Rita and Seymour M. Lipset. 1992-93. "Racial and Ethnic Conflicts: A Global Perspective." *Political Science Quarterly*. Vol. 107 No. 4:588-606

Kourvetaris, Andrew and George A. Kourvetaris. 1996. "Attitudes Toward European Integration: The Cultural and Ethnic Dimensions" in *The Impact of European Integration*. Edited by George A. Kourvetaris and Andreas Moschonas. Westport: CT Praeger

Kriesberg, Louis. 1992. *International Conflict Resolution*. New Haven Yale University Press.

Linz, Juan J. 1978. *The Breakdown of Democratic Regimes: Crisis, Breakdown, and Reequilibration*. Baltimore: Johns Hopkins University.

McKay, James. 1982. "An Exploratory Synthesis of Primordial and Mobilization Approaches of Ethnic Phenomena." *Ethnic and Racial Studies* Vol. 5, No. 4 (October): 395-420

Meštrović, Stjepan G. with Slaven Letica and Miroslav Goreta. 1992. *Habits of the Balkan Heart: Social Character and the Fall Of Communism*. College Station, TX: Texas A and M University Press.

Mihailovic, Kosta. 1986. *Regional Development: Experiences and Prospects in Europe*. United Nations Research Institute for Social Development, Geneva. The Hague: Mouton

Mirac, Jovan. 1984. *Sistem i kriza: Prilog kritickoj analizi i politickog sistema Jogoslavije. Zagreb: Cekade.*

Moskos, Charles C., Jr. 1976. *Peace Soldiers: The Sociology of a United Nations Military Force*. Chicago: University of Chicago Press.

Nagel, Joane. 1993. "Ethnic Nationalism's: politics, Ideology, and the World Or Order." *International Journal of Comparative Sociology*. Vol. 34, Nos. 1-2:103-12

Olzak, Susan. 1983. "Contemporary Ethnic Mobilization." *Annual Review of Sociology* Vol. 9 (355-74).

Petcovic, Ruza. 1986. Migracije u Jugoslaviji. Beograd: 11CSSO.

Premdas, Ralph R., S.W.R. de A Samarasinghe and Alan B. Anderson. 1990. *Secessionist Movements in Comparative Perspective* New York: St Martin's Press.

Ramet, Pedro. 1985. "Contradiction and Reform in Yugoslav Communism: A Conclusion." In Pedro Romet, ed. Yugoslavia in the 1980s.

__________. 1992. *Nationalism and Federalism in Yugoslavia 1962-1992.* Bloomington: University of Indiana Press

Roudometof, Victor. 1996. "The Consolidation of National Minorities in Southeastern Europe" in *Journal of Political and Military Sociology*, Vol. 24, No. 2 (Winter 1996): 187-207.

Rusinow, Dennison. 1968. The Macedonian Question Never Dies. New York: American University Field Staff.

Samarasinghe, S.W.R D.A. 1990. Introduction. *Secessionist Movements in Comparative Perspective*, ed. Ralph R. Premdas S.W.R. de A. Samarasinghe and Alan B. Anderson. New York: St. Martins

Sekelj, Laslo. 1993. *Yugoslavia: The Process of Disintegration* translated from The Serbo-Croat by Vera Vukelic, Social Science monographs, Boulder, CO, Atlantic Research and Publications, Highland Lakes, N.J. Distributed by Columbia University Press, New York.

Sekulic, Dusko, Garth Massey, and Randy Hodson. 1994. "Who Were the Yugoslavs? Failed Sources of a Common Identity in the Former Yugoslavia." *Amer. Soc. Rev.* Vol 59, No 1 (February) 83-97.

_________. 1977. "O izviorima moci u organizaciji." *Julturni radnik* 30(5): 91-107.

Smith, Anthony D. 1986. *The Ethnic Origins of Nations*. New York: Basil Blackwell.

_________. 1991. *National Identity*. Reno, NV: University of Nevada Press.

_________. 1992. "National Identity and the Idea of European Unity." *International Affairs 68 (1): 55-76.*

_________. 1996a. "Opening Statement: Nations and Their Pasts." *Nations and Nationalism* 2 (3): 358-365.

_________. 1996b. "Memory and Modernity: Reflections on Ernest Gellner's Theory of Nationalism." *Nations and Nationalism* 2 (3): 371-388.

_________. 1998. *Nationalism and Modernism*. New York: Routledge.

Stalin, Joseph. 1942. *Marxism and the National Question*. New York: International Publishers.

Stavrianos, Lefteris S. 1958. *The Balkans since 1453*. New York: Harper and Row.

Tilly, Charles. 1978. *From Mobilization to Revolution*. Reading: Addison-Wesley.

Tsoukalis, Loukas. 1981. *The European Community and its Mediterranean Enlargement*. London: George Allen and Unwin.

_________. 1983. *The European Community: Past, Present and Future*. Oxford: Basil Blackwell

Vujacic, Veljko and Victor Zaslavsky. 1991. "The Causes of Disintegration in the USSR and Yugoslavia" in *Telos*: *A Quarterly Journal of Critical Thought*. No. 88.

Weber, Max. 1948. *From Max Weber: Essays in Sociology*. New York: Routledge & Kegan Paul. Translated and edited by H. H. Gerth and C. Wright Mills.

Woodhouse, C. M. 1992. "Recognizing Macedonia Defies History." *The Christian Science Monitor*. Vol. 84, No. 235 (Oct. 28).

CHAPTER 2
NATIONAL MINORITIES, NATION-STATES, AND EXTERNAL NATIONAL HOMELANDS IN SOUTHEASTERN EUROPE*

Victor Roudometof
Miami University

The "ethnic revival" of the 1990s has provided the background for the disintegration of Yugoslavia and led to the bloodshed in Croatia, Bosnia-Herzegovina, and Kosovo. The NATO forces intervened militarily twice in the region and their involvement led to a large NATO military presence in Bosnia, Kosovo, and the Republic of Macedonia. Part of the rationale for the deployment of NATO forces was the threat of ethnic conflict in the region. Practically all observers agree that ethnonational disputes are the main cause for the proliferation of violence in the Balkans (see, for example, Shoup 1990; Larrabee 1994). My discussion in this essay inquires into the conditions leading to the consolidation of national minorities in Southeastern Europe and the irredentist or secessionist claims that often accompany them.

For the purposes of this discussion, a *minority group* is defined as a group using cultural markers (such as language or religion) to distinguish itself from majority outsiders (Barth 1969). In contrast, a *national minority* establishes itself as such through an identification of its members with cultural symbols that belong to an "imagined community" living outside the boundaries of the particular nation-state the minority inhabits. Political mobilization is a requirement for the transformation of a minority group into a national minority. The characterization of a minority group as a national minority offers the possibility of outside intervention regarding this group's rights. In the Balkan context and for reasons that will be discussed later in this essay, such a proclamation is viewed as an immediate threat to state sovereignty. Furthermore, if a minority group views itself as a national minority it is inclined to ask for international recognition of its rights as well as an open acknowledgement of its cultural difference. It thus constrains attempts at ethnic homogenization especially if the nation-state builds its own public persona as a "cultural" rather than "political" nation. In the following, I discuss (a) the long term structural factors that helped formulate the issue of national minorities in the Balkan

---

* This essay is a heavily revised and updated version of the author's article, "The Consolidation of National Minorities in Southeastern Europe," *Journal of Political and Military Sociology* 1996 [24] 2, pp. 187-209.

context, and (b) the politicization of minority membership as expressed during the late 1980s and 1990s.

THE FORMATION OF NATIONAL MINORITIES: STRUCTURAL FACTORS

The Balkan system of states that emerged out of the Balkan wars of 1912-13 and the subsequent World War I (1914-1918) formed a *political field* with the issue of national minorities as one of the important factors shaping their interstate and intrastate relationship. As Brubaker (1996) argues, this political field consists of three mutually linked entities: the national minorities, the nation-states in which these minorities inhabit, and the external national homelands of these minorities. The interactive processes set in motion by this triadic relationship lead to the vicious circle of mutual animosity. One only needs to recall the motto that proliferated during the disintegration of Yugoslavia in the 1990s: "Why should *I* be a minority in your state if *you* can be a minority in my state?" In the period after World War I but also for most of the twentieth century, no Balkan nation-state was able to incorporate all of its potential nationals into its territory. Minority groups remained scattered in Greece, Bulgaria, Albania, Romania, and the kingdom of Serbs, Slovenes, and Croats. Indeed, the emergence of the so-called "first Yugoslavia" (1917) was an explicit but ultimately futile attempt to manage the complicated cluster of issues surrounding the coexistence of Serbs, Croats, Slovenes, and a host of other smaller South Slavic groups within the boundaries of a single state (Djilas 1991; Banac 1984; Lampe 1996).

Within this system of states, the completion of nation building required a considerable degree of centralization and homogenization. For the Balkan lands, however, ethnic heterogeneity has been the rule rather than the exception. Although, following World War I, a number of population exchanges among Bulgaria, Greece, and Turkey helped the ethnic homogenization of these states; they failed to totally solve the issue. Additionally, the concept of the nation-state has been historically linked with the ethnic homogenization of a particular population (McNeill 1985; Weber 1976). Subsequently, during the inter-war period, the minority groups in the Balkan nation-states became the subjects of state-sponsored policies of cultural homogenization (for a review of individual cases, see Roudometof 2002). In turn, such policies further alienated the minorities from their nation-states, helping the gradual transformation of the minority groups into national minorities. Although this interpretation explains the historical trends in most Balkan states, it is important to take notice of the

rationale behind such policies of cultural homogenization. These policies were an expression of the conceptualization of the nation-state as a monolithic, culturally integrated community, whereby membership to the nation is defined in terms of cultural membership to an ethnic community (Roudometof 1999). It is a foregone conclusion that this conceptualization of the nation-state is far from universal. On the contrary, in countries like the US or even France citizenship has provided the means for the successful incorporation of generations of new immigrants (Lipset 1963; Brubaker 1992). But in Eastern and Southeastern Europe, the absence of a democratic tradition of citizenship rights has been compounded by a strong emphasis on ethnic or collectivist nationalism (Seton-Watson 1977; Smith 1986; Greenfeld 1991). Under these conditions, nation-building most often took the form of emphasizing *nationhood*—that is, membership to a nation in terms of religious, linguistic, or ethnic ties—as the most important component of the national idea (for further discussion, see Roudometof 2001).

In this respect, the "ethnic" character of the nation-state provides the basic rationale for policies of cultural homogenization. The application of these policies into the tapestry of minority groups in the Balkans provides a long term structural predisposition on the part of the minorities to mistrust state authorities. All Balkan states have historically pursued their nation-building process on the basis of collectivist "ethnic" nationalism.[1] Throughout the nineteenth century, they systematically attempted to enlarge their territory by incorporating as many of their proclaimed "nationals" as possible. Their historical traditions, public institutions, national histories, and literatures all emphasize nationhood rather than citizenship as the single most important component of the nation-state (for details, see Roudometof 1999; 2001, especially Chapters 4 & 5).

Under these conditions, a minority group is increasingly put into a position in which its "special status"—in terms of institutional separation from the majority in the fields of education, religion, and language—is viewed as representing a threat to the very stability of state boundaries. The situation can be formulated in terms of Hirschman's (1970) famous choice between exit and voice. The minority group can attempt to "exit" the state—that is, secede—or it might attempt to cooperate within the state structure—that is, to claim a "voice" within the political system of the nation-state. Hirschman has pointed out the importance of loyalty as a determinant between exit and voice. If the minority group is loyal to the state, it tends to opt for participation whereas if loyalty is low it might attempt to exit the state through extended autonomy or secession. Loyalty, however, is established with great difficulty when common bonds of solidarity between minority and majority are absent. When ethnic nationalism

prevails, the acknowledgment of difference represents hubris to the essential unity of the nation.

Table 1 below presents an account of the minority groups in Southeastern Europe during the last decade of the twentieth century.

TABLE 1. MINORITY GROUPS IN THE BALKANS CA. 1990-2000

MINORITY GROUP	NATION-STATE	% OF POPULATION
Greeks [a]	Albania	8-12
Turks	Bulgaria	8.5
Gypsies [b]	Bulgaria	6.0
Macedonians [c]	Bulgaria	2.75
Muslim Pomaks [d]	Bulgaria	5.0
Serbs [e]	Croatia	11.6
Serbs	Bosnia	32
Croats	Bosnia	18.4
Albanians	Republic of Macedonia	20
Serbs	Republic of Macedonia	2.2
Gypsies	Republic of Macedonia	2.4
Albanians [f]	Serbia	17.2
"Muslims" [g]	Republic of Macedonia	4.8
"Yugoslavs" [h]	Serbia	3.4
East-Orthodox Albanians	Albania	8-12
Roman-Catholic Albanians	Albania	10
Albanians	Montenegro	6.5
Turks/Pomaks [i]	Greece	1-2
Hungarians [j]	Serbia (Vojvodina)	6.1
Hungarians	Romania	8-10

[a] The total number of Greek-Orthodox Albanians, Greeks, and Vlachs is close to 20% of the population. Greeks routinely consider the approximately 200,000 Vlachs part of the minority whereas Albanian sources consider them a separate group. Each group (i.e. Orthodox Albanians and Greeks) is estimated between 8-12% but given the significance of religion as a cultural marker and the inadequate knowledge of Greek by many of the ethnic Greeks, it is difficult to accurately differentiate the two groups. For studies of the electoral behavior of the minority and attempts to estimate its numerical strength, see Berholli et. al. (1994: 427-34) and Dodos (1994: 115-44).

[b] According to data presented by the Romani leaders the Gypsies number between 800,000 and 1,000,000 (Simonov 1990:13). If this estimate is correct, then Poulton's (1991:116) number of 576,926 should be revised.

[c] This figure was reported in the *World Directory of Minorities* (1990). In all likelihood, it overestimates the Macedonians. The population in the Pirin region of Macedonia (Bulgaria) might consider themselves both Macedonians and Bulgarians, while some of them consider the two identities mutually exclusive. For a quantitative and qualitative research on the issue of ethnicity in the region, see Boneva, Nikolov, and Roudometof (2000).

[d] The World Directory of Minorities (1990) estimates 150,000 Pomaks (1.7% of the population) and 900,000 Turks (10% of the population). The Pomaks are Muslim Slavs adhering to Islam in terms of religion, but they are Slav speaking. Poulton (1991:111) reports a figure of 268,971 Pomaks as given by local authorities at the end of 1990. Because of the importance of religion as a cultural marker, it is quite likely that at least some of them might want to consider themselves "Turks."

[e] The Serb population of Croatia lived in Eastern Slavonia and the Khin region (the so-called Serb Republic of the Krajina). The Republic included less than 250,000 inhabitants in the early 1990s, and soon its population further diminished because of immigration into Serbia. While the Serbs of Krajina held on to their territory in the first half of the 1990s, they succumbed to the Croatian Army's Operation Flash and Operation Storm in May and August of 1995. Subsequently, this population was ethnically cleansed from their territory and resettled in Vojvodina, Serbia proper, and Kosovo.

[f] This percentage refers to the Albanian population of Kosovo as part of the Republic of Serbia. Of course, Kosovo was autonomous prior to the late 1980s, and the Albanian population made up close to 90% of the total population of the province. It was the attempt by the Milosevic regime to ethnically cleanse Kosovo of its Albanian majority that prompted the NATO strike against the rump Yugoslavia in the spring of 1999. Subsequently, the majority of the Albanians returned to the region under the protection of the NATO troops. However, the result was a reverse ethnic cleansing whereby the Serb minority had to flee the region or fortify themselves in ethnic enclaves. In most cases, the NATO troops have to intervene in order to maintain peace and security in the region.

[g] It is unclear how many of the "Muslims" are Turks. According to the 1981 census, there were 86,691 Turks constituting 4% of the population. But these numbers have fluctuated during the last 20 years (in 1953, 203,938 were recorded as "Turks"). More recently, it appears that a number of the people previously declared as "Turks" have switched their identification to "Roma" (Gypsies) or "Albanian" (Petrovic 1992; also, Poulton 1991: 91-93).

[h] The category of "Yugoslavs" was created in the 1961 census. The number of people declaring themselves as "Yugoslavs" increased during the last two decades in an uneven pace with significant percentages in Bosnia-Herzegovina, Serbia, and Vojvodina, but small percentages in Slovenia, Kosovo, and Macedonia (Poulton 1991:98; see also Gordy 1999).

[i] According to the Greek government there are only Muslim Greeks (but no Turks). The World Directory of Minorities (1990) gives the estimate of 1-2%. It is more likely that the 120,000 people estimated to belong to this category constitute approximately 1.3% of the Greek population recorded officially as "Muslim" (HFDFP's Review, 1992).

[j] According to the statistics compiled by Lydanyi (2002), this number has remained stable (around 400,000) for most of the twentieth century. In 1981, there were 385,000 and by 1991 they were 339,000. The Serb population of Vojvodina increased almost three-fold from 382,000 in 1910 to over a million in 1961. During the later 1990s, Serb authorities began the resettlement of Serb refugees into the region, thereby altering the population ratios in cities that were previously mixed or dominated by the Hungarian minority.

Sources: HFDFP's *Southeastern European Yearbook* (1992), *The Review of Defense and Foreign Policy* (1992; 1999), *World Directory of Minorities* (1990), Poulton (1991), Lydanyi (2002), Allcock et. al. (1998), and Petrovic (1992).

Note: A "minority group" is listed in this table insofar it constitutes 2% of the population in a state. Smaller groups do exist within the Balkans, but for current purposes they are ignored. Whenever statistical information was contradictory (for example, Greeks in Albania or Turks and Pomaks in Greece), there was an attempt to reconcile different estimates by encompassing the whole range of these estimates.

As the reader will observe, reliable counts of the minorities are extremely difficult to obtain because of the local authorities' desire to minimize the official appearance of ethnic fragmentation, but also because of the interplay between ethnicity and religion. That is, the dividing lines between Pomaks and Turks (or between Orthodox Albanians and ethnic Greeks or between Gypsies and Turks) are hazy. In these cases religion establishes a more important link than language, a feature that testifies to the extent that modern Balkan nations trace their origins to the disintegration of the millet system of the Ottoman empire (cf. Roudometof 2001). Hence, the gradual consolidation of national minorities operates through the identification of some of these "intermediate" groups within one or another national minority.

Moreover, geography plays an important role: if the minority group is not in close proximity with a rival nation-state that can be realistically perceived as an alternative homeland, it is more likely that it will be co-opted within the existing nation-states. A number of minority groups in the Balkans have followed such a fate with the Vlachs being the most prominent example of successful strategies of assimilation (for details, see Poulton et. al. 1989:29-36; Poulton 1991:95-96, 189-92; Minority Rights Group 1990: 130-31). The Vlachs

are mainly pastoral nomads dispersed among the states of Yugoslavia, Bulgaria, Greece, Albania, and Romania. Since they are Orthodox Christians, they have mostly become part of the predominantly Eastern Orthodox nation-states in which they live.[2]

In contrast, minority groups that can look to a highly visible external national homeland (a land perceived as the minority's "natural" fatherland) in close proximity to their own territory are the ones most likely to be transformed into national minorities. This tendency is most often cultivated via school textbooks, religion, language, and political-cultural mobilization. Economic reasons can intensify or inhibit this process as well. Close geographical proximity to an external national homeland makes "exit" a more tenable choice since it "only" requires the alteration of state boundaries.

Of the minority groups located to close proximity to a potential external national homeland, only the Serbs and Croats in Bosnia-Herzegovina were dispersed. In 1991, they constituted 31.4% and 17.3% of the republic's population respectively. Serbs constituted the absolute majority in parts of Eastern Bosnia-Herzegovina and the majority or relative majority in parts of Western Bosnia. The Croats and Muslims were dispersed throughout the region, with more Croats living close to the coastline and more Muslims living in the interior of the country. In other regions, the pattern of concentration is more pronounced. The Turks of Bulgaria live in the Kardzhali region in southeastern Bulgaria and the Razgrad-Shumen area in northeastern Bulgaria, whereas the Pomaks inhabit the Rhodope Mountain area of southeastern Bulgaria and the Lovech-Tetever region in central Bulgaria. Most Albanians in the former Yugoslavia were concentrated in Kosovo, while the Albanians in Macedonia live in the western part of the republic, in close proximity to the Albanian state. Also, the Greeks of Southern Albania or Northern Epirus live close to the Greek-Albanian border.[3]

Finally, the consolidation of national minorities in the region has been partially influenced by the groups' demographic rates. Over the post-World War II period, the Albanians' high birth rate resulted in their increase from 67.25% of Kosovo's population at the 1961 census to 77.4% at 1981 and almost 90% at 1991 (Cviic 1991: 67). A high birth rate also helped Albanians in the Republic of Macedonia to increase their numbers from 19.8% of the population in 1981 to 21.0% in 1991. According to unofficial estimates this percentage is even higher, and by the late 1990s, it must be at least 25% of the population. In Bosnia-Herzegovina, the Muslim population also increased from 39.5% in 1981 to 43.7% in 1991 (Petrovic 1992: 3-24). According to the 1992 census in Bulgaria, the population decreased by 5.3% compared to the 1985 census—but the minorities' birth rates clearly surpassed the birth rates of ethnic Bulgarians

(Nikolaev 1992; Poulton et. al. 1989: 9-10). The high birth rates are not necessarily beneficial for the minority groups. Often, local nationalists portray the minorities as engaged in a demographic warfare whereby a group uses a high birth rate to ensure the ultimate domination of a particular region.

Taking into consideration the factors mentioned in the discussion thus far, Table 2 presents an account of the groups most closely resembling national minorities, including the nation-state in which they are located and their potential external national homelands.[4]

TABLE 2. POTENTIAL NATIONAL MINORITIES IN THE BALKANS *

NATIONAL MINORITY	NATION-STATE	EXTERNAL HOMELAND
Greeks	Albania	Greece
Turks	Bulgaria	Turkey
Albanians	Republic of Macedonia	Albania
Albanians	Serbia (Kosovo)	Albania
Serbs	Croatia	Serbia
Serbs	Bosnia	Serbia
Croats	Bosnia	Croatia

Source: Compiled from Table 1.

* In this essay, attention is focused on the minority groups in the Southern Balkans (Albania, Macedonia, and Bulgaria). Hungarian minorities within Yugoslavia have been excluded from this discussion. For an analysis of the Hungarian minorities' status, see Lydanyi (2002).

The discussion thus far has focused on the structural factors acting to intensify the "minority question" in the Balkans. The close proximity between a group's location and a potential external homeland, demographic trends, and the importance of nationhood as a cultural barrier with respect to the incorporation of minorities within the states' political body are all factors that tend to promote "exit" rather than "voice" in the Balkan context. All of these are long term structural factors leading to the consolidation of the groups listed in Table 2 as potential national minorities. Turning these groups into actual national minorities involves attributing political significance to their cultural markers, a feature that is generally absent when cultural differences are used as categories of classification rather than as categories of subjective identification (Rothschild

1981). In the Balkans, the end of Cold War offered the opportunity of politicizing ethnic differences.[5] During this mobilization, minority groups became increasingly identified with external national homelands, thus providing the context for the outbreak of ethnic conflict in the peninsula. Yugoslavia provides the most widely known example of this regional trend.

THE MINORITY QUESTION AND THE COLLAPSE OF YUGOSLAVIA

To understand the developments in Yugoslav politics during the 1980s, one has to take into account the fact that nationalist tensions were present during the Titoist era as well. The communist regime was successful in employing the party apparatus as a means to prevent nationalist tensions among the different republics. Moreover, the establishment of a federal structure offered at least a minimal recognition for the independent political entities representing the major "nations" of the federal Yugoslavia. Thus, although Croatia, Slovenia, Serbia, Macedonia, and Bosnia-Herzegovina were not sovereign states, the federal structure provided at least a space where concerns over "autonomy"—conceived mainly as independence from Serb domination—could be articulated. Therefore, the federal structure was an important vehicle for the defusion of nationalist aspirations (Ramet 1992).

During the 1960s, however, these issues became threatening once again. Under the leadership of Rankovic, Serbianization policies were put in place in Kosovo, Bosnia-Herzegovina, and Vojvodina. This caused the reaction of the other national groups leading to a series of frictions during the 1966-1972 period (Ramet 1992; Rusinow 1977; Cohen 1993: Ch. 1). Largely in response to this situation, the 1974 Constitution attempted to fracture even more the federal structure by significantly expanding the autonomy of the provinces of Vojvodina and Kosovo. The autonomy of the provinces was first established in 1947, but the 1974 constitutional expansion of this autonomy was seen as a "carving" of the Serb territory and served as the first basis for future grievances (Ramet 1992:73-78; Dragnich 1989). Additionally, the new constitution recognized the Muslims as one of the sovereign nations in Bosnia providing the legal basis for the development of national identification on the basis of religious difference. This was to a considerable extent a movement to accommodate the rising Muslim nationalism during the 1969-71 period. In light of the fact that Serbs and Croats had advanced nationalist theories claiming the Muslim inhabitants as "their own," the assertion of a new national group offered—at least for some time—the possibility for a "consociational" model of democracy to advance in Bosnia (Rusinow 1982).

Although the peripheral nationalism expressed in the constitution reforms undertaken by Slovenia, Croatia, Macedonia, and Bosnia-Herzegovina are responsible for aggravating the nationalist tensions in the political scene of Yugoslavia (see Hayden 1992b: 654-73), the role of Serb nationalists should also be taken into account. During 1986, the Serb resentment against the 1974 restructuring of the federal structure was openly voiced in the Draft Memorandum of the Serbian Academy of Sciences as well as in a petition signed by 200 prominent Belgrade intellectuals. Both documents argued against the partition of Serbia proper into three parts under the 1974 constitution; and in favor of putting an end to the Serb "genocide" carried out in Kosovo by Albanian "separatists" (Cviic 1991: 65; Poulton 1991: 19). The Serb Orthodox Church allied itself with those opposing the Serb "genocide" in Kosovo, thus adding a religious element to the conflict (Kaplan 1993).

The post-1974 recognition of Kosovo's autonomous status led to a proliferation of Albanian nationalist activity that took the form of organizations, literature, etc. spreading over its territory. In 1981, Albanian nationalism expressed itself in a series of demonstrations, arson, and terrorist activities. The University of Pristine—with a population of approximately 37,000 students—served as the principle site for the nationalist activity. Through the blatant use of military force, the Yugoslav armed forces crashed the rebellion. By no means, however, did this oppression put an end to nationalist activity. Throughout the 1980s, a number of underground organizations were uncovered, and during the 1981-87 period, the local authorities brought criminal charges against 5,200 Kosovar Albanians (Ramet 1992:195-98).

Up until the mid-1980s, Yugoslavia appeared to be stable, because the threat to centralization was coming from "peripheral" republics and not from the center (Serbia). In fact, the possibility of fragmentation remained rather remote given the control of the communist party over the federal apparatus and its commitment to the federal idea. This was to change with the appearance of the new leader of Serb communists Slobodan Milosevic in the political scene. But Milosevic did not operate in a vacuum. Through the 1970s and 1980s economic conditions worsened causing a widening of the economic gap between the country's rich north provinces and the south (Rusinow 1988; Woodward 1995). Concomitant with it was the legitimization crisis of the communist regime. Milosevic offered a way out to the communist elites by endorsing the Serb orthodox Church and becoming the leader of Serb nationalism (Ramet 1992:225-30; Glenny 1992).

Milosevic exploited the Albanian "threat" in order to build popular support for the communist party. In the spring of 1987 Milosevic visited Kosovo in order to take part in the celebration of the battle of 1389, the most important

national holiday of Serbia. In a 1389 battle that took place in Kosovo, the Turks defeated the Serb forces, leading to Serbia's occupation by the Ottomans for the following 400 years. Despite the negative outcome, the Kosovo battle has become a mark of Serb national identity, and Milosevic played out the national themes with reference to the contemporary situation. He promised Kosovo Serbs that "nobody would ever beat them again." Within a few months, he used their alleged suffering to attack the previous leadership in Serbia and carried a purge throughout Serbia resulting in the consolidation of his position. In October 1987, more federal police units were dispatched in Kosovo. Milosevic staged a number of protests and demonstrations that led to the fall of the local governments in Vojvodina and Montenegro (in 1988 and 1989) bringing the control of these regions under the auspices of his followers.

In Kosovo, a general strike in February 1989 led to military oppression that crushed the Albanian protests within a week claiming a reported number of 24 deaths. In March 1989, 44 ethnic Albanians were arrested and charged with inciting rebellion. On March 23, 1989, Kosovo's Assembly ringed by Yugoslav army tanks gave its consent to the constitutional changes demanded by Belgrade (Cviic 1991:67-8). On March 28, 1989, Serbia's Assembly adopted them giving the Serb authorities in Belgrade control over Kosovo's police, courts, and territorial defense (a similar strategy was followed in Vojvodina as well). All of the above events raised Milosevic's popularity to unprecedented heights and resulted in his reelection as President of Serbia in December 1990. Milosevic appeared to be the protector of all Serbs within Yugoslavia.[6]

Moreover, the Kosovo affair—and to a lesser extent the similar developments in Montenegro and Vojvodina—acted as warnings for Croatia and Slovenia that the Serb program of "centralized democratization" meant the return of Serb supremacy. As pluralism within and outside the communist party lines came to the forefront of politics during the late 1980s, politicians in both countries used the national question as a means for attracting the votes of the population. Additionally, the desire of the federal government to revise the federal constitution in an effort to produce a different arrangement among the republics provided them with the context in which to assert their desire to exit the federation.

The major event that led to the official collapse of the second Yugoslavia was the Slovenian crisis of 1989 (Hayden 1992a; Cohen 1993:177-81; Andrejevich 1990a:23-26; Ramet 1992:221). Slovenia's desire to break its ties with the federation was greatly facilitated by the increasingly centralized and nationalist policies of the Serb president Slobodan Milosevic. The Slovenes opted for the option of a loose confederation whereas the Serbs opted for a centralized federation. The difference between the two sides and the Slovenian

insistence on rejecting a compromise led to the crisis of 1989-90. There are no significant national minorities within the Slovenian territory but this affair was of great strategic importance, because it provided a frame of reference for the Croatian attempt to break ties with the Yugoslav federation. The Slovenian route for establishing independence was to amend the republic's constitution in a way inconsistent with the guidelines of the federal structure. The crisis was intensified when, following the elections of 1990, the victorious nationalist coalition of five parties (DEMOS) pursued a strategy of debating the options of a confederation or a complete succession. The Serb government reacted by cutting its commercial ties with the republic, an action that forced the option of "exit" for the Slovenes and hurt the remaining of Yugoslavs more than the Slovenes (Andrejevich 1990b). On July 2, 1990, Slovenia declared its "sovereignty," setting the stage for similar developments in Croatia, Bosnia-Herzegovina, and Macedonia.

Following the Slovenian declaration, Croatia was fast to follow the same route. During the first multi-party elections in April/May 1990, the right wing and nationalist party of Franjo Tudjman emerged as the winner. The party promised to break its ties with the old arrangement, but the way that this would take place remained open. Tudjman's victory was seen as a return to World War II Croatian nationalism raising fears among the Croatian Serbs regarding their future in the new state. The new regime attempted to balance the non-proportional character of most civil service positions through the hiring of Croats and the firing of Serbs, and this intensified the feeling of persecution among Croatian Serbs. Additionally, the Croatian constitution was amended in order to provide for the adoption of the traditional Croatian symbols—a coat of arms, flag, and national anthem—as the official insignia of the republic. The Latin script was also adapted as the official alphabet (Cohen 1993:131). The new ethnic symbolisms emphasized the explicit ethnic character of the proposed new state. The adoption of the old (World War II) nationalist symbols by the new regime acted as a reminder to a large portion of the Serb minority of the horrible events that occurred during the establishment of the Croat fascist regime. During the Ustasa regime, tens of thousands of Serbs were killed in concentration camps (although, to this day, historians keep debating the exact numbers). Fear acted as a stimulus leading to the mobilization of the local Serb community around a nationalist program.

On August 1, 1990, Croatian Serbs in the Kihn area east of the Adriatic staged an armed rebellion, conducted their own referendum on the issue of autonomy, and proclaimed themselves an autonomous region (the so-called Krajina republic). Supported openly by the Belgrade regime, the Croatian Serbs proclaimed themselves to be "the Serbian region of Krajina in Croatia" on

January 4, 1991, and a part of Serbia in March 1991 (Poulton 1991:27; Cviic 1991: 73-74; Glenny 1992: Ch. 1). During the second half of 1990, a stalemate was reached with the two northern republics and Serbia (with Motenengro) between peace and war. Finally, on June 25, 1991, the two republics seceded, setting the stage for the Serbo-Croatian Civil War. Although the Croatian Serbs were able to maintain their territorial units for a considerable period of time, they were eventually overcome when in 1995 the Croatian forces rushed into their enclaves. The ultimate outcome of their attempt at secession was that they became refugees, resettling into Vojvodina, Kosovo, and Serbia proper (for further discussion on the Serb minority in the 1990s, see Zakosek 2000).

In Bosnia-Herzegovina, the democratization process intensified the ethnic rivalries among Croats, Bosnian Muslims, and Serbs. When the crisis of 1989-90 occurred the parties participating in the elections in Bosnia were organized mainly according to ethnic lines. The few attempts to create parties that would transcend the ethnic factor failed due to inadequate popular support, and the Serb and Croat ethnic parties pursued a strategy aiming toward the eventual partition of the republic (Hayden 1993). Despite rising ethnic tensions, Bosnia remained calm until October 1991, when the Croats and Muslims within the government coalition declared their intention to secede and correspondingly, to hold a referendum on the issue. Both Serbs and Croats worked against the establishment of a strong central authority, but the Croats viewed an independent republic as a means to their goal of secession (or extended autonomy) while the Serbs viewed an independent republic as a direct threat to their status. The Bosnian Serbs' anxiety over their future heightened in February 1992 when the plans for the referendum were announced and the Muslim-Croatian leadership adopted the "one man, one vote" solution. Fear of exclusion from the political process pushed the Serbs to boycott the referendum. Bosnian Serb officials working in cooperation with the Yugoslav Army started preparations for hostilities. On March 1, 1992, when gunmen fired on members of a Serb wedding party at Sarajevo, the signal was given: within hours, barricades were erected, and soon the fighting spread to the rest of the republic (Cohen 1993: 237). The war persisted up until the 1995 Dayton Accord, which set out to maintain the status quo while simultaneously proclaiming the principle of territorial sovereignty of Bosnia-Herzegovina. In many respects, the net result has been legal fiction: Bosnia is not unified, but rather a patchwork of independent and semi-independent units and mini-fiefdoms.

The former Yugoslav Republic of Macedonia proclaimed its independence from Yugoslavia on September 17, 1991. Its disassociation from the Yugoslav federation was peaceful, yet the republic's claim to be the official of the Macedonian nation revitalized the centuries old Macedonian Question. Greece

opposed the state's declaration of independence and led an effort to prevent the state's official recognition by most states and international organizations (for reviews, see Roudometof 1996 and Pettifer 1999). It was only in 1995 that Athens and Skopje were able to sign an agreement that led to an improvement of inter-state relations between the two states. During the first part of the 1990s, the declaration of Macedonian independence was accompanied by a protracted debate on the issue of Macedonian minorities in Greece and Bulgaria. It soon became evident, however, that the most important minority issue was that of the Albanian minority within the newly created republic.

Throughout the 1980s, the authorities have alleged that the educational mechanism, the radio programs, and literature circulated among the members of the Albanian population are of an irredentist nature (Poulton 1991; 1992). During the 1990s, the gap between Albanians and Macedonians increased, leading to fears of civil war in the new state. Ultimately, the two main political parties representing the two major groups were able to form a coalition in 1997 (Perry 2000; Kohl & Libal 1997). It did appear as if this would be a short-lived experiment, but the Kosovo Crisis of 1999 changed the entire situation. The Kosovo Crisis was initiated by the gradual shift of the Kosovo Albanians toward radicalism. After more than a decade of peaceful protests and civil disobedience, radical Albanians formed the Kosovo Liberation Army (KLA or UCK in Albanian). The guerilla warfare initiated by this group signaled a hardening of the Serb forces that proceeded with plans to ethnically cleanse at least part of the province. This effort led to yet another NATO intervention in the spring of 1999. The net result was the withdrawal of the Serb forces and the establishment of a peculiar type of protectorate, whereby the Albanians won in practice their freedom, yet they did not achieve either statehood or unification with the Albanian state. Just as with the Bosnian intervention, the NATO forces' presence in the region "freezes" the situation, postponing discussion on Kosovo's ultimate status for the future.

POLITICIZING ETHNICITY IN THE SOUTHERN BALKANS 1989-1999: A SUMMARY

Internal problems with respect to minorities also plagued Yugoslavia's neighboring states as well. Albania's most important minority issue had to do with the Greek-Orthodox minority that lives in the south of the country (Southern Albania or Northern Epirus to the Greeks). The territory had been occupied by Greece twice in the past—during the Balkan wars of 1912-13 and during World War II (1940)—both times raising the prospect of incorporating the territory to the Greek state. Officially, Greece maintained the state of war

with Albania until 1987. During the inter-war period, Albania proceeded to shut down all Greek language schools (Roudometof 2002). The post-World War II communist regime isolated the Greek minority and subjected it to harsh repression—especially with respect to religious practices. This repression was, however, part of the state's general policy of atheism and thus it targeted all religious groups within the state (Muslim, Catholic, and Orthodox). By the mid-1980s the regime's attitude was softened.

Following the collapse of the communist regime, at least 300,000 Albanians immigrated illegally to Greece, transforming Greece into a host country to immigrant workers (Triandafyllidou and Mirkakis 1998). Not surprisingly, the immigration wave led to growing xenophobia, which in turn was directed primarily toward the Albanian workers. These developments influenced greatly the Greek-Albanian relationships. During the first free elections in Albania, the Greek minority was organized in the "Omonia" (Harmony) Party and attempted to compete in the elections. This did not go unopposed since the Ministry of Justice attempted to restrict parties that organize themselves according to an "ethnic" basis. The Omonia Party was successful in electing five deputies to the new Albanian Parliament (U.S. Country Reports on Human Rights 1991; Zanga 1992).

During 1993, the political situation deteriorated when Albanian authorities expelled Archmadrite Chrysostomos, a Greek clergy working with Anastasios, the Archbishop of the Albanian Orthodox Church. The reason for this action was the alleged "nationalist propaganda" of this cleric against the Albanian state. In this context, it is important to note that the boundaries differentiating Orthodox Albanians from Greeks are unclear. Many members of the Greek minority have only an elementary knowledge of Greek and look to the Orthodox Church as the basic cultural marker for their own cultural differentiation from the rest of the population. Hence, an emphasis on the "Greek" character of the Albanian Orthodox Church can be seen as an attempt to "acculturate" members of the Albanian Orthodox community into Hellenism. The Greek minority demonstrated against the deportation and the protesters clashed with the police. The minority rallied behind the Archbishop whereas the Albanian authorities treated the situation as a nationalist provocation.

The Albanian government, led by the Democratic Party of prime minister Sali Berisha, argued that the Archbishop's own position was rather precarious. According to the government's position, the higher posts of the Albanian Orthodox Church should be reserved for Albanian nationals alone. In sharp contrast, Archbishop Anastasios (just like Chrysostomos) is a Greek, not an Albanian, citizen. Against this argument, the Orthodox clergy protested that the revitalization of the Orthodox Church required the temporary appointment of

higher clergy that were not Albanians. They argued that the Church had suffered extensively under the communist regime, and by the early 1990s there were very few priests who had survived the communists' religious persecution.

In the meantime, the Greek authorities were quick to react. They sought to send some of these Albanian immigrants "back to Albania." Although there was a legal basis for such an action, Greece had abstained from doing so as a gesture of goodwill towards Albania. In the days following the Chrysostomos' deportation, some 5,000 Albanians were sent to Albania. Given the inadequate control of the border, there was little doubt that most of them would be back within a few days, but the purpose of these actions was to "remind" Albania of its financial dependence on the income from Albanian workers in Greece. In an interview in the Greek journal *Economic Review* (August 19, 1993) the Greek Premier Constantinos Mitsotakis made clear that Albania could not afford to react to the deportations of Albanians from Greece since its weak economy made the state dependent upon the remittances of Albanians from Greece.

In the aftermath of this affair, the Greek Premier declared that the status of the Greek minority in Southern Albania (or Northern Epirus) should be equated with that of the Albanian population in Kosovo, and if autonomy was to be given to them, then the same should apply to the Greeks in Albania. In the post-1993 period, the socialist governments of Andreas Papandreou and Costas Simitis moved gradually away from this confrontational strategy. Of crucial importance to the restructuring of Greek-Albanian relations was the Greek government's swift persecution of the Northern Epirus Liberation Front (MAVI), who was accused in 1994 and 1995 of orchestrating attacks on Albanian military posts and personnel.

But the Greek state's actions or foreign policy does not solely determine the position of the minority. Equally important is the interplay among Albanian domestic politics, the Albanian tribal division between Ghegs and Tosks, and religious affiliation. All these factors have shaped the Greek minority's position in the 1990s, and will undoubtedly continue to do so in the future (for a review, see Pettifer 2000). The Greek minority's status remains uncertain: its official speakers voice the need for financial support in order to keep the educational institutions running and emphasize the importance of religious identification for the preservation of ethnic consciousness.

In practical terms, the minority question seems to have been solved by economic means. Just as with the rest of the Albanian population, the Greeks of Albanian did not hesitate to immigrate into Greece in search of better economic opportunities. Indeed, it is hard to imagine that the majority of them will ever return to Albania. Thus, although the minority is likely to remain a source of

friction in Greek-Albanian relationships, both states have a vested interest to maintain open borders and interstate dialogue on a whole host of issues such as economic development, interstate cooperation, the Albanian immigrants, and so on. During the second half of the 1990s, the Greek authorities instituted a permanent residency status (similar to the US "green card") in an effort to transform the illegal immigrants (many of whom are Albanians) into a legally recognized group of workers, and thereby decrease their exploitation by employers. Furthermore, the Greek government did not hesitate to castigate racist and xenophobic sentiments, albeit with little success.

Bulgaria's major thorny issue concerns the fate and mode of incorporation of the large Turkish and Muslim minorities in southeastern Bulgaria. During the last years of the communist regime (1984-1989) there was a deliberate attempt made by the authorities to forcefully "acculturate" the Muslims into Christian Bulgarian culture.[7] This took the form of forcing a change of names from Muslim to Christian and delivering new identification papers to the minority. For those who avoided the change, the local bureaucracy denied the validity of their old papers. In effect, this created serious problems in all dealings with authorities. Additionally, the free operation of religious institutions was restricted, and there were accusations regarding alleged prohibition of speaking Turkish and accusations regarding job discrimination. The campaign was met with sporadic small-scale protests by the Turks, resulting in a number of people being imprisoned.

By 1989 a Turkish civil rights group was formed, and mass protest started including hunger strikes, demonstrations, etc. As a result the authorities increased their pressure and began expelling a number of Turks—mainly activists in the beginning—to Turkey. Soon this took the form of an exodus with at least 60,000 refugees crossing the border during the first half of the year. By late August the number climbed to 300,000. The collapse of the communist regime in 1990 and the democratization of the Bulgarian political system also resulted in a diffusion of the ethnic crisis. On December 29, 1989, the Bulgarian government revoked the assimilation campaign. A number of the refugees returned, discovering that in many cases government officials and local people had taken advantage of their absence in order to sell movable and immovable property for profit. During the summer of 1990, the central authorities instructed the local government to make efforts to resettle the returning group. Muslims continued to suffer from public discrimination in housing, education, and health care, but the gradual liberalization of political life resulted in a general improvement of the human rights for the minority group.[8] In October 1990, the first Islamic institute teaching Muslim culture was founded in Sofia, and in February 1991, the first Turkish language newspaper appeared.

The attempt to reverse the assimilation policy did not go unopposed. Organized by local nationalists in the city of Karbzhali in December 31, 1989, the Committee for the Defense of National Interests called for a plebiscite on the government's decision. By January 4, 1990, demonstrations opposing the reversal of this policy had been reported in Sofia, Plovdiv, Haskovo, Pleven, Shumen, Ruse, Targovishte, Sliven, and other places (Perry 1991). Attempting to defuse the situation, the government brought together in a Social Council of Citizens both sides involved in this affair. The Council voiced its demand for guarantees of Bulgaria's "national interest and security." It recommended that separatist and autonomist organizations be banned and conceded to Bulgarian nationalist opinion by calling for the banning of public displays of the Turkish flag and confirming Bulgarian as the only official language. Subsequently, on January 15, 1990, the Bulgarian National Assembly approved a declaration reiterating the main points agreed by the Council (Ashley 1990). There were two major reasons leading to this intense backlash. First, many individuals had profited through the selling of the Turks' property and were afraid of their return. Second, the Bulgarian public was afraid that the minority would be given political and cultural rights and a type of autonomy that would be the first step toward the carving of Bulgarian territory.

Soon after the collapse of the communist regime, the Muslim minority organized itself into the Movement of Rights and Freedoms (or DPS). The movement eventually mutated into a political party, thanks to tacit support by former communist, Bulgarian Socialist Party (BSP). Despite an official ban on electoral participation for organizations based on religious and ethnic platforms, the Muslim minority's political party did survive throughout the 1990s, and has secured its participation in Bulgarian politics (for a review of the party's trajectory in the 1990s, see Ilchev 2000). In the 1990s, the Turkish minority party has been a regular partner in government coalitions—although xenophobic and anti-Turkish sentiments have remained prevalent among the Bulgarian public (Grekova 1999). For example, in a 1992 survey a reported 83.8% of the Bulgarian public considered the Turks to be "religious fanatics," and, subsequently, refused to marry them (80.8%) or even to be friends with them (38.7%) (Hopken 1997: 77).

CONCLUSIONS

In order to arrive to a better understanding of the dynamics of the minority question within the Balkan mini-system of states, a differentiation between *necessary* and *sufficient* conditions is required. That is, the structural factors

outlined in this essay are responsible for the origins, maturation, and social significance of the minority question in Balkan politics. The state-sponsored organization of the Balkan societies on the basis of nationhood—that is, ethnic and religious considerations—rather than citizenship has made very difficult the incorporation of minority groups within these nation-states (cf. Roudometof 1999). Additionally, the close geographical proximity of minority groups to potential external national homelands as well as demographic considerations have added strain in majority-minority relations throughout the region. But all these conditions are not sufficient to either clearly articulate national minorities as organized political entities or to account for the proliferation of violence in the area during the 1990s.

As the Yugoslav experience as well as the Albanian and Bulgarian cases illustrate, political mobilization provides the sufficient condition for such an outcome. Of special importance is mobilization at the religious and educational levels since the preservation of an ethnoreligious identity provides the most visible cultural markers of difference between the minority groups and the local majority population. Hence, educational and religious institutions have often become focal points of controversy within the region. Disputes over educational and religious rights are *not* solely an issue of human rights as such (Gurr and Scarritt 1989), and it is at least simplistic to view these affairs only from the moral standpoints of the average citizen in Western democracies or that of human rights advocates. These issues are always accompanied by the silent (or vocal) assumption that the assertion of communal rights by the minority group *de facto* transforms the group into a national minority and thus provides the context for a possible restriction to the sovereignty of a particular nation-state.

Moreover, politics provide the final and indispensable component to this process. In Yugoslavia, it was the deliberate political action undertaken by Milosevic and his supporters that helped shape the nature of the rising Serb nationalism. To a considerable extent, the same holds for the peripheral nationalisms expressed in the Republic of Macedonia, Croatia, and Slovenia. During the 1990s, the horrors of the war in Bosnia-Herzegovina and the more cautious policies of Bulgaria and the Republic of Macedonia—and to a lesser extent, Albania as well—helped the containment of the Balkan crisis. Of course, none of these short-term political strategies of crisis management could remove the structural strain from the political field, let alone provide for a permanent solution to the minority question.

With the exception of Serbs and Croats in Bosnia-Herzegovina and the Greeks in Albania, the remaining minority groups in the region are Muslim, thus creating religious tension between Orthodox states (Bulgaria, Serbia, Greece, the

Republic of Macedonia) and Muslim minorities. The existence of these minorities is related historically to the process of the creation of the Balkan states themselves during the nineteenth and twentieth centuries. By and large, the Muslim population of the Balkans failed to develop a national consciousness parallel to the one of its Christian counterpart (Irwin 1989). Being mostly in a position of privilege and also because of their relative isolation from the West, the Muslim communities have been rather passive recipients of social changes. Their status underwent dramatic changes in the course of the twentieth century as they found themselves surrounded by Christian majorities and living in nation-states that tend to emphasize ethnic and religious identity as the major component of membership in each nation-state. Asserting their "cultural rights," however, is not a simple matter because the shadow of Ottoman-Turkish rule has marked the Balkans to such an extent that the incorporation of a Muslim element into the local societies represents a very difficult task. Moreover, during the 1980s and 1990s, the Muslim minorities provided excellent scapegoats for ex-communists turned nationalists.

The preceding analysis has to be placed within the context of the broader post-1989 European trends. As Brubaker (1995: 108-10) points out, post-communist Europe confronts a potentially explosive dynamic interplay among ethnically heterogeneous, yet conceived as homogeneous nation-states. Indeed, the Balkan nation-states provide ideal examples of this interplay. Just as elsewhere in Europe, the Balkan states' dominant elites promote (to varying degrees) the language, culture, demographic position, economic flourishing, and political hegemony of the state-bearing nation thereby clashing with the substantial, self-conscious, and (to varying degrees) organized and politically alienated *minority groups*. As these groups' political mobilization proceeds, they are gradually (and to varying degrees) transformed into *national minorities* whose leaders demand cultural or territorial autonomy and resist actual or perceived policies or processes of assimilation or discrimination. These national minorities are becoming permanently fixated to their *external national homelands*, whose elites (again to varying degrees) closely monitor the situation of their co-ethnics in the neighboring states, vigorously protest real or alleged violations of their rights, and assert the right, even the obligation, to defend their interests.

Despite the initial containment of the ethnic conflict in Bosnia-Herzegovina and Croatia, the long-term structural strain caused by this dynamic interplay was not removed from the political field. Nor was there any political action to shift the bases of inter-state rivalry in the region. Indeed, political events alone could sparkle the fire of war in other parts of Yugoslavia—and eventually they did.

The 1999 Kosovo Crisis aptly demonstrated these long-term structural factors. The net result was another round of NATO-led military intervention, leading to the stationing of even more NATO troops in the region. The maintenance of the status quo and rationale of crisis management prevailed with little attention paid to more long-term trends—or indeed, to the lesson delivered to minority groups throughout the region.

The collapse of the Milosevic regime in the fall of 2000 might be a major turning point. The international community is currently willing to recognize Serbia as a potential partner in peace and security strategies throughout the region. Similar trends toward inter-state cooperation have been observed in the rest of the Balkans (Dannopoulos 2001), thereby raising the possibility that the circle of violence could be reversed in the visible future. The development of common policy guidelines and principles that would govern the political behavior of all Balkan states should serve as a deterrent to the proliferation of ethnic violence. To a considerable degree, such an endeavor includes the redesigning of local nation-states in ways that accommodate minority groups and thus can prevent the consolidation of national minorities. Whether the promise of European membership will make it possible for the local states to follow such a strategy remains to be seen.

ENDNOTES

[1] For accounts of the emergence of the Balkan nation-states in the 19th century, see Stavrianos (1958), Jelavich and Jelavich (1977) and Jelavich (1983). On the importance of nationhood as a defining characteristic of these states, see Smith (1986; 1991), Kitromilides (1983), and Roudometof (1998). The relationship between religion and nationalism in Yugoslavia is explored in Ramet (1989: 299-327).

[2] The Gypsies (or Roma) are another group that is most often identified with the Muslims or Turks. There is a movement toward the opposite direction as well. In 1993, Macedonia's Roma political party addressed a letter to the United Nations calling for the creation of a separate "nation" constituency (see Troxel, 1992; Poulton, 1991: 90-93; Ilchev and Perry, 1993: 35-41).Additionally, a number of Muslim Roma, apparently desiring to disassociate themselves from the Turks, have formed an association proclaiming Egypt as their historical homeland and asking for recognition of their minority group as "Egyptians." It

is doubtful, nevertheless, that these attempts will be successful. It is not surprising, however, that this declaration came from the Macedonian Roma, who are the most prosperous group among the Balkan Gypsies. The high rates of illiteracy, the relative absence of educational systems in the Romani language, the migratory lifestyle, and their dispersion makes it unlikely for the Roma to transform themselves into an influential constituency.

[3] This discussion will not discuss the issue of Macedonian national minorities in Bulgaria and Greece. The existence of such minority groups is undisputed, however, it is likely that initial estimates have greatly exaggerated their numerical strength. For further discussion on the Macedonian issue, see Roudometof (1996) and Boneva, Nikolov, and Roudometof (2000).

[4] This does not mean that irredentist visions are confined only to the groups listed in Table 2. For example, Macedonian nationalists claim the existence of "enslaved brothers" within the neighboring states despite the fact that estimates of these minorities are often less than 2% of the population. Similarly the Muslim and Pomak minority in West Thrace within Greece can be considered as a potential national minority if a successful "Turkish" identification prevails. As with the Macedonians however, the numbers are not in their favor. Even when combined, the Pomak and Turkish minority groups account only for 1.3% of the total population with most of the minority concentrated in two counties (Xanthi and Rhodopi) in West Thrace (Poulton, 1991:182-4; also HFDFP's Yearbook 1992). In this particular case, geopolitics could favor the consolidation of a national minority, but geopolitics alone provide an insufficient basis.

[5] Some Western observers have confused ethnic conflict among peoples with feelings of prejudice or animosity on an individual basis. Such feelings are certainly absent in the Yugoslav case, as evidenced by survey research results cited by Gordy (1999: 2-6).

[6] This description refers only to the circumstances that led to Milosevic's rise to power. Over the 1990s, his regime ruthlessly destroyed political & cultural alternatives in order to maintain an artificial isolation from the rest of the world and thereby convince the population of its own righteousness. See Gordy (1999) and Ramet (1999) for further discussion.

[7] For detailed descriptions of the campaign, see the reports of Amnesty International (1988, 1989,1990), Poulton et. al. (1989), Poulton (1991), the Ass. Press reports of August 31and March 6,1989, and the 1987 CSCE hearings (Part

I). For the history and status of the minority—presented from the Turkish point of view—see Karpat (1990). For a third party analysis, see Neuremberg (1997).

[8] See the U.S. Country Reports on Human Rights (1990:1108) and the Amnesty International Report (1992). See also the 1991 U.S. Country Reports on Human Rights regarding details on the Turkish minority party.

REFERENCES *

* Sources in Greek indicated by (G)

Allcock John B., Marko Milivojevic, and John J. Horton (eds.). 1998. *Conflict in the Former Yugoslavia: An Encyclopedia*. Denver, CO: ABC-Clio Press.

Andrejevich Milan. 1990a. "The Dispute between Serbia and Slovenia," *Report on Eastern Europe*. Jan. 19: 23-26

Andrejevich Milan. 1990b. "Slovenia Heading Toward Independence," *Report on Eastern Europe*. March 30: 36-40

Amnesty International. 1988-95. Annual Reports. New York: Amnesty International.

Ashley Stephen. 1990. "Bulgaria: Ethnic Unrest During January," *Report on Eastern Europe* 9 February : 4-11

Banac Ivo. 1984. *The National Question in Yugoslavia: Origins, History, Politics*. Ithaca: Cornell University Press.

Barth F. (ed.). 1969. *Ethnic Groups and Boundaries: The Social Organization of Culture Difference*. London: Allen and Unwin.

Berholli, Arqile, Seifi Protara, and Kristaq Prifti. 1994. "The Greek Minority in the Albanian Republic: A Demographic Study," *Nationalities Papers* (22) 2: 427-34.

Boneva Bonka, Stephan E. Nikolov, and Victor Roudometof. 2000. "In Search of 'Bigfoot': Competing Identities in Pirin Macedonia, Bulgaria," pp. 237-58 in Victor Roudometof (ed.), *The Macedonian Question: Culture, Historiography, Politics*. Boulder, Co: East European Monographs, distributed by Columbia University Press.

Brubaker, Rogers. 1992. *Citizenship and Nationhood in France and Germany*. Cambridge: Cambridge University Press.

Brubaker, Rogers. 1995. "National Minorities, Nationalizing States, and External National Homelands in the New Europe," *Daedalus* 124 (2): 107-32.

Brubaker, Rogers. 1996. *Nationalism Reframed: Nationhood and the National Question in the New Europe*. Cambridge: Cambridge University Press.

Cohen Lenard J. 1993. *Broken Bonds: The Disintegration of Yugoslavia*. Boulder: Westview Press.

Commission on Security and Cooperation in Europe—100th Congress. 1987. Hearings. Part I: National Minorities in Eastern Europe, The Turkish Minority in Bulgaria. Washington: G.P.O.

Cviic Christopher. 1991. *Remaking the Balkans*. London: Royal Institute of International Affairs.

Dannopoulos, Constantine. 2001. "Toward Cooperation in Post-Cold War Southeastern Europe?" *Mediterranean Quarterly* (forthcoming).

Djilas Aleksa. 1991. *The Contested Country: Yugoslav Unity and Communist Revolution 1919-1953*. Cambridge, Mass: Harvard University Press.

Dodos, Dimosthenis Ch. 1994. *Electoral Geography of Minorities: Minority Parties in South Balkans, Greece, Bulgaria, Albania*. Athens: Exantas (in Greek).

Dragnich, Alexis N. 1989. "The Rise and Fall of Yugoslavia: The Omen of the Upsurge of Serbian Nationalism," *East European Quarterly* 26 (2): 183-198.

Glenny, Misha. 1992. *The Fall of Yugoslavia: The Third Balkan War*. New York: Penguin.

Gordy, Eric D. 1999. *The Culture of Power in Serbia: Nationalism and the Destruction of Alternatives*. University Park, PA: Pennsylvania State University Press.

Greenfeld Liah. 1991. *Nationalism: Five Roads to Modernity*. Harvard: Harvard University Press.

Grekova, Maya. 1999. *The Turkish Minority in Bulgaria*. Paper presented in the First International Symposium on Ethnic Identities and Political Action in Post-Cold War Europe, Demokretus University of Thrace, Xanthi, September 1-3, 1999.

Gurr Ted R. and James R. Scarritt. 1989. "Minorities at Risk: A Global Survey," *Human Rights Quarterly* (11): 375-405

Hayden Robert M. 1992a. *The Beginning of the End of Federal Yugoslavia: The Slovenian Amendment Crisis of 1989*. Pittsburgh: Carl Beck Series in Russian and East European Studies, Center for Russian and East European Studies, University of Pittsburgh.

Hayden Robert M. 1992b. "Constitutional Nationalism in the Formerly Yugoslav Republics," *Slavic Review* 51 (4): 654-73

Hayden Robert M. 1993. "The Partition of Bosnia and Herzegovina," *RFE/RL Research Report* 2 (22) May 28: 1-14.

Hellenic Foundation for Defense and Foreign Policy (HFDFP). 1992. *The Southeastern European Yearbook 1991*. Athens: ELIAMEP.

Hellenic Foundation for Defense and Foreign Policy (HFDFP). 1992 & 1999. *Review of Defense and Foreign Policy* (G). Athens: ELIAMEP.

Hirschman Albert O. 1970. *Exit, Voice, and Loyalty: responses to decline in firms, organizations, and states*. Cambridge: Harvard University Press.

Hopken W. 1997. "From Religious Identity to Ethnic Mobilization: The Turks of Bulgaria, before, under and since Communism," pp. 54-81 in H. Poulton and S. Taji-Farouki (eds.), *Muslim Identity and the Balkan State*. New York: New York University Press.

Ilchev Ivan and Duncan Perry M. 1993. "Bulgarian Ethnic Groups: Politics and Perceptions," *RFE/RL Research Report*. 2 (12) 19 March. 35-41

Ilchev, Ivan. 2000. "Emigration and the Politics of Identity: The Turkish Minority in Bulgaria," pp. 237-68 in Jonathan P. Stein (ed.), *The Politics of National Minority Participation in Post-Communist Europe: State-Building, Democracy, and Ethnic Mobilization*. Armonk, NY: M.E. Sharpe.

Irwin Zachary T. 1989. "The Fate of Islam in the Balkans: A Comparison of Four State Policies," pp. 379-407 in Pedro Ramet (ed.), *Religion and Nationalism in Soviet and East European Politics*. Durham: Duke University Press.

Jelavich Barbara. 1983. *History of the Balkans, Vol. 1: 18th & 19th Centuries*. Cambridge: Cambridge University Press.

Jelavich Charles and Barbara. 1977. *The Establishment of Balkan Nation-States*. Seattle: University of Washington Press.

Kaplan Robert D. 1993. *Balkan Ghosts: A Journey through History*. New York: St. Martin's Press.

Karpat Kemal H. 1990. *The Turks of Bulgaria: The History, Culture, and Political Fate of a Minority*. Istanbul: Isis Press.

Kitromilides Paschalis. 1983. "The Enlightenment East and West: A Comparative Perspective on the Ideological Origins of the Balkan Political Traditions," *Canadian Review of Studies in Nationalism*. 10 (1): 51-70

Kohl, Christine von and Wolfgang Libal. 1997. "Kosovo, the Gordian Knot of the Balkans," pp. 3-104 in Robert Elsie (ed.), *Kosovo: In the Heart of the Powder Keg*. Boulder, Co: East European Monographs, distributed by Columbia University Press.

Lampe, John. 1996. *Yugoslavia as History: Twice There Was a Country*. London: Hurst.

Larrabee, F. Stephen (ed.). 1994. *The Volatile Powder keg : Balkan security after the Cold War*. Washington, D.C.: American University Press.

Lipset Seymour M. 1963. *The First New Nation*. New York: Basic.

Lydanyi, Andrew. 2000. "The Fate of Hungarians in Vojvodina." In Steven B. Vardy and Hunt Tooley (eds.), *Ethnic Cleansing in 20th Century Europe*. Boulder, Colo.: East European Monographs, distributed by Columbia University Press.

McNeill, William H. 1985. *Polyethnicity and National Unity in World History*. Toronto: University of Toronto Press.

Minority Rights Group (eds.) 1990. *World Directory of Minorities*. London: Longman.

Nikolaev Rada. 1992. "Bulgaria's 1992 Census: Results, Problems, and Implications," *RFE/RL Research Report* 2(6). 5 February. 58-62

Neuremberg, M. 1997. "Bulgaro-Turkish Encounters and the Re-Imagining of the Bulgarian Nation (1878-1995)," *East European Quarterly* (31) 1: 1-19

Perry Duncan M. 1991. "Ethnic Turks Face Bulgarian Nationalism," *Report on Eastern Europe* 15 March. 5-8

Perry Duncan M. 2000. "Conflicting Ambitions and Shared Fates: The Past, Present, and Future of Albanians and Macedonians," pp. 259-99 in Victor Roudometof (ed.), *The Macedonian Question: Culture, Historiography, Politics*. Boulder, Co: East European Monographs, distributed by Columbia University Press.

Petrovic Ruza. 1992. "The National Composition of Yugoslavia's Population, 1991," *Yugoslav Survey* XXXIII (1): 3-24

Pettifer, James (ed.). 1999. *The New Macedonian Question*. London: Macmillan.

Pettifer, James. 2000. "The Greek Minority in Albania: Ethnic Politics in a Pre-national State," pp. 167-88 in Jonathan P. Stein (ed.), *The Politics of National Minority Participation in Post-Communist Europe: State-Building, Democracy, and Ethnic Mobilization*. Armonk, NY: M.E. Sharpe.

Poulton Hugh. 1991. *The Balkans: Minorities and States in Conflict*. London: Minority Rights Group.

_________. 1992. "The Republic of Macedonia after UN Recognition," *RFE/RL Research Report* 2 (23). 4 June. 22-30

Poulton Hugh with the Minnesota Lawyers International Human Rights Committee. 1989. *Minorities in the Balkans*. London: Minority Rights Group. Report No 82.

Ramet Pedro. 1989. "Religion and Nationalism in Yugoslavia," pp. 299-327 in Pedro Ramet (ed.), *Religion and Nationalism in Soviet and East European Politics*. Durham: Duke University Press.

Ramet Pedro. 1992. *Nationalism and Federalism in Yugoslavia 1962-1991*. Bloomington: Indiana University Press.

Ramet, Sabrina P. 1999. *Balkan Babel: The Disintegration of Yugoslavia from the Death of Tito to the War for Kosovo*. Boulder, Co: Westview Press.

Rothschild, Joseph. 1981. *Ethnopolitics: A Conceptual Framework*. New York: Columbia University Press.

Roudometof, Victor. 1996. "Nationalism and Identity Politics in the Balkans: Greece and the Macedonian Question," *Journal of Modern Greek Studies* (14) (2): 253-301.

_________. 1998. "Invented Traditions, Symbolic Boundaries, and National Identity in Southeastern Europe: Greece and Serbia in Comparative-Historical Perspective, 1830-1880," *East European Quarterly* (32) 4: 429-71.

__________. 1999. "Nationalism, Globalization, and Eastern Orthodoxy: 'Unthinking' the 'Clash of Civilizations' in Southeastern Europe," *European Journal of Social Theory* (2) 2: 234-47.

__________. 2001. *Nationalism, Globalization, and Orthodoxy: The Social Origins of Ethnic Conflict in the Balkans*. Westport, CT: Greenwood Press.

__________. 2002. "Ethnic Heterogeneity, Cultural Homogenization, and State Policy in the Inter-war Balkans," in Steven B. Vardy and Hunt Tooley (eds.), *Ethnic Cleansing in 20th Century Europe*. Boulder, Colo.: East European Monographs, distributed by Columbia University Press.

Rusinow Dennison. 1977. *The Yugoslav Experiment 1948-1974*. London: Hurst.

Rusinow Dennison. 1982. "Yugoslavia's Muslim Nation," *University Field Staff International Report* (8): 1-8

Rusinow Dennison (ed.). 1988. *Yugoslavia: A Fractured Federalism*. Washington: Wilson Center Press.

Seton-Watson, H. 1977. *Nations and States: An Inquiry into the Origins of Nations and the Politics of Nationalism*. London: Methuen .

Simonov, Simon. 1990. "The Gypsies: A Reemerging Minority," *Report on Eastern Europe* 25 May: 12-5.

Smith, Anthony D. 1986. *The Ethnic Origins of Nations*. Oxford: Basil Blackwell.

Smith, Anthony D. 1991. *National Identity*. Rheno: University of Nevada Press.

Shoup, Paul S. (ed.). 1990. *Problems of Balkan Security: Southeastern Europe in the 1990s*. Washington: Wilson Centre Press.

Stavrianos, Lefteris S. 1958. *The Balkans since 1453*. New York: Harper and Row.

Triandafyllidou, Anna and Antonis Mirkakis. 1998. "A Ghost Wonders Through the Capital," pp. 164-79 in Brend Baumgartl and Adrian Favell (eds.), *New Xenophobia in Europe*. London: Kluwer.

Troxel, Luan. 1992. "Bulgaria's Gypsies: Numerically Strong, Politically Weak," *RFE/RL Research Report* 6 (March): 58-61

U.S. Department of State. 1989-1992. *Country Reports on Human Rights Practices*. Reports submitted to the Committee on Foreign Affairs, House of Representatives and the Committee on Foreign Relations, U.S. Senate. Washington: U.S. Government Printing Office.

Weber, Eugene. 1976. *Peasants into Frenchmen: The Modernization of Rural France 1870-1914*. Berkeley: University of California Press.

Woodward, S. 1995. *Balkan Tragedy. Chaos and Dissolution After the Cold War*. Washington DC: Brookings Institution.

Zakosek, Nenad. 2000. "Ethnic War and Disempowerment: The Serb Minority in Croatia," pp. 213-36 in Jonathan P. Stein (ed.), *The Politics of National Minority Participation in Post-Communist Europe: State-Building, Democracy, and Ethnic Mobilization*. Armonk, NY: M. E. Sharpe.

Zanga, Louis. 1992. "Albanian-Greek Relations Reach a Low Point," *RFE/RL Research Report* 1 (15) 10 April: 18-21.

CHAPTER 3
PARDON? A CONFLICT FOR A NAME? FYROM'S DISPUTE WITH GREECE REVISITED

Demetrius Andreas Floudas*
Anglia Polytechnic University
England

I. INTRODUCTORY REMARKS

The entanglement between Greece and the Former Yugoslav Republic of Macedonia (FYROM), over the issue of the recognition of the latter and the name under which this recognition would take place, has served as a potent reminder of the considerable influence that nationalistic divides have always exerted in the Balkan region. For Greece, this dispute animated passions and stimulated a nationalist fervor that had been unseen for decades and, remaining a not fully resolved issue, it may contain a number of elements that could serve as a focus of regional conflict in the future. For the fledgling FYROM, the entanglement constituted a matter of paramount importance not merely in defining its external policy but it was also perceived as a matter influencing both its existence as a nation and its future status in Southeastern Europe.

This article will attempt an analysis of the dispute between Greece and FYROM, from its beginnings up until the present day. In the first instance, it will trace the origins of the controversy and portray the current dispute as the latest stage in evolution of the Macedonian Question of the past. Furthermore,

---

* Parts III and IV of this paper are based on a presentation given at Trinity College University of Cambridge in May 1994. The author wishes to thank the Legal Office of the Ministry for Foreign Affairs in Athens, the Ministry for Macedonia and Thrace in Thessalonik the Press and Information Office of the Greek Embassy in London and particularly M. Papademetriou for the material provided; Dr. E. Divani of the University of Athens and M. N. Ziogas of ELIAMEP for their assistance with the sources; Dr. L. Prabhu, Associate of the BDICFA, for his comments; Dr. H. Tzimitras of the Panteios University, Athens for h feedback on the version presented at the London School of Economics and Political Science in November 1994; Dr. E. Kofos for his expert advice; and the former Greek Government Ministers Dr. M. Papakonstanlinou, Mr. S. Papathemelis and Mr. A. Samaras for their time and valuable personal insights into the lesser-publicized aspects of the issue.

the diplomatic strategies of the two countries involved will be examined for the 1991-1995 period. In addition, the content and significance of the contentious issues of this debate will be scrutinized. Finally, the factors which contributed to the diplomatic exacerbation of the issue and caused a failure of both countries involved to secure a resolution to the dispute that they would consider "positive" will be analyzed and the repercussions for the Balkan region's short- and long-term geopolitical status quo will be outlined.

The focus of the article is the dissection and analysis of the Foreign Policy of Athens regarding the Macedonian question in the post-war period, with particular attention to the years 1991-1995. As such, its ultimate objective is to provide a contribution to the scholarly investigation of the factors influencing Greek Foreign Affairs in the 1990s.

II. *"MACEDONIA NOSTRA"*: THE HISTORICAL BACKGROUND OF THE MACEDONIAN QUESTION.

The geographical term "Macedonia" is a Greek word and was used in antiquity to designate the area inhabited by the Macedonians, "the tall ones," apparently on account of the distinguishing physical height of this tribe.[1] It was thus the inhabitants who gave their name to the region and not the other way round.

For most of their earlier history, the Macedonians appear to have led a relatively peripheral existence and were accordingly slow to partake in the intellectual, social and cultural progress of southern Greece.[2] The kingdom of Macedonia reached a peak under Philip II (359-336 BC), when it was enlarged considerably through a series of successful military campaigns and included a large part of the southern Balkan peninsula. At the time of death of Philip's son, Alexander the Great, the Macedonians had created a vast empire in Asia and Africa, after spearheading an astounding military and ideological crusade against the Persians "on behalf of all Greeks."[3]

Slavs first appeared in the region in the 6th century A.D. during the great migrations of the period, whilst in the Middle Ages various other populations started moving in the area.[4] Under Byzantine and Ottoman rule, the term was used in its geographical sense, i.e. it covered the boundaries of the former four Roman administrative regions of "Macedonia."[5] This was in fact larger than "historic Macedonia," the core domain of the 4th century B.C. Macedonian Kingdom, and was inhabited by a multitude of different Balkan ethnic groups, Turks, Serbians, Bulgarians, Greeks, Vlachs, Jews and Albanians.

In the crumbling 19th century Ottoman Empire, the increasing breakdown of central authority led to growing interest in occupied Macedonia amongst the surrounding Balkan nation-states. The respective national ideologies of these newly-independent countries, in the form of accurate or arbitrary historical, ethnological and political claims, began to converge on the heterogeneous province and the ensuing tension precluded any hope of consensus when the time to redraw the borders of that "microcosm of Balkan complexities"[6] would come. The eventual annexation of the largest possible portion of geographic Macedonia became thus pivotal in the nationalist and irredentist plans of Bulgaria[7], Greece[8] and Serbia and a fundamental consideration of their national consciousness. Chronologically, the Macedonian Problem in its original form may be said to begin with the founding of the Bulgarian Exarchate in 1870.[9] This was perceived as an initial step to establish a distinct Bulgarian national identity for the Slav-speaking populace and it was further pursued by the founding of schools and by indulging in vigorous propaganda.[10] The growing activity of the Bulgarians alarmed Serbia and Greece, which decided in turn to mobilize in this cultural cold war. By 1900 educational indoctrination had given way to more acute measures as the Bulgarian-backed I.M.R.O.[11] embarked on an armed campaign with bands of guerrillas, the *komitadjis*.[12] The other two countries responded by organizing combatant groups of their own,[13] and from 1903 to 1908 a ruthless and protracted struggle took place amongst the Balkan Christians in territory belonging formally to the Turks, who had limited success (and, arguably, equally limited interest) in containing the conflict.[14]

The Balkan Wars of 1912-1913 ended the Ottoman rule.[15] After successfully stripping the Ottoman Empire from almost all her European possessions, the Balkan alliance broke up and Bulgaria attacked Serbia and Greece in a clash over the spoils. The Bulgarians were severely defeated in the Second Balkan War and the Treaty of Bucharest (August 1913) confirmed the final partitioning of the Macedonian region amongst the Balkan neighbors. Greece annexed 51.5% of geographic Macedonia,[16] Bulgaria gained 10.1% and the remaining 38.4% became part of the kingdom of Serbia, under the name Southern Serbia.[17]

In the meantime, a curious twist to the original "Macedonian Question" evolved. Until that time the term "Macedonian" had never been used by any of the three countries involved,[18] or any segment of the actual population, as anything other than a geographic definition.[19] In the interwar period however,[20] the term began to be put to use for the first time as an ethnic description[21] serving as a fabrication to promote Comintern's aspirations to increased regional influence.[22]

The crucial step was taken in 1944 by the Yugoslav leader Tito, when he implemented the decision to create a new federal state consisting of six republics. He gave to the southernmost province, previously known as *Vardarska Banovina* (i.e. District of [the river] Vardar), the new name of People's Republic of Macedonia.[23] This republic was made a constitutive of federal Yugoslavia and its Slavic inhabitants, known until then as ethnic Bulgarians or Serbs, were recognized as its "titular nation"[24] under the name *Makedontsi* (Macedonians). Their language, which was until then held to be a western Bulgarian dialect, was christened "Macedonian"[25] and became one of Yugoslavia's official languages.

This was a political masterstroke on behalf of Tito. He managed to safeguard for Yugoslavia a region which had been claimed by Bulgaria ever since the Second Balkan War,[26] and at the same time to create a Piedmont that could facilitate the unification of the remaining Macedonian territories into the Yugoslavian federation.[27] An extensive "Macedonization" process was initiated so as to instil a distinct national identity in the awareness of the population; numerous Greek and Bulgarian historical and cultural elements were appropriated,[28] whilst the younger generations started to be systematically infused with irredentist views of a Greater Macedonia and of their as yet "unliberated brothers." Tito's immediate plans for annexation of the Bulgarian and the Greek parts of Macedonia were respectively thwarted by the clash with Moscow in 1948[29] and the termination of the communist-induced ferocious civil strife in Greece in 1949.[30]

At the same time, the reaction of Greece to this attempted provocation was remarkably lukewarm and remained so for more than four decades. The reasons for this lie in the following:

a) From 1944 until 1949, the internal situation in Greece was hardly suitable for the planning and implementation of a coherent foreign policy due to the instability caused by the civil war that was ravaging the country.

b) In the final phase of the civil strife, Tito's decision to close the Greek-Yugoslav border and discontinue the aid to the insurgents proved a major factor in ending the conflict in favor of the Athens-based government. Even though this was not a result of any deference on Belgrade's part towards the Greek government but for other reasons, the latter had a strong incentive not to stress the point of the southernmost province's name at the time.[31]

c) After Yugoslavia broke with the Eastern Bloc and adopted a non-aligned stance in the 1950s, Greece came under fierce pressure by the U.S.A. to normalize relations with her northern neighbor and refrain from stirring up

mischief in the future, as Yugoslavia was perceived to be a strategically important buffer state in the soft underbelly of the Warsaw Pact.[32]

d) As the tension with Turkey escalated in the postwar period, it was important for Greece to secure its "northern front" in order to focus on the *periculum ex oriente*.

e) Furthermore, as Orthodox Serbia had been the traditionally friendly agent for Greece in the otherwise insecure Balkan peninsula, a rapprochement with the (Serb-dominated, after all) Yugoslavia would seem inevitable in order to ensure at least one ally in the area. Thus for example, Belgrade's positions on the Cyprus issue were always recognized as "encouraging" by the Greek side.

f) With the state of war against Albania perpetuated and Bulgaria technically an enemy country, Greece's only overland connection with mainland Europe passed through the territory of the Federal Republic of Yugoslavia.[33]

g) "The alien Slav element, as a result of its role during the Occupation and the civil war, had left [Greece] *en masse* and the prospect of its manipulation by a neighboring country to threaten the security and territorial integrity of [Greece] had been removed."[34]

h) Greece could operate as a strategic dyad with Yugoslavia, blocking the approach of Warsaw Pact troops to the Mediterranean in the event of widespread hostilities, thus manyfold enhancing the vital bargaining potential of either country individually.[35]

Thus, Greek reaction in so far as the new "Macedonian Question" was concerned remained, until the end of the 1980s, (at best) restrained, and after 1950 the standard cliché about the "traditional friendship" of the two peoples was reiterated at every opportunity by any public statement or analysis concerning bilateral Greek-Yugoslav relations.[36] Abroad, however, a major cultural campaign was launched, capitalising on Yugoslavia's privileged position in the non-aligned movement.[37] A significant program of translations from Macedonian into the most important world languages was initiated, along with the organization of international conferences and the generous dissemination of S.R.M. books in prestigious academic institutions,[38] especially in countries with multicultural credos such as Canada and Australia.[39]

Hence, a de facto recognition of a Macedonian ethnic entity had been attained internationally by 1970 already.[40] And, in spite of the occasional irritated protest from the Greek public opinion in the late 1980s, the inescapable conclusion was now that this "newly-established "Macedonian" nation could rightfully stake a claim to everything Macedonian; i.e. everything of, or pertaining to the region of Macedonia and its inhabitants."[41]

III. THE DIPLOMATIC STRUGGLE FOLLOWING THE DISSOLUTION OF YUGOSLAVIA

In the post-Tito Yugoslavia it soon became apparent that the initiative had passed to the individual republics and the delicate balances that had held the system together for forty years had been upset. The collapse of the Iron Curtain in 1989 and the arising turmoil accelerated the centrifugal tendencies.[42] On December 23, 1990 a referendum in Slovenia supporting independence, triggered off the chain of events that led to the dissolution of the Federal Socialist Republic of Yugoslavia. In a similar referendum on September 8, 1991,[43] a large majority in the Yugoslav Republic of Macedonia[44] voted in favor of independence and the Republic duly declared its sovereignty on September 17, 1991.[45] At the same time, it started seeking international recognition as the "Republic of Macedonia." The Greek government had been expecting this eventuality, after the eruption of fighting in the north of Yugoslavia earlier in the year had signalled that the federation's days were numbered.[46] But for the Greeks in general it was a tremendous jolt, as they suddenly realized in 1991 that a new state was about to appear at their northern frontier with a name which they had thought to be unquestionably theirs. Greece had spent the last two years entangled in a paralysing internal squabble and successive general elections that had nurtured severe introspection and had delayed the readjustment of foreign policy to the novel exigencies of post-iron-curtain realities in Europe. So, the Greek public opinion arose excitedly in a forceful campaign against the new state intended to compel it to relinquish all linguistic and symbolic connections with Greek history; and the "Macedonian issue" entered a new chapter of its history.

On December 16, 1991, the Council of Ministers of the European Community met to consider the *de jure* recognition of the breakaway former Yugoslav republics in Brussels. The Foreign Minister A. Samaras put forward the position of the Greek side concerning FYROM,[47] centering on objections against the use of the name "Macedonia," the likelihood of future territorial claims and the hostile propaganda emanating from certain circles in Skopje.[48] At the time, with attention focused on the recognition of Slovenia and Croatia and the convoluted negotiations regarding the Treaty on European Union,[49] Samaras, at the end of a marathon session, had little difficulty in persuading the Council to adopt the Greek views and include them in the resulting declaration.[50] After this initial success, the favorable opinion of the Badinter Commission, which endorsed FYROM's recognition,[51] was also set aside and a ferocious diplomatic struggle commenced between Athens and Skopje. Both

President Karamanlis and Foreign Minister Samaras engaged in correspondence with the European partners outlining Greece's argumentation,[52] whilst north of the border it was realized that this was going to be a hard fight.

Amidst intensifying Greek passions towards FYROM's unyielding stand, the Foreign Minister clarified the Greek views at the Lisbon EC Foreign Minister Council on February 17, 1992. The Portuguese EC Presidency that undertook to explore the prospects of resolving the impasse, came up with a draft deal (the so-called "Pineiro package"),[53] which was rejected as there was no agreement on the name (New Macedonia had been put forward). Later, at the Guimaraes Council of Ministers it was decided that the Member States "are willing to recognize [FYROM] as a sovereign and independent state, within its existing borders, and under a name that can be accepted by all parties concerned."[54]

The zenith of the Greek Foreign Policy's effectiveness during the dispute with FYROM was achieved at the European Council of Lisbon on June 27, 1992. The past semester of intense Greek diplomatic activity had been fruitful and the Community finally formulated a position whereby it was to recognize FYROM in accordance with the December 1991 declaration and only "under a name which does not include the term Macedonia."[55] In Greece, public opinion was jubilant, but in Skopje the blow toppled the government. The hardliners emerged vindicated and during the rest of 1992 the situation was methodically exacerbated by both sides: in August, FYROM adopted the 16-point Star of Vergina as the emblem on the national flag and in September, the new school textbooks that were circulated were laden with irredentist references to "Greater Macedonia" and claims on hellenic cultural heritage; on the other hand, Greece intensified a selective embargo on fuel and commodities.[56]

As the European front appeared unreceptive at the moment, the FYROM government decided to seek recognition elsewhere and on July 30, 1992 applied directly to the United Nations for recognition.[57] But time was running against the Greeks now. The European press was starting to rally clearly in support of the little fledgling state, whilst Skopje was using every conceivable diplomatic means to curtail Athens' international backing. The EC Member States were not hiding their uneasiness and possible second thoughts over the "Macedonian issue" and a break in the solidarity of the EC seemed forthcoming[58] as the Edinburgh European Council gave a very watered-down assurance of continued support to the Lisbon declaration.[59] The situation was declining rapidly in FYROM, which was facing problems with the large Albanian minority and dreaded a southward expansion of the war raging in Bosnia-Herzegovina. Besides, the economy was in a dismal state, caught in a stranglehold between the U.N. sanctions against the rump Yugoslavia to the north and the Greek measures to the south, and with no hope of securing World Bank/International

Monetary Fund aid without prior recognition. However, these weaknesses were exploited successfully as a bargaining chip, since the last thing that anyone wanted was an additional crisis in the Balkan region.[60] In anticipation of the United Nations decision on the admission of FYROM, Athens resumed diplomatic efforts in the final months of 1992, seeing FYROM's U.N. membership as inevitable but attempting to avert the worst.[61] In January 1993 the Greek Government submitted a 16-point memorandum to the Security Council[62], denouncing FYROM's intransigence and "destabilising influence in the region." It also contained attachments of the "Greater Macedonia" maps printed in FYROM, of the Vergina Star on its flag etc. Gligorov's government duly counter-attacked on February 3 with a memorandum accusing Greece of recalcitrant behavior and of "exerting destabilising influence in the region. . ."[63]

The Security Council accepted the new republic's application by resolution 817/1993 and recognized it under the provisional name "Former Yugoslav Republic of Macedonia." For the first time in the history of the Organization a state had been admitted under a temporary name, especially in view of the fact that all the federative states of the former Soviet Union and Yugoslavia which had recently become independent members had retained the name which they had within the federations. Greece also managed to hinder the flying of the offensive FYROM flag at the U.N.[64] and to secure a recommendation that the difference over the name be resolved "in the interest of the maintenance of peaceful and good-neighborly relations in the region."[65] The decision produced a lot of disapproval in the Greek public opinion and it was regarded as a failure by the increasingly vociferous nationalists. The Government was caught in a cul-de-sac trying to abate the national fervor that had been unleashed at home[66] and to improve the by now increasingly tarnished image of the country abroad.[67]

In implementation of the 817/1993 resolution, a round of negotiations intended to devise Confidence Building Measures was initiated by the Co-Chairmen of the Steering Committee of the International Conference on the former Yugoslavia, C. Vance and Lord Owen. On May 14 they submitted a draft plan for an agreement on the contentious issues (emblems, constitution, propaganda), but this fell through again on account of the suggested name (Nova Makedonija: unacceptable to both sides).[68] Later the same month, the Greek Government extended a compromise proposal with the name "Slavomakedonija," the first time that the firm position against the use of any compound name to include "Macedonia" was waived.[69] This was equally unsuitable for FYROM, since its inhabitants are far from being homogeneously slavic, and further mediation was deferred until after the Greek elections in October 1993.[70]

IV. IN HOC SIGNO DISPUTATUR: THE ELEMENTS OF CONTENTION

An appraisal of the elements of contention between Greece and FYROM can be helpful in elucidating the extent to which the historical components of the Macedonian question commingled with current geopolitical and strategic necessities in order to formulate the issues of the dispute. Both sides had certainly demonstrated few signs of coming to a compromise over these issues, but often inflamed the situation further instead. Greece had been taking exception with fluctuating rigor to the use of the Macedonian name and the promulgation of a "Macedonian" nation since the end of the war, but it was during the December 4, 1991 meeting of the Government cabinet in Athens that the objections to FYROM's recognition took their final form.[71]

1. *The controversial articles of the FYROM Constitution.* In November 1991, FYROM adopted a new constitution containing clauses that Greece found objectionable. The drafting of the constitution was strongly influenced by the strongest party in the Parliament, the nationalist VMRO, and subscribed to a number of the proclamations in its electoral manifesto.[72] In particular, the Preamble to the Constitution[73] underlines its ideological affinity to the principles of the Krushevo Republic (1903)[74] and of the Antifascist Assembly of the National Liberation of Macedonia (A.S.N.O.M., 1944), regarded as the first steps towards the creation of an independent "Macedonian nation." In these declarations direct reference is made to the annexation of Macedonian territory belonging to Greece and Bulgaria and to the resistance of the people against the Balkan imperialists who carved up Macedonia in the early part of the century.[75] Art. 3 of the Constitution was also a major point of contention.[76] It originally referred to FYROM's territory as being indivisible and inalienable but, in the amendments made on January 6 1992, paragraphs (c) and (d) were added in an effort to conform to the Badinter Commission's criteria. Paragraph (c) was held by Greece to imply territorial claims against neighboring states as, in conjunction with the Preamble, it could supply the legal basis for the annexation of territories in the future. This however should be read in light of paragraph (d), which expressly rejected any such claims. Finally, Art. 49 was seen as nurturing a climate of irredentism in FYROM as well as creating an excuse for the Republic to interfere with the internal affairs of Greece under the pretext of a constitutional duty to assist a "Macedonian" minority.[77] Again, the 1992 amendments explicitly renounced any such prospect.

To an outside observer, the arguments of Greece as regards the 1991 Constitution did not appear very convincing. Assuming that there was ground

for fear that these expansionist claims were being harbored by FYROM's basic charter, the 1992 amendments had adequately removed it, on paper at least. If on the other hand, as the Greek Government maintained, Balkan politics are hardly straightforward and even an express claim of non-interference should not be taken at face value, then why bother about constitutional provisions at all? As long as Athens remained convinced that the malevolent intent of Skopje was going to manifest itself in the future despite the "express safeguards" originally introduced by the 1992 amendments, the logic of still pursuing constitutional alterations escaped the outside observer. This is not to say that it FYROM's undertaking in the 1995 interim agreement to amend the controversial articles once again was not a significant step forward, but in retrospect, if Skopje had in a sense managed to create the perception that any claims on Greece had already been absolved by the 1992 amendments, then the insistence in convoluted legal-historical arguments effectively weakened the overall Greek position.

2) *Symbols, Propaganda and the Minority Issue.* Numerous maps, car stickers and posters had been circulated in the new Republic, portraying a "Greater Macedonia," i.e. the whole of geographic Macedonia stretching south to Mt. Olympus, as the historic homeland of the "Macedonians" in FYROM.[78] These had been issued by private or semi-official sources (e.g. the V.M.R.O.) and were used by Greece as proof of the territorial aspirations against her northern provinces. The FYROM government authorities however have always disavowed themselves from this and tried to diffuse the matter as either the work of a few extremists or the direct popular reaction to Greece's relentless attempts to smother FYROM. More troublesome, because of its official origin, appeared to be the inclusion of similar maps in the school textbooks of history published in 1992 and 1993. These created the impression that all Macedonian heritage belongs rightfully to FYROM and that there exist unliberated territories within the boundaries of Bulgaria and Greece that have been stolen from the motherland.[79]

One of the main weapons in the bilateral propaganda struggle was the vexed issue of the existence of a Slavic minority in Greek Macedonia. The policy of Athens in the last five decades has been a staunch denial of the existence of any such minority, however small. Especially after independence however, FYROM repeatedly raised the matter in international fora, demanding that Greece respect the fundamental human rights of this long-suffering minority[80] and recognize its "Macedonian" status.[81] The existence and the numbers of the Slav minority in Greece[82] became one of the major issues in the ensuing bedlam,[83] especially as Skopje was fleet to employ the Greek objections to Art. 49 of the

Constitution as implied evidence for the real numerical strength of the minority.[84]

Finally in August 1992, the Parliament of FYROM adopted as an emblem on their flag the sixteen-pointed Star of Vergina, the symbol of the ancient Macedonian dynasty.[85] This move was not only historically questionable but was also regarded as a gross national slur by the incensed public opinion in Greece.[86] It had been suggested at the time that what prompted the adoption of the Vergina Star was a desire from Skopje's part to advance maximalist objectives in order to barter with them for other concessions at the negotiating table when the time comes.[87] The bilateral negotiations that followed the 1995 interim accord justified this view.

3) *The use of the name.* Undoubtedly, all the above points of friction were accessory and appurtenant to the crux of the whole dispute, the name of the new state. The bases for the Greek reasoning were historical, ethnological and geographical and have been broadly outlined above. Indeed, if strict archaeological and historical exactness is sought, one may regard as an oxymoron the use of the term "Macedonian" by a slavic people. Moreover, the heritage and culture of the much wider geographic region runs the risk of becoming soon monopolized, even without any further action from FYROM, since it will be almost natural to associate it with the only country which contains the Macedonian name in the state denomination.[88] But it would be wrong to assume that the argument exhausted itself there; what appeared to be at issue was not only national pride but also long-term Greek national security. This may sound exaggerated in view of the weakness of the new state, but the Greeks could not easily forget that Balkan politics are notoriously volatile and susceptible to defy predictions. As Athens saw it, regional powers like Turkey or Bulgaria may seek to take advantage of this feebleness, with a view to achieving an "encirclement" that could prove detrimental for Greece. This could be accompanied by renewed territorial claims on Greek territory, founded on historical and geographical claims to a "Greater Macedonia," since by that time in the future this legacy might be regarded as belonging, partly at least, to FYROM.[89] Foreigners, failing to appreciate the possibility of such a turn of events, tended to misinterpret Greek security anxieties[90] in relation to the name as originating from fear of future secessionist movements of the Slav minority in the north of the country.[91]

It is imperative to note Skopje's arguments justifying their use of the name: They have been centered around the view that FYROM is the only state situated integrally in Macedonia, therefore it is well justified to use this name as far as geographical considerations go. In parallel, FYROM emphasizes that it does not

claim for itself a monopoly on the name nor is it concerned with the Greek province named Macedonia.[92] Their sole objective remains to stop Athens operating a monopoly over Macedonia and to allow FYROM to exercise its right of self-determination in the choice of its name. To this effect, FYROM stressed the following points: that the Greek Consulate in Skopje addressed the authorities using the name Socialist Republic of Macedonia as late as the beginning of 1992;[93] that for the first time in history a segment of geographic Macedonia came under Greek administration in 1913;[94] that FYROM was the first to use the name officially, after 1944, whilst Greece never used it in an official form until 1988, therefore the *prior tempore potior jure* rule must be applied;[95] and that, most importantly, the change of the Republic's name is against the will of the people and it "will unconditionally destabilize the country."[96] Nevertheless, whether there was indeed substance in the claims of FYROM that their citizens feel members of a distinct Macedonian nationality appeared to go unquestioned in Greece. To answer this appropriately, neither the decades of persistent indoctrination should be left out of consideration nor Greece's violent struggle since 1991 in contrast to her complacency for the 45 years before this. If it was a common bond for the people that the government in Skopje wanted, they found it by claiming this name and rallying the whole population in a united resistance front under a common cause against the pugnacious Greeks.[97]

V. *DÉNOUEMENT*: RECOGNITIONS, COUNTERMEASURES, THE EUROPEAN COURT OF JUSTICE, THE 1995 INTERIM ACCORD AND THE STALEMATE.

The first country to recognize FYROM, under the name "Republic of Macedonia," was Bulgaria in January 1992. Sofia preferred an independent state that should be easier to influence than the previous Yugoslavian federative republic, which had engaged in strong anti-Bulgarian policies.[98] At the same time however, true to its long-standing position, Sofia denied the existence of a separate "Macedonian" nation, choosing to consider FYROM's population as a close relative instead.[99] Shortly afterwards Turkey recognized FYROM, again as "Macedonia," and was the first country to establish full diplomatic relations with Skopje. Given that FYROM could provide fertile ground for Ankara's moves to extend its influence in the post-Yugoslavia Balkans and that Greece was vehemently opposed to such a recognition, this move was hardly surprising.[100] Until its admission in the United Nations in 1993, the only other

countries to recognize the state had been Russia, Slovenia and Croatia. Despite U.N. membership, the European Union and all major Western countries refrained from establishing full diplomatic relations with Skopje but with 1993 coming to a close it was apparent that this was not going to last for long, as mass media in the West were increasingly turning against the Greek positions.[101] The October 10 general elections brought the Socialists to power, and (the generally considered as uncooperative) A. Papandreou back to premiership. The new government was determined to initiate a tougher approach to the Macedonian issue and had repeatedly confirmed these intentions during the electoral campaign.[102] In a letter to the U.N. Secretary-General, the new Foreign Minister K. Papoulias stated that Athens was willing to proceed with the Vance-Owen mediation only as long as FYROM would quit its deliberate procrastination tactics and acquiesce to some basic Greek demands.[103] This move prompted six EU Member States (Denmark, France, Germany, Italy, the Netherlands, United Kingdom) to accord full diplomatic recognition to Skopje, only a few days before the semester of the Greek Presidency of the Community was about to begin.[104] Greece protested against this action on the grounds that it constituted a breach in the unity of the Common Foreign and Security Policy of the Union, and that it opened the floodgates for a wave of recognitions which would automatically resolve the issue in FYROM's favor and allow it to be even more inflexible at the bilateral negotiations. When the United States followed suit in February 1994,[105] Greece replied by severing diplomatic ties with Skopje and imposing a blockade on FYROM goods moving to and from the port of Thessaloniki with the exception of humanitarian aid on February 16.[106] An unprecedented condemnation followed in the whole of Europe, as the international community reacted with indignation to what was seen as Greek hysteria. Serious opinion-makers questioned openly the suitability of Athens running the European Union affairs for the first semester of 1994 and even suggested the removal of Greece from the Union altogether.[107] In a flurry of tense diplomatic activity, the Greek government tried to explain its position amidst growing allegations that the countermeasures constituted flagrant breach of the country's obligations under international law[108] and under European Community law, as a Member of the E.U.[109] The matter was discussed by the Council at Ioannina, where the Greek government again came under attack for the measures, but no final decision was reached. On April 22 the Commission brought an action under Art. 225.2 of the EC Treaty, alleging that the Hellenic Republic had made improper use of Art. 224 of the Treaty in order to justify the unilateral measures adopted on February 16. Art. 225 provides for an accelerated procedure for the Commission to bring a Member State directly before the European Court of Justice for making improper use of the powers it

has under Art. 224 to take emergency measures in the event of serious internal disturbances, war, threat of war, or for maintaining peace and international security.[110] The matter caused serious consternation in Greece, with wild speculation about "extensive antihellenic conspiracies" becoming rife.[111]

At the same time, the Commission filed an application for interim measures under Art. 186 EC, requiring Greece to suspend the trade blockade pending judgement on the main action. Greek efforts were mobilized and on May 24, 1994 the government submitted a 65-page document (along with a massive annex) containing its written observations on the interim relief application. The document consisted of two parts, one outlining the historical background and the other refuting the Commission's legal claims.[112] The European Court considered the legal arguments and came up with a carefully worded decision rejecting the Commission's application for interim measures on the basis of insufficient proof on what regards the harm caused to Community competition. The Court also underlined the fact that a number of considerations innate to the matter were of political and not legal nature.[113] The June 29, 1994 decision was welcomed with approval as "Greece's full vindication."[114]

Even if this was not necessarily the case, the dispute was obviously coming to a close, one way or the other. The deteriorating situation in Bosnia-Herzegovina further north, meant that the Greece-FYROM dispute was rapidly becoming demoted to less than a side-show. After several months of relatively low-level activities, with both sides remaining entrenched in their former positions, the breakthrough was precipitated by the Advocate-General's opinion on the legality of the Greek countermeasures, issued in April 1995.[115] In fact, the Advocate-General was suggesting to the European Court that, under the circumstances of the case in question, a ruling could not be made by the Court on the essence of the dispute. Although this was far from vindicating the Greeks for the imposition of trade sanctions, it was certainly one of the arguments heavily relied upon by the Greek side. In Skopje, a Foreign Ministry statement described the opinion as "an attempt to exert political pressure" and expressed the hope that the ECJ would still go on and adopt the "correct" ruling.[116] At the same time however, it was becoming increasingly clear in FYROM that the embargo was not going to be declared unlawful by the European Community and thus the only way to avert further damage to the already reeling economy led to the negotiating table. A summer of intense bilateral diplomatic activity followed, culminating in an agreement aimed at normalizing relations, signed on September 13, 1995 by the Foreign Ministers of the two countries. The essence of the interim accord was the lifting of the trade sanctions against Skopje in exchange for the FYROM's undertaking to change its national flag, refrain from using symbols "linked to Greece's cultural and historical heritage" and amend

the "offending" articles of its Constitution.[117] In response to the interim accord, the European Commission decided to drop the legal action against Greece, before the final decision of the Court was due.[118] Nevertheless, the accord did not clarify the most important of the disputed issues, the name of the new country, stating instead "that the Parties will continue negotiation under the auspices of the Secretary-General of the United Nations with respect to the outstanding difference between them."[119] The dispute was far from over.[120]

Lengthy rounds of negotiations have followed the interim accord in order to reach an agreement on the issue of the name. Both sides indicated[121] that they would be looking towards a single name for FYROM, instead of a double one, to be used in all occasions both internally and internationally.[122] In 1998 elections, the former communists in Skopje lost power to a right-wing alliance which included a bloc of Albanian parties. Kiro Gligorov was replaced in presidential elections the following year by nationalist VMRO candidate Boris Trajkovski. During the Kosovo crisis of 1999 FYROM's economic woes were worsened by UN sanctions against its main trading partner, Serbia, and a massive influx of Albanian refugees whilst NATO launched its Kosovo peacekeeping operation from FYROM. The country's large Albanian minority remains a source of severe ethnic tension which erupted violently in 2001, prompting the insertion of a separate NATO peace-keeping force.

VI. AN ANALYSIS OF THE FACTORS WHICH AFFECTED GREEK FOREIGN POLICY DECISIONS DURING THE DISPUTE: 16 POINTS.

The factors that contributed to the escalation and exacerbation of the dispute between Greece and FYROM could make a matter for disagreement on themselves. The strategic planning of the Greek Foreign Policy during the 1989-1995 dispute was influenced by a variety of different considerations, some of them historical, some practical, some purely academic and even some attributable to chance. Nevertheless, in an attempt to evaluate critically the information outlined previously, a number of observations (16 as in the beams of the Vergina Star!) can be made:

1) "There is NO Macedonian issue": if one is looking for the single most important reason that influenced Greek foreign policy during the dispute with FYROM, this should be it. This standard, unchanging Greek position for 45 years, immersed the whole issue in silence and allowed Tito's Yugoslavia to proceed unperturbed. Constant statements from official sources to the effect that for Greece there is no such thing as a Macedonian Problem, created a profound ignorance of the Greek points of view in the public opinion internationally (since

there did not seem to exist *any* point of view). Similarly, the treatment of federative Skopje as a kind of diplomatic juvenile delinquent, against whom no suppressive measures should be attempted but mild protests to "parent" Belgrade made instead, demonstrates how mistaken Greek diplomacy was in assessing and handling the situation. And it was with belated ardor that Greece started to address the issue abroad and initiate home-spun "Macedonization" schemes.[123]

2) As a consequence of Greek apathy, the game of outside impressions had already been won by FYROM even before the diplomatic struggle for recognition began in 1991. Decades of Macedonian conferences and volumes of special Macedonian monographs in Institutions, Universities and libraries all over the planet had remained undisputed. Thus, by 1991-1992 when the whole world was hearing that "Macedonia" wanted to gain independence but Greece was vehemently denying it recognition because of objections to its name, it was never a question of *whether* this new state should be called like this but only on *why* the Greeks do not allow it to be called like this.

3) The inflexible position of Greece over the issue is also a factor that needs further evaluation. On one hand, the intensity of the public reaction demonstrated that, right or wrong, the population held adamant views on the subject.[124] On the other hand, the widely-publicized antagonism between FYROM and a country superior economically, politically and militarily, produced instinctive reactions and allegations that Greece was intimidating her neighbor. A point of further debate ought to be whether Athens should have accepted a compromise derivative name once it had become evident that its support in Europe was ebbing. As it happens, both major political parties in Greece were entangled in the imbroglio caused by the fierce public reaction and in order to affirm their national credentials, they had to adopt volens-nolens the position that the term "Macedonia" would not be acceptable in any form in FYROM's name, conceding to the views aired publicly by the Greek socialist MP S. Papathemelis during a 1991-1992 tour of awareness-raising speeches.[125] Certainly, as the dispute progressed, the intransigence of both sides did not permit many face-saving options.[126]

4) Greek foreign policy proved catastrophically unready to stand up to the new challenges that the dissolution of the Eastern Bloc and the redistribution of regional power demanded. The pre-1990 constant refutation of any Macedonian problem and the content of the relations with Yugoslavia and S.R.M. indicated that Greece did not consider even remotely that the possibility of a challenge in the status quo in Macedonia would ever arise. Conceding that the end of the cold war was certainly not something easily forecast in the eighties, Greece's preoccupation with Turkey did not allow for even basic preparations to ensure

a coherent Balkan policy in the event of a break-up of Yugoslavia, and disregarded the warning signs that such an eventuality was probable. One should not forget the use of the term (S.R.) Macedonia by the Greek Consulate to address the Skopje government as late as 1991.

5) Cultural haughtiness and arrogance on behalf of the Greeks contributed to the unfamiliarity with their positions both at home and abroad.[127] For a long time there was little else for a reaction than a disdainful attitude against both FYROM, for attempting to usurp the Hellenic heritage of Macedon, and against some "hapless barbarians" around the world who could be ignorant enough to give credence to "FYROM's fabrications." And this was coupled with the loftiness of the Greeks being certain of having right in what they claimed, a fact that (in their eyes) made any need to actually attempt to prove the legitimacy of these assertions redundant.[128] Even after Athens had embarked in the diplomatic struggle to hinder recognition, there were hardly any attempts made to use the media in the West to attain a favorable influence, although in the home front the newspapers were overflowing with pointless philippics against FYROM.[129]

6) The dispute over Macedonia should not be examined separately from the Yugoslavian conflict and the countless side-issues and problems that this caused. Greece's wishes and interests in most aspects of the Yugoslavian crisis ran contrary to the interests of almost all other Western powers. To start with, Athens was in favor of the preservation of Yugoslavia (even advocating this as late as 1993), which brought her immediately at odds with Germany, Italy and Austria, who for historical reasons and in order to increase their regional influence, sought to dismember Yugoslavia. This of course gave to the individual federative republics the chance to proclaim their sovereignty and pursue their own policies. Furthermore, Greece's support for Serbia, her only historical ally in the region, did not exactly enhance its international reputation, given Serbia's status at the time as an international bully and a pariah state.

7) The Yugoslavian crisis was a major dent in the prestige of the embryonic Common Foreign and Security Policy of the European Union. The federalists' aspiration to create a new axis of security in the shape of the E.U. was shattered as Europe tried ineffectually to avert the severest conflict on European soil since W.W. II (a conflict in whose creation it had played a major role in the first place). Greece's hostility against the poorest of the former Yugoslav Republics was correctly perceived as a potential threat to its existence and a potential cause for further expansion of the war southwards. Irrespective of how good or convincing Athens' arguments were going to be, Europe was not going to allow Greece to exert pressure and strangulate FYROM, as this could mean facing a new embarrassing failure to safeguard peace in the region.[130] The Macedonian

problem was seen as a pointless aggravation of an already inflamed situation and respect for Greek sensitivities could not last for long. FYROM also knew this as well and did a good job of reminding it to anyone listening. Hence, the Union ultimately broke its solidarity in supporting Greece.

8) Along similar lines can the U.S. involvement and reaction be explained. After the failure to hinder the outbreak of hostilities in Bosnia, America saw FYROM as a way of giving "politicians and the voters a feeling of painlessly contributing to the Yugoslav crisis."[131] Not wanting to be accused of interfering in internal European Union matters, the U.S. waited until the break in the Union's ranks became manifest in order to recognize FYROM. In addition, as the Balkans started to be divided into spheres of influence, the U.S. sought to secure one of these new countries under its wing, i.e. FYROM. This obviously paid handsome dividends later during the 1999 crisis, when FYROM was used as a staging ground for NATO troops moving into Kosovo.[132]

9) Further to pursuing their own very real interests, a number of European countries showed a rather superficial appreciation of the real essence of the dispute between Greece and FYROM, dismissing it often in a high-handed manner as childish hysteria[133] or impenetrable Balkan peculiarities.[134] In this way, Greece was torn between a need to apply occidental foreign policy standards so as to display that she is a worthy member of the Western world, and the insufficiency of these policy measures to bring forth the desired results within the highly complex Balkan diplomatic theatre.

10) As a consequence, Athens' foreign policy was often oscillating between cultural and pragmatic arguments. After the realization that a debate over heritage rights, the ethnicity of the ancient Macedonians, the concepts of cultural patrimony of mankind etc. would not be adequate to persuade the world opinion, an attempt was made to formulate a *realpolitik* by justifying Greek views by means of more "rational" and interest-oriented arguments.[135] These however were not necessarily more successful as they presupposed that the listening parties possessed special knowledge of the Balkan area, its history and its specific idiosyncrasy.

11) The 1992 decision of the Council in Lisbon not to recognize FYROM with a name containing the term "Macedonia" was certainly a high point in E.U. solidarity, but it should also be born in mind that the Europeans were responding in this fashion to the Greek conservative government's warnings that, in the opposite case, the return to power of "trouble-making" A. Papandreou would be very likely.

12) A range of different factors caused the balance to finally turn in favor of FYROM during the crucial second semester of 1992. Athens rested on the

laurels of the Lisbon declaration and dramatically slackened diplomatic activity during the summer, whilst the FYROM government was steadily increasing its influence. Skopje augmented its strategic status because of the need to enforce the U.N. embargo against Serbia and also attracted the support of islamist and philocroat circles. The change of Council Presidency was also very positive for the Skopje side, as the British started to systematically undermine the Lisbon declaration with a view to amending it. The summer of 1992 might have been an opportunity for Athens to achieve a favorable outcome at a time when FYROM's situation had come to an all-time low.

13) FYROM gained international sympathies by projecting an underdog image, oppressed by its irritable neighbor. Notwithstanding the extent to which this reflected a true situation, Greek Foreign Policy felt obliged to take into consideration the public opinion's disapproval of "the evident tolerance and acceptance displayed by the international community toward the image of the "poor underdog" that President Kiro Gligorov [adeptly and possibly rightfully] applied to himself and his state. [. . .] The President of FYROM [is seen] as a Balkan "Jean Valjean" who was caught stealing a small loaf of bread, the Sun of Vergina, in order to feed his family: that is to give his "oppressed" and "misunderstood" people a sense of pride. [. . .] His aim was to cast Greece in the role of the inhuman "Javert."[136]

14) The Greek positions suffered from feeble attempts to gain influence in Western mass media and thus adopt a positive media image. On the other hand, it appears that from 1992 there was a concerted effort in certain European countries to consolidate FYROM's position through official instructions to newspapers and television channels to adopt an "antihellenic" stance. In the meantime, oceans of ink were aimlessly flowing in both FYROM and Greece preaching to the converted.[137] Finally, even foreigners agree that the Greek lobbying in Europe was not sufficiently energetic.[138]

15) Geopolitical, strategic and sentimental reasons aside, FYROM also became a valid cause on humanitarian grounds. Possibly even because it was far less dangerous to intervene in FYROM than further north where they were really needed, several individuals and NGOs stressed the need for immediate action in Skopje's favor, in order to avert a humanitarian catastrophe. For the same reasons, the Greek countermeasures of February 1994 were seen in a very dim light by the international community. Macedonia had become "a black stain in the conscience of Europe" as the Danish Foreign minister U. Jenssen said.[139]

16) In conclusion it should be noted that apart from the national and international foreign policies described above, a number of private or semi-official interests also became entangled in the issue of FYROM's recognition,

e.g. Islamic unity organizations and the Soros Foundation, which tended mostly to support Skopje (and Tirana) both materially and by means of lobbying.

VII. CONCLUSION: MACEDONIA CUIUS?

The traditional "Macedonian Question" underwent drastic changes in the 1990s as a result of the dissolution of Yugoslavia and the emergence of an independent state under the provisional international name of Former Yugoslav Republic of Macedonia. This analysis has demonstrated that the dispute between Greece and FYROM concealed no hidden agenda, but it really did revolve around the issue of the name that the new state was going to adopt. Whether this country would be named Macedonia or not was not a side-question but, for the Greek side at least, the crux of the argument. On a dialectic level, one is led to the conclusion that the diplomatic struggle over which entity has the right to use for itself the name Macedonia is an illustrative undercurrent of a dispute between the proponents of two nationalist ideologies over the possession of national identity,[140] history and culture, all of which, from a nationalist perspective, are considered to be the property of the nation.[141] It is a dispute over the ownership of cultural property in which each of two countries has attempted to place a trademark on what it considers to be its name, its national emblems and its famous ancestors. Since a state's culture is as much its possession as its territory, the appropriation of this culture by another country has thus been construed as a threat to national integrity. The fundamental to agree on the very status of the contested name of the land and its people seems to be a product of the use of entirely different criteria in defining basic terms: for Greece, the word "Macedonia" and all that it symbolizes in racial and cultural continuity is the critical issue; the goal of FYROM is recognition of its ethnospecificity.[142]

After being marginalized in the strategic chessboard of the "New World Order" because of the collapse of the U.S.S.R. and the end of the cold war, Greece managed to become seriously isolated internationally in the struggle against FYROM and alienate herself from her most important allies.[143] For a period of several years after 1992, Athens was seen as a "second bully of the Balkans," an accomplice almost of Serbia and unworthy of European and international support or even, in the extreme cases, membership. In retrospect, Greece missed a chance that the power vacuum in the Balkans provided to emerge as a leading regional power and present a pole of development in the south of Europe. It could also be argued that, to a certain extent, Greek reaction against FYROM undermined the potentially privileged position that she would have in influencing the young state[144] allowing Turkey to deploy itself with

less hindrances in the geostrategic chessboard of the Balkan peninsula and substitute Greece as the regional power.[145]

At the same time, the Former Yugoslav Republic of Macedonia, although initially successful in preventing a spill-over of the armed conflict in ex-Yugoslavia towards its own territory, was obliged to go through the first four years after its independence entangled in a bitter dispute, one that seemed capable to threaten its very existence. It was with great diplomatic skill and courage that the complete collapse of the small state was prevented. By the end of 1994 it was becoming apparent to both sides that the continuing dispute had run out of steam and was resulting only in further embarrassment and losses,[146] and the interim accord of September 1995 did not come as a surprise to many. Moreover, the issue was (deliberately?) allowed by both sides to remain unresolved during the interminable UN negotiations, thereby strengthening the status quo in favor of a generalized usage of the name "Republic of Macedonia."[147]

Finally, the inherent instability of FYROM (name or no name) due to its volatile ethnic mix, was greatly exacerbated (as it was for the whole of the Balkan region) by the 1999 NATO intervention in Kosovo, and further came into stark contrast by the low-level civil conflict fought in FYROM in 2001. The future of FYROM as an independent state in its current form, name and borders does not appear universally guaranteed and will presumably be influenced by the final outcome of the situation in the currently "limbo"-suspended issue of the Kosovo province and the likely reactions of the Albanians. Although a steadfast focus of Greek foreign policy throughout the last decade has been the at all costs preservation of the territorial integrity of its northern neighbor, it is conceivable that the time may have come for Athens to sacrifice this holy cow of hellenic diplomacy and reconsider whether such a heretical approach might be in the long run advantageous to the Greek positions.

Endnotes

[1] The ethnic name is derived from the adjective *μακεδνὺς* occurring already in Homer (Odys. *η* 106). See Andriotes (*History of the Name "Macedonia"*) at p. 143. For a discussion of the ethnic origin of the Macedonians see Andriotes (*The Language and Greek Origin of the Ancient Macedonians*). Using arguments based on linguistic analysis to support the Greek side of the argument, Hadjidakis (Du Caractère Hellénique de la Macèdoine).

[2] The ethnicity of the ancient Macedonians has been a matter of heated debate for some time. Based on "Demosthenes" philippics (where Philip was denounced as an uncouth semi-barbarian) some sources have denied any ethnic connection between the Macedonians and other Greeks. Nevertheless, it appears that currently most serious researchers do not seem to question the hellenism of the Macedonians, as members of the Doric tribe. For an exposé of the argument: Nystazopoulou-Pelekidou, p. 3 *et seq.*; with detailed discussion, Wardle; also Sakellariou pp. 44-47; Martis at p. 20 *et seq*; *cf.* also fn 3 *infra*. With details, the book by Poulton (Who are the Macedonians?).

[3] See *inter alia* Martis, pp. 53-71; Ellis & Walbank; but also Pribichevich, pp. 37-64.

[4] For more see Libal, p. 15 *et seq.*; Pribichevich, pp. 65-93; Christophilopoulou; Bucar, p. 8 *et seq.*

[5] The Ottomans never used the name Macedonia as an administrative (or ethnic) appellation; *cf.* Papazoglou;

[6] Kofos E., (*National Heritage and National Identity in Nineteenth- and Twentieth-Century Macedonia*), p. 4.

[7] E.g. the book by Tachiaos.

[8] See concluding chapter by Veremis; also Kitromilides; Kofos, (*Dilemmas and Orientations of Greek Policy in Macedonia: 1878-1886*).

[9] Zotiades at p. 13.

[10] See Klok, (*De Macedonische Kwestie*).

[11] Internal Macedonian Revolutionary Organization, as the *Vatresna Makedonska Revoljucionenna Organizacija* (V.M.R.O.) is internationally known.

[12] For a Slav-Macedonian view of IMRO, the "Macedonian Revolution" and the Macedonian Struggle (cultural and military), see Pribichevich, pp. 106-135; also Bucar, pp. 90-104.

[13] *Cf.* Koliopoulos; for a chronological account see Papakonstantinou, (I Makedonia meta ton Makedoniko Agona), pp. 38-53.

[14] Kofos, (*The Fight for Freedom 1830-1912*); see also Dakin p. 73 *et seq.*

[15] For a fascinating contemporary description of the ethnic and religious mix of peoples in Macedonia right after the end of Ottoman rule, see the 1913 *National Geographic* report of Villari.

[16] It must be noted that Greece secured not only the largest part of the geographic region of Macedonia, but also approximately 90% of the historic core of ancient Macedonia; Voros, (*The Macedonian Question of our Neighbors*).

[17] Zotiades, p. 29, fn. 73.

[18] Bulgaria, aligning with the Central Powers in WWI and with the Axis in WWII, occupied Serb and Greek Macedonia on both occasions; *ibid.*, pp. 72-76; See e.g. Klok, (*De tweete Macedonische Kwestie*).

[19] Recapitulating Voros, (Different uses of the term Macedonia in the Centuries of History); for the Greek side) see Mackridge & Yannakakis (*The development of a Greek Macedonian Identity Since 1912*).

[20] The Bulgarian part never assumed the Macedonian name. During the interwar years it was known as the Pirin district, whereas after the Second World War it was given the administrative name of the Blagoevgrad Okrug.

[21] See the article by Kofos, "The Macedonian Question: The Politics of Mutation."

[22] "The struggle for a united and independent Macedonian republic of the working people is a worthy cause," *Resolution of the Communist International on the Macedonian Question and the IMRO (United), 1934*, in: Kondis B. et al (eds.), p. 23; see also Papakonstantinou M., (*I Makedonia meta ton Makedoniko Agona*), p. 13 *et seq*; Voros, (*Macedonian Question of Neighbors*), p. 39 *et seq.*; but from the Bulgarian point of view, see Misirkov.

[23] Zotiades, pp. 77-82; Kofos, (*The Making of Yugoslavia's People's Republic*

of Macedonia). In 1963 the "People's Republic of Macedonia" was renamed "Socialist Republic of Macedonia."

[24] On the notion of "titular nation," see Bremmer & Taras (*eds.*), p. 5.

[25] Until the mid-20th century, linguists understood under "Macedonian language" the ancient dialect spoken in the area, widely considered to be a form of "pre-Greek." See *inter alia* the (celebrated as co-discoverer of Linear Script B) J. Chadwick (*The Prehistory of the Greek Language*).

[26] And reinforced by military occupation during both wars; about the Macedonian policy of Bulgaria in the period after World War II, see Zotiades, pp. 94-100; on Serbia see Michailidis (*Serbian Claims in Macedonia Between the Wars*).

[27] "The fighting Piedmont of Macedonia has fiercely proclaimed that it will not stint on support or sacrifice for the liberation of the other two segments of our nation and for the general unification of the entire Macedonian people," Report of the Organizing Committee of the Anti-Fascist Assembly of National Liberation of Macedonia (ASNOM) concerning its activity from its foundation to its first session (2.VIII.1994), Kondis *et al* (*eds.*), p. 35; See Zotiades, pp. 83-90; Leontaritis, p. 21; Pribichevich, p. 145 *et seq.*

[28] Kofos, (*National Heritage and National Identity*), p. 20, comments on the "Yugoslav Macedonian historiographers, who could labor with equal ease in the annals of history and the world of fantasies."

[29] Zotiades, pp. 91-93.

[30] For the influence of the Macedonian Controversy on the Greek civil war, see Kofos, (*The Impact of the Macedonian Question on Civil Conflict on Greece*); also Kondis; informative background to be found in Hammond.

[31] See Klok, (*De tweete . . .*), p. 4.

[32] For the Greco-Yugoslav relations in the 1950s, see Zotiades, pp. 101-107; also Stefanidis, (*The US, GB and the Greek-Yugoslav Rapprochement*).

[33] Giakoumis, p. 443.

[34] This is a manifestly untrue statement of course but it remained one of the mainstays for Greek propaganda for almost half a century. It is quoted here as found in the "Statement by the Head of the Greek Delegation" in: Reply of the Yugoslav Intervention at the Plenary Session of June 22, 1990; C.S.C.E., Conference on Human Dimension, Offprint, Athens: ELIAMEP, 1991, at p. 355.

[35] Kofos, (*Greece and the Balkans in the '70s and '80s*), p. 8.

[36] *Ibid.*, p. 7.

[37] Bilateral cultural agreements of third countries with Yugoslavia were sure to include a pro-Macedonia proviso; see Kofos (*National Heritage and National Identity*), p. 29.

[38] With details, Martis, p. 104 *et seq.*

[39] Kofos, (*National Heritage and National Identity*), p. 32.

[40] An illuminating personal anecdote is mentioned by Martis, at p. 101.

[41] Kofos, (*Politics of Mutation*), at p. 170.

[42] An example of the slackening of central control and the consequent unleashing of hitherto latent nationalist trends are the sharp clashes between the Greek and Yugoslav delegations during the C.S.C.E. conferences on Human Dimension (Copenhagen 1990, Moscow 1991) over allegations of maltreatment of the "Macedonian" minority in northern Greece; statements by the Head of the Greek delegation in: Valinakis & Ntalis (*eds.*), at pp. 23, 43.

[43] For the results of the referendum, *ibid.*, p. 38.

[44] In March 1991 the Socialist Republic of Macedonia had dropped the "Socialist" from its name and remained, as the "Republic of Macedonia," a part of the Yugoslav federation.

[45] Declaration of Independence of the Yugoslav Republic of Macedonia, in Valinakis & Ntalis (*eds.*), p. 40.

[46] The President of the Republic of Macedonia, the former communist Kiro Gligorov, had been initially favorable to association within a "New Yugoslavia," a fact that had seemingly reassured Athens too much.

[47] To avoid confusion through the use of varied nomenclature, the Yugoslav Republic of Macedonia will be subsequently referred to as FYROM (Former Yugoslav Republic of Macedonia), a name it officially adopted however only *after* its recognition by the United Nations in 1993.

[48] In the November 1990 elections in FYROM the notoriously nationalistic V.M.R.O. (resurrected I.M.R.O.) emerged as the largest party in Parliament and, although it remained in the opposition, its stalwart antihellenic outlooks were to become a notable influence on Skopje's policy.

[49] For some of the background of this meeting, see Axt; Alendar, pp. 1009-1011.

[50] "The Community and its Member States also require a Yugoslav Republic to commit itself, prior to recognition, to adopt constitutional and political guarantees ensuring that it has no territorial claims towards a neighboring Community State and that it will conduct no hostile propaganda activities versus a neighboring Community State, *including the use of a denomination which implies territorial claims*" (our italics); Extraordinary EPC Ministerial Meeting: Declaration on Yugoslavia, Brussels, 16.XII.1991, in Valinakis & Ntalis (*eds.*), p. 50.

[51] This Commission was to consider the conformity of the individual Yugoslav Republics to the conditions that the Community had set for recognition; see FYROM's reply to the Badinter Commission questionnaire, 29.XII.1991, *ibid.*, p. 54; Badinter Commission Report No. 6 (Re: FYROM), 11.I.1992, *ibid.*, p. 65.

[52] See letters of Karamanlis to the EC Heads of Government, 3.I.1992, *ibid.*, p. 63; and to Italy's PM G. Andreotti, 21.I.1992, *ibid.*, p. 83; letter of Samaras to the EC Foreign Ministers, 17.I.1991, *ibid.*, p. 72.

[53] From the name of the Portuguese Foreign Minister who negotiated it; "Pineiro package," *ibid.*, p. 87.

[54] Council of Ministers, Guimaraes decision, *ibid.*, p. 94.

[55] Lisbon European Council, Conclusions of the Presidency, Annex II, 26-27.VI.1992, *ibid.*, p. 100. It appears that in exchange for EC support on the Macedonian issue, Greece promised to ratify the Maastricht treaty, participate in sanctions against its traditional ally Serbia, and ratify the EC financial protocol with Turkey.

[56] *Cf.* Perry (*Une crise en Gestation? La Macédoine et ses voisins*).

[57] See FYROM's Reaction to the Lisbon European Council Decision, 3.VII.1992, in Valinakis & Ntalis (*eds.*), p. 103; and President Gligorov's Letter to the U.N. Secretary General, *ibid.*, p. 106.

[58] See e.g. Karamanlis' Letter to the Heads of Government of the EC, 24.X.1992, *ibid.*, p. 108, where he professes his surprise over "the incomprehensible tendencies within the Community towards a review of the Lisbon decision."

[59] Edinburgh European Council, Conclusions of the Presidency, Section D, External Relations, 11-12.XII.1992, *ibid.*, p. 123.

[60] Although this was later eclipsed by the events in 2001 (Operation "Necessary Harvest"), it is useful to be reminded that already in December 1992, 1000 UNPROFOR soldiers (including 300 U.S. troops) were moved to FYROM in order to prevent "possible developments which could undermine confidence and stability in the Former Yugoslav Republic of Macedonia or threaten its territory"; Security Council Resolution 705(1992) of 11.XII.1992, authorizing establishment of an UNPROFOR presence in FYROM.

[61] For a behind-the-scenes overview of this mobilization see the article by the then Foreign Minister Papakonstantinou, (*I Eisdohi ton Skopion ston OIE*).

[62] Memorandum of Greece concerning the Application of the Former Yugoslav Republic of Macedonia for Admission to the United Nations, 25.I.1993, A/47/877 (agenda item 19), S/25158; published with attachments, Athens: ELIAMEP, 1993.

[63] Memorandum regarding the admission of the Republic of Macedonia in the

U.N. and the Greek Memorandum trying to prevent it, 3.II.1993, in: Valinakis & Ntalis (*eds.*), p. 138.

[64] Letter of the President of the Security Council to the U.N. Secretary-General, 7.IV.1993, *ibid.*, p. 149.

[65] Security Council Resolution 817(1993), S/25855.

[66] See e.g. Papakonstantinou, (*I Eisdohi ton Skopion. . .*), p. 26 *et seq.*

[67] The U.N. recognition of FYROM was one of the factors that contributed significantly to the fall of the Nea Dimokratia government.

[68] Papakonstantinou, (*Ellada kai Skopia, Metra Oikodomisis Empistosynis*) suggests that this plan would have been a very positive outcome for Greece at the time; see rejecting letter to the U.N. Secretary-General by Gligorov, 29.V .1993, in: Valinakis & Ntalis (*eds.*), p. 162.

[69] Letter of G. Papoulias (re: the Vance-Owen plan), 27.V.1993, S/25855/add. 1.

[70] Vance announcement: U.N. Press release SG/SM/5111, 28.IX.1993.

[71] Libal, p. 132.

[72] Compare the disputed articles of the Constitution with some of the principles contained in the V.M.R.O. manifesto, November 1990 in: Valinakis & Ntalis (*eds.*), p. 34.

[73] "Resting upon the historical, cultural, spiritual and statehood heritage of the Macedonian people and upon its centuries long struggle for national and social freedom as well as for creation of its own state, and particularly upon the statehood-legal traditions of the Krushevo Republic and the historical decisions of the Antifascist Assembly of the People's Liberation of Macedonia and the constitutional-legal continuity of the Macedonian state as a sovereign republic within Federal Yugoslavia, upon the freely manifested will of the citizens of the Republic of Macedonia on the referendum of September 8, 1991, as well as upon the historical fact that Macedonia is established as a national state of the Macedonian people . . .," as quoted *ibid.*, p. 47.

[74] *Cf.* the sources in: Bozhinov & Panayotov (*eds.*), p. 498 *et seq.*

[75] Manifesto issued at the First Session of A.S.N.O.M. to the People of Macedonia, 2.VIII.1944, in Kondis *et al* (*eds.*), p. 36; FYROM's President Gligorov has signed the A.S.N.O.M. declarations as a member of the Organization.

[76] a. The territory of the Republic of Macedonia is indivisible and inalienable.
b. The existing borders of the Republic of Macedonia are inviolable.
c. *The borders of the Republic of Macedonia could be changed only in accordance with the Constitution, and based on the principle of voluntariness and generally accepted international norms.*
d. *The Republic of Macedonia has no territorial claims against neighboring states.*," Art. 3 of the FYROM Constitution as quoted in Valinakis & Ntalis (*eds*), p. 47; the January 1992 amendments are in italics.

[77] a. The Republic takes care of the status and rights of the members of the Macedonian people in neighboring countries, as well as of emigrants from Macedonia, assists their cultural advancement and promotes the links with them. *The Republic shall not interfere in the sovereign rights of other states and their internal affairs.*
b. The Republic takes care of the cultural, economic, and social rights of the citizens of the Republic abroad," Art. 49 of the FYROM Constitution as quoted *ibid.*, p. 47; the January 1992 amendments are in italics.

[78] See a collection in "Borders, Symbols, Stability," Athens: Citizens' Movement, 1993.

[79] An examination of 12 new textbooks of history and geography is made by Kofos, (*The Vision of a "Greater Macedonia."* Remarks on FYROM's new school textbooks).

[80] "The politicization of Slavo-Macedonian language, legends, folklore, songs, dances and rituals has rendered this culture so sensitive a political issue that it can no longer be permitted to exist" Karakasidou (*Politicising Culture*), p. 28; also Karakasidou (*National Édeologies*).

[81] A history of the Slav-Macedonian minority in Greece after World War I

can be found in Bucar, pp. 203-240; for a recent rendition and an anthropological case-study see the book by Karakasidou (*Fields of Wheat, Çills of Âlood*).

[82] The estimates found in the bibliography range from 2,300 in Munuera, at p. 47, fn. 112; 20,000 to 50,000 in Perry, (*La Macédoine et ses voisins*), at p. 190; "20,000 and 50,000 Macedonian speakers [. . .] of which 10,000 have a Macedonian national identity" in Danforth, (*The Macedonian Conflict*) at p. 78; 45,000 "at most" in Libal, at p. 137; more than 50,000 in Bucar, at p. 239; 100,000 in Pribichevich at p. 237.

[83] See e.g. "Macedonian Minorities: The Slav Macedonians of Northern Greece and the Treatment of Minorities in the Republic of Macedonia," Oxford: The British Helsinki Human Rights Group, 1994. *Cf.* Kozyris (*The Macedonians of Greece*).

[84] Included in the Memorandum regarding the admission of the Republic of Macedonia in the U.N. and the Greek Memorandum trying to prevent it, 3.II.1993, in Valinakis & Ntalis (*eds.*), p. 138.

[85] Found in 1977 on the lid of a gold larnax attributed to Philip II, father of Alexander the Great; with details Andronikos, (*Art during the Archaic and Classical Periods*) p. 100 *et. seq.*; Andronikos, (*Vergina, the Royal Tombs and the Ancient City*).

[86] See *inter alia* Coughlin C., "Red Flag is Red Rag to Greeks," *The Sunday Telegraph*, 27.II.1994.

[87] *Cf.* Derala.

[88] Thus, Greek arguments in Memorandum of Greece concerning the Application of the FYROM for Admission to the U.N., point 10; "Macedonia: More than a Difference over a Name," Secretariat General for Press and Information, Athens, 1994.

[89] Klok, (*De tweete . . .*), p. 5; Giakoumis, at p. 456.

[90] The rather absurd proposal that the minuscule FYROM may conceivably represent a territorial threat to Greece has justifiably raised eyebrows with most

non-Greek analysts; nevertheless, arguing in favor of the possibility that this state may one day be used as a basis for claims against Greece, Kentrotis (*Echoes from the Past*), p. 99.

[91] See Perry, (*La Macédoine et ses voisins*), at p. 190; Munuera, at p. 48.

[92] Memorandum regarding the admission of the Republic of Macedonia in the U.N. and the Greek Memorandum trying to prevent it, in Valinakis & Ntalis (*eds.*), p. 138.

[93] *Ibid.*

[94] *Ibid.*; i.e. under administration of the post-independence modern Greek state.

[95] *Ibid.*; this is an untrue statement as it applies to the renaming of the Greek Ministry for Northern Greece to Ministry of Macedonia-Thrace in that year but disregards the use of the name to denote the administrative area for many other purposes ever since 1913.

[96] *Ibid.*

[97] Further on nationalism as a nation-building force in FYROM, Troebst, (*Makedonische Antworten auf die "Makedonische Frage"*); see also Pope H., "Macedonia seeks to evade hawk's claws," *Sunday Independent*, 27.II.1994.

[98] On the Bulgarian-Yugoslavian conflict over Macedonia, see Troebst, (*Die bulgarisch-jugoslawische Kontroverse um Makedonien* 1967-1982).

[99] Comment entitled "Bulgarien: Die Anerkennung Makedoniens," *Südosteuropa* 41 (1992), p. 236; Nelson, p. 53.

[100] Mazower; Derala, p. 8.

[101] See Barber L. & Hope K., "EC-Greek row over Macedonia worsens," *Financial Times*, 14.I.1994; Palmer J., "EU States plan links with Macedonia," *The Guardian*, 30.XI.1994.

[102] Papandreou had stressed that he would never recognize FYROM as

"Macedonia" or with a name containing this term in several televised interviews, e.g. September 28 and November 5, 1993.

[103] This letter is dated November 4, 1994; *cf.* Reply of the U.N. Secretary-General to the Foreign Minister K. Papoulias, 8.XI.1994 in Valinakis & Ntalis (*eds.*), p. 172.

[104] On December 16, 1993; see Perry, (*Crisis in the Making? Macedonia and Its Neighbors*), p. 31; Algieri, p. 3.

[105] White House Announcement regarding the Recognition of FYROM in: Valinakis & Ntalis (*eds.*), p. 176; see also the Reply of President Gligorov to President Clinton, *ibid.*, p. 178.

[106] Decision of the Cabinet of Ministers to cease the Movement of Goods to and from Skopje, 16.II.1994, *ibid.*, p. 180; further expounded in (internal) *Circular of the Ministry of Economics to the Greek Customs Regarding the Movement of Goods to and from Skopje*, 18.II.1994, p. 183.

[107] For the press reaction to the Greek countermeasures, see *inter alia* Tett G., "Blockade by Greece puts EU on the spot," *Financial Times*, 18.II.1994; "Time for Greece to rethink," The European, 25.II.1994; Mortiner E., "Southern Discomfort," *Financial Times*, 3.III.1994; Theodoracopulos T., "Greece defies its own Great Legacy," *The Wall Street Journal*, 21.IV.1994.

[108] On the validity of the claims that Greece contravened International Law by denying to landlocked FYROM access to the port of Thessaloniki, the essay by Syrigos.

[109] Outlining, "Written Observations of the Hellenic Republic regarding the Application for Interim Measures, case C-120/94 R, Commission v. Hellenic Republic," pp. 18-19 [uncirculated]; see also Argumentation regarding the adoption of measures by the Hellenic Republic against the Republic of Skopje, 21.II.1994 in: Valinakis & Ntalis (*eds.*), p. 185; Letter of J. Delors to A. Papandreou, 22.II.1994, *ibid.*, p. 192; Memorandum of the Greek Government to the European Commission, 26.II.1994, *ibid.*, p. 194; Letter of J. Delors to A. Papandreou, 21.III.1994, *ibid.*, p. 213.

[110] Article 224 EC

Member States shall consult each other with a view to taking together the steps needed to prevent the functioning of the common market being affected by measures which a Member State may be called upon to take in the event of serious internal disturbances affecting the maintenance of law and order, in the event of war, serious international tension constituting a threat of war, or in order to carry out obligations it has accepted for the purpose of maintaining peace and international security.

Article 225 EC

If measures taken in the circumstances referred to in Articles 223 and 224 have the effect of distorting the conditions of competition in the common market, the Commission shall, together with the State concerned, examine how these measures can be adjusted to the rules laid down in this Treaty.

By way of derogation from the procedure laid down in Articles 169 and 170, the Commission or any Member State may bring the matter directly before the Court of Justice if it considers that another Member State is making improper use of the powers provided for in Articles 223 and 224. The Court of Justice shall give its ruling in camera.

[111] *Cf.* "Etsi mas parapempoun se diki oi etairoi mas [Thus bring us to Court our Associates], to Pontiki, 11.V.1994; Mardas D., "Skopia-embargo: to kostos tis diethnous ypokrisias" [Skopje-embargo: the cost of international hypocrisy], *Kyriakatiki Eleftherotypia*, 24.VII.1994.

[112] "Written Observations of the Hellenic Republic regarding the Application for Interim Measures," a document provided by the Legal Office of the Ministry for Foreign Affairs in Athens.

[113] Order of the Court in case C-120/94 R, *Commission v. Hellenic Republic*, 29.VI.1994.

[114] A. Papandreou, quoted in "European Court rejects Commission appeal, "Greece vindicated," *Bulletin* (Athens News), 30.VI.1994; see also Wolf J., "EC Court declines to move against Greece's Embargo," *The Wall Street Journal*, 30.VI.1994; Statement by the Government Spokesman E. Venizelos in Brussels, 29.VI.1994, supplied by Press Office of the Greek Embassy in London; Statement of T. Pangalos in New York, 29.VI.1994, supplied by Press Office of the Greek Embassy in London.

[115] See *Greece Information, News from Greece*, No. 10, 13.IV. 1995, Greek Embassy London, Press and Information Office.

[116] As quoted *ibid.*

[117] *Greece Information, News from Greece*, No. 20, 20.IX. 1995, Greek Embassy London, Press and Information Office. Enlightening is also the report on the debate on the Greek Parliament regarding the interim accord, *ibid.*, No. 24, 10.XI. 1995.

[118] For an analysis of the action brought against Greece from a European Community law point of view, see Stefanou & Xanthaki.

[119] *Ibid.* On September 27, 1995 FYROM was admitted as a member of the Council of Europe.

[120] Moreover, in January 1996, both countries opened liaison offices in their capitals. *Greece Information, News from Greece*, No. 29, 23.I. 1996, Greek Embassy London, Press and Information Office.

[121] In December 1999, C. Vance was succeeded by M. Nimets as UN envoy in charge of the bilateral negotiations.

[122] The name issue has continued to surface in additional contexts; for example, in October 1997, the Polish president, A. Kwasniewski, refused to sign the text of a joint declaration with his counterpart K. Gligorov containing the name "Republic of Macedonia," insisting on the internationally recognized designation FYROM.

[123] E.g. the renaming of the Ministry for Northern Greece in 1988, the addition in the name of the Aristotelian University of Thessaloniki, minting of coins with the Vergina Sun, the creation of the Macedonian Press Agency in Thessaloniki in 1991, the establishing of the Vergina Star as a Greek national symbol in 1993.

[124] "Were the two million people who demonstrated in Thessaloniki last month really all hysterical? Or might it not be that, in light of historical experience, they were articulating fears we do not yet fully appreciate?," Pflueger F., "A face-saving solution exists," *The Wall Street Journal*, 21.IV.1994.

[125] It appears that a position firmly advanced by diplomatic circles of the Greek Foreign Ministry was to accept the name "*Novamakedonija.*"

[126] Munuera, *passim.*

[127] "The responsible politicians and intellectuals, who had the possibility to know what is happening across the border, faced the situation phlegmatically and I would say with a certain modicum of arrogance. For the intellectuals, all these are but gross concoctions, unable to influence the most naive of humans. Why must they occupy themselves with a worthless fabrication?" Martis, at p. 114.

[128] See Millar P., "Laying claim to the Legacy of Alexander," *The European*, 7-13.IX.1995.

[129] Even the more serious articles were often not directed towards the public outside of Greece by virtue of where they were published, e.g. Sfetas & Kentrotis, (*Skopje: In search of an Identity and International Recognition*).

[130] *Cf.* Munuera, p. 58 *et seq.*

[131] Perry, (*Crisis in the making?*), at p. 57.

[132] See the 1997 book by Shea (*Macedonia and Greece*).

[133] "When Vance and I visited Athens in September we had found Prime Minister Mitsotakis wrestling with a major political problem which some other EC governments dismissed too lightly" Lord Owen (*Balkan Odyssey*), p. 75.

[134] Rivolta D., "Attenti all iredentismo macedone," *Il Giornale*, 31.V.1994; Mazower, *passim.*; Kofos E., "Introduction" in: Valinakis & Ntalis (*eds.*), p. 15.

[135] See Marinos, p. 3; *Cf.* Clogg R., in the *London Review of Books*, 18.VIII.1994.

[136] Kofos (*The vision of Greater Macedonia*), at p. 7.

[137] See Marinos, at p. 7.

[138] "Ció che si puo rimproverare ai greci é di non aver saputo fare la giusta lobby a Bruxelles e Strasburgo," Rivolta D., "La Macedonia si salve senza pregiudizi," *Il Giornale*, 25.VI.1994.

[139] Quoted in Valinakis & Ntalis (*eds.*), p. 142.

[140] Danforth, (*The Macedonian Conflict*), *passim*.

[141] Danforth, (*Claims to Macedonian Identity*), p. 10.

[142] "A Macedonian is defined as "a person by inheritance who speaks a Slavonic language coming from that area of Europe known as Macedonia whether such is part of Greece, Yugoslavia, Bulgaria, or Albania," *ibid.*, p. 44.

[143] Someritis, p. 8; in addition, with arguments that the Greek policy between 1991-1995 failed to produce the desired outcome or to resolve the issue and precipitated a costly rift between Greece and her allies, the article by Zahariadis.

[144] Munuera, at p. 49.

[145] Perry, (*Crisis in the Making?*), at p. 54.

[146] See Marakis N., "Strofi tis Athinas sto Makedoniko"[Athens shifts its position over Macedonia], To Vima, 4.IX.1994; "Syzitame kai Onoma me ta Skopia"[We are also discussing the name issue with Skopje], *Kyriakatiki Eleftherotypia*, 11.IX.1994; Diamantis T., "Gligorov: To Onoma ehei kleisei" [Gligorov: the issue of the name has been settled] *Eleftherotypia*, 12.X.1994.

[147] Konstantakopoulos D., "A last chance to resolve the issue of the name of the FYROM," *Ependytis*, 25.XIII.2001; Iordanidis K., "Greece and FYROM: Challenges and Opportunities," *Kathimerini* (English Edition), 14.V.2001; Ligeros S., "Greece to pay," *Kathimerini*, 7.IX.2001; Marakis N., "The New Opportunity for the Name," *To Vima*, 6.V.2001; Couloumbis T. & Tziampiris A., "Unheralded, a New Foreign Policy Emerges for the Balkans," *Kathimerini* (English Edition), 9.VII.2001; Kartalis J., "The Price of the Impasse," *To Vima*, 26.XIII.2001.

REFERENCES

Official Memoranda, Government Letters, Reported Court Cases, Press Announcements and Newspaper Articles are referred to in full in the footnotes and are not included in this list. Likewise with unpublished government sources and diplomatic memoranda that the author was given access to.

Alendar, B. "The European Community and the Yugoslav Crisis," *Review of International Affairs* (Belgrade), 1009.

Algieri, F. 1994. "A Problem of Recognition—The Controversy About Macedonia," *CFSP Forum*, 1, 3.

Andriotes, N. 1960. History of the Name "Macedonia," *Balkan Studies* 1, 143.

__________. 1978. *The Language and Greek Origin of the Ancient Macedonians*. Thessaloniki: Institute for Balkan Studies.

Andronikos, M. 1992. "Art During the Archaic and Classical Periods" in Sakellariou (*ed.*), *Macedonia: 4000 Years of Greek History and Civilization*. Athens: Ekdotike Athenon, 100.

Axt. H. 1993. "Hat Genscher Jugoslawien entzweit?" *Europa-Archiv*, 351.

Bozhinov, V. and Panayotov, L. (*eds.*) 1978. *Macedonia: Documents and Material*, Sofia: Bulgarian Academy of Sciences.

Bremmer, I. and Taras, R. (*eds.*) 1993. *Nations and Politics in the Soviet Successor States*. Cambridge: University Press.

Bucar, V. 1979. *La Macedonia e i Macedoni*. Florence: Olschki.

Chadwick J. 1963. *The Prehistory of the Greek Language*, Cambridge: CUP.

Christophilopoulou, A. 1992. "From the Sixth to the Ninth Century: Political History" in Sakellariou (*ed.*), *Macedonia: 4000 Years of Greek History and Civilization*. Athens: Ekdotike Athenon, 250.

Dakin, D. 1961. "British Sources Concerning the Greek Struggle in Macedonia, 1901-1909," *Balkan Studies* 2, 71.

Danforth L. 1993. "Claims to Macedonian Identity: The Macedonian Question and the Breakup of Yugoslavia," *Anthropology Today* 9, 3.

_________. 1995. *The Macedonian conflict. Ethnic nationalism in a Transnational World*, Princeton: Princeton University Press.

Derala, J. 1994. "Macedonia at the Crossroads," *War Report* 3/4, 8.

Ellis, J. and Walbank, F. 1992. "Zenith and End of the Macedonian Kingdom: Political History" in Sakellariou (*ed.*), *Macedonia: 4000 Years of Greek History and Civilization*. Athens: Ekdotike Athenon, III.

Giakoumis, P. 1992. "Hellas und die Makedonische Frage," *Südosteuropa* 41, 443.

Hadjidakis, G. 1992. *Du caractère Hellénique de la Macèdoine, Heracleion: Société des Études Historiques Crètoises.*

Hammond, N. 1993. *The Allied Military Mission and the Resistance in West Macedonia*. Thessaloniki: Institute for Balkan Studies.

Karakasidou, A. 1993. "Politicising Culture: negating Ethnic Identity in Greek Macedonia," *Journal of Modern Greek Studies*, 11, 1.

_________. 1994. "National Ideologies, Histories and Popular consciousness: a Response to Three Critics," *Balkan Studies*, 35. 113.

_________. 1997. *Fields of Wheat, Çills of Âlood*. Passages to Íationhood in Greek Macedonia 1870–1990, Chicago: The University of Chicago Press, 1997.

Kentrotis, K. 1994. "Echoes from the Past: Greece and the Macedonian Controversy," *Mediterranean Politics*, 1, 85.

Kitromilides, P. 1990. "'Imagined Communities' and the Origins of the National Question in the Balkans," in Blinkhorn, M. & Veremis, T. (*eds.*). *Modern Greece: Nationalism and Nationality*. Athens: SAGE-ELIAMEP, 23.

Klok, K. 1992. "De Macedonische Kwestie," *Kleio* 6, 3.

_________. 1993. "De Tweete Macedonische Kwestie," *Kleio* 2, 3.

Kofos, E. 1991. *National Heritage and National Identity in Nineteenth- and Twentieth-Century Macedonia*. Athens: ELIAMEP.

_________. 1980. "Dilemmas and Orientations of Greek Policy in Macedonia: 1878-1886," *Balkan Studies* 21, 45.

_________. 1992. "The Fight for Freedom 1830-1912" in Sakellariou (*ed.*), *Macedonia: 4000 Years of Greek History and Civilization*. Athens: Ekdotike Athenon. 444.

_________. 1986. "The Macedonian Question: The Politics of Mutation," Balkan Studies 27 (1986), 157.

_________. 1962. "The Making of Yugoslavia's People's Republic of Macedonia." *Balkan Studies* 3. 375.

_________. 1989. *The Impact of the Macedonian Question on Civil Conflict on Greece*, (1943-1949), Athens: ELIAMEP.

_________. 1991. *Greece and the Balkans in the '70s and '80s*. Athens: ELIAMEP.

_________. 1994. *The Vision of a "Greater Macedonia": Remarks on FYROM's New School Textbooks*, Thessaloniki.

_________. 1994. "Introduction" in: Valinakis & Ntalis (*eds.*). *To Zitima ton Skopion: Episima Keimena 1990-1994* [The issue of Skopje: Official Sources 1990-1994]. Athens: Sideris, 15.

Koliopoulos, J. 1990. "Brigandage and Irredentism in Nineteenth-Century Greece" in Blinkhorn, M. & Veremis, T. (*eds.*). *Modern Greece: Nationalism and Nationality*. Athens: SAGE-ELIAMEP, 67.

Kondis, B. 1987. "The Macedonian Question as a Balkan Problem in the 1940s," *Balkan Studies* 28, 151.

Kondis, B. et al (*eds.*) 1993. *Resurgent Irredentism: Documents on Skopje "Macedonian" Nationalist Aspirations (1934-1992)*. Thessaloniki: Institute for Balkan Studies, p. 23.

Kozyris, P. 1996. "Book Review: The Macedonians of Greece: Denying Ethnic Identity," *Journal of Modern Greek Studies* 14, 147.

Leontaritis, G. 1993. "The Macedonian Question" in *On Scientific Truth About Macedonia*. Athens: National Technical University of Athens, 21.

Libal, W. 1993. *Mazedonien zwischen den Fronten*. Vienna: Europaverlag, 1993.

Mackridge, P. & Yannakakis, E. (*eds.*). 1997. *Ourselves and Others: The Development of a Greek Macedonian Identity Since 1912*, Oxford: Berg.

Marinos, G. 1994. "O heirismos ton ethnikon thematon" [The Handling of National Matters], *Oikonomikos Tachydromos*, 6.X., 3.

Martis, N. 1984. *The Falsification of Macedonian History*, Athens.

Mazower, M. 1994. "The Bigger Balkan Conflict," *War Report* 3/4, 3.

Michailidis, I. 1995. "Traditional Friends and Occasional Claimants: Serbian claims in Macedonia between the wars," *Balkan Studies* 36, 103.

Misirkov, K. 1978. "The Nationality of the Macedonians" [II.V.1924], in: Bozhinov, V. & Panayotov, L. (*eds.*), *Macedonia: Documents and Material*. Sofia: Bulgarian Academy of Sciences, 759.

Munuera, G. 1994. "Preventing Armed Conflict in Europe: Lessons From Recent Experience." Paris: Institute for Security Studies WEU.

Nelson, D. 1993. "A Balkan Perspective" in *European Security Toward the Year 2000*. Washington DC: National Defence University, 53.

Nystazopoulou-Pelekidou, M. 1993. "A Historical Survey of the Macedonian Question" in *On Scientific Truth about Macedonia*. Athens: National Technical University of Athens, 3.

Owen, D. 1995. *Balkan Odyssey*, London: Victor Gollancz.

Papakonstantinou, M. 1991. *I Makedonia meta ton Makedoniko Agona* [Macedonia after the Macedonian Struggle]. Athens: K.P.E.E.

__________. 1994. *I Eisdohi ton Skopion ston OIE* [Skopje's Admission to the U.N.], Diethnis Epitheorisi 18 (March), 21.

__________. 1994. *Elladakai Skopia-Metra Oikodomisis Empistosvnis* [Greece and Skopje-Confidence Building Measures]. Athens: K.P.E.E.

Papazoglou, P. 1992. "Macedonia Under the Romans: Political and Administrative Developments" in Sakellariou (*ed.*), *Macedonia: 4000 Years of Greek History and Civilization*. Athens: Ekdotike Athenon, 192.

Perry, D. 1994. "Une crise en Gestation? La Macédoine et ses voisins," *Politique Étrangère* 1, 179.

__________. 1994. "Crisis in the Making? Macedonia and Its Neighbors," *Südosteuropa* 43, 31.

Pettifer, J. 1995. The New Macedonian Question, London.

Poulton, H. 1995. *Who Are the Macedonians?*, London, 1995.

Poulton, H. & Taji-Farouki, S. (*eds.*). 1997. *Muslim Identity and the Balkan State*. London: Hurst.

Pribichevich, S. 1982. *Macedonia-Its People and History*, Pennsylvania State University Press.

Sakellariou, M. 1992. "The Early Years: The Inhabitants," in Sakellariou, M. (*ed.*), *Macedonia: 4000 Years of Greek History and Civilization*. Athens: Ekdotike Athenon, 44.

Shea, J. 1997. *Macedonia and Greece: the Struggle to Define a New Balkan Nation*. London: McFarland.

Sfetas, S. & Kentrotis, K. 1994. "Skopje: In search of an identity and international recognition. A critique of the recent publication by the Skopje Academy of Sciences and Arts: Macedonia and its relations with Greece (Skopje, 1993)," *Balkan Studies* 35, 337.

Someritis, R. 1994. "Greece: Alone at Last!" *War Report* 3/4, 8.

Stefanidis, Y. 1986. "The United States, Great Britain and the Greek-Yugoslav Rapprochement, 1949-1950," *Balkan Studies*, 27, 315.

Stefanou, C. and Xanthaki, H. 1995. "Article 224 of the Treaty of Rome and the Repercussions of Case C-120/94," 3 Web Journal of Current Legal Issues.

Syrigos, A. 1994. "Land-Locked States and Access to the Sea: The Greek Blockade of the Former Yugoslav Republic of Macedonia," Presentation at the Research Centre for International Law, University of Cambridge, [unpublished]

Tachiaos, A. 1990. *The Bulgarian National Awakening and its Spread into Macedonia*. Thessaloniki: Society for Macedonian Studies.

Troebst, S. 1992. "Makedonische Antworten auf die 'Makedonische Frage' 1944-1992: Nationalismus, Republiksgriindung, nation-building," *Südosteuropa* 41, 423.

__________. 1983. Die bulgarisch-jugoslawische Kontroverse um Makedonien 1967-1982. Munich: Oldenbourg.

Valinakis, G. 1992. *Greece's Balkan policy and the "Macedonian Issue,"* Entenhausen: Stiftung Wissenschaft und Politik.

Valinakis, G. and Ntalis, S. (*eds.*). 1994. *To Zitima ton Skopion: Episima Keimena 1990-1994* [The issue of Skopje: Official Sources 1990-1994]. Athens: Sideris.

Veremis, T. 1990. "From the National State to the Stateless Nation 1821-1910" in Blinkhorn, M. & Veremis, T. (*eds.*). *Modern Greece: Nationalism and Nationality*. Athens: SAGE-ELIAMEP. 9.

Villari, L. 1913. "The Races and Religions of Macedonia," *National Geographic*, 23, 1118.

Voros, F. 1993. "Different Uses of the Term Macedonia in the Centuries of History: A Possible Source of Misunderstanding" in *On Scientific Truth about Macedonia*. Athens: National Technical University of Athens, 49.

__________. 1993. "The Macedonian Question of our Neighbors" in *On Scientific Truth about Macedonia*. Athens: National Technical University of Athens, 31.

Wardle, K. 1992. "The Early years: The Cultures" in Sakellariou, M. (*ed.*), *Macedonia: 4000 Years of Greek History and Civilization*. Athens: Ekdotike Athenon, 30.

Zahariadis, N. 1996. "Greek Policy toward the Former Yugoslav Republic of Macedonia 1991-1995," *Journal of Modern Greek Studies* 14, 147.

Zotiades, G. 1961. *The Macedonian Controversy*. Thessaloniki: Institute for Balkan Studies.

__________. 1992. "Bulgarien: Die Anerkennung Makedoniens," *Südosteuropa* 41, p. 236.

__________. 1993. Memorandum of Greece Concerning the Application of the Former Yugoslav Republic of Macedonia for Admission to the United Nations, 25.1.1993, A/47/877 (agenda item 19), S/25158; published with attachments, Athens: ELIAMEP.

__________. 1993. Borders, Symbols, Stability, Athens: Citizens' Movement.

__________. 1994. *Macedonian Minorities: The Slav Macedonians of Northern Greece and the Treatment of Minorities in the Republic of Macedonia.* Oxford: The British Helsinki Human Rights Group. 1994.

CHAPTER 4
THE BOSNIAN WAR, 1992-1995: A STRATEGIC ANALYSIS

Harry Papasotiriou
Panteion University

The purpose of this chapter is to analyze the political objectives and the strategies of the three opponents in the Bosnian War, i.e. the Serbs, the Croats, and the Muslims as well as the involvement of the international community. The complex series of events in that conflict will be dissected in terms of the central strategic decisions of the main actors and their consequences.

The chapter attempts to provide a detached strategic analysis of this recent conflict. It is not a piece of advocacy; it seeks not to defend or condemn actors and actions on the basis of moral or legal principles, but to explain the causes, the course, and outcome of the Bosnian War on the basis of a quadrangular set of dynamically interacting strategies. This does not mean that I wish to minimize the human suffering in that conflict or to absolve the perpetrators from responsibility. But since the moral aspects of the Bosnian War are very extensively covered in the literature, I have chosen the different angle of strategic analysis, which allows me to place the atrocities in their strategic context and assess their strategic consequences.

Strategy is the interaction of adversaries who threaten to use force to secure their conflicting political objectives.[1] While strategic problems are usually analyzed in the context of conflicts between states, the concepts of strategic analysis also apply in wars involving one or more sub-state actors (such as civil wars and wars of national liberation). The strategic analysis of a war consists of the examination first of the conflicting political objectives of the adversaries and second of the means, the moves and counter-moves—i.e. the strategic interaction—by which they sought to secure them against each other. Thus, the strategic analyst is primarily interested in the effectiveness rather than the morality of a strategy. He does not assess a strategy according to moral criteria, but according to whether it achieved its political objectives. This does not mean that morality is unimportant to strategic analysis. Strategies that are perceived grossly to violate moral standards may evoke such a strong reaction, by the adversaries or third parties, as to fail to attain their objectives. Internal and international legitimacy is an important aspect of strategy, indeed sometimes the most important factor determining the outcome of a war, as the cases of Vietnam and Afghanistan demonstrate.

The Bosnian War was part of the broader series of events that resulted from the violent break-up of the Socialist Yugoslav federation in 1991-92. Bosnia's

peculiarity was that alone among Socialist Yugoslavia's republics it had no dominant majority. In 1991, 43.7% of its population was Muslim, 31.4% Serbian, and 17.3% Croatian, while a farther 5.5% identified themselves as "Yugoslavs."[2] The surge in Serbian and Croatian nationalism that had led to the violent disintegration of the Socialist Yugoslav federation in 1991 swept the Serbian and Croatian communities in Bosnia, who thus on the whole felt no loyalty to Bosnia as a political entity and identified with their respective neighboring motherlands.

It is therefore reasonable to assume that in early 1992 a majority of Bosnia's inhabitants did not wish to end up in an independent Bosnian state: the Serbs wanted to unite with Serbia and the Croats with Croatia. Only the Muslims were in favor of Bosnia's independence as an ultimate objective. The Bosnian elections of November 2000 indicate that this is probably still true today.

Yet the desire of Bosnia's Serbs and Croats to unite with their respective motherlands faced the complication that Bosnia's three ethnic groups were geographically mixed. This complication was worst for the Serbs, since most of the local districts *(opstinas)* in which they dominated numerically were located in the north-western part of Bosnia, which is surrounded by Croatia in four fifths of the compass and is furthest away from Serbia.[3] For the Bosnian Croats, the situation was less unfavorable because their largest concentrations were in Bosnia's south-west, neighboring Croatia. Central Bosnia and much of its eastern territory neighboring Serbia was marked by local districts that were either mixed, with none of the three ethnic groups having an absolute majority, or had Muslim majorities, though the eastern strip along the border with Serbia also had significant pockets of local districts dominated by the Serbs.[4]

A peaceful tripartite partition of Bosnia at the outset was thus very difficult; it would have required an agreement on the new borders and a voluntary exchange of populations. The alternative for the Serbs was to try to prevent the secession of Bosnia from the Yugoslav federation. In this matter, though they were opposed by a different majority of Bosnia's population. Since remaining under Serbian domination within the Yugoslav federation was the worst possible outcome for Bosnia's Croats, they joined the Muslims in supporting secession. They saw Bosnian independence as a first step towards their ultimate objective of seceding in turn from Bosnia and uniting with Croatia.

The Bosnian Serbs sought to thwart the will of Bosnia's circumstantial Muslim- Croatian secessionist majority through the consociational structure of Bosnia's constitutional scheme, which was designed to maintain its tripartite ethnic equilibrium through explicitly anti-majoritarian provisions. On central

issues such as independence and inter-ethnic relations, Bosnia's constitution required tripartite consensus.[5]

The Muslims and the Croats were able to circumvent these constitutional restrictions on the basis of new rules of the game that were introduced by the international community, i.e. the European Union (EU) to which the United States deferred on Yugoslav matters until the spring of 1992. It will be necessary at this point briefly to summarize the EU's policy in the Yugoslav question in late 1991 and early 1992.

Prior to the Yugoslav crisis, the international community was in principle opposed to violent secessionist movements. The secessionist objective of Croatia and Slovenia in 1991 conflicted with the principle of the inviolability of borders and the territorial integrity of sovereign states, which is central to international stability. From the point of view of international order, this principle overrules self-determination; if the reverse were true, countless states would be destabilized by minority secessionist movements.[6] The international community's approach to secessionist movements is that they should be "killed by kindness,"[7] i.e. that states should guarantee minority rights and pursue inclusive policies towards minorities in order to remove legitimate grievances that fuel secessionisms.

In the course of the Yugoslav crisis in 1991, the international community moved to the new position of allowing one exception to the principle of the inviolability of borders and the territorial integrity of sovereign states. In the case of a federal state like the Socialist Federal Republic of Yugoslavia, the secession of federal units is internationally accepted, if the federation has clearly fallen apart. In such a case, the successor states are internationally recognized on the basis of their old borders within the defunct federation. The theory behind this approach is that a federation is in some sense a voluntary union of autonomous units, so that if this union disintegrates the units simply break apart and become independent.

This was the finding of the Badinter Commission that was set up by the European Community (subsequently EU[8]) in September 1991 as an arbitration body to resolve differences amongst the Yugoslav republics. The key criterion for independence and international recognition that the Badinter Commission stipulated was that a majority of a Yugoslav republic's population vote for independence in a referendum.[9]

The position of the Badinter Commission was opposed by Serbia on two grounds. First, the Serbs argued that the internal borders of Yugoslavia's republics were arbitrary and did not reflect the geographic distribution of Yugoslavia's nationalities. They saw themselves as victims of a double standard, which allowed the secession of Croatia and, later, Bosnia from the Yugoslav

federation, but not the secession of the Serbian areas from Croatia and Bosnia. The war in Croatia and, later, Bosnia took place because Serbia wanted to change these internal federal borders so as to incorporate the main concentrations of Serbs in these two former Yugoslav Republics.[10] Second, and more specifically related to Bosnia, the Serbs argued that the majoritarian referendum that was stipulated as a condition for independence and international recognition contravened Bosnia's consociational, consensus-requiring constitutional scheme.

When the EU recognized the independence of Croatia and Slovenia in mid-January 1992, without having first secured an overall agreement between the Yugoslav republics on the terms of Socialist Yugoslavia's dissolution, it spelled the doom of Bosnia. The precedent of the first two republics' successful secession promptly fueled the secessionist urge amongst the Muslims and the Croats of Bosnia, who were not prepared to remain in a Serbian-dominated rump Yugoslavia. Since they proceeded on the basis of the referendum principle stipulated by the EU's Badinter Commission, the EU could hardly resist them. The referendum took place on 28 February 1992, and some 65% of eligible voters supported independence. (Since the Bosnian Serbs abstained from the referendum on the basis that it violated Bosnia's consociational constitutional scheme, the percentage of actual votes in favor of independence reached 99.7%). On 1 March 1992, sectarian violence broke out in Sarajevo, resulting in the erection of the first Serbian barricades dividing the city."[11]

In March 1992, the EU made an urgent attempt to mediate between Bosnia's three ethnic groups by proposing a tri-cantonal constitutional arrangement. At first this proposal was accepted by all three sides. It is unlikely that the scheme would have provided a lasting peace, since the Bosnian Serbs—and hence the Croats in their wake, too—were likely at some opportune moment to launch their own secessionist moves from an independent Bosnia in order to unite with their motherland. However, it was the Muslims who backed away from the tri-cantonal scheme, a mere two weeks after they had agreed upon it. Yet it is upon a tri-ethnic principle that Bosnia is organized today, according to the Dayton agreements. The Muslim leader Alia lzetbecovic miscalculated badly in thinking that he could have an independent Bosnia organized upon unitarian, majoritarian principles. In 1995, he ended up with a tri-ethnic scheme not very different from the one he rejected in March 1992, but only after his people suffered the worst destruction that Europe has seen since 1945.

The roots of Izetbecovic's miscalculation are not difficult to discern. He correctly assumed that the international community was about to recognize the independence of Bosnia on the basis of the referendum. From this, he over optimistically deduced that the international community would intervene

militarily to protect Bosnia from Serbia's designs. He also seems to have misinterpreted as support the Croatian pro-independence vote in the referendum, but he soon discovered that the Croats had their own anti-Muslim agenda. It took almost two years for the international community to coerce the Croats into co-operating with the Muslims against the Serbs, and then another year and a half for the international community to intervene military.[12]

Full-scale warfare broke out in Bosnia at the beginning of April 1992, immediately after the EU and the United States proceeded with an ill-conceived "preventive" recognition of Bosnian independence. Far from preventing the war, Bosnia's international recognition probably fueled it, since it took place before a mutually acceptable constitutional scheme had been agreed upon by Bosnia's three ethnic groups. Henceforth, the Serbs lost trust in international mediation and pursued their objectives by military means. Shortly afterwards, the Bosnian Croats followed the same path, though somewhat less visibly.

In launching the war, the Serbs had three operational objectives: First, they sought to place the Serbian population pockets in Bosnia beyond the Bosnian government's control. Second, they sought to expand these pockets and to link them territorially, so as to create one continuous Serbian territorial unit. This objective required major offensives in order to expand the territory under Serbian control. Third, they sought to control a continuous strip of Bosnian territory that would link Serbia via northern Bosnia with the Serbian pocket in Krajina (Croatia) at the northwestern borders of Bosnia. Thus, at stake was the fate not only of the Serbian population in Bosnia but also of the Serbs in Krajina, who in the Croatian War in 1991 had achieved their de facto independence from the Croatian state, but whose position would become untenable unless a line of communications with Serbia via northern Bosnia was secured.

Bosnia's international recognition constrained the Serbian strategy in Bosnia, since Milosevic decided not to involve the Yugoslav army directly, in order formally to maintain the fiction that Yugoslavia was not a participant in the Bosnian War. He had strengthened the Yugoslav forces in Bosnia in the months prior to its international recognition in an unsuccessful attempt to intimidate the Muslims and the Croats. After the international recognition, the Yugoslav army formally withdrew from Bosnia, but it left behind tens of thousands of troops (ostensibly only Bosnian Serbs), as well as large amounts of military equipment and ammunition in the hands of the Bosnian Serbs. Moreover, the army of the Bosnian Serbs was led by generals and officers of the Yugoslav army. It was assisted by irregular groups of Serbian volunteers who were motivated by a mixture of nationalism and greed and who financed their operations through looting, smuggling, and organized crime.[13]

Having thus secured at the outset of the war a decisive military superiority over the as yet scarcely formed forces of the Bosnian government, the Bosnian Serbs proceeded within twelve months to displace the government and gain control over approximately 70% of Bosnia's territory. In their offensives, the Serbs sought to expel not only the government forces and administrators but also the Muslim and Croatian populations. Thus populations that had lived in ethnically mixed areas for centuries were forcibly uprooted. This process of "ethnic cleansing," as it was euphemistically called, involved the most massive human rights violations that Europe has seen since 1945. Indeed, even from within the ruthless logic of "ethnic cleansing," the torture, rape, and murder of civilians took place on an unnecessarily large scale, well beyond what was needed to force populations to migrate, and far worse, for example, than what happened in Kosovo in 1998 and 1999.[14]

In strategic terms, the excessive brutality of the "ethnic cleansing" that attended the Serbian military advances in 1992 and 1993 was counterproductive. It may have facilitated the speed and thoroughness of the Serbian advance, but it led to a collapse in Serbian international legitimacy, which eventually brought about the international intervention. However legitimate and persuasive some of the Serbian political arguments might have been, they were drowned in the shock and the horror that the massive atrocities evoked in world opinion.

The Serbian offensives of 1992 and early 1993 by-and-large attained their operational objectives, though not in a fully satisfactory way. The large Serbian population pockets in Bosnia's north-western corner, which neighbored the Serbian pocket of Krajina in Croatia, were linked with the Serbian territories in eastern Bosnia that neighbored Serbia, but at one point the link consisted of a very thin strip of land in northern Bosnia. Serbian efforts to enlarge that strip and make it less vulnerable failed, in the face of very strong Muslim defensive positions. Moreover, in spite of the "ethnic cleansing" that took place, several urban centers in eastern Bosnia remained under Muslim control and were placed under UN protection with its "safe areas" policy. These Muslim urban islands, which were surrounded by Serbian territory, remained an obstacle to the formation of a homogeneous Serbian territorial unit within Bosnia.

After the spring of 1993, the Serbian strategy consisted mainly of demonstrations of strength and harassment actions, the objective of which was to convince the Bosnian government to accept an agreement on Serbian terms. These limited military operations continued to defy world opinion and to contribute to the collapse of Serbian international legitimacy. This was particularly the case in regard to the siege of Sarajevo, which limited the city's supplies to a trickle, made difficult any international access to the Bosnian government's seat,[15] and made life dangerous for the city's inhabitants through

the almost constant small-scale bombardments that lasted until February 1994. The world media focused on Sarajevo and provided a steady stream of news and images that were detrimental to the Serbian side. Thus, in strategic terms, the Serbian siege of Sarajevo on balance benefited the Muslim side (in spite of the hardship that the Muslim inhabitants of the city suffered), since it advanced its objective of bringing forth an international military intervention.

The Croatian objectives at the outset of the Bosnian War were similar to those of the Serbs. From July 1992, when the Bosnian Croats declared their "independence" from the Bosnian government, they sought to secure, expand, and "ethnically cleanse" the main pockets of the Croatian population in Bosnia, particularly in the south-west neighboring Croatia, where their local opponents were mostly Muslims. The Croatian methods of ethnically homogenizing the territories under their control were quite as brutal as those of the Serbs, though on a smaller scale and with less international visibility.[16]

While the Croatian forces on the ground created a de facto independent Croatian zone within Bosnia, Croatia's president Franjo Tudjman faced a difficult strategic dilemma. On the one hand, he was tempted to make a deal with Milosevic to partition Bosnia; indeed, the two sides held talks on partition in 1991 and again in 1992.[17] This option would secure Croatian irredentist objectives in Bosnia, but it would pit Croatia against the international community, which after Bosnia's international recognition was committed to a solution that would maintain Bosnia's territorial integrity.

On the other hand, Tudjman had an incentive to cooperate with the international community in order, at some future opportune moment, to be able to overrun and eradicate the Serbian pockets within Croatia, which defied his state's authority. Without international support, or at least acquiescence, he could not hope to circumvent the arms embargo that the international community imposed on all the former Yugoslav republics, and thus he could not hope to reverse the military balance within Croatia so as to be able to conquer the Serbian pockets.

In effect, Tudjman had to choose between his objectives in Bosnia and in Croatia itself; he could not have it both ways. After some prevarication, in early 1994 under the pressure of the United States, he came down firmly in favor of the second option. Thereafter, the Croats and the Muslims overlooked their profound differences in Bosnia and began to cooperate against the Serbs.[18]

The Muslims found themselves in the weakest position at the outset of the Bosnian War. Unlike the other two ethnic groups, they had no neighboring motherland to support them with arms and troops. Since they inherited very little of the strength of the old Yugoslav Peoples Army, they found themselves hopelessly outgunned on the battle-fields. The arms embargo that the

international community imposed on all the former Yugoslav republics worked specifically to their disadvantage, since they were more in need of new weapons than the Serbs and the Croats. Moreover, up to March 1994, they faced simultaneous assaults from both the Serbs and the Croats. Their only hope for securing Bosnia's independence and territorial integrity was an international intervention.

It is a tragic irony that the very atrocities that the Muslims suffered in the hands of the Serbs were the most potent factor in their favor in the international community. The leading Western governments were very reluctant to be drawn militarily into a war in the mountains and valleys of the inner Balkans. Their attitude was summarized by President Bush, who declared in July 1992, "I am not interested in seeing one single United States soldier pinned down in some kind of guerrilla environment," and who explained that Bosnia was different from Kuwait, since it did not involve "the overt invasion of one country by another."[19] However, the Western governments were confronted internally by a storm of indignation, outrage, and shame at Western inactivity in the face of the worst humanitarian disaster witnessed by Europeans since World War II. Moreover, the West also had to face an Islamic world that was united as rarely before by the slaughter of the Muslims in Bosnia. "Not a drop of Kuwait's petroleum must be spilled. But the blood of the Muslims in Bosnia may flow in rivers," the Turkish newspaper Sabah maintained in 1992, echoing arguments that were made across the Islamic World.[20]

The leading Western governments tried to charter a course that would avoid a direct Western military involvement in what many feared would become a Balkan Vietnam, but at the same time would respond to the spreading sentiment of failure and humiliation in their domestic publics. At first, the international community restricted itself to purely humanitarian goals, such as operating under UN protection food convoys to besieged Muslim cities, and deploying UN blue helmets in the UN "safe areas." In February 1994, the Bosnian Serbs were compelled, under threat of a NATO bombardment, to withdraw their heavy artillery from the vicinity of Sarajevo, ending the near-constant bombing harassment of the besieged Bosnian capital.[21]

But with no end to the conflict in sight, in 1994 the Clinton administration took steps to alter the military balance on the ground. The Croats and the Muslims were pushed to an alliance against the Serbs. Violations of the arms embargo were tolerated, in order to facilitate a military build-up by both the Croatian and the Bosnian governments. Moreover, the United States secretly tolerated the infiltration of Islamic volunteers and arms into Bosnia, even from anti-Western states such as Iran.[22]

The rising military strength of the Muslims was demonstrated by the initial success of their Bihac offensive in late 1994, in which for some time they overran one hundred square kilometers of traditionally Serbian territory. They now had a chance (not their first) to demonstrate that they were quite as capable as the Serbs and the Croats in committing brutal atrocities to secure the "ethnic cleansing" of conquered territory."[23]

Yet the Bosnian Serbs failed to discern the full extent to which the military balance had changed, eroding their local military superiority. In July 1995, they overran the UN "safe area" of Sebrenica, expelled the women and children, and slaughtered an estimated 8,000 of the town's men.[24] The mass murder in Sebrenica, probably the worst single crime in all the Yugoslav wars of the 1990s, was an act of breath-taking defiance. By brutally destroying the "safe area," the Bosnian Serbs made a mockery of the United Nations and dealt a major blow to the prestige of the United States, NATO, and the EU. The most powerful alliance in the world was directly and unmistakably challenged by a minor Balkan force.

The retribution was swift and forceful. It consisted of an apparently carefully orchestrated triple set of moves. The Croatian army quickly overran the Serbian pockets in Krajina and expelled their Serbian populations, in what amounted to the most massive single "ethnic cleansing" operation in the Yugoslav wars up to that time[25] (only the later Serbian campaign of mass expulsion of the Albanians from Kosovo in late March and early April 1999 was larger in scale for a comparably short period). Next, the Bosnian Croats and the Muslims launched offensives against the Bosnian Serbs, forcing them to abandon almost a third of the territory that they held hitherto. Finally, NATO launched a major bombardment on the positions of the Bosnian Serbs, facilitating the military advance of the Muslim-Croatian coalition.

The assault on the Bosnian Serbs ended when they had retreated almost precisely to 49% of Bosnia's territory, which was the portion allotted to them in the various peace plans that were being discussed since 1993.[26] In the subsequent Dayton conference, a Bosnian settlement was devised on tri-ethnic grounds. The Bosnian Serbs constitute one unit in the Bosnian confederation, with substantial autonomy. The Muslims and the Bosnian Croats constitute the second unit, which is itself divided into a Muslim and a Croatian part. This arrangement is not much different from the one rejected by Izetbecivic in March 1992.

Post-Dayton, Bosnia has been relatively peaceful, though local violence has broken out, particularly between the Muslims and the Croats. The peace is maintained by the international peace-keeping force, which has been in Bosnia since Dayton, but it seems unlikely that the combined majority of Serbs and

Croats will develop a genuine allegiance to Bosnia in the foreseeable future. In the Bosnian elections of November 2000, five years after the end of the war, the Serbs and the Croats voted in favor of hard-line nationalist parties whose ultimate objective is union with their respective motherlands. Only the Muslims voted in favor of moderate parties that favor an integrated and tolerant Bosnia.[27] It is hard to escape the conclusion that this state exists by international fiat, and that it will collapse once more should the peace-keepers depart.

This is a very meager result for a war in which an estimated two hundred and fifty thousand humans lost their lives and a farther two million were displaced from their homes. With its decision to support the secessions only of federal Yugoslav republics. But not of sub-republic population blocks, the international community is stuck with a state that is unviable without an indefinite international military protectorate. The liberal idealist dream of fostering a multi-cultural society in Bosnia seems Utopian, especially in the light of the vivid memories of the recent slaughters that divide Bosnia's ethnic groups. The international community might have prevented the worst of the slaughter, and created a more stable long-term situation, if it had promoted a tripartite division of Bosnia in 1992 or even in late 1993 when the EU's mediator Lord Owen actually floated the idea but such an approach derives from the practical pragmatism of Realpolitik. At the time, people were influenced by the legalistic utopianism of Liberal Idealism that prevailed in the Western approach to the Yugoslav question.

ENDNOTES

[1] Note also General Andre Beaufre's definition of strategy as "the art of the dialectics of wills that use force to resolve their conflict," in his *Introduction a la strategic* (1963), p. 16.

[2] Cohen, Lenard, *Broken Bonds: The Disintegration of Yugoslavia* (1993), p. 139. These figures do not add up to 100%, since Bosnia's population also included small groups from Socialist Yugoslavia's other ethnic groups.

[3] Crnobrnja, Mihailo, *The Yugoslav Drama* (1996), pp. 22-23.

[4] For a detailed map of the local districts and their ethnic composition, see Owen, David,
Balkan Odyssey (Nov. 1995), pp. 64-65.

[5] Crnobrnja, Mihailo, *The Yugoslav Drama* (1996), p. 174.

[6] For a short but very informed examination of these matters, see Hoffman, Stanley, "New International Disorder," *New York Review of Books*, 9 April 1992.

[7] The phrase was used to describe the Irish policies of Salisbury's and Balfour's Unionist governments in the later nineteenth and early twentieth centuries. That it failed to appease the Irish Nationalists who strove for Home Rule is an early indication, that the international community's approach is not a panacea in dealing with secessionist movements.

[8] The name was changed from "European Community" to "European Union" by the Treaty of European Union (Maastricht), which was signed by the member governments in December 1991, but only came into force two years later after a lengthy ratification process in the member states. Nonetheless I will use the term EU throughout this chapter for the sake of uniformity.

[9] See Caplan, Richard, "International Diplomacy and the Crisis in Kosovo," *International*
Affairs (October 1998), p. 747-48.

[10] In terms of the two conflicting principles of territorial integrity versus self-determination, Serbia's overall position was internally contradictory, since it supported the self-determination of the Serbs in Croatia and Bosnia, but denied self-determination to the Albanian Kosovars. Milosevic used exactly the same arguments about majority rule to deny self-determination to the Kosovo Albanians, that Tudjman used to deny self-determination to the Serbs in Krajina. Cohen, Lenard, *Broken Bonds: The Disintegration of Yugoslavia* (1993), pp. 274-75.

[11] *Ibid.*, pp. 236-37.

[12] On lzetbecovic's miscalculations in March 1992, see Crnobrnja, Mihailo, *The Yugoslav Drama* (1996), p. 177-78. The Muslims and the Croats briefly co-operated from April to June 1992, but from July 1992 to March 1994 were at war with one another.

[13] Malcolm, Noel, *Bosnia: A Short History* (1994), pp. 235-44.

[14] For an in-depth journalistic account of the atrocities, see the influential series of articles by Mark Danner that appeared in the *New York Review of Books* in 1997 and 1998. The *Wall Street Journal-Europe*, 4 January 2000, summarizes evidence on the Kosovo conflict which suggests, that the atrocities there were much more limited than in the Bosnian War.

[15] Three of Richard Holbrook's aids were killed in 1995 on the way to Sarajevo, when their vehicle fell off the dangerous mountain road that led to the Bosnian capital. This was the only road outside Serbian control that was available for international access to Sarajevo. Serbian forces were apt to fire at or near UN vehicles on that road in order to demonstrate their military presence and intimidate the UN troops. See Holbrook, Richard, *To End a War* (1996), ch. 1.

[16] Boyd, Charles, "Making Peace with the Guilty: The Truth About Bosnia," *Foreign Affairs* (Sept./Oct. 1995), makes the point that the Croats and, indeed, the Muslims were as bad as the Serbs in terms of a propensity to commit atrocities, but had less power to do so on the same scale.

[17] Malcolm, Noel, *Bosnia: A Short History* (1994), pp. 231-32.

[18] Sharp, Jane, "Dayton Report Card," *International Security* (Winter 1997/8), pp. 111-12.

[19] *USIS* bulletin, 2 July 1992.

[20] Omar Erzeren, "Kreuzzug gegen den Islam: Die Reaktion der Turkei und der islamischen Welt aufden Krieg in Bosnien," *Krieg aufdem Balkan* (1992).

[21] For an account of the UN engagement in Bosnia, see Ekwall-Uebelhart, Barbara & Raevsky, Andrei, *Managing Arms in Peace Process: Croatia and Bosnia-Herzegovina* (1996).

[22] Boyd, Charles, "Making Peace with the Guilty: The Truth About Bosnia," *Foreign Affairs* (Sept./Oct. 1995), pp. 30-32.

[23] *Ibid.*, pp. 29-33.

[24] Andreatta, Filippo, "The Bosnian War and the New World Order: Failure and Success of International Intervention," Occasional Paper, *The Institute for Security Studies* (1996), p. 21. The same number is cited in Sharp, Jane, "Dayton Report Card," *International Security* (Winter 1997/8), p. 112.

[25] This at any rate is the assessment in Owen, David, *Balkan Odyssey* (1995), pp. 353, where Lord Owen states that the "Croatian government attack on the Krajina in early August 1995 created the biggest single flood of refugees—over 150,000 Croatian Serbs—since the break-up of Yugoslavia."

[26] Owen, David, *Balkan Odyssey* (1995), pp. 336-37.

[27] *Wall Street Journal-Europe*, 13 November 2000.

REFERENCES

Andreatta, Filippo. 1996. "The Bosnian War and the New World Order: Failure and Success of International Intervention," Occasional Paper, *The Institute for Security Studies*, Paris: West European Union.

Beaufre, Andre. 1963. *Introduction a la strategic*, Paris: Librairie Armand Colin.

Boyd, Charles. 1995. "Making Peace with the Guilty: The Truth About Bosnia," *Foreign Affairs*, Vol. 74 No. 5 (Sept./Oct).

Caplan, Richard. 1998. "International Diplomacy and the Crisis in Kosovo," International Affairs (The Royal Institute of International Affairs), Vol. 74, No. 4 (October).

Chandler, David. 2000. *Bosnia*, London: Pluto Press, Second Edition.

Cohen, Lenard. 1993. *Broken Bonds: The Disintegration of Yugoslavia*, Boulder, Colorado: Westview.

Crnobrnja, Mihailo. 1996. *The Yugoslav Drama*, Montreal: McGill-Queen's University Press, Second Edition.

Ekwall-Uebelhart, Barbara & Raevsky, Andrei. 1996. *Managing Arms in Peace Process: Croatia and Bosnia-Herzegovina*, Geneva: United Nations Institute for Disarmament Research, Disarmament and Conflict Resolution Project.

Erzeren, Omar. 1992. "Kreuzzug gegen den Islam: Die Reaktion der Turkei und der islamischen Welt aufden Krieg in Bosnien." From Eric Rathfelder, ed., *Krieg auf dem Balkan*, Reinbeck bei Hamburg: Rowohit Taschenbug Verlag GmbH.

Hoffman, Stanley. 1992. "New International Disorder," *New York Review of Books*, 9 April 1992.

Holbrook, Richard. 1996. *To End. a War*, New York: Random House Trade.

Malcolm, Noel. 1994. *Bosnia: A Short History*, New York: New York University Press.

Owen, David. 1995. *Balkan Odyssey*, London: Victor Gollancz.

Sharp, Jane. 1997. "Dayton Report Card," *International Security*, 22:3 (Winter).

SUGGESTED FURTHER READINGS

For the internal political dynamics in the Socialist Yugoslav federation which led to its violent collapse and resulted in the Bosnian War, particularly useful is the analysis of Crnobrnja, Mihailo, *The Yugoslav Drama*, Montreal: McGill-Queen's University Press, Second Edition (1996). The international community's involvement in the Bosnian War is most immediately presented by two protagonists, the EU's representative Lord Owen in his *Balkan Odyssey*, London: Victor Gollancz (1995), and the Clinton Administration's Richard Holbrook in his *To End a War*, New York: Random House Trade (1996). These two books are an invaluable source on the international diplomacy regarding the Bosnian War, and will probably only be superseded when the related European and American archives become available to researchers. On the Dayton agreement, its implementation, and its prospects, the most useful analysis is in Chandler, David, *Bosnia*, London: Pluto Press, Second Edition (2000).

CHAPTER 5
CROATIA–SERBIA: ISSUES OF CONTENTION

Kleomenis Koutsoukis, Panteion University
Pantelis Sklias, Democritus University

1. INTRODUCTION: BRIEF THEORETICAL CONSIDERATIONS

It is vital not to detach the issues of contention from the overall framework of political conflict, which destabilised South Eastern Europe. Separatism is one of three types of destabilizing events.[1] Separatism involves a certain degree of challenge to the authority of the state. "Separatism often is the expression of ethnolinguistic disagreements for which no solution is evident aside from changes in the jurisdiction of the state as it applies to various racial, ethnic and linguistic groups residing within its borders."[2] Eventually, destabilizing events are a direct threat to the legitimacy and the capability of the state to determine the allocation of resources to its citizens. In this case, political activity and behavior may include "unilateral declarations of autonomy or succession, interposition or exception to the administration of law, and rejection or assertions of allegiance or rights and responsibilities of citizenship."[3]

The objective of this brief analysis is the examination of the Serbian-Croat issues of contention within the framework of comprehending separatism as a sequence of destabilizing events. In other words, we will examine how the demand for separatism has been expressed and finally realized in the case of Croatia. In this analysis we examine the main issues of the contentious relations between the two states. Emphasis is put on the historical basis of the contention that provides the background for understanding the contemporary situation. In this analysis, we are assessing the legal aspects raised by the Serbian side insofar as the autonomy and the recognition by the international community of the independent Croatian state are concerned. The role of the contemporary territorial issues including the one of Eastern Slavonia and the Pravlaka Peninsula and the issue of human rights mainly with regard to the return of Serbian refugees in Croatia. Finally, we stress the "modern propaganda" means and the influence of the Internet as a contemporary way of raising and preserving the contention issues between the two states.

2. THE PAST REVISITED: THE SECOND WORLD WAR AND THE ISSUES OF CONTENTION

In the last decade events between the two states resulted in the re-emergence of the Second World War perceptions concerning the role of these two nations and their collaboration links with the Nazi regime. Additionally, it is not possible to understand the events that took place in the territory of the Former Republic of Yugoslavia (FRY) without in-depth historical analysis. This is the only way to perceive the essence of the conflicts and give an international explanation of the events, that have been influential in the international legal relations and international legal order. Most of the current issues of contention come out of the perceptions and prejudices that have their roots in the WWII period.

These are long-standing issues, which are still valid. Nevertheless, recent political developments in both countries (as a result of the death of President Tudzman in Croatia) the consequent change in government (as a result of the January 27, 2000 elections), and the defeat of President Milosevic in the latest elections in Serbia, seem to create the background for a change of the environment between the two countries.

Recently, Mrs. Vesna Cvjetkovic-Kurelec, Deputy Minister of Foreign Affairs of the Republic of Croatia stated that:

> Elections in January this year marked a democratic maturity of Croatian society, and a new beginning. A chance was long due and we intend to use it to its full potential. . . . We believe that from being a part of a problem Croatia became a part of a solution, an agent of stability and security bordering a region burdened with instability and insecurity. But many tasks still remain to be accomplished. . . .[4]

The recent meeting of Croatian and Yugoslav businessmen is also an indication towards the development of a positive climate.[5]

However, Croatia has a long way to go because the historical background makes any positive move towards reconciliation quite complicated. Traditionally, the Croats' efforts for independence have been considered by the Serbs an issue of secession against the motherland, Serbia. Serb presence in the region is seen as legitimatizing the existence of a united Yugoslavia, independently from the political regime (monarchy or democracy).

The presence of Serbs in Croatia has been seen as an occupation by the Croats, and they have never accepted it. Separatist efforts are very well documented and put in a chronological order in the Croatian Constitution itself.

The Preamble of the Constitution of Croatia follows a historical sequence of efforts of the Croatian people to independence starting with the formation of the Croatian municipalities in the 7th century, and the foundation of the independent medieval state of Croatia in the 9th century. The Constitution also documents the foundations of state sovereignty during World War II through decisions of the Anti-Fascist Council of the National Liberation of Croatia (1943), to oppose the proclamation of the Independent State of Croatia (1941), and subsequently in the Constitution of the People's Republic of Croatia (1947), and the several subsequent constitutions of the Socialist Republic of Croatia (1963-1990). It seems that the Croats have made considerable effort to convince the international community that the Croatians deserve an independent state.

The events during the Second World War demonstrate the huge differences between the Serbian and Croatian nations. The role of the two nations during the War is also questioned by both. Based on the Serbian literature, Serbs suffered from a genocide as a result of the "separatist tendencies" by the Croats and their collaboration with the Nazi regime during the Second World War.[6] Ustashi actions are also under historical investigation because Serbs accused them of inhuman activities.[7]

On the other side, Croats have their own explanation concerning the events during the Second World War. More precisely, Ustashe is seen as an extremist organization whose function was permitted by the Nazi administration. Indicative is the following statement:

> In 1941, despite security agreements with Britain and France Yugoslavia was invaded by German, Italian, and Hungarian forces. Nazi Germany permitted an extremist Croatian organization, the Ustashe, to set up the Independent State of Croatia (NDH) including Croatia and all Bosnia, under their leader, Ante Pavelic. The NDH, in turn, contributed Croatian units to the Nazi war effort, primarily to the Russian front. Macek was interned in a village outside of Zagreb, and many HSS activists (Croatian Peasants Party) jailed. Also, imprisoned were other regime opponents and ethnic undesirables; the concentration camp (actually a series of camps) at Jasenovac was particularly infamous. The number of persons who perished at Jasenovac is still in dispute. . . . The Communist-led forces proclaimed a new Yugoslavia at Jajce, in Bosnia, in 1943, and with their victory in 1945, set up a federal state of six republics, substantially restoring the old borders between Bosnia and Croatia. . . . Tito's new authoritarian government, suppressed any sign of ethnic nationalism, with all power given to the multi-ethnic (in theory, non-ethnic) communist party. . . .[8]

These are two contradictory views of the same historical events. However, the events in the period between 1941-1945 always had negative effects on Serbian-Croat relations especially to the extent that these perceptions and prejudices have been revisited during the period between 1990-1995 and the extent to which they remain valid till today. These contemporary issues are now assessed.

3. CONTEMPORARY ISSUES OF CONTENTION

The contemporary issues of contention between Croatia and Serbia can be summarized as follows:

1. The dispute concerning the legitimacy of the independence of Croatia and the extent to which this is in accordance with international law? This is an issue of relevant importance because Croatia is a *de facto* and *de jure* independent state.

2. The territorial disputes concerning Eastern Slavonia and the Pravlaka Peninsula. These issues are very much connected with the role of the UN peace keeping-forces and the actions of the Great Powers.

3. The return of the refugees to Croatia and the respect of their rights, including property issues and educational rights.

3.1 The appearance of an independent Croatian state: secession or independence?

The "Croatian crisis" as it appeared in 1971 is closely related with the post-1990 events. The crisis was caused by new economic policies that provided for a decision-making mechanism by the central government instead of a decentralized system of power, favored by the richer democracies of FYR (Croatia and Slovenia).[9] In this framework which remained almost the same until 1990 the issues of Serbian-Croatian contention have been determined by:

- The wish of Croats to exploit the economic resources of the region for the benefit of their own democracy. Their main concern focuses on the Dalmatian beaches and the tourist industry which produces an important part of the hard currency in FYR to be used exclusively for the development of infrastructure in Croatia.

- The individuality and different character of the Croat language and the cultural habits of the nation;

- The desire to develop decentralized structures instead of a Serbian dominated territorial, political, and economic system;

- The revival of the role of nationalities during the Second World War, which has always been a serious drawback in the relations between the Serbs and the Croats.

These points show that the Serbian-Croat issues of contention can be considered under the theoretical framework developed in Part one of this article.

However, we can argue that Croatia cannot be considered as being neglected in the ex-FYR economic system. On the contrary, as Table 1 demonstrates, investments in the region are among the highest in the country. Eventually, neglect and isolation cannot be considered as the origins of contention issues and separatism.

TABLE 1

Economic indicators of different FYR regions (FYR average = 100)

	Investments /	Exports /	Average
Yugoslavia	100	100	100
Slovenia	168	189	156
Croatia	104	86	107
Serbia	94	100	90
Voivodina	90	82	90
Kosovo	98	42	68
Bosnia Herzegovina	83	92	84
Montenegro	73	76	74
FYROM	50	79	68

Source: *Courier des pays de l' Est*, No. 331, 7-8/1988.

Serbs always have seen Croatian efforts for independence as secessionist tendencies that were dormant for almost half a century. Based on this assumption, the death of Josip Broz Tito was a signal that the time was right to dismember Yugoslavia. At the federal level, it was proposed that a referendum

be held in the entire territory of Yugoslavia to determine its fate and constitutional set-up but Croatia and Slovenia refused. Croatian Republican leaders with obvious secessionist ambitions came to the fore. An attempt to find a solution through dialogue among them did not bring any result.

The Assembly of the Republic of Slovenia made the first step toward autonomy on July 2, 1990 by adopting a Declaration on the sovereignty of the "State of the Republic of Slovenia" and declaring that republican laws took precedence over the federal ones. Six months later, after the referendum was held, a decision on secession was made.[10]

Croatia followed suit. The Assembly (Sabor) of the Republic of Croatia adopted on December 22, 1990 the Constitution of the Republic of Croatia whereby "the Republic of Croatia is established as a national State of the Croatian people."[11] After the referendum in which the Croatian people opted for secession, the Sabor made a decision on the sovereignty and independence of the Republic of Croatia, on the same day as Slovenia, on June 25, 1991. The official recognition of Croatia as an independent state by the European Union was made on January 15, 1992. Recognition by the United States came much later on April 7, 2000.

Croatian independence in this case as well as that of the Second World War has also been supported or even imposed by external factors and the international community. However, it should be noted that the recognition of Croatia was not without disagreement among the EU members. More precisely, Germany recognized both Croatia and Slovenia unilaterally on 23/12/1991, and that caused a clash among the EU members. Characteristically, the French *Figaro* stated that: "EC members are German sheep. . . . The findings of Arbitration Commission which assisted Europe in making up its mind, are an exercise in legal hypocrisy." In these dramatic moments, UN Secretary General Peres de Guellar warned the EC's hasty action "would certainly be conductive to escalation of violence which might derail the peace negotiations."[12] France followed Germany[13] while Van den Broek openly advocated the position that "it was impossible to maintain a unified Yugoslavia."[14]

The USA, which stayed on the sidelines but verbally supported Yugoslav unity, also changed its opinion in the wake of pressures by Germany, while Baker, US Secretary of State, said that : "Serbia will be expelled from Europe by the international community for the next or a few more generations."[15]

The historical sequence of events is described below.[16] The Preamble of the 1990 constitution[17] aims at securing the nation of Croatia as a national independent state with the characteristics of a "millennial national identity of the Croatian nation, confirmed by the source of its entire historical experience in

various political forms and by the perpetuation and growth of state-building ideas based on the historical right to full sovereignty of the Croatian nation."

- June 15. 1997: With 61%, Franjo Tudjman starts another five-year term as President. The OSCE judges the elections as "below minimum democratic standards" for countries wanting to be members of European institutions.
- Nov 21, 1995: the Dayton Peace Agreement[18] is signed
- Oct 29, 1995: Tudjman's party HDZ winds early parliamentary elections
- Aug 4, 1995: President Tudjman conducts a successful three day Blitzkrieg against Krajina Serbs and occupies Krajna region. 150,000 Serb refugees cross the border to Bosnia and Serbia.
- May 1, 1995: Croatia starts re-occupation of Western Slavonia and establishes its sovereignty in the "Krajina" and the city of Knin.
- 1992: HDZ wins absolute majority in parliamentary elections required by the new constitution.
- 1991-1995: Serbia occupies one third of Croatia and forms the Republic of Srpska Krajina. They also conquer 70% of Bosnia-Herzegovina.
- July 1991: Eastern Slavonia is ethnically cleansed within three months.
- Dec 1990: The first Croatian constitution is adopted.
- May 30, 1990: The Republic of Croatia is proclaimed.
- Spring 1990: Croatia holds its first democratic elections and ousts the Communist system; HDZ (Croatian Democratic Party) of Franjo Tudjman wins; Serbia threatens war.
- 1989: During the 60th anniversary of the battle of Kosovo celebration Milosevic directly announces Serbia' s policy of founding Greater Serbia against the interests of other Republics.
- 1988: The Serbian communist party under the leadership of Slobodan Milosevic adopts the plan of creating Great Serbia.

The right to self-determination and sovereignty is also stated:

Proceeding from the above presented historical facts and from the generally accepted principles in the modern world and the inalienable, indivisible, non-transferable and inexpendable right of the Croatian nation to self-determination and state sovereignty, including the inviolable right to secession and association, as the basic preconditions for peace and stability of the international order, the Republic of Croatia is hereby established as the national state of the Croatian people and a state of members of other

> nations and minorities who are its citizens: Serbs, Muslims, Slovenes, Czechs, Slovaks, Italians, Hungarians, Jews and others. . . .

The acts of these two republics were actually unilateral acts of secession that meant the end of the FYR. Their acts were followed by Bosnia-Herzegovina and FYROM, as a prelude to an inter-ethnic war of unprecedented results.

Throughout all these events, the position of Serbia and Montenegro was quite clear. Their position was that the unity of the FYR had to be preserved. The Federal authorities responded by having the Constitutional Court of Yugoslavia, as the highest court in the country, declare the acts of secession of Slovenia and Croatia null and void.[19] On the basis of the Constitution of the FRY according to which the territory of the FRY is "single and made up of the territories of the socialist republics, while the borders of the FRY cannot be changed without the approval of all republics and autonomous provinces." Based on the Constitution of the FRY, the decisions of the Constitutional Court according to the Article 394 are binding and valid.

Eventually, the autonomy of Croatia and Slovenia came to be considered as actions against the Unity of the Federation. Events in Croatia are characterized as being similar to those of 1941 and the Second World War. Indicative is what Professor Ivan Cukalovic states:[20]

> Croatia and Slovenia failed to heed the decisions of the Constitutional Court and instead were engaged in setting up para-military forces. In Croatia, the same as in 1941, the anti-Serb campaign broke out. On 2 March 1991, the police of the Republic of Croatia opened fire on the JNA members in Pakrac, on 31 May in the Lakes of Plitvice while on 8 April the Military Court in Zagreb came under attack. The situation between the members of the Croatian police and para-military forces on the one hand and the Yugoslav army on the other became tense. The President of Croatia, Franjo Tudjman, on 5 May 1991 called upon the Croats to stage demonstrations in front of the Command of District Military-Naval Headquarters. On that occasion, several JNA vehicles were set ablaze, while fire was opened on the members of JNA. It was exactly in those crucial moments that, in line with the principle of rotation under the FRY Constitution, a Croat, Stipe Mesic, became the President of the FRY. He openly stated: "My mission is accomplished. . . . Yugoslavia is no more.[21]

Opinions held by the two sides are quite opposite. The Croatian state is seen by the Serbian side as an event of secession while the Croats claim that they

have a right for independence. The legal aspect of this issue of contention is assessed below.

It is absolutely clear that the Serbian side:

1. Declares that the 1991 clashes between the Croatian and Serbian forces are between the legitimate and the non-legitimate, the formal military forces and the para-military forces; a civil war in the territory of the FRY was caused by the forcible secession of Slovenia and Croatia. In this case, such acts of secession are invalid from the legal point of view both in terms of international and national law because they are contrary to the FRY Constitution and decisions of the Constitutional Court. On the other side, Croats claim that the whole situation was an issue of independence and state sovereignty, as well as that of self determination, an issue that was highly emphasized those days in the international scene.

2. Sees the developments of 1991 as similar to those of 1941, and this view revives the sentiments concerning the role of the two nations during the Second World War. Serbs usually refer to the statements of Goebels in 1941 and Genscher in 1991 concerning the recognition of Croatia and the dismemberment of Yugoslavia. Serbian literature accentuates this issue and makes parallel comparisons between events and personalities, but these do not help an independent approach at all. "On 6 April 1941, Goebels emphasized that Yugoslavia existed no more in the wake of secession of Croatia and that on public occasions the word Yugoslavia or Yugoslav people could not be used any more, since those did not exist," while in 1991 Genscher stated that "an act of secession of Croatia is fait accompli on the basis of which the future policy of the Balkans should be formulated."[22]

3. Considers the Arbitration Commission established as legally powerless because it has no legal basis. Eventually, the borders proclaimed between the republics for inter-State (international) borders are obviously not accepted and a result of pressures. That commission was not an arbitration commission but an advisory body that overstepped its mandate. According to them, the new states emerged first, and then Yugoslavia disappeared, which puts the validity of their conclusions under question.[23]

4. The acceptance of the newly formed Republic in the United Nations system has also been an unacceptable event for the Serbs. Based on the Serbian point of view: "the ensued acts which followed have been totally

incompatible with the international law. Secessionist republics were admitted to the membership of the United Nations during the Presidency of Austrian Ambassador. In order to become a UN member, a State has to prove that it is a peace-loving country and fulfill general preconditions in line with international law, that the State controls territory, has population and exercises a sovereign power. In the territory of Croatia, the civil war was already emerging and therefore the basic precondition for admission in UN was not met, i.e. that the state was a peace--loving one. The recognition granted to Croatia was given by a certain number of countries, although the issue of territory was not resolved, i.e. the issue of borders, population or sovereign power, since the territories populated by the Serbs remained outside Croatian control because the Serbs did not agree to the prepared scenario, the same as in 1941."[24] Based on the above framework, the establishment of an independent Croatian state is completely unacceptable from the point of view of the international law and as such it is a severe violation of the right to self-determination.

Based on the above disputes as a result of the independence of Croatia we will now examine the territorial questions that form the second aspect of the contemporary issues of contention between the two states.

3.2. Territorial disputes: the issue of Eastern Slavonia and Pravlaka Peninsula

The view of the "common state" among the Serbs, as developed also in the case of the Croatian Serbs, cannot be seen independently from the one which had been adopted between the Communist party organization in the JNA and the SPS of Milosevic. This view can also serve as the background for the understanding of both the territorial disputes arisen after the independence of Croatia as well as the Serbian stance towards Kosovo after 1990. "The generals believed that YU could survive as a state with 'social orientation', and that those believing the country could be transformed into a 'civic and western type European state' were only leading it into a civil war. The proponents of parliamentary democracy simply did not understand the national question in YU. The Serbian Communists and the JNA generals agreed that Yugoslavia Union (YU) was possible only as a Communist party state. They further agreed, ominously, that the 'anti-Communist and anti-socialist front' in the other Republics was 'anti-Serb.' And they also agreed that YU as a confederation of the six republics was unacceptable, because this was not a proper state, while

the Serbs wished to live in a single state with single citizenship, borders, leadership, army, market and currency."[25]

On July 25, 1990, almost one month after the proclamation of the Republic of Croatia, the Serbs met in the town of Srb and decided to set up a Serb Sabor (Assembly). Their leader, Dr Jovan Raskovic, said in his speech: "The Serb Sabor was formed out of necessity. It does not want a fight, nor does it want any friction or strife. We only want to show that Serbian people live in these territories and beyond and that they seek their rights and their dignity."[26] A few months later, on December 21, 1990, the Autonomous Region of Krajina was proclaimed in Knin. It was defined as "a territorial autonomy within the Republic of Croatia and within federal Yugoslavia." Even the Serbs of Slavonia and Baranja, regions remote from Knin, which had also declared themselves as two autonomous regions, participated in the Serb National Council.

After the promulgation of the Constitution of the Republic of Croatia, in which the Serbian people had been made an ethnic minority, and following the decision on secession of Croatia, the Serbian people living in Croatia passed a resolution on non-recognition of acts by the Sabor of the Republic of Croatia concerning disassociation. Paragraph 7 of the resolution establishes that the Serbian people in Croatia organized as the Autonomous Region of Krajina "remain to live in the State of Yugoslavia, i.e. in their common State with the Republic of Serbia and the Republic of Montenegro as well as with the Serbian people living in Bosnia and Herzegovina and other peoples in the republics accepting the common State." Consequently, the Serbian people expressed their wish to remain to live in the common State, but when it was indicated that Croatia would be recognized and that the Yugoslav army would withdraw, Croatian Serbs proclaimed the Republic of Serbian Krajina on 19 December 1991.

The Eastern Slavonia issue has resulted in atrocities by both sides. The UN role is also an issue of dispute among the Serbs and the Croats. A review of both literatures is indicative.

The Serb side claims that peace forces not only have never accomplished their tasks properly but at the same time have contributed towards the fulfillment of the Great Powers interests which has also led to violations of human rights and crimes from the side of the Croats.[27] Thousands of Croatian Serbs were expelled from Croatia including thousands of women and children, all fleeing to Serbia. This is another very serious issue of contention that is assessed in the next part of this article.

On the other side, Croats claim that the UN missions have been successful: "Current peace operations upon the territory of Croatia—UN Transition Authority in Eastern Slavonia (UNTAES) and UN Mission of Observers in

Prevlaka (UNMOP)[28]—are considered successful by my Government. Under the Basic Agreement signed between the central authorities of the Republic of Croatia and the Serbs from the Croatian Danubian Region, and pursuant to relevant Security Council resolutions, the two-year UNTAES mandate expires on January 15, 1998. Croatia holds that at this moment there are no reasons whatsoever for any prolongation of the UNTAES mandate beyond January 15, 1998. We are also firmly convinced that this mission will be fully completed on time and will go down in history as one of the most successful UN peacekeeping operations. Just yesterday, the Croatian Government submitted a detailed report to the President of the Security Council setting out the substantive achievements and costs of the steps that Croatia has taken in fulfilling its commitment to the peaceful reintegration of the Croatian Danubian region.

The results achieved under the auspices of the UN with the full cooperation of the Croatian authorities can be described as highly satisfactory. Demobilization has been completed. Local elections have been held through which the Croatian Danubian Region has been reintegrated into the legal and political system of the country. Local government has largely been transferred to the newly elected and constituted bodies.

Rules have been defined and prepared in cooperation between the Republic of Croatia, UNTAES, and UNHCR to enable a dignified, safe, and organized return of displaced persons and refugees to their homes in and out of the Croatian Danubian Region. So far about 2,000 formerly displaced non-Serbs, almost all of them Croats, have returned to the Croatian Danubian Region and more than 6,000 Croatian Serbs have returned from the region to their homes elsewhere in Croatia. The return of displaced persons and an international presence will continue after the departure of UNTAES. At the invitation of the Croatian authorities, OSCE has undertaken to monitor the developments in the Croatian Danubian Region after January 15, 1998.

The reintegration of the Croatian Danubian Region has never been an easy or simple process. The Republic of Croatia and all its citizens, especially the population of the Croatian Danubian Region, including the persons expelled from it, owe a debt of gratitude to UNTAES and all the States whose troops have participated in this highly successful operation.

The UNMOP mandate, tasked to monitor the demilitarization of the area from both sides of the southernmost border between the Republic of Croatia and FRY, has been helpful in stabilizing the security in that area and creating conditions for a lasting settlement through bilateral talks. The Republic of Croatia has shown full understanding of FRY's interests concerning the security of the Boka Kotorska Bay, while being concerned for its own security in the Dubrovnik hinterland. In this regard, UNMOP has played an important role, but

it will not be possible to deal with the outstanding problems through endless prolongation of the UN mandate.

Croatia believes that by now the developments have reached a stage where an agreement on permanent demilitarization of this border area can be made along the lines of reciprocity and with full respect for the territorial integrity of both States and their internationally recognized borders. The UN observers may be replaced by bilateral control mechanisms designed to ensure compliance with what has been agreed. This will save the United Nations precious funds which may be put to better and more purposeful use elsewhere."[29]

It should be said that the mission of UNTAES was terminated on 15/1/1998, which means that Eastern Slavonia, Baranja, and western Srem are completely re-integrated in the constitutional and legal system of the Republic of Croatia.

Finally, the issue of the Prevlaka Peninsula is a contemporary aspect of the contention between the two states. Prevlaka Peninsula is important to FRY as it controls access to a vital FRY naval base on the Adriatic Sea in Kotor, Montenegro.

Croats consider the Peninsula as being integrated in their territory.

> During the last several years, we have often heard and read in the media the pronounced Greater Serbian claims that the peninsula Prevlaka in southern Croatia had in fact always belonged to them giving eastern Herzegovina access to the sea. Since Prevlaka, along with the rest of Konavle, has, since the Middle Ages, belonged to Dubrovnik, Dalmatia, and Croatia geographically, cadastrally, administratively, judicially, ecclesiastically, religiously, and nationally, eastern Herzegovina has its own two hundred and fifty year-old access to the sea in Sutorina with which Prevlaka and the rest of Konavle were never politically joined. Prevlaka never belonged to Montenegro nor does was it ever needed by the Montenegrins, as representatives of the Montenegrin liberal opposition claim, and Serbia has an exit to the sea directly and indirectly through Montenegro. Diplomats and politicians should know and should take into account historical and natural rights and the fundamental human rights of the centuries-old farmers and today's land owners on Prevlaka, on which they live and from which they have been departing for half a century, as well as the interests of the Croatian state for this its most southern region whose inhabitants they are. With the break-up of the former Yugoslavia, this region became the meeting place of two new state realities: the Republic of Croatia and the Republic of Montenegro and it would be best for both sides if this area were to become in the future an oasis of peace, a factor of stability and a heaven-

sent area for domestic and foreign tourists and not a potential war zone which neither people want.[30]

United Nations observers were first deployed in the Konavle Prevlaka region in October 1992, in accordance with UN Security Council Resolution 779 (1992) and the Vance Plan (S/23280, Annex III—United Nations peace-keeping plan for Croatia—approved by Security Council Resolution 740 (1992)). The Vance Plan called for the demilitarization of the UN-designated Protected Areas in Croatia. It also stated that "all JNA forces deployed elsewhere in Croatia would be relocated outside that republic." Subsequently, the Croatian and Yugoslav presidents, Franjo Tuðman and Dobrica Æosiæ, signed, on September 30, 1992 in Geneva, a Joint Declaration (S/24476) by which they agreed that "the Yugoslav army will leave Prevlaka by October 20, 1992, in accordance with the Vance Plan." They further agreed that "[T]he overall security of Dubrovnik and Boka Kotorska will be resolved through subsequent negotiations."

The Secretary-General, in a letter to the Council (S/24710) on October 26, 1992, stated that "(T)he last remaining units of the Yugoslav Army completed their withdrawal from the Prevlaka Peninsula on 20 October 1992" and that "[W]ith the final departure of the Yugoslav Army from Croatian soil, a crucial element in the United Nations peace-keeping plan approved by the Security Council (S/23280, Annex III) has been fulfilled." In his report pursuant to Resolution 779 (1992) (S/24848), the secretary-general stated that "the Yugoslav Army had now completed its withdrawal from all Croatian territory in compliance with the plan approved by the Council, and UNPROFOR military observers were stationed on Prevlaka peninsula" (emphasis added).

Following the restructuring of the United Nations Protection Forces (UNPROFOR) in March 1995, the functions of the UN military observers were transferred to the UN Confidence Restoration Operation in Croatia (UNCRO) [Security Council Resolution 981 (1995)]. In his report pursuant to Resolution 981 (S/1995/320), the Secretary-General stated that "[I]n order to monitor the demilitarization of the Prevlaka peninsula, UN military observers will patrol and maintain a permanent presence on the most southerly portion of the peninsula. They will also monitor the area 5 kilometers on either side of the border and report on the presence of any military forces" (emphasis added).

With the termination of the UNCRO mandate in January 1996, the Security Council, by its Resolution 1038, (1996), authorized UN military observes to continue to monitor the demilitarization of the Prevlaka. The United Nations Mission of Observers on Prevlaka (UNMOP) became an independent mission of 28 observers on February 1, 1996. In his report pursuant to UN Security

Council Resolution 1038, (S/1996/180) the secretary-general reiterated that he had noted in his report S/24600 that the proposal elaborated by UNPROFOR was accepted by both sides, and that under the agreement the

> Yugoslav Army would withdraw completely from Croatia, Prevlaka would be demilitarized and heavy weapons would be removed from neighboring areas of Croatia and Montenegro. The agreement was based on a concept of the establishment of a demilitarized zone on either side of the Croatian/Montenegro border." In his subsequent report S/1996/502, the secretary-general clearly indicated border delineation by stating that "[T]he withdrawal of Croatian military personnel and the partial removal of mines in the United Nations-controlled zone on the Croatian side of the border . . . are positive developments (emphasis added).

The temporal mandate of UNMOP was subsequently extended on July 15, 1996 [Security Council Resolution 1066 (1996)], on January 14, 1997 [Security Council Resolution 1093 (1997)], on July 14, 1997 [Security Council Resolution 1119 (1997)], on January 13, 1998 [Security Council Resolution 1147 (1998)], and on July 15, 1998 [Security Council Resolution 1183 (1998)]. Prevlaka is routinely discussed in the Security Council under the Agenda Item "Situation in Croatia."

Successive reports of the UN secretary-general have found that the situation in Prevlaka does not represent a threat to international peace and security, but it sees the UN presence there as "providing conditions conducive to bilateral negotiations" (S/1998/578, S/1998/939, S/1998/16). The UN mission has been extended till mid December 2000. However, no permanent solution has been found yet which maintains the Pavlaka question valid.

Both the Eastern Slavenia and the Pravlaka Peninsula questions are two vivid issues of contention among the two states. Highly interconnected with those two issues is the big question of the return of the refugees.

3.3. The return of the refugees: an issue of continuous contention

Another issue of contention which seems to be a lasting one is that of the respect of human rights of the refugees which have now started going back as a result of the fierce events that took place between 1991-1995.

The issue of the return of the Serbian Croats is still a questionable point. The diminishing numbers of registration of Serb students in the schools is an indicative factor of the diminishing numbers of Serbs living in the areas in question: "Following the passing of the enrollment deadline for elementary and

secondary school pupils for the 1998/99 school year in Eastern Slavonia (the Croatian Danube Region), and particularly in the Vukovar-Sirmium county, enrollment results are disheartening: the enrollment of students of Serb nationality has drastically decreased in comparison to last year."

Data collected by the Board of Education and Culture of the Joint Council of Municipalities in Vukovar show that not a single student of Serb nationality has enrolled in the first grade in the elementary schools in Lovas, Tovarnik, Šidski Banovci, Ilok and Sarengrad, while only one such student has enrolled for first grade in Èakovci. Additionally, the number of students enrolled in general has decreased by 15 percent (the percentage is even greater in some schools) from the number of students in those same schools during the recently completed school year.

It is worth noting that this problem is occurring in those same areas in which there has been an intensified return of Croat displaced persons, the consequence of which, judging from the data, seems to be a worsening state of affairs for the Serb population in this county.

The situation is even more serious when one realizes that the actual number of students who will attend classes beginning in the fall is much less than the present number enrolled because students continue to leave the area.

Data from the Vukovar Customs Branch office show that from the 16th of January 1998, 1500 students who registered have definitely moved out of Croatia. These numbers encompass only those who have moved away with all of their belongings. Initially, families leaving the country were, for the most part, those who had, following the military actions "Flash" and "Storm," moved into the abandoned homes of displaced Croats; however those leaving in the past two months are natives of the area, and particularly from those places where the return of displaced Croats has been intense."[31]

The Serbian Unity Congress states similar concerns. Based on figures produced by the Joint Council of Municipalities[32] in Vukovar, Croatia, SUC claims that the Serb population of Eastern Slavonia, Baranja, and Western Srem continues to decline at an alarming rate. "The figures for the Serb population of this region since 1991 are:

1991: 80,000
1995: 130,000 (including refugees from the Krajina region of Croatia)
January 1998: 67,000 (including 15,000 Krajina refugees)
April 1998: 60,000

The reason for this continuing exodus is attributable mainly to intimidatory pressure from the Croatian authorities who assumed control of the region on

January 15, 1998 following the end of the United Nations Transitional Administration in Eastern Slavonia (UNTAES) mandate. In the eyes of the Serbs, this pressure takes the form of:

- Dismissal of Serbs from jobs and their replacement by Croats;
- Administrative and financial obstacles to the registration of Serb companies;
- Manipulation of agricultural prices to damage Serb farming entities;
- Failure to provide proper legal and financial resources to the Joint Council of Municipalities in violation of the Croatia Government letter of intent of January 13, 1997;
- Dismissal of Serbs from the police force and their replacement by Croats;
- Nationalist intimidation from the Croatian media;
- Secret indictment of Serbs for unknown crimes.

These actions by Croatia violate the November 12, 1995 Erdut Agreement. This Agreement made provision for the return of Eastern Slavonia to Croatian administration on the understanding that Croatia would guarantee the rights of Serbs living there and of those who wished to return.

Croatia's actions have had the effect of reducing the Serb population of Croatia from approximately 16% in 1991 to 3% today. It appears that the Croatian intention is to "cleanse" all Serbs from Croatia.

The Serbian Unity Congress protests these Croatian actions strongly. First and foremost, they are morally repugnant. American involvement in the Bosnian war came about in part because of opposition to "ethnic cleansing." This is now taking place on a massive scale in Croatia and in the Croat-dominated area of the Bosnian Federation where an elderly Serb couple was murdered on April 15. Following this outrage, the UN Spokesman in Bosnia accused the Croatian authorities of "nationalistic Croatian violence against Serbs."[33]

The human rights issue has been an important aspect of the newly established Republic of Croatia with the rest of Europe. The EU has condemned human rights violations and the authoritarian regime of Franjo Tudzman. In 1995, the relations between the EU and Croatia ceased. Only after the latest political events and the reaffirmation of the newly elected Croatian government has the EU reviewed the relations with the country. This evolution creates now hopes that in the frame of this new political environment the refugee issue will be resolved.

3.4. Use of modern technology in contention

The issue of contention still continues. This time Serbs and Croats do not only use guns and other "traditional" ways of contention. They also use modern technology and Internet. As Reuters reported on November the 2nd 1998, a group of Serbian hackers called "Crna Ruka" (Black Hand) broke onto the web site of Croatian state-owned daily *Vjesnik*, and wrote slogans like "We are fighting for the truth and for Serbia." Croatian hackers retaliated the next day, blocking the site of the Serbian National Library. "Read Vjesnik and not Serbian books" the message said. "This has nothing to do with politics. This is simply our reply to their propaganda. We wanted to show them we are better hackers," said a member of the Croatian Mind Hackers who rang the daily. "If they break into Croatian cyberspace one more time we will hack their government's server" he said. In the meantime Crna Ruka gained publicity the same month when they entered the site of the Kosovo Information Center, run by ethnic Albanians who fought for independence from Serbia. It is undoubtful that even cyberspace has borders for Croatians and Serbs.

4. Conclusions

The Serbian movements for independence "fall" into the theoretical considerations concerning separatism. Following a historical sequence of events, we can conclude that Croats have always challenged the authority of the state. Such challenges were based on the expression of ethnolinguistic disagreements, unilateral declarations of autonomy or secession, interposition or exception to the administration of law, and rejection or assertions of allegiance or rights and responsibilities of citizenship. The issue of independence has been formalized while other issues of dispute still remain alive.

The issues of contention between Serbs and Croats are deep-rooted. They can be summarized as follows:

1. The fact that the Serbs consider the act of the independent Croatia as a secessionist one and not as an act of independence, which eventually leads to the violation of international law and the UN Charter, especially to what concerns the development of the self-determination notion and principle.

2. The fact that Serbs consider the international community as being prejudiced against them, going on with acts and actions that fulfill the interests of the

Great Powers against the interests of the Serb populations and Serbia, in general.

3. The issue of Eastern Slavonia and the respect of the human rights of the Serbian population, especially to what concerns the return of the refugees and their rights, with property rights being a starting point. It should be noted that based on the 1997 Human Rights Report of the USA State Department, the Croatian governments is to blame for serious violations of human rights against the Serbian population in the country.

4. The issue of the Pravlaka Peninsula, which is still under question and unresolved.

Democracy has a long way to go in the Balkans. Corruption is pervasive, and ethnic animosities are great. Not all-political opposition is democratic. Mr Milosevic has had a number of ultra-nationalist rivals. In Croatia, many anti-Tudjman elements are still sympathetic to his blocking of the return of the Serb refugees, but a large proportion of the Serbian and Croat people want something better than their current fate. Everybody hopes that recent democratic changes in both Croatia and Serbia will contribute to the direction of peace and stability in the region as well as the prosperity of their people away from frustrations and contention.

This analysis might not be the one that covers all issues. However, we attempted to integrate all different issues in one chapter. Additionally, we have made an effort to present both sides' opinions in order to conceive the deep-rooted issues of contentions. We hope that this chapter will serve as a basis for additional research and will serve at least to create a framework of understanding between the two states.[34]

ENDNOTES

[1] The other two types of destabilizing events being decolonization and transnational disputes. Separatism is defined as "a type of behavior that has as its objective withdrawal or disaffiliation from the jurisdiction of a nation state by part of its population," see Edward A. Ziengenhagen and Kleomenis S. Koutsoukis, *Political Conflict in Southern Europe: Regulation, Regression and Morphogenesis*, (Praeger: New York 1992), p. 35.

[2] *Ibid.*

[3] *Ibid.*, p. 64.

[4] Transition and Integration: Prospects for Partners and Candidates in Europe, 46th General Assembly of the Atlantic Treaty Association, Croatian contribution to the regional stability, Presentation by Mrs Vesna Cvjetkovic-Kurelec, Deputy Minister of Foreign Affairs of the Republic of Croatia, Budapest, 31 October 2000.

[5] Representatives of more than 500 Yugoslav companies and 450 Croatian firms opened talks in Belgrade on the 16th of November 2000 resuming business cooperation, non-existent for ten years. "Yugoslav Chamber of Commerce Vice-President Drago Sofranac welcomed the businessmen and wished them success in resuming business cooperation. Sofranac said the job that lay ahead was to institutionalize mutual relations and sign accords on free trade and on liberalizing the visa regimen, so as to attain the desired level of trade. "This could be our joint message to the competent state bodies," he told in the plenary session. He noted that the two countries' economies were largely compatible, their production and other capacities having been developing within the same economic space for decades. Croatian Chamber of Commerce President Nadan Vitosevic, in turn, said it was Croatia's strategic national target to join the European Union, which could be achieved by "placing complete peace in the region and economic cooperation with Serbia. "Our markets are inter-dependent," according to Vitosevic." Source: Tanjug Media Agency, 16/11/2000.

[6] Serbs argue that in this way "the separatist tendencies" in Croatia surfaced immediately after the outbreak of the Second World War. As early as 10 April

1941, the leaders of the Ustashi movement (separatist movement in Croatia) proclaimed an Independent State of Croatia. That act coincided with the entrance in Zagreb of the 14th German armored division, while Vlatko Macek, a Croat, former Deputy Prime Minister of the Yugoslav Government, invited Germany to recognize the Independent State of Croatia. German General Kuhn stated that Zagreb welcomed troops with such enthusiasm that he felt as though he was in Linz. See SS Veesmayer to the Foreign Ministry, Telegram No. 41 of 5/4/1941.

[7] Serbs argue that, with a view to totally annihilating them in the territory of Croatia, several extermination camps were set up where Serbs were killed in planned fashion and individually. Former commander of Jasenovac camp Ljuba Milos, at a trial in Belgrade after the war, said that it was impossible to determine the number of people killed, but that the number was huge. It is also claimed that in Jadovno camp, Serbs were killed tied to one another. According to the Yugoslav Encyclopedia, in Jadovno alone 35,000 Serbs were killed while the total number of people killed exceeded 1,000,000. According to the number of victims, the Jasenovac camp was the most notorious, with around 700,000 Serbs, Jews and Gypsies killed. Around 400 Orthodox churches were also destroyed. See *Spiritual Genocide*, Slobodan Mileusnic, Mitropolija Zagrebacko Ljubljanska 1997.

[8] Croatia net: Croatian History, http://www.croatia.net/html/history2.html, p. 1, 2.

[9] Krulic J., *Histoire de la Yougoslavie*, Ed. Complexe, 1993.

[10] *Official Gazette of the Republic of Slovenia*, No. 26/1990 and 1/1991.

[11] *People's Papers*, No. 56/1990.

[12] *International Herald Tribune*, 12 December 1991, p. 2.

[13] *Le Monde*, Vendredi, 13 September 1991, p. 2.

[14] Wynaendts H., *L'engranage Chronique Yugoslaves*, Juillet, 1991-1992, Paris, 1993, p. 14.

[15] Baker J., *The Politics of Diplomacy*, New York, 1995, p. 481.

[16] As stated in ICL-Croatia Index, http://www.uni-wuerzburg.de/law/hr_indx.html, p. 1, 2.

[17] As adopted in 18 December 1990.

[18] The agreement was initialled by the Republic of Bosnia-Herzegovina, the Republic of Croatia, and the FRY. It was witnessed by the Contact Group nations—the USA, Britain, France, Germany and Russia and the EU Special Negotiator. According to the terms of the Agreement, a sovereign state known as the Republic of Bosnia-Herzegovina will consist of two entities: the Bosnian Serb Republic and the Federation of Bosnia (Croats and Muslims). Source: http://www.state.gov/www/regions/eur/bosnia.

[19] Official Gazette of the FYR 23, 89/1991.

[20] In an interview with Dr. Pantelis Sklias on 25/10/2000.

[21] Jovic B., The Last Days of FYR, Belgrade 1995.

[22] More on the subject (Avramov, *Postheroic War of the West Against Yugoslavia*, Belgrade 1997, pp. 189/190).

[23] More on the subject: Kreca M., Badinter Commission, Critical overview, 1993.

[24] Interview with Ivan Cukalovic, Professor of International law in the University of Kragujevac, Kragujevac, 25/10/2000.

[25] Source: http://www.barnsdle.demon.co.uk/bosnia/serbia2.html, p. 2.

[26] Radulovic S., *The Fate of Krajina*, Belgrade, 1996, p. 19.

[27] See daily media like Nasa Borba, August 6, 1995, p. 4, Politika, August 5, 1995, p. 7. as well as Smilja Avramov, The West's Post-Heroic War against Yugoslavia, Belgrade, 1997, p.365. In all cases, the UN Peace-Keeping forces are considered to be in full cooperation with the Croatian site, while Great Powers, namely the USA, are accused of fully supporting the atrocities of the Croatian troops against the Serbian population of the region concerned.

Comparisons are also made with the 1941 period mentioning that detention camps have been erected and developed for the Serbs.

[28] UN Transition Authority in Eastern Slavonia and UN Mission of Observers in Prevlaka respectively. The Basic Agreement between the parties was signed on November 12, 1995 and came into force with the passage of UN Security Council resolution 1037 (1996) dated January 15, 1996. It provided for the establishment of a Transitional Administration to govern the region during a 12 month-period, extendible for an additional 12 months at the request of one of the parties. The agreement and its enabling resolution covers, inter alia, demilitarization, establishment of police forces, population movement, restoration of property and assistance in reconstruction. A UN mission entitled UNTAES (UN Transitional Authority in Eastern Slavonia) comprised of a 5000-person military force, a UN Civilian Police force together with supporting UN civilian staff is to be set up to assist the Administrator in carrying out the mandate. The UN has appointed an American, Mr. Jacques Klein, as the Transitional Administrator, and Major General Schoups of Belgium as the military commander.

[29] Statement by H. E. Dr. Mate Graniæ, Deputy Prime Minister and Minister for Foreign Affairs of the Republic of Croatia, General Assembly, Fifty-Second Session, UN, NY, 25/9/1997.

[30] Prof. Dr. Stjepo Obad, http://www.dalmatia.net/croatia/politics/prevlaka.htm.

[31] Croatian Helsinki Committee for Human Rights Bulletin, No. 10, July 28, 1998.

[32] The Joint Council of Municipalities is a legal entity under Croatian law. It was established by written agreement with the Government of Croatia on May 23, 1997, signed in the presence of UN Deputy Administrator Jacques Klein. It is based on the Erdut Agreement of November 12, 1995 and UN Security Council Resolution 1037 (January 15, 1996). Its purpose is to represent the Serbian ethnic community in Eastern Slavonia, Baranja, and Western Srem. It acts as an advisory body to the Croatian Government.

[33] Serbian Unity Congress, Press Release, April 23, 1998.

[34] For a recent and broader socioeconomic perspective of the region see: Pantelis Sklias, *International Political Economy: The Balkans, Central and Eastern Europe, The Members of the Former USSR and Their Relations with European Union*. Athens: Papazissis, 2001.

REFERENCES

A. Primary Sources

1. Croatian Helsinki Committee for Human Rights Bulletin, No. 10, July 28, 1998.
2. HE Dr. Mate Graniæ, Deputy Prime Minister and Minister for Foreign Affairs of the Republic of Croatia, General Assembly, fifty-second Session, UN, NY, 25/9/1997.
3. International Herald Tribune, 12 December 1991, p.2
4. Le Monde, Wednesday, 13 September 1991, p.2
5. Nasa Borba, 6 August 1995, p.4,
6. Official Gazette of the FRY 23, 89/1991
7. Official Gazette of the Republic of Slovenia, No. 26/1990 and 1/1991.
8. People's Papers, No. 56/1990
9. Politika, 5 August 1995, p.7.
10. Serbian Unity Congress, Press Release, April 23, 1998.
11. Source: Courier des pays de l' Est, No. 331, 7-8/1988.
12. SS Veesmayer to the Foreign Ministry, Telegram No. 41 of 5/4/1941.
13. Tanjug Media Agency, 16/11/2000.
14. Transition and Integration: Prospects for Partners and Candidates in Europe, 46th General Assembly of the Atlantic Treaty Association, Croatian contribution to the regional stability, Presentation by Mrs. Vesna Cvjetkovic-Kurelec, Deputy Minister of Foreign Affairs of the Republic of Croatia, Budapest, 31 October 2000.

B. Theoretical Works and Secondary Sources

1. Andreas Papandreou Institute of Strategic and Development Studies, *Balkans Observatory*, Croatia, 1999, Athens.
2. Andreas Papandreou Institute of Strategic and Development Studies, *Balkans Observatory*, Slovenia, 1999, Athens.

3. Andreas Papandreou Institute of Strategic and Development Studies, *Balkans Observatory*, Bosnia and Herzegovina, 1999, Athens.
4. Avramov, A., *Postheroic War of the West Against Yugoslavia*, Belgrade 1997, pp. 189/190.
5. Baker J., *The Politics of Diplomacy*, New York, 1995, p. 481.
6. Jovic B., *The Last Days of FRY*, Belgrade 1995.
7. Kreca M., *Badinter Commission: Critical overview*, 1993.
8. Krulic J., *Histoire de la Yougoslavie*, Ed. Complexe, 1993.
9. Mileusnic S., *Spiritual Genocide*, Mitropolija Zagreba~ko Ljubljanska 1997.
10. Papasotiriou X., *The Balkans After the End of Cold War*, in Greek, Athens, Papazisis, 1994.
11. Radulovic S., *The Fate of Krajina*, Belgrade, 1996, p. 19.
12. Sklias, Pantelis. *International Political Economy: The Balkans, Central and Eastern Europe, The Members of the Former USSR and Their Relations with European Union*. Athens: Papazissis, 2001.
13. Wynaendts H., *L'engranage Chronique Yugoslaves*, July 1991-1992, Paris, 1993, p. 14.
14. Yallouridis X and Alifantis S. (eds.), *The Balkans in the Crossroads of Developments*, in Greek, Athens, Roes, 1988.
15. Ziengenhagen A. E. and Koutsoukis S. K., *Political Conflict in Southern Europe: Regulation, Regression and Morphogenesis*, New York, Praeger,1992.

C. Internet Sources

1. http://www.croatia.net/html/history2.html,
2. http://www.uni-wuerzburg.de/law/hr_indx.html
3. http://www.state.gov/www/regions/eur/bosnia
4. http://www.dalmatia.net/croatia/politics/prevlaka.htm

CHAPTER 6
CROATIA'S NATIONAL INTEGRATION: PASSING THROUGH THE 19TH TO THE 21ST CENTURY

Dimitrios Koukourdinos
London School of Economics and Political Science

INTRODUCTION

"WAR made states and states made war": Charles Tilly's observation on the formation of modern nation-states in Europe could very well describe the dramatic events that took place in the Western Balkans after 1989. During the last decade, in the area of former Yugoslavia, the world has witnessed the violent collapse of a state, the creation of at least five new states in its place, and the struggle among themselves and with the various para-states inside their contested borders. All these took place in a war with human and material losses of a magnitude that Europe has not experienced since the end of WWII. In this process of simultaneous disintegration and creation of a new regional order, the concept of "state" holds a central place. More than anything else, the conflict that started in the Western Balkans after 1991, and continues till today, is a war over the control of territories and the creation of new nation-states.

Apart from Slovenia, Croatia was the only former Yugoslav republic that had managed to exit the turmoil with relative success. In sharp contrast to its northern neighbor, Croatia's bid for independence had been challenged for a long period, both externally and internally. It took this country five years of open conflict till it managed to secure its sovereignty and territorial integrity. The impact of war on the development of Croatian statehood and democracy during these and subsequent years cannot be overestimated. The relation between the war and the formation of the new state is more than obvious. Once fighting started, "warmaking and statemaking reinforced each other, indeed remained practically indistinguishable until states began to form secure, recognized boundaries around substantial contiguous territories."[1]

Since the signing of the Dayton Agreement, Croatia ceased to be an immediate part of the Yugoslav conflict. A second phase started during which the task was how to achieve democratic consolidation and economic prosperity, rather than how to secure the existence of the state itself. Yet, this was not an easy process. While the state-building policy pursued by the first President of Croatia, Franjo Tudjman, was successful in establishing the sovereignty of the

country, its political, ideological, and institutional implications hindered the consolidation of full democracy well after the war ended.

State-building itself is a rather neutral term. Its essence, its direction, and its evolution are immediately related to the socioeconomic, institutional, and political conditions present at the moment of its initiation as well as to the ideas that underpin its goals. More importantly, state-building depends largely on the ideas, the policies and the will of the leadership that undertakes the execution of this tremendous task. Nationalism and historical legacies were significant factors in Croatia's transition, however, not independently, but through their influence on the choices and decisions of leaders regarding the creation of the state.

Therefore, the examination of Croatian national integration in the 1990s should include the description of older issues related to its statehood and past attempts to create an independent state; the real problems that such an evolution had to face and solve in the 1990s; the actors and their political goals; and finally the policies followed in order to achieve these aims.

THE 1000 YEAR EXISTENCE OF A SEMI-STATE: CROATIAN STATEHOOD BEFORE 1989

The first paragraph of the 1990 Croatian Constitution leaves no doubt as to what is considered to be the foundations of the new state. The new state is based on "the millennial identity of the Croatian *nation and the continuity of its statehood*, confirmed by the course of its entire historical experience in *various state forms* and by the preservation and growth of the idea of a national state, founded on the historical right of the Croatian nation to full sovereignty."[2] Such a grandiose and bold statement comes as no surprise; the manifestation of the centuries-old historical continuity of the nation holds a central place in most nationalist political agendas, and Croatia is no exception to that. Of course, such a belief ignores the fact that modern nations and their institutional expression, the nation-state, are the outcome of a much more recent process, which, in the case of Eastern Europe, started no earlier than the 19th century.[3] However, in the case of Croatia, these claims deserve close attention, for they were not just part of a nationalistic rhetoric attempting to legitimatize the new state but they also served as political agendas. Moreover, a brief examination of the historical notions and attributes of Croatian statehood and nationhood helps us to understand the general problems underlying its state-building in the 1990s.

1. Croatia as an old state

The most extraordinary claim of Croatian historiography is the existence of a continuous *state* tradition that goes back to the 10th century. In the Middle Ages, Croatia emerged under king Tomislav as a regional power in the Balkans, but two centuries afterwards it lost its sovereignty under the Magyars. However, this was done in a formal manner, under an agreement that offered the orphaned Croatian throne to the Hungarian king (Pacta Conventa). It is interesting to note that to Croatian historians this development was the "least of evils," the only alternative of Croatia's nobility to preserve some kind of autonomy in the face of serious external threats. Although Croatia's *de facto* individuality and autonomy are questionable, there existed a *juridical* foundation of Croatian statehood based on the agreed subjection first under the Hungarian and later under the Habsburgs crown. However thin, this arrangement allowed the survival of a notion of Croatian *statehood* until the 19th century.

Of course the *de jure* recognition of Croatia's existence was not a guarantee for the behavior of the all-powerful imperial centers. Thus, during the last centuries of foreign domination, there was a constant struggle for affirmation and respect of this status. Due to this, the Croatian elite developed a tradition of constant bargaining and political obstructionism in a continuous attempt to secure as much autonomy as possible from an external power center (Vienna or Budapest) and a belief that bargaining can bring results.[4]

However, the relatively positive element of the legal recognition of Croatian statehood was weakened by the fact that there was no political unity among Croatian-populated areas. In fact, territorially, Croatian lands included at least six distinct regions and sub-regions, namely the Zagreb region, Slavonia, Dalmatia, Istria, Vojna Krajina, and the city of Dubrovnik, as well as the Croatian populated areas of Western Herzegovina. All the aforementioned lands had diverse historical experiences, as they formed parts of different states (Austria, Hungary, Venice, Ottomans) and developed strong regional identities. The tendency for high territorial centralization, so obvious in Tudjman's state-building policy, should be viewed also under the light of this fact.

The third and certainly the most important element in Croatian statehood tradition is the *"Serbian question."* Large scale Serbian presence in Croatia started in the 16th century, when many Serb families were invited by the Habsburgs to settle along Austrian borders with the Ottoman Empire to serve as border guards in exchange for special privileges and relative autonomy. Since then, this region was known as the Military Frontier (*Vojna Krajina*), and it was put under the immediate control of Vienna. The independence of the Military

Frontier—although significant for Croatia's defense—generated what were perhaps the first disputes between Zagreb authority and the Krajina Serbs.[5] In this respect, the "Serbian question" started not so much as an ethnic but rather as a territorial problem; most of the time, Krajina was a region beyond Zagreb's direct control. Moreover, in times of dispute between Croatian nobility and the imperial center, the latter was following a policy of "divide and rule" and tried to mobilize the Krajina Serbs as a balance to Croatian demands.[6] Hence, the beginning of a tradition where the Serbs, in their attempt to secure their status, are used as checkers of Croatian emancipation aspirations.

2. Croatia as a modern nation

When the messages of the French Revolution reached the confines of Zagreb, Croatian state identity was already a fact. At this point Croatian intellectuals undertook the task of defining the contents of modern Croatian *nationhood*. During the subsequent decades, two major strands of thought influenced this development. The first had to do with the emergence of ideas about South Slavic unity. The so-called "Illyrian movement" that later developed into "Yugoslavism" had as its founders and main supporters two prominent Croats, Ljudevit Gaj and bishop Josip Juraj Strossmayer. It was an idea that advocated mainly the linguistic but also the ethnic unity of Croats and Serbs. Still, its real content was political. In fact, the Illyrian idea appealed for South Slav solidarity as a reaction to Budapest's attempts at Hungarization. As a romantic movement, "Illyrianism" was for a long time limited to certain Croatian intellectual circles and did not penetrate the wider population in large scale.

However, while the Croats did indeed lay the basis for the Yugoslav idea, Illyrianism was not the only Croatian national project. The 19th century saw the formulation of an alternative Croatian vision in which Croats were seen as clearly and unmistakably different from the Serbs.[7] The main promoter of this alternative was Ante Starčević and his Croatian Party of Rights. His slogans were "Croatia for the Croats" and "Neither Vienna nor Budapest." His persistent refusal of any connection with the Austro-Hungarian Empire, but other than the person of the King, had a strong appeal among the people.[8]

For a long time, the two political projects remained antagonistic, and the dispute was never fully settled. Nevertheless, what accounted for the success of the Yugoslavia the Croation separatism was neither its correspondence to "reality" nor its popularity. It was mainly the result of elite choices, having to do with external conditions. Immediately after WWI and under territorial threats

from a revisionist Hungary, a bitter Austria, and an offensive Italy, the majority of the Croatian elite opted for Illyrianism and cooperation with Serbia. The connection with Belgrade could provide a vital defense.

3. Croatia in Yugoslavia

The political considerations of the time prevailed. The Croats decided to join what was till then a typical nation-state under the umbrella of a precarious national identity that overemphasized just one element, language, and downplayed the significance of history and religion. More importantly, the two major nations that would constitute the new South Slavic state had very different perceptions of what "Yugoslavism" meant, with the Croats recognizing some differences (and thus demanding differentiation at state level) and the Serbs ignoring them altogether (and hence standing in favor of centralization).

It soon became obvious that the unity of a state cannot be based only on the presence of external threats. The Kingdom of Serbs, Croats, and Slovenes, as the first Yugoslavia was initially called, was a state of convenience based on serious mutual misperceptions on the part of both Serbs and Croats; these misconceptions were exacerbated by differences of style and aspirations derived from different historical experiences.[9] The Croatian reaction to Serbian unitary trends took the form of two different policies. The one advocated by the prominent politician Stjepan Radić included a temperate but uncompromising demand for decentralization, typical of the previous legalistic and obstructionist traditions of the Croatian elite. The second, initiated by Ante Pavelić and his fascist Ustaša movement, was extremist, reactionary; and supported outright independence and armed resistance.

The assassination of Radić on the floor of the parliament deteriorated relations between all parties concerned. To take control of the situation, King Alexander attempted a *coup d'etat*, but the imposition of a royal dictatorship and the change of the state's name to Yugoslavia was dangerous for Croats for it denied their tradition of statehood all together. Conflict of interests continued well into the 1930s when a last attempt was made to improve the situation. The Agreement of 1939, known as *Sporazum*, proposed an enlarged Croatian entity inside the state, the so called Croatian *Banovina*, that would include all Croatian territories plus the Croat-inhabited part of Bosnia, but the arrangement came too late to have an effect.

After subduing Yugoslavia in 1941, the Germans installed an independent Croatian State (NDH-Independent State of Croatia) under the authority of their ally, Ante Pavelić and his Ustaša organization. Echoing the ideas of Starčević

about the Croatian origins of Bosnian Muslims, the state incorporated Bosnia and Herzegovina, but left out many Croatian regions in Dalmatia that were given to Italy. It was during this period that the biggest problem of Croatian statehood, the status of Croatia's Serbs, acquired enormous dimensions. Although historiography from both sides tried to manipulate the number of victims for political purposes, it is beyond doubt that the Ustaša regime launched a policy of extermination against the Serbian minority.[10] The usual clashes of interests, which were serious in the past but never resolved in such a violent way, were now transformed into deep distrust, even hatred.

As a reaction, Croatian Serbs, together with antifascist Croats, joined Tito's partisan forces. Thus, when the war was over, the Serbs of Croatia emerged as the winners in the new order. Due to their large numbers in the partisan army, they were over-represented in the Croatian Communist Party and in the means of coercion. Their participation in the party and the army were to guarantee that Serbs of Croatia would never again be menaced by fascist genocide.[11]

On the other hand, the federal structure of the second Yugoslavia meant that Croats, as well as other Yugoslav nations should gain their republic and thus recognition of statehood. The Bosnian territories formed the Socialist Republic of Bosnia and Herzegovina, but Croats gained Istria and the part of Dalmatia occupied by the Italians, a move that brought most Croat lands under Zagreb's authority. However, inside the republic, the status of the Serbs was elevated to that of a constituent nation. It was an arrangement typical of Tito's balancing policies: according to the Constitution of the Socialist Republic of Croatia, the latter was defined as "the nation state of Croatian people, and the state of the Serbs living in Croatia." There were actually thoughts of establishing an autonomous province of Krajina along the model of Serbian autonomous provinces, but these plans were abandoned. Instead, Croats got again a *de jure* recognition of their statehood and the Serbs were given anew the role of checkers of the expression of Croatian nationalism. If Kosovo and Vojvodina were formed in order to curtail Serbian hegemonism, Croatian Serbs would serve as the bulwark to Croatian national aspirations.

Many explanations have been suggested as to the causes the led to Yugoslavia's disintegration. Some emphasize "objective" factors, like economic failure, ethnic structure etc, while others focus on the role of "subjective" elite decisions and choices. From the point of view of state-building and state-failure, Yugoslavia's disintegration started gradually in the 1970s, due to its weakness at two levels: first, the institutional weakness of the federal center vis-à-vis the republics, and second, the fragility of "Yugoslav" identity that never managed to replace the existing national identities.

As far as the institutional weakness of the federal center is concerned, the adoption of the 1974 Constitution was a point of no return. The initial idea was to create a system of collective governance by all the republics that would take over power after Tito's death. The bond would be provided by the League of Communists, and its guardian would be the federal army. The republics increased their competence in many policy fields and also got a powerful veto in the decision-making at the federal level. In fact, what the Constitution achieved was to make the republics the real loci of power in a largely confederal arrangement.[12]

Yet, this weak settlement could have been functional if it had been based on solid identity grounds, but "Yugoslav" identity was again a compromise at the lower common denominator. As Schöpflin noted, "Yugoslavism as a doctrine was too closely bound up with communism and, given the propensity of communists to centralize power, it was associated with Serbian power. This made it hard for non-Serbs to see a genuinely all-Yugoslav identity as attractive to them."[13] Hence, the collapse of communism in 1989 raised all these problems to the peak. If Yugoslavia was to survive, it had to change. It could be that the Yugoslav political elites of the 1980s were short of political imagination, but the issue of centralism versus decentralization reappeared and was exacerbated by republican leaders' policies.

The main parts in this conflict were initially Slovenia and Serbia. The pretext of an economic crisis was given. The reformist communist elite of Slovenia wanted more liberalization and decentralization. The die-hard communist leader of Serbia with Yugoslavia-wide ambitions, Slobodan Milošević, was adamant that only further centralization could solve Yugoslavia's problem. A compromise between the two was extremely difficult from the very outset. The Croatian branch of the League of Communists was caught in the middle. Its absence from the flow of events that transpired in late 1980s is remarkable. The reason is to be found in what took place in the early 1970s. After a brief period of ambivalence, Tito launched a policy of purges in order to suppress reformist-*cum*-nationalist ideas that started spreading in Croatia in the late 1960s. Starting as a movement of intellectuals for the affirmation of Croatian cultural distinctiveness, the so-called MASPOK (masovan pokret-mass movement) expressed clear political goals and even made demands for a republican army and a seat for Croatia in the UN. The suppression of the "Croatian Spring" in late 1971 had far-reaching consequences. First, after the purges, the Croatian League of Communists (SKH) became the most conservative and loyal branch of the federal communist party. Hence, their inability to have a more constructive role once the crisis broke up. Second, the

already high presence of Serbs in the SKH leadership became even more pronounced. As for the MASPOK participants, after two decades of persecution, some of them were to reappear as important political figures in 1989. In any case, from 1972 until 1989, Croatia was indeed Yugoslavia's "Silent republic."[14]

CROATIA'S ROAD TO INDEPENDENCE: STATE-BUILDING *ÜBER ALLES*

1. "God and Croatia": Tudjman's rise to power

The figure that has shaped Croatia's postcommunist development is undoubtedly that of Dr. Franjo Tudjman. Seen respectively by friends and foes as the Croatian Bismarck or the personification of Machiaveli's authoritarian Prince, Croatia's first President was indeed a formidable personality. Starting his career as a partisan and later as the youngest general in the Yugoslav People's Army, he soon developed a strong interest in history. This was an important step in the development of his personality, as his preoccupation with what he perceived as the falsification of Croatian history by the communist regime led to his utterly "historicist" understanding of the political present. For example, his belief that there was a deliberate exaggeration of WWII crimes committed by the Ustaša regime, combined with the downplaying of Croatians' contribution in the antifascist struggle, became a central theme in his political program. His commitment to the nationalistic Croatian cause led to his periodic persecution and imprisonment.

In early 1989, when it became obvious that the communist party's monopoly would not last long, Tudjman founded the Croatian Democratic Community (HDZ-Hrvatska Demokratska Zajednica). As many similar organizations in Eastern Europe at the time, HDZ was not a party in the strict meaning of the term. It was rather an umbrella-movement that brought together people of different political and ideological origins. Indeed, from the very beginning, one could detect two distinct groups, the first formed by ex-communists and persons of partisan background who had been purged back in 1971, and the second formed by people of clearly nationalistic convictions, many of whom were coming from the anti-communist, anti-Yugoslav and pro-Ustaša circles of the Croatian diaspora. Tudjman himself had visited Croatian communities abroad, and, although as a former partisan, he was received with suspicion by many, he managed to convince the majority to support his plan for an independent state.[15]

Tudjman's political agenda was clearly anti-communist, anti-Yugoslav, and nationalistic. Democracy was mentioned, but, as Yugoslavia and communism had become two indistinguishable terms, it was assumed that whoever was anti-Yugoslav was also a pro-democrat. The pursuit of independence of course presupposed that Tudjman had clear thoughts as to how to address the main problems connected with the legacies of Croatian statehood. Two related issues arose here, namely the justification of previous attempts for national emancipation and a proposal regarding the status of Serbs inside Croatia.

Regarding the former, Tudjman's political program made explicit references to ideas made famous by Croatian national figures, especially Starčević and his struggle for Croatia's state right, as well as Radić and his democratic republicanism.[16] His model for the state that he wanted to establish was the *Croatian banovina* of 1939, that is, an enlarged Croatia that would incorporate a part of Bosnia. This had fascinated Tudjman since the 1960s, and he considered it to be an acceptable model for a future solution of the Yugoslav question.[17] Moreover, Tudjman was in favor of the French model of a highly centralized state. Any idea of strong regional authority or federalism was unconditionally rejected; in fact, strong regional parties like the *Istrian Democratic Assembly* were deemed just as dangerous as the Serbs.[18]

Nevertheless, at the core of Tudjman's political vision lay the idea of "*reconciliation*" between Croatia's Partisan and Ustaša past. For the Croatian leader, the policy of national reconciliation was the only solid ground on which he could build an independent Croatian state, without any fear of "Yugoslavism" backlash, so typical of modern Croatian history. Indeed, any mention of figures like Gaj and Strossmayer, the representatives of the pro-Yugoslav concept of Croatian nationhood, was suppressed by Tudjman, and Yugoslavism was certainly not included in his reconciliation concept.[19]

It is clear that "national reconciliation" was an idea conceived by Tudjman to enhance pan-Croatian solidarity, but such a Croato-centric policy would automatically exclude the Serbian minority. Especially the attempt to whitewash the WWII regime provoked Serbs' sentiments and fears, yet Tudjman felt no need to calm Serbian anxiety. On the contrary, through his speeches, he did his best to alienate the Serb population even more. Tudjman's reconciliation policy set in motion the dual process of bridging the differences between Croats by increasing the chasm between them and Serbs.

Reasonably, the only counterweight to Tudjman's political program could be provided by the Croatian League of Communists (SKH). The latter had served for decades as a conflict management institution between Croats and Serbs. But, after 1971, the compromising and conformist SKH rapidly lost its

legitimacy as an institution that could defend effectively Croatian interests vis-à-vis Milošević's centralizing agenda. Thus, there was an urgent necessity for the Croatian leadership of the party to convince the population of its Croatian pedigree. Facing an extremely assertive Serbian leader, no significant part of the Croatian political elite would be able to defend Croatia's pro-unitary side and argue in favor of a reconstituted new "Yugoslavism."

Indeed, Milošević's growing power was the determinant factor in the victory of HDZ policy in Croatia. Other anti-communist parties, like the Croatian Social Liberal Party (HSLS) under the former 1971 dissident Dražen Budiša, were also arguing in favor of democratization and the right of Yugoslav nations to self-determination. The difference was on the relative emphasis that HDZ and HSLS put on democracy and national emancipation. For the HSLS democratization came first. The HDZ, however, wanted national emancipation from Yugoslavia as its main goal; the establishment of democracy was expected to be an automatic consequence of national emancipation. Nevertheless, Milošević's pressure on Croatia and the complete absence of any adequate response from the part of Croatian communist elite left the Croatian voters with a growing feeling of impotence and anger. Thus, the politician that could provide voters with a forceful defense of Croatia's endangered sovereignty would win,[20] and the favorite in this competition was Franjo Tudjman.

2. State-building begins

In the first multiparty elections held in April 1990, HDZ won 42 per cent of the votes; thanks to the majoritarian electoral system, it won 58 per cent of seats in the legislature (205 seats out of 356). Former Communists, now Social Democrats, were the second party with 30% of the votes. HSLS was the third with 20% of the votes but very few seats. In May, Tudjman, having gained 281 votes, was elected by the parliament as the President of Croatia. His legitimacy was boosted by this electoral victory, so Tudjman was quick to start the crucial task of state formation.[21] Each one of his moves, at every level, broadened the chasm between the Croatian majority and the Serb minority.

First came the change of the constitutional basis of the state. The new Constitution, put in force in December 1990, explicitly stated that Croatia was the *nation-state* of the Croatian nation. The Serbs were mentioned as a minority, along with other less numerous ethnic groups. Although Serbs were nominally granted equal rights with the majority nation, this was a serious lessening of their previous status as a constituent nation of the republic. After the fall of the monopoly of SKH, where Serbs were well represented, this move decreased

their political leverage even more. Then, at the level of symbolism, the new government decided to restore old national emblems, to change the names of towns and streets, and to remove every sign connected with the recent communist past. Although the insignia, the flag, and other symbols of statehood had origins dating back to the Middle Ages, the fact that they were also used by the Ustaša regime triggered the Serbs' deepest fears that the dramatic experience of WWII would be repeated. Last but not least, Tudjman sought to Croatianize state institutions and public administration. Serbs were indeed over-represented in the public sector, the judiciary, the media and especially in the institutions of coercion (an estimated 67 per cent of the Police were staffed by Serbs).[22] This over-representation was a major obstacle in the pursuing of a Croatian nation state. Thus, together with negative symbolism and loss of political status, Serbs feared for their jobs and their general economic survival in a Croation nation state.

Their deeper fear, however, was Tudjman's determination to cut off Croatia from the Yugoslav state. In the 1990 elections, Croatia's Serbs, the children of WWII Partisans, voted mainly for the familiar League of Communists, expecting that this party would represent their interest in remaining in a united Yugoslavia. However, as already noted, the Croatian communist elite, being under fierce attack both internally (by nationalist parties) and externally (by Milošević), sought to transform the SKH into an organization committed to the advancement of Croatian interests.[23] In no way did they want to be perceived as an effectively "Serbian" party. The Serbs were particularly traumatized by the fact that the reformed SKH voted in favor of and contributed to the enactment of the new Constitution. Thus, they turned their loyalty massively to the newly formed Serbian Democratic Party that was arguing in favor of Serbs staying in Yugoslavia. Encouraged by Milošević, the Krajina Serbs started to challenge Croatia's sovereignty in Serb-populated lands; they launched a policy of creating a "state inside the state." During the summer of 1990, the Serbs announced their intention to hold a referendum on the question of autonomy. They simultaneously erected barricades, blocking all main roads to Krajina. The Croatian government then moved quickly to prevent what was essentially the division of Croatian territory under two jurisdictions.

3. Croatia: A State of War

The conflict over the control of Krajina soon escalated into open war with the involvement of the Yugoslav Peoples' Army (JNA). At the outset, this was a clash between two clearly defined camps, the Croats and the Serbs. However, this image is only partly true for the conflict in Croatia resembled more what

Brubaker has described as a triangle between a *nationalizing state*, a *national minority*, and *an external national homeland.*[24]

Tudjman knew that the key to the solution of the problem was not in Knin, Krajina's capital, but in Belgrade. Before the declaration of independence and the subsequent intervention of the JNA, Tudjman believed that there was still room for a settlement. He was convinced that the federal army would not intervene after all.[25] The Croatian President had a clear "grand strategy" concerning the ultimate goals of Croatia's state-building, still he had not rejected the possibility of a new *Sporazum* with the Serbian leadership. The infamous Karadjordjevo meeting between Tudjman and Milošević, where they allegedly discussed a possible partition of Bosnia, was indicative of such expectations.

Putting aside their mutual and deep distrust, it was possible that Milošević and Tudjman could strike a deal. However, the deal was never realized, and the reason for that was the decision of Slovenia to speed up the declaration of its independence. This movement upset the balance of power and obliged Tudjman to push for Croatia's independence as well, in order not to remain alone in a very difficult situation. Indeed, it has been argued that Milošević allowed the Slovenes to leave without problem in order to concentrate his war efforts on the Croatian front.

The Croatian war lasted for 4 years. During the first phase, Croatia lost 30 per cent of its territory to the Krajina Serbs and JNA. After the Serajevo ceasefire in January 1992, a second phase started during which a UN mission (UNPROFOR) was deployed between the warring parties. Then, in the summer of 1995, after 3 years of military build up, Croatia launched the Operations Flash and Storm that brought the territories under Zagreb's control and sent 180,000 Serbs into exile. Croatia had secured its sovereignty and territorial integrity, but a closer look at its policies and goals is necessary to understand the outcome of this dramatic struggle.

i. Unity in Power, Power in Unity: the Croatian camp

Tudjman's state-building strategy was based on a high centralization of power inside Croatia. The combination of different strands of Croatian politics under the umbrella of his party was the first step. When war started, the Croatian President moved to create a Government of National Unity and bring all major parties into it. As Cohen noted, "once open hostilities broke out with the JNA and the Krajina Serbs, strong pressure developed for Croatians of all political stripes to support the regime."[26] The truth is that each Croatian party would prove a strong supporter of Croatian independence.[27] In sum, since the

sovereignty and territorial integrity of the Croatian state was at stake, there was a real "unity of purpose" between all Croatian political forces. However, Tudjman's intentions over Bosnia led to what Pusic described as the awakening of the Croatian opposition.[28] Bosnia represented the limits of Croatia's state-building consensus.

The war situation helped Tudjman to create a highly centralized decision-making process where the President was the real locus of power. Constitutionally, Croatia established a semi-presidential system. The Government is accountable both to the legislature and to the President of the Republic. Its head is the prime-minister, but the President presides during the work of the executive when present.[29] Essentially, he was the head of the government as well, for there was no case in which a serious decision was made in his absence. But the government was not even the real locus of decision-making. On the contrary, the Presidential Council, which is described by the Constitution as an advisory body, was the institution making serious decisions. If we take into account the fact that Tudjman was the leader of the majority party in the parliament, we can have a clear image of the extend of his power. It would not be an exaggeration to say that the Croatian state, in its first steps, was like the famous Russian dolls with the Croatian President at the core. Finally, Tudjman prevented the emergence of powerful and potentially dangerous rival centers inside his party or the government, and he was the balancing force between the various strands in his catch-all party. For example, in 1992, he did not hesitate to remove one of his close associates, Josip Manolic, from the post of the head of intelligence services when Manolic started acquiring too much power.[30]

Tudjman was also successful in centralizing the control of the means of coercion. Although Croatia started the war having a clear military handicap, it was soon able to mobilize 200,000 soldiers. Tudjman held strict control of the command system through the appointment of the members of the General Staff and the promotion policy. He was responsible for the appointment of commanders down to the battalion level.[31] Twice he faced a crisis, but he was able to solve it without problems. The first was the disagreement with his Chief of Staff, general Špegelj, over military policy during the first phase of the conflict. Tudjman overcame Špegelj's disagreement by replacing him. The second was a more serious threat posed by HOS, the paramilitary wing of the ultranationalist Croatian Party of Rights. The latter had managed to mobilize great numbers of volunteers, and it was becoming very caustic as regards to what it perceived as Tudjman's soft policy on Slavonia. This problem was more difficult to solve. The commander of the HOS paramilitaries was shot dead under mysterious circumstances, and the political leaders were arrested and tried. By the end of 1992, according to the then Chief of Staff, all paramilitary

units and party-armies were brought under the unitary command of the Croatian Army.[32]

ii. "Only Unity Saves the Serbs": the Serbian Camp[33]

Although one would expect the opposite, in the Serbian side one does not observe the same consistency concerning the focus of demands. On the contrary, each actor in the Serbian side seemed to have a rather diverse agenda as to what the goals of struggle were. Three separate actors can be detected. First, there was the leadership of the Serbian minority in Krajina. Second, one finds the leaders of the Republic of Serbia, namely Milošević and his close associates. Thirdly, there was the former Yugoslav Peoples Army (JNA). The relationship between the Croatian government and the other parts of the Croatian political elite had been regulated, however imperfectly, through the elections. Thus, there was less controversy as to who was in charge of the policy-making in the Croatian side. On the contrary, the existence of three relatively autonomous actors from the Serbian side created a real problem of coordination of goals and actions that would prove fatal for the final achievement of Serbian national goals.

Moreover, the leadership of the Autonomous Republic of Krajina represented just a part of the overall Serbian population of Croatia, albeit the more vocal one, but in no way could it be perceived as representative of the whole minority. In fact, as secession of Serbian-inhabited lands became the main consideration of the minority's leadership, the urban Serbs were largely left outside these plans and their position was effectively ignored. The "Republic of Krajina" itself was a patchwork of different regions, without even territorial sequence. This territorial dimension was to prove very important. The leadership of the Knin area proved to be more difficult to control for Milošević, while the one in Slavonia was closer to his authority. Each of these regions had its own political and military leadership. Thus, they became an additional obstacle to the policy-making from the Serbian side which made decision making harder and more inflexible.

Regarding their political goals, the Krajina Serbs started off by evoking cultural autonomy. As Croatian independence was becoming more and more probable, Serbian minority leaders raised the stakes by claiming their right to remain in Yugoslavia. This coincided with a change in the Serbian leadership, with the hard-liner mayor of Knin, Milan Babić, taking power from Jovan Raskovic, a non-communist, largely out of Milošević's grip. Then there was a covert split between those who wanted the preservation of Yugoslavia and those

who were in favor of Krajina's inclusion in a Serbian nation-state. As the two tasks seemed increasingly to coincide, this dimension lost its value, but it reappeared later when Karadzic replaced Milošević as the champion of the Serbian national cause.

Finally, Krajina political leaders had no absolute control on the armed units in their territory. Apart from the highly decentralized Krajina militia, neither JNA nor paramilitaries were taking orders from Knin. As Glenny reports, the last Chief of Staff of the Krajina Army was sent there by Milošević in order to organize evacuation rather than defense.[34] Just before the 1995 events, the split between those who were looking to Belgrade and those who were seeking cooperation with Bosnian Serbs and Karadžić turned into open clash. The words of the last President of Krajina are revealing of the tension that existed in the Serbian camp. In response to the question why Serbs left Krajina, he says: "This was the consequence of a secret agreement between Tudjman and Milošević. Army commanders were linked to Belgrade; they ordered the troops to retreat and forced people to run away.'[35]

As for the JNA, it started the conflict as an autonomous actor. After the disintegration of the LCY, it had remained the sole federal institution. Its initial involvement in the Croatian crisis was as a neutral mediating power between the warring parties. Since this position was actually preventing the Croatian government from resuming control of the Serbian territories, it was immediately perceived as an enemy power by the state-seeking leadership in Zagreb. Relations between JNA and the Serb population were not always conflict-free, and there were complaints that the army was not helping as it should. The disintegration of the federal institutions turned the JNA into an army without a state. Lacking clear political goals, confused, and outside formal civilian control, the Yugoslav army soon fell under the absolute influence of Slobodan Milošević.

Milošević was the catalyst and the real center of power in the Serbian side. He was granting and withdrawing his support from the various Krajina leaders, according to his needs, either to destroy any opposition to his role as the leader of the Serbian nation, or to win credit with the international community as a possible peacemaker. His political goals were never clearly expressed. Apart from his famous quotation "all Serbs in one state," there is no other clear declaration of intentions. In fact, this last statement was a very convenient one as it could be interpreted to fit all expectations. It was both a call for Greater Serbia and a call for a unified Yugoslavia, which meant a Serbia-dominated federation. This may not be significant, but it was a crucial tactic in order to nullify the nationalist opposition at home and to co-opt the last pro-Yugoslav elements, namely the army. Milošević was resolute at claiming that Serbia was not at war with anybody. In fact, during the whole crisis, his primary focus was

the power struggle in Belgrade rather than the frontiers of the Serb nation in Croatia or Bosnia.

This confusion of goals, actors and policies stood in sharp contrast with Croatia's determination to win back its lost sovereignty. Perhaps the final outcome of the war was due to several factors, but the difference between the "unity of purpose" in the Croatian side and the "feudal" controversies in the Serbian camp had a great impact. Lord Owen, one of the main international negotiators in the conflict, gave a brief but telling description of the Croatian war: "the victors of the Yugoslav wars of 1991-5 have been the Croats and President Tudjman. The losers have been the Croatian Serbs and their useless leader, Martić as to Milošvić, he has beaten off Karadžić's challenge to be the King of the Serbs."[36]

CONCLUSION: FAREWELL TO THE 19TH CENTURY

For the last two centuries, Croatian national integration can be seen as a pendulum between South Slav cooperation (due to external pressure) and Croatian independence (due to internal pressure). In the early 1990s, Croatia under Tudjman's leadership launched a campaign of nation-state building. The war-making and state-building efforts of Croatia led to the creation of a sovereign state. Moreover, Croatia is today more homogeneous than it has ever been at any other point in its history, but Croatia paid a very high price for an irregular evolution of its democratic political system. High-centralization, due to the war, stood in sharp contrast to the necessity of power dispersion, so important for a smooth transition to democracy.

In early 2000, there was a total change in power in all branches of government. The death of Tudjman, the Croation charismatic leader, has led to the dismantling of the informal nexus of power that he had built around himself and the HDZ. As for the institutionalized aspects of centralization, there will probably be some conflict as to which elements of the political system should change. The recent conflict between premier Račan and President Mesić, concerning the control of the Army and the intelligence services, shows that this will not be an easy task.[37]

However, institutional rearrangement is not the most important element in Croatia's second round of transition. The real challenge for Croatian leadership is the need to address the misdeeds of the "successful national integration," mainly the treatment of its Serbian minority especially after the 1995 military operations. We could say that one way or another, Croatia passed the 19th century's state-building stage. Now it has to adapt to the 21st century.

ENDNOTES

[1] C. Tilly, *Coercion, Capital, and European States, AD 990-1992* (Oxford: Blackwell Publishers, 1992), p. 97.

[2] *The Constitution of the Republic of Croatia* (Zagreb: Narodne Novine, 1998), chapter 1, emphasis added.

[3] The relationship between "state" and "nation" in the emergence of the modern nation-states has been a major subject in political science literature. Opinions differ from those that focus on the paramount role of the state in the creation of modern nations, to the ones that emphasize the existence of an "ethnic core" prior to the creation of the state. It is generally accepted, however, that *modern nations* are, as their title reveals, a recent phenomenon. For a short account on the issue see A. Smith, "State-Making and Nation-Building," in Hall, J. A. ed, *States in History*, (Oxford: Blackwell, 1986), pp. 228-263.

[4] G. Schöpflin, "The rise and fall of Yugoslavia," in McGarry J & O'Leary B. eds, *The politics of ethnic conflict regulation: case studies of protracted ethnic conflicts*, (London: Routledge, 1993), p. 177.

[5] Z. Isakovic, *Identity and Security in former Yugoslavia*, (Aldershot: Ashgate Publishers, 2000), p. 39.

[6] For example the attempt of the Magyar governor Khouen to encourage Serbian nationalism in order to direct it against the Croats. See S. Gazi, *A History of Croatia*, (New York: Barnes & Noble, 1973), pp. 189-200.

[7] G. Schöpflin, "Yugoslavia: State Construction and State Failure," in Bianchini S & Schöpflin G. eds, *State-Building in the Balkans: dilemmas on the eve of the 21st century*, (Ravenna: Longo, 1998), p. 241.

[8] It is interesting to note that Starčevic, apart from underlying Croatian differences, also concluded that actually all South Slavs, except Bulgarians, were Croats. During this period similar ideas were expressed by Serb intellectuals. The Serb writer Vuk Karadžić believed that all South Slavs were Serbs. This is

indicative of the fluid status of modern national identities in the region in mid-19th century.

[9] G. Schöpflin, "The rise and fall of Yugoslavia," p. 176.

[10] Estimation of the victims in the infamous concentration camp of Jasenovac varies between 45,000 (Croatian estimates) to 700,000 (Serbian estimates). More accurate figures would be about between 90,000-200,000. See M. Glenny, *The Fall of Yugoslavia* (London: Penguin Books, 1996), p. 81; C. Bennet, *Yugoslavia's Bloody Collapse: Causes, Course and Consequences*, (London: Hurst & Co, 1995), pp. 44-5.

[11] G. Schöpflin, "The rise and fall of Yugoslavia," p. 179.

[12] For a thorough analysis on the impact of institutions in the disintegration of communist federations see V. Bunce, *Subversive Institutions: the Design and the Destruction of Socialism and the State*, (Cambridge: Cambridge University Press, 1999).

[13] G. Schöpflin, "Yugoslavia: State Construction and State Failure," p. 247.

[14] For an analysis of the underpinnings of the "Croatian Spring" see A. Cuvalo, *The Croatian National Movement 1966-1972*, (New York: Columbia University Press, East European Monographs, 1990).

[15] Interview of the then Minister of Defence Gojko Šušak in *Hrvatsko Slovo*, 27 December 1996.

[16] I. Goldstein, *Croatia: A History*, (London: Hurst & Co, 1999), p. 205.

[17] *Ibid.*, p. 206.

[18] Interview of President Tudjman in *Hrvatski Vojnik*, 4, 68 (15 July 1994), p. 5.

[19] S. P. Ramet, *Balkan Babel: The Disintegration of Yugoslavia from the Death of Tito to Ethnic War*, (Oxford: Westview Press, 1996), p. 210,

[20] I. Goldstein, *Croatia*, p. 210.

[21] L. Cohen, "Embattled democracy: postcommunist Croatia in transition," in K Dawisha & B Parrot (eds.) *Politics, power and the struggle for democracy in South-East Europe* (Cambridge: Cambridge University Press, 1997), p. 81.

[22] S. Markotich, "Croatia: Stalemate over Krajina," in *RFE/RL Research Report*, 3, 26 (July 1994), p. 19.

[23] L. Cohen, "Embattled democracy," p. 77.

[24] R. Brubaker, *Nationalism Reframed*, (Cambridge: Cambridge University Press, 1996), pp. 55-76.

[25] N. Cigar, "Croatia's War of Independence: The Parameters of War Termination," in *The Journal of Slavic Military Studies*, 10, 2, 1997, p. 48.

[26] L. Cohen, "Embattled democracy," p. 85.

[27] V. Pusić, "Croatia at the Crossroads," in *Journal of Democracy*, 9, 1 (January 1998), p. 113.

[28] V. Pusić, "Croatia at the Crossroads," p. 114-5.

[29] *The Constitution of the Republic of Croatia* (Zagreb: Narodne Novine, 1998), Articles 94-106.

[30] M. Milivojevic, "Croatia's Intelligence Services," *Jane's Intelligence Review*, September 1994, p. 405-6.

[31] *Constitution*, Article 100 and *Law on Defence, National Gazette*, no. 49/91, Article 52.

[32] J. Gow, "Military-Political Affiliations in the Yugoslav Conflict," in *RFE/RL Research Report*, 1, 20, (May 1992) p. 19.

[33] A famous Serbian proverb, whose initials (the four "S") was the emblem of Serb nationalists, those in Krajina included.

[34] M. Glenny, *The Fall of Yugoslavia*, (London: Penguin Books, 1996), p. 283-4.

[35] Interview of Milan Martić, in *FBIS-EEU-96-224*.

[36] D. Owen, *Balkan Odyssey,* (London: Indigo, 1996), p. 387.

[37] I. Pukanic, "Zašto je došlo do otvorene eskalacije sukoba Mesića i Račana" (Why have we arrived to open conflict escalation between Mesić and Račan), in *Nacional*, no 229, 06/04/2000.

REFERENCES

Cohen, Lenard. 1997. "Embattled democracy: postcommunist Croatia in transition," in Karren Dawisha & Bruce Parrot eds. *Politics, Power and the Struggle for Democracy in South-East Europe* (Cambridge: Cambridge University Press), pp. 69-121.

Goldstein, Ivo. 1999. *Croatia: A History* (London: Hurst & Co)

Irvine, Jill. 1997. "Ultranationalist Ideology and State-Building in Croatia, 1990-1996, in *Problems of Post-Communism*, vol 44, no 4, July/August 1997, pp. 30-43.

Isakovic, Zlatko. 2000. *Identity and Security in former Yugoslavia* (Aldershot: Ashgate Pbs).

O'Shea, Brendan. 1998. *Crisis at Bihac* (Stroud, Gloucestershire : Sutton).

Pusić, Vesna. 1998. "Croatia at the Crossroads," in *Journal of Democracy*, vol 9, no 1, January 1998, pp. 111-124.

Tanner, Mark. 1997. *Croatia: A Nation Forged in War* (New Haven, CT : Yale University Press).

Tatalović, Siniša. 1996. "Military and Political Aspects of the Croato-Serbian Conflict," in *Politička Misao*, vol. 33, no. 5, 1996, pp. 166-190.

Žunec, Ozren. 1998. "Rat u Hrvatskoj 1991-1995, 1 Dio: Uzroci Rata i Operacije do Sarajevskog Primirja (War in Croatia 1991-1995, part 1: War reasons and Operations till the Sarajevo Armistice)," in *Polemos*, vol.1, no.1, 1998, pp. 57-87.

CHAPTER 7
THE IDEA OF SELF-DETERMINATION: LESSONS FROM THE FORMER YUGOSLAVIA

Raju G. C. Thomas
Marquette University

THE PROBLEM AND ITS IMPLICATIONS

In September 2000, at the United Nations summit in New York, President Bill Clinton of the United States, Prime Minister Tony Blair of Britain, and Prime Minister Jacques Chretien of Canada, supported by the U.N. Secretary-General, Kofi Anan, endorsed the idea of humanitarian interventions within sovereign states. They proposed the setting up of a permanent U.N. Peace-Keeping force to undertake such actions. Anan declared that states cannot hide behind the principle of sovereignty when indulging in "evil" within its borders. Anan and Western leaders were, of course, referring to events in Bosnia, Kosovo, East Timor, Rwanda, and Sierra Leone. By contrast, during the summit, China, Russia and India invoked the principle of state sovereignty, the rejection of the right of self-determination beyond decolonization as provided by the U.N. Charter, and non-interference in the internal affairs of states. These are principles embodied in the U.N. Charter, although the original terms of the Charter had already eroded with the passage of the 1948 Genocide Convention, the 1948 Universal Declaration on Human Rights, and other multilateral agreements on individual and minority rights.

Undoubtedly, the promotion of the self-determination principle and the enforcement of human rights world wide are noble and worthy goals. Self-determination appears to be an extension of the principles of democracy and freedom, and who could object to humanitarian intervention by the international community to stop genocide and ethnic cleansing by state authorities within its national borders? However, there is a problem that is usually overlooked. Often, the threat and willingness to intervene militarily by the "international community" (which in reality means the United States and not the United Nations) in the internal affairs of sovereign states in support of the self-determination principle, actually provokes and causes further bloodshed and human rights violations that may not otherwise have occurred. Further, where the territorial integrity of the state is violated and territorial secessions are encouraged, it leads to more demands by other ethnic or ideological groups for the same right of self-determination and secession leading to more violence, more death and destruction, and greater human rights violations. Disgruntled

minorities and ethnic groups seeking secession then have a vested interest in provoking the state authorities into massive human rights violations in order to invite "humanitarian interventions" by the "international community." Where such problems were restricted and localized at one time, they now become more massive and widespread.

Indeed, the encouragement of the right of self-determination, an unwillingness to respect the sovereignty of the state, and the willingness to indulge in humanitarian interventions would create the conditions where such an active international policy posture would become necessary. A standing or threatened policy of humanitarian intervention by the United States and the West then becomes the cause of human rights nightmares. Although NATO and their supporters now claim routinely that they attacked Serbia in violation of the U.N. Charter in order to return the one million Albanians driven out of Kosovo, it was the illegal assault that caused the flight. During the year prior to that attack some 2,000 Albanians and Serbs had died, some 300,000 Albanians had been internally displaced, and another 70,000 may have moved out of Kosovo to Albania and safer areas abroad, because of the overreaction of Serbian security forces against the Kosovo Liberation Army. It is not an unusual phenomenon for the insurgents and terrorists to be unknown and hidden within the civilian population, e.g., Chechnya, Kurdistan,and Kashmir. Allegations have been made that the expulsion of all Albanians had been planned by Milosevic before NATO's assault and that the assault provided the needed excuse to do so. However, as a paper by an M.I.T. scholar presented at the American Political Science Association in September 2000 demonstrated, there is no evidence that such a "Horseshoe Plan" existed.[1] (Greenhill, Kelly 2000.) The Serbian expulsion of Kosovo Albanians during NATO's bombing campaign occurred in those regions where the KLA was actively conducting a ground campaign in support of NATO.

Following NATO's war against Serbia, efforts were made to sever Kosovo from Serbia and to encourage the secession of Montenegro from the rump Yugoslavia. Such actions do not lead to fewer human rights violations but more of them, with the one time victims conducting further violations against their former oppressors. Thus, a US-led NATO, with a pliant United Nations and Secretary-General in tow, have set themselves up for an active role in world affairs. They face no challenge from the defunct Soviet-led Warsaw Pact countries, and indeed little challenge from anywhere to anything that they may choose to do in the name of high morality.

Such a policy posture could undermine the unity and stability of multi-ethnic states, which will in turn contradict the other noble Western goal of promoting inter-ethnic tolerance and co-existence in states with different linguistic,

religious, and cultural groups. Human rights violations could reach epidemic proportions and keep the proposed U.N. peacekeeping force busy indefinitely, which will further increase the need for even more peacekeepers. Thus, two large bureaucracies, the U.N. and NATO, by creating new roles for themselves, become self-serving and self-perpetuating. Besides, the lofty declarations and proposals made at the U.N. summit in September 2000 by Clinton, Blair, Chretien, and Anan, are applicable only to small and weak states, not to states such as Russia, China, and India. It would also appear somewhat cynical and hypocritical for the United States and Canada especially, to enforce such high human rights standards in the rest of the world when their own records of racial tolerance and co-existence have only been resolved in the last couple of decades. People in the rest of the world are expected to reach their high moral standards immediately now that the U.S. and Canada are able to meet these standards themselves.

Ironically, with the fall of Milosevic, the West has reversed itself on the question of the right of self-determination for various ethnic groups within Yugoslavia and the territorial integrity of the rump Yugoslavia. After having rushed to enforce the Slovenian, Croat, and Bosnian Muslim right of self-determination and secession, the US and NATO have made no further moves to allow these rights to Montenegrins and Kosovo Albanians in the rump Yugoslavia. The implication here appears to be that NATO countries have the right to destroy the territorial integrity of states as long as the US disapproves of the leaders or the countries which they still consider "communist." Democracy has been redefined as electing leaders that the West approves or removing leaders of whom the West disapproves even through mob actions in the streets as in Serbia in September 2000. Self-determination will be encouraged and enforced only for those ethnic groups that the US media favors, but will be rejected in large and/or friendly countries that do not advance US government interests. A nationalist is defined as anybody who questions, let alone protests, Washington's arbitrary and destructive policies against other states and their leaders. Being pro-West, even if it is at the expense of the territorial integrity of states, is the essential character of a democratic and non-nationalist leader.

The new "humanitarians" in the United States and the West have declared that the sovereignty of states is now virtually obsolete, the era of the Westphalian state has come to an end, and concepts of realism and neo-realism that emphasize the pursuit of state power or security, can no longer be sustained. These new rules of the game have been declared by American leaders, journalists, and scholars as essential for world peace and security and for the promotion of individual rights and human dignity. However, the

undermining of the sovereignty of states beyond voluntary multilateral economic and military agreements (such as the World Trade Organization, the Non-Proliferation Treaty, the Biological Weapons Convention, and the Chemical Weapons Convention), could lead to more "Yugoslavias" in the rest of the world as more ethnic groups resort to insurgency and terrorism to secede from existing multi-ethnic states with the expectation of political and military support from the West.

The rising tide of insurgency and terrorism in Chechnya in Russia, Xinjiang in China, and Kashmir in India, all Muslim majority areas no different from Kosovo in Yugoslavia, are indicative of the problem. If the Kosovo Liberation Army can be so easily reclassified from being terrorists and drug traffickers to being freedom fighters by the US State Department, then other terrorist separatist groups may hope for the same. Dislodging East Timor from Indonesia by the Fall of 1999, has since provoked other violent secessionist movements in Aceh, Ambon, and the Moluccan Islands. Writing in the *New York Times* on October 22, 1999, Barbara Crossette advised that the US now turn its attention to Kashmir following the successful severance of Kosovo from Serbia and East Timor from Indonesia.

Against such American tendencies, Prem Shankar Jha, a leading Indian journalist and former advisor to Prime Minister Inder Kumar Gujral, noted in the *Hindustan Times* on November 5, 1999, that "two days ago, the Congress of the United States began a hearing on human rights. It was not an enquiry into the state of human rights in America but in Kashmir, in a country that did not elect them, over which it does not have the remotest jurisdiction, and where even the most calamitous events would not affect America's political or economic well-being."[2] (Prem Shankar Jha 1999)

SECESSIONIST MOVEMENTS AND STATE SOVEREIGNTY

In 1992, during the Clinton-Gore presidential campaign, Strobe Talbot, who subsequently became Deputy Secretary of State, wrote that ". . . within the next hundred years . . . nationhood as we know it will be obsolete; all states will recognize a single global authority. . . . A phrase briefly fashionable in the mid 20th century–citizen of the world–will have assumed real meaning by the end of the 21st."[3] (Trifkovic, Srdja 2000) In September 1999,Talbot went further stating that the United States in its current form may cease to exist in the 21st century because nationhood will have been rendered obsolete, and will be replaced apparently by "globalhood" (my term). This new American concept of globalhood does not mean an egalitarian community of all humankind but a

system dominated by and controlled by the rich Western capitalist states for the promotion of multinational corporate interests.

A major test case of nationhood versus globalhood was evident in the former Yugoslavia where the right of self-determination was granted by the West to Slovenes, Croats, Bosnian and Albanian Muslims, but not to the Serbs. The United States and the West proceeded to tear Yugoslavia apart between 1991 and 1999 by recognizing new states based on the former internal provinces and boundaries of the old state of Yugoslavia. Once this was done, the new Serbian minorities were denied the right of national self-determination to secede from these new states. The sovereignty and territorial integrity of the new states were to be preserved at all costs even if it resulted in the expulsion of all Serb minorities. At the time of the 1995 Dayton Agreement, Croatia had become virtually an ethnically pure nation-state (although the post Franjo Tudjman government under Stipe Mesic offered to accept all Serbs who fled, back into Croatia). On the other hand, the Bosnian Muslim ethnic group who refused to be part of a multiethnic Yugoslavia where they would be a minority, was granted a multiethnic "mini Yugoslavia" where they would be a majority. Bosnia was held up as the prototype of a state based on multi-ethnicity, tolerance, and harmony. In reality, it consists of three ethnically pure mini-states within a state held together by NATO.

Some disturbing international precedents were set in the Yugoslav case that could lead to more chaos and injustice rather than political stability in the rest of the world, especially India. Traditionally, the unwritten rules of the "old world order" were as follows:

1. When the right of self-determination is invoked by secessionist ethnic groups, the state almost always invokes the principles of the territorial integrity and sovereignty and the inviolability of its borders. This invariably leads to civil war. It is a violation of international law to recognize unilateral declarations of independence by secessionist groups and territories against the wishes of federal or central governments engaged in resisting the separatists.

2. The notion of state sovereignty in the past meant that other states did not have the right to interfere in its internal matters. While multilateral economic and arms control treaties, signed voluntarily for the mutual benefits they provide, have increasingly placed limitations on state sovereignty, such self-limitations do not extend to the right of external interference in the internal struggle between the state and the secessionists.

3. The state's "standard operating procedure" in dealing with secessionist demands and accompanying insurgency or terrorism is the attempt to crush it through counter-insurgency and counter-terrorist means. The level of violence by the state then invariably exceeds that of the separatists. Human rights

violations are committed by both sides. The justification for such state actions is that in the long run it produces less tragedy and suffering by deterring other separatist movements and preventing the collapse of the state. This is hardly a satisfactory condition but the policy of humanitarian interventions may be less desirable.

4. Apart from the long standing states of Europe and a few others elsewhere such as Japan, Thailand, Iran, and Ethiopia, most states came about haphazardly with the end of empires: the end of the Spanish and Portuguese empires in the Americas in the 18th and 19th centuries; the Austro-Hungarian and Ottoman empires in Europe and the Middle East at the end of the First World War; and the end of all European empires in Asia and Africa over a period of decades after the Second World War. There is no serious rationale for the existence of large states such as the United States or India, and small states such as Trinidad or Tuvalu, the latter, with a population of 9,000, being the most recent state to be admitted to the U.N. The formation of new states from an existing state through successful separatist violence aided by outside powers, or through mutual agreement between the state and the secessionists, have been rare, e.g., Bangladesh from Pakistan, Eritrea from Ethiopia, and the several states born out of the former Soviet Union and Yugoslavia. However, the reference to the right of self-determination in the United Nations Charter applies only to decolonization, although state formation as the result of decolonization may carry no logic or consistency. Most states are accidents of history.

5. When a state attempts to crush secessionist movements through military force, the term "aggression" as defined by the United Nations Charter does not apply. This is civil war, and not war among states. A state has the legal right to preserve its territorial integrity by force with a moral obligation to minimize human rights violations. While the state may be accused of "crimes against humanity" under conditions of civil war, this does not give outside powers the right to dismantle and destroy the state.

6. According to the Guidelines of the Montevideo Convention of 1933, new states are to be recognized on the empirical evidence that they possess clearly demarcated territorial boundaries, a stable population, and a government in control. Preference and moral considerations are less relevant.

7. If parts of an existing state manage to secede, the rights of the old state are retained by the remnant state, if this part still remains the equal or greater part of the single or each of the several parts that seceded from the old state. There are precedents establishing this rule as in the case of India when Pakistan seceded in 1947, Pakistan when Bangladesh seceded in 1972, and Russia when the rest of the Soviet Republics seceded in 1991. In 1947, independent India assumed the rights of British India and was thereby a member of the United

Nations and earlier of the League of Nations. Pakistan was declared the successor state in 1972 although, at that time, the population of Bangladesh was greater than that of Pakistan. Russia's population in 1991 was less than the combined population of the all the 15 republics that seceded.

8. Secession may be considered immoral when it leads to the denial of past benefits to the rest of the country, when it compels other units also to secede leading to state disintegration, and where such actions lead to war, chaos, and human tragedy.

The above principles and practices were discarded in cavalier fashion by the "international community" in the case of the former Yugoslavia, and this set precedents elsewhere in the world that will generate more violence and instability. In retrospect, it is difficult to believe that the sudden media-generated hysterical hate and mass prejudice against the Serbs that swept the West could have led to such a transformation of the rules of the international system. Earlier, the international response was different in the case of Nigeria's crushing of the Ibo secessionist movement in Biafra; China's suppression of Tibet's secession; India's suppression in Kashmir, Punjab and Assam; Pakistan's crushing of secessions by Baluchistan and Sind, and its unsuccessful attempt to do the same in East Pakistan; Sri Lanka's war against Tamil separatists; Philippines in the Muslim Moro areas; Indonesia in East Timor; Turkey in "Kurdistan"; Britain in Northern Ireland; and Spain in the Basque areas. In the case of Russia's crushing of the Chechnya separatist movement and reducing the province to near rubble, the problem, crisis, and reaction were far greater than Serbia's problems in Kosovo. NATO conducted no humanitarian intervention here. The consistent principles and practices applied in these comparable cases were denied to the remnant Yugoslavia.

Serbia's claim to Kosovo was no different than the claims in most of the above cases, or even the claim the United States had to Texas, New Mexico, and California, which were states wrested from Mexico by force in the 19th century. Kosovo was annexed by Serbia in 1912 during its quest to consolidate historic Serb territories and unite the Serbian people into a single state. This goal was no different from the unification of Italy in the 1860s and Germany in the 1870s. Moreover, Serbia could have had its "Greater Serbia" for the asking at the end of the First World War for having fought and sacrificed enormously on the side of the victorious Entente Powers. Efforts to carve out a "Greater Serbia" after the unilateral declarations of independence from the newly recognized states of Croatia and Bosnia involved keeping within the rump Yugoslavia as much of the old territories of Yugoslavia where Serbs lived. This was not the same thing as Nazi Germany's attempts to annex the German inhabited territories of the Sudetenland in Czechoslovakia or Silesia in Poland.

Serbia did not seek to annex by force the territories of Austria, Hungary, Rumania, Bulgaria, or Albania. Indeed, if the rules applied to the former Yugoslavia were applied elsewhere in world, few of the existing state boundaries would survive, especially those in Africa and the Americas. It would open up a pandora's box leading to civil wars, refugee flows, and global chaos.

Countries with secessionist problems such as China in Tibet, Russia in Chechnya, India in Kashmir, Turkey in "Kurdistan," and Indonesia in East Timor, are big countries or allied with the West. These states would not tolerate the kind of intervention and destruction of their territorial integrity that Yugoslavia suffered. Therefore, the Western powers were careful not to recognize the independence of Tibet, Chechnya, Kashmir, Kurdistan and, until recently, East Timor, territories which these major states consider part of their sovereign state, right or wrong. Amidst political turmoil in Indonesia following the overthrow of President of Suharto, East Timor has now been dislodged from Indonesia by the "international community" (or Western dictated U.N.) encouraging violent demands to secede in Aceh, Ambon, Irian Jaya, and the Moluccan Islands.

Apart from peaceful or violent decolonization movements for independence, and except for the peaceful dissolution of Czechoslovakia and the violent but successful movements for independence by Bangladesh in 1971 and Eritea in 1993, virtually all past secessionist movements have been prevented through massive force by central government forces or have simply dissipated over time. They included Biafra from Nigeria; Katanga from Zaire; the Kurdish areas from Turkey and Iraq; South Yemen from North Yemen (a union which had only been forged in 1990); Punjab, Assam, Nagaland and Mizoram from India; Baluchistan and Sind from Pakistan; Tamil Ealam from Sri Lanka; Shans and Kachins from Burma; and the Moros from the Philippines. Even Abraham Lincoln chose civil war to prevent the Confederate South from seceding from the United States.

DEMOCRACY, FREEDOM AND THE SELF-DETERMINATION PRINCIPLE

In dealing with the various conflicting demands and rights of self-determination and territorial integrity in the former Yugoslavia, the international community embarked on a confused and contradictory set of goals and policies. Hurst Hannum writes: "Perhaps no contemporary norm of international law has been so vigorously promoted or widely accepted as the right of all peoples to self-determination. Yet the meaning and content of that right remain as vague and imprecise as when they were enunciated by President Woodrow Wilson and

others at Versailles."[4] Hannum, Hurst 1990) Is there a universally accepted international norm that "nations" have the right to "secede" from an existing sovereign state under the principle of national self-determination? There is none.

Allen Buchanan warned against confusing democratic rights with secessionist rights based on the principle of self-determination.[5] (Buchanan 1991) He pointed out the need to view the two concepts and their objectives together to understand their differences and to avoid the likely adverse consequences of confusing the two concepts. While there is "widespread, unambivalent endorsement of the goal of democratization," there are serious doubts about destroying the state itself through secessions in advancing this goal of democratization. "There is good reason to be apprehensive. Attempts at secession, and the efforts of states to resist them, have frequently led to severe economic dislocations and massive violations of human rights. Ethnic minorities have won their independence only to subject their own minorities to the same persecutions they themselves formerly suffered."[6] (Buchanan 1991) Buchanan further points out the misleading parallels between democratization and secession. "Both democratization and secession, it may seem, are exercises of the right of self-determination. If democracy is popular sovereignty—participation in government by the people—then secession may be seen as the effort of various peoples to govern themselves, to be politically self-determining, in the most literal sense, by forming their own independent, fully sovereign states." Buchanan provides two reasons for rejecting self-determination and secession as an extension of democracy. First, secessionist struggles have generated massive human rights violations on all sides and economic destruction and deprivations. Second, "as Abraham Lincoln argued, secession can pose a lethal threat to democracy: If a discontented minority can exit the polity whenever it is outvoted by the majority on an issue it deems of great importance, then the majority does not rule. In addition, if secession is considered as a real option, then a minority group may use the threat of "exit" as a form of "voice" that serves as an effective veto on majority rule."[7] (Buchanan 1991)

This raises the basic question of whether "nations" have the right to "secede" from a sovereign state under the principle of national self-determination. In the more liberal interpretation of freedom, subject ethnic groups within a state are considered to have the right to hold referendums to determine whether they wish to remain part of the state or secede from it. This right of national self-determination is, however, mentioned only obliquely and in passing reference in Article 1 (2) of the United Nations Charter which reads: "To develop friendly relations among nations based on respect for the principle of equal rights and self-determination of peoples, and to take other appropriate

measures to strengthen universal peace." Articles 73 to 91 essentially deal with "Non-Self-Governing Territories" and the "Trusteeship System" but have nothing to do with granting self-determination to peoples within existing sovereign independent states. The 1970 "Declaration on Friendly Relations" elaborated on the Charter and went beyond to declare that the principle did not only apply to colonial territories but also to "all peoples" "the right freely to determine without external interference, their political status."[8] (Franck 1992) The principle was emphasized in Article 1 of the "International Covenant on Civil and Political Rights" passed in 1976 and ratified by 113 continues by the end of 1991. However, the rights of minorities to self-determination, according to the Covenant, did not include the right to secede. It implied the right of peoples in all states "to free, fair and open participation in the democratic process of governance freely chosen by each state."[9] (Franck, Thomas M. 1992) A 1990 meeting of the Conference on Security and Cooperation in Europe (CSCE) in Copenhagen went far in affirming democratic rights and human rights of peoples but did not go as far as to endorse the right to secede.

From the standpoint of equity and fairness, two related questions may be asked. If the principle of national self-determination with the meaning of "the right to secede from a state" could be granted to Slovenians, Croatians, Bosnian Muslims, and Macedonians, then why cannot the same principle be granted to the Serbs of the newly recognized states of Croatia and Bosnia? And, if the Serbs demand this right, then why should not the Albanians of Kosovo demand the same right? If national self-determination extending to the right to secede is the new overriding norm of world politics today, then it surely must also be granted to new minorities created by state secessions. Or, some logical explanation must be provided as to why the principle of the right to secede was applied selectively to Slovenia, Croatia, and Bosnia but not to other ethnic groups demanding secession elsewhere in the world. Domestic political disputes, minority ethnic grievances, and armed secessionist struggles have been far more intense and prolonged elsewhere than in the former Yugoslavia.

From a global-comparative perspective, it is difficult to justify Slovenia and Croatia being allowed to "jump the queue" ahead of other self-proclaimed nations demanding the right to secession and international recognition. As regards the claim of Serbian domination, it is not unusual for dominant ethnic groups to insist on more centralized political arrangements which they control. Such complaints have been made in the past against the English in Britain by the Irish, Scots, and Welsh; against the English speaking settlers in Canada by the French speaking settlers in Quebec province; against the WASPs (White Anglo-Saxon Protestants) in the US by African-Americans and Hispanics; against the Punjabis in Pakistan by Bengalis, Sindhis, and Baluchis; against the Hindi-

speaking Hindus of India by other linguistic and religious minorities; and against the Russians in the former Soviet Union and the new Russia by other linguistic and religious minorities. Majority versus minority nationalist politics have taken place in all of these countries. What was different about the former Yugoslavia was that Germany, Austria, and the Vatican pushed the European Union to recognize the independence of Slovenia and Croatia; and then the United States pushed the rest of the world to recognize the independence of Bosnia. The criteria of recognition here was selective and arbitrary. All the internal "republics" of the former Yugoslavia were then granted the right to secede which led to the recognition of the remaining province, Macedonia. Other would-be independent secessionist nations elsewhere in the world did not receive such powerful and influential patronage.

LESSONS AND PROSPECTS

The fundamental issue in the former Yugoslavia was the violation of Yugoslavia's territorial integrity and sovereignty, the rush to advance the principle of self-determination, and the reckless use of massive force in violation of the U.N. Charter on humanitarian grounds. These constitute the underlying causes of the problem in the former Yugoslavia with lessons for the rest of the world. Recognition or the promise of recognition led to the unraveling of Yugoslavia and to widespread bloodshed and ethnic cleansing. There was no violence before the unilateral declarations of independence by Slovenia, Croatia, and Bosnia in defiance of the Serbs and Serbian dominated federal authorities in Belgrade. Slovenes, Croats, and Slav Muslims were not being oppressed by Serbs. Indeed, the Serbian complaint was that Tito had run the state on the principle that "A weak Serbia made for a strong Yugoslavia." Likewise, the promise of independence encouraged the Albanians of Kosovo to provoke the Serbian security forces into committing human rights violations in order to invite NATO military intervention.

In choosing between the principle of the right of self-determination and the principle of the territorial integrity of sovereign states, the "international community" has now established the following self-contradicting and dangerous precedent and principles in the Yugoslav case: (1) The internal boundaries of a sovereign state will automatically become international frontiers without change if that sovereign state is taken apart through new state recognition policy. (2) These newly recognized international frontiers of the newly-created sovereign states that have been recognized will be preserved and enforced at any price, thus contradicting the earlier decision to take the international frontiers of the

pre-existing sovereign state apart based on the right of self-determination and secession.

ENDNOTES

[1] Greenhill, Kelly. 2000. "People Pressure: The Coercive Use of Refugees in the Kosovo Conflict." Paper presented at the American Political Science Association Convention, Thursday, September 1st, 2000, Marriot Wardman Park Hotel, Washington, D.C.

[2] Prem Shankar Jha, "The Making of a Rogue State," *Hindustan Times*, November 5, 1999.

[3] From "The Birth of the Global Nation," in *Time*, July 20, 1992. Quoted by Srdja Trifkovicin *Kosovo Under NATO: Anatomy of an Unjust War*, Chicago and London: The Lord Byron Foundation for Balkan Studies, 2000

[4] Hurst Hannum, *Autonomy, Sovereignty and Self-Determination: The Accommodation of Conflicting Rights*, Philadelphia: University of Pennsylvania Press, 1990, p. 27.

[5] See For a detailed study of the moral arguments for and against secession, see Allen Buchanan, *Secession: The Morality of Political Divorce from Fort Sumter to Lithuania and Quebec*, Boulder, Colorado: Westview Press, 1991, pp. 27-125.

[6] Allen Buchanan, "Democratization, Secession and the Rule of International Law." MacArthur Foundation Program in Transnational Security, Working Paper Series, 1995, pp. 2-3. Center for International Studies, Massachusetts Institute of Technology and the Center for International Affairs, Harvard University.

[7] Buchanan, p. 4.

[8] Cited in Thomas M. Franck, "The Emerging Right to Democratic Governance," *American Journal of International Law*, vol. 86, no. 4, 1992, p. 58.

[9] Thomas Franck, p. 59.

REFERENCES

Buchanan, Allen. 1991. *Secession: The Morality of Political Divorce from Fort Sumter to Lithuania and Quebec*, Boulder, Colorado: Westview Press, 1991.

__________. 1995. "Democratization, Secession and the Rule of International Law." MacArthur Foundation Program in Transnational Security, Working Paper Series, 1995, pp. 2-3. Center for International Studies, Massachusetts Institute of Technology and the Center for International Affairs, Harvard University.

Franck, Thomas M. 1992. "The Emerging Right to Democratic Governance," *American Journal of International Law*, vol. 86, no. 4, 1992.

Greenhill, Kelly. 2000. "People Pressure: The Coercive Use of Refugees in the Kosovo Conflict." Paper presented at the American Political Science Association Convention, Thursday, September 1st, 2000, Marriot Wardman Park Hotel, Washington, D.C.

Hannum, Hurst. 1990. *Autonomy, Sovereignty and Self-Determination: The Accommodation of Conflicting Rights*, Philadelphia: University of Pennsylvania Press, 1990.

Jha, Prem Shankar. 1999. "The Making of a Rogue State," *Hindustan Times*, November 5, 1999.

Trifkovic, Srdja. 2000. *Kosovo Under NATO: Anatomy of an Unjust War*, Chicago and London: The Lord Byron Foundation for Balkan Studies, 2000.

CHAPTER 8
THIRD PARTY INVOLVEMENT IN ETHNIC CONFLICT: THE CASE OF THE KOSOVO WAR*

Edward A. Tiryakian
Duke University

"Sociology, as all the sciences, has as a function to unveil hidden things" –
Pierre Bourdieu, *On Television*.

Although conflict models have been a noted feature of sociological interpretations of modern society (Collins 1994), one of the oldest and most ubiquitous forms of conflict, war, has received little concentrated attention by sociologists. Recently, Hans Joas has taken to task one macro sociological perspective, modernization theory, for its failure to deal with war and its collateral problem of violence (Joas 1999). This neglect of war as an integral feature of modernity is not peculiar to modernization analysis but may be extended to competing paradigms (Tiryakian 1999). A moment's reflection will indeed bring to the fore the centrality of war for the modern world: in the definition and construction of collective identity (national anthems, monuments, holy days commemorating those killed in battle), as one instance, or in the periodization of history (the War of Independence, the Napoleonic Wars, the *ante-bellum* South, the two World Wars and the interwar period, the Cold War). While war, once it is engaged, has become in the modern world the largest collective mobilization of a population (technically, except for conscientious objectors, modern wars make no allowance for "free riders"), how this mobilization takes place and sustains itself has received scant attention, if any, in the social movement literature.

Related to the question of mobilization, while critical theory has reopened the crucial problematic of legitimation of the modern state (Habermas 1975), the focus of legitimacy analysis has largely avoided dealing with wars having

---

*Revised version of a paper presented at the Military Session, annual meeting of the American Sociological Association, Washington, DC, August 12-16, 2000. I would like to thank Duško Sekulić, Charles Moskos and Keith Doubt for thoughtful comments.

democratic states as primary actors. The problem of legitimation here seems solved by the disclaimer: "democracies do not fight each other." Such a proposition, while appealing, is simplistic, and particularly so if it implies that "democracies" are less prone to engage in bellicose actions than non-democracies. One must be conscious of two fine points: first, who defines "democracy" and second, some countries that consider themselves "democracies" may erase a "war deficit" against other "democracies" by fighting (even if they do not start) wars against countries defined as "non-democracies." So, for example, Great Britain, considered "civilized" at the beginning of the 20th Century, began that century with an imperialist war that used concentration camps against prisoners from the two Boer republics.

Obtaining legitimacy for the engagement of war is an important state endeavor in the modern world, especially if the democratic state initiates the bellicose action. To achieve this, both for the sake of mobilizing its own population and receiving support from world public opinion, the state engaging in internal and/or external wars may seek a variety of ways to treat the other as "barbaric," "despotic," "totalitarian," "subversive" and the like. If this is achieved satisfactorily, legitimacy is obtained to utilize various means of destruction on the other (and equivalent privations and sacrifices for the regime's own population). Legitimation, however, is not a fixed condition of a social order; it is an on-going process which, as any complex of social interaction, may be halted or interrupted, leading to a legitimation crisis—as happened in the course of the Vietnam War. Increasingly, the legitimation process (and of course its obverse, delegitimation) of state action is mediated by the media and by television in particular, which has come to be a primary source of information for the general public.

What this paper seeks to do is bring out some of the complexities and ambiguities of war, democracy, and modernity, by analyzing the war at the close of this past century, which was initiated by the United States. The Kosovo War closed the century when the United States took the initiative to protect an oppressed population (ethnic Albanians), that was perceived to be threatened with genocide, by a so-called "rogue" state (the Federal Republic of Yugoslavia).

By doing a structural-functional analysis as an entry point, this paper seeks to bring out certain features that make what really happened in Kosovo more complex than the one-dimensional lofty depiction of the war presented by the general North American media. In this respect, the analysis complements the sociological perspective already given by Horowitz (1999) and his insightful comparison of Kosovo with Vietnam. It also provides materials for a new line of inquiry in studies of nationalism and ethnic conflict: how to account for the

internationalization of an intrastate conflict by the intervention (or lack thereof) of third parties (Carment and James 2000).

After an initial discussion of the war in Kosovo and its relation to modernity and modernization, I will seek to provide a broader framework to account for the war, one that will point out ambiguities as to what was involved. A concluding section will consider the consequences of the Kosovo War, for the United States, for the region, and for the larger Europe.

THE KOSOVO WAR: MODERNIZATION AND MODERNITY

The Balkan (from the Turkish, meaning "Mountain") region of Southeastern Europe has had a long-standing image as a backwater of European modernity (Kaplan 1993; Todorova 1997). It has also been the scene of political liberation movements—an important aspect of political modernity—in the form of wars of independence of Christian Orthodox subjects (Serbs, Greeks, and Bulgars) from mainly Ottoman subjection in the 19th Century. In particular, the movement for Greek independence in the 1820s had a general if not romantic appeal for the West and may be regarded as a prototype of later nationalist movements in Europe (Dakin 1973; Howarth 1976). Balkan struggle for autonomy also involved armed struggles of other state actors engaging in power politics too complex to be detailed here, but suffice it to say that, in the century just ended, the Balkans have been the setting for no less than four multinational wars, two in the years immediately preceding WWI and two in the 1990s (Mazower 2000). In the last of these in 1999, during March-June,[1] the United States/NATO waged a 78-day war on the Former Republic of Yugoslavia to restore autonomy to the Kosovo region from Serbia and resettle displaced ethnic Albanian refugees.

What renders the Kosovo War different from its predecessors is a series of things: First, the major protagonists were not Balkan nations fighting one another or seeking autonomy from an alien power outside the Balkans. A nation-state within the Balkans—Yugoslavia/Serbia—was the target of external collective action, a NATO alliance initiated and led by the United States. Second, the nature of warfare for the Western combatants gave emphasis to maximal use of high technology warfare so as to minimize the possible loss of lives for allied forces. The modernization of the military in the digital age has in the past two decades meant a commitment to making war *capital intensive rather than labor intensive.*[2] The progressive substitution of hi-tech warfare for open field combat warfare (which characterized World War I) certainly reached a peak in the Kosovo War: no NATO/American troops were killed by the enemy

in the 78 days of the campaign and no NATO aircraft was lost in combat. The war was fought and won from the air, and the fighting was controlled by computers.

Michael Ignatieff has lucidly captured an essential aspect of the modernity of this war by calling it a "virtual war," one whose paradoxical reality was played out by countries whose technological omnipotence skillfully played in the hands of risk-adverse political cultures (Ignatieff 2000: 163).[3] Ignatieff also points out that the theatre of operations of the war in Kosovo was not only the *air* over Serbia/Kosovo, but it was also the *air* provided by the key role played by television. The television coverage of the war provided a "construction of reality" via images (Albanian refugees streaming into Macedonia and Albania) beamed through cable channels to a world whose support for the bombardment was necessary to legitimate the NATO action. NATO closely controlled what the civilian population at home saw via its briefings to Western journalists. That tight control of television, the medium of modernity par excellence, was considered essential and this was shown in NATO's air strike of the Serbian/Yugoslav television broadcasting system in Belgrade, though this was not a military target and in fact led to civilian casualties. In modern wars, total control of the media of information becomes an imperative. To the extent that television becomes the medium through which the reality of war is experienced by the civilian population, the war itself becomes a sort of spectator sport, a virtual reality extravaganza offering "the pleasure of a spectacle with the added thrill that it is real for someone, but not, happily for the spectator" (Ignatieff 191). It might be said that, for the spectators at home, the medium of television mediates immediately.

Further in this vein, developing electronic manipulation in the United States took a new turn from experimental video processing technology into a new means of conducting warfare, essayed in Kosovo in automatically detecting moving Serbian military vehicles (Amato 2000); this new technology could just as readily make refugees (or other figures) appear or disappear from a background field on the television screen of viewers outside the playing field. Moskos has epitomized Kosovo as "the first postmodern war" (2000) because of the role played by technology. Thus, this paper may be viewed in part as an attempt to deconstruct the Kosovo War, which was presented by the media as a "humanitarian effort."

In the 1990s, the Balkans had little strategic interest for American security, nor did the region possess critical energy resources like the Persian Gulf did. What then accounts for the scale and nature of American involvement in its dramatic intervention in Kosovo and Serbia? The United States had not

intervened unilaterally in previous ethnic conflicts in the region (with the exception of its intervention in the 1946-49 Greek civil war). Nor had the United States intervened in similar situations in the 1990s where an ethnic minority was at risk of mass destruction by repressive government action, as in the case of Ruanda, Turkish Kurdistan, or Indonesia's East Timor. It is at this point that we must consider both the manifest and the latent functions of the action initiated by the United States, deriving such an analysis from Merton's classic paradigm (1967). This will bring out the applicability of the quote from Bourdieu at the beginning of this paper.

THE KOSOVO WAR: MANIFEST FUNCTIONS

With the emergence of the Kosovo Liberation Army (KLA) engaging in armed struggle against the Yugoslav state's endeavor to reassert domination over its Kosovo region, a new cycle of "ethnic cleansing" had been taking place in Kosovo in 1997-1998. In an earlier cycle in the 1970s and early 1980s, the number of Albanians living in Kosovo, from both significant natural increase and from immigration through the porous border, had greatly increased to an absolute majority (90% of the Kosovo population).[4] Benefiting from the autonomy granted by anti-Serb Tito, they had taken over control of local councils and regional institutions, with a net effect being a bloodless "ethnic cleansing" of Serbians, which resulted in thousands of indigenous Serbs leaving Kosovo. After the Dayton Peace Accords in 1995 put an end to the Third Balkan War, Serbs from Bosnia-Herzegovina were encouraged to resettle in Kosovo, and Belgrade turned its attention to the "reconquest" of Kosovo. By 1998, Kosovar Albanians were in defiance of Belgrade rule. They had elected their own president (Ibrahim Rugova), refused to attend state schools where Serbian was the language of instruction, and refused to pay local taxes to Serbian authority. Both the civilian and the armed factions of Albanian resistance sought an independent Kosovo. In effect, Western countries sought to avert another Bosnia by threatening to use military sanctions if forcible ejection of ethnic Albanians did not cease; in the face of continuing and intensifying KLA terrorist action, Serbian military and paramilitary forces countered with escalating repression, especially on villages and ethnic Albanians suspected of aiding the KLA.

To greatly condense, a compromise brokered by the United States in October 1998 came to an end with renewed KLA action, leading to further Serb action. French diplomatic effort led to the various parties (including after much bickering the two major Albanian factions), the United States and its NATO allies coming to the historic French castle of Rambouillet, where protracted

discussions took place in February 1999, in the hope that agreements for autonomy for Kosovo with a planned timetable could be drawn. Serbia/Yugoslavia, under strong pressure (a virtual ultimatum), was willing to sign an agreement that would provide for protection and eventual restoration of the Tito era autonomy of the ethnic Albanian population but balked at a clause (inserted at the end of the talks) which provided for 28,000 NATO troops having direct access to Kosovo to supervise the accord. President Clinton ordered NATO to launch its aerial attack, which it did starting on March 24 and which continued for eleven weeks, rejecting in the process a Serbian proposal for a truce during Easter.

What, then, were the manifest functions of the action of the United States/NATO as stated to the world by President Clinton and the State Department?[5] They were:

(1) a compelling "moral imperative" to provide humanitarian assistance in preventing a human catastrophe,
(2) protecting America's national interests in a strategic part of Europe where we have old and new allies that could be engulfed in a major war, and
(3) maintaining the credibility of NATO.

The *legitimation* of the massive air bombardment given to the tactics faced a complex challenge. Serbia/Yugoslavia (FRY), unlike Iraq in 1990, had not attacked any other surrounding state. Nor had the United States and Serbia ever fought in an armed conflict against each other earlier in the century. Further, there was widespread popular opposition in Europe to a NATO engagement against a European country, especially one that had fought two world wars on the side of the Allies. And lastly, the Serbs were, like the great majority in the Balkan region, Orthodox Christians while the Albanians were predominantly Muslim, a cultural difference that might mean little in the West but one that touches upon long memories of Ottoman rule in Europe.

The legitimation strategy to justify the attack served three purposes: first, it caused the *demonization* of Serbian action by blaming its leader, Slobodan Milosevic; second, it showcased the *victimization* of ethnic Albanians in Kosovo; third, it stressed the *disinterestedness* of the United States' intervention, which claimed that securing a free Europe would provide the foundation "on which the security of our children will depend." The strategy was embodied in several ways.

The demonization of Milosevic was carried out in public pronouncements of heads of states allied to the United States through the mainstream mass media. President Clinton best showed the effective use of rhetoric in his address of March 24 denouncing Milosevic as "a dictator in Serbia who has done nothing since the cold war ended but start new wars and pour gasoline on the flames of ethnic and religious divisions." If tanks and artillery were shooting in cold blood fathers and sons in Kosovo, this was due to the same Milosevic who was responsible for the ravages in Bosnia in 1995 on innocent people, killing a quarter of a million people, and turning two million Bosnians into refugees. To heighten the demonization, Milosevic and the Serbs became linked to Hitler and the Nazis through such references as "Sarajevo . . . is where World War I began. World War II and the Holocaust engulfed the region. . . . This was genocide in the heart of Europe, not in 1945 but in 1995. . . . let's not forget what happened: innocent people herded into concentration camps. . . ." The association of Milosevic with Hitler continued through the length of the aerial war and even well beyond, reflected widely in statements of leaders and in the Western press and television (Simic 2000).[6]

The victimization of ethnic Albanians was forcefully dramatized by repeated television showing of refugees—mainly women and children—streaming across Kosovo into Macedonia or Albania, and/or being brutalized and beaten by Serb military and paramilitary. Television also covered the accusations of rape by Serbian military personnel. Estimates of more than a million being driven from their homes were humanized even more dramatically by various portraits of individuals and their families forcefully driven out by Serbs seeking revenge for NATO raids. As *Newsweek* reported (April 19 1999, p. 28), the situation of the Albanian refugees uprooted from their homes was critical in the public acceptance of the war against the Serbs, as the State Department early in the war warned of the disappearance of 500,000 ethnic Albanians. Moreover, there were various reports of Serb atrocities, of concentration camps, etc.

The disinterestedness of the NATO allies and the moral basis of the war were stressed by eminent public figures in addition to Clinton. Thus, British Prime Minister Tony Blair declared,

> We need to enter a new millennium where dictators know that they cannot get away with ethnic cleansing or repress their peoples with impunity. In this conflict we are fighting not for territory but for values (cited in *Newsweek*, April 19,1999: 40).

This sentiment was further refined by Václav Havel, President of the Czech Republic, in addressing the Canadian Senate and House of Commons. The Kosovo War marked a new beginning in which human rights have taken priority in international relations over the sovereignty of the nation-state, or, as he put it,

> this is probably the first war that has not been waged in the name of 'national interests,' but rather in the name of principles and values (Havel 1999).

THE KOSOVO WAR: LATENT FUNCTIONS

Merton's seminal discussion of *latent functions* is heuristic in uncovering aspects of the Kosovo War that seem to have escaped public awareness and media analysis during the actual war period. Recall that Merton in proposing the concept of latent function indicated that this takes us beyond the simplistic moral evaluation of action based on a white or black moralization by pointing out consequences which take on "additional complexities usually involved in responsible social decisions" (Merton 1967: 122). There is no question, of course, that Serbian repression of ethnic Albanians was odious and reprehensible (and Yugoslavia was already subject to an economic embargo imposed as a consequence of its invasion of Bosnia in the mid-90s). Still, if invoking latent functions "precludes the substitution of naïve moral judgments for sociological analysis" (Merton 1967: 124), what else was involved or conveyed as consequences of the United States/NATO intervention?

Leaving aside that taking action against an external foe might be thought to provide a beleaguered government or an administration with domestic support,[7] the following latent functions of the Kosovo war initiative may be entertained as pertaining to the foreign relations of the United States:

1. Revalidation of the necessity of NATO at a time of crisis for NATO;

2. Demonstration to the Islamic world that the United States was not fundamentally anti-Islamic in conflict situations where one of the parties was an Islamic nation;

3. Demonstration to European countries, inside and outside the European Union, that the presence of the United States and its military technology is vital to European security.

Let us briefly discuss these in turn.

First, the year 1999 was to be marked as a celebration of the fiftieth anniversary of the North Atlantic Treaty that established NATO as a defense organization. What muted the celebration was whether NATO should continue given the demise of what had brought it into existence, the Soviet Union as a military threat to the survival of Western democracies. As students of organizations have long ago established (Zald and Denton 1963), the ultimate challenge to a voluntary organization is the solution of the task for which it was designed; those having a stake in it will be prone to find a new challenge not in the original mission statement. In 1998-1999, NATO (as a military organization designed to intervene in the defense of any of its parts if attacked by a country outside the alliance) was seeking to justify itself by expanding eastward by bringing into the alliance former Soviet republics. This elicited protest from Russia, which saw with trepidation an eastward expansion of a military organization on its borders. Russian opposition was also shared by many in the West who felt this was a time to bring Russia into the Western fold, rather than to marginalize it. *Consequently, NATO's attack on Serbia/Yugoslavia had as latent function to show Russia that NATO was not seeking aggressive activity against Russia but only to maintain stability in a danger zone of Europe removed from Russian frontiers.* Or stated in alternative terms, *the Kosovo War enabled NATO to "reinvent" itself as a necessary European peacekeeper.*

Second, as if to give credence to the Huntington thesis regarding the "clash of civilizations" in advanced modernity replacing the clash of nation-states (1993), the United States in particular had attacked, bombed, or taken military action in the 1980s and 1990s a disproportionate number of countries that could be identified as part of Islamic civilization: Lebanon, Somalia, Iraq, Iran, and the Sudan. At the same time, Western European countries such as France, Belgium, Switzerland, Austria and Germany, while not engaging in external armed conflict with Islamic countries, had nevertheless experienced severe ethnic tensions and new nationalist parties whose targets were mainly immigrant populations from Islamic countries. *Consequently, the Kosovo War, as a follow-up to intervention on behalf of Bosniak Muslims, was important in demonstrating to the Islamic world that the United States and its Western allies could take the side of an Islamic population in a conflict with an Orthodox Christian population.* In this context, for NATO to refuse Milosevic's offer to suspend hostilities during the long Easter season was a sign to the Islamic world that religion would not trump the humanitarian concerns of the West. As a further sign, the United States and NATO welcomed the military, economic, and other forms of direct airlift assistance provided by Islamic countries such as Turkey,

Kuwait, Palestine, and Saudi Arabia to Albanians in both Albania and Kosovo (Qusti 1999). All in all, then, direct intervention in Kosovo, along with the Dayton Peace Accords and American pressure on the European Union to accept the candidacy of Turkey, sent an important signal of a more benign American foreign policy toward the Islamic world, at least toward Islam in Europe (Esposito and Nasr 2000).

Third, as the decade was coming to an end, many Europeans felt that the defense and security of Europe should become more of a European affair than an American military one, either through NATO or the Western European Union. The Kosovo War demonstrated the progress in aerial combat technology that the United States had achieved since the Gulf War; it provided a convenient terrain in which to try out strategic bombing and new combat technologies for the new century. *Consequently, the Kosovo War demonstrated to Western allies and to the rest of the world the undisputed military might of America. This in turn made clear the merit of remaining clients to American military technology and the value of letting the United States retain charge of NATO.*

THE KOSOVO WAR: UNFORESEEN CONSEQUENCES

Merton's seminal paradigm of functional analysis highlights the distinctive contribution of sociology in the study of unintended as well as intended consequences of social practices. Merton identified the former as latent functions and the latter as manifest (1967: 120). In a neo-functional vein (Colomy 1990; Alexander 1998), one may propose that while latent functions may be hidden from view at the time or in the time period (t_1) during which the overt action or practice occurs, unintended consequences may also occur at a later time (t_2) as having been brought into being by the original action. In other words, while latent functions may be treated as unintended (in the sense of motivation not publicly recognized), there are other unintended or unanticipated consequences of purposive action which appear only later. The sociological study of war can show numerous instances of this effect. For example, a victorious country may face greater global competitiveness from its defeated foes, if the latter's destroyed infrastructure leads a new regime there to invest heavily in new and more productive industries and technologies.

What can be said about outcomes of the Kosovo War? This depends on the temporal horizon in terms of which consequences are laid out and assessed.

The *immediate* outcome was a vindication of the manifest intentions of the United States and its allies. The power and ability of NATO to wage a war without combat casualties of NATO troops firmly established its credibility as

an incredibly efficient military organization made up of different commands. The outflow and brutal handling of ethnic Albanians came to an end, and refugees could be resettled in their traditional homeland, even within days of the cessation of hostilities. The humanitarian rescue in scope and size was monumental, perhaps unique in history.

The short-term outcome fell somewhat short of the intentions of the United States and its allies. In going to war, the expectation was that the aerial attacks on the Serbian capital would turn the Serbs against Milosevic and greatly weaken his regime support, making it easier for his domestic opposition to overthrow him. In rallying Serbians of various persuasion against NATO, the bombings had a contrary effect, in line with Simmel's classic insight that conflict against an external foe tends to enhance group cohesion because patriotism tends to be generated even if the regime is authoritarian. The prime target of the Kosovo war, Slobodan Milosevic, survived in office for more than a year after the cessation of the bombardment. While Vojislav Kostunica's Democratic Opposition of Serbia took over the government by winning 64% of the vote in the September 2000 elections against 14% for Milosevic's own Socialist Party, up to this writing at least the new Serbian government has not extradited Milosevic to a war crimes international tribunal of justice. Equally vexing to the United States and its allies has been the shattering of the expectation of Kosovo becoming a democratic multiethnic autonomous region in which Albanians, Serbs, and other ethnic groups would live side by side, along the lines of the Dayton Peace Accords for Bosnia.

In effect, the ethnic Albanians in Kosovo, prodded more by militant KLA (UCK) leadership than by its more moderate civilian Ibrahim Rugova, have taken a "winner-take-all" attitude. Despite KFOR peacekeepers (too few to maintain effective control), wide-spread violence against Serbs and other minority ethnic groups (such as Roma) have taken place continuously since June 1999 as justified retribution, with a new round of equally brutal "ethnic cleansing" clearing large areas in central and southern Kosovo of Serbs (Dérens 2000: 14; Ash 2000). It is awkward for understaffed KAFOR peacekeepers to be hard on the KLA, which had been enlisted by NATO in its fight against Milosevic, even if training in guerilla warfare had also been reported done in northern Albania with funds from the drug trade and support from Hezbollah and other anti-Western organizations. In the post-war setting, the KLA has vied for power with the more moderate Democratic League of Kosovo (LDK) by use of strong-arm tactics and racketeering, directed against both Serbs and civilian Albanians (Ash: 50; Dérens 2000: 14).[8] In the aftermath of this war, lambs have turned into lions, or as the veteran observer Timothy Garton Ash put it

> . . . young Kosovars manifest a thirst for revenge that sickens not just foreigners but also many among the older generation of Kosovars. . . . it is entirely fitting to speak, in this context, of reverse ethnic cleansing (which) has been carried out under the very noses and tank barrels of more than 40,000 international troops (Ash 2000: 48).[9]

Ash noted that, while Kosovo was being unilaterally Albanized (as in the previous ten years Milosevic had sought to Serbianize it) and increasingly becoming prey to politico-mafia groups, many of which were not Kosovar Albanians but who crossed the porous border from Albania (Dérens, *ibid.)*, the external agencies sent to reconstruct a viable multiethnic society were only succeeding in Balkanizing themselves (Ash: 50).

Long-term outcomes are necessarily harder to envisage. From the point of view of the United States and Western nations, at least of political elites, eradicating a "demon" in the Balkans—Slobodan Milosevic—may be viewed as both a goal and a solution to much of the region's political ills. The stabilization of the region could in the new century be further brought about by the gradual integration of the republics of the former Yugoslavia into the European Union and into NATO. Although this scenario fits in with Gurr's recent evaluation of the secular decline in ethnic conflict (Gurr 2000), I would posit several caveats before concluding that we have seen the last of Balkan wars.

The fate of Kosovo is very uncertain. This uncertainty is partly created because internally it is hard to discern (a) what would ensue if the NATO and UN peacekeeping forces (KFOR, UNMIK) depart and (b) what might result from the first elections for a national assembly (scheduled for November 2001). This is also partly created by the fact of Kosovo's proximity to two states, Albania and Macedonia, with all three having a fast-growing Muslim-ethnic Albanian population, while the other groups are not growing (Tables 1, 2, 3).[10] The irredentist desire of a "Greater Albania" that would bring into a single political fold Albania, Kosovo and Albanian Macedonia may appear as a chimera to Westerners because this could destabilize the Balkan region anew, yet the history of the Balkans is replete with visions of a "Greater" nation; a "Greater Albania" may well be an appealing vision for an ethnic group with strong population growth.[11] Derivatives or relatives of the Kosovo Liberation Army such as UCPMB (Liberation Army of Preseva, Medvedje and Bujanovac) and NLA (National Liberation Army) have launched guerilla attacks, the former in the Presevo valley region in southern Serbia , the latter more recently in mountainous regions of Macedonia (easily accessible from Kosovo). The NLA has engaged in a guerilla war in regions in Macedonia where they can draw in

support from the ethnic Albanian population, still a minority relative to the majority Slav population but one with a much higher rate of natural increase (see Table 4).

Macedonia, with its long contested past in seeking to carve (if not invent) a modern national identity while being coveted by various neighbors (Kofos 1990; Danforth 1995; Poulton 1995), is a very fragile democratic state, with an equally fragile Macedonian Slavic-Albanian coalition government. Its breakup over demands for autonomy by the radicalized Albanian minority, in a scenario that bears similarities to the one in Kosovo, is unfortunately a real possibility unless the very Western states that intervened in Kosovo would send and continue to send unwavering signals that they would strongly oppose such a break up, from within or from without. Speedy integration into the European Union and/or the external provision of significant resources to make up for economic deficits unwittingly inflicted on Macedonia by the Kosovo War are also critical to the democratic survival of this country. The violent break up of Macedonia might well provoke a new round of Balkan unrest and destabilization, drawing Greece and Bulgaria into the Macedonian fray, at one end, and providing a negative model of integration for multiethnic relations in Bosnia.

In brief, neither short-term nor long-term outcomes of the Kosovo War can, at present, be viewed unequivocally as a positive prognosis.

THE KOSOVO WAR: ULTIMATE CONSIDERATIONS

Since this paper begins with a citation from Bourdieu, it is appropriate to close by referring again to his short but insightful work pertaining to television, the privileged medium in terms of which the world sees itself and others. Bourdieu points out that television is, for a large proportion of the population, the unique source of information, but television also tends to focus on trivial things, diverting the public away from information that could make them exercise their rights as citizens. Furthermore, says Bourdieu, television can paradoxically *hide in showing* ("cacher en montrant"), by showing something other than what it should show if it did what it was supposed to do, which is provide information (Bourdieu 1996: 17f).

By providing genuine investigative reports about the background to the Kosovo conflict, as television and other media had done in the later stages of the Vietnam conflict, by allowing Kosovar Serbians a voice, by indicating that a Serbian opposition to Milosevic existed within the Serbian national assembly, by encouraging negotiations over a possible partition of Kosovo which would have given the majority of the territory to ethnic Albanians and provided for minority

enclaves in some parts of the symbolic heartland of Serbia (Massey, Hodson and Sekuliæ 1999), the media might have played a constructive role in this war and created the possibility of a non-violent intervention (Chomsky 2000).

What the Western media opted for was a certain dualism that Moskos has well captured in pointing out that the Kosovo War "presented two diametrically opposed paradigms of military-media relations" (2000: 53). NATO's bombardment campaign was conducted with unquestioned acceptance of briefings—a "return to the pattern of official manipulation of news information." The Western media were party to a sharp dualism as reporters glossed over NATO's failure to live up to "international humanitarian law" (Amnesty International 2000). The media provided no images of the civilian damage due to cluster bombings (Wiebe 1999) or utilization of depleted uranium casings that may well be a factor in the incidence of leukemia in target areas. On the other hand, the media had uncontrolled access to those perceived as victims of Serb atrocities, the ethnic Albania refugees in camps. Moskos points out that this dualism in media-military relations (essentially "we won't investigate your military conduct if you let us investigate human drama") provides the rationale (or rationalization) for "how the term 'humanitarian war' could enter the international vocabulary without being regarded as an oxymoron" (Moskos 2000: 53).

If Kosovo was indeed a "postmodern war," it may be hopeless to find a moral, especially since the postwar situation of chaos, absence of civil society, and brutal attacks on Serbs, Roma, Turks and other non-Albanians—de facto a new and equally deplorable "ethnic cleansing"—make it difficult to say that democratization is replacing authoritarianism (Rohde 2000). There is a role for state intervention in ethnic conflict; however, waging war as a form of intervention is in itself no assurance that the outcome will be long-term what was intended. State intervention in this ethnic conflict may have won the war but lost the peace, or to invoke an ancient adage, the road to hell is too often paved with good intentions.[12]

ENDNOTES

[1] The dating of the Kosovo War from March to June is based on the entry of NATO into the armed conflict within Kosovo that had been going on for two years, with the emergence of the Kosovo Liberation Army (UCK) engaging in various acts of violence that provoked equally violent reactions by the Serbian/Yugoslav military and paramilitary. One can trace the conflict back further to 1989-90 when the formal autonomy of Kosovo granted by Tito was abrogated by Milosevic, leading to the setting up of a "parallel" government in ethnic Albanian hands called the "Albanian Republic of Kosovo," recognized by Albania but not by Belgrade. For succinct background materials on the war see Drezov, Gokay and Kostovicova (1999).

[2] A consideration of minimizing fatalities for one's troops does not, of course, mean that enemy targets, inert as well as human, are to be treated with equal caution, since war retains its basic objective of destroying the enemy.

[3] In effect, it is First World democracies that combine the two features of a high technology and risk-adverse political cultures. Where these countries engage in peacekeeping efforts involving potential loss of lives of their troops, recruits will increasingly come from Third World countries. Perhaps the use of Hessian troops in the War of Independence was prototypical.

[4] I have not been able to obtain population time series for Kosovo, including differential growth rates for the various nationalities. It is uncertain whether these exist since I was told that the Albanians refused to answer the 1991 Yugoslav census.

[5] The following is taken from the speech of President Clinton carried in *The New York Times* March 25, 1999, A15; see also the Department of State Fact Sheet, "U.S. and NATO Objectives and Interests in Kosovo", March 26, 1999. The presidential address also expressed these intentions as a mission statement seeking the restoration of peace: to demonstrate the seriousness of NATO's purpose; to deter an even bloodier offensive against innocent Kosovar civilians, and to seriously damage the Serbian military's capacity to harm Kosovars.

[6] Thus, Joschka Fisher, Germany's Foreign Minister, stated in an interview with *Newsweek* (April 19, 1999, p. 30), "I see a parallel to that primitive

fascism (of the Nazi era). Obviously, the '30s are back, and we cannot accept that... my generation was brought up with two experiences. The first is "Never Again War." And the second is "Never Again Auschwitz." It means standing up against genocide... If we accept Milosevic as a winner, it would be the end of the Europe I believe in . . ."

[7] "Depending on the interaction effects between variables [ethnic composition and institutional political constraints], certain leaders may prefer policies that lead to confrontation because of domestic payoffs," (Carment and James, 2000: 180).

[8] In Kosovo's first democratic elections held in October 2000, Rugova's Democratic League (LDK) got 58% of the vote, while two offshoots of the KLA, the Democratic Party of Kosovo (PDK) and the Alliance for the Future of Kosovo (AAK) received 27% and 8%, respectively.

[9] This might have been foreseen in the grim findings of a 1989 survey that "Albanians, whether in Kosovo, where they are the majority, or in Macedonia, where they are the principal minority, have the greatest intolerance toward other groups of any national group in the former Yugoslavia," (Hodson, Sekulić and Massey, 1994: 1551).

[10] I have not been able to get population data for Kosovo by ethnic group. However, one source suggests that a combination of Serbian emigration, Albanian immigration and higher ethnic Albanian birth rates led to a rise in the Albanian share of the Kosovo population from about 50% in 1946 to 80% in 1991 ("Kosovo", *Encyclopedia Britannica Online* <http://www.eb.com:180/bol/topic?eu=47187&sctb=1>).

[11] In Macedonia in March 2000 I was informed by an Albanian that the solution to the region was "1+1+1=1" by which he meant the union of Albania, Kosovo and most of Macedonia to create a unified Albania.

[12] After completing this paper, a recent sociological interpretation of Bosnia and Kosovo came to my attention: Keith Doubt's *Sociology after Bosnia and Kosovo* (2000). While the author also makes use of Merton's functional analysis, his interpretation of the Kosovo War (leaving aside the question of Bosnia which I do not treat) is very different from mine.

REFERENCES

Alexander, Jeffrey. 1998. *Neofunctionalism and after*. Malden, MA: Blackwell.

Amato, Ivan. 2000. "Lying with Pixels," *Technology Review* 103 (July/August): 60-66.

Amnesty International. 2000. "NATO/Federal Republic of Yugoslavia 'Collateral Damage' or Unlawful Killings?" *Violations of the Laws of War by NATO during Operation Allied Force*. AI Index: EUR 70/18/00. June 2000. Online http: www.amnesty.org/ailib/ainpub/2000/SUM/47001800.htm.

Ash, Timothy Garton. 2000. "Anarchy and Madness," *New York Review of Books*, February 10: 48-53.

Bourdieu, Pierre. 1998 (1996). *On Television*. Translated by Priscilla Parkhurst Ferguson. New York: New Press.

Carment, David and Patrick James. 2000. "Explaining third-party intervention in ethnic conflicts: theory and evidence," *Nations and Nationalism*, 6 (April): 173-202.

Chomsky, Noam. 2000. "Au Kosovo, il y avait une autre solution," *Le Monde Diplomatique*, no. 552 (March): 10-11.

Collins, Randall. 1994. *Four Sociological Traditions*. New York: Oxford.

Colomy, Paul, ed. 1990. *Neofunctionalist Sociology*. Aldershot, Hants (England) and Brookfield, VT: Edward Elgar Publishing.

Dakin, Douglas. 1973. *The Greek Struggle for Independence*. Berkeley: University of California Press.

Danforth, Loring M. 1995. *The Macedonian Conflict. Ethnic Nationalism in a Transnational World*. Princeton: Princeton University Press.

Dérens, Jean-Arnault. 2000. "Adieu au Kosovo Multiethnique," *Le Monde Diplomatique*, no. 552 (March): 14.

Doubt, Keith. 2000. *Sociology after Bosnia and Kosovo*. Lanham, MD: Rowman & Littlefield.

Drezov, Kyril, B. Gokay and D. Kostovicova, eds. 1999. *Kosovo: Myths, Conflict and War*. Staffordshire, UK: Keele European Research Centre, Keele University.

Esposito, John and Vali Nasr. 2000. "Rethinking U.S. Foreign Policy and Islam after Kosovo," *Georgetown Journal of International Affairs*, Online. Winter/Spring premier issue: 1-11.

Gurr, Ted Robert. 2000. "Ethnic Warfare on the Wane," *Foreign Affairs*, 79 (May/June): 52-64.

Habermas, Jürgen. 1975. *Legitimation Crisis*, T.McCarthy, trans. Boston: Beacon Press.

Halimi, Serge and Dominique Vidal. 2000. "Médias et désinformations," *Le Monde Diplomatique*, no. 552 (March): 12-13.

Havel, Václav. 1999. "Kosovo and the End of the Nation-State," *The New York Review of Books* (June): 4-6.

Hodson, Randy, Duško Sekulić, and Garth Massey. 1994. "National Tolerance in the Former Yugoslavia," *American Journal of Sociology* 99 (May): 1534-58.

Horowitz, Irving Louis. 1999. "The Vietnamization of Yugoslavia," *Society*. 36 (July-August): 3-10.

Howarth, David. 1976. *The Greek Adventure*. New York: Atheneum.

Huntington, Samuel P. 1993. "The Clash of Civilizations?" *Foreign Affairs* 72 (Summer): 22-49.

Ignatieff, Michael. 2000. *Virtual War: Kosovo and Beyond*. New York: Metropolitan/Henry Holt

Joas, Hans. 1999. "The Modernity of War.Modernization Theory and the Problem of Violence," *International Sociology*, 14 (December): 457-72.

Kaplan, Robert D. 1993. *Balkan Ghosts: A Journey through History*. New York: St. Martin's.

Kofos, Evangelos. 1990. "National Heritage and National identity in Nineteenth- and Twentieth-Century Macedonia." Pp. 103-41 in M. Blinkhorn and T. Veremis, eds., *Modern Greece: Nationalism and Identity*. Athens: Eliamep.

Massey, Garth, Randy Hodson and Duško Sekulić. 1999. "Ethnic Enclaves and Intolerance: The Case of Yugoslavia," *Social Forces*. 78 (December): 669-91.

Mazower, Mark. 2000. *The Balkans: A Short History*. New York: Modern Library.

Merton, Robert K. 1967. "Manifest and Latent Functions," in *On Theoretical Sociology*. New York: Free Press/Macmillan.

Moskos, Charles C. 2000. *The Media and the Military in Peace and Humanitarian Operations*. Chicago: Robert R. McCormick Tribune Foundation.

Poulton, Hugh. 1995. *Who are the Macedonians?* Bloomington: Indiana University Press.

Qusti, Hussein Saud. 1999. "Unsung Heroes," *Aramco World*, 50 (July/August): 2-15.

Rohde, David. 2000. "Kosovo Seething," *Foreign Affairs*. 79 (May/June): 65-79.

Simic, Charles. 2000. "Anatomy of a Murderer," *New York Review of Books*, January 20: 26-29.

Todorova, Maria. 1997. *Imagining the Balkans*. New York and Oxford: Oxford University Press.

Tiryakian, Edward A. 1999. "War, the Covered Side of Modernity." *International Sociology*, 14 (December): 473-89.

Wiebe, Virgil. 1999. "Cluster Bomb Use in the Yugoslavia/Kosovo War," Mennonite Central Committee. Online http://www.mcc.org/misc/CbinYugo.html. 15 pp.

Zald, Mayer N. and Patricia Denton. 1963. "From Evangelism to Social Service: The Transformation of the YMCA," *Administrative Science Quarterly*, 8: 214-34.

Table 1. Rates of Natural Increase (per 1000), Selected Balkan Countries, 1971-1980

Year	Country	Rate of Natural Increase
1971	Albania	25.2
1980	Bulgaria	3.6
1979	Greece	7.2
1980	Hungary	0.3
1979	Romania	8.7
1980	Yugoslavia	8.0

Source: United Nations, *Demographic Yearbook 1980*, New York: 1982, pp. 149-150.

Table 2. Rates of Natural Increase, Albania and the Republics of the Former Yugoslav Federation, 2000

Country	Population (in millions)	Births/1000	deaths/1000	annual natural increase (%)
Albania	3.4	18	5	1.3
Bosnia-Herzegovina	3.8	13	8	0.5
Croatia	4.6	11	12	-0.1
Macedonia	2.0	15	8	0.6
Slovenia	2.0	9	10	-0.1
Yugoslavia	10.7	11	11	0.1

Source: Population Reference Bureau, *2000 World Population Data Sheet*. Washington, D.C.: 2000, p. 9.

Table 3. Rates of Natural Increase (per 1000), Serbia, Kosovo, FYR Macedonia, 1995-1997.

Region	Year	live births	Deaths	growth rate
Serbia				
	1995	63,737	66,756	-0.5
	1996	60,924	69,218	-1.4
	1997	59,071	69,422	-1.8
Kosovo				
	1995	44,776	8,671	17.1
	1996	45,343	8,142	17.3
	1997	42,920	8,624	15.7
Macedonia				
	1996	31,403	16,063	7.7

Source: Barry Turner, ed., *The Statesman Yearbook 2000*. New York: St.Martin's Press, 2000, pp. 1959f.

Table 4. Population of Macedonia, Major Ethnic Groups, 1961-1991.

Ethnicity	1961	percent of population (1961)	1991	Percent increase 1961-1991	percent of population (1991)
Total of population	1,406,003	100.0	2,033,964	44.7	100.0
Macedonian	1,000,854	71.2	1,328,187	32.7	65.3
Albanian	183,108	13.0	441,987	141.4	21.7
Muslims	3,002	0.2	31,356	944.5	1.5
Serbs	42,728	3.0	42,775	0.1	2.1
Turks	131,484	9.4	77,080	-41.4	3.8
Roma	20,606	1.5	52,103	152.9	2.6

Adapted from: *1993 Statistical Yearbook of Macedonia* (Skopje: Government of Macedonia, 1994), p. 80, courtesy of the Population Reference Bureau, Washington, D.C.

PART II
ECONOMIC DEVELOPMENT AND CIVIL SOCIETY

CHAPTER 9
SOUTHEASTERN EUROPE IN TRANSITION

Eleftherios N. Botsas
Oakland University

I. INTRODUCTION

We are dealing here with inexact concepts. To a certain extent, every country is in transition. As Heracletos said a long time ago, everything changes from one state to another. However, change is not always welcomed. It introduces uncertainty, and uncertainty may reward only those who anticipate the future correctly. There are powerful econometric models that may approximate reality, but they are only approximations or even, sometimes, informed guesses. So what does being in transition mean? Change may be at the margin without affecting the systemic foundations. However, when we talk about transitional economies we mean more than reforms or changes at the margin. In today's parlance, the word "transitional" is reserved for those countries which moved from central planning to a system of market determined economic outcomes. This is how the International Monetary Fund (IMF) uses the term, and it is also the meaning of the term as used in this essay. IMF (2000, 271) states that "One common characteristic of these countries is the transitional state of their economies from a centrally administered system to one based on market principles."

We are still left with the problem of determining which countries make up South Eastern Europe (SEE) and which do not. Even geographic names like "Balkan" countries have lost their historical classification. As long as they were part of Yugoslavia, Croatia and Slovenia were Balkan. After their breakaway, some authors include them in an inquiry of Balkan affairs and others do not. In this essay on South Eastern Europe in transition, the emphasis will be on the countries that were traditionally classified as Balkan. That would include all of the former Federal Republic of Yugoslavia, Bulgaria, Romania, Turkey, and Greece, although, as a member of the European Union, Greece is no longer classified as Balkan by any multilateral entity. Moreover, Hungary and Poland, two central European economies (CEE), will be to some extent included in SEE for comparative analysis.

Studying the economic development of Eastern Europe, Nicolas Spulber (1996:18) observed, that "The three very small countries of the area . . . Rumania, Serbia, and Bulgaria developed essentially as food producing and food exporting countries." Central planning attempted to transform all of them to

industrial powers, but with the possible exception of the former Yugoslavia, the forced transformation failed. To this day, the Balkan countries (except Slovenia) still allocate disproportionate amounts of labor in agriculture.[1] Planners tried to force labor out of agriculture by turning the terms of trade against this sector, but again they failed to develop light industries that could become sources of technological change. The fall of the Berlin Wall in 1989 revealed the failures of central planning. Industries and countries that were advertised as pioneers on the technological fronts came out to be wastelands of concrete and steel. In addition, the collapse of the system released forces that were destined to change the make up of the Balkans and put some of the Balkan economies into a path of cumulative movement away from convergence with the international economy. The impact of divergence is directly related to the degree of taut planning before the collapse of the Soviet system and its support of the satellite economies through subsidies.

II. SYSTEM TRANSFORMATION

We knew even before the fall of the Berlin Wall that central planning had failed to meet even the most fundamental targets of its own proclamations. On the other hand, central planning developed badly needed social overhead, gave direction to social efforts, and increased the supply of skills of labor through training and education. In spite of all these, central planning also failed to create self-sustained growth. Moreover, in the peripheral countries (and that is what South Eastern Europe has historically been), central planning created resistance to changing conditions in the world markets. Therefore, the symbolism of the fall of the Berlin Wall was welcomed, but we knew that transition would be difficult. However, the extent of difficulties was underestimated. Even those who claimed specialized knowledge of the era were dramatically wrong. Academicians, reporters, and administrators, underestimated the difficulties of transition. We had some knowledge of the problems faced by market economies suddenly turned to centrally planned economies, but, simply stated, there was no historical prototype to which we could turn for guidance in the opposite direction. A taut command system turned to the anarchy of the market for guidance in things in which neither the market nor planning had any valid experience. Basically, the advisers saw a dichotomous process. (1) A gradual adaptation of the market system through privatization and legal reform, or (2) shock therapy: a return to the market forces unconditionally. We now know that all centrally planned economies (CPEs), which adopted the market system, even in a limited form, experienced substantial fall in their economic welfare. As Table 1 makes clear, while certain formerly centrally planned economies like

those of Poland, Hungary, and the Czech Republic were able to reverse the early fall in economic activity, but others were not. South Eastern Europe's transition turned into a painful exercise with no end in sight. Table 1 shows in summary form the movement of real gross domestic product (GDP), or gross material product (GMP) in South Eastern Europe.

It is evident that the European countries in transition exhibit two distinctly different adjustment paths. Countries like Poland, which applied "shock therapy" early in the transition process, were able to adjust to the market at a lower cost in terms of unemployment and falling GDP than countries that delayed the adjustment process. There are two groups of country behavior to adjustment here: one exhibits the expected J-curve adjustment and the other does not.

TABLE 1. PERCENT CHANGE IN REAL GDP AND PER CAPITA GNP IN 1999

	Average 1982-91	1992	1993	1994	1995	1996	1997	1998	1999	1999[α] US $
Albania	-2.6	-7.2	9.6	9.4	8.9	9.1	-7.0	7.9	7.2	870
Bosnia & Herzegovina	NA	NA	NA	NA	32.4	85.8	39.9	12.8	8.6	920
Bulgaria	0.3	-7.3	-1.5	1.7	2.2	-10.9	-6.9	3.5	2.4	1380
Croatia	NA	NA	-8.0	5.9	5.7	5.9	6.8	2.5	-0.3	4580
Czechoslovakia	0.3	-8.5								
Czech Republic	NA	NA	0.1	2.2	5.9	4.8	-1.0	-2.2	-0.3	5060
FYROM	NA	NA	-7.5	-1.8	-1.1	1.2	1.4	2.9	2.7	1690
Hungary	-0.4	-3.1	-0.6	2.9	1.5	1.3	4.6	4.9	4.5	4650
Poland	0.2	2.6	3.8	5.2	7.0	6.0	6.8	4.8	4.1	1520
Romania	-0.8	-8.8	1.5	3.9	7.1	3.9	-6.1	-5.4	-3.2	1390
Slovak Republic	NA	NA	-.37	4.9	6.9	6.6	6.5	4.4	1.9	3590
Slovenia	NA	NA	2.8	5.3	4.1	3.5	4.6	3.9	4.9	9890
Turkey	4.8	5.0	7.7	-4.7	8.1	6.9	7.6	3.1	-5.0	2900
Greece	1.9	2.3	0.7	-1.6	2.0	2.1	2.4	3.4	3.7	11770

[α]GNP World Bank (2000a) Atlas methodology
NA= not available or not applicable
Sources: IMF *World Economic Outlook 2000*, II (September), Appendix Table7.
World Bank, World Development Indicators, 8/2/2000.

J-curve adjustment says that in sudden and dramatic changes, such as devaluation of a currency or the economic revolutions experienced in 1989, the economic variables we want to influence the economy in a positive way may initially move in the opposite direction. Since we want to study the change in the economies after the fall of the Berlin Wall, we can let, each country's GDP

equal 100 in 1989, the base period, and see the relative change in the GDP indices for the rest of the period under study. The initial impact of the drastic change in policy fundamentals on the economy will be negative for some time before it turns to positive. Note that we study each group's time path of adjustment independently of the other group. It describes the catching-up process with respect to its initial position. In other words, we examine the changing real GDP of each group versus itself, not one group versus the other.

Let's follow the United Nations Economic Commission for Europe (UNECE) classification here. The first group consists of the central European economies in transition (CETE), that is, the Czech Republic, Hungary, Poland, Slovakia, and Slovenia. The second group, SETE (south-eastern transition economies), consists of Albania, Bosnia-Herzegovina, Bulgaria, Croatia, Romania, the Former Yugoslav Republic of Macedonia (FYROM), and the federal Republic of Yugoslavia. As Figure 1 shows the GDP of CETE behaved as the J-curve hypothesis would predict. Originally, real GDP fell below its pre-transition path, but it reversed the fall and more than caught up with a positive trend. Still, CETE had to wait for seven years before it could reach the 1989-GDP-level. From the economic point of view, the discount rate and the dynamic effects of privatization affect the present value of the lost output. All we can say here is: there is no free lunch.

The second group, which consists of the Balkan countries in our study, moved farther away from convergence. It was better off under the old regime than under the free-market conditions. One may say that a ten-year period is too short, but as Keynes is supposed to have said, in the long run we are all dead. In comparison to pre-1989 output, all European economies in transition experienced a decline in real GDP in the early stage of transition. However, Poland, Hungary, and the Czech Republic recovered from the early fall. Their per capita GDP presents what economists call a J-curve: a fall below the 100 base-line levels in 1989 followed by a gradual increase above the base line. In South Eastern Europe, only Slovenia presents a similar picture. The Balkan transitional economies do not. A report by the World Bank (2000b:6) assessing the difficulties of SEE states that: "The past decade of transition and conflict has been exceptionally difficult for the people of South Eastern Europe. . . . Conflict, an absence of a political consensus for reform, shallow democratic traditions and weak institutions have all combined to constrain economic and political development in most countries of South Eastern Europe." The World Bank's definition of SEE consists of Albania, Bosnia and Herzegovina, Bulgaria, Croatia, the Federal Republic of Yugoslavia (FRY), Former Yugoslav Republic of Macedonia (FYROM), and Romania. That is, the same as UNECE's SETE.

The pessimism about progress in the Balkans is more generalized. However, the pessimism about the Balkans is reflected in the general literature on Balkan transition. Even when there were very few data to draw conclusions, authors draw historical analogies that support their pessimism. This is also reflected in the general literature on the Balkans, and the general tendency is to assign blame on historical hatreds. For example, lack of democratic tradition has been blamed for the divergence in transition. Yet one has to ask, for example, in what sense has Hungary been more democratic than Romania? More fundamentally the question is: is there empirical evidence that democracy leads to higher rates of economic growth? Has India achieved higher rates of economic growth than China? Are all other things equal? Pessimists like Shlomo Avineri argue that South Eastern Europe lacks democratic traditions that promote market activities. According to Avineri (1992:15), "1989 and ensuing developments suggest that the best predictive indicator of a country's post-communist future is its past."

There is no empirical evidence that democracy leads to higher rates of economic growth, but it is true that the state, whether democratic or not, have played important role in both retardation and growth of the region.[2] The usual comparison is between the Balkan countries on one hand and Hungary, Poland, and the Czech Republic on the other. However, unless one also refers to the infusion of capital from the developed West into Central Europe, the comparison is incomplete. In more general terms, we know that the imprints of empire rules remain long after the imperial powers have died. In our case, we can say that the Balkan countries and SEE reflect economically the long heritage they acquired from their master occupiers. Those who were under Austro-Hungarian rule are much more advanced than those who were under Ottoman rule. Their masters have been gone for a long time, but the seeds of progress or backwardness have deep roots. The two sets of rulers left behind them institutional and ideological legacies that are still relevant today, in spite of the progress of modern Turkey. I do not wish to discard history and animosities as important players in Balkan developments, but one has to look beyond historical appearances to see the forces of economic growth or retardation.

The United Nations Economic Commission for Europe splits the transitional economies of Europe into central European transitional economies (CETE), southeast European transitional economies (SETE), and Baltic States and CIS.[3] We shall analyze CETE and SETE here. SETE countries are the Balkan transitional economies. Have the two subsets of transitional European economies performed differentially? A priori one would expect an affirmative answer. First of all, CETE countries were more industrialized than SETE countries. Secondly, even if the initial conditions in 1989 were the same, CETE countries were closer, geographically and structurally, to the European center of economic

activity. Starting with an index of GDP =100 in 1989, we see that CETE countries did behave according to behavior specified by the J-curve hypothesis. They caught up with their pre-1989 GDP. This does not mean that they are catching up with the European Union, but unleashing the market forces led to gradual recovery of very depressed economies. Ten years after the fall of the Berlin Wall, the South Eastern European countries had not even caught up with their 1989 GDP. To this date, they remain fragmented and basically agricultural.

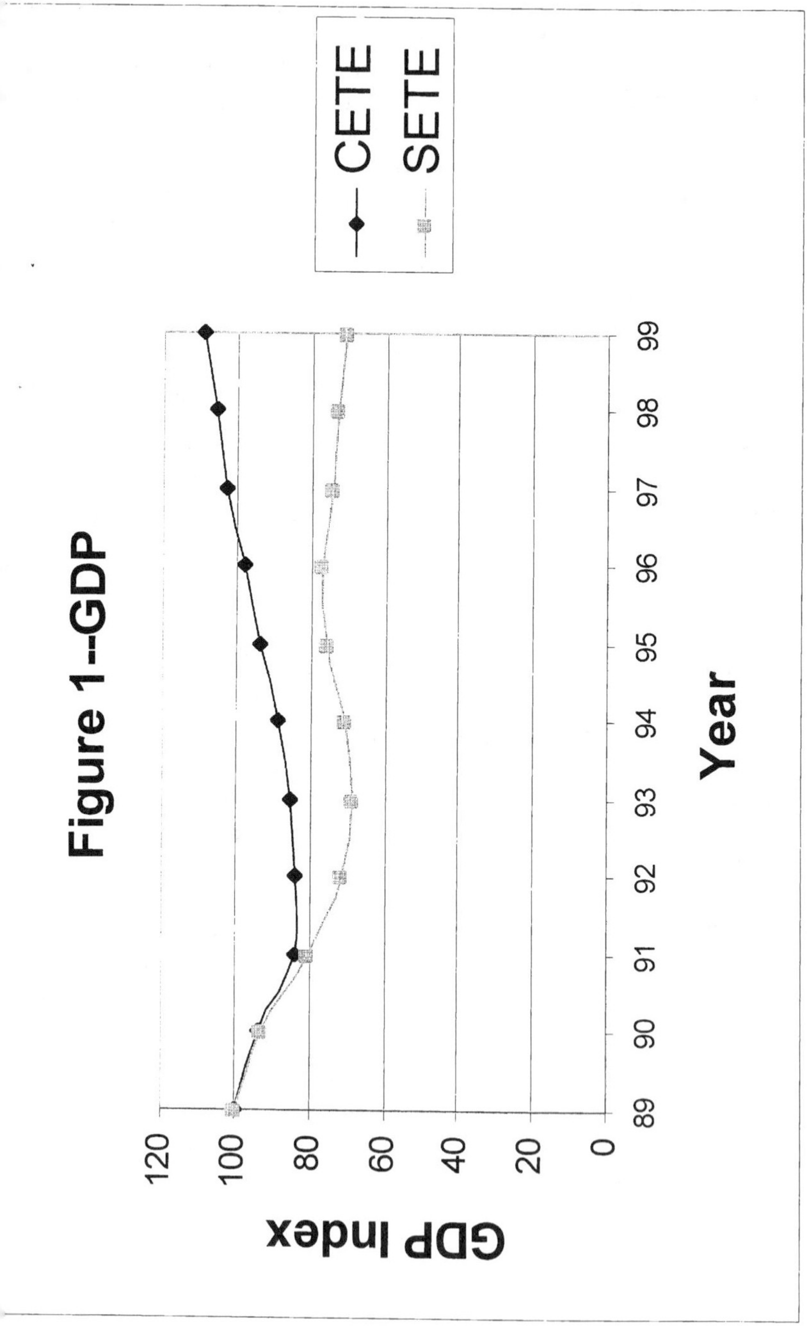
CETE
SETE
GDP Index
120
100
80
60
40
20
0
89
90
91
92
93
94
95
96
97
98
99
Year

Figure 1--GDP

Figure 1 shows that as a group CETE surpassed the level of 1989 GDP in 1997. EU moved, of course, further ahead, but the catching up process has started. Since CETE countries are scheduled to join the EU earlier than SETE countries, there is likely to be a speeding up process for central Europe and a wider gap for South Eastern Europe. All formerly centrally planned economies of Europe were affected by the west's embargo on trade and investment with the Soviet Union and its satellites. Therefore, the small economies of the East were deprived of the ability to borrow technology from the West. We know now that the embargo's intent to maximize the damage to the East was successful. However, since CETE countries developed stocks of knowledge, their assimilation to the center of the EU will pose no problems except for the periphery within EU. In other words, accession of the CETE countries presents a competitive challenge to Greece, Portugal, and Ireland, but not to the EU center. We now know that the CETE countries lost, on the aggregate, about fifteen percent of their pretransition output, but the loss of the SETE countries is larger and the time period longer. Moreover, the Kosovo war distorted trade and transportation networks to such an extent that trade among former members of the Federal Republic of Yugoslavia has been almost totally eliminated. Interregional trade is the first index of integration. The World Bank's study *The Road to Stability* (2000b6) concluded, "The past decade of transition and conflict has left the region with a legacy of mediocre growth and declining living standards."

In order to estimate the time distance that central and east European countries (CEE) need to catch up with the EU, Stanley Fischer, Ratna Sahay, and Carlos A. Vegh (IMF/WP/98/53) looked at the income gap of CEE and western European countries in 1937 and 1992 and found that, for the most advanced CEE country of 1992, Czechoslovakia, it would take 18 years (:35), while for Albania it may take forever. The authors found that "it would take the Czech Republic only 15 years to catch up with the low-income western European countries."(IMF/WP/98/53:35) In relative terms, all CEE countries lost income under socialism. The authors estimate that, "on average, the CEE countries gave away about one generation worth of income during the 40 years of socialism." (IMF/WP/98/53:10) Of course, it was not only the socialist countries of Europe that lost relative rank versus the western European average. Greek and Turkish per capita GDP dropped from 70 and 32 percent of the average to 67 and 29 per cent, respectively (IMF/WP/98/53:10). So, in spite of their post-World-War II economic growth, Greece and Turkey were, in relative terms, closer to the European average in 1937 than they were in 1992. All Balkan economies grew between the two periods, but Europe grew faster and

left the Balkans behind. However, it was the former socialist countries in the Balkans that suffered the most. The income gap between them and the rest of Europe increased. Romania and Bulgaria dropped from 28 and 39 percent, respectively, to 17 and 26 percent of the western European average (ibid). Socialism was brought to the Balkans at a high price. Yet, many ideologues question Greece's choice of the market rather than socialism in the 1950s and 1960s. Nostalgia for a world that never existed can be found allover contemporary Greek writings. The historical record shows, however, that most of the Balkans are poor and grow poorer through time.

Foreign direct investment (FDI) has been the most important vehicle of technological innovations and economic growth in many of the formerly peripheral countries of Asia or Europe. The ability of Spain and Ireland to close the gap between themselves, on one hand, and the center of EU could not be possible in the absence of FDI. It can take the form of mergers and acquisition (M&A) or Greenfield operations. Since mergers and acquisitions change ownership from domestic to foreign, they may or may not introduce technological innovations. This is the main reason why developing countries prefer Greenfield operations to M&As. Still, whatever the form it may take, FDI has been credited with the globalization of the markets. Depending on the industry in which firms operate, the size of the market, rate of growth of GDP, availability of critical human and non-human resources, and political stability are the usual magnets of attractions of FDI. In standardized mass-produced products like shoes and clothing, labor cost may determine FDI inflow. But even in such a case, political stability that enhances the firm's ability to predict is very important. European economies in transition are new in the game of FDI. Therefore, they are of minor importance to the global strategies of the firms as markets for products. However, they possess highly skilled labor and have proximity to the core of the European Union, variables that can give competitive advantage to multinationals. Moreover, multinational corporations tend to cluster more than national firms do.

Except for Russia, central and east Europe was not viewed as a hospitable place for FDI. It lacked natural resources or effective markets for products of advanced technology. Therefore, FDI was of limited scope before the fall of the Berlin Wall. Some writers argue that one decade after the 1989 revolutions, FDI is still anemic for the region. Table 2 shows the flow of FDI in 1997-99 as well as the stock of FDI at the end of 1999 for some countries. Because the region is a newcomer to the field of international finance, it is, of course, obvious that the stock should be expected to be low. However, even in its best year, 1999, central, east, and southern transitional economies attracted only three percent of

the global FDI. The bulk of FDI goes to other advanced economies and SE Asia.

TABLE 2. FOREIGN DIRECT INVESTMENT, 1997-1999, MILLION US$

	1997	1998	1999	1999 stock in billions
Albania	48	45	41	
Bosnia Herzegovina	NA	100	60	
Bulgaria	505	537	806	
Croatia	530	898	1408	
FYROM	16	118	301	
Romania	1215	2031	1041	
Yugoslavia	740	NA	NA	
Slovenia	375	248	181	
Czech Republic	1300	2720	5108	16
Hungary	2173	2036	1944	19
Poland	3077	5129	6471	30
CETE-5	7087	10641	14034	
SETE-7[α]	2313	3629	3326	

[α] Excludes Bosnia and Herzegovina and Yugoslavia.
Source: UNECE, *Economic Survey of Europe 2000*, Table 1.2.14

We can draw certain conclusions from Table 2. First, within the group of European economies in transition, the Czech Republic, Hungary, and Poland are the main recipients of FDI. Secondly, for a plethora of reasons, the Balkan economies in transition are not the favorites of international investment. Some of the reasons have to do with general social perceptions reinforced by journalistic overkill, and some have to do with governmental pronouncements in the investing countries. Thirdly, most of these countries are candidates for European Union membership. Looked at from the point of view of convergence or proximity to the European Union average, one finds a very long distance between the Balkans in transition and Brussels. The three central European countries are likely to be the first to join. Will they lengthen the distance between Brussels and the Balkans? Given the economic and political distance between Balkan and central Europe, the answer would be in the affirmative. That's one of the reasons why Greece has become a strong advocate of further assistance to SEE to join the family of European economies. Greece has provided foreign assistance of about $500 million to the Balkans, much more

than the rich EU or USA. In spite of all the rhetoric about integration, the Balkan countries in transition remain isolated. While Hungary, Poland, and the Czech Republic had powerful voices in the United States and European business and intellectual communities, the Balkan transitional economies had no voice. Preoccupied with the demonization of Slobodan Milosevic, NATO and the State Department were not in the mood for looking at the area objectively. Secretary of State Madeleine K. Albright and NATO pursued the complete destruction of any economic or military Serbian power. The Kosovo war objectives, which were never stated or understood, could not be compromised for economic development. The strategy was to remove Mr. Milosevic and the Yugoslav army from any power in the Balkans. Even today, when Mr. Milosevic is out of power, the US insist on his transfer to The Hague before it delivers the promised $100 million in economic aid. The fact that this is likely to increase nationalist and anti-American feelings in Yugoslavia seems to be of no interest to policy makers in Washington. For example, on March 10, 2001, *The New York Times* on the web reported that, "The United States has told the new democratic government in Belgrade that if it expects American aid to continue, it should arrest and imprison former President Slobodan Milosevic by the end of March." This may cause unrest in Yugoslavia. Sometimes, powerful countries are not concerned with the reactions of defeated minor powers.

All armed conflicts increase the risk to foreign investors. The risk could be destruction of the firms' property, expropriation, or simply control of the firms that are based in NATO countries. Moreover, foreign investment tends to cluster in the same areas. There is a "herd" phenomenon in foreign investment. Like humans migrating to places where they have "friends and relatives," FDI tends to follow the investment by other nationals. Low levels of previous investment mean low stock, and low stock may prevent substantial flows. The stock of foreign establishments in the Balkan transitional economies was very limited. Since those countries did not posses resources critical to the profitability of FDI, corporate decision makers bypassed them. As the UNCTAD press release 2859 (3 October 2000) stated, "The Kosovo conflict influenced some potential investors interested in south-eastern Europe to postpone decisions." Contrary to the Marxist rhetoric on economic imperialism, there is no evidence that war and FDI go hand-in-hand. And since NATO succeeded in maximizing the damage to the civilian economy of Yugoslavia, FDI in the Balkans may be postponed for long periods of time. Furthermore, the Balkans will be in an inferior position to compete with the Baltic countries in EU eastward expansion. EU-based multinational corporations are the principal investors in the European transitional economies.

In addition to wars in the former Yugoslav republics, many commentators, especially the in influential US press, accuse the Balkan countries of being nationalistic. Nationalism can be peaceful. Pride in one's nation, history, or culture is a universally shared characteristic. It can also be an aggressive way of imposing one's historical, political, or cultural values on others. Commentators on the Balkans imply the latter without ever saying anything about the former. Yet nationalism is a public good, a good of collective consumption. The World Bank (2000b:3) tells us "The past decade of transition and conflict has been exceptionally difficult for the people of South Eastern Europe. . . . Conflict, an absence of a political consensus for reform, shallow democratic traditions and weak institutions have all combined to constrain economic and political development in most countries of South Eastern Europe." This is a common refrain in discussions of the Balkans. Somehow, history and nationalism have been blamed for every action or reaction of the Balkan people. Yet we know that nationalism is a public good that may be consumed for the betterment or worsening of a society. As Isaiah Berlin (1997: 251) has observed, "nationalism is responsible for magnificent achievements and appalling crimes." It is present in one form or another in all societies. The expression the 'American Way' is a symbol of nationalism. Moreover, restrictions or controls of business enterprises or their technology according to nationality is another form of nationalism. The United States has a long history of restricting the activities of foreigners in industries that are critical in high technology or defense. Yet, we observe that such restrictions may affect the direction of FDI, but not its volume. Critics of nationalism may point out that the laws in the United States, combined with the power of U.S. institutions like the judiciary and Congress, safeguard the integrity of foreign investment. Legal procedures establish a degree of predictability of final outcomes.

Borders define property rights of the sovereign, and no power is likely to exist during the investment-planning horizon to challenge the US borders. On the other hand, the Balkan states seem to have endless border disputes. Such disputes introduce unpredictable variables in the investment calculus. The absence of a benchmark makes predictions about the future more difficult. Unpredictability of basic givens is one of the strongest obstacles to FDI. As I have argued elsewhere (Botsas. 1999)

> The struggle for more is a universal phenomenon and a condition of human existence, and "more" does not have to be in terms of measurable material things. More can be in air space, in nationalism, in seawater, in useless swamps that are symbols of national strength. For example, Greece and Turkey almost had a catastrophic war over the Imia islet in eastern Aegean.

> Since at least the rise of the nation state, national territories have come to symbolize exclusive property rights. Violation of such property rights is enough cause for war.

In spite of two world wars, South East Europe has not been able to settle the border issues. This creates uncertainty that shifts the political risk in favor of solid borders, although foreign investors wish there were no borders at all. Many writers view nationalism in the poorer countries as the main source of conflict that prevents foreign investment. Critics frequently view it as an irrational force that has enslaved both the leadership and the populace of SEE. Yet, nationalism is a public good that is present, in various forms, in every society. Moreover, nationalism may work as a benchmark, a point of reference in decision-making. According to Isaiah Berlin (256), "Nationalism is the direct product of wounds inflicted on a sense of common nationhood, or common race or culture." In such a case, Balkan nationalism can be viewed as a reaction to the way the Balkan countries have been treated.

Both East and West have done their best in driving co-operation out of the Balkan lexicon. Healing old wounds becomes impossible when new wounds are inflicted in the process. In the hope of getting a Serbian revolution against Milosevic, NATO destroyed the productive capacity of Yugoslavia and encouraged the creation of states in every neighborhood. The process of destabilization will continue at least until the whole area joins the European Union. Even then, as the case of the Spanish-Basque conflict shows, the Balkans may remain hostile to the idea of an international community. NATO created a monstrous situation in the Balkans. First, it encouraged and supported logistically and militarily the creation of an independent Kosovo, and then it discovered that it had created a source of instability in southern Serbia and the Former Yugoslav Republic of Macedonia (FYROM). As *The New York Times* reported on the current problems in FYROM (March 11, 2001), "The influx of hundreds of thousands of Kosovo Albanian refugees during NATO's war with Yugoslavia in 1999 brought ethnic tension to a boiling point and revealed the Slavs' deep fears of being inundated by Albanians and the Albanians' bitter resentment at decades of repression. . . . And Albania, which shares its long western border, offered little more than instability and chaos for years." Given the chaotic conditions of Albania, massive economic aid may be the only solution to the problem.

In cases where there is some balance of power, or where higher adherences to acceptable international-law standards exist, border disputes are resolved peacefully. The split between Slovakia and the Czech Republic, or between

Sweden and Norway in the beginning of the 20th century, or the proposed separation of Quebec from the rest of Canada exhibit such constraints to unilateral ambitions. The settlement between Romania and Hungary on the issues of minorities and borders also comes to mind as a rational cost-benefit evaluation of alternatives. In the cases of the former Yugoslavia and Turkey versus Greece, however, international law has been ignored. In such cases, inclusion in a more powerful bloc, like the European Union, may be the only way of moving ahead with cooperation in SE Europe.

Foreign investment may take the form of portfolio short-run capital inflow or long run direct investment in productive capacity. Portfolio investments are in an even worse shape than FDI in the Balkan economies in transition. Bulgaria's declaration of a moratorium on servicing previous foreign debt in March 1990 made finance of development through the international credit markets more difficult. In the final analysis, foreign investors invest in a country in the hope of making profits convertible to their own currencies. The declaration of a moratorium scared foreign capital. Still, foreign capital could be attracted in the form of foreign direct investment (FDI), but in the absence of resources critical to the international economy there are neither portfolio nor FDI inflows.

In the case of all three formerly centrally planned economies, FDI has been anemic. In these three countries, FDI has been lagging far behind the flow into other European countries in transition. This is so in spite of the reforms that Bulgaria and Romania introduced. According to the OECD (1997:125) economic survey, "Bulgaria was actually among the first of the central and eastern European countries to allow foreign direct investment on its territory, passing a joint venture law in 1980." Moreover, "At the outset of economic transition, Bulgaria was again among the first countries of the region to adopt legislation to attract foreign investors."(ibid). As Table 2 shows, FDI declined the invitation.

Profitability and safety of capital are the primary concerns of investors, both domestic and foreign. Investment decisions require analysis of estimated costs and revenues in the long run. Such an evaluation requires accurate information before funds are committed. Because of the prolonged adherence of the centrally planned economies (CPEs) to taut central planning, the amount of accurate information for investment analysis is limited. That, however, is the case for all former CPEs. Yet, of all European countries in transition only Russia and Ukraine received lower levels of FDI than Bulgaria. Because of its inter-ethnic wars and international embargoes, Yugoslavia could not expect substantial inflow of FDI. However, Turkey has been experiencing inter-ethnic war and substantial inflow of FDI. The difference is that the West classifies the Kurds

as terrorists, but the Bosnians, Croats, and other former Yugoslavs as freedom fighters. Investors are mindful of how the United States, Germany, and France deal with international upheavals.

The abrupt systemic changes (shock therapy) of the Balkan CPEs could not overcome the established inefficiencies of the central planning legacies. The hostility to competition was present in all the economies in transition, not just the Balkan ones. Since the Soviet Union provided the Council for Mutual Economic Assistance (CMEA) countries with energy at priced far below world prices in the 1970s and 1980s, the CPEs of Europe had no incentives to economize on energy consumption. For example, evaluating Bulgaria's application for membership, the European Commission found that until mid-1996 Bulgaria was using two to four times more energy per unit of output than the average in countries of the European Union.[4] The CMEA countries had developed energy intensive industries that reflected technology and prices of the 1960s rather than the 1990s. Compared with EU and some other economies in transition, the Romanian economy, too, presents high-energy intensity industries. Since the Bulgarian economy was the most integrated with the Soviet Union, it faced more severe difficulties in the process of adjustment, especially when Europe is concerned more with Poland, Hungary, and the Czech Republic than with the Balkans. Throughout the 1990s, the Commonwealth of Independent States (CIS) remained the main destination of Bulgarian exports.

III. EU CANDIDACY

There are thirteen candidate countries for EU accession. The candidate countries (CCs) are spread from the Baltic Sea to the eastern Mediterranean. Their per capita GDP varies from 81percent to 22 percent of the EU15 average. Cyprus is the richest and Bulgaria the poorest. Albania is much poorer than Bulgaria, but Albania is not a candidate. However, in this section, we shall deal with the Balkan countries only. It suffices to say here that Greece is the poorest EU country, but only Cyprus has a per capita GDP higher than the poorer EU country. Slovenia's per capita GDP is about the same as Greece's (although some estimates show it slightly higher and some slightly lower). Albania showed signs of lawlessness and disintegration, but it seems to be on the road to recovery. Its rate of real GDP growth from 1995 to 1999 is a healthy average of just over seven percent per year. Still as Table 3 shows, Albania is the poorest and most agriculture- based economy of the Balkans. Its main trade partners are Italy and Greece. These two countries are also the main markets of migration for Albania's excess supply of labor. Its fertility rate, at 2.6 children per woman, is the highest in Europe.

Bulgaria, the former Yugoslav Republic of Macedonia (FYROM), and Romania are the next poorest countries of Southeastern Europe. Both Bulgaria and Romania delayed their privatization reforms and are paying the price now. The current armed disturbances of Albanian minorities in both southern Serbia and FYROM are creating further delays in economic cooperation and development. "The influx of hundreds of thousands of Kosovo Albanian refugees during NATO's war with Yugoslavia in 1999 brought ethnic tension to a boiling point and revealed the Slavs' deep fears of being inundated by Albanians and the Albanians' bitter resentment at decades of repression," reported *The New York Times* (March 11, 2001). "And Albania, which shares its long western border, offered little more than instability and chaos for years." From the economic point of view, the main criticism on Romania and Bulgaria is the delayed reforms. The IMF country report (IMF 2000/159:5) has spelled out the problems, but in the absence of capital inflows the two formerly CPEs will find the catching-up process difficult. "Romania's progress in stabilization and reform compares unfavorably with that of many other transition economies, not withstanding some catching-up in recent years." (*Ibid*). Moreover, it has to be remembered that Ceausescu's obsessive aversion to foreign debt during the 1980s starved the economy of imports of necessary inputs to facilitate technological change and future growth. Throughout the 1980s Romania, in order to reduce the external debt, had an excess of exports over imports by reducing imports.

As said before, both are candidates for accession to the European Union. Ranked by dependence on agriculture, Bulgaria, Romania, and Turkey have only one-third of Albania's dependence. Yet all of them, as well as Greece, have very inefficient agriculture. For example, the percentages of labor-force employment in agriculture are 20% for Greece and 42% for Turkey. Thus, as the International Monetary Fund *World Economic Outlook* (IMF 2000:2: 252) puts it, "In comparison with most of the other EU candidates, apart from Bulgaria and Romania, Turkey's economic structure is weighted relatively heavily toward agriculture: as in Romania, this sector generates around 16 percent of value added and accounts for about 40 percent of employment."

The Slovenian economy is much more developed than the rest of SEE. Still, FDI is not optimized, but the Slovenes do not seem to be concerned about this. They are doing rather well because of the manufacturing expansion of the 1970 and 1980s created by the workers' self-management program under the old Yugoslav system. Moreover, although their FDI is sizable, they express no particular desire to increase it. As Professor Mencinger has expressed it, "foreign investment is an emergency solution and nothing else. If you cannot

manage your own resources as well as foreigners can, you need foreigners."[5] Still there is a conflict between the politicians who wish to keep the state enterprises state-controlled and the businesses that desire faster privatization so they can expand business activities. No matter how the Slovenes see it, multinational firms do have a better record than national firms on productivity and profitability. Joining the European Union is, however, the goal of both politicians and business people. Slovenia's advantage is also in the fact that outsiders perceive it as a non-Balkan and non-corrupt developed country.

TABLE 3. BALKAN PROFILES

Country	1998 GDP origin			life expectancy	trade[β] % of GDP	PCs[+]	phone main♦ lines	exports to EU % of total
	Agric.	industry	services					
Albania	63	18	19	72	11	NA	31	93
Bulgaria	21	29	50	71	23	2.7	329	53
Croatia	NA	NA	NA	73	45	11.2	348	49
FYROM	12	27	61	73	NA	NA	199	
Romania	18	41	41	69	13	2.7	162	
Slovenia	4	38	58	73	66	25.1	375	77
Turkey	16	27	57	69	19	2.3	254	84
Greece*	9	24	67	78	19	5.2	522	γ

[β] Trade as percent of GDP, purchasing power standards, World Bank, years 1995-98.
*Greek distribution from Roberto Barcellan, *Greece: the twelfth member of the euro-zone*, p. 4.
[+]Per 100 people
♦ Per 1,000 people
γ Greece's trade with EU is considered domestic.
Sources: UN *Human Development Report* 1999; Eurostat (1999), *Key data on Candidate countries*, Memo 10/99; World Bank, *World Development Indicators*; IMF, *Direction of Trade Yearbook*

Perceptions of corruption affect the willingness of multinational enterprises to make long-term commitments in the form of FDI. Whether Balkan politicians are more corrupt than others is not a relevant issue. We are talking here about perceptions that affect the flow of FDI. For example, Transparency International

ranks 99 countries according to perceived corruption. Of all SEE countries, only Slovenia is perceived to be among the developed countries in terms of perceived corruption. In 1999, it ranked 25th, together with Japan. The Czech republic ranked 39, Poland 44, Slovakia 53, Turkey 54, Bulgaria and FYROM 63, Albania 84, and Yugoslavia under the Milosevic regime 90. Even *The Wall Street Journal*, a strong supporter of Turkey, sees corruption as a disease of the Turkish economy. Because of Turkey's financial crisis, the *Journal* published a rather lengthy article, written by James Dorsey, on March 1, 2001, in which Turkish businessmen and academicians discussed corruption on Turkey. There is no doubt that corruption increases the cost of doing business and may prevent foreign capital inflow. All countries face the problem of corruption, but SEE cannot afford to lose in terms of capital inflow. The World Bank (2000b:3)study on SEE emphasizes that "Much of economic development, social inclusion and regional stability in South Eastern Europe will depend on strengthening of institutions, governance and a lowering of the level of corruption." As Table 3 shows, from the point of trade relations, all these Balkan economies are already integrated with EC, but they lag far behind EU in the use of informational technologies. The number of personal computers per 100 inhabitants is low in all candidate countries except Slovenia. Even in the three "fast track" countries, the use of personal computers per 100 inhabitants is very low. Hungary's rate at (7.4), Poland's at (6.2), and the Czech Republic's at (10.7) personal computers per 100 persons also fall short of the EU average of 24.8.

One final aspect of the relative stagnation of SEE is the cost of conflict. Military expenditures as percent of GDP are given in Table 4. The collapse of the Warsaw Pact freed some resources for the civilian-goods industries. All formerly centrally planned economies of Europe reduced their relative shares of military spending. The Balkans are an exception again because, as the outside dangers decreased, the inside conflicts increased in the former Yugoslavia. Each republic now has to provide for its own security. Moreover, ethnic minorities now aspire to build empires. So, again central Europe received a peace dividend, but SEE has to increase its defense spending.

The collapse of the Soviet Union created opportunities for the Turkish military to project itself as the guardian of the secular Turkish state as well as a regional power. The United States under the continuing instrumentalist policies encouraged Turkey to build a more powerful military, although the Turkish people are the only threat to its power. The economic crisis of 2000-2001 has been put aside in favor of a purchase spree for bombers, fighters, submarines and so on.

TABLE 4. BALKAN MILITARY EXPENDITURES AS PERCENT OF GNP (1987-1997)

Year	Bulgaria	FYROM	Greece	Hungary	Romania	Slovenia	Turkey
1987	14.4c		5.2	7.0c	7.2c		3.3
1988	12.2c		5.2	7.0c	6.2c		2.9
1989	11.9c		4.6	6.3c	6.1c		3.1
1990	8.6		4.6	2.0	3.7		3.5
1991	4.0		4.2	2.2	4.0		3.7
1992	3.3		4.4	2.1	3.3	2.3	3.8
1993	2.9		4.4	1.9	2.1	1.7	3.9
1994	2.8	2.2	4.4	1.9	2.5	2.2	4.0
1995	2.7	2.9	4.4	1.5	2.5	2.3	3.9
1996	2.5	3.3	4.5	1.6	1.9	4.0	4.1
1997-	3.0	2.5	4.6	1.9	2.4	5.2	4.0

Source: US Department of State, *World Military Expenditures and Arms Transfers* 1998.

IV. CONCLUDING REMARKS

The transition from central planning to market has been much more painful for the former CPEs of Europe than anticipated. Moreover, there are two distinct paths of adjustment: the economies of Central East Europe and South East Europe have diverged, with the South falling far behind. Attempts at catching up with the pre-1989 economic conditions have been successful in the former case and a failure in the latter. The dichotomy can be explained by certain characteristics of the two regions. First, the initial economic levels were unequal in 1989. The South was economically further behind the rest of Europe. Secondly, and more importantly, the South delayed the introduction of reforms. Unsure about the effects of removing the protection of the state, both Romania and Bulgaria delayed the adjustment process. This fact, combined with the intellectual support of Hungary, Poland, and the Czech Republic in the capitals of Western Europe and North America, discouraged foreign direct investment in the Balkans. The civil strife that followed the dissolution of Yugoslavia, border disputes, and Turkey's ambition to become a regional superpower further delayed the adjustment process. European Union accession is the only hope of lifting the living standards of the area.

ENDNOTES

[1] Disproportionate in terms of the European Union average. Such a comparison is meaningful because all of them aspire to become EU members.

[2] See for example, Botsas 1992 and 1998. "The State and the Market: The Greek Economy on the Eve of Maastricht," in *Balkan Studies*, vol. 33(No. 2), 1992, pp.323-337.

[3] CETE consists of Czech Republic, Hungary, Poland, Slovakia, and Slovenia. SETE consists of Albania, Bosnia and Herzegovina, Bulgaria, Croatia, Romania, The former Yugoslav Republic of Macedonia and Yugoslavia.

[4] The Commission's evaluation can be found in its Agenda 2000 (http://europa.eu.int/comm/dg1a/agenda2000/en/opinions/bulgaria/b21.htm.

REFERENCES

Avineri, Shlomo. 1992. "The End of the Soviet Union and the Return to History," in Michael Keren and Gur Ofer (eds), *Trials of Transition*. Boulder, Co: Westview Press.

Barcellan, Roberto. 2001. *Greece: the twelfth Member of the euro-zone*. Brussels: Eurostat 2/2001

Berlin, Isaiah. 1997. *The Sense of Reality: Studies in Ideas and History*. New York: Farrar, Straus and Giroux.

Botsas, Eleftherios. 1992. "The State and the Market: The Greek Economy on the Eve of Maastricht," *Balkan Studies*, 33, 2: 323-337.

__________. 1998. "The Balkans in Transition," *Balkan Studies*, 39,2:305-322.

__________. 1999. "State Sovereignty, Tribalism, and the Balkan War," George Lasker and Vladimir Lomeiko, Eds. *The Culture of Peace*. International Institute for Advanced Studies, University of Windsor, Windsor, Ontario.

Dorsey, James. 2001. "Success to Anti-Corruption Drive Could be the Key to Turkish recovery, *The Wall Street Journal*. March 1.

Eurostat. 1999, *EU Enlargement: Key Data on Candidate Countries. (Memo 10/99)*. Brussels: Eurostat.Financial Times. 2000. *Country Briefs: Slovenia*.

Fischer, Stanley. 1998. *How Far is Eastern Europe from Brussels?* IMF, Working Papers WP/98/53. Washington, D.C.: The International Monetary Fund.

International Monetary Fund. 2000 (October). *World Economic Outlook*.

____________ (b). 2000. *Direction of Trade Yearbook*.

New York Times. 2001

Organization for Economic Cooperation and Development (OECD). 1998. *Economic Surveys: Romania*.

__________. 1998. *Bulgaria*.

Spulber, Nicolas. 1996. *The State and Economic Development in Eastern Europe*. New York: Random House.United Nations Conference on Trade and Development (UNCTAD). 2000. *World Investment Report: Cross-border Mergers and Acquisitions and Development*. New York: United Nations.

United Nations Economic Commission for Europe (UNECE). 2000. *Economic Survey of Europe*. New York: United Nations.

United Nations Development Programme. 1999. *Human Development Report*. New York: Oxford University Press.

United States State Department. 1998. *Military Expenditures and Arms Transfers*. Washington, D.C.: Government Printing Office.

World Bank (a). 2000. *World Development Report 2000/2001*. New York: Oxford University Press.

__________ (b). 2000. *The Road to Stability and Prosperity in South Eastern Europe: A Regional Strategy Paper*. Washington, D.C.: The World bank.

__________ (c). 2000. *World Development Indicators*.

CHAPTER 10
SOUTHEASTERN EUROPE: PROSPECTS FOR INCREASED ECONOMIC INTEGRATION

Bob Donnorummo
University of Pittsburgh

INTRODUCTION

For the last two centuries, the concepts of Southeastern Europe (SE E) and integration have rarely been linked. Indeed, given the history of conflict in this region, and more recently the violence of the 1990s, SE E and integration seem to be oxymoronic notions. Nonetheless, this chapter asks if changes in the last two decades have created circumstances whereby increased economic integration is more probable. These changes are: (1) Greece's entry, and the consideration of other countries in the region for entry, into the European Union (EU); (2) the revolutions of 1989 which began the transformation to democracy and capitalism for the former communist countries in the region, with exception of Yugoslavia whose transformation was delayed until 2000; and (3) the continuing advance of technology and its impact on changing the conditions necessary for developing countries to reach sustainable economic development.

The position taken in this chapter is that these changes have increased the likelihood of greater economic cooperation despite the region's historic lack of economic integration and the significant political and cultural differences and tensions that exist among the countries involved. Nonetheless, increased economic integration, technological change, and economic development do not exist in a political vacuum. The principal threat to expanded economic integration is political, or more specifically, the inability to sustain improvement in Greek-Turkish relations and the presence of a large unstable area in the middle of Southeast Europe, namely Yugoslavia. While, the recent electoral victory of Vojislav Kostunica (October 2000) and subsequently the popular uprising which removed Slobodan Milosevic from power have given raise to hopes that Yugoslavia will be a positive force in the reconstruction of the region's political stability and economic development, the situation in Kosovo and Macedonian-FYROM remains very fluid.

Ten countries are included in this particular definition of Southeastern Europe. There is no need to be unduly rigid in determining which countries are in part of SE E and which are not since this type of debate tends to be rhetorical and detracts from the principal arguments about economic integration. The ten countries selected for analysis are: Croatia, Macedonia-FYROM, Bosnia-

Herzegovina, Yugoslavia, Albania, Romania, Bulgaria, Greece, Turkey and Cyprus.

The principal motivation for including these ten countries is that they are contiguous and have sufficiently common economic agendas; that is, they are neighbors and face similar challenges and opportunities. It was *not* because they have similar cultures and a history of cooperation. Re-arranging the members of this regional identification on the basis of similar cultures and friendly relations can be justified for some purposes, but this discussion is limited to economic integration and therefore other criteria were employed.[1] For example, Catholic Croatia could be excluded and paired with Slovenia and central Europe for a number of reasons, but Slovenia is already well on its way to integration with the European Union (EU), and Croatia has close economic, linguistic, and cultural ties to other countries in SE E. One could reasonably include Moldova in this group. Also, Greece, Cyprus, and Turkey are included because of their shared economic interests, not their level of political cooperation. I would suggest that while one must certainly be aware of and account for historical traditions and political relations, geography and common issues of economic development are the paramount variables. The fires that swept through SE E in the summer of 2000 did not consider whether they were destroying Catholic, Orthodox, or Muslim properties. They were the result of similar weather patterns and geographic proximity. The reasoning for defining SE E as the above noted ten countries is similarly based on geography and the needs of these ten countries for sustainable economic development.

Selecting countries by primarily geographic and economic factors opens the door to criticism that political-economic analysis is sometimes insensitive to critical cultural differences. This criticism has been justifiably leveled at Marxists and neo-liberals alike. My own beliefs come closest to the neo-liberal camp, but do not ignore the importance of cultural differences in assessing the needs of a country or region. My neo-liberal views are going to favor free trade and open borders for Foreign Direct Investment, but they are not going to diminish the role of specific historical determinants nor the power of individual states. The author's positions do not posit undue faith in the market and thus advocate the presence of weak political entities in the misguided belief that economic development should be only the work of non-state actors. It is held that economic development in SE E will be assisted by the presence of strong and effective governments, the continued enhancement of free market activities, a closer relationship with the EU (and eventual membership for many of these countries), and enhanced regional economic integration.

GLOBALIZATION AND REGIONALISM

The undeniable presence of increasing global economic integration has given raise to several misconceptions about its impact. It is often incorrectly assumed that globalization will lead to economic homogenization (for a thoughtful rejection of this idea, see Gray 1998). Also, discussions of the global economy usually do not give sufficient focus to cultural, political, and economic backlashes (Friedman 1999). Furthermore, there is sometimes a tendency to overstate the demise of the powers of the nation-state and unduly enhance the power of regionalism. As is usually the case, there are elements of truth in each of the above misconceptions, but they are exaggerated to the point of distortion.

Global economic integration as measured by the levels of foreign trade, Foreign Direct Investment (FDI), the activities of multinational corporations, and technologically driven connectedness is indeed a powerful actor in the world today. Furthermore, regional economic zones transcend some aspects of the Westphalian concept of the sovereign state. These regional associations and "the emergence of a new global economy raise(s) the specter that the old bases of territorial affiliation will be shattered" (Kaplan 1999: 42). While the state remains, and will remain for some time to come, the most relevant political entity, the trend is that some of the powers previously held as a monopoly of the state are being ceded to regional common markets and global forces (multinational firms and advanced technology) and that some traditional attitudes and identities may have to be altered in order to accommodate affiliations which extend beyond the individual state. One example would be the controls over its economy that Greece relinquished when it entered the European Monetary Union (EMU) on 1 January 2001.

It would be unwise to discuss the economic integration of SE E without noting the central role of the European Union (EU) and its planned expansion. Furthermore, the saliency of the EU, as well as the impact of the global economy, will increasingly be critical variables in the future. Heightened regionalism within Europe, the presence of transition economies with open markets and privatized assets which facilitate foreign trade and investment, as well as advanced technologies that have little respect for geographic boundaries have all converged to make economic integration in SE E more probable, and more necessary.

A world in which e-mail and the Internet connect billions of people, products, and ideas in different countries with a speed that past generations could not have imaged is indeed a new development. For example, in the mid-1980s, there were several thousand computers connected to the Internet, but by the end of the century that figure was over 50 million. The relative importance

of foreign trade and FDI (for both advanced and developing countries) has grown to reach uncharted territory in the 1990s. While foreign trade rose throughout the 19th century from about 4% to 11% of the world's GDP, the trade barriers following World War I caused that figure to drop significantly and only to return to pre-1914 levels by 1970. However, since 1980 foreign trade has grown to equal 15.5% of the world's GDP, despite the fact that the GDP has itself increased six-fold (Scott 1998, 25-29). The lowering of tariffs as a result of the World Trade Association and the growth of regional custom unions (EU, NAFTA or MERCOSUR) has had a positive impact on the level of foreign trade, as has the expanded presence of multinational firms. In the 1980s, there were roughly some 7,000 multinationals in the world's 15 most developed countries, but by the end of the 1990s this figure reached 40,000 (United Nations, 2000, 8, 10). The largest 38,000 multinational firms in the G-7 countries tripled in value (in dollars) between 1985 and 1994, and their intra-firm foreign trade levels are significant. Some scholars (Dunning 1998) estimate that multinationals are directly and indirectly responsible for over one-half of all foreign trade. Surely the impact of 63,000 multinational corporations in 1999 is too great to be ignored.

There is also a connection between advanced technology and multinationals in the area of FDI. The significantly up-graded quality of relatively inexpensive, almost instantaneous information available to corporations enables them to place production and services at multiple sites, often in other countries, manage these facilities at low costs,[2] be closer to customers, thereby reduce transportation expenses, and generally maximizing efficiencies and profits. Their investments are likely to have important economic ramifications (directly and indirectly via domestic suppliers and technological spin-offs) for the host countries, specifically for the emerging or developing economies of SE E. FDI and intra-firm trade have a positive impact on increasing the developing host country's ability to export more "human-capital intensive" goods. It has been estimated in 1996 that over three-quarters of Hungary's exports of manufactured goods were from foreign owned firms (Smith 2000: 182).

Today's high level of global economic integration is readily apparent from the stunning increases in FDI. FDI in-flows increased seven fold between 1980 and 1995; accumulated FDI stock has expanded from $700 to $1.7 tr., becoming "the principal vehicle of the deeper integration of the world economy" (Rienicke 1998: 3). This upward trajectory has been maintained in the last seven years despite the unfavorable investment climates in developing and emerging markets since the "Asian crisis" beginning in the fall of 1997 and the melt down of the Russian economy in August 1998. In 1999, total global FDI inflows reached $865 billion, which was a 27% increase over 1998 (United Nations 2000: 3).

In 1980, global outflows and inflows of FDI stocks was 10% of the world's GDP, but in 1999 it tripled to 31% (United Nations 2000: 17).

While 37.2% of all FDI in-flows went to developing countries in 1997, this was dominated by a few countries, especially China and Brazil. Given the increasing importance of technological and communication infrastructures to the profitability of FDI, there is no guarantee that this money will continue to flow into developing economies like those in SE E. In fact, the percentage of FDI (but not the absolute value) targeted for developing countries has sharply decreased since 1997. Also, FDI will not be a "kick-start" for economic development unless host countries are prepared for its effective utilization (Meyer 1998). Nonetheless, developing economies have increased annual FDI in-flows from $12 bl. in 1986 to $108 bl. in 1995 (Meyer 1998), and $208 bl. in 1999 (United Nations 2000: 3). In terms of the transforming economies of eastern Europe and the former Soviet Union, FDI was modest in the early 1990s, but has since become an increasingly important factor in the transition process (United Nations 1998:162, and Financial Times Survey 1998a). FDI in SE E will be discussed in greater detail below, but at this point suffice it to say that FDI is an important aspect of the new constellation of forces which determine the ability of developing and emerging markets to reach sustainable economic growth and which also leads to increased regional and global integration.

ECONOMIC INTEGRATION IN SOUTHEASTERN EUROPE

The economic advantages of regionalism and the powerful presence of the EU and its planned expansion, the newly opened markets and privatized assets of SE E, the generally enhanced conditions for FDI in the 1990s, as well as technology advancements which serve to increase trade and the reach of multinational firms all point to the probability of enhanced economic integration in SE E.

The strongest economy in the region, Greece, has been a member of the EU since 1981. While it has experienced economic growth since joining the EU, Greece's relative lack of restructuring and the continued dominant role of the state in the economy has not allowed it to experience the exceptional growth enjoyed by Ireland or Spain after their entrance (World Bank 1999: 18). However, Greece's membership in the EU, and especially its drive to join the EMU in January 2001, have placed restrictions on the leadership's previously undisciplined approach to managing the economy and provided Greece with a strong market for its exports, agricultural stability, and significant funds for infrastructure projects.[3] In sum, Greece has become more of a regional player

and since the early 1990s it has become a leading force in the economic development of SE E.

The spirit and letter of the rules governing EU membership do not only affect Greece, even though it is presently the only SE E country in the EU. Of the ten countries included in this discussion, Cyprus is in the first tier of countries slated for inclusion, while Bulgaria, Romania, and Turkey are in the second tier and will probably soon be joined by Croatia. Hence, six of the ten countries of the region will someday (but, except for Greece and Cyprus, probably not before 2010) be members of the EU. The entrance date is important, but one cannot under estimate the magnitude of the impact of the accessional process on these economies while they are in the process of satisfying EU rules for membership. The impact of the EU includes: pressure on the aspiring members to maintain strict monetary policies; access on equal footing to the large EU market for their goods and services; the need to restructure their industries to become more competitive, which will include expanding the privatization process as well as increasing efficiencies, often requiring a reduction in the number of workers at a firm; modernizing the agricultural sector in order to compete with EU countries; and the continued opening of their economies to external trade and investment. EU membership should also allow the relevant countries of SE E to take advantage of agricultural subsidies and increased funds for needed infrastructure improvements, although the present status of the EU's Common Agricultural Policy and Structural Funds will probably be altered and the conditions for the entering countries is not known at this time.

It is necessary to make three points about the relationship between the EU and SE E. First, the level of economic integration within SE E is presently very low (Cetinic 1999). In the mid-1990s, relatively little foreign trade of the countries of SE E was intra-regional, while most depended on the EU for anywhere from about 30% (Romania) to over 60% (Greece) of their imports and exports (Gianaris 1996: 143). Second, while Greece is the strongest economy in the region, it is still a relatively small emerging market; the impact of its economic leadership on the region cannot equated with the impact of Germany throughout eastern Europe nor with Scandinavia on the Baltic countries. Third, the EU may be important for the countries of SE E since it receives from one-quarter to two-thirds of their exports, depending on the country, but SE E is *not* economically important to the EU for whom trade with SE E makes up less than 1% of its total foreign trade (Tsoukalis 1994). Therefore, while the impact of the EU is and will continue to be very important, the key basic ingredients for

sustainable economic growth in SE E will remain internal restructuring (as is usually the case) and increased intra-regional cooperation.

OBSTACLES TO ECONOMIC INTEGRATION

The first and most critical set of obstacles to economic integration are political, often connected to long standing and continuing conflicts and feelings of mistrust that exist among the peoples of SE E. If these conflicts, real and potential, cannot be neutralized, or if feelings of aggregate mistrust cannot be reduced (Gallagher 2000), ordinarily persuasive arguments for increased integration based on economic rationality will have little saliency. While analyses of the prospects for sustainable economic growth in emerging or developing countries have not sufficiently focused on the damaging impact of nationalism which has been a primary motivating factor for conflicts and mistrust (Donnorummo 2000), this chapter is not the appropriate place for an extended discussion of this important variable. Yet it must be noted that the need for intra-regional political stability in SE E is an undeniable prerequisite for increased economic integration.

SE E, and especially the term Balkans, have become synonymous with conflict, and the media has been quick to conclude that this is an area of the world where people have fought with each other throughout history. This is far from a full and accurate picture since the various peoples of SE E have also shown an ability to cooperate and live together, or at least co-exist. Furthermore, scholars like Misha Glenny (2000) have noted the important role of the West in exploiting and fanning the flames of mistrust among the peoples living in the region. Recognition of nationalistic differences in SE E is needed to underscore its continued importance, but it is also important to note that its existence is not necessarily an intractable condition which will forever prevent increased economic integration.

It is clear that serious issues of internal and trans-national conflicts remain on the agenda for SE E. The tensions (albeit seemingly reduced of late) between Greece and Turkey over a number of issues and particularly Cyprus, as well as the deep scars left from the recent fighting in Croatia, Bosnia-Herzegovina, and Kosovo are acute obstacles to integration. The spill-over effects from potential internal conflicts in Yugoslavia (Montenegro), Bosnia-Herzegovina, Macedonia-FYROM, or the Kurds in Turkey could also produce dangerous, negative centrifugal forces negatively impacting the entire region. One of the most serious obstacles to regional economic integration, sanctions against an ostracized Yugoslavia, has been greatly reduced since the removal from power of Slobodan Milosevic. Prior to the dramatic events in the autumn of 2000, Yugoslavia was

accurately described as a blank spot on the canvas of a painting attempting to envision increased regional integration (Wagstyl and Buchan 2000). Now that dangerous blank spot is being replaced by numerous hopeful signs which suggest that, while the difficulties for Yugoslavia and the region are far from over, at least the foundation for increased political and economic stability and interaction with Europe and SE E is now in place (Kaplan 2000).

One can point to several additional signs which suggest that politics might not stand in the way of increased economic integration in the coming decades. For example, a regime change through the ballot box in Croatia in 2000 produced a more integrative-friendly climate for cooperation with the EU and neighboring states (Financial Times Survey 2000c). The decision of Greece and the EU to place Turkey on the list of accession countries is also encouraging. It has been insightfully noted that, in the long run, it is in Greece's best interest if Turkey is Euro-centered rather than an Islamic state isolated from Europe (Tsoukalis 1994). Greece has also shown that disruptive bilateral disputes can be resolved, as was the case with its sanctions against Macedonia-FYROM. Furthermore, as discussed below, intra-regional trade and FDI, while modest, are growing.

In addition to political obstacles, there are important barriers to increased economic integration which stem from the fact that these are poor countries and, in some cases, economies where agricultural production represent a large share of the GDP, thereby generally reducing the variety of goods and services available for foreign trade. While these factors are not going to disappear in the near future, they need not impose insurmountable barriers to expanded integration.

In terms of GDP per capita, these are poor countries relative to the EU (about 25% of the EU average). Their GDP per capita wealth ranges on a US dollar exchange rate basis in 1997 from the very wealthy to extremely poor. The wealthiest country in the group is Cyprus, excluding the Turkish section, followed by Greece (the poorest of the existing EU countries with a per capita GDP of about $9,000), the Turkish part of Cyprus and Croatia (about $4,000), Turkey (at $3,500), Romania, Bulgaria, Macedonia-FYROM and Bosnia-Herzegovina between ($1,000 and $1,500), Yugoslavia (estimated at $800 but maybe actually closer to $500), and Albania (with only $700). There are also high levels of unemployment in all the states of the former Yugoslavia, as well as Albania, Romania, and Bulgaria. Inflation has long been a serious problem in Turkey. Inflation can be reduced much easier than the high rates of unemployment because many of these countries have significant redundant industrial labor forces which need to be reduced as their firms are modernized and restructured. Also, Albania, Bosnia-Herzegovina, Macedonia-FYROM, and

Turkey have rapidly growing populations. This makes the need for job growth even more essential. The Croatian economy has been stagnate for two decades, and in the last decade the former communist countries of SE E have lost a significant part of the GDP. Between 1989 and 1997, the Romanian economy shrunk by about 18% (but even more since 1997), Albania by 21%, Macedonia-FYROM by 32%, Bulgaria by 37%, and Yugoslavia by 50% (but again more since 1997) (United Nations 1998).

This low level of economic development signifies that these countries have a weak position relative to EU countries in terms of non-farm goods available for export, level of technology, as well as transportation, financial, and other infrastructures. It also reflects inefficiencies in their industrial facilities, services, and farms that will be forced to complete on the European and global markets. This lower level of wealth and economic development increases the urgency of continuing to trade with and seek investments from the EU, while *at the same time* developing additional intra-regional networks where they will have the advantages of geographic proximity and fewer of the disadvantages of competing with more efficient economies of the EU.

In terms of the structures of the economies of the region, there is again a wide range but one that is generally much more heavily weighted toward agriculture than is the case with the existing EU countries. While less than 10% of Croatia's economy is dependent on agriculture, in 1997 the figures were higher with Bulgaria (14%) and Turkey (15% but a very large 46% of the people are employed in an inefficient and heavily subsidized agricultural sector), Greece (17%), Romania (19%), and continues up the scale with Bosnia-Herzegovina, Macedonia-FYROM, and Albania. Yet it should be noted that there has been a steady decline in the relative importance of agriculture in these economies over the last half century. Except for Albania and Bosnia-Herzegovina, the majority of people in the region live in urban areas, and in some cases (Bulgaria, Greece, Croatia, and Macedonia-FYROM) over 60% live in cities (Bogosavljevic 1999: 106). Nonetheless, the large farm populations in countries like Turkey and Romania, which may have negative feelings about opening their domestic market to imported foreign goods, might cause the push for entrance into the EU to result in spirited political debates. Conversely, the EU is justifiably concerned about the expense associated with adding poor, agricultural exporting countries to their ranks.

Outside of agriculture, several other conditions should be noted. Much of the industrial base of the former communist countries is in general disrepair and in need of either liquidation or technological modernization. Also, as discussed briefly below, the countries of SE E, especially Turkey, are energy deficient.

On the positive side, they have well educated work forces whose strengths have not yet been effectively utilized. Furthermore, Cyprus has developed a niche for itself in the financial service sector, and Cyprus, Greece, Turkey, and Croatia have developed tourism as an important and profitable part of their economies, for example, 25% of the Croatian GDP in 2000. Also, people in these four countries possess strong market oriented skills. However, these same skills are just beginning to surface in Bulgaria, Romania, Albania, and Macedonia-FYROM where they were not employed under communism. The economies of Kosovo and Bosnia-Herzegovina are heavily dependent on foreign aid which cannot be a long range solution to their underdevelopment. On balance, the problem is one of relatively low economic development and the presence of large agricultural sectors which produce similar goods not conducive to high levels of foreign trade.

MEASURING ECONOMIC INTEGRATION

In this section the focus will be on foreign trade and FDI as measures of economic integration. Both are very useful indicators, but do not reflect the entirety of economic integration. As noted above, historically and at present, there is surprising little trade amongst these contiguous countries. Relative poverty, large agricultural sectors, war, and political divisions have all worked to keep intra-regional trade low. However, the tearing down of the Berlin Wall in 1989 set in motion a series of important developments for many of the countries of the region and these developments are having a generally positive impact on foreign trade and FDI. Yet, following the collapse of communism in the region, there remain severe disruptions in foreign trade patterns in the region and these disruptions have had a negative impact on particular national economies. For example, Bulgaria was no longer able to depend on the Soviet Union to buy its often inferior goods. Almost one-third of Bulgaria's exports of value-added machinery and equipment in the 1980s was in the form of poor quality computers sold to the Soviet Union (Smith 2000: 157). With the collapse of the Soviet Union, this market no longer existed, and Bulgaria lost its market for computers and many other goods. This was a severe blow to its economy, but one which also begs for enhanced economic relations with the other countries in SE E. In addition to rearranging trading patterns from east to west, the former communist countries, as well as Greece and Turkey, but for different reasons, began to privatize their economies. The end of the restrictive former communist trading bloc and the privatization of enterprises in SE E have contributed to expanded foreign trade and FDI in the 1990s.

Examples of expanded foreign trade include Greece's trade with Albania which was a mere $12.2 ml. in 1991 but quickly reached $221 ml. in 1994 (Gianaris 1996: 58). While second in importance to Italy, by 1998 Greece's share of Albania's foreign trade had grown to the point that almost 30% of all Albania's imports came from Greece (Financial Times Survey 2000a). Greece's total trade with the Balkan countries jumped from only $240 ml. in 1989 to $1.4 bl. in 1996 (Triantaphyllou 1999), and represents about 20% of its total foreign trade. While the economies of eastern Europe have been opened up in the 1990s with a doubling of their foreign trade levels between 1991 and 1997, these are nonetheless small and relatively poor countries and the sums involved are not large.

Table 1. Foreign Trade, 1997, in millions of US dollars

	Exports	Imports	Major Trading Partners, %
Albania	.2	.7	Italy (47%), Greece (21%)
Bosnia-Herzegovina	.6	2.2	Croatia (34%), Slovenia (16%)
Bulgaria	4.9	4.6	EU (43%)
Croatia	8.2	11.4	Italy (21%), Germany (18%)
Greece	5.4	23.7	East Europe (21%), Germany (19%)
Macedonia	1.2	1.6	EU (43%), Ex-Yugoslavia (28%)
Romania	9.8	12.4	Italy (22%), Germany (17%)
Yugoslavia	2.7	4.8	East Europe (33%), Bosnia-H. (19%)

Source: Cetinic (1999: 125-126)[4]

There is not a single country of the region for whom trade within the region was larger than its trade with the EU in 1997, including then sanctioned Yugoslavia (see Table 1). The general pattern was 60% of foreign trade with the EU, and an average of only about 25% with other SE E countries (Cetinic 1999: 126-127). It has been justifiably conclude that "the Balkans as an economic region is practically non-existent" (Cetinic 1999:128).

The trade between the countries of SE E and the EU is rather heavily weighted in favor of the EU. In 1997, only Bulgaria had more exports than imports with the EU, and this was largely the result of Bulgaria's post-1996 economic downturn which caused it to lack the funds to import goods from the EU. In 1997, Turkey, for example, imported $10.5 bl. more than it exported

to the EU. Countries like Croatia, which had a $3 bl. negative trade balance with the EU (all trade data from Cetinic 1999: 127), would do well to increase its trade with SE E countries in order to help address this foreign trade imbalance. Increasing exports to the EU is both necessary and possible, but will not become a reality until a number of conditions develop in SE E countries: internal restructuring resulting in more efficient firms; increased FDI expanding trade within and between larger multinational companies; developing niche activities which would include tourism and shifts in the agricultural sector to more specialized production of such items as perhaps olive oil in Croatia, wines in Bulgaria, Croatia, and Romania, or organic foods in Turkey.

Intra-regional FDI is a very important ingredient for increasing intra-regional trade. Although FDI is aided to a limited degree by cultural similarities (Meyer 1998), the more salient variable is the degree of political risk involved. This means that while there are positive geographical and cultural reasons for Greece's relatively aggressive FDI in SE E (Financial Times Survey 1998b), reduced political risks are the paramount factor, in allowing for the expansion of FDI which is a decision based on the ability to enhance profits, which in turn requires political stability. The combination of somewhat reduced political risks and the lure of the large Turkish market (70 million people) has led to an increase in Greece's trade activity with Turkey. Greece's trade with Turkey increased from $221 ml. in 1995 to over $1 bl. in 2000. While the growth is impressive, it still represents less than 4% of Greece's total exports and a mere 1.5% of its imports. Nonetheless, the trend is encouraging, and there exists the possibility for expanded Greek FDI in banking, energy, and infrastructure projects in Turkey (Financial Times Survey 2000d). Turkey has also become a more active participant in outward FDI, and again political stability is a key factor. An empirical study of Turkish firms that invested abroad showed that while Turkey's cultural ties with Central Asia were important,[5] the most important factor in deciding whether to invest was the potential for profit and the quality of governmental relations; both were more important than cultural or linguistic similarities (Demirbag, Gunes, & Mirza 1998). This type of decision making underscores the fact that if political risks can be reduced, the opportunities for increased intra-regional FDI will be based on the prospects for profit, not traditional likes or dislikes.

FDI flow into the transforming former communist countries of eastern Europe is another component of the regional prospects for enhanced economic integration. The level of FDI in eastern Europe was modest in the first half of the 1990s, but grew substantially in the second half of the decade. At first, only Hungary and to a lesser extent the Czech Republic were attracting significant amounts of FDI, but after 1998, Poland became the area's leader in absolute

terms. In 1997, Hungary was number one in terms of FDI per capita ($1,548), followed by the Czech Republic ($838) and Estonia ($760). The comparable per capita figures for SE E are Croatia ($259), Bulgaria ($105), Romania ($97), Albania ($97), and Macedonia ($24) (United Nations 1998: 163). The only large investor, besides Greece, in SE E is the South Korean carmaker Daewoo which invested over $550 ml. in Romania in 1996. However, given Daewoo's severe financial problems at the end of the 1990s, their position in SE E is a very doubtful base for further investments. The principal investors in the countries of eastern Europe are Germany, US, and Austria. While in 1994 the FDI stock in eastern Europe represented only .7% of United States' FDI and 2.3% of Germany's, Austria has a much more focused eastern European approach since this region is responsible for 30.9% of its outward FDI stock (Meyer 1998: 35). There is not much intra-regional investment in SE E. For example, while Greece is the second largest investor in Albania in 1997 (Italy is first), the six largest investors in Bulgaria are all from outside SE E, and the seven largest investors in Romania also are outside the region (Meyer 1998: 12). Some improvements in intra-regional FDI are noticeable in the data for 1999. Greece moved up to be the fourth largest foreign investor in Bulgaria; Croatia was the second largest foreign investor in Bosnia-Herzegovina, and Cyprus was the largest and Greece the fifth largest foreign investor in Macedonia-FYROM. Yet Croatia had virtually no FDI from other SE E countries; and while Cyprus was the third largest foreign investor in Romania,[6] the only other SE E countries investing in Romania were Turkey (10th) and Greece (13th) (United Nations 2000: 226).

As with foreign trade, Greece's FDI in SE E has increased dramatically throughout the 1990s. These are interconnected phenomena. By 1996, there were over 3,000 Greek firms investing in SE E. In that same year, over 1,000 Greek firms had invested in Bulgaria and were responsible for about 10% of that country's FDI, yet that was well behind the level of German investment. Greece's relatively small $65 ml. investment in Albania did, however, represent 27% of that country's total FDI in 1996. Also the 300,000 Albanians living in Greece send home about $400,000 in remittances (Triantaphyllou 1999).

While the levels of intra-regional FDI are modest, there is a base being formed and Greece's total investment of about $3 bl. is leading the way (Financial Times Survey 1999b; 2000d). While Greece has provided public funds for aid and incentives for external investments, the main players are private firms; especially telecommunications, led by the Hellenic Telecommunications Organization (OTE), which have committed about $1.5 bl. to Bulgaria, Romania, and Yugoslavia. The dispute over the name Macedonia did not stop Greece's largest bank, National Bank of Greece, from investing in Macedonia-FYROM's largest bank or Hellenic Petroleum from building a

pipeline connecting Thessaloniki to Skopje. Another component of Greece's FDI in SE E, and beyond, is its participation in the Black Sea Trade and Development Bank located in Thessaloniki. Greece, Russia, and Turkey are the largest shareholders in this bank.

Putting Greek FDI in SE E in perspective, one should note that it is a sensible and substantial initiative by the Greek government and its private sector, and that it is part of the puzzle for constructing a foundation for increased economic integration for the region. Nonetheless, it should also be recognized that the Greek economy is not capable of shouldering the entire burden and that other factors need to play a positive role in order to make expanded integration a reality. One such factor is the region's absence of energy sources. In the process of supplying Turkey and the other countries of SE E with oil and natural gas, a large number of regional energy and infrastructure projects will be realized that will increase external and intra-regional FDI and will contribute to increased foreign trade and interdependence of energy sources.

A focus on the energy issue itself would move the present discussion beyond SE E, specifically to the east, the Caspian Sea. It would also require an emphasis on foreign policy and pipeline plans. Since these issues are beyond the scope of this chapter, this discussion will be limited to a few salient points and examples.

The energy needs of SE E are critical because the region has limited domestic sources. This situation is compounded by several other related developments. Bulgaria gets about 40% of its energy from a dangerous source, the outdated and unsafe nuclear facility at Kozlodui. Greece's energy is dependent on natural gas from Russia via the Yarmal-Europe pipeline and wants to secure alternate suppliers. Yet the largest single determinant of the region's energy future is the seemingly unsatiable appetite for oil and gas of the rapidly growing Turkish population. The almost 70 ml. people of Turkey are increasing their energy consumption 7% per year. In 20 years, it will expand more than four fold. Presently, primary domestic energy production accounts for 38% of Turkey's needs, but by 2010 domestic sources will meet only 29% of its needs. Turkey's consumption is now equivalent to 76 million tons of oil per year, but this will increase to 179 million by 2010 (Arikan 2000: 194). In sum, Turkish hydro-powered electricity and coal (predominantly low quality lignite) will not be able to service the needs of its growing population and modernizing economy. Hence, a variety of external factors will become increasingly important, and this could be directly and indirectly positive for increased economic integration in SE E.

Electrical grid connections between Turkey and Europe are not yet in place, but feasibility studies exist, and there is hope for Turkey's inclusion in the

future. Presently, Turkey has an agreement to purchase electricity from Bulgaria in return for Turkish infrastructure investments in Bulgaria (Arikan 2000). Turkey is also at the center of a variety of plans for oil and gas pipelines. In addition to the proposed Baku-Tbilisi-Ceyhan pipeline, there is a Turkmenistan-Turkey-Europe gas line and the "Blue Stream" project which would bring gas from Russia to Turkey via lines underneath the Black Sea. This movement of oil and gas from the Caspian Sea to Europe places Turkey and SE E in a very pivotal position.

Greece is also involved in the transmission of oil out of the Caspian Sea. This involves the movement of Caspian oil along the existing pipeline to Novorossiysk in Russia to Burgas, Bulgaria, to be connected via a $1 bl. pipeline to Alexandroupolis. Greece also plays an important role in the integration of SE E via the construction of two highways in northern Greece that would more conveniently link people and goods throughout SE E and the region to central Europe. In addition to EU support for highways, it also contributes to the construction of the new airport in Athens which will serve as a transportation hub for the region. The new airport, Eleftherios Venizelos, began its operation in the spring of 2001.

CONCLUSION

The catalysts to economic integration in SE E are the EU, Greece, and Turkey. The principal mechanisms for increased economic integration will be intra-regional FDI, which will be an important component for expanded intra-regional foreign trade. There has been a modest expansion of cooperative economic activities in the 1990s, but enhanced future intra-regional activity is necessary and quite probable. The efforts and impact of the EU and Greece in the 1990s have been encouraging, but continued and deepened integration will to a large extent depend on the ability of Greece and Turkey to restructure and make their own economies more efficient, to jointly reduce bi-lateral tensions, and to play major roles in the rebuilding of the economies of the region.

In addition to the importance of Greek-Turkish relations, there must be political stability and expanded cooperation between countries inside and outside of the region with Yugoslavia. The outcomes of both situations will be largely determined by the people of Greece, Turkey, and Yugoslavia, but it is advisable for external actors (US, Russia, EU, and NATO) to be involved and pro-active. The economic carrots held out by accession to the EU are providing incentives for changes that encourage increased economic regional integration, which is seen as the most effective vehicle for SE E's chances of prosperity and stability in the future.

ENDNOTES

[1] These ten countries suggested as a Southeastern European unit are both similar and different from variety of organizational lists and schema. For example, the establishment in 1996 of the US inspired Southeast European Cooperative Initiative (SECI) includes Hungary, Slovenia, and Moldova, but not Cyprus and, for political reasons, not Yugoslavia. The US Overseas Private Investment Corporation's business development fund includes Slovenia and Montenegro, but not Yugoslavia, and excludes Cyprus and Greece. Two points need to be made. The inclusion of countries in Southeastern Europe as defined in this chapter is not based on domestic or international political concerns, and the list is subject to reasonable changes.

[2] Horst Siebert (1999: 8) employs a dramatic example to demonstrate technology's impact on reducing costs for the multinational firm in the global economy. In 1930 a three minute telephone call to London cost $250, in 1950 that call cost $50, but in 1990 in was only $3.32. In 2000 e-mail and internet usage has reduced even that low figure.

[3] Greece's net contribution from the EU presently totals about 4% of its GDP.

[4] Taken from Cetinic (1999), Tables 1, 2 and 3, 125-126, who used data from Deutsche Bank Research.

[5] The data are from Demirbag, Gunes & Mirza (1998) and were based on a comprehensive survey of Turkish firms. The data also show that despite the focus on Turkey's FDI in Central Asia, in 1994 its external investments were substantial only in Kazakhstan and that Turkey's primary location for foreign investment was the UK. Besides the UK, Turkey invested more heavily in Germany, the US and the Netherlands than in any other Central Asian state besides Kazakhstan.

[6] The original source of much of the money invested by financial entities in Cyprus was from some other country. This is referred to as "round-tripping." About 4% of all FDI in central and eastern Europe are from financial institutions based in Cyprus, but a higher percentage for SE E and still higher for Russia.

REFERENCES

Arikan, Y. 2000. "Energy Issues and Opportunities for Turkey." In F. Altmann & J. Lampe, eds., *Energy and the Transformation Process in Southeast Europe*. Gutershol: Bertelsmann. 193-204.

Bogosavljevic, Srdjan 1999, "South Eastern Europe and Demographic Ethnocentrism." In J. Melinic, ed., *South Eastern Europe 2000: A View from Serbia*. Belgrade: Stubovi kulture. 105-121.

Cetinic, Goran 1999. "Distortions in Trade Flows." In J. Milinic, ed., *South Eastern Europe 2000: A View From Serbia*. Belgrade: Stubovi kulture. 123-134.

Demirbag, M., R. Gunes & H. Mirza 1998. "Political Risk Management: A Case Study of Turkish Companies in Central Asia and Russia." In H. Mirza, ed., *Global Competitive Strategies in the New World Economy: Multilateralism and the Transnational Firm*. Cheltenham, UK: Edward Elgar. 284-309.

Donnorummo, Bob 2000. "Emerging Markets and the Process of Globalization." In M. McMullen, B. Donnorummo and J. Mauch, eds., *Higher Education and Emerging Markets*. New York: Routledge Former. 3-24.

Dunning, John, ed. 1998. *Globalization, Trade and Foreign Investment*. Oxford, UK: Elsevier

Financial Times Survey. 1998a. "Investing in Central and Eastern Europe," *FINANCIAL TIMES*, 8 May.

__________. 1998b. "Greece and South-East Europe," *FINANCIAL TIMES*, 1 June.

__________. 1999a. "Turkey: Finance and Industry." *FINANCIAL TIMES*, 22 November.

__________. 1999b. "Greece," *FINANCIAL TIMES*, 21 December.

__________. 2000a. "Albania," *FINANCIAL TIMES*, 23 February.

__________. 2000b. "Turkey: Infrastructure." *FINANCIAL TIMES*, 5 April.

__________. 2000c. "Croatia," *FINANCIAL TIMES*, 22 June.

__________. 2000d. "Greece," *FINANCIAL TIMES*, 13 December.

Friedman, Thomas. 1999. *The Lexus and the Olive Tree*. New York: Farrar, Starus and Giroux.

Gallagher, Tom. 2000. "Nationalism and Democracy in South-East Europe." In Geoffery Pridham and Tom Gallagher, eds., *Experimenting with Democracy: Regime Change in the Balkans*. London: Routledge. 84-111.

Gianaris Nicholas. 1996. *Geopolitical and Economic Change in the Balkan Countries*. Newport, CT: Praeger.

Glenny, Misha. 2000. *The Balkans*. New York: Viking.

Gray, J. 1998. *False Dawn: The Delusions of Global Capitalism*. New York: The New Press.

Kaplan, David 1999. "Territorial Identities and Geographic Scale." In Herb Gutman and David. Kaplan, eds., *Nested Nationalities: Nationalism, Territory and Scale*. London: Rowman and Littlefield Publishers, Inc. 31-49.

Kaplan, Robert. 2000. "Yugoslavia's Fate, and Europe's," *THE NEW YORK TIMES*. 6 October, A31.

Meyer, Klaus. 1998. *Direct Foreign Investment in Economies in Transition*. Cheltenham, UK: Edward Elgar.

Minic, Jelica., ed. 1999. "Reconstruction and Development Programme for South Eastern Europe." In J. Minic, ed., *South Eastern Europe 2000: A View From Serbia*. Belgrade: Stubovi kulture. 7-24.

Reinicke, W. 1998. *Global Public Policy: Governing Without Government*. Washington, D.C.: Brookings Institute.

Scott, A. 1999. *Regions and the World Economy: The Coming Shape of Global Production*. Oxford, UK: Oxford University Press.

Siebert, Horst. 1999. *The World Economy*. London: Routledge.

Smith, Alan. 2000, *The Reintegration of Eastern Europe into the European Economy*. London: MacMillan Press.

Triantaphyllou, Dimitri. 1999, "The Greek Approach to the Balkans." In Thanos Veremis and Dimitri Triantaphyllou, eds., *The Southeast European Yearbook, 1997-1998*. Athens: Hellenic Foundation for European and Foreign Policy. 203-215.

Tsoukalis, Loukas. 1994. "The European Community and the Balkans." In F. Stephen Larrabee, ed., *The Volatile Powder Keg: Balkan Security After the Cold War*. Washington, D.C.: The American University Press. 219-231.

United Nations Economic Commission for Europe. 1998. *Economic Survey of Europe*, no.1. Geneva: United Nations.

United Nations, Conference on Trade and Development. 2000. *World Investment Report 2000: Cross-Boarder Mergers and Acquisition and Development*. New York: United Nations.

Veremis, Thanos. 1994. "Greece: The Dilemmas of Change." In F.Stephen Larrabee, ed., *The Volatile Powder Keg: Balkan Security After the Cold War*. Washington, D.C.: The American University Press. 119-133.

Wagstyl, D. and D. Buchan. 2000. "Starting From Scratch," *FINANCIAL TIMES*. 29 May.

World Bank 1999. *Slovenia: Economic Transformation and EU Accession*. Washington, D.C.: WorldBank.

CHAPTER 11
THE DEVELOPMENT OF CIVIL SOCIETY IN SOUTHEASTERN EUROPE

Dr. Tina Mavrikos-Adamou
American College of Thessaloniki
Thessaloniki, GREECE

I. INTRODUCTION

The aim of this Chapter will be to contemplate the possibility of some form of a civil society developing in South-eastern Europe (SE E). As used in this Chapter, civil society is defined as those institutions, organizations, and practices that are not controlled directly by the state but which help to support and lend legitimacy to the political system. The above may include voluntary groups, professional organizations, environmental activists, and other interest groups. It appears that some form of a civil society needs to be created so that the countries of SE E can sustain a democratic government and create legitimacy for the state (see Donnorummo, this volume). For our purposes, when referring to "South-eastern Europe," the countries which are referred to include the former Yugoslav Republics—(Former Yugoslavian Republic of Macedonia—FYROM, Slovenia, Croatia, Serbia, Bosnia-Herzegovina), Romania, Bulgaria, Albania, Greece and Turkey. Space does not allow a lengthy discussion of all; therefore, only Albania, Bulgaria, FYROM, what has remained of Yugoslavia, and Greece will be examined in some detail.

II. THE MERITS OF CIVIL SOCIETY

There remains much contention in contemporary literature concerning the merits of civil society and whether it has contributed or can contribute to the maintenance and consolidation of a democratic political system where it has developed or where it is in the process of developing (see Diamond 1997 in general and Schmitter 1997 in particular for a discussion of civil society and its effects on the consolidation of democracy). Those on one side of the argument claim that civil society should not be seen as the panacea for the problems that the nation-state is now facing, and therefore can not be perceived as the solution for those problems (see Rieff 1999: 11-22; see also Carothers, et al. 1999/2000:18-22). Others are more optimistic and point to the potential of a strong civil society enhancing democracy and its accompanying political and social institutions (see for example, Hall 1998: 32-41; for another look at how

civil society can help consolidate democracy, see Diamond 1999). The discussion gets more complex when the issue turns to the relevance of civil society in those countries which have very diverse historical, cultural, and political experiences from those of the West (Bunce 2000; see also Tempest 1997, for a skeptical view of the ability of civil society to develop in East European countries).

When referring to the countries of SE E, for example, one can easily perceive the dangers of adopting a western notion of civil society and trying to apply it unchanged to the region. Even in Greece, generally viewed as the SE E country which has adopted western practices more thoroughly than its Balkan neighbors, the popular understanding of civil society differs substantially from that of its EU partners to the north and west. Thus, the concept of civil society does not seem to "fit" comfortably within the context of society that exists within these countries (see Haynes 1997 for a description of the development of civil society in Third World countries where the concept likewise does not "fit" comfortably). Yet, there is sufficient evidence to believe that without some form of civil society the SE E countries will not be able to sustain their political systems and institutions, especially those countries which have most recently (since 1989) ventured to form some kind of "democratic system" which did not exist previously.[1] Citizens need to have avenues to express their interests and demands besides simply voting, and they need to find ways to affect political outcomes in nonviolent ways (see Di Palma 1991).

What does seem clear is that the development of some form of civil society in SE E will have to go hand in hand with the development of democratic political and social institutions provided by the state. The idea that civil society can alone create a bulwark for a democratic form of government indeed appears to be shortsighted and erroneous. Only with an accompanying strong democratic state supporting the groups and practices found within a mature civil society can civil society contribute to cementing a democratic form of government. Therefore, any prescription for SE E countries encompassing the role of civil society will have to receive the strong backing of the state, both financially and morally. There remain several predictions, however, as to how long it takes for a fully developed civil society to form. If one was to rely on Dahrendorf's (1990) forecast, then it might take as long as sixty years for such social change to occur.

Other more optimistic predictions contend that the formation of a civil society in Eastern Europe need not be so lengthy if these countries are able to imitate civil society formations in the west, or simply let civil society flourish where it was previously existent but suppressed by authoritarian regimes (see Delli Zott 1995). In any case, civil society is something that needs to be

invented in most SE E countries, and this process inevitably will take some time, the duration of which will obviously depend upon the particular country under examination (Engelbrekt 1997).

How can civil society assist SE E countries in developing democratic practices? First, by allowing previously stifled voices to be heard, the government can create an arena where citizens' interests and concerns can be expressed. If citizens' interests and concerns are properly channeled and organized in such an arena, it is possible to envision a democratic forum for discussion. If citizens can form groups and associations to air their concerns and avoid the pitfalls of expressing only narrow-minded, short-sighted issues, then conceivably such groups can support a democratic system.

Second, political parties should not be seen as the sole vehicles acting as locomotives for the development of civil society, since a strong and balanced civil society requires individuals to form interest groups of all kinds, from cultural organizations to professional groups to business associations. Needless to say, the larger question is whether the societies of SE E, which have very diverse cultural and historical backgrounds from those of the west, will be able to ignite such citizen participation. These societies will likewise need to cultivate the idea of human rights, i.e., the notion that all citizens have inalienable rights. Adam Seligman has perhaps put it aptly when he mentions that the ideas of trust and mutuality, which are found in western societies, are inhibited in those societies of the east because their citizens have ethnic, religious, and cultural differences (Seligman 1992:150).

The role of the former communist leadership and those who wielded political and economic power, the power elite (formerly known as *nomenklatura*) in these countries, must also be taken into consideration. The continuing presence of these individuals within the political and social life of these countries is formidable and enduring. In many ways, they have prohibited the development of a civic culture to form among average citizens because they monopolize the avenues available for citizen expression, including those of political parties, the mass media, and economic enterprises (see Bugajski 1997).

On a more practical level, one must take into consideration that civil society flourishes once citizens can look to the future and see the importance of developing associations and groups which can build towards established goals. Citizens have to be able to secure the material aspects of life, however, to be able to come to this realization. Unfortunately, in most of the countries here under discussion, citizens are still trying to maintain their everyday subsistence, and have little time or inclination for developing the social structures and

organizations needed to support a robust civil society (see Drakulic 1996 for a description of everyday life in the Balkan countries).

III. CIVIL SOCIETY AND THE QUESTION OF LEGITIMACY

A further issue which needs to be explored is the question of legitimacy of the state and how this relates to civil society. If one was to separate out formal legitimacy from social legitimacy, then it becomes clearer how civil society becomes one of the dimensions of the question of legitimacy. Formal legitimacy concerns the legal aspects of the formation of the political system and its institutions, and that the law is observed. Social legitimacy pertains to the subjective component of legitimacy, where society comes to accept the political system and supports it (Weiler 1992:19).

Both formal (or political) legitimacy and social legitimacy can be enhanced by civil society and its accompanying associations and practices which feed into the question of legitimacy. Put simply, a democratic state needs a strong civil society to be perceived of as legitimate, and civil society needs a strong democratic state to support its organizations and associations. So clearly the issue is not one or the other, but rather both are needed for democracy to grow, each backing and supporting each other so that they lead to both formal and social legitimacy (Hefner 1998:16-28).

When one applies these concepts of civil society and legitimacy to the countries of SE E, particularly ex-communist societies, what stands out is the lack of appropriate conceptual tools (and even vernacular) to relate these issues to these societies. It appears inappropriate to simply apply western concepts and notions to SE E countries without stepping back to acknowledge the vast differences which remain between "east" and "west." However, it is as equally erroneous to believe that these SE E societies which were under the yoke of a non-democratic system cannot develop their own version of civil society and citizenship which will aid them in establishing democracy at home. Obviously, an indigenous movement is needed to propel the forces of change, and to develop the prerequisites for the civil society. One can not simply transplant into these societies unfamiliar and foreign concepts and expect them to take root immediately. But with the development of the notion of citizenship in these ex-communist states, replacing the previous notion of subject/servant, there is reason to believe that a civil society can form, advanced by active citizenship (Nelson 1996: 345-369). However, citizenship has to come to mean actively participating in society, but by working within the framework of the state and its institutions, and not against these.

Furthermore, it is necessary that western commentators take under consideration the relative lack of good knowledge about the histories of many of these ex-communist states (particularly the case of Albania, for example), and the lack of western familiarity with their political culture and its practices. Moreover, we have not come to comprehend the degree of complexity of many of the issues and dilemmas that these states face internally. These are highly ethnically diverse societies, and they can also be viewed as violent societies. A look at the number of wars that the countries in the Balkans have been involved in seems to insinuate that indeed there has been much violence in these countries (for a brief history, see Mazower 2000; see also Roudometof 2001).

In this regard, there is a connection between low levels of interpersonal trust and societies of violence. Where one witnesses a substantial degree of internal hostilities among citizens or between the countries themselves, there appears to be low levels of trust and mutuality found among citizens and vice versa. These intricacies, however, need to be examined for each particular country under investigation. The campaign launched by NATO in Kosovo in April of 1999, however, is just one of many examples revealing the west's inability to understand just how complex and inter-related problems are in the Balkans.

Having remarked upon the many difficulties and intricacies of applying the concept of civil society to the countries of southeastern Europe, an attempt will be made to relate something briefly about each of the aforementioned countries which comprise southeastern Europe. Where information is available, nongovernmental organizations (NGOs) will be used as the source of empirical data to compare and contrast the countries under consideration, and as a means by which to gauge the degree of civil society formation and activity.

IV. THE DEVELOPMENT OF CIVIL SOCIETY IN SE E COUNTRIES

Albania

As the most closed of all former communist countries, Albania can be seen as having the least experiences with the notion of civil society. Albania's political culture - or at least what is known of it - appears to have come from what could be described as the exact opposite of civil society, namely, total repression by the state. For example, there was not a single known autonomous group activity in the country until the fall of communism in 1990. Hence Albania as a country has practically no cultural experiences to draw upon in order to establish the basis for civil society. Having recognized that fact, however, Albania has witnessed, albeit slowly, the formation of political organizations independent of the government, but these are not adequate enough

to express the ideas and concerns of the average Albanian. Albania continues likewise to be plagued by economic woes and remains one of the poorest and most underdeveloped countries in Europe today. Therefore, what one witnesses here is a weak democratic state lacking both political and social institutions to support the development of civil society. Clearly a major effort will be needed on the part of the Albanian people to form organizations and interest groups which could provide a forum for discussion leading to the development of some sort of a democratic environment supporting civil society.

One such effort, the Society for Democratic Culture (SDC), a US sponsored organization, began creating programs aimed at igniting some form of a civic spirit in Albania at the beginning of the 1990s. Primarily focused on voter education and mobilization, the SDC also attempted to promote citizen participation in the political and economic affairs of the country. The National Democratic Institute, the organization which helped establish SDC, aimed at working with the newly formed Albanian parliament to promote a dialogue between lawmakers and their constituents (Biberaj 1998).

Another organization, the Helsinki Committee, which was formed to oversee human rights violations, fell victim to infiltration by former communist party members and thus was less effective in acting as an organization of civil society. Other organizations have been unable to act as real voices of the Albanian people because they too have been dominated by former communist party members who do not allow for a democratic and open political environment to grow.

The NGOs in operation in Albania presently are found in Tirana, and therefore do not involve over half of Albania's population which is rurally based. Figures from the Albanian Civil Society Foundation reveal that women's organizations seem to be some of the most active, as are those of culture and art which are nearly all Tirana-based (see Tables 1 & 2). However, as mentioned previously, there is little if any tradition in Albania of active citizen participation through the organizations and structures of civil society. Where mass public participation has occurred, it has tended to be violent and destructive, such as the civil unrest in 1997 which occurred in the aftermath of economic scandals.

In the case of Albania, an additional consideration worth emphasizing is that the non-profit sector is heavily supported by foreign sources, especially after the Kosovo crisis in 1999. There does appear to be some resentment among Albanian, indigenous NGOs, that have become more the helpers of international agencies rather than autonomous organizations. Likewise, there is speculation that foreign supported NGOs do not positively affect Albanian society to the degree that would be expected, and that funds often go astray, either due to corruption or money-pocketing on the part of unscrupulous partners.

Hence, for Albania to develop a culture supporting civil society, major steps are needed to secure an environment for democracy to progress and allow for the input of citizens into the policy-making process (see Pano 1997). Law and order need to be firmly established and maintained; legitimacy, both political and social, are prerequisites for development of a civil society. Albania needs much assistance from the international community to confront the immediate challenges the country faces both politically and economically. Likewise, an indigenous movement is necessary to support democratic consolidation in the country. Albania needs to maintain peace with its neighbors and avoid at all costs confrontations leading to destabilization and chaos.

Table 1: Comparing & Contrasting NGOs—Civil Society Organizations

	Number of Registered NGOs	*Characteristics of NGOs*
Albania	500 (250 active)	Service oriented but Tirana based; women's organizations are some of the strongest in the country in terms of activities
Bulgaria	8,000 (1,000 active)	Well-established NGOs which do not always work together well. They are dominated by intellectual, policy, cultural and professional organizations
FYROM	458 (domestic) 87 (foreign)	Underdeveloped; many NGOs engage in a broad range of activities and are service oriented
Serbia	2,000 (700-1,000 active)	Strong humanitarian issue oriented sector; political orientation
Montenegro	150 (50 active)	Small; centered around a single person; underdeveloped

Source: Based on Jenny Hyatt's (2000) research on NGOs in the Balkans.

Table 2: Types of Civil Society Organizations

Albania	Women's organizations, such as that of "Rural Women" and "Useful to Albanian Women Association" are some of the strongest, as are arts/cultural organizations, and those of youth, health, and environmental issues.
Bulgaria	More professional organizations operating here than in other Balkan countries; leisure and entertainment represent approximately 18.3% of NGOs operating in Bulgaria. NGOs involved in culture & arts amounting to 11.2% of the total of NGOs registered.
FYROM	Due to the underdeveloped nature of the non-profit sector in FYROM, no data is available describing fields of activity where civil society organizations are found. Some associations supporting women's issues, such as that of "Humanitarian Association for the Emancipation, Solidarity and Equality of Women," are more organized than others.
Serbia	Ecological organizations and social/humanitarian organizations represent 40% of NGOs in operation in Serbia. Youth and student associations and those concerned with community development account for a further 20% of NGOs in operation.
Montenegro	Due to the small population of Montenegro (estimated at 650,000), there are few associations/organizations in operation. Those that exist are mostly found within the fields of women's issues, human rights/ democracy, environment, and youth organizations.

Source: Jenny Hyatt (2000).

Bulgaria

What distinguishes Bulgaria from its other Balkan neighbors is that it has a tradition of cooperation that dates back to the period of Ottoman rule. Bulgarians created "chitalishta's," or reading clubs, which encouraged reading, the development of music groups, and amateur theatre which were supported by volunteers. Some of these organizations still survive today in a modern guise. Thus, it is not surprising that today Bulgaria continues to have a large percentage of NGOs, approximately 11%, whose activities are involved in culture or the arts. There are also a large percentage of professional organizations, amounting to approximately 20% of registered NGOs, and since 1989, the Ecoglasnost organization went beyond being an environmental movement and adopted political and social issues as well. Thus, the traditional intellectual trend in Bulgaria remains an underlying pattern for the establishment

of NGOs today, whereby a large number of highly educated individuals are involved in their activities and organization.[2]

However, under communism, all those organizations in which people did not support or pledged their allegiance to the communist party were banned. Since the fall of communism, and under a great deal of political and economic instability, the development of civil society in Bulgaria has experienced difficulties, partially due to high levels of crime and corruption, and partially due to a large black market and high unemployment, particularly among the Roma minority.

What characterizes the NGO sector presently in Bulgaria is that there are a small number of large, well established NGOs, but these do not always cooperate with one another to enhance pluralism. As with Albania, most NGOs are concentrated in the largest cities and towns, thus not reaching that percentage of the population residing in the countryside. Government funding for NGOs is quite limited, and thus the non-profit sector relies heavily on foreign donors, amounting to approximately 93% of their total income. Some of these foreign donors include the Charles Stewart Mott Foundation, the National Endowment for Democracy, and the Volkswagen Foundation (Hyatt 2000:68). Indigenous companies do not amount to a major source of economic support for the non-profit sector due to the poor economic environment and the still underdeveloped market economy.

Thus Bulgaria still has a long road to travel before it can develop the foundations for a strong civil society. For organizations to grow and flourish in Bulgaria, public participation and awareness is necessary. Bulgaria needs likewise to sustain a stable economy and to develop the infrastructures necessary to support a vibrant civil society for which there does appears to be the basis of development. And unlike many of its Balkan neighbors, Bulgaria has no serious threat of violence, either internally or externally, which puts it in a more advantageous position, comparatively speaking, for the consolidation of democracy and the development of civil society.

FYROM: Former Yugoslav Republic of Macedonia

Similar to Bulgaria, FYROM has a tradition of civil society organizations which can be traced to the period before the Second World War and which took on a national character when the Yugoslav state was established. Prior to the Second World War these took the form of charity associations, sports and women's clubs, and cultural societies. At the close of the war, however, things changed. As Jenny Hyatt describes:

> After the war, during the establishment of the Yugoslav state, new systems were developed which effectively resulted in the nationalization of civil activity. Structures called *optestveni organizaci* (societal organizations) brought people together in groups such as Second World War veterans, women, youth, children, students, disabled people, scouts, writers and musicians. They were organized at the local, national and federal levels, so Macedonian organizations had delegates in the Socialist Federal Republic of Yugoslavia (SFRY) 'unions' of these organizations. All organizations were collective members of the Socialist Union of the Working People. During the 1970s and 1980s this framework continued (although the late 1980s were marked by a decline of enthusiasm and trust among their members) and only ceased with the end of communism (Hyatt 2000: 107).

Since FYROM became independent in 1991, many diverse style NGOs have developed such as the Forum for Human Rights, the Helsinki Citizens' Assembly Chapter in Macedonia, First Children's Embassy "Megjashi," and the European Movement. However, these organizations operate in an environment which is economically, socially, and politically weak. There remains a very high unemployment rate in FYROM (estimates range between 40-50%), and there are social problems such as drug abuse, prostitution, domestic violence and crime which reek havoc on the social fabric of society.

Although FYROM managed to escape war with Serbia, it experienced severe economic hardships due to the Kosovo crisis of 1999 when an influx of some 360,000 refugees entered into the country seeking shelter and assistance. This resulted in an economic crisis for the country, a crisis that is still being felt at present. However, FYROM's most recent dilemma is with its indigenous Albanian minority and with Albanian extremists in Kosovo, who have ignited new tensions in the country's northwestern border with Kosovo. These could jeopardize the political stability that the country has enjoyed since independence (for a review, see Perry 2000).

The prospects for the development of a vibrant civil society in FYROM will hinge on its ability to maintain peace and stability in the region and to confront its multi-ethnic character. However, FYROM must likewise secure a political and economic climate to support the institutions and associations that civil society needs to grow. As yet, the media in FYROM have been unable to become a truly independent voice of the public. They are still owned and operated by the state and are heavily party oriented (Perry 1997). More avenues

for citizens' views and opinions need to develop for a democratic arena to grow allowing for free exchanges of ideas among the multi-ethnic population.

Economically, although no longer strangled by embargoes and commercial blockades, the influx of refugees from Kosovo in addition to slow privatization and marketization have resulted in severe economic hardships for FYROM. Recent unrest with Albanian extremists will crush tourism in the country as well as hinder foreign investments, which have been rising since 1996 and which contributed to the development of a more robust economy. Thus, the recent events in FYROM do not augur well for the development of civil society in the country, although no predictions should be made as to what lies ahead in the future for the country.

Yugoslavia: Serbia and Montenegro

Yugoslavia poses perhaps the most difficulty in considering whether some form of a civil society can take root in this country (for an overview, see Perry 1997 and Gordy 1999). Up until September of 2000, the government of Slobodan Milosevic stifled any independent form of citizen organization that did not directly support his government. As such, it is indeed difficult to speculate as to the prospects, in the post-Milosevic era, of civil society growing in Yugoslavia. Given these circumstances, some preliminary observations can be made as to the history of citizens' movements in the country in the post World War Two era, and what political culture the Serbs and Montenegrins have inherited as a foundation for building civil society now in a more democratic environment.

At the close of the Second World War, Tito created citizen's associations as a way to bolster his version of communism, allowing citizens to participate in some 20,000 associations, mostly engaged in sports, folk, art, and hobby activities (Hyatt 2000: 153). Whoever was not a member of the Communist Party was automatically made a member of the Socialist Alliance of Working People, and thus Tito created his own version of civil society, one which was closely monitored by the Party and whose activities had to conform to supporting Yugoslav communism.

In the post-Tito era, and with the disintegration of the federation, new organizations were created, mainly concerned with humanitarian causes, but they still operated within a very hostile political environment which did not allow for the free expression of citizens' views and opinions. NGOs were perceived to be the only alternative to the government and the only pro-democratic force that attempted to push out Milosevic. Therefore, the Milosevic government was extremely hostile to these newly forming NGOs which created formidable challenges for the operation and continuation of NGOs in the country. When the

NATO campaign against Serbia occurred in April of 1999, many NGOs had to close down operations or move to neighboring countries. However, once the hostilities ceased, they resumed operation and in fact became more determined to act as a voice for citizens who wanted change for the country. At this time, NGOs have gained more favorable media coverage internationally and have been recognized as the focus for those who sought an end to the Milosevic era.

As Table 1 notes, there are approximately 700-1000 active NGOs in Serbia and 50 active in Montenegro. In Serbia, the vast majority of NGOs remains very politically oriented. The NGOs are involved in humanitarian causes, ecological issues, and youth and student concerns. It comes as no surprise then, that the student movement in Yugoslavia was the force behind the parliamentary takeover which brought down the Milosovic government in what can be described as a "people's" movement. One can trace a political tradition of citizen participation and determination to effect change and the policy-making process. Under a democratic rubric, there is the possibility that the citizens' interests and opinions might find more constructive avenues by which to press for civic rights. If the organizations and associations which support civil society can secure a legitimate environment in which to operate, and are given due consideration by the new government, then there is hope in believing that a civil society can help cement and consolidate democracy in Yugoslavia. By the same token, one must be cautious in jumping to any conclusions about the political future of the country given the newness of the present political situation and the continuing position of Yugoslavia in the Balkans.

As with the previous examples, most NGO activity in Yugoslavia tends to be based around the capital city, Belgrade, although over the last several years a number of NGOs have begun to form in other parts of the country. However, these organizations have a hard time securing the material needs for their operation; until recently they operated covertly, and got little support from international agencies. UN sanctions against Serbia and embargoes against the country have left Yugoslavia in a paralyzed state economically in terms of resources and everyday needs. Hence the operation of NGOs has been affected by these circumstances which has limited their ability to function effectively and achieve their stated goals. There have been some NGOs which have operated outside the country, such as the "Balkan Community Initiatives Fund," based in the UK. These NGOs supported NGOs in Serbia, Kosovo, and Montenegro. However, these organizations are few in number and have not been able to reach a very large percentage of citizens throughout the country. Most of the other international organizations have focused on refugee issues, such as OXFAM, for example.

To focus more specifically on the situation in Montenegro, here one views a more limited tradition of citizen activity than in Serbia. However, like other organizations in Serbia and the other republics under Tito's communism, Montenegrin associations were mouthpieces of the state and their activities were closely monitored and controlled. When Yugoslavia disintegrated, Montenegro was the only republic to remain in the federation. In the 1990s, Montenegro did see some NGO activity concerned with human rights, youth, peace, and women's issues. However, due to its small population and its lack of a real political culture that can act as a foundation for building a civil society, Montenegro remains underdeveloped when compared with her Balkan neighbors. In the post-Milosevic era, there remains uncertainty about Montenegro's relationship with Serbia and whether Montenegro might seek independence in the near future. These political circumstances make it indeed difficult to speculate on the possible formation of a civil society in Montenegro and its ability to help build a democratic system in the country. Internally, Montenegro has a high unemployment rate, an active black market, and high levels of corruption. These characteristics do not create a favorable environment for citizens' associations and interest group activity. If the Montenegrins become preoccupied with gaining independence from the federation, this will further delay the possibility of a civil society developing quickly and could even bring in political instability or even worse, civil war.

Thus, Yugoslavia at present has numerous challenges to face in the post-Milosevic era and these to a great extent will determine her future political make-up and thus the possibility a civil society developing within. Yugoslavia is economically devastated due to war and embargoes, but it is also politically volatile as the new president, Vojislav Kostunica, is tested for his commitment to democracy. Furthermore, ethnic tensions in Kosovo, Montenegro, and neighboring FYROM, all amount to formidable obstacles for the country. Whether a true democratic transition in the country can occur remains to be seen, while peace is tenuous and the outbreak of war hovers on the horizon. If an indigenous political culture can form to include ethnic minorities, and civic organizations are allowed to play a constructive role in expressing citizens' opinions, then one can remain marginally optimistic about the future of Yugoslavia and its ability to cultivate a civil society to enhance democracy. Much at present remains uncertain, however, and this makes one heed caution in any predictions about the future.

Greece

Greece can be perceived as the most "westernized" of all the countries in SE E, and has enjoyed a democratic system which was restored in 1974.

However, when compared with her northern EU partners, Greece has an underdeveloped, weak civic environment. This can be partially explained historically because Greece did not experience the effects of 19th century liberal political and ideological morements that were responsible for introducing modern civil society (and its structures and institutions) to the rest of western Europe (Diamandouros 1983). As a legacy of the Ottoman past, Greece inherited an omnipresent state that perpetuated patron-client relationships that stifled the development of other voluntary institutional forms and structures that could have acted as counterbalances.

One can enumerate at least four main features characteristic of civil society in Greece. First, Greece continues to be characterized by a highly centralized state in which the central government holds the reigns of power and assigns and distributes precious state resources, which continuously feeds the patron-client system. Since the locus of power is at the center, it is here where the decision-making process occurs and where the negotiations and deal-making take place.

Second, there are entrenched patron-client networks still in operation. Greece inherited those from her Ottoman past. The patron-client networks have resulted in a commingling of the "private" versus "public" spheres. Structurally, this can be seen through the lack of separation between church and state. The Greek Orthodox religion is taught in the public schools in Greece, and thus Hellenism is still identified with Orthodoxy. Recently, a major disagreement erupted between church authorities and the present PASOK government of Kostas Simitis over the government's decision to remove religion as a category listed in the Greek identification cards (ID) necessary for all public transactions. Church authorities began a campaign to get signatures for a petition to pressure the government to call a referendum for the Greek people to decide whether or not the carrier's religious designation should be removed from ID cards or not. In short, a major rift occurred between the Greek Orthodox church and government officials attempting to create a more secular civic environment in Greece.

The commingling of the private and the public spheres on a day to day basis can be witnessed in public offices (banks, tax offices, etc.) as well as in the allocation of pressumably public services. For example, in utilities and hospitals, preferential treatment is dispensed to those who have a "messo" (literally translated as a go-between, meaning a *connection* or personal contact) and who can, therefore, expedite the bureaucratic red tape that leads to delays and squandered time. The large number of self-employed people in Greece also indicates this coalescing of private and public domains, in which family businesses are still very widespread in Greece.

Third, there is immature associational and interest group formation, partially due to the over-riding position that the *political* environment (i.e. the political party system) has over the *social* in terms of organizational power. As Dimitri Sotiropoulos (1993: 51) has accurately described:

> There are only a few ethnic and linguistic minorities in Greece; the church is bound to the state; voluntary associations are sparse and social service organizations are sanctioned by the state; gender groupings, peace movements, and environmental groups do not enjoy a long life, and they usually fall under the tutelage of one of the political parties. In short, many private or independent associations and institutions in Greece are unable to support a strong civil society.

Finally, the state bureaucracy, best characterized as a bloated public sector, is an administrative state apparatus that serves the government (i.e. the party) in office, thereby perpetuating the patrimonial nature of the Greek state. Since each party that comes into office places into the bureaucracy *its own people* (which means that it creates more positions in the bureaucracy because a majority of public sector jobs are permanent positions), it has become difficult for the bureaucracy to formulate a plan for modernization and put it into practice in the time period during which that party holds the reigns of power.

Thus, the main avenues of political participation in Greece operate through the political parties. The parties are the main actors, especially due to the absence of interest groups and voluntary associations. During the last thirty years, Greek governments have been unable to transform the onerous socio-economic structures that perpetuate the patrimonial state. Neither of the two main political parties, the socialist PASOK and the conservative New Democracy, have effectively put into practice a successful modernization program to bring about real structural changes.

The Greek educational system is another institution in need of extensive revitalization. Antiquated means of teaching are still employed within a system that puts a premium in passive learning, memorization, and the status quo. The mass media have established an independent voice with the opening up of state TV and radio to private entrepreneurs since 1989, but those who have acquired these TV and radio stations are few (since the starting up costs are enormous and some "families" have monopolized broadcasting). Therefore, the airways have not escaped political tutelage.

Hence Greece, although seemingly more advanced in its development of civil society than the other countries of SE E mentioned here, still has a long

way to go before it can claim to have a robust civil society. Greece, having consolidated democracy since 1974 while being a member of the EU, finds itself comparatively in a more favorable position than its southeastern neighbors. However, it too has been unable to create an environment in which the associations and groupings of civil society can strive and act as a representative voice of the Greek people.

V. CONCLUSION

The constitution of a civil society in SE E appears to be a formidable task in many of these aforementioned countries, but it is a necessary condition for the establishment and maintenance of a democratic government. Each of these societies faces the challenge of consolidating democracy (with the exception of Greece). Without the establishment of a civil society, this seems indeed quite difficult. However, one has to acknowledge that civil society alone can not secure all the sufficient conditions necessary for a democratic government. Other political, social, and economic structures and institutions will have to be established to exercise control over state power. These must be created by social forces indigenous to each individual society. For example, constitutional reform is necessary for maintaining law and order and for securing legitimacy, and therefore must be accomplished as swiftly as possible.

Furthermore, there is no simple recipe for establishing a civil society in these countries, and henceforth maintaining it. Each of the SE E countries will have to create its own version of civil society in keeping with the unique patterns of social and political development it has experienced. Therefore, social forces promoting civil society must be indigenous and relative to each distinct society. Yet these forces must be kept in check by the state, to safeguard and ensure the freedoms and initiatives on which civil society depends. A free press can play a vital role in these societies, allowing for citizens' opinions and views to be heard and considered.

Finally, it needs to be noted that civil society as it is developing in SE E will have uneven and mixed success within each particular country. The ultimate success or failure will depend upon many forces, both internal and external. Political stability needs to be maintained, and war and violence avoided at all costs. At present, the Balkan states lack a comprehensive plan or program for the structural transformation of their economies and societies, and those eastern states found farthest from the EU market will have less exposure to western institutions and practices. Those states found closest to the west, either geographically or economically, may fair better in the long-run. In any case, the destinies of these countries shall remain a concern for both east and west, and

much research needs to be done to understand and interpret how the forces of civil society can be decisive in determining their future.

ENDNOTES

[1] Likewise, many feel that a market economy can not exist without a civil society to support it. Therefore, the economic sphere, that of a free market and private enterprise, is perceived to be a prerequisite around which a new civil society can be constructed. See Bob Donnorummo's Chapter in this volume.

[2] See Bell (1997), for a discussion of political participation in post- communist Bulgaria.

REFERENCES

Bell, John D. 1997. "Democratization and Political Participation in 'Postcommunist' Europe." From Karen Dawisha and Bruce Parrott, eds. *Politics, Power, and the Struggle for Democracy in South-East Europe.* Cambridge, UK: Cambridge University Press.

Bermeo, Nancy & Philip Nord eds. 2000. *Civil Society Before Democracy: Lessons From Nineteenth Century Europe.* Lanham, Maryland: Rowman & Littlefield Publishers, Inc.

Biberaj, Elez. 1998. *Albania in Transition.* Boulder, Colorado: Westview Press.

Bugajski, Janusz. 1997. "The Balkans: On the Brink Again." *Washington Quarterly* 40 (4) : 211-230.

Bunce, Valerie. 2000. "The Historical Origins of the East-West Divide: Civil Society, Political Society, and Democracy in Europe." From Nancy Bermeo et al eds. *Civil Society Before Democracy: Lessons From Nineteenth Century Europe.* Lanham, Maryland: Rowman & Littlefield Publishers, Inc.

Carothers, Thomas et al. 1999/2000. "Civil Society." *Foreign Policy*. (Winter): 18-22.

Dahrendorf, Ralf. 1990. *Reflections on the Revolution in Europe*. NY: Crown Publishing Group Inc.

Delli Zott, Giovanni. 1995. "Problems of Change, the Growth of Civil Society, and the Role of the West." From Alberto Gasparini, ed. *Social Actors & Designing the Civil Society of Eastern Europe*. Stanford: JAI Press Inc.

Diamandouros, Nikiforos P. 1983. "Greek Political Culture in Transition: Historical Origins, Evolution, Current Trends." From Richard Clogg ed. *Greece in the 1980's*. London: MacMillan.

Diamond, Larry. 1999. *Developing Democracy Toward Consolidation*. Baltimore/London: The John Hopkins University Press.

Diamond, Larry, ed. et al. 1997. *Consolidating the Third Wave Democracies*. Baltimore/London: The John Hopkins University Press.

Di Palma, Giuseppe. 1991. "Legitimation From the Top to Civil Society: Politico-Cultural Change in Eastern Europe." *World Politics*. (October): 49-80.

Drakulic, Slavenka. 1996. *Cafe Europa: Life After Communism*. NY: Penguin Books.

Engelbrekt, Kjell. 1997. "Unfinished Democracy." *Problems of Post-Communism*. (November/December): 3-13.

Gordy, Eric D. 1999. *The Culture of Power in Serbia: Nationalism and the Destruction of Alternatives*. University Park, Pa.: Pennsylvania State University Press.

Hall, John. 1998. "The Nature of Civil Society." *Society*. (May/June): 32-41.

Hall, John. ed. 1995. *Civil Society*. Cambridge, UK: Polity Press.

Haynes, Jeff. 1997. *Democracy and Civil Society in the Third World.* Cambridge, UK: Polity Press.

Hefner, Robert W. 1998. "Civil Society: Cultural Possibility of a Modern Ideal." Society. (March/April): 16-28.

Hyatt, Jenny. 2000. *An Introduction to the Non-Profit Sector in the Balkans.* Kent, Maine: Charities Aid Foundation.

Mazower, Mark. 2000. *The Balkans: A Short History.* NY: The Modern Library.

Nelson, Daniel N. 1996. "Civil Society Endangered." *Social Research.* (Summer): 345-369.

Perry, Duncan M. 1997. "The Republic of Macedonia: Finding its Way." From Karen Dawisha and Bruce Parrott, eds. *Politics, Power, and the Struggle for Democracy in South-East Europe.* Cambridge, UK: Cambridge University Press.

Perry, Duncan M. 2000. "Conflicting Ambitions and Shared Fates: The Past, Present, and Future of Albanians and Macedonians." From Victor Roudometof (ed.), *The Macedonian Question: Culture, Historiography, Politics.* Boulder, Colo.: East European Monographs, distributed by Columbia University Press.

Pano, Nicholas. 1997. "The Process of Democratization in Albania." From Karen Dawisha and Bruce Parrott, eds. *Politics, Power, and the Struggle for Democracy in South-East Europe.* Cambridge, UK: Cambridge University Press.

Rieff, David. 1999. "The False Dawn of Civil Society." *The Nation.* (February 22): 11-26.

Roudometof, Victor. 2001. *Nationalism, Globalization, and Orthodoxy: The Social Origins of Ethnic Conflict in the Balkans.* Westport, Conn.: Greenwood.

Seligman, Adam B. 1992. *The Idea of Civil Society*. Princeton, NJ.: Princeton University Press.

Schmitter, Philippe C. 1997. "Civil Society East and West." From Larry Diamond, ed. et al. *Consolidating the Third Wave Democracies*. Baltimore/London: The John Hopkins University Press.

Sotiropoulos, Dimitiri A. 1993. "A Colossus with Feet of Clay: The State in Post-Authoritarian Greece." From Harry J. Psomiades and Stavros B. Thomadakis, eds. *Greece, The New Europe, and the Changing International Order*. NY: Pella Publishing Co.

Tempest, Clive. 1997. "Myths from Eastern Europe and the Legend of the West." From Robert Fine and Shirin Rai, eds. *Civil Society: Democratic Perspectives*. London: Frank Cass.

Weiler, Joseph. 1992. "After Maastricht: Community Legitimacy in Post-1992 Europe." From *Singular Europe*. William Adam, ed. Ann Arbor, Michigan: The University of Michigan Press.

CHAPTER 12
"WE BELONG TO THE WEST"? REPRESENTATIONS OF EASTERN AND WESTERN EUROPE IN THE GREEK PRESS AND THE POSITIONING OF THE "WE"

Anna Triandafyllidou
European University Institute

GREECE AND ITS SOUTHEAST EUROPEAN CONTEXT

Greece's history and politics have been marked by its ambivalent position, at the crossroads between East and West. This ambivalence is reflected on its national-cultural identity (Roudometof 1999; Tsoukalas 1994), foreign policy, and relations with other countries (Heraklides 1995). Greekness is Janus-faced. On the one hand, it looks to the East, to the Byzantine tradition and the Christian Orthodox heritage. However, the East is also a source of worry for modern Greece; it represents Turkey (earlier, the Ottoman Empire) and the Muslim world. On the other hand, the West has been a source of nationalist inspiration and support for the young Greek state in the 19th century and the country's political and cultural referent throughout the 20th century. The pro-Western attitude of Greece has been confirmed by its accession to the European Union in 1981. However, Greeks also look at "Europeans"[1] with suspicion; modern Western European culture is alien to the Greek traditions. Even though the nationalist narrative managed to incorporate classical Greece with the Byzantine heritage and construct a national past without ruptures, the ambivalence between East and West remains an important feature of Greek identity and politics even nowadays. As a matter of fact, Europe has constructed its view of modern Greece with reference to its ancient civilization, neglecting the two thousand years in-between. Greeks have thus found themselves trapped between Hellenism and Romiosyne (Tziovas 1994), uncertain themselves of who they really are.

Fellow EU member-states also perceive the "marginality" of Greece in the context of Europe. The fact that Greece has no common frontiers with any other EU country has important political and military implications concerning relations with third countries, migration control, and the creation of a no-internal-border zone for free trade and movement. Even though high school curricula in most Western European countries include a large section on the history and literature of classical Greece, modern Greece is often regarded as an outsider in the European context. The confrontation between Greece and its fellow partners in the EU on the "Macedonian issue,"[2] their mutual lack of understanding, and

Greece's unpleasant position as the only country that tried but could not make it to the first phase of the European Monetary Union are but two of the most obvious expressions of the ambivalent position of Greece, at the fringes of the united Europe.

Moreover, Greece has important historical, cultural, and religious affiliations with southeastern Europe and is geographically located in the Balkans, an area that has been the target of much international attention as well as military intervention by UN and NATO forces during the 1990s. During the last decade, the Balkans and, in particular, the republics of former Yugoslavia have been torn by ethnic conflict, which led to bloodshed, political instability and economic decline. Greece is the only EU member-state located in this unstable area. It is culturally and religiously close to the other Balkan countries, but it is geo-politically distant from them.

This geo-political and cultural specificity—uniqueness, one may say—of Greece is however counterbalanced by a number of common features that the country shares with its southern European neighbors, notably Italy and Spain. The three countries make part of a larger cultural space that could be termed "Mediterranean,"[3] which is structured around traditional notions of family, community, and honor. Furthermore, their economies are characterized by a relatively weak industrial sector with the prevalence of tertiary and agricultural activities and a large informal economy. National politics are dominated by clientelistic patterns of relations between politicians and voters. Besides, all three countries were major emigration poles, experiencing large outgoing flows, even after the Second World War, towards the U.S., Australia, Canada, and northern Europe (Belgium, France, Germany, Sweden) but have been suddenly converted to hosts in the late 1980s (Baldwin Edwards and Arrango 1998; King *et al.* 1999).

It is against this theoretical and historical background that I shall study the representations of the European Union, Europe, and other member states, as well as Central and Eastern European countries (CEEC) and Russia in the Greek press and their intertwining with images and understandings of the ingroup identity, namely the Greek nation(-state). The aim of this study is twofold. First, it will highlight the complex relationship of Greek identity with its "Eastern" and "Western" components and explore the positioning of the country between "East" and "West," as a Balkan country and as a modern EU member-state. Second, it will examine how the representation of Greece, Greek identity, and/or Greekness in the press is re-elaborated and re-defined in relation to the process of European integration.

THE PRESS DISCOURSE: DATA AND METHODOLOGY

The following section concentrates on the analysis of the Greek press discourse in four distinct historical moments, during the past twenty years. The press is not taken to represent the public opinion but is seen as the discursive arena in which public and political debate develops and personal opinions and attitudes are formed. The analysis of the mainstream press discourse, namely of two large, moderate newspapers with a national circulation, will reveal the representations, issues, symbols, values, and interpretative frames prevalent in the public and political debate on the nation(-state), relations with EU and CEEC, and its overall positioning within the European (both Eastern and Western) geopolitical and cultural context.

Eleftherotypia (ELT) and *Eleftheros Typos (TIPOS)* are the two newspapers analyzed, on the basis of two sampling periods (the last week of February[4] and October) in the years 1983, 1989, 1993 and 1999. These years cover four important phases in the European integration process. 1983 represents the Cold War era. Although at the time, the European Economic Communities had been consolidated and their enlargement to the South had started, the European scene was largely marked by the East-West opposition and the related nuclear armament competition. 1989 marks the collapse of the Communist regimes in Central and Eastern Europe and the opening of Central and Eastern European countries' borders towards the West, which allowed for the gradual "re-connection' of Europe (Spohn 2000) and also a sudden increase of population flows between Eastern and Western Europe. 1993 is marked by the process of ratification of the Maastricht treaty and may be considered the year of creation of a European Union. Finally, 1999 reflects the current situation. It is the year of the Helsinki summit meeting and also the year in which the common European currency, the Euro, came into force.

The material analyzed includes a total of 1105 articles: 657 articles have been selected from ELT and 448 from TIPOS; they refer either to Greece as a country/nation/ingroup or to the EU (and earlier EEC), Central and Eastern European countries, Russia or a combination of these countries and/or transnational units. The database includes all articles referring to EEC/EU affairs, foreign policy concerning Eastern or Western Europe,[5] and migration, while articles referring to domestic matters or news were retrieved selectively. Among those, only articles that included a reference to the country, the people, the nation, Greece, the Greeks and/or some representation of any of the previous as an ingroup and referred to issues such as the national economy/currency, welfare policy or employment were selected. Table 1 represents the distribution

of the articles over time and table 2 refers to their reference to Greece, "Western" and "Eastern"[6] Europe. Tables 3 and 4 show the distribution of articles over time in relation to Greece, other countries and the EU, and in the two newspapers separately.

TABLE 1. ARTICLES CODED—DISTRIBUTION OVER TIME

	1983	1989	1993	1999	Total
Eleftherotypia (ELT)	151	129	189	197	657
Eleftheros Tipos (TIPOS)	111	83	138	116	448
Total	262	212	327	313	1105

TABLE 2. ARTICLES CODED—DISTRIBUTION IN RELATION TO REFERENCES TO GREECE, EEC/EU AND CENTRAL AND EASTERN EUROPE

	ELT	TIPOS	Total
Reference to Greece	368	241	609
Reference to EU, other member state or Europe	298	241	539
Reference to Central and Eastern European countries or Russia	245	153	398
Reference to Greece *and* EU or other member state or Europe	146	124	270
Reference to Greece *and* Central and Eastern European countries or Russia	88	46	134
Reference to EU/member state/Europe *and* CEEC/Russia	44	31	85

TABLE 3. ARTICLES CODED—DISTRIBUTION IN RELATION TO REFERENCES TO GREECE, EEC/EU AND CENTRAL AND EASTERN EUROPE AND OVER TIME

	1983	1989	1993	1999
Reference to Greece	174	47	186	202
Reference to EU, other member state or Europe	139	80	156	164
Reference to Central and Eastern European countries or Russia	95	113	131	59
Reference to Greece *and* EU or other member state or Europe	78	23	75	94
Reference to Greece *and* Central and Eastern European countries or Russia	59	5	58	12
Reference to EU/member state/Europe *and* CEEC/Russia	21	15	29	8

TABLE 4. ARTICLES CODED—DISTRIBUTION IN RELATION TO REFERENCES TO GREECE, EEC/EU AND CENTRAL AND EASTERN EUROPE, OVER TIME FOR EACH NEWSPAPER

	1983		1989		1993		1999	
	ELT	TIPOS	ELT	TIPOS	ELT	TIPOS	ELT	TIPOS
Reference to Greece	119	55	24	23	101	85	124	78
Reference to EU, other member state or Europe	66	73	39	41	90	66	103	61
Reference to Central and Eastern European countries or Russia	59	36	70	43	76	55	40	19
Reference to Greece *and* EU/other member state or Europe	47	31	4	19	39	36	56	38
Reference to Greece *and* Central and Eastern European countries or Russia	44	15	5	0	29	29	10	2
Reference to EU/member State/Europe *and* CEEC or Russia	10	11	9	6	18	11	5	3

The articles were indexed into a Microsoft Access database where their identifying features (name of newspaper, date of publication, page number) were inserted. The title, subtitle, lead, and comments on the article's content including its representation of specific countries and the relations between them were typed in text variables. The database included also a number of numeric and character variables for the coding of references to EU member states, EEC/EU, Europe, CEEC, Soviet Union/Russia, and other countries. These variables were useful for retrieving selectively and performing simple quantitative operations in the data set. The content of the text variables was analyzed qualitatively, concentrating on representations of ingroup/insiders vs. Others, the connection between specific countries and issues, recurrent themes, and relations between the Greek nation(-state) and minorities/immigrant communities. The methodology adopted in this research is that of unstructured, qualitative discourse analysis, namely "a general analytic approach whose precise implementation depends upon the particular theoretical issues at hand" (Reicher and Hopkins 1996: 359) rather than as a set of rules for processing data. Hence, the analysis undertaken concentrates on the specific issues of concern in the study.

FINDINGS

The analysis of the newspaper material concentrates on the evolution of the discourse in time and with particular reference to the international and national context that characterizes each of the years studied. The analysis will seek to address two main themes. First, it will study the representation of the Greek nation and nation-state in the press discourse and its positioning in its immediate southeastern geopolitical and cultural context. I shall thus highlight the specificity, if not uniqueness, of Greece as an EU member state located in the Balkans and in close proximity to Eastern Europe and Turkey. Attention will be paid to the intertwining of these two elements with Greek national history and perception of nationhood as well as their strategic use by politicians. The second part of the analysis will concentrate on the Western European context of Greece, the representation of the EEC, and later the EU and its relations with the country, and also the strategic use and interplay of "European" and "national" elements in the discourse.

GREECE: AN ETHNIC NATION AND A BALKAN LEADER

This section will present the main features of the debate on Greece as a nation(-state) and, in particular, its positioning in relation to its Balkan neighbors

as well as Central and Eastern European countries, so as to sketch its "southeastern profile."

Clearly most of the articles that referred to Greece as a nation(-state)[7] referred also to some other country; hence, it is difficult to speak of representations of the nation as such but rather of representations of the nation in contrast or in relation to some other nation(-state). Some of the features that characterized the discourse on the nation related to the national history or present situation. First, in all four years studied, there were references[8] to anniversaries of important events in the national history, like the day of the patron saint of Thessalonike (26 October), the anniversary of Ioannina's liberation[9] from the Ottomans (22 February) and 28 October, the anniversary of the Greek government's refusal to surrender to Mussolini.[10] These celebrations provided the occasion for venerating the national heroes, remembering past glories, boosting the national pride but also drawing lessons for the present. Such anniversaries fulfilled the basic function of systematically reminding the Greek people of "who we are."

A second theme that strikes mostly for its limited importance rather than for its presence regards economic issues, the state of the national economy, and its role in the positioning of the country in the international community. Several articles[11] concentrated on unemployment, the progress of industry and/or the national economy, as well as the delayed development and poor performance of the country. However, these issues were not all together important for Greece's representation. Newspaper reports covered such issues, but they rarely related them to the state of the nation. This finding is in conformity with earlier research concerning Greece's poor performance in international comparisons and its emphasis on cultural or transcendental values in order to affirm its importance and superiority (Tsoukalas 1993).

Another issue reported marginally but still present in all four years was the question of minorities, both Greek minorities abroad and ethnic or cultural minorities in Greece. In either case, this was a matter of bitter controversy. In 1983, there were still some references to Greek emigrants in Germany, testifying to the long emigration tradition in the country. Similarly, in 1983 and 1989, the issue of Greek returnees from the Soviet Union was a matter of concern, mostly with regard to the protection of their welfare rights. After 1989, numbers of returnees increased and included both post-war political refugees who wanted to return to Greece and Pontic Greeks.[12] Articles on these newcomers expressed concerns with regard to their marginalization in Greek society (ELT #112, #510) but more recently (1999) they emphasized their Greekness (TIPOS #372, ELT #630). Concerns were expressed with regard to the fate of ethnic Greeks residing in Albania (Vorioepirotes) (TIPOS #22, #279,

#298, ELT #290, #302) in 1983 and in 1993; these articles may be said to reflect Greek-Albanian relations.

The press coverage on ethnic or cultural minorities in Greece included the Turkish Muslim and Pomak minorities in Thrace and in northeastern Greece, the Rom community which is dispersed throughout continental Greece, and the Slav Macedonian minority that mobilized more recently, in the mid to late 1990s. Reports on these communities were very rare and mainly referred to crimes committed within them (ELT #39, #69, #185, TIPOS #264, #361). In 1999, concerns about the mobilization of the Slav Macedonian minority provided the opportunity for some debate on the positive or evil nature of ethnic diversity within a country (ELT #515, #558, #573).

Limited attention was paid to immigration in 1993 and 1999, although it has become an important public issue in the 1990s. Most articles in 1993[13] referred to Albanian immigrants in Greece and were largely negative, equating clandestine migration with criminality and distinguishing between "good" Voriepirotes and "evil" Albanians. However, in October 1999, a series of racist murders of immigrants by a young Greek gave rise to a more articulated debate on racism, xenophobia, migration, and "our" tradition. Although the murders and any kind of racist violence were condemned and newspapers expressed their outrage, the racist character of the action was generally downplayed and the murders were attributed to the deranged personality of the perpetrator rather than his ideas.[14] In ELT, a critical debate[15] took place which paid attention to racism and xenophobia as social problems, emphasized the need for immigrant integration, and promoted a positive representation of aliens residing in Greece. In TIPOS, in contrast, the publication of opinion surveys and the related analysis of the phenomenon suggested that more control was needed: people might lose their temper and attack immigrants because there are too many foreigners in the country (TIPOS #428, #439).

The above general features of the representation of the Greek nation(-state) in the press confirm the ethnic, transcendental character of Greek nationhood (Kitromilides 1983; 1990; Tsoukalas 1993) and the exclusion of immigrants from Greek society (King *et al.* 1998; Psimmenos 1995; Triandafyllidou 1999). The emphasis on the national history, ethnic origins, and purity of the nation provides not only the basis for anti-immigrant and anti-minority discourse but also a tool-kit of symbols, images, and myths that are used in the public debate to deal with (real or perceived) national challenges or threats. The strategic use of this set of national images and symbols can be seen in three versions of the nationalist discourse developed in 1983, 1993 and 1999.

The first of these discourses, identified in articles[16] published in 1983, I have called the "national growth and foreign policy" discourse. This discourse was developed deliberately by the then Socialist government and Prime Minister Andreas Papandreou. Apart from promoting his own party interest, Papandreou constructed a nationalist vision of the country's position and destiny at the national and international level. Greece was represented as a small but independent and important country, a leader in the Balkans. The key position of Greece between Europe/the West and the "Eastern Block," its being the only "Western" country in the Communist Balkans, and its links with the Mediterranean countries of Italy and Spain were emphasized. The country's pivotal East-West geopolitical location and Balkan context were transformed into a competitive edge in the international scene. While attention was paid to Greece's membership in the EEC, its contacts and co-operation with Bulgaria, Yugoslavia, and the Soviet Union were given major visibility. Some attention, albeit limited, was paid to economic growth and the expansion of industry.[17] Papandreou and his supporters mixed the small size, long history, and geopolitical particularity of Greece in a cocktail of national pride and glory. Thus, the ambivalence of Greek identity and geopolitical position was transformed into a point of strength and a vision of national grandeur. This discourse was pertinent to the Cold War context where mediation between East and West was sought to slow down the nuclear armament competition between USA/NATO and USSR. After 1989, this Janus-faced East-West orientation of Greece took a different form in line with the changing international context.

The two nationalist discourses identified in 1993 and 1999 were triggered by two events that were perceived as national threats or challenges for Greece. In 1993, the key issue was the "Macedonian question" and, more particularly during the sample period, the Greek-FYROM negotiation in the context of the United Nations. Talks between the two countries aimed at reaching an agreement concerning the FYROM's claim to the "Macedonian" name and symbols, which the Greeks considered their own "cultural property" (Triandafyllidou *et al.* 1997). In 1999, the challenge and threat came from the Kurdish leader's (Ochalan) arrest by the Turkish authorities; Greece found itself involved in an unfortunate and rather clumsy way in this event, causing embarrassment to its EU partners and tension in its relations with Turkey.

The "Skopje[18] discourse"[19] was built upon references to the classical heritage, Alexander the Great, the genealogical origins of the Greek nation, its long and glorious history and great culture. It emphasized the sacredness of national symbols and heroes and affirmed their belonging to Greece. The press constructed the national image in opposition to the "thieves" (σφετεριστές),

namely the FYROM people and government, who were represented as chauvinists, extremists, and rigid. Greece, in contrast, was presented as moderate, reasonable, and flexible. However, the Skopje discourse was not limited to the Greek-FYROM relations. It included the overall position of Greece in the Balkans and, as I shall argue in the following section, conditioned Greece's relations with its EU partners. A typical example of this discourse was found in an article titled "Close relations with USA, Balkan bridge. The Prime Minister described the foreign policy of its government" (ELT, #315, 25/10/93, p. 14). In this article, the ethnic conflict and political instability of the Balkan region and the end of the Cold War were presented as a challenge and an opportunity for Greece to assume its leading role in the Balkans. This however, it was argued, could only be possible when the "Macedonian issue" was resolved. This would allow Greece to prosper and become a strong and independent country. The Skopje discourse involved a new national(ist) vision for Greeks but also highlighted the advantage of being a European Balkan country. This seems to be a distinctive feature of modern Greece.

The "Ochalan discourse,"[20] named after its main protagonist, involved another revival of the nationalist discourse. The unhappy handling of the case by Greece was compensated by a nationalist rhetoric on Greek honor (*φιλότιμο*), the long and glorious history of "our race" (*φυλή*), and the national pride and dignity of Greeks, which override concerns for economic stability and dependence on the EU. An intelligence colonel involved in the case became a national hero because, according to the press, he stood faithful to the country's tradition of honor and pride. This discourse involved by definition the Greek-Turkish relations, which represent a whole separate issue beyond the scope of this study. Not surprisingly, the Ochalan discourse was entrenched in Greece's relations with its Balkan neighbors. Greek relations with Bulgaria, FYROM, Serbia, and Turkey were elaborated in this context, and lines were drawn between friends and foes, namely between allies of the Turks and "our" allies. The country's anchoring in the Balkans was emphasized, perhaps also in contrast to its increasingly European/EU orientation.

Two features that these two discourses share in common are worth noting. Firstly, in both cases, the handling of what was perceived as a "national issue" (*εθνικό θέμα*), which in 1993 was the "Macedonian question" and in 1999 the Ochalan case, became the primary criterion on which to judge the government's performance.[21] All internal, economic, social, or political issues faded away in front of the national ones. This view risks giving a competitive edge to parties that adopt extreme nationalistic viewpoints and exploit the national sensibility of the voters. In both cases, the dominant nationalist discourse was partly counteracted by a moderate and critical account of the events,[22] which

appealed to realism against "ideological terrorism" and distinguished "real" patriotism from "pseudo-patriotism" that was represented as unrealistic and harmful to the country's interests.

Taking a closer look at the press discourse on Central and Eastern European countries (CEEC)—including the Balkans—and the Soviet Union/Russia, the complementarity between the nationalist discourse and the representation of CEEC and relations with them becomes evident. Greek relations with the Soviet Union and Balkan countries like Yugoslavia and Bulgaria were given prominence[23] in 1983 and 1989. They were part of the "national growth and foreign policy" discourse of the early 1980s but also reflected Greece's concerns for peace in Europe during the Cold War and in the Balkans in 1989. During the ethnic tension within Yugoslavia in 1989, newspapers reported events, especially in Kosovo, without taking sides or making judgements. In 1993 and 1999, representations of Balkan countries, Bulgaria, FYROM, and Serbia in particular, reflected the "Skopje discourse" (in 1993) and also the geopolitical and cultural links between these countries.

The historical links between Serbia and Greece were emphasized in the 1993 and 1999 debate, when NATO and the UN threatened the former with military intervention for reinstalling peace in the region. The Greek press presented[24] events in a neutral manner, and the important political and economic role of Serbia in the Balkan context was emphasized (ELT #446, #520). Overall, there were both critical and favorable representations of Serbia in the two conflicts. However, the prevalent feature of the reports was that of understanding and moderacy. Some articles preached for multi-national, multi-cultural societies in the Balkans (ELT #537, #539, #569). A typical feature of the discourse was once more Greece's leading role in the Balkans for promoting peace and stability (ELT #315, #317, #283, #301, #454).

Reports on Albania and Greece's relations with that country[25] referred less to the Balkan context and more to bilateral links. The Greek minority in Albania and the Albanian immigrants in Greece were two matters of concern that brought about a negative representation of the Albanian government and people. This view was enhanced by reports on political disorder and instability in this country. However, more recently, in 1999, Albania's struggle to become "westernized" and come closer to Greece both politically and economically was recognized. In this context, Greece was seen to represent Europe or the West, in contrast to backward, ex-communist, "Eastern" Albania. This differentiation further highlighted the pivotal role of Greece in the Balkan context.

Relations with USSR/Russia, although flourishing in 1983 after Papandreou's effort for an independent foreign policy, later declined. The Greek press discourse largely followed the line drawn by international press agencies

and other Western European countries' coverage (Triandafyllidou 2001). It promoted a positive view of Gorbachev and his reforms, and later represented Russia as a chaotic country, constantly in political crisis and social upheaval, with an ill-functioning democracy and overall alien to "the West" or "Europe."

The discourse on CEEC too followed the Western press pattern (Triandafyllidou 2001) of Cold War and threat discourse in the 1980s, including spy stories (TIPOS #30, #44) and the nuclear NATO and Warsaw Pact missile controversy.[26] In 1989, reports on political reforms in Central and Eastern Europe occupied a large part of the foreign news in the Greek press; however, attention concentrated on four countries: Czechoslovakia, DDR, Hungary, Poland, and to a lesser extent Romania. The coverage[27] was generally ambivalent and mainly hesitant concerning the depth of the change. Mostly, attention was paid to the repression of opposition by the Czechoslovak, East German, and Polish governments. Only Hungary was represented positively as a democratizing country. Reports referred almost exclusively to politics. Little was said about the economic transition to capitalism except for its social costs with regard to Poland (TIPOS #194). The Greek press largely ignored former Soviet republics with the exception of Georgia's civil war and the interference of Russia and Armenia in it.

This brief overview of the Greek press discourse on CEEC and Soviet Union/Russia confirms the importance of the Balkan context for Greece's national identity and geopolitical position. Greece adopted a pivotal role as the mediator between East and West and a leader in the region. This emphasis reflected the ambivalence of Greek national identity and culture, which includes both "Western" (European) and "Eastern" (Balkan) features and traditions. Nonetheless, the grand foreign policy of Papandreou and related nationalist discourse during the Cold War were transformed, in line with the post-1989 international context, to a representation of a modern, developed, European country with a leading role to play for stability in the Balkans. The extent to which Greece has been successful in this mission is, of course, a matter of IR and political science research that goes beyond my scope here. However, the emphasis of the press on the country's uniqueness and specificity is worth pointing out. Thus, apparently contradictory elements such as the ethno-genealogical, absolute view of nationhood and a pre-modern economic behavior interacted with the modernizing and Europeanizing tendencies in a fundamentally explosive Balkan context, producing a relatively coherent picture of a "unique" nation.

GREECE AND THE "UNITED" EUROPE

From a total of 1105 articles included in the database, 539 referred to the EEC/EU, (Western) Europe[28] in general, or some EEC/EU member-state.[29] The qualitative analysis of the debate and its evolution over time reveals a number of *threads* that organize discourse on EU and Europe. I use the term thread to emphasize the continuity of a specific theme, issue, or representation in time. Some of these discourse threads survive and evolve in all four phases studied while others die out and/or are resurrected later on.

Two important threads were the representation of the EEC and later EU as an international economic actor and as an international political entity.[30] The image of a unitary political actor was more often than not used in contrast to the U.S.A. but also to Islam, in the case of the Rushdie affair (ELT #94, #198). In 1993 and 1999, the EU was seen to intervene as a transnational political unit in the ethnic conflict in former Yugoslavia and also in relation to the Kurdish leader's arrest by Turkey. The Ochalan arrest, in particular, led to an extensive debate in the Greek media concerning relations between Greece, the EU, fellow member-states, and third countries. The unity and the fragility of the EU as a transnational power were highlighted by the Greek newspapers.

Another set of "discourse threads' referred to the relationship between EEC/EU and Greece. In the period studied, three distinct threads have been identified which can be schematically classified in terms of the issues involved in each case. Hence, I shall distinguish between the "social issues," the "political relations," and the "economic" thread.

The "social issues thread"[31] was overall positive. EEC/EU was seen as a factor of progress in social issues, at least in relation to the situation in Greece. Concerns related mainly to (un)employment, welfare provisions, and social policy. In 1999, attention was also paid to social protest at the European level. The "pan-European" mobilization of farmers and their demonstration in Brussels were reported in both newspapers. Social issue coverage reflected a deepening European integration.

The "economic thread"[32] was an interesting and controversial one because it captured much of the gist of the overall debate on the EEC/EU. There were two main sub-discourses in this area, which indirectly touched upon the political realm too. First, there was a set of arguments, frames, and images that referred to Greece's economic integration into the EEC/EU, the prosperity and progress that this would bring to the country, and the modernization and further development of whole sectors of the national economy, (as a result of the overall positive influence of the EEC/EU policies and, in particular, of subventions or

other funding coming from the EEC/EU). In 1989 and 1993, TIPOS privileged a representation of the EEC as a "river of gold" from which money poured into the Greek economy. Critical views of EEC funding, (which was said to be ill-distributed among member states,) and the limitations placed by EEC on Greek production and exports were also discussed in the press (mainly by ELT). Overall, positive representations prevailed and EEC/EU was seen as a vehicle for progress and prosperity for Greece. This positive image was changed mainly in 1999, when this thread of discourse was merged with the one below to an overall integration discourse around the Agenda 2000 (EU's comprehensive set of policies for the period 2000-2006).

Already in 1989 an integration discourse emerged in the economic realm, which concentrated on the economic development of EEC as a whole and on the harmonization between member-states. This thread gained new impetus in 1993 with the debate on the Maastricht treaty ratification and its implications for the future of the Community. Emphasis was put on the "ever closer Union" objective, but important criticisms were recorded concerning the kind of Europe that was to be created. On the occasion of the Greek presidency of the EEC in 1993, the relationship between the country and the Community was re-elaborated by the press. Attention was drawn to the Greek government's vision of a Europe with a social profile, promoting employment, welfare policies, and growth (see in particular ELT #300, #354, #362, #326). The integration thread took a new turn in 1999: the Union was taken for granted but was in crisis. The crisis representation was pervasive in the debate on Agenda 2000 and the reform of the Common Agricultural Policy. Although member-states were seen as interdependent, the perception of crisis and rigidity on the part of some countries was strong. The perception of an institutional and commercial European reality was however put forward through the publication of financial news that referred to EU in its totality, especially after the introduction of the Euro.

The second branch of the economic thread was cross cutting to the first and referred to the relationship between the Greek economy and the unified European market and/or other member-states' economies. This line of argumentation included a pro-European view, in which the authority and legitimacy of the EU to set the criteria and guidelines for economic development and public finance were fully endorsed. Greece was seen as subordinated to the EEC/EU decisions, fully in agreement, with them and striving to comply with the pre-requisites for entering the Single Market and the European Monetary Union. In this view, notions such as "compromise," "harmonization," "co-operation," "negotiation," "reaching a consensus" prevailed when reporting disagreement between member-states. Moreover, EEC/EU experts' authority and legitimacy to judge Greece's performance and also to set the criteria that would

decide the country's present and future were uncontested. This line of argumentation existed in all four periods studied and was enhanced in 1999, on the eve of Greece's integration into the European Monetary Union (EMU).

An opposite set of arguments, namely an anti-European view, questioned the advantages that Greece had to gain from participating in the Common Market, saw Greece's interests as antagonistic to those of other member-states or EU as a whole, and criticized EEC/EU decisions. In 1983, this type of argument was put forward concerning the need to protect the Greek market from free competition within the EEC. This discourse temporarily disappeared in 1989 but re-surfaced in 1993 and 1999. In 1993, emphasis returned to the balance of power between countries, a balance reflected, according to the press, in the funding received by smaller and weaker countries. Perhaps not surprisingly, since more integration and interdependence sharpens disagreements and contrasts, the perception of national antagonisms was more pronounced in 1999. The EU was seen as a superordinate unit to which Greece and other member-states incontestably belonged, but there was also a high awareness of the antagonistic national interests and the strategies adopted by member states to protect them and influence EU policies. This line of argumentation put into question the very essence of the integration process.

Quite distinct from the other two, a "political relations" thread was also identified in the newspaper discourse. This thread reflected not only the progress of political integration and the evolution from the European Economic Communities to a European Union but also the changing international environment and the re-shuffling of the East-West relations. In 1983, the debate was organized in Cold War terms of Western "good guys" and Eastern "bad guys." In this period, the EEC was mainly seen as an economic alliance; its relevance in East-West relations, according to the Greek press discourse, was limited. The contrast between the two "blocks" was represented as a broadly European, not EEC, matter. Europe, as a geographical area, was seen as the arena of the nuclear missile controversy (TIPOS #69, #91, #95, #98, ELT #218, #236, #239). Greece's relations with Turkey, for instance, were mediated by the Council of Europe and not the EEC (TIPOS #20, #32, ELT #257, #196). The framing of political discourse remained more or less unchanged in 1989, when changes in CEEC were contrasted to (Western) Europe (TIPOS #185, ELT #64)[33] and/or specific member-states that had special links with CEEC, like (Western) Germany (related to the DDR) or Finland (in relation to the USSR).

The political character of the Community became relevant in 1993 with reference to the "Macedonian question." The controversy between Greece and FYROM led to an extensive debate concerning "us" and "them." Greece's relations with other member-states were represented as ambivalent, and

connected to the latter's recognition of FYROM as an independent republic (ELT #379, #390, TIPOS #262). The issue involved the symbolic negotiation of Greece's relation and position within the Community. The EEC was at times represented as the ingroup and in other articles as the outgroup, closer to Turkey, FYROM or the USA rather than Greece. It also remained doubtful to what extent Greece was bound by its membership to the EEC in the political realm. Priority was given to what was perceived as the national interest, independent of Community decisions.

In 1999, in contrast, with reference to the Ochalan issue, the press discourse changed. The perception of Greece as part of a transnational *political* unit was, clear and that emphasis shifted to solidarity and interdependence[34] between member-states. The Prime Minister of Greece reportedly explained to fellow EU partners the mishandling of the issue by Greece and apologized for not having informed them in advance. Even though in some articles the EU was represented as torn by internal disagreements, it was overall seen as inextricably related to Greece in this matter, sharing responsibility with this last. Greece appealed to its partners and the EU as a whole to take action towards Turkey, as if the Union was a unitary, compact political entity.[35] The same framing of Greece-EU relations was adopted when the status of Turkey as an applicant for membership to the EU was discussed. The matter came up later in 1999, and Greece found itself in a delicate position, given its historically hostile relations with Turkey. The press coverage on this issue was organized in terms of interdependence among member-states, solidarity, and compromise (ELT #524, #559, #531, #578, #580, #476, TIPOS #429). This view reflected the Greek government's policy while the opposition insisted on representing Turkey as Other and asking for a more rigid stance on Greece in the EU (TIPOS #424-5, #401). However, even in this viewpoint, the political unity of the EU was not contested.

The analysis of the representation of the EEC/EU, Europe, and the fellow member-states in the Greek press has highlighted the multi-dimensional character of European integration and the gradual reinforcement of the political perspective, which complements and supports the economic unification. The discourse included both positive and negative views and varied in time, in relation to the issues that were topical in each of the four periods studied. In my opinion, two of its characteristics are worthy of particular attention. First is the nearly total subordination of the national government (and the press coverage) to EU experts' authority and legitimacy in the economic realm. Second is the emergence of a sense of solidarity and interdependence with other member-states and the EU as a whole. This reciprocal dependence was seen as compatible with

and supportive of national interests and identity. This is a rather recent phenomenon. During the Greece-FYROM controversy in 1993, the press presented the issue as a national matter to which European mediation was welcome, but it was seen as external to the nation. In the Ochalan case, on the contrary, six years later, the role and responsibility of Greece, the EU and/or other member-states were represented as inextricably related. Feelings of solidarity and interdependence within the EU context were mobilized in the discourse to make up for what was perceived as national humiliation and a threat to the image of the nation.

CONCLUSIONS

This chapter has studied the representation of Greece, fellow EU member states, EEC/EU and Europe as well as CEEC and USSR/Russia in the Greek press during the past twenty years. The scope of the analysis has been twofold. First, I aimed at exploring the positioning of Greece between West and East and the representation of Greece's identity and geo-political role in its double function as a small Balkan country and as a modern state, partner in the EU. Second, my objective was to study the relationship between representations of Greece and the EU, Europe, or other member-states and the extent to which national interests and identity were seen as incompatible to European integration. Apart from having paid little attention to identity and discourse issues (Triandafyllidou and Spohn 2000), approaches to European integration tend to see a feeling of identification with Europe as either non-existent and/or non-desirable or as incompatible to national identity, hence bound to eventually replace this last or create some kind of superordinate political loyalty.

The representation of the Greek nation(-state) in the press confirms the findings of earlier research that emphasized the transcendental ethnic character of Greek identity. National history and myths were used to deal with (real or perceived) national challenges or threats. Moreover, they were strategically used by political parties to gain votes. National issues were seen as of a higher order than any other social, economic, or political concerns. This nationalist discourse was inscribed into the Balkan context to which Greece was seen as belonging. Greece was represented as standing-in-between East and West, in conformity with its Janus-faced identity (Tziovas 1994). In the 1990s, cultural and political links with the Balkans were integrated into the European vocation of the country. The pivotal position of Greece was thus emphasized to reconcile apparently contradictory elements such as the ethno-genealogical, absolute view of nationhood with a project of modernization and Europeanization. This

discourse confirms the perception of uniqueness or, at least, particularity of Greece in the European context.

The analysis of the discourse on the EEC/EU points to the established authority and legitimacy of the EU in economic and social matters. However, it also highlights the deepening of the political integration among member-states and eventually the intertwining of national politics and identity with the EU. Although Greek national identity remains important and, as said earlier, national issues were given priority over all other concerns, awareness of Greece's interdependence with other member-states and EU as a whole proved to be high. The press emphasized solidarity and sharing of responsibility with the Union and fellow members in international relations. National sovereignty was seen as partly belonging to the European level. Thus, identification with Europe appeared as complementary and even supportive to national identity even though it did not and cannot, in the immediate future at least, replace this last.

ENDNOTES

[1] In colloquial Greek, the joke "we have become Europeans" is commonly used to denote Greece's integration into the European Union but also to delineate in a subtle way the perceived difference between Greece and Europe.

[2] I.e., the question of recognition of the Former Yugoslav Republic of Macedonia as an independent Republic, the name that this last would take as well as its nationalist claims to what the Greeks deemed as "their" national heritage.

[3] The author is aware of the problematic character of the term "Mediterranean" (Goddard *et al.* 1994: 4-23) but she uses it to denote the higher level of cultural proximity between these three countries in comparison to their looser links with western or northern European countries.

[4] For *Eleftheros Typos*, the last week of April instead of February was selected for the year 1983 because the newspaper started being published only in that month.

[5] Articles referring to non-European countries (or socio-political actors) such

as USA, Japan, Arabic countries, Latin America and others were excluded from the database.

[6] I shall use as shorthand expressions the terms "Western Europe" to refer to the European Union or EEC and/or a member-state, and "Eastern Europe" to refer to Central and Eastern European countries or Russia.

[7] I use the terms "nation" and "nation-state" or "nation(-state)" interchangeably with regard to Greece to denote the perceived unity of the nation with its state. In the Greek language, the word "εθνικός" (ethnikós) *means both "ethnic" and "national."*

[8] Given the large number of articles analyzed in the study, I shall cite the most representative ones for each issue, using abbreviations: ELT = *Eleftherotypia*, TIPOS = *Eleftheros Typos* and numbers (e.g. #7, #218) that refer to the ID number of the record in the database. Articles are cited randomly, not following the numerical order, as they appeared in my notes. ID number reflects order of insertion into the database not date of publication of the article. The full data on each record may be made available upon request to the author.

[9] Ioannina is a medium-size, by Greek standards, city in northwestern Greece and the capital of the region of Epirus. Thessalonike is the second largest Greek city with over one million inhabitants. It is the economic, political, and cultural centre of northern Greece.

[10] ELT #85, #199, #223, #285, #601, TIPOS #110, #133, #328, #329, #331, #332, #411-413.

[11] ELT #136, #263-5, #30, #49, #289, #548-550, #524, #368, TIPOS #417, #352, #377, #250, #330, #61, #78, #87, #151, #156.

[12] Ethnic Greeks who had migrated from the region of Pontos (in the southern coast of the Black Sea) to Russia in the beginning of this century later were deported to Central Asia (Kazakhstan, Georgia, Armenia) and after the collapse of the Soviet Union "returned" to Greece, which they saw as their homeland.

[13] TIPOS #212, #229, #291, #298, #322, ELT #307.

[14] TIPOS #425-7, #389, #398, #436-8, #441, ELT #529, #491-5, #481-2, #474, #495, #577.

[15] ELT #570, #572, #574, #576, #588, #588-9, #590-1.

[16] ELT #147, #264, #193-4, #197, #211, #216, #231, #251, #256, #188, #180-1, #176, #179, #161-2, #165, #167, #140-1, #151-3, #145, #137, #122, #154, TIPOS #21, #46, #58, #49, #72, #89, #97, #103.

[17] TIPOS #61, #78, #87, ELT #30, #49, #136, #263-5.

[18] I use the term "Skopje discourse" to hint to the Greek government's and media's obstinate decision to refer to FYROM as "Skopje" (from the name of its capital) and to the FYROM citizens as "Skopjans."

[19] TIPOS #198, #200, #215, #214, #227, #262, #256, #273, ELT #316.

[20] TIPOS #336, #344, #363, #373, #354, #362, ELT #631, #640, #627, #596, #516, #648, #511, #646, #658.

[21] On defence of the national interest and "Hellenic" spirit of the political parties, see ELT #459, #436, #319, #454, #387, TIPOS #222, #275, #280, #286, #304, #305, #307.

[22] In 1993: TIPOS #272, ELT #451-2, #434, #420-1, #416, #397 and in 1999: ELT #616-7, #655, #463, #465.

[23] TIPOS #54, #57-8, #46, #72, #96-7, #103, #152, #139, #144, ELT #76, #89, #73, #60, #70, #180-1, #188, #177, #176, #179, #170, #161-2, #165, #167-8, #151-4, #144-5, #148, #251, #256, #231, #235, #211, #197, #193.

[24] TIPOS #289, #296, #357-8, #374, #359, #379, ELT #388, #328, #433, #384, #340-1, #355, #630, #647, #621, #636, #657, #466, #569, #537, #539.

[25] References to Albania appear only in 1993 and 1999 when the Communist autarchic regime of that country collapsed.

[26] TIPOS #13, #68, #91, #80, #81, #98, ELT #121, #124, #239, #218, #190.

[27] TIPOS #121, #128, #155, #160, #129, #139, #136, #142, #157, #162, #168, #174, #187, ELT #115, #103, #77, #55, #25, #33, #21, #12, #2, #17, #113, #114, #105.

[28] I refer to Europe and the European Union as two separate though closely related concepts. The term European Union refers to the material reality of the social, political, and economic entity called European Union. This reality includes of course culture and identity elements but these are demarcated by the institutional forms and geo-political boundaries of the Union. The term Europe, in contrast, refers to the more general idea of Europe, or better to the ideas of what is Europe (a political, cultural, geographical, or other type of entity) that may be used in the press.

[29] Current member-states (EU15) were included in this count throughout the period studied (1983-1999) so as to take note of any evolution on the press coverage and representation of these countries.

[30] For EEC/EU as international economic actor, see 1983: ELT #172, TIPOS #52; 1989: ELT #118; 1993: ELT #442, #282, TIPOS #206; 1999: ELT #472, #592. As international political actor, 1983: ELT #259, #247, #230, TIPOS #94; 1989: TIPOS #123, #194, ELT #198, #94; 1993: ELT #393, #308, TIPOS #263, #312, #323; 1999: ELT #583, #596, #599, #614, #653, #618, #626, #628, #645, TIPOS #337, #333, #347-8, #345, #343, #356, #366.

[31] In 1983: TIPOS #67, ELT #224; in 1989: TIPOS #118-9, #165; in 1993: TIPOS #239, ELT #335, #320, #304, #293; in 1999: ELT #519, #551-2, #470, #473, #608, TIPOS #334.

[32] In 1983: TIPOS #31, #39, #79, #93, #100-1, #111, #4, #8-4, #63, #102, #105-7, ELT #131, #228, #261, #266-7, #252, #220, #212, #208, #219; in 1989: ELT #28, #68, #99, TIPOS #120, #171, #192, #116, #125-6, #131-2, #141, #159, #134, #145-6, #149, #156, #164, #173, #181; in 1993: ELT #314, #402, #342, #383, #367, #353, #276, #407, #353, TIPOS #234, #317, #308, #314, #259, #290; in 1999: TIPOS #350, #346, #371, #377, #400, #399, #390-1, #351, #369, #377, #383, ELT #624, #627, #524, #512, #574, #549, #534, #553, #547, #592, #593, #638, #650-1, #654, #606-7, #625, #497.

[33] Representations of the CEEC and their relations with Greece or the EU were discussed in the previous section.

[34] ELT #464, #600, #598, #627, #643-4, #463.

[35] TIPOS #337, #333, #347-8, #343, #345, #356, à366, ELT #596, #599, #614, #618, #626, #628, #645, #653.

REFERENCES

Baldwin Edwards, M. Arrango, J. 1998. Eds. "Immigrants and the informal economy in southern Europe." South European Society and Politics, special issue, 3, 3.

Goddard, V. Llobera, J. and Shore, C. 1994. "Introduction. The Anthropology of Europe." From V. Goddard, J. Llobera and C. Shore, *The Anthropology of Europe. Identity and Boundaries in Conflict*, Oxford: Berg.

Heraklides, A. 1995. "*Οι εικόνες του εθνικού 'εαυτού' και του 'άλλου' στις διεθνείς σχέσεις: η περίπτωση της ελληνικής εξωτερικής πολιτικής*" (Images of the national "self" and the "other" in international relations: the case of the Greek foreign policy), *Sighrona Themata*, 54: 27-36.

King, Russell Lazaridis, Gabriella and Tsardanidis, Charalampos. 1999. Eds. *Eldorado or Fortress? Migration in Southern Europe*. London: Macmillan.

King, Russell Iosifides, Theodoros and Myrivili, Lena. 1998. "A migrant's story: from Albania to Athens." *Journal of Ethnic and Migration Studies*, 24(1): 159-175.

Kitromilides, Paschalis. 1983. "Το Ελληνικό κράτος ως εθνικό κέντρο." From Demetris Tsaousis. Ed. *Ελληνισμός-Ελληνικότητα: Ιδεολογικοί και Βιωματικοί Άξονες της Νεοελληνικής Κοινωνίας* (Hellenism and Greekness. Ideological and Biographical Axes of Modern Greek Society). Athens: Estia.

Kitromilides, Paschalis. 1990. "'Imagined Communities' and the Origins of the National Question in the Balkans." From M. Blinkhorn and T. Veremis. Eds. *Modern Greece: Nationalism and Nationality*. Athens: Eliamep.

Psimmenos, Iordanis. 1995. "*Μετανάστευση από τα Βαλκάνια: Κοινωνικός Αποκλεισμός στην Αθήνα*" (Immigration from the Balkans: Social Exclusion in Athens). Athens: Glory Book and Papazisis.

Reicher, Stephen Hopkins, Nick. 1996. "Self-category constructions in political rhetoric; an analysis of Thatcher's and Kinnock's speeches concerning the British miners' strike (1984-5)." *European Journal of Social Psychology*, 26: 353-371.

Roudometof, Victor. 1999. "Unthinking the "Clash of Civilizations' in Southeastern Europe." *European Journal of Social Theory*, 2(2): 233-47.

Spohn, Willfried. 2000. The European Union's Eastern Enlargement and Changes in Collective Identities. A Western and Eastern European Comparison. European Forum, European University Institute, Seminar Paper EUR/23, February 2000.

Triandafyllidou, Anna. 1999. "Racists? Us? Are you joking? The discourse of social exclusion of immigrants in Greece and Italy." From Russell King, Gabriella Lazaridis and Charalampos Tsardanidis. Eds. *Eldorado or Fortress? Migration in southern Europe*. London: Macmillan.

Triandafyllidou, Anna. 2001. *National Identity Reconsidered: Images of Self and Other in a United Europe*. Lampeter, U.K.: Edwin Mellen Press, forthcoming.

Triandafyllidou, Anna and Spohn, Willfried. 2000. *Representations of Europe and the nation in current and prospective member-states: media, elites and civil society* (EURONAT). Project proposal funded by the European Commission Research DG. European University Institute, Florence, June 2000.

Triandafyllidou, Anna. Mikrakis, Andonis and Calloni, Marina. 1997. "New Greek Nationalism." *Sociological Research Online*, 2(1), www.socresonline.org.uk/2/1/7.html

Tsoukalas, Constantinos. 1993. "Greek National Identity in an Integrated Europe and a Changing World Order." From H. Psomiades and S. Thomadakis.

Eds. *Greece, the New Europe and the Changing International Order*. New York: Pella.

Tsoukalas, Constantinos. 1994. "Ιστορία, *μύθοι και χρησμοί*. Η *αφήγηση της ελληνικής συνέχειας*" (History, myths and oracles.(History, myths and *oracles. The narrative of the Greek continuity). From Επιστημονικό Συνέδριο Εθνος-Κράτος-Εθνικισμός (Scientific Congress on Nation-State-Nationalism)*, V.A.. Athens: Εταιρεία Σπουδών Νεοελληνικού Πολιτισμού και Γενικής Παιδείας.

Tziovas, D. 1994. "Η *δυτική φαντασίωση του ελληνικού και η αναζήτηση του υπερεθνικού*" (The western imaginary of Hellenism and the search for transnationality). From *Επιστημονικό Συνέδριο Εθνος-Κράτος-Εθνικισμός (Scientific Congress on Nation-State-Nationalism)*, V.A. Athens: Εταιρεία Σπουδών Νεοελληνικού Πολιτισμού και Γενικής Παιδείας.

PART III
GEOPOLITICS AND SECURITY POLICIES

CHAPTER 13
THE BALKANS AND A TRANSFORMING NATO

S. Victor Papacosma
Lemnitzer Center
Kent State University

Critically situated at a strategic geographic crossroads, the Balkan peninsula has, apart from the numerous wars among its indigenous occupants, attracted numerous conquerors and invaders over the centuries. Because of the heavy involvement of stronger outsiders, Balkan inhabitants have infrequently been in the position to determine their own destinies; however, direct military confrontation between rival Great Powers in this area has been minimal. During the Cold War, neither the United States nor the Soviet Union effectively deflected the overriding nationalist concerns and strategic attention of allied states in the Balkans toward broader alliance objectives in the superpower confrontation. Thus, NATO stepped cautiously but accomplished little in trying to reconcile the differences between Greece and Turkey and, obviously, alliance solidarity and planning suffered. Concurrently, the Soviet Union moved warily and suffered even greater setbacks in maintaining what was initially and briefly a solid Communist wall of four states in southeastern Europe.[1]

ROUND I: BOSNIA[2]

As the 1980s drew to a close and the new decade began, dramatic developments in the Soviet Union and Eastern Europe combined to topple Communist party domination and to bring an end to the Cold War. Soviet hegemony in Eastern Europe crumbled, the Warsaw Pact officially ended its existence on July 1, 1991, and the Union of Soviet Socialist Republics formally died in December 1991. Superpower rivalry ceased and NATO justified its existence handsomely by defending Western interests and deterring aggression from the East for four decades. No one knew, however, what NATO's post-Cold War calling would be.

Balkan problems, fundamental to the origins of the Cold War and laterally to the consequent founding of NATO, would contribute, in a tortuous manner, to the Atlantic Alliance's evolving mission after 1989. The proclaimed "new world order" proved short-lived and, if anything, not very "new" for southeastern Europe. Many old problems, with pre-1939 origins, revived vigorously along with new variables to create an updated Balkan morass. Nationalism was replacing communism as the dominant ideology, and the world

was reminded once again of the durability and regenerative volatility of ethnic hatreds and regional rivalries. Communism and the superpower confrontation had simply muted these sentiments in certain areas.

The fall of communism in and rapid superpower retreat from Eastern Europe essentially left the region's peoples to their own devices, a rare condition with good and bad consequences. The region could no longer consider itself an area of contention between rival Great Power/superpower interests. Hostilities in the Balkans, if they did not directly involve neighboring Greece and Italy could ostensibly remain localized between the disputants, but the balkanization of Yugoslavia compelled governments in Europe and the United States to reevaluate such initially optimistic assumptions.

The complex process of transition from communism to regimes and institutions more resembling those of democratic and free-market Western Europe was not smooth: it encountered, dependent upon the country, varying degrees of political, economic, and social difficulties. In the Balkans, as in some republics of the former Soviet Union, ethnic issues dominated and gave direction to post-Communist developments. Yugoslavia, which had implemented a moderate form of Communist rule and which had played with its nonaligned foreign policy a positive role in maintaining regional stability, has had a bloody post-Cold War experience. Worsening economic and political conditions during the 1980s and the fall of Communist regimes elsewhere intensified centrifugal separatist forces in Yugoslavia. Attempts to dismantle Communist hegemony, while maintaining the federal structure, faltered and then failed, as each national group in the multiethnic state had its own agenda. The Yugoslav People's Army (JNA), with its Serbian-dominated officer corps, remained the only important organization still committed to the maintenance of the federation.[3]

Tensions within Yugoslavia increased in 1990-91, and widespread fighting erupted after the JNA moved to counter the secessions of Slovenia and Croatia, proclaimed on June 25, 1991. Slovenia, largely because of its very small Serbian minority and geographic position, saw its struggle with the JNA end rather quickly, but fighting in Croatia, with its relatively large and concentrated Serbian population, increased in intensity. The Federal Republic of Macedonia voted to assert its sovereignty in September, but no bloodshed resulted from this pronouncement. Such would not be the case following an early March 1992 referendum, boycotted by its Serbian population, when the Federal Republic of Bosnia-Herzegovina declared its independence. Bosnian Serbs, in turn, proclaimed the Serbian Republic of Bosnia-Herzegovina later that month and began to shell Sarajevo, the Bosnian capital, on April 5.

Yugoslavia, with its declining state of affairs, attracted attention, but the United States and its allies during the late summer of 1990 were concentrating

on a response to Iraq's invasion of Kuwait. European Community member-states appeared preoccupied with advancing European integration. The future of the Soviet Union also concerned Western policymakers who hoped to take advantage of pending opportunities to downsize defense budgets. Just a few years earlier, Yugoslavia's disintegration, with the accompanying shock to the regional status quo, probably would have created a Cold War crisis and might well have invited the intervention of one superpower—with an inevitable counterresponse from the other. This did not happen now since the security of NATO members did not appear to be involved. NATO's alliance was based on collective defense and conceived for the different international challenges of the Cold War; it had no prescribed charge in the Yugoslav situation. Consequently, a redefinition of its mission had to be proposed and accepted to justify its existence. With its structure, forces, equipment, and overall military capabilities, NATO was, however, the organization that could doubtlessly produce the most conclusive results if it were called on to act assertively by its members. Notwithstanding many differences and the utilization of intra-alliance pressures and compromises in arriving at a common policy, the Soviet threat had provided the crucial unifying focus for NATO allies for four decades. New criteria for determining threats to security and accompanying responses had to be established for the alliance that had succeeded so well in another era and that generated few calls for its dissolution in the present.[4]

NATO was by no means ready or willing to involve itself in the worsening Yugoslav situation when fighting broke out in mid-1991. The constraints were many and included the reluctance of the United States to intervene and its preference to have Europe respond to the crisis.[5] The European Community (EC), the Conference on Security and Cooperation in Europe (CSCE), the Western European Union (WEU), and the United Nations all entered into the diplomatic campaign to arrange an end to the Yugoslav fighting before the close of 1991. These efforts all faltered in trying to contain the fighting that spread to Bosnia-Herzegovina in the early spring. The situation then became even more complicated as a triangular conflict involving Muslims, Serbs, and Croats in shifting alliances further plagued those actively seeking resolution to the conflicts. By the summer of 1992, world opinion generally singled out the Serbs as the prime culprits in a war of aggression that viciously and deliberately claimed thousands of innocent civilians among its victims.

Western diplomatic initiatives, chronically reactive to worsening conditions and increased bloodshed, lacked the coercive potential of armed forces or the will to use them, largely because governments considered the political, military, and financial stakes too great. European and American leaders deliberately avoided the prospect of consigning the large number of troops necessary to

impose peace in such a hostile setting. Traditional appraisals of the Balkans as a quagmire dominated military-political assessments in Western capitals, and the Serbs understandably became emboldened by the prospect of a continued tepid response by the world community.

Within the context of the reordered Europe, the major decisionmaking states did not perceive their national interests to be directly threatened by this otherwise dreadful war in the Balkans, but the press and television diligently exploited the news-making developments and horrors so that neither voters nor their leaders could ignore them. If aggressors remained unchallenged, the use of force to change borders and the genocidal practice of "ethnic cleansing" threatened to destroy a people before the world's eyes on the television screen. Moreover, the mushrooming numbers of refugees in Europe, at unprecedentedly high numbers for the period since the late 1940s, portended sensitive domestic problems for European states. This Balkan war, therefore, had a potential impact on developments in other regions and for continued instability.

Shortly after the outbreak of fighting in Yugoslavia in late June 1991, the EC brokered its first cease-fire and sent observers to monitor conditions. Many other mediated cease-fires followed, only to be broken by the belligerents. Brussels reacted to the ongoing crisis by dispatching EC observers to the area of fighting, establishing a peace conference for the conflicting parties, imposing an arms embargo, and freezing EC aid to Yugoslavia. The EC then called upon the United Nations in September 1991 to join in the peacemaking process. The UN responded with a succession of Security Council resolutions, with peacekeeping forces, sent first to Croatia (March 1992) and then to Bosnia, with a smaller monitoring force to the Former Yugoslav Republic of Macedonia (FYROM), and with humanitarian aid to relieve suffering in Bosnia-Herzegovina. The CSCE also participated in the manifold initiatives to end the fighting. The deployment of UN peacekeeping units to Croatia facilitated the establishment of relative quiet, although Croats were hardly ready to accept the militarized occupation of about one-third of their territory by Serbs as a permanent condition.

NATO, for its part, began the process of mission redefinition for the post-Cold War era in June 1990 at its London summit and continued it at the Rome summit in November 1991, several months after fighting had broken out in Yugoslavia. Adopting a new strategic concept and calling for associated new force structures, NATO was reorganizing and reorienting itself for changes occurring in Europe. Importantly, provision was made for the new force structures to assume a greater role for multinational formations in support of UN or CSCE peacekeeping missions. The Atlantic Alliance now had the authorized capability to operate out-of-area and not solely in response to a direct threat to

one of its member-states. The North Atlantic Council resolved at Oslo in June 1992 that NATO would be prepared to support CSCE peacekeeping activities on a "case-by-case" basis, a position declared jointly with the WEU at the Helsinki CSCE summit the following month. At its ministerial meeting in Brussels in December 1992, NATO confirmed its readiness to support on a case-by-case basis peacekeeping operations under the authority of the UN Security Council, which had the primary responsibility for international peace and security. Underlying this approach was the evident prospect, according to a NATO official, that "NATO is not prepared to undertake a peacekeeping operation on its own initiative; it is unlikely that such an approach would find consensus among the Allies."[6]

With the greatest capabilities at its disposal but essentially sharing many of the same policymakers participating in the other involved institutions, NATO in July 1992 began its slow and incremental participation in efforts to contain and end hostilities in the former Yugoslavia.[7] Even before its December 1992 decision regarding support for UN peacekeeping operations, NATO joined with the WEU in air and sea operations to enforce UN Security Council Resolutions 713, 757, and 787 preventing unauthorized shipping from entering the territorial waters of the reconstituted and downsized Federal Republic of Yugoslavia (FRY), now made up of only Serbia and Montenegro. Initially, there was no authorization to stop, board, and search vessels suspected of breaking sanctions, but in November the decision was made to uphold UN Security Council resolutions imposing an arms embargo on all republics of the former Yugoslavia and an economic embargo on Montenegro and Serbia.[8] The alliance in early April 1993 responded with Operation Deny Flight to UN Security Council Resolution 820 allowing NATO aircraft to shoot down planes violating the no-fly zone imposed on Bosnian airspace in October 1992 and monitored since then by NATO aircraft. The first flights by American, French, and Dutch fighter jets on April 12, 1993, represented a momentous act, if only in symbolic terms, because the alliance assumed a combat mission in a nondefensive capacity and out-of-area. The North Atlantic Council in early July adopted plans offering close air support to UN troops and other personnel in Bosnia if they were attacked and requested air strikes. Concurrent with these developments, NATO also agreed in early June to back with air power the UN Security Council resolution for the creation and security of six safe areas (in Sarajevo, Tuzla, Zepa, Gorazde, Bihac, and Srebrenica). Bosnian Serb forces were required to leave these cities and to allow UN peacekeepers unrestricted access. As the strangulation of besieged Sarajevo tightened, NATO on August 2 threatened to bomb Bosnian Serb forces unless they relented. A barely nominal retreat followed.[9]

Despite all the attention directed toward peacekeeping units, even larger numbers of peacemaking forces appeared necessary to create the conditions appropriate for the effective disposition of peacekeepers whose mission was limited and constantly threatened. With no coherent political strategy to unify the disparate positions of NATO members, truly effective military measures could not be implemented to influence the warring parties—primarily the Bosnian Serbs—to end their fighting and to arrive at a lasting settlement. The complex situation had become even more difficult when Croats began fighting Bosnian Muslims, their former allies, in early April 1993. The concern of the international community translated into diplomatic, economic, and humanitarian approaches.

The quest for an honorable diplomatic solution to the multifaceted crisis also fell victim to the passing of time. In particular, UN mediator Cyrus Vance and European Community negotiator Lord David Owen worked tirelessly but unsuccessfully to draft a plan for peaceful resolution of outstanding issues and for a restructured Bosnia-Herzegovina. Alliance measures to reinforce UN resolutions for pressuring the Bosnian Serbs, who controlled about 70% of the countryside, fell far short of their intended purpose. Pursuing brutal tactics essentially directed at creating an ethnically divided Bosnia associated or federated with Serbia, the Bosnian Serbs were succeeding in their attempts to carve out the largest share for themselves, although they comprised only about one-third of Bosnia's prewar population. Despite the condemnation of world opinion, aggression had provided rewards for the Serbs even as they refused to accept the share of about half of Bosnia's territory allotted to them as too small. Borders were being changed by force, the principle of partition seemingly had been accepted, and thousands of refugees would never be able to return to their ancestral homes.

Decisive military action to force an end to these patterns, advocated by many politicians and journalists, found few supporters among decisionmakers. Apart from the general unwillingness of NATO allies to supply the extensive commitment of troops considered necessary to implement effective ground strategy, Britain and France, which provided the largest contingents for UNPROFOR (UN Protection Force) in Bosnia, opposed measures such as widespread air strikes, fearing that their lightly armed peacekeeping units would become easy victims or hostages of the Bosnian Serbs. Generally advocating increased air activity, the Clinton administration, too frequently erratic in its own positions, experienced difficulties arriving at some sort of consensus with European allies. Moreover, Washington maintained that it would provide American troops for peacekeeping purposes only after a definitive cease-fire and peace had been agreed to. The three Western members of the UN Security

Council also had to consider the concerns of Russia still in the process of developing post-Soviet foreign policy, in an area of its traditional interest, southeastern Europe.

While a number of measures to bolster the image and mission of NATO predominated at the Brussels summit of January 10-11, 1994, the Bosnian imbroglio was approached carefully so as not to disrupt unity. NATO leaders confirmed all previous decisions and reaffirmed the alliance's readiness to execute air strikes to prevent the strangulation of Sarajevo and other threatened areas in Bosnia. By the end of the month, intensive discussions in Brussels centered increasingly on utilizing air attacks against Bosnian Serb forces to relieve UN peacekeepers in captive areas and to help free designated safe havens from the suffocating grip inflicted upon them.[10]

A challenge to demonstrate NATO's resolve came shortly afterward in formulating a response to the mortar-shell attack of Sarajevo's marketplace on February 5 that resulted in sixty-eight dead and more than two hundred wounded. Blamed on the Serbs, this carnage heightened outrage in Western capitals and forced an emergency meeting of the North Atlantic Council, which announced its ultimatum on February 9. It condemned the ongoing siege of Sarajevo, called for the Serbian withdrawal of or placing under UN control by February 20 all heavy weapons located in an area within twenty kilometers of Sarajevo's center, and sanctioned NATO support for UNPROFOR in carrying out its task of identifying heavy weapons that were not withdrawn or regrouped in conformity with the listed demands. NATO also authorized air strikes in response to UN requests, against targets in violation of these terms. NATO's quickly fashioned firmness appeared to work, as virtually all heavy weapons in and around Sarajevo—including those of the Muslims—were withdrawn or placed under UNPROFOR control by the deadline.

When six Serbian aircraft violated the no-fly zone over Bosnia on February 28, NATO planes shot down four of the intruders. This brief encounter not only provided another opportunity to display NATO's stiffened posture but also corresponded to a veritable "baptism in the Balkans": These were the first shots ever fired in combat by NATO forces in the alliance's forty-five years of existence. Coupled with the announcement in late February of a U.S.-brokered cease-fire between the Bosnian Croats and Muslims, these developments raised hopes for a lasting solution.

Such prospects dimmed quickly. Although conditions in Sarajevo eased, the Bosnian Serbs resumed provocative actions on several fronts to confront the Muslims, to harass UNPROFOR, and to test the resolve of NATO. In the process, divisions glaringly reappeared in the ranks of those seeking peace. UN officials expressed concern in March that the momentum for peace was faltering

and that countries were unwilling to provide strong military and political support and, especially, the thousands of troops necessary for policing cease-fires throughout Bosnia.

A pattern of sorts did seem to set in, with little progress toward establishing conditions for a final peace. NATO continued to involve itself in combat activity on a highly selective basis and at the request of UN authorities during 1994, but these intermittent, pinprick actions against Bosnian Serb forces contributed little to change the course of the battlefield struggle or to influence diplomatic maneuvers for arranging peace. During the spring, a "Contact Group" of Britain, France, Germany, Russia, and the United States formed to forward new peace proposals. The terms, announced on July 5, allocated 51% of Bosnia-Herzegovina's territory to the nascent Muslim-Croat federation and the remainder to the Bosnian Serbs, with both parts remaining in a single state. The former begrudgingly accepted the provisions, but the Bosnian Serbs balked, claiming that the plan called for an inequitable slashing of the 70% of the land area controlled by them and that it denied them the right to form a separate state or to join Serbia. Importantly, Russia backed the proposal, as did Serbia's Slobodan Milosevic, who urged the truculent Bosnian Serbs to accept. When they did not, Belgrade imposed a trade embargo on the Bosnian Serbs in August. In return for this reversed stance toward its Bosnian compatriots, Serbia's leadership hoped for an easing of the UN-imposed economic sanctions that had taken their toll on its economy.

Among the Contact Group states, the United States alone outspokenly advocated the lifting of the arms embargo for the Bosnian Muslims as a means of eliminating the Serbian superiority in weapons and creating conditions for a more equal confrontation. The Clinton administration also pushed for more extensive and intensive NATO air strikes against Bosnian Serb targets. These positions, seen as a means to compel the Bosnian Serbs into accepting the Contact Group's peace proposals, ran counter to the views of other group members. As the countries providing the largest numbers of troops to the UN peacekeeping units in Bosnia, Britain and France contended that lifting the arms embargo would only intensify and broaden the conflict and endanger their lightly armed forces. Rather than face such a prospect, London and Paris would pull out their troops before they became battlefield casualties or hostages. Such a move also augured a vital setback to the critical humanitarian aid engineered locally by the UN detachments, whose replacements from other UN member-states would be hard to produce. In the meantime, the Bosnian Serbs continued to demonstrate in varied ways that they controlled important lifelines for Sarajevo and other designated safe havens. The impasse persisted on the battlefield, among decisionmakers, and between institutions.

NATO's redefined role as a subcontractor in support of UN peacekeeping missions on a case-by-case basis had become increasingly awkward, and the precarious UN-NATO relationship worsened during the fall of 1994. Meeting in New York in late October, NATO and UN negotiators drafted an accord for a tougher policy in Bosnia. NATO air strikes were now to be conducted on a "timely basis," and "while general warning may be given to an offending party, tactical warning of impending air strikes, in principle, will not." Under normal circumstances, several targets were to be authorized for each air strike to be carried by NATO in close coordination with UNPROFOR. The joint statement also referred to "dual key" arrangements remaining in effect to ensure that "decisions on targeting and execution will be taken jointly by UN and NATO military commanders."[11]

Battlefield and diplomatic developments during November would contribute to significant policy shifts on the part of the outside powers. Bosnian Muslim-Croat forces had launched an offensive in late October against the Bosnian Serbs and made important gains. Initially cheered by this turnaround, groups sympathetic to the Bosnian Muslim cause soon became disheartened when the Bosnian Serbs regrouped and succeeded in their counteroffensive against Muslim fighters and civilians in the Bihac enclave of northwestern Bosnia—an officially designated UN safe area whose status was to be secured with NATO support. Then on November 11 the United States announced that it had ordered American forces in the Adriatic to stop enforcing the arms embargo against the Bosnian Muslims.[12]

The impact of "contradictions" intensified. The UN on November 21 authorized NATO air strikes on the Udbina airfield in Serb-occupied Croatia, from which Serb planes attacked Muslim positions in nearby Bihac. UN officials, however, limited the choice of targets. The mission's thirty-nine aircraft, constituting the biggest military operation by NATO in its forty-five-year history, fired only on the runway, a taxiway, antiaircraft guns, and a surface-to-air missile site. UN commanders argued against targeting Serb planes on the airfield in order to avoid casualties, but ultimately they sought to avert Serb reprisals against UN troops, particularly the ill-equipped Bangladeshi contingent trapped in Bihac. When NATO planes followed on November 23 with two more raids against Serb antiaircraft systems, the Serbs retaliated by rounding up UN personnel, spurring additional fears that UN soldiers might be killed.[13] Despite public protestations of UN-NATO resolve in executing these air strikes, it had become evident that Bosnian Serb forces recognized, and appreciated, the missions for what they were: pinprick strikes that would only have pinprick consequences on their side carried out by stronger powers unable to agree upon common, decisive, and forceful measures.

With allies sharply criticizing each other and with NATO solidarity fraying markedly, the Clinton administration undertook sharp modifications in American policy in late November. Limited bombing had failed to pressure the Serbs into accepting the Contact Group's peace plan. Unsuccessful in budging Britain and France from their policy positions toward the Bosnian conflict, Washington now concluded that it was more important to reestablish NATO unity, albeit at a potential price for America's leadership role. The United States had been unable to impose its will on allies with troops in Bosnia, in large part because of its own unwillingness to commit soldiers to the region until after the cessation of fighting. A number of commentators referred to the worst crisis within NATO ranks since Suez nearly four decades earlier.[14]

In determining that a diplomatic route toward arranging peace in the thirty-two-month Bosnian conflict should now be increasingly emphasized, Washington, in conjunction with other Contact Group members, offered the Bosnian Serbs the possibility of a "special relationship" with Serbia. The Serbs first had to accept Bosnia's sovereignty "in principle" and the group's original proposal for territorial division (51% of which would fall under Muslim-Croat control). There were no evident assurances that this new tack would provide better results or, for that matter, contribute to vastly improved relations among the allies. In playing their hand boldly, the Bosnian Serbs by early December stalled the entire UN military and aid delivery operation in the most vulnerable Bosnian regions with hostage-takings, beatings of UN troops, and blockades of overland fuel and food convoys. The Serbs, concerned about possible NATO air attacks, declared that they could not assure the safety of any aircraft flying in Bosnian airspace and informed UN sources that they linked the release of UN peacekeepers to NATO. Despite continued Serb provocations and violence against UN units, UN commanders refused to call on NATO for countermeasures and protection.[15]

Concurrent with these developments and the increasingly untenable conditions for UNPROFOR, officials projected a possible UN withdrawal from Bosnia with the participation of NATO. The impact of such a move on the warring parties and region would be manifold, with no side reaping great benefits. If withdrawal of the UN's approximately twenty-three thousand troops were to occur, the United States committed itself to provide up to half of the personnel of the projected NATO support force of fifty thousand. At this critical juncture, the Bosnian Serb side contacted former president Jimmy Carter to assume a mediatory role. In a mission fraught with controversy, Carter flew to Sarajevo and succeeded in arranging a temporary cease-fire between the Bosnian Serbs and Muslims that began on December 23. UN mediators then took over

and worked out a subsequent agreement for a four-month cessation of hostilities starting on January 1, 1995.[16]

The first months of 1995 indicated few departures from ongoing patterns and, if anything, focused greater attention on flaw-ridden attempts to establish peace in Bosnia. The tenuous Carter cease-fire broke down completely during the spring, and in late May the Serbs defied UN orders to bring heavy weapons under UN control and to remove all heavy weapons around Sarajevo. In response to a NATO attack on a Serb ammunition depot, the Serbs shelled designated safe areas and, on the following day, began rounding up UN peacekeepers as hostages, eventually seizing more than 350 troops. Air strikes were then halted. For its part, the Bosnian government utilized safe areas to launch raids on Bosnian Serb forces, and in mid-June began an offensive to break the seize of Sarajevo. The Bosnian Serbs retaliated by stepping up their shelling of the capital and safe areas. Milosevic, evidently trying to separate Serbia's policy from that of the Bosnian Serbs, helped negotiate the release of UN hostages. In June, NATO stepped up its potential involvement by authorizing the formation of a "rapid-reaction force" of 12,500 troops to UNPROFOR and by approving a plan for the despatching of 60,000 troops to Bosnia if UNPROFOR units had to be evacuated.

July events intensified pressure on NATO for some long overdue action on the provocative tactics of the Bosnian Serbs. In overrunning the safe area of Srebrenica and then Zepa, the Bosnian Serbs took more UN hostages; according to later reports, they also expelled 42,000 Muslims and massacred thousands of Muslim men. These developments heightened world outrage against the Bosnian Serbs and increased criticism of the manifest incapacity of the UN and NATO to thwart these horrors.[17] Following a Contact Group meeting in London on July 21 and in still another attempt to ratchet up its capabilities, NATO warned the Serbs against attacking Gorazde and other safe areas, simplified procedures for conducting air strikes, reduced the impediments in the dual key policy with the UN, and considerably increased the targets for strikes. NATO actions finally seemed ready to go beyond threatening rhetoric and pinprick attacks. Moreover, the Clinton administration began assuming a more active role in coordinating policy with London and Paris.

The Serbian juggernaut lost its momentum in August. Croatian forces, which had received covert aid from America, stormed the Serbian-controlled Krajina area of Croatia and retook the area for Zagreb in just three days, forcing thousands of Serbs to flee. Belgrade did nothing to come to their assistance. When the Bosnian Serbs sent a mortar shell into a Sarajevo market, killing 37 people, and then rejected UN and NATO conditions for a heavy-weapons withdrawal from around Sarajevo, NATO responded on August 30 with 15 days

of extensive strikes against Bosnian Serb military targets. Considerable damage to their military infrastructure and battlefield retreats in the face of a Bosnian Muslim and Croat offensive forced the Bosnian Serbs to yield to demands for removing heavy weapons around Sarajevo and other safe areas. Once again, Belgrade did not come to the aid of fellow-Serbs in Bosnia, and territory under Bosnian-Serb control shrank to around the level offered in earlier peace plans and now in revived peace efforts sponsored by the United States and actively advanced by Richard Holbrooke, assistant secretary of state for European and Canadian affairs.

President Clinton on October 5 announced that all combatants would honor a cease-fire, which, after a two-day delay, came into force on October 12. The cease-fire would continue for sixty days or until the completion of "proximity peace talks" in the United States. Many analysts could agree with Lord David Owen's judgment that "Richard Holbrooke deserved much credit for the breakthrough, and American political muscle and ability to fine-tune NATO's air strikes had been crucial."[18] A coalition of stronger forces, so long in the making and so long in demonstrating its ability to act assertively, had finally compelled the Bosnian Serbs to yield in the face of superior might.

A continued NATO role was deemed critical in subsequent efforts to bring peace to Bosnia. In anticipation of such a function, the North Atlantic Council in October approved the formation of an Implementation Force, termed IFOR, for deployment in Bosnia following an agreement upon peace terms. The "peace proximity talks" convened on November 1 in Dayton, Ohio, during which the United States and fellow Contact Group states arrived at a hotly-bargained settlement agreed to by the Republic of Bosnia and Herzegovina, the Republic of Croatia, and the Federal Republic of Yugoslavia (which represented the Bosnian Serbs). Initialed on November 21, the peace agreement with its military, civic, and political sections became effective upon its formal signing on December 14 in Paris. The terms allocated 49% of Bosnia's territory to a Serb Republic and 51% to a Muslim-Croat Federation. Bosnia was to be "one state, with one capital [Sarajevo], but two entities."[19] Despite initially widespread pessimism in many quarters about the viability of the controversial accord, it did provide basic guideposts for the road toward more stable and peaceful conditions.

The critical military aspects of the Dayton accord depended on NATO for successful implementation. IFOR, conceived as a multinational force, would fall under the command of NATO with a grant of authority from the United Nations. In an evident attempt to avoid conflicts, including over the rules of engagement, between NATO and the UN, the commander of UN peace forces transferred authority over 17,000 troops to the IFOR commander on December 20, 1995.

Apart from the heavy involvement of the United States, Britain, and France, which provided the bulk of the forces, the remaining NATO states participated in varying degrees, as well as sixteen non-NATO states, of whom twelve had Partnership for Peace (PfP) status, including Russia. Under NATO command with a multinational force approaching 60,000 (United States with 18,000, EU countries with 29,000, and about 10,000 from non-NATO members), IFOR operated under NATO rules of engagement with the authorization to respond to situations with "robust use of force, if necessary." Thus, the NATO-led Operation Joint Endeavor in Bosnia represented "NATO's first-ever ground force operation, its first-ever deployment 'out-of-area,' and its first-ever joint operation with NATO's Partnership for Peace and other non-NATO countries."[20]

Within the context of its designated military mission in the Dayton accord, IFOR achieved a number of objectives by the end of its 12-month mandate in December 1996. With only a few, essentially accidental, deaths, IFOR's presence contributed to the termination of fighting. Dayton's military timetable was met with the pullback of Bosnia's armies from confrontation lines and with IFOR supervision of the withdrawal and storing of heavy weaponry. The former warring parties also ceded lands assigned to others in the Dayton pact. On December 20, 1996, the Stabilization Force (SFOR) succeeded IFOR, assuming the mission of maintaining the security environment to facilitate Bosnian efforts to reconstruct its economy and society. SFOR's efforts in assuring military and personal security have been generally effective and accomplished with a multinational force, still led by NATO, numbering 20,000 by late 2000.

Of continuing concern, however, is the daunting challenge of developing conditions for a truly democratic, multiethnic, and economically viable Bosnia. In these areas there have been marginal accomplishments, despite extensive and intensive involvement of, among other international bodies, the United Nations, the Organization for Security and Cooperation in Europe (OSCE), the European Union, the World Bank, and the International Monetary Fund. Just one indicator of limited progress is manifest in the strong showing of the Serb, Croatian, and Muslim nationalist parties in Bosnia's November 2000 elections, even as more moderate political parties came to power in neighboring Croatia and Serbia. Bosnian society remains fragmented, and, it has been argued, international guardianship is unwittingly contributing to the condition rather than truly promoting conciliatory politics. "The dynamic of the Dayton process has been to award greater mandates to international institutions, increasingly disempowering the Bosnian people and their representatives."[21]

ROUND II: KOSOVO

NATO's belated intervention in the summer-fall of 1995 brought an end to the fighting in Bosnia, set the stage for the uneasy peace that followed, and contributed, with its relative success, to a new, if not controversial, strategic mission for the Atlantic Alliance. The Balkan region, notorious for its uncanny ability to produce problematic conditions, next served up another challenge for NATO members in the Kosovo province of FRY with its large concentration of Albanians (about 90% of the population).

Conditions had worsened significantly for the Albanians after Serbia's Milosevic ended the province's autonomy in 1989, and in 1991 they responded with a campaign of nonviolent resistance against Belgrade's harsh policies. The high level of violence characterizing neighboring Bosnia after April 1992 did not extend into this corner of the former Yugoslavia, in part attributable to President George Bush's late December 1992 warning to Belgrade (and reiterated by the successor Clinton administration) that the United States was prepared to take unilateral military action, without European cooperation, if the Serbs spread their aggression to Kosovo or FYROM. However, after the Bosnian conflict ended, the situation turned noticeably for the worse in 1996 with the launching of reprisal attacks against Serbian police and state officials by the Albanian Kosovo Liberation Army (KLA). The level of violence escalated in 1997; in the winter of 1998, serious encounters occurred as Serb forces sought to eliminate the KLA.[22]

The international community condemned Serbia's strong-arm tactics against the ethnic Albanian population with many press references to renewed tactics of ethnic cleansing on the part of Serbs. Calls for substantive dialogue between the disputants, including UN Security Council Resolution 1160 (March 31, 1998), brought no substantive results, as the tempo and involvement of individual countries and international groups, such as the European Union and Contact Group, increased during 1998. On their part, NATO planners during the late spring and summer began formulating military options. Still another series of initiatives to reverse the intensifying conflict met with no success. A Kosovo Diplomatic Observer Mission (KDOM), involving the Contact Group, began official monitoring in July, but the Serbian forces succeeded in crushing a number of KLA strongholds during August. Serbian advances in September forced thousands of Kosovar Albanians to flee their homes, and the ensuing humanitarian crisis fueled the concern of the international community. UN Security Council Resolution 1199 on September 23 called for, among other directives, a cease-fire and the withdrawal of Serbian forces sent to Kosovo to crush the rebellion. The following day NATO formally declared its initial steps

for possible military intervention in Kosovo by sanctioning two contingency plans, one for air strikes and another for maintaining a cease-fire agreement. Thus, as with the Bosnian crisis, NATO had incrementally voiced its concern along with other international organizations and then declared plans for possible intervention. On this occasion, however, NATO was signaling its readiness to act well before the magnitude of casualties and human dislocation reached the levels of the earlier crisis.

In response to the concerted pressure and Richard Holbrooke's persistence, Milosevic agreed to a cease-fire, the presence of 2000 unarmed members of a Kosovo Verification Mission (KVM) from the OSCE, and aerial reconnaissance by NATO. The Serbian leader also promised to withdraw forces and to propose a political solution for ending the crisis. To reinforce the diplomatic efforts, NATO on October 13 issued an activation order for air strikes that could be implemented at the discretion of Secretary General Javier Solana. Just before the termination of a deadline extension, Belgrade demonstrated compliance with the departure of special police troops from Kosovo. The KLA sought to reap advantages from the Serbian withdrawal by reclaiming territory and launching small-scale attacks. A low-level of fighting continued despite the cease-fire and the presence of KVM observers, who now sought to avert armed conflict with mediation and negotiations.

The new year brought with it a flare-up of hostilities in Kosovo and reports of massacres and atrocities, largely attributed to the Serbs. Responding to the latest round of fighting, the Contact Group in late January demanded that the warring parties meet with mediators in France, and the North Atlantic Council on January 30 backed up this call by once again authorizing the secretary general to order air strikes, if required. A first round of extended negotiations met at a chateau in Rambouillet near Paris from February 6 to 23 and attempted to formulate a peaceful interim settlement and political framework for Kosovo. Held under the auspices of the Contact Group and co-chaired by the French foreign minister and his British counterpart, three co-mediators representing the United States, Russia, and the European Union presided over the meeting. Secretary of State Madeleine Albright actively involved herself in the last stages. For differing reasons, neither the Kosovar Albanians nor the Serbs were ready to endorse the cobbled agreement. Albright candidly remarked on February 21 that if both sides refused to sign, "there will not be bombing of Serbia."[23] Cumulative pressure on the Kosovar Albanians, who were divided due to the intransigent positions of the KLA, brought tentative acceptance from the Albanian delegation, which agreed in principle to sign the accord but first requested to consult advisers in Kosovo. A follow-up session was called for March 15 in Paris.

In the interim, the Pentagon released reports that the Yugoslav army was massing armored troops on the Kosovo border. Talks resumed, and the Albanian delegation on March 18 endorsed the peace plan, while the Serbian representation did not sign. Belgrade refused to accept Rambouillet's provision for a referendum in Kosovo after three years, which would have assuredly resulted in a vote for independence by the Albanian majority. Additionally, Milosevic opposed the terms that would have allowed NATO forces movement through all of Yugoslavia.[24]

In the immediate aftermath of the Paris meeting's closure, Yugoslav and KLA forces stepped up their campaigns in Kosovo, and the OSCE withdrew its KVM observers on March 20. Richard Holbrooke was again sent to Belgrade in a last-ditch attempt to salvage peace efforts but found Milosevic unwilling to yield. NATO then set procedures in motion to launch its military response. Secretary of State Albright later commented that "Signing Rambouillet was crucial in getting the Europeans two things. . . . Getting them to agree to the use of force and getting the Albanians on the side of this kind of settlement." She also added that if the signing had not been forced at that time "we would be negotiating while they [the Serbs] were carrying out their 'village a day keeps NATO away.'"[25] NATO commenced Operation Allied Force, its bombing campaign of Serbian forces in Kosovo, on the evening of March 24, thereby launching its first ever military operation against a sovereign state.

When contrasted to the strung out and belabored response to the Bosnian conflagration, NATO this time demonstrated a readiness to react quickly—too much so, some critics would maintain—to impose peace in the Balkans. Many alliance members, embarrassed by the price of earlier inaction, did not wish to see a repeat of the previous conflict's ethnic cleansing with its accompanying loss of life and mass waves of refugees—thousands of whom sought sanctuary in Western Europe. Even though conditions in Kosovo by no means approached the deplorable levels seen earlier in Bosnia, enough NATO leaders evidently believed that quick, decisive action against Milosevic would result in his rapid concession to NATO demands based on Rambouillet. A senior NATO official remarked that "There were a lot of Milosevic watchers who said a few bombs might do it."[26] Such would not, however, be the case. In turn, Milosevic boldly resisted despite NATO's overwhelming military superiority and ever intensifying bombing, largely, it is speculated, in his anticipation that the cohesion of the NATO alliance would wither once the bombing campaign brought no dramatic results.[27] In this projection, the Serbian leader miscalculated, although there were noticeable, but not debilitating, fissures in the alliance during the seventy-eight days of bombing.

In a move to reassure the American public regarding the involvement of the United States in NATO's campaign, President Clinton in his televised address announcing the start of bombing promised: "I do not intend to put our troops in Kosovo to fight a war."[28] With declared parameters placed on America's role, it was quite unlikely that any allies would volunteer to dispatch land forces into the combat zone, an emergent situation akin to that which plagued NATO planning during the Bosnian crisis. Public support for a campaign that brought body bags home would rapidly disappear. These imposed limits on NATO's attack mission facilitated Serbia's stepped-up offensive to crush the KLA, forcing more than one million Albanians to flee their homes and seek sanctuary in neighboring countries, particularly Albania and FYROM.

Instead of quelling hostilities, NATO intervention contributed to their intensification and to further regional destabilization In response to the Serbian advances on the ground, air attacks, which had initially focused on Serbian units and military installations in Kosovo, expanded to include targets in Serbia after April 3 when NATO missiles struck the defense and interior ministries in central Belgrade. NATO justified its campaign on the basis of humanitarian necessity, and the North Atlantic Council issued a statement on April 12 to emphasize this stance:

> The crisis in Kosovo represents a fundamental challenge to the values of democracy, human rights, and the rule of law, for which NATO has stood since its foundation. . . . The FRY has repeatedly violated United Nations Security Council resolutions . . . [which] has created a massive humanitarian catastrophe which also threatens to destabilize the surrounding region. . . . These extreme and criminally irresponsible policies . . . justify the military action by NATO.[29]

The events surrounding NATO's fiftieth anniversary at the Washington Summit on April 23-24 were less celebratory than originally intended because of the uncertain direction of Balkan developments. The extended bombing had not delivered the anticipated results, and prospects of a possible ground war, fraught with controversy and division among NATO member-states, loomed ominously on the horizon. Among larger allies, Italy and Germany were especially concerned about the prospect of sending troops into Kosovo. In Greece, large public demonstrations voiced strong opposition to the bombing of Serbia, a fellow Orthodox Christian nation, and the Greek government called for renewed diplomatic efforts to halt the fighting. While not participating in any military actions, Greece stated that it would not prevent NATO from such

missions and allowed its port of Thessaloniki to be used for the resupply of forces in FYROM.[30]

Notwithstanding the backstage gloom in Washington, public proclamations of unity and renewed commitments to NATO's mission dominated media coverage. The Kosovo experience contributed to the amended definition of NATO's mission for the 21st century. The alliance affirmed its traditional objectives, among others, of assuring collective defense, the transatlantic relationship, and stable security environment in Europe. Significantly, it also endorsed NATO's burgeoning roles in crisis management and stability through partnerships with other nations and organizations such as the OSCE and EU. In a specific "Statement on Kosovo" the alliance confirmed its commitment to support "a peaceful, multi-ethnic and democratic Kosovo where all its people can live in security and enjoy human rights and freedoms on an equal basis." The statement also declared that "It is our aim to make stability in Southeast Europe a priority of our transatlantic agenda."[31]

Achieving this aim supplied many uncomfortable moments as Serbian forces managed to make gains, the mass exodus of fleeing Kosovar Albanians continued unabated, and intensified NATO bombing, which at times struck unintended targets such as the Chinese Embassy in Belgrade and civilians, failed to force Milosevic to his knees. The alliance's political and military leaders heatedly debated the dreaded option of a land invasion of Yugoslavia if the air campaign brought no conclusive results. Despite extensive planning and preparations, NATO leaders would never grant the final political authorization for an invasion.[32] Importantly, however, the possibility of a ground engagement was never totally excluded in public pronouncements, and this would play in NATO's favor.

Unlike NATO's air campaign in Bosnia, its bombing of Yugoslavia in spring 1999 did not constitute a mission officially sanctioned by the UN Security Council. The United States and other NATO allies sought to avert a likely veto from Russia and probably China for authorization of military action against Yugoslavia. As an avowed friend of Serbia, Russia, hardly in the position to extend effective military aid, offered Belgrade diplomatic support, expressing its vocal opposition to the bombing and general NATO policy. In a mediatory role, Moscow advocated a reduced future role for NATO in Kosovo, an objective sought by Belgrade. The North Atlantic Council's statement of April 12 had called for Milosevic to "agree to the stationing in Kosovo of an international military presence," an implicit reference to NATO. The document also demanded that the Serbian leader "provide credible assurance of his willingness to work on the basis of the Rambouillet Accords in the establishment of a political framework agreement for Kosovo . . . ."[33]

Subsequent negotiations and proposals worked around these and related issues, as NATO intensified its bombing of Serbia during May. The basis for serious discussions centered around a statement of principles released by the foreign ministers of the G-8 nations on May 6. The wording allowed some wiggle room for compromise by suggesting, for example, that the UN was to be granted a key role in Kosovo at war's end. Ultimately, the cumulative effect of the bombing, the continued solidarity of NATO's member states, the possibility of a NATO land campaign, and Russia's diplomatic pressures forced Belgrade to yield officially on June 10, 1999. NATO, the G-8, EU, UN, and Russia all played critical roles in the hammering out of final terms with Yugoslavia. Operation Allied Force came to an end without a single NATO fatality after more than 38,000 sorties, nearly 11,000 of which were strike sorties.

The peace plan emerged as a basic compromise solution to break the stalemate. Serbian military and police forces were to withdraw from Kosovo, the KLA was to disarm, Albanian refugees were to return to their homes, and a multinational military force with NATO at its core, but also including Russian and Ukrainian troops, would move into the province for peacekeeping purposes. Significant for Belgrade was the stipulation securing the territorial integrity and sovereignty of Serbia. A civilian administration would be set up in Kosovo under the UN, which became the overarching political authority. UN Security Resolution 1244 of June 10 affirmed the basic guidelines of the agreement. Two days later, the international peacekeeping mission, Kosovo Force (KFOR), with NATO forces in the lead, moved into Kosovo from staging points in FYROM and Albania. An initial standoff between NATO and Russian troops, which had arrived in Pristina several hours earlier on that first day, did not seem to bode well for future cooperation, but several days of hard negotiating defined the areas of responsibility and confirmed unity of command.[34]

By the end of September 1999, KFOR had succeeded in demilitarizing Kosovo, and the former combatants had complied with the deadline for handing in weapons. Hundreds of thousands of refugees returned to their homes. In its political role, the UN Interim Administration Mission in Kosovo (UNMIK) based itself on four pillars. The UN supervised civil administration, including the UN International Police (UNIP), the UN High Commissioner for Refugees (UNHCR) provided humanitarian relief, the OSCE set out to encourage democracy and institution building, and the EU embarked on promoting economic recovery.[35] The missions for all were laden with difficulties.

NATO's publicly avowed premise for its Kosovo intervention had rested on the need to curb the humanitarian disaster and threat to regional stability.[36] Despite NATO's proclamations of success, some quite opposite results had

become manifest. NATO's bombings had actually helped the Serbs to drive the Albanians out of Kosovo. Moreover, embarrassing revelations appeared after the conflict as news releases claimed that original estimates of Serbian killings of Albanians were misleading, inflated, and by no means of genocidal proportions.[37] The resulting human dislocation also undermined regional stability, the consequences of which assumed unanticipated forms.

The agreement ending the fighting had not outlined the future political disposition of the Kosovo province, whereas the abortive Rambouillet process had made some specific proposals. In a stinging critique of NATO's policy, one analyst points out that the Albanians had fought for independence based on the right to national self-determination, while NATO insisted that Kosovo be regranted autonomy and remain part of Yugoslavia. Further, "The alliance had . . . intervened in a civil war and defeated one side, but embraced the position of the party it had defeated on the issue over which the war had been fought."[38] Countering this contention, however, it has to be pointed out that, had NATO backed the KLA program for independence, it would have established an unfortunate precedent for encouraging guerrilla and breakaway movements around the world—or as close as in neighboring FYROM with its sizeable and restive Albanian minority.

KFOR deployed some 46,000 military personnel from thirty-nine countries, contributed to the establishment of relative peace, and facilitated the activities of other international organizations operating in Kosovo. However, concurrent with the return of around one million refugees to their homes in Kosovo, many Albanians welcomed the opportunity to pressure the remaining Serbian minority, already considerably downsized, to flee. Included in the exodus were other minorities, such as Roma Gypsies. Although KFOR could claim that it successfully implemented the demilitarization of the KLA and transformed it into the Kosovo Protection Corps, a civilian emergency unit under the direction of the UN interim administration, other Albanian insurgent groups emerged to disturb the peace and extended operations into Albanian-populated areas of southern Serbia.[39]

Still another, this time positive, twist in regional dynamics occurred when the Serbian electorate in late September 2000 voted Milosevic out of office. After initial attempts to deny the victory to the opposition, Milosevic succumbed to mounting popular pressures and the resulting loss of support from the security and military forces. On October 6, he conceded defeat, and Vojislav Kostunica headed the broadly-based coalition that now assumed power. Long NATO's bête noire, Milosevic, who had also been indicted in May 1999 by the International Criminal Tribunal for the Former Yugoslavia, bequeathed a myriad of problems to the new leadership.

For all the difficulties endured under his policies, Kosovar Albanians had more recently benefitted from Milosevic's international notoriety and the UN-NATO presence in their province. The prospect, however, of a more democratic Serbian regime with a rehabilitated image presaged a potential setback for the aspirations of Albanians for independence, an objective supported now even by moderate leaders in their ranks. With the ouster of Milosevic, renewed international talk of a possible rapprochement between Serbs and Kosovar Albanians so as to perpetuate Belgrade's sovereignty over the province was quite reprehensible for the Albanians.

Indeed, the image of the Albanians declined as that of the Serbs received a positive jump-start with their new government. Albanian extremist elements, which called themselves the Liberation Army of Presevo, Medvedja, and Bujanovic, moved into the three-mile wide buffer zone of Serbia bordering on Kosovo that had been created with the end of NATO's bombing campaign. NATO's original intention in setting up the Ground Safety Zone (GSZ) was to distance Yugoslav forces from KFOR units, but by late 2000 Albanian insurgents were attacking Serbs and seeking to consolidate the positions of the local Albanians.[40]

These developments contributed to what a few months earlier would have been considered a quite fanciful scenario: A Yugoslav foreign minister visited NATO Headquarters in Brussels on January 10, 2001, and openly stated that "NATO and the FRY are no longer enemies." Lord George Robertson, NATO's secretary general, subsequently revealed that "NATO and Yugoslavia are working on a daily basis towards a common purpose: preventing extremists from causing more violence in the Presevo Valley [a section of the GSZ]."[41] The reversal of roles now fashioned the Serbs as a force for stabilization, and discussions began on arranging for a return of Yugoslav forces to the GSZ.

Albanian extremist elements next set their sights on FYROM with its estimated Albanian minority in the neighborhood of 30% of the population. With men and supplies spirited across the border from Kosovo, this self-proclaimed National Liberation Army fomented disturbances in FYROM early in 2001 in areas with heavy concentrations of Albanians. Up to this juncture, FYROM's situation had been relatively stable despite battling in the other former Yugoslav republics. Although Tirana consistently maintained a political distance from Albanian militants in Kosovo and now FYROM, the objective of the insurgency was to consolidate a broad band of Albanian-controlled areas in Kosovo, sections of southern Serbia, and FYROM—even if it were to exist separately from independent Albania in the short-term.

Concern over this latest destabilizing turn in the southern Balkans reflected itself in the widespread condemnations of the Albanian militants, but an overt

response on the part of NATO to stem the uprising was not forthcoming. Reports on the prevailing mood in Brussels indicated that "there was no appetite for the West to get involved in sorting out another Balkans war."[42] Instead, NATO strategy focused on providing support to the weak military and government in Skopje. KFOR troops also moved to seal the border between Kosovo and FYROM. On March 8, NATO approved the return of Yugoslav security forces to a nine square mile strip of the GSZ along the border of FYROM, a policy initiative labeled as the first phase of the controlled reoccupation of the entire zone by the Yugoslavs.

The situation remained unsettled during April and May. Although sporadic fighting continued, particularly in FYROM, NATO's policy of isolating the Albanian insurgents seemed to have some effect. Symbolic of NATO's reoriented policy direction, the North Atlantic Council on May 14 announced that the controlled return of Yugoslav security forces into the larger area of GSZ would begin on May 24 "as the final step in a phased and conditioned process."[43] To reinforce NATO's support of the reconstituted government in Skopje, the NATO secretary general signed an agreement with it on May 21 governing the status of and arrangements for KFOR troops in FYROM. On the same day, Albanian rebels in the GMZ agreed to terminate their 16-month campaign against Yugoslav forces. NATO's special envoy to southern Serbia, Pieter Fieth, stated that the peace deal "sends a strong signal to the region as a whole, especially to the Albanian community in and around Kosovo, that armed violence has no future and that it is best to pursue political aspirations through peaceful means."[44]

CONCLUSION

Balkan conflicts have played a critical function in the process of NATO's mission redefinition in the post-Cold War era. During the Cold War, the attention of the superpowers focused on the central front, but, after its closure, Southeastern Europe with the violent dissolution of former Yugoslavia surfaced as a prime area of concern on continental Europe, albeit without the prospect of any serious involvement by rival outside powers. Institutionally, NATO became drawn into this area as the EC/EU, CSCE/OSCE, and the United Nations proved unable to bring an end to fighting in Bosnia. The Atlantic Alliance's new role did not evolve smoothly and is reflective of outstanding problems emanating from the revamped security environment in Europe and, more broadly, the world. NATO's task can be seen to have shifted from an earlier role of primarily deterring superpower confrontation and providing collective defense "to crisis management, peacekeeping, and support for collective security."[45]

The nonmilitary, political dimensions of NATO, often underemphasized, in tandem with its superior military organization and capabilities have tried to adjust to new security conditions as a means to justify the alliance's ongoing importance. The preeminence of NATO is maintained in large part by default, since other organizations have faltered in their efforts to handle crises such as those in the former Yugoslavia. Thus, the European Union has experienced difficulties in its post-Maastricht attempts to develop a viable "Common Foreign and Security Policy." Alternatively, NATO, with the critical presence of the United States, continues to accommodate, by dint of necessity, the sometimes uncomfortable relationship between European members and the world's sole superpower.

As the preceding commentary attempts to establish, NATO's response to what were seemingly unprecedented security challenges in Bosnia and Herzegovina and then Kosovo resulted in decision making and policies that were at times fallible and certainly controversial. Ultimately, NATO can be only as strong as the collective will and objectives of member-states allow it to be. The Bosnian situation provided an important test, and the NATO performance was initially indecisive and delayed and then somewhat effective in bringing an end to the fighting. The NATO states responded more quickly and decisively in the spreading Kosovo crisis, although probably not with the best military strategy. Despite the involvement of other international organizations in both crises, NATO prevailed as the determining force in bringing an end to fighting on a major scale. Overall, however, the results are inconclusive because attempts to restore true stability, reconciliation, and peace in the region are still very much in process. The policies to advance these objectives are multipronged and involve numerous nations, organizations, and billions of dollars. One of the major components in this effort is the Stability Pact for Southeast Europe that was signed by forty nations in Sarajevo on July 30, 1999.[46] But the persistently recurring threats to consolidating stability and security, as for example the incidents engineered by extremist Albanians in Kosovo and FYROM, offer a symptom of chronic regional ailments. Unless there is a dramatic turn for the better that reverses recent patterns, the peacekeeping role of NATO-backed units such as SFOR and KFOR will have to be maintained.[47]

In the broader scheme of things, there have been advances under the aegis of NATO to extend continent-wide security. NATO, as the EU, launched a long-term program for enlargement to integrate states from the East with those of the traditionally more prosperous and stable West. Initially, the Clinton administration devised the Partnership for Peace (PfP) and in early 1994 invited nonmember states to participate in the program for developing new security relationships with the Atlantic Alliance. Romania was the first to sign on in late

January 1994, followed quickly by Bulgaria, Albania, and Slovenia, which indicated the strong desire of Balkan area states to advance their ties with Western Europe and to link their security concerns in this preliminary manner with NATO. FYROM joined the following year. Three of the early signatories—Poland, Hungary, and the Czech Republic—were subsequently approved for full membership, which commenced just days before the start of the bombing campaign against the Serbs in March 1999. The Balkan PfP states, aspiring to a similarly elevated status, provided important services to NATO during the bombing campaign but also received, out of necessity, important security assurances from Brussels.[48] Of considerable significance, also, is the acquisition of PfP status for Croatia in May 2000, a development associated with the bolstering of democratic practices there following the death of Franjo Tudjman in December 1999. And in May 2001, Belgrade, which had established lines of cooperation with NATO in the GMZ, formally expressed its wish to join the PfP, a development considered most improbable just months earlier.

All states in the Balkans, including Bosnia, now have links with NATO and work with it. As events have shown, such relationships do not, however, assure stability and peace because of the continued existence of volatile and divisive issues among them. The two remaining states with a Balkan location, Greece and Turkey, NATO members since 1952, have maintained a troubled relationship for more than four decades and on several occasions have come close to war. NATO's attempts at mediating their disputes have been marginally successful, and, despite recent initiatives aimed at rapprochement, outstanding issues still separate them.[49]

With the collective defense calling of the Atlantic Alliance approaching dormancy, increased attention in the transforming NATO is being devoted to nontraditional missions. The Balkan peninsula has offered NATO opportunities to justify its continued existence, but the region has not served itself up as "user friendly" in the process. Such, however, has been historically and pejoratively a characteristic of the Balkans. Among the many writers who have commented on this phenomenon, Professor William M. Sloane of Columbia University offered just one critique in his volume with the most apt title, *The Balkans: A Laboratory of History*. His preface, written less than four months before the assassination of the Archduke Franz Ferdinand on the streets of Sarajevo, states: "In prophecy it [his book] does not indulge because the experiments making in the historical laboratory are absolutely without previous indication or trial, and the elements entering in are difficult beyond measure to test and define."[50] NATO can certainly provide testimony for this judgment.

ENDNOTES

[1] For a discussion of superpower policy in the Balkans during the Cold War, see S. Victor Papacosma, "NATO and the Balkans," in *NATO in the Post-Cold War Era: Does It Have a Future?* ed. S. Victor Papacosma and Mary Ann Heiss (New York: St. Martin's Press, 1995), 245-55.

[2] A significant portion of this section has appeared in S. Victor Papacosma, "NATO in the Post-Cold War Balkans," *Journal of Political and Military Sociology* 24, No. 2 (Winter 1996): 233-52.

[3] For a succinct analysis, see Steven L. Burg, "Why Yugoslavia Fell Apart," *Current History* 92 (November 1993): 357-63.

[4] F. Stephen Larrabee concludes: "The idea that the only real security threat is an attack on the members of N.A.T.O. is outdated now." "Recent Developments in the Balkans: External and Security Aspects," *The South East European Yearbook 1992* (Athens: Hellenic Foundation for Defense and Foreign Policy, 1993), 91.

[5] One U.S. official reportedly stated in late June 1991: "After all, it's not our problem, it's a European problem." Quoted in James R. Steinberg, *The Role of European Institutions in Security after the Cold War: Some Lessons from Yugoslavia* (Rand Note N-3455-FF) (Santa Monica: RAND Corporation, 1992), 13.

[6] John Kriendler, "NATO's Changing Role—Opportunities and Constraints for Peacekeeping," *NATO Review* 41, No. 3 (June 1993): 18.

[7] Unless otherwise cited, basic information on NATO's involvement in the former Yugoslavia in the following section is drawn from newspaper accounts and several sources available electronically from NATO: Henk Vos, "Co-operation in Peacekeeping and Peace Enforcement," NATO Public Data Service, NATODATA%BLEKUL11.BITNET@PSUVM.PSU.EDU (October 21, 1993); Sir Russell Johnston, "The Yugoslav Conflict—Chronology of Events from 30th May 1991-8th November 1993," ibid. (November 29, 1993); Bruce George, "After the NATO Summit," ibid. (May 26, 1994); and Henk Vos and James

Bilbray, "NATO, Peacekeeping and the Former Yugoslavia," ibid. (July 15, 1994).

[8] During the period from November 22, 1992 to June 18, 1996, NATO and WEU forces challenged about 74,000 ships, inspected almost 6,000 at sea, and diverted more than 1,400 to port for inspection. After June 15, 1993 the mission was called "Operation Sharp Guard." "NATO-WEU Operation Sharp Guard–Fact Sheet," NATO Public Data Service, NATODATA@CC1.KULEUVEN.AC.BE (October 2, 1996).

[9] "Operation Deny Flight," NATO Public Data Service, NATODATA%BLEKUL11.BITNET@PSUVM.PSU.EDU (December 29, 1994).

[10] The chairman of the North Atlantic Military Committee during the winter of 1994 stated that the NATO integrated forces made the single largest contribution to the international involvement in the former Yugoslavia. Apart from the forces serving directly under UN control, there were over one hundred aircraft, more than a dozen ships, and around ten thousand men and women from alliance states conducting NATO integrated maritime and air operations in support of the UN effort. Alliance members also directly contributed an additional fifteen thousand personnel to UNPROFOR operations. Field Marshal Sir Richard Vincent, "The Brussels Summit—A Military Perspective," *NATO Review* 42, No. 1 (February 1994): 10.

[11] NATO, "Press Statement Issued Jointly by UN and NATO," Press Release (94) 103 (October 28, 1994). One alliance source candidly remarked in the accord's aftermath: "What we have here is an agreement papering over the cracks between two bureaucracies with fundamentally different views on peacekeeping and on how to implement broadly the same mandate." "U.N.-NATO Accord Masks Difference—NATO Sources," Reuters, October 28, 1994.

[12] "NATO Retains Embargo, Europe Dismayed by U.S. Move," Reuters, November 11, 1994. A NATO official tersely remarked: "What is happening is that contradictions which have existed for a long time within NATO with regard to Bosnia are now being exposed as a consequence of U.S. domestic policies." "Pentagon Details Embargo Plans," ibid.

[13] "Serb Planes Could Fly Again Despite NATO Strike," Reuters, November

21, 1994; "Bombed Croatian Serb Airfield Repaired and Possibly in Use," *Washington Post*, December 5, 1994.

[14] "In Policy Switch, U.S. Puts Bosnia Aside to Preserve Alliance," *Washington Post*, November 30, 1994; "U.S. and Bosnia: How a Policy Changed," *New York Times*, December 4, 1994; Michael Kelly, "Surrender and Blame," *New Yorker*, December 19, 1994, 50.

[15] "Not Quite the End in Bosnia," *Economist*, December 10, 1994, 46.

[16] "What happens to Bosnia after the U.N. Withdraws?" *Boston Globe*, December 16, 1994; "The Consequences of Pulling Out," *Economist*, December 17, 1994, 53; "Bosnia Cease-Fire to Start Today," *Washington Post*, December 24, 1994; "U.N. Says Bosnia is Quiet as Cease-Fire Starts," *New York Times*, December 25, 1994; "And So to Belgrade," *Economist*, December 24, 1994, 48; "Bosnian and Serb Commanders Meet as Cease-Fire Begins," *New York Times*, January 2, 1995.

[17] Radovan Karadzic, the brassy leader of the Bosnian Serbs, boldly remarked: "NATO threats don't mean anything to us." "The Impotence of the West," *Economist*," July 15, 1995.

[18] David Owen, *Balkan Odyssey* (London: Victor Gollancz, 1995), 340.

[19] *Economist*, 25 November 1995, 23.

[20] "IFOR - Fact Sheet,"NATO Public Data Service, NATODATA@CC1. KULEUVEN.AC.BE. (September 7, 1996).

[21] David Chandler, "Bosnia: The Democracy Paradox," *Current History*, 100, No. 644 (March 2001): 119. See also, Ivo H. Daalder and Michael B. G. Froman, "Dayton's Incomplete Peace," *Foreign Affairs*, 78, No. 6 (November/ December 1999): 106-13; Gerald Knaus and Marcus Cox, "Whither Bosnia?" *NATO Review* 48 (Winter 2000-2001): 6-11. A harsher appraisal, "Today, Bosnia is a Potemkin state run by legions of autocratic international bureaucrats," is offered by Ted Galen Carpenter, "Jackboot Nation Building: The West Brings 'Democracy' to Bosnia," *Mediterranean Quarterly* 11, No. 2 (Spring 2000): 21.

[22] Details on the Kosovo conflict in the form of annotated chronologies can be found in: BASIC, "Kosovo: The Long Road to War: A Chronology 1998," www.basicint.org/eur_kosovo_chron3.htm (March 15, 2001) and "A Chronology 1999," www.basicint.org/eur_kosovo_chron4.htm (March 15, 2001); also Department of State, "Kosovo Chronology," www.state.gov/www/regions/eur/fs_kosovo_timeline.html (March 15, 2001).

[23] Quoted in Ivo H. Daalder and Michael E. O'Hanlon, *Winning Ugly: NATO's War to Save Kosovo* (Washinton, DC: Brookings Institution Press, 2000), 83. For extensive coverage of the Rambouillet meetings, see pp. 69-89.

[24] A former Canadian diplomat, who had served as ambassador in three Balkan states, observed: "Rambouillet was a classic example of diplomatic negotiations under the threat of force. . . . It was an ultimatum to the Serbs—sign or be bombed. It was an ultimatum to the Albanian Kosovars—sign or be left to continue the struggle alone against the Serbs." James Bisset, "NATO's Balkan Blunder," *Mediterranean Quarterly* 12, No. 1 (Winter 2001): 48.

[25] Quoted in Elaine Sciolino and Ethan Bronner, "Crisis in the Balkans: The Road to War—A Special Report," *New York Times*, April 18, 1999.

[26] *Ibid.*

[27] For extensive discussion of Serbian policy, see Barry R. Posen, "The War for Kosovo: Serbia's Political-Military Strategy," *International Security* 24, No. 4 (Spring 2000): 39-84.

[28] Quoted in Dana Priest, "The Commanders' War: The Threat to Invade Serbia," *Washington Post* (September 19, 1999).

[29] "The Situation in and Around Kosovo: Statement Issued at the Extraordinary Ministerial Meeting of the North Atlantic Council Held at NATO Headquarters, Brussels, on 12th April 1999," www.nato.int/docu/pr/1999/p99_051e.htm (March 15, 2001).

[30] For a country-by-country breakdown of positions regarding the campaign, see Alan Cowell, "It's a Wonder This Alliance Is Unified," *New York Times*, April 25, 1999.

[31] "Statement on Kosovo," *NATO Review* 47, No. 2 (Summer 1999): D1-D2. For the complete text of all publicly signed documents of the summit, see pp. D1-D16.

[32] "The Commanders' War," *Washington Post*, September 19, 1999.

[33] "Statement on Kosovo," *NATO Review*, D1.

[34] Among the many discussions of the peace agreement, see: Posen, "The War for Kosovo," 75-81; Daalder and O'Hanlon, *Winning Ugly*, 165-181, 274-278 (for text of UN Resolution 1244); William H. Lewis, "Peace Operations—Crossing the Rubicon? *Pas Encore*," *Mediterranean Quarterly* 11, No. 1 (Winter 2000): 11-14; Spyridon Sfetas, "Kosovo: The Beginning and End of the Yugoslav Crisis," *Defensor Pacis* 4 (January 2000): 83-88.

[35] Bernard Kouchner, "The Challenge of Rebuilding Kosovo," *NATO Review* 47, No. 3 (Autumn 1999): 12-15.

[36] NATO Secretary General Javier Solana stated that for the first time "a defensive alliance launched a military campaign to avoid a humanitarian tragedy outside its own borders" and that "an alliance of sovereign nations fought not to conquer or preserve territory but to protect the values on which the alliance was founded." Javier Solana, "NATO's Success in Kosovo, *Foreign Affairs* 78, No. 6 (November/December 1999): 114.

[37] Ronald Scott Mangum, "NATO's Attack on Serbia: Anomoly or Emerging Doctrine?" *Parameters* 30, No. 4 (Winter 2000-01): 47-48; Bissett, "NATO's Balkan Blunder," 40-42.

[38] Michael Mandelbaum, "A Perfect Failure," *Foreign Affairs* 78, No. 5 (September-October 1999): 5.

[39] General Klaus Reinhardt, "Commanding KFOR," *NATO Review* 48, No. 2 (Summer-Autumn 2000): 16-19.

[40] Bernard Kouchner, UNMIK's head, remarked on the altered images prior to departing his post in late 2000: "The Kosovo Albanians have already damaged their reputation in the eyes of the world and undercut international sympathy by the culture of impunity and tolerance for reverse ethnic cleansing and violence."

Quoted in Lenard J. Cohen, "Post-Milosevic Yugoslavia," *Current History* 100, No. 644 (March 2001):105.

[41] Lord George Robertson, "European Security in the 21st Century," January 25, 2001, www.nato.int/docu/speech/2001/s010125b.htm (May 10, 2001).

[42] Jane Perlez, "As Strife in Macedonia Rises, U.S. and NATO Shun Fight," *New York Times*, March 19, 2001.

[43] NATO Press Release (2001)066, "Statement by the Secretary General: Return of Yugoslav Security Forces to Sector B of the Ground Safety Zone," May 14, 2001, www.nato.int/docu/pr/2001/p01-066e.htm (May 15, 2001).

[44] Balkan Information Exchange Daily News, "Albanian Guerrillas Lay Down Arms in Presevo," May 22, 2001, www.balkan-info.com (May 23, 2001).

[45] Karl Kaiser, "Reforming NATO," *Foreign Policy*" No. 103 (Summer 1996): 138.

[46] For extensive analysis of international economic efforts, see the special issue, "Balkan Reconstruction," *Journal of Southeast European and Black Sea Studies* 1, No. 1 (January 2000).

[47] NATO's supreme allied commander Europe, General Joseph Ralston, responding in late May 2001 to discussions over downsizing SFOR in Bosnia, emphasized that "We need a functioning system of law and order [in Bosnia]. . . . I want those conditions as soon as we can get them, but I don't have a time frame for it." Michael R. Gordon, "Despite Pentagon Pressure, NATO Plans Modest Cutback in Bosnia," *New York Times*, May 27, 2001.

[48] NATO announced on April 23, 1999 that "we will not tolerate threats by the Belgrade regime to the security of its neighbors. We will respond to such challenges by Belgrade to its neighbors resulting from the presence of NATO forces or their activities on their territory during this crisis." Quoted in Daalder and O'Hanlon, *Winning Ugly*, 129.

[49] For discussion of Greek-Turkish problems, see S. Victor Papacosma, "NATO and Internal Disputes," in *NATO after Fifty Years* ed. S. Victor

Papacosma, Sean Kay, and Mark R. Rubin (Wilmington, DE: Scholarly Resources, Inc., 2001), 199-225.

[50] William M. Sloane, *The Balkans: A Laboratory of History* (New York: Eaton and Mains, 1914), viii.

REFERENCES

Burg, Steven L., and Paul S. Shoup. *The War in Bosnia-Herzegovina: Ethnic Conflict and International Intervention*. Armonk, NY: M. E. Sharpe, 1999. This study covers the dissolution of Yugoslavia and the Bosnian conflict in a comprehensive and authoritative fashion.

Clark, Wesley K. *Waging Modern War: Bosnia, Kosovo, and the Future of Combat*. New York: Perseus Book Group, 2001. Having served as NATO's Supreme Allied Commander, Europe, General Clark offers a detailed account of the Kosovo campaign and critical commentary of the political constraints imposed on it.

Daalder, Ivo H., and Michael E. O'Hanlon. *Winning Ugly: NATO's War to Save Kosovo*. Washington, D.C.: Brookings Institution, 2000. The authors provide important insights into the diplomatic prelude of the Kosovo campaign and the subsequent policy debates and decisions associated with NATO's controversial bombing mission.

Holbrooke, Richard. *To End a War*. New York: Random House, 1998. A driving force in bringing about the Dayton Peace Accords, Richard Holbrooke details his version of the complex developments, including coverage of NATO's role.

Papacosma, S. Victor, Sean Kay, and Mark R. Rubin, eds. *NATO after Fifty Years*. Wilmington, DE: Scholarly Resources, Inc., 2001. Individual articles in this volume cover aspects of NATO's post-Cold War adaptation during the 1990s.

CHAPTER 14
INSTITUTIONALIZED RESTRAINT AS POLICY: THE EUROPEAN UNION AND THE DISINTEGRATION OF YUGOSLAVIA

Kostas A. Lavdas
University of Crete, Greece

INTRODUCTION

The end of the Cold War was formally declared in November 1990 at the CSCE meeting in Paris. The Charter of Paris made it clear that "the era of confrontation and division in Europe ha[d] ended." As the Cold War ended, so did the certainties associated with Cold War stability. The attainment of a new level and a new quality of stability was now becoming dependent on the emergence and sustainability of new institutional arrangements mitigating the stressful aspects of interstate interaction. The functioning of relatively stable interstate systems over long periods of time testifies to the role of norms, routines, and organizations institutionalizing international relations (cf. Keohane 1989; Rosenau 1992; Hoffmann 1995: 284-285). Conflict situations develop in periods of transition and uncertainty, when highly institutionalized systems dissolve in junctures involving the redefinition of roles by the major players, and before new institutionalized equilibria have been reached. Conflict in that interregnum helps determine subsequent arrangements, although resilient elements of the previous institutional design are also influential in shaping outcomes.

It is certainly not surprising that the collapse of the bipolar certainties would lead to at least the potential for intensified regional conflicts, as the Cold War bloc rivalries receded. The European security system found itself in a period of transition, which appeared to leave open a number of different future possibilities. Aspects of the uncertainty which distinguish a period of transition have been the coexistence of a highly institutionalized Western Europe and a disintegrating Eastern and Southeastern Europe, the instability accruing from traits such as the revival of nationalism, and the emerging global debates about the role of the United Nations (UN) and the composition of its Security Council. Regional conflicts have fueled debates about the role, legitimacy, and limits of UN "humanitarian intervention" in particular (for an analysis see Wheeler 1993: 133-157). Such debates have been associated with a certain relativization of the principle of non-intervention in the internal affairs of states, a principle enshrined in the UN Charter. The weakening of the principle of non-intervention

can be supported from a liberal theoretical standpoint by pointing to possible links between a state's authoritarian features at home and aggressive policy abroad. Liberal theorists of international relations from Kant onwards have insisted that democracy is a prerequisite of international peace. Irrespective of one's theoretical viewpoint, the fact that non-intervention becomes relativized as an international norm is, in itself, an indication of uncertainty. Although non-intervention is anchored in the traditional conception of statehood which originates in the Peace of Westphalia, its role in post-World War II international relations helped create a bridge between the sovereignty-oriented structure of international relations and the contemporary international society which is characterized by dense interactions and close cooperation. As Cassese argues, non-intervention "currently plays the role of a necessary shield behind which States can shelter in the knowledge that their more intense international relations will not affect their most vital and delicate domestic interests" (Cassese 1986: 144).

In the case of Southeastern Europe, the prospects for future stability will depend on the form and content of the re-institutionalization of regional governance structures and the emergence of a new set of transnational linkages (Lavdas 1996). The EU is bound to be a key factor in the re-institutionalization process, and yet the EU's recent record in dealing with the Yugoslav conflict has been mediocre. In view of the EU's relative weakness in foreign and security policy, its role in the Yugoslav conflict has concentrated more on the creation of a framework for arbitration and the regulation of conflict and less on intervention by the EU as a coherent actor. The EU has been required to develop policies which will at once contain the spread of conflict and stabilize the former Yugoslav polities, appeal to the European publics whose support is needed in the context of Economic and Monetary Union (EMU), while managing to avoid offending national foreign policy sensitivities. The task appears formidable in part because the EU currently finds itself in a situation in which it faces and tries to resolve basic problems of legitimacy, participation, and administrative capacities, problems which are central to all evolving political systems (Lavdas 1997).

The juncture at which the EU currently finds itself made it particularly difficult for the European system to cope with disintegrating Yugoslavia. But even if we bracket the issue of the current juncture in EU's development, the particular case of the Yugoslav conflict would still appear to be too demanding a test for the evolving EU foreign policy and security capacities. The major European powers have a record of rivalries in the historical Balkans, while the differences among European foreign policies have been compounded by the particular East-West balance mix which had been underlying Yugoslavia's

domestic structure and international position since World War II. In view of the difficulties emanating from the Yugoslav conflict as well as the inherent weaknesses of the developing European common foreign and security policies, the EU record can be regarded moderately successful in an admittedly minimalist but crucial sense, i.e., in regulating and restraining the most divisive elements of European national foreign policies, thereby helping control the spread of conflict beyond the Balkans.

A FRAMEWORK AS POLICY

By the time Yugoslavia started disintegrating, the European foreign policy and security framework had acquired certain important but still transitional features. It is commonplace to suggest that the foreign policy and security cooperation structures of the EU remain weak. This is particularly true if we consider foreign policy and security against a background of an advanced and complex system of common policies in a number of other areas, from internal market and competition to structural policies and environmental protection. Foreign policy cooperation emerged in the form of the European Political Cooperation (EPC) as a result of an agreement which was reached in The Hague Summit in 1969 and was aiming to relaunch European integration while proceeding with the enlargement of the EC.

Briefly put, the EPC was conceived as a compromise institution and also, therefore, as an institution with a basically intergovernmental structure. However. the involvement of EC institutions and the interweaving of EC and EPC processes became significant at an early stage, and were strengthened by the fusion of political and economic negotiations in the context of the so-called Euro-Arab dialogue in 1974. In the 1970s the EPC became closely involved in the Conference on Security and Cooperation in Europe (CSCE) and the relationship proved mutually advantageous because the CSCE provided the framework within which the EC states could tentatively try the ground for a distinct European foreign policy cooperation system. The EPC was formally brought closer to the EC institutional system with the Single European Act (SEA) of 1986, which in part confirmed and formalized actual developments of the previous years without seriously challenging the intergovernmental nature of cooperation. The SEA also spelled out a commitment of the member states to consult and try to achieve common policies. But the limitations of the EPC persisted, including the difficulties in legitimizing the EPC system. Indirectly, the European Parliament "gained a real foot inside the mechanisms of Community foreign policy" with the power of assent in relation to association and enlargement agreements, institutionalized with the SEA (Bonvicini 1998:

68). The collapse of Communism in Eastern Europe found the EC/EPC invested with considerable potential in terms of foreign policy coordination, but with little if any capacity to set common policy targets and enforce them.

On paper, the *lacuna* could be dealt with partly through mechanisms of common security and defence policies, but Paris had consistently shown a preference for foreign policy cooperation coming first. The Western European Union (WEU), an organization which was established back in 1954 as an alternative to the stillborn attempts to create a European Defence Community and was subsequently disabled by the Cold War realities of intra-bloc superpower dominance, was revived in 1984 as a result mainly of French and Italian initiatives. The WEU has acquired a mixed role as the defence cooperation aspect of European integration and, at the same time, a European aspect of NATO (Van Eekelen 1992). By establishing the Common Foreign and Security Policy (CFSP) as one of the three pillars of the institutional edifice of the EU, the Treaty on European Union (TEU) confirmed and extended the increased interest in a European defence and security policy. But it also expressed a compromise perspective between those who urged an independent European defence dimension and the staunch Atlanticists (see *Financial Times*, 11 December 1991: 2). The WEU became part of both the CFSP and of NATO, and this was reflected in the twin objectives of "build[ing] up WEU in stages as the defence component of the European Union" and "develop[ing] WEU as a means to strengthen the European pillar of the Atlantic Alliance" (Declaration on Western European Union, TEU). The WEU's operational role has been under development and includes a joint Franco-German force launched in 1991. The actual procedures followed by the member states in this area "have been designed to bring about coordination of the policies of the member states rather than a truly integrated European policy," and this has not been changed significantly with the TEU (Edwards and Nuttall 1994: 99). The still rather unimpressive profile was partly due to the particular combination of continuity and change which has marked the transformation of world politics since 1989. The ensuing uncertainty was reflected in the ways in which strategy, domestic politics, and institutional enabling and constraining mechanisms interact in shaping national positions on the future role of security policy in Europe.

THE DISINTEGRATION OF YUGOSLAVIA

A brief and unavoidably schematic account of the evolution of the Yugoslav conflict from the perspective of EU involvement between 1991 and 2001 would suggest a periodization in six phases. The first phase is dominated by the

German-led EC recognition of Slovenia and Croatia. Having played a major role in the early phase of the Yugoslav conflict, German foreign policy resumed the back seat after 1992. The second phase, between 1992 and the Gorazde crisis in April 1994, is dominated by considerable fragmentation and a number of centrifugal forces at work. The third phase, which can be said to have begun in mid-1994, was characterized mainly by the emergence of a series of Anglo-French initiatives and increased Russian involvement, while various centrifugal tendencies remained significant. The fourth phase, which began in the summer of 1995 and can be said to include 1996-97 (before the Kosovo crisis erupted), was marked by increased US involvement and the emergence of a new equilibrium: the weakening of the Bosnian Serbs and the defeat of the Krajina Serbs were accompanied by a certain—temporary—rehabilitation of Belgrade's role in international negotiations. The fifth phase includes the conflict in Kosovo and the increased military role for NATO with the bombing of Yugoslavia. Finally, the sixth phase begun in the aftermath of the bombing of Yugoslavia has been marked by the regime change in Belgrade and is still evolving in 2001.

The breakup of federal Yugoslavia has been a dramatic chapter in the international politics of post-Cold War uncertainty brought about by the collapse of bipolar stability and aggravated by the resurgence of ethnic conflict and the competing aspirations of emerging regional players. Following the collapse of one-party rule in the Socialist Federal Republic of Yugoslavia (SFRY), the presidents of the six Yugoslav republics (Slovenia, Croatia, Serbia, Montenegro, Bosnia, Macedonia) engaged in high-level talks aiming to define a new political order for Yugoslavia. Conflict and disintegration ensued as a result of the stalemate of these talks, which were undermined by Slovenia's determination to achieve independent statehood and by the nationalist policies of the Serb president Milosevic and the Croat president Tudjman (for different accounts of the breakup of Yugoslavia see Glenny 1993; Pavkovic 2000a; Ramet and Adamovich 1994; Gow 1994; Vickers 1998; Zametica 1992; Zimmermann 1995).

While the disintegration of Yugoslavia was to some extent the result of structural deficiencies of the institutional system and the balances on which it rested, it is clear that the secession of Slovenia and Croatia (25 June 1991) constituted the starting point of the conflict. The conflict then took the form of recursive secessions, which became variations on the "secede and damn the others" theme (Pavkovic 2000b). Slovenia's secession was critical. The Croatian nationalist leadership was distinguished by strong commitment to the creation of an independent Croat state, which could possibly include parts of Bosnia-Herzegovina. The last US ambassador to SFRY reports a conversation with Tudjman, in which the Croatian president suggested that "Bosnia has never had

any real existence. . . . it should be divided between Serbia and Croatia" (Zimmermann 1995: 15; cf. Glenny 1993: 149-150, 82-86; Hoare 1997). Still, the Croats left open the possibility of a new Yugoslavia until it became clear that Slovenia would go ahead with the independence declaration, and Croatia decided to follow for tactical reasons (Glenny 1993: 86-87). In the words of the last US ambassador to the SFRY, the Slovenes'independence declaration, which had not been preceded by even the most token effort to negotiate, effectively put under their control all the border and customs posts between Slovenia and its two neighbors, Italy and Austria. This meant that Slovenia, the only international gateway between the West and Yugoslavia, had unilaterally appropriated the right to goods destined for other republics, as well as customs revenues estimated at some 75 percent of the Yugoslav federal budget (Zimmermann 1995: 12).

The reaction of the Serb-dominated Yugoslav Army (JNA) was prompt. Yet agreement for a cease-fire was reached within weeks, and Slovenia was soon spared the fighting. This was in part due to European mediation, on which I will concentrate below, but it was mainly an indication of the critical role played by ethnic minorities in determining the course of the Yugoslav conflict. While there were no Serb communities in Slovenia, the situation was very different in Croatia, and when fighting broke out between Serb and Croat communities in Croatia and the JNA intervened, in effect against the Croat government forces, the stage was set for a protracted conflict (Glenny 1993: 101-111).

The timing of the German-led EC recognition not only of the two secessionist republics but of "all Yugoslav republics" provided they expressed a wish "to be recognized as independent states" (16 December 1991) proved to be a major flaw in the European approach to the Yugoslav crisis. It was a flaw which affected also a number of other policies and initiatives in the region (cf. Owen 1995; Zimmermann 1995: 15-17; Glenny 1993: 111-112, 188-192, 236-238). The conflict spread into Bosnia-Herzegovina in 1992, partly as a result of the European Community's decision to declare, in effect, the collapse of federal Yugoslavia, and also with the help of Belgrade's manipulation of the Bosnian Serbs' anxiety over the erosion of the trinational parity (Moslems-Croats-Serbs) in Bosnian political life. The fighting between the Moslem-dominated Bosnian government, Bosnian Serbs, and Bosnian Croats revealed the significance of the national lines along which political life of the Bosnian communities was organized (Glenny 1993: 141-173). The war led to the weakening of any remaining elements binding together the different communities in Bosnia (Glenny 1993: 142-143). The development of better relations between the Bosnian government and Bosnian Croats, let alone Bosnian Serbs, was for most of the

time between 1993 and 1995 dependent upon the existence of strong peacekeeping forces (*The Independent*, 5 March 1994: 8).

In view of the significance of national demarcating lines in the Yugoslav conflict, and of the tenacity and persistence of the fighting and the atrocities committed, it is tempting to argue that Serb disregard for the preestablished internal borders which were inherited from Tito's federal structure does not appear irrelevant or indefensible. The EU / UN position, however, has been that the preestablished internal borders in Yugoslavia (between the six republics) should become international borders and should not be allowed to be challenged at the time of independence (Weller 1992), a position rejected by Belgrade at least until 1995. In December 1994, the European Council reiterated its emphasis on "early mutual recognition between all States of the former Yugoslavia within their internationally recognized borders" as "essential for the future stability of the region" (Bull. *EU* 12-1994, point 1.3.11). In other words, the EC—even after having issued the invitation to the Yugoslav republics to state whether they wished to be recognized as independent states—restricted recognition to federal units and refused to recognize the secession of any sub-federal unit or region in Yugoslavia (see Pavkovic 2000b: 485). The problem with the Serb approach is that, as Wheeler (1993: 147-148) notes, the international community accepts territoriality, not ethnicity/nationality as the criterion for admitting new states; accepting the right to national self-determination of ethnic Serbs in Croatia and Bosnia would question territoriality as the criterion of statehood in international society.

On the other hand, however, it should be clear that the EC/EU has been ambivalent in its treatment of the principle of the inviolability of borders: the recognition of the independence of Slovenia and Croatia was based on the combination of a reading of the CSCE human rights provisions (concerning a state's treatment of its minorities) and a primacy accorded to internal borders (between the six republics) in the particular case of the SFRY. In 1991 the German position gave precedence to "self-determination" arguments (combined with an initial preference for the CSCE as the appropriate forum), while most other EC states attached greater importance to the integrity of the federal Yugoslav state. As the EC was eventually dragged along in recognizing breakaway Slovenia and Croatia, the emphasis on federal Yugoslavia's internal borders became necessary in the attempt to reconcile an "interventionist humanitarian" approach with a more general interest in the stability of borders.

Given the lack of an effective international approach to the conflict at an earlier stage, a factor to which we will now turn, the attempts at negotiated settlement which took place in November 1995 with the help of a US initiative

had to take into account the fact that, despite the strengthening of the Croat and Bosnian government positions earlier in 1995, Serb gains in Bosnia (but not Croatia) remained considerable.

CENTRIFUGAL FORCES, CENTRIPETAL TENDENCIES, AND INSTITUTIONAL RESTRAINTS IN EU POLICY

Against the background of the dramatic changes that were taking place in Eastern Europe and the potential destabilization of European international relations, the Yugoslav crisis conjured up disturbing images of historical rivalries among the major EU partners. The early phases of the Europeans' approach to the Yugoslav crisis appear to suggest that national foreign policy traditions, coupled with domestic political pressures and commitments, did play significant roles. While the US government was advocating democratic unity or negotiated development for Yugoslavia (Zimmermann 1995: 6, 11-12), by December 1991 the Europeans were under pressure from Germany to recognize Slovenia and—more controversially—Croatia. Slovenia had been spared the fighting by August 1991, but Croatia was a very different case in terms of both position in the conflict and domestic political features. The European Badinter Commission, which had been set up to report on the former Yugoslav republics' institutional and democratic credentials for diplomatic recognition, was far from being satisfied that the domestic situation in Croatia (including the position of minorities) was acceptable. At a critical stage, in late November 1991, Germany was joined by Italy in stepping up pressure for the recognition of Slovenian and Croatian independence *(Financial Times*, 29 November 1991: 2). As mentioned, the timing of the recognition of the secessionist republics was a disaster.

The EU's role in the Yugoslav conflict has been influenced by four interconnected but analytically distinct categories of factors: the foreign policies of EU member states, member states' calculations of long-term benefits accruing from participation in the process of European integration, the independent impact of EU institutional norms and processes, and the evolving external relations of the EU with the US and with the former Communist states. The modest results of EU involvement in the Yugoslav conflict have been offered as evidence supporting the view that the EU's record in this context should be examined along realist or neo-realist lines. It can be argued that the difficulties in reaching a common policy testify to the often conflicting objectives, while at the same time revealing the intergovernmental aspects of the EU system. Also, certain member states have responded to aspects of the crisis in ways that

suggest the combined influence of domestic pressures and a degree of national foreign policy continuity.

By and large, however, developments since 1991 indicate that participation in the EC/EU institutional system mitigated the most divisive and stressful effects of historical foreign policy traditions, geostrategic concerns, and domestic pressures. While the EU has failed to pursue, let alone enforce, a coherent policy, it can be argued that (a) learning from past participation in the EU, (b) the internalization of European norms as well as (c) calculations of long-term benefits associated with continuing participation have resulted in an equivalent to "negative integration" in the foreign policy field: restraint in the pursuit of national foreign policies and at least a minimum effort to achieve coordination. The internalization and institutionalization of restraint is one aspect of the broader phenomenon of the influence exercised by the emerging European norms of cooperation and integration on the very process of national preference formation in the member states (Risse-Kappen 1994). The internalization of restraint has been manifest on several occasions and has operated at the levels of national preference formation as well as supranational policy coordination. Externally, the EU has indicated a common position vis-a-vis the UN Security Council, although there has been no implication that its members at the Security Council ensure the defence of EU positions (see, e.g., *Bull. EC* 1/2-1993, points 1.4.5, 1.4.10), despite the fact that the CFSP provisions in the TEU offer this opportunity (Art. J.5.4 TEU).

The Early Phases

When military conflict broke out in Yugoslavia in June 1991, the Europeans reacted swiftly through the institutional means of the EU, by dispatching to Belgrade the "Troika" of European foreign ministers. The "Troika's" early optimism, reflected in the Brioni Accord, was based on the notion that the Yugoslav crisis could be tackled on an *ad hoc* basis, beginning with the Slovene issue and, if necessary, dealing with other issues as they emerge (Glenny 1993: 98-101). By failing to address the Croatian issue and, more generally, the question of minorities in the crumbling Yugoslavia, the EC lost the opportunity of an early approach to the Yugoslav crisis in a comprehensive and negotiated way. The worsening of the situation in 1992 was addressed by the EU with the appointment of a special mediator, first Lord Carrington and then Lord Owen, the use of economic inducements (including sanctions: *Bull. EC* 1/2-1993, point 1.4.5), as well as the deployment of peacekeeping forces (EU Monitors). The institutions of the EC—especially the Commission—had played an important role

in coordinating policy towards the Eastern European states after the changes in the late 1980s, and the Commission's response to the challenges had been largely successful. Economic inducements constitute a major aspect of EU policy in the Yugoslav crisis, and the role of EU institutions in formulating and implementing economic measures is critical. Slovenia has been supported with a series of economic, financial, and trade cooperation agreements *(Bull. EC* 718-1993, point 1.3.24-26), and the Commission has recently recommended to the Council that similar agreements should be negotiated with Croatia *(Bull. EU* 1/2-1995, point 1.4.85).

The EU cooperated with the UN in sponsoring two major conferences, the London Conference of August 1992 and the Geneva Conference of January 1993, as well as the standing working groups in Geneva. The commitment to Bosnian sovereignty was accompanied by careful attempts to prepare a Bosnian map that would be acceptable to all sides by referring to their legitimate concerns about their communities. The plans prepared by Lord Owen and his UN counterpart, first Vance and later Stoltenberg, were repeatedly rejected by the Bosnian Serbs, the Moslem dominated Bosnian government, and the Croats.

The main feature of the first phase has been the attainment of a degree of European policy coherence, albeit of a hegemonic-asymmetrical nature: member states followed Germany in recognizing Slovenia and Croatia and, in effect, declaring the collapse of Yugoslavia. The fact that member states other than Germany calculated long-term benefits of a coherent European foreign policy or more general benefits from avoiding strains in European policies as being more significant than differences in national foreign policy positions indicates the effects of participation in a developing scheme of coordination and integration of policy goals and policy instruments. It also demonstrates, on the other hand, the possibility that institutional norms can be manipulated by the most powerful parties in the arrangement when these parties calculate that benefits from an action will outweigh possible losses in external support. This calculation was in fact atypical of German foreign policy, which had generally managed to pursue a successful course between the Scylla of inward-looking isolationism and the Charybdis of quick and unrestrained assertion of leadership.

In the second phase, fragmentation created obstacles to pro-active decision-making, as the national foreign policies assumed precedence over the requirements of a coherent European approach to the crisis. A number of European states have pursued national foreign policies with little consultation at EU level. Italy has been pursuing an active role in Eastern Europe in general as well as in the Southeastern region, aiming to re-cultivate or extend linkages. Italian foreign policy has often developed in the absence of consultation with

other EU member states, causing occasional frictions with Italy's partners (for different accounts cf. Tsakaloyannis 1992: 191; Mastny 1995; Pavkovic 2000a). On other occasions, groupings of Yugoslavia's neighbors, including Italy and Germany but also Austria and Hungary, consulted on matters of diplomatic recognition of former Yugoslav republics and worked towards common positions (Altmann 1992: 163-165).

The EU's only member state in the region, Greece, was initially pursuing a policy in the Yugoslav conflict that was at odds with the policies of several other member states (on Greece cf. Featherstone & Ifantis 1996 and Lavdas 1997). Three factors have been mainly responsible for this. First, domestic pressures in Greece associated with perceptions of the country's history of good relations with Serbia. On the one hand, these relations presented a problem for the formulation of a common European approach. On the other hand, Greece tried to act as a broker on a number of occasions, as it did, for example in the negotiations aiming to diffuse the crisis resulting from the Bosnian Serbs' hostage-taking tactics in May-June 1995 (*The Times*, 6 June 1995: 1, 16; *The Times*, 7 June 1995: 12). Second, to the extent that one of the main objectives of Greek foreign policy in the region had been to limit the expansion of the influence of Turkey, whose foreign policy since the end of the Cold War has been driven in part by an often unsuccessful endeavor to establish herself as a regional power (cf. Yilmaz 1995), Greece's policy choices were often bound to diverge from those of other EU states. Finally, Greece's initially tense relations with the Former Yugoslav Republic of Macedonia (FYROM) increased the appearance of a rift between Greek foreign policy and a presumed EU policy. The issues involved in the Greek approach to FYROM are complex, and a fuller examination would be beyond the scope of this chapter. Greece made a number of unsuccessful attempts to diffuse the crisis after assuming the EU Council presidency in the first half of 1994 (see, e.g., *The Guardian*, 15 February 1994: 11). Greece opposed the use of Western military force in Bosnia, and used EU fora in attempts to find diplomatic solutions and avoid NATO air raids (*The Independent, 17* February 1994: 11). That such attempts were largely unsuccessful was mainly due to the same factors which compromised most international efforts to reach a settlement from the beginning of the conflict, although Greek-EU tensions over FYROM weakened further the chances of Greek initiatives. By 1994, Western fragmentation had presented a window of opportunity for Russian foreign policy which, in consultation with Serbia and Greece, achieved concessions from the Bosnian Serbs in return for the deployment of Russian peacekeepers in Sarajevo and the temporary withdrawal

of the threat of air strikes *(The Independent* 19 February 1994: 1, 7; *Suddeutsche Zeitung*, 23 February 1994: 4, 8).

While the use of NATO air power under the command of the United Nations Protection Force (UNPROFOR) against the parties in the conflict remained an option throughout 1994 and played a key role in the summer of 1995, both the threat and actual use of air raids have been envisaged in a number of different ways. Over Sarajevo in February 1994, NATO threats led to the unanticipated consequence of increased Russian involvement and a temporary settlement, agreed through Russian mediation and with US assurances to the Russians for Western control of the Bosnian government's heavy weapons in the exclusion zone *(Suddeutsche Zeitung*, 23 February 1994: 1). It is questionable whether there has been any clear strategic thinking behind the use of air strikes in the Yugoslav conflict before the summer of 1995 (cf. Barber 1994). For the Clinton administration, a seemingly tough line on enforcing agreed policies in Bosnia, mainly through air strikes, could be used to assuage pressure from the powerful pro-Bosnian lobby in Congress for a unilateral US decision to lift the UN arms embargo against Bosnia-Herzegovina *(Financial Times*, 23 September 1994: 1). In view of the certainty that a unilateral US move in that direction would sour transatlantic relations, air strikes could under certain circumstances be used to avoid tensions between the US and the EU, and both sides have occasionally resorted to or accepted the use of air power with such considerations in mind. Russia's role, on the other hand, has been constrained by difficult foreign policy choices between an internally unstable situation (aggravated by the electoral results of Zhirinovsky's ultra-nationalists) and broader strategic interests in establishing a working relationship with the West, including pro-Croat Germany. Russian opposition to the use of NATO air power (e.g., *Financial Times*, 11 April 1994: 3) has been firm but usually couched in mild terms, although Russian policy has linked the future of the NATO inspired Partnership for Peace to broader developments in Southeastern Europe. The deployment of Russian peacekeeping forces in the Serb sector of Sarajevo in February 1994 represented an attempt by Russia to enter the Yugoslav crisis as a major power. From that point onwards, the EU appears to have endorsed the view that Russian interests in the area had to be taken into account more seriously (cf. *The Independent*, 24 September 1994: 9).

In asking NATO to authorize air strikes to protect "safe areas" in Bosnia, the UN Secretary-General accepted the US and British view that Security Council Resolutions 824 and 836 were sufficient for the authorization of the use of air power against forces threatening the seven designated "safe areas" (the previous use of air power in February 1994 had concerned protection of UN

personnel under threat). By contrast, the Russian view was that a new Security Council Resolution was needed (*The Independent*, 20 April 1994: 10). What role did NATO military capabilities play in the Bosnian equation in 1994? By and large, air strikes for the protection of "safe areas" proved ineffective in a strategic sense while also seriously jeopardizing the UN's appeal to the Serbs (for a different view see Gow 1994). By extending the scope (from the protection of UN personnel to the protection of designated "safe areas") while maintaining strict limits to the use of force, the UN produced three policy failures: it (a) lost credibility (with the very damaging result of UN forces being treated as hostages or potential hostages), (b) gave the impression that the use of force for purposes of enforcing UN agreements would be inadequate, while (c) in fact it avoided taking the next step of actually enforcing UN-sanctioned agreements such as the London Conference agreement.

By contrast, the hypothetical combination of more extensive use of force for a narrower set of objectives (protection of UN personnel) might have been more effective and from a long-term perspective less demoralizing. In fact, the Bush administration's early reluctance to get involved militarily was the result of an accurate reading of a situation in which specific threats might lead to the need for escalation (cf. Gompert 1994: 39-40). Although the Gulf War had shown that the Bush administration was capable of using "decisive force," the complexities of the Yugoslav conflict and the transatlantic and intra-European divisions, along with the lack of domestic support in the US, precluded any similar scenario being played on European ground. Greater US involvement and bolder use of force in the summer of 1995 were aimed at achieving Bosnian Serb concessions in order to increase the likelihood of successful political negotiations.

The apparent differences of view between the UN military commanders and the diplomats in charge (e.g., *The Independent*, 18 April 1994: 8) and between the French overall head of UN operations in Yugoslavia and the British UN commander for Bosnia (*International Herald Ttibune*, 23 February 1994: 1, 9) have also weakened NATO's position or, if they were more apparent than real, have failed to function as a deterrent against Bosnian Serb advances. Before the summer of 1995, the actual function of the threat and limited use of air strikes had been in terms of the application of a stimulus, predictably provoking retaliatory responses: over Gorazde and then Bihac in April and November 1994, over Sarajevo in May 1995. The one exception, over Sarajevo in February 1994, led to unanticipated consequences (greater Russian involvement), and only indirectly and temporarily to Bosnian Serb withdrawal.

As the UN policy on "safe areas" appeared to be increasingly difficult to manage, more conspicuously in April 1994 when the Bosnian Serbs successfully attacked Gorazde despite the threat and eventual limited use of NATO air strikes, the Europeans became convinced that a non-political solution would be either impossible or it would have to include arming the Bosnian side. Neither Britain nor France would contemplate arming the Bosnians, and the Russians were obviously strongly against it. In Gorazde's case, the fate of a designated UN "safe area" underlined the limitations of a number of available policies. All general pessimism in European foreign ministerial meetings was due to the sense of such limitations being due to differences between the US and Europe, among the Europeans themselves, and the desire not to upset the Russians (*The Independent*, 18 April 1994: 9).

Following the Gorazde debacle, the meeting of EU foreign ministers in Luxembourg in April 1994 centered on an "Anglo-French appeal for a united diplomatic front to halt further Serb territorial aggression" *(Financial Times* 19 April 1994: 1). The potential for closer Franco-British defence cooperation has been noted by Balladur and Major on previous occasions and with reference to a wider range of issues. On Yugoslavia in particular, the French and British foreign ministers had met separately before to consult at critical moments, for example after the Russian diplomatic coup of February 1994 and in advance of the general EU-US-Russian meetings *(Financial Times*, 21 February 1994: 1). Now, the EU proposed a streamlined approach coordinating the EU, US, and Russian diplomatic efforts. Furthermore, the EU called for an immediate and unconditional cease-fire in Gorazde, for extra troops to be deployed with the UN peacekeeping force in Bosnia, and for the resumption of negotiations for a new map for Bosnia. The EU initiative saw a degree of temporary convergence with Russia as the latter criticized the Bosnian Serbs for failing to honor their word over Gorazde. At the same time, the Europeans were expressing frustration that the US was unwilling to assist the UN with forces on the ground.

While issues concerning the use of military force, mainly in the form of air strikes, continued to appear prominently in EU-UN-US-Russian exchanges, the diplomatic equation began to change in view of increasing differences between Belgrade, on the one hand, and Pale (in Serb-held Bosnia) and Knin (in Serb-held Croatia), on the other. Such differences were mainly due to Belgrade's reassessment of the costs and benefits of the situation, partly in view of the EU/UN-imposed economic sanctions on the Federal Republic of Yugoslavia (Serbia and Montenegro). In October 1994, the EU and UN mediators announced that the border between the self-styled "Republic of Serbia" and the Federal Republic of Yugoslavia (FRY) had been closed. The shifts in Belgrade's

position have been facilitated on the one hand by increased Russian involvement, and on the other by European pressure, pushing Belgrade to isolate the Bosnian Serbs as a condition for the gradual lifting of sanctions against FRY *(Bull. EU* 9-1994, point 1.3.11).

Against this background, the escalation of conflict in May 1995 brought about new developments. The use of NATO air strikes has been the main stimulus once again, this time leading to the capture by Bosnian Serbs of UN troops. The ensuing diplomatic activities presented three points of interest. First, the UN Secretary General's position offered a straightforward choice between a lightly armed UN humanitarian operation or a multinational military force which would intervene in the war but which would remain outside the UN structure. Second, the French and British governments, who remained skeptical about strong intervention throughout the conflict, were put under immense pressure since their troops figured prominently among the hostages. Last but not least, Russia responded with a certain detachment, confirming opposition to NATO air strikes while at the same time criticizing Serb tactics. The European response to the new situation was a further development along the Anglo-French cooperation line. The Franco-British Rapid Reaction Force (RRF), announced in early June, consisted of two brigades in national uniform but operating under UN command and aiming to "carry out missions to enhance the protection of UNPROFOR and to assist in the proper execution of its mandate" *(Financial Times,* 5 June 1995: 2; *The Independent*, 5 June 1995: 11). The RRF indicated a response which tried to avoid the clear-cut alternatives suggested by the UN Secretary General, insofar as it was designed to retain the link with UN operations while upgrading considerably the operational capabilities. The RRF initiative was important because it encouraged a degree of flexibility in dealing with the situation in Bosnia, avoided the dangerous scenario of UN withdrawal, and indicated that Anglo-French cooperation in this area may develop considerably.

The creation of the RRF also raised a number of questions. Up to the summer of 1995, and although the WEU could theoretically offer a military vehicle, the EU's role had been primarily diplomatic, economic, and peacekeeping. At the diplomatic level, the EU had intervened through the special mediator and the relevant Commissioner, in cooperation with the Contact Group, holding regular meetings and trying to broker a diplomatic solution. The multiple-layer diplomatic involvement in the crisis had been matched by a complex structure of military command, linking the UN and NATO forces. That structure now included the Anglo-French RRF, which was designed to be under

the operational control of the UN commanders on the ground, without being fully integrated in the UN forces.

EU-NATO-US Involvement During the Fourth Phase

The fourth phase in the conflict, beginning in the summer of 1995, was marked by a US initiative which succeeded in changing the balance of military forces on the ground while bringing considerable diplomatic pressure to bear on the leaders of Bosnia, Croatia and Serbia. The EU was gradually side-stepped after the escalation of fighting in May 1995 because it lacked both the policy and the instruments that would enable it to retain a leading role in breaking the deadlock. By 1995, the EU and UN mediators were joined by a five-nation Contact Group aiming to integrate the EU (France, Britain, Germany), US, and Russian perspectives. The latest proposed plan therefore had the apparent backing of all powers involved. But it soon became evident that the US role would be critical. The plan promoted the creation of a Moslem-Croat federation in Bosnia, and allowed a link between that federation and Croatia. Within the framework of a Bosnian state, a similar link could be offered to the Bosnian Serbs (linking them to Serbia), on the condition that they accept to remain in the Bosnian state and retain control of 49 per cent of the territory. Although the Bosnian Serbs were slow to accept the plan, the US-backed Croat offensive and the US initiative in the summer and autumn of 1995 persuaded Belgrade to put pressure on them to do so.

The US-sponsored peace agreement signed in Dayton, Ohio, in November 1995 preserves Bosnia as a state made up of two parts, a Bosnian-Croat Federation and a Bosnian-Serb Republic, and pledges that a "strong international force" led by NATO not the UN will enforce the agreement *(Financial Times*, 22 November 1995: 1-2; 23 November 1995: 3). The maps finally created with the Dayton accords made few changes to the battle lines that had formed by November 1995 that would allow the plan to be easily implemented. The *sui generis* state form envisaged by the agreement may prove a long-term solution or it may share the fate of a number of failed power-sharing experiments in divided multi-ethnic states.

Following the Dayton agreement in November 1995, there remained crucial areas in which the EU could play a key role. Although the implementation of the agreement depended on NATO troops, European contributions would be important and could take various forms. The contribution of the RRF, in particular, can be assessed with reference to crisis management in Yugoslavia, but also in terms of its role in the evolving European defence cooperation

structures. As regards the latter, it should be remembered that the RRF has been the response to an emergency, not an outgrowth of the evolution of the CFSP. Ideas of contingency planning within a EU-NATO framework had been discussed on various occasions before, but disagreements between Paris and London over the link of the envisaged force to NATO had stalled developments. The WEU Franco-German corps was a potentially significant initiative, but it was also made possible at the time thanks to rather than despite of a situation that imposed constitutional constraints to German deployment abroad. The exact position of the RRF in the EU/WEU framework has not been defined, and one of the issues that will have to be addressed concerns German participation. So long as they existed, constitutional constraints postponed a number of questions. As Kinkel noted, Germany's civilian role and "the politics of holding back" *(The Guardian*, 12 July 1994: 1) contributed to German and European growth and stability. German integration into schemes of UN-sanctioned European military involvement abroad is of paramount importance, and if that requires a slower pace, then a slower pace might be appropriate.

In this context, the RRF's role in the Yugoslav conflict would have to be evaluated less with reference to specific military objectives and more in terms of its contribution to overall European stability. It was of course unlikely that RRF would be able to provide the military capability required for the military solution of major crises in the absence of full US involvement. The main question therefore concerns the role of such initiatives in the context of developing and clarifying the relations between the EU, the UN, and NATO while creating the conditions for the re-institutionalization of international relations in Southeastern Europe. The latter depends not only on the enforcement of peace deals but also on the creation of an appropriate diplomatic and economic framework. In the Bosnian case, the main way in which the EU may secure the consent of the different parties to the operation of a power-sharing political system is through the parallel intensification of its economic and diplomatic efforts, including economic and diplomatic sticks as well as carrots and utilizing the Union's image as Europe's center of stability and economic advancement.

The Bombing of Yugoslavia and the Real and Symbolic End of the Cold War

The next step in the Union's involvement came in the late 1990s, with the Amsterdam Treaty, the change in British policy, and—dramatically—the conflict in Kosovo. In the areas of foreign and security policy, Maastricht had institutionalized provisions not just for "cooperation" but for a "common

policy." Amsterdam moved a little further, creating the post of a "Mr. CFSP," although the new Treaty "did not substantially alter the nature of CFSP" (Bonvicini 1998: 73). But in meetings in October and December 1998, Britain proceeded to what amounted to a major policy turn, with the Blair government declaring the need for a more autonomous European defence.

Once again, Yugoslavia (on this occasion, Kosovo) became a test that proved too demanding. The enormous responsibility of the Milosevic regime in increasing tensions and violating the rights of Albanians within Kosovo has been well documented and does not require a detailed rehearsal here. The special status of Kosovo within Yugoslavia was abolished by the Milosevic regime in 1989-1990 (see Roudometof, this volume). Serbia's new constitution "subordinated all of the province's organs, including its legislature, to those of Serbia and removed its legislature's power to make laws, thus severely reducing its previous legislative and political autonomy" (Pavkovic 2000b: 491). On the other hand, certain crucial aspects of the story—such as the exact conditions and circumstances surrounding the emergence and strengthening of the Kosovo Liberation Army (UCK)—remain obscure and will have to await the fruits of future research. In any case, the growth of the UCK and the side-stepping of the moderate leadership of Ibrahim Rugova went hand-in-hand with increased US involvement in the region and increased tensions in domestic politics in Albania: the nationalist Democratic Party became increasingly identified with Albanian irredentism (for balanced accounts of the Kosovo crisis see Vickers 1998; Veremis and Kofos 1998).

Yugoslavia under Milosevic became cognizable as the last remaining case of a Cold War regime in Europe (Cuba, N. Korea are non-European cases) and at the same time as a test case for the application in Europe of the emerging norm of humanitarian intervention. As John Spellar, Britain's Defence Minister, put it: the countries of Eastern and Southeastern Europe wished to become part of "European society," while Yugoslavia under Milosevic was a "black hole" which represented a threat to the region (BBC TV 2, *Newsnight*, 28 May 1999). Contributing to the debate over the relative weight of the established principle of non-intervention versus the emerging norm of human rights protection through humanitarian intervention, UN Secretary—General Kofi Annan declared that "no government has the right to hide behind national sovereignty in order to violate human rights" (*The Guardian*, 7 April 1999). At the same time, the fragility of the emerging norms was underlined by the cautious and occasionally openly critical remarks of UN Human Rights Commissioner Mary Robinson. One month into the air campaign, she stated her concern "that there isn't a focus

to this bombing campaign . . . that this campaign has lost its moral purpose" (*The Guardian* / www.newsunlimited.co.uk/Kosovo/Story, April 1999).

The failure first of the US-brokered agreement with Milosevic in October 1998 and then of the Rambouillet plan led to the most extensive bombing campaign ever undertaken by NATO. The Alliance began its bombing campaign against Yugoslavia on 25 March 1999. The campaign ended 11 weeks later, when NATO troops finally entered Kosovo. The province has been governed since by a UN—led administration, but ethnic Albanian groups hope it will eventually become independent of Yugoslavia. The military-technological superiority of the US within NATO reasserted itself in the clearest possible way. While in the years before 1999 it had become possible to talk about the "Europeanization of NATO" (see Varwick and Woyke 1999), the crisis itself underlined the critical role of the US when it came to the use of force. Yet as Stanley Hoffmann notes, the war resulted in a situation and a climate "that gave a very strong push to the idea of a CFSP" and "reinforced the continental Europeans' desire for greater diplomatic and strategic autonomy" (Hoffmann 2000: 194-195). Finally, the sixth phase in the Yugoslav conflict, beginning with the withdrawal of Serb forces from Kosovo in late June 1999, eventually led to the regime change in Belgrade in October 2000 and the formation of a new government under Vojislav Kostunica. Hopes for the re-integration of Yugoslavia in the European system were raised especially after the Organization for Security and Cooperation in Europe (OSCE) invited the country—which was expelled from the Organization in 1992—to join.

FROM FRAMEWORK TO A SYSTEM BASED ON INSTITUTIONALIZED AND INTERNALIZED RESTRAINT

It is still early to say whether the period of conflict in Yugoslavia has come to an end. The regime change in Belgrade is definitely a step in the process of integrating Yugoslavia in European society. At the same time, the early months of 2001 witnessed the stirrings of Albanian nationalism in FYROM, the violation of FYROM borders by Albanian irregulars based in Kosovo, and clashes between Albanians and FYROM security forces. These developments do not augur well for the future stability of the region. But while it may be early for an assessment of the role of the EU in the Yugoslav conflict, we may venture a number of tentative conclusions on points of broader significance.

In view of the collapse of bipolar certainties and the need to tackle crises like the Yugoslav conflict, the elaboration of mechanisms which will restrain the re-nationalization of European foreign policies appears to be a key requirement

for further development of the CFSP. In this light, the obvious difficulties in generating outcomes which would demonstrate the existence of an advanced stage of foreign policy and security cooperation should not be allowed to conceal certain significant indications of an evolving European governance structure. European governance emanates from the acceptance of norms of governance which rely on shared understandings and routinized practices (cf. Rosenau 1992: 4-8; Risse-Kappen 1994). Such norms and routinized practices aim to regulate the high density of contemporary international relations, although they are not necessarily associated with a particular normative agenda for institutional design, such as the federalist agenda (for a different view see Pinder 1994: 117-118, 121-122). The CFSP, the role of which is moving from a coordinating one to one involving the pursuit of common policies (cf. Bonvicini 1998; Hoffmann 2000), can have significant prospects only in relation to the development and expansion of the broader governance structures nurtured by European integration and involving a variety of policy areas.

This does not necessarily require a hasty effort to establish a single foreign and security policy. The perils of extreme intergovernmentalism often lead to calls for a strengthened CFSP based on majority voting. Wistrich, arguing from a European federalist standpoint, suggests that policy failures will be with us so long as European foreign and security policy depends on a minimalist intergovernmental consensus instead of being pursued by EU institutions taking decisions in the common interest and using majority voting (*The Independent*, 25 February 1994: 17). This appears to be close also to the view held by the former foreign affairs spokesman of the German CDU (Lamers 1995: 37-38). Of course, it is difficult to find fault with the view that post-Cold War challenges require a better defined CFSP and more systematic thinking about the potential of the pulling of sovereignty in foreign policy and defence. Yet the pressing issue concerns the conditions for further institutionalization of regional and international behavior, rather than the hasty creation of a single European foreign policy and defence voice with the help of extending majority voting in the Council to more sensitive areas and making EU institutions responsible for common policies.

Debating weaknesses should not be allowed to conceal the fact that, in principle, a number of EU policies in the Yugoslav crisis have been appropriate. The emphasis on territoriality and the unwillingness to allow borders to be challenged have been a consistent EU policy line from 1991 onwards, even if the treatment of the SFRY was in itself problematic. The policy was meant to constrain the weight and spread of nationalism. Indeed, Serb nationalism in Bosnia and Croatia, Albanian nationalism in Kosovo and FYROM, and Croat

nationalism in Bosnia could set the stage for a large-scale confrontation over borders. The opposing view suggests that, "had the 'trapped minorities' in all of the [Yugoslav secessionist] cases been allowed to secede, they would have achieved peacefully the secession they in fact attempted to secure by the force of arms" (Pavkovic 2000b: 500). This view ignores two important parameters: (a) not all "trapped minorities" limit their claims to a "natural" space and a justified course of development—some become "trapped" by the ambitions and longer-term aspirations of their own leaderships; and (b) it is difficult to defend the general application of such a policy without risking world-wide confrontations over borders.

Which brings us to the reasons used to legitimize policies. Over Kosovo in particular, NATO intervention was legitimized through the appeal to an "ethical foreign policy" which would aim to enforce respect for human rights. The scholarly defence of this approach has underlined the need for the concept of external security to incorporate humanitarian intervention and international law enforcement, aiming at the defence of civilians from human rights violations in different parts of the world (Kaldor 2000: 58). The issue has been extensively debated, but it should be noted—from the perspective of our analysis in this chapter—that the implications of using this particular legitimatory scheme rather than another one need to be examined more carefully. Unlike the established nation states, the EU cannot—for the foreseeable future—become the recipient of "thick" affinities and feelings of loyalty. It will have to resort to "thin" sentiments (for the distinction see Walzer 1994). That is why the debates over "constitutional patriotism" and civic loyalties have a particular significance in the emerging EU political system (see Lavdas 2001). In this context, the resort to "ethical criteria" which transcend national boundaries and national loyalties and the notion of "humanitarian intervention"—even if we are inclined to view them as elements of legitimatory discourse—may play various and multiple roles in the process of (a) re-institutionalizing international relations in the periphery of the EU system while at the same time (b) shaping the perceptions of this emerging system by European citizens.

It is evident that the issues involved in debating the question of European regional crisis management range from strategic considerations to problems of legitimation and direction for the emerging EU political system. On the one hand, the strengthening of the CFSP will further integrate France's security perspective and military capabilities in the western European mainstream. And this is becoming more likely in view of recent British policy rethinking in this area. Despite the co-existence of different views in US thinking about the future military capabilities of the EU, US officials have on several occasions criticized EU inaction when confronted with European crises—such as the one involving

the dispute and near confrontation between Greece and Turkey over Imia in 1996 (see McCormick 1999: 207). At the same time, however, the negotiation of an advanced idea of a common security policy involving the extension of majority voting in this area will be complicated by attempts by France to preserve her autonomous nuclear capability. While Germany's integration in a system of collective defence which would include the control of European nuclear forces has been debated for some time now (Bull 1982: 159-160), it is to be expected that French policy will continue to regard as optimal a combination that includes a common control of conventional forces and sufficient contingency planning while allowing France the possibility to retain her nuclear independence.

A more effective approach to crises in the EU periphery will therefore depend on the outcome of internal EU debates about the future direction of the Union. This, in turn, relates to the use of the prospect of EU associate membership and eventual full membership as a negotiating tool. In view of the possibility of increased US detachment, coupled with the improbability of a strong European military presence in the near future, this approach, which underlines the significance of an *institutional* regional crisis management, is becoming the best way of dealing with European conflicts generated with the long and tortuous transition to post-Communist and post-authoritarian politics. The Union is already playing a major role in shaping the future of the countries of Central and Eastern Europe (CEECs). As Sedelmeier suggests, an important factor influencing EU policy is the notion of a "special responsibility" vis-à-vis the CEECs. Accordingly, EU policy is inclined towards an accommodation of CEECs demands and "proscribing a policy that appears purely oriented towards narrow self-interest." But the extent to which CEECs can actually be accommodated will depend on the policy paradigms which underpin EU policies (Sedelmeier 2000: 219-220).

Eventually, the EU's overall capacity for institutional regional crisis management will be a major factor determining the extent and form of further institutionalization of European international relations. In turn, the EU's overall capacity will depend on three parameters. Firstly, on the pace and characteristics of the process of incorporating the CEECs in an enlarged EU. Secondly, it will depend on the consolidation of a policy paradigm in the enlarged EU which would ensure that issues of political integration remain on the EU agenda. Finally, it will also depend on the evolving security policy of the Union and its relations with NATO's Partnership for Peace and Russia's evolving role. During the Kosovo crisis it became evident that, despite occasional tensions, Russia had given up the idea of supporting the Milosevic regime in Belgrade. There is no

doubt that the creation of some capacity for the EU enforcement of internationally negotiated agreements and arbitration outcomes will be necessary. Against the background of apparent change in the British position, the EU after Amsterdam, seems to be moving in the direction of the consolidation of a European rapid reaction force.

But EU's role is bound to be dependent in the foreseeable future, by the Union's very nature as a predominantly "civilian power," on its medium and long-term capacity to expand the perimeter of its institutionalized governance structures without significantly diluting their content. In other words, it is still the case that the main issue is conditioned by developments in the debates on relations between deepening and widening the EU, debates that have helped shape the evolving European agenda at least since the 1969 Summit in The Hague. From this perspective, the main issue concerns the processes favoring institutionalization and the various economic, political, and cultural factors that influence or prohibit developments in that direction. It is in relation to these developments that the movement from "negative" to "positive" integration in the CFSP will be decided. The movement is from policy as institutionalized and internalized restraint (avoiding the re-nationalization of foreign policies) to policy as the coherent pursuit of common European goals.

REFERENCES

Altmann, Franz-Lothar. 1992. "Ex-Yugoslavia's Neighbors: Who Wants What?." *The World Today*, August/September: 163-165.

Bonvicini, G. 1998. "Making European Foreign Policy Work."In M. Westlake, ed. *The European Union after Amsterdam*. London: Routledge.

Bull, Hedley. 1982. "Civilian Power Europe: A Contradiction in Terms?" *Journal of Common Market Studies* 21: 149-164.

Bull. EC / EU, 1/2-1993, 7/8-1993, 5-1994, 6-1994 9-1994, 12-1994, 1/2-1995.

Cassese, Antonio. 1986. *International Law in a Divided World*. Oxford: Clarendon Press.

Edwards, Geoffrey and Nuttall, Simon. 1994. "Common Foreign and Security Policy." In A. Duff et al., eds., *Maastricht and Beyond*. London: Routledge.

Featherstone, Kevin & Ifantis, Kostas, eds. 1996. *Greece in a Changing Europe*. Manchester: Manchester University Press.

Financial Times, various dates.

Glenny, Misha. 1993. *The Fall of Yugoslavia*. London: Penguin Books.

Gompert, David. 1994. "How to Defeat Serbia." *Foreign Affairs* 73: 30-47.

Gow, James. 1994. "Towards a Settlement in Bosnia: The Non-Military Dimension." *The World Today*, May: 96-99.

The Guardian, various dates.

Hoare, A. 1997. "The Croatian Project to Partition Bosnia-Herzegovina, 1990-1994." *East European Quarterly*, 31: 87-105.

Hoffmann, Stanley. 1995. "Balance, Concert, Anarchy, or None of the Above." In S. Hoffmann, *The European Sisyphus: Essays on Europe, 1964-1994*. Boulder: Westview Press.

__________. 2000. "Towards a Common European Foreign and Security Policy?."*Journal of Common Market Studies*, 38. 2: 189-198.

The Independent, various dates.

International Herald Tribune, various dates.

Kaldor, Mary. 2000. "Europe at the Millennium."*Politics*, 20: 55-63.

Keohane, Robert. 1989. *International Institutions and State Power*. Boulder: Westview Press.

Lamers, Karl. 1995. "Alle Wollen Dazugehoren." *Der Spiegel* 23: 37-38.

Lavdas, Kostas A. 1996. "The European Union and the Yugoslav Conflict: Crisis Management and Re-Institutionalization in Southeastern Europe." *Journal of Political and Military Sociology*, 24: 209-232.

_________. 1997. *The Europeanization of Greece: Interest Politics and the Crises of Integration*. London: Macmillan.

_________. 2001. "Republican Europe and Multicultural Citizenship." *Politics*, 21: 1-11.

Mastny, Vojtech ed. 1995. *Italy and East-Central Europe: Dimensions of the Regional Relationship*. Boulder: Westview Press.

McCormick, John. 1999. *Understanding the European Union*. London: Macmillan.

Noel, Emile. 1994. "From the Maastricht Treaty to the Enlargement of the Community." In G. Parry, ed., *Politics in an Interdependent World: Essays presented to Ghita Ionescu*. Cheltenham: Edward Elgar.

Owen, David. 1995. *Balkan Odyssey*. London: Victor Gollancz.

Pavkovic, Aleksandar, 2000a. *The Fragmentation of Yugoslavia: Nationalism and War in the Balkans*. Second edition. London: Macmillan.

_________. 2000b. "Recursive Secessions in Former Yugoslavia: Too Hard a Case for Theories of Secession?" *Political Studies*, 48: 485-502.

Pinder, John. 1994. "Interdependence, democracy and federalism." In G. Parry ed., *Politics in an Interdependent World: Essays presented to Ghita Ionescu*. Cheltenham: Edward Elgar.

Ramet, Sabrina Petra and Adamovich, Ljubisa, eds. 1994. *Beyond Yugoslavia*. Boulder: Westview Press.

Risse-Kappen, Thomas. 1994. "The Long-Term Future of European Security: Perpetual Anarchy or Community of Democracies?" In W. Carlsnaes and S. Smith, eds., *European Foreign Policy: The EC and Changing Perspectives in Europe*. London: Sage.

Rosenau, James. 1992. "Governance, order, and change in world politics." In J. N. Rosenau and E.-0. Czempiel, eds., *Governance Without Government: Order and Change in World Politics*. Cambridge: Cambridge University Press.

Sedelmeier, Ulrich. 2000. "East of Amsterdam: The Implications of the Amsterdam Treaty for Eastern Enlargement."In K. Neunreither & A. Wiener, eds. *European Integration After Amsterdam*. Oxford: Oxford University Press.

Suddeutsche Zeitung, various dates.

Tsakaloyannis, Panos. 1992. "Risks and opportunities in the East and South." In A. Pijpers ed., *The European Community at the Crossroads*. Dordrecht: Martinus Nijhoff.

Van Eekelen, Willem. 1992. "The bridge-building functions of WEU." In A. Pijpers, ed., *The European Community at the Crossroads*. Dordrecht: Martinus Nijhoff.

Varwick, J. & Woyke, W. 1999. *NATO 2000: Transatlantische Sicherheit am Ausgang des Jahrhunderts*. Opladen: Leske und Budrich.

Veremis, Thanos & Kofos, Evangelos, eds. 1998. *Kosovo: Avoiding Another Balkan War*. Athens: Hellenic Foundation for European and Foreign Policy.

Vickers, Miranda. 1998. *Between Serb and Albanian: A History of Kosovo*. London: Hurst.

Walzer, Michael. 1994. *Thick and Thin: Moral Argument at Home and Abroad*. Notre Dame, IN: University of Notre Dame Press.

Weller, Marc. 1992. "The International Response to the Dissolution of the Socialist Federal Republic of Yugoslavia." *American Journal of International Law* 86: 569-607.

Wheeler, Nicholas. 1993. "The Human Rights and Security Agenda: Beyond Nonintervention?" In G.W. Rees, ed. *International Politics in Europe: The New Agenda*. London: Routledge.

Yilmaz, Bahri. 1995. "Regionalmacht Turkei: Hat sie ihre Fuhrungsrolle verpasst?" *Intemationale Politik* 5: 37-42.

Zametica, John. 1992. "The Yugoslav Conflict." *Adelphi Papers* 270. London: IISS.

Zimmermann, Warren. 1995. "The Last Ambassador: A Memoir of the Collapse of Yugoslavia.' *Foreign Affairs* 74: 2-20.

CHAPTER 15
THE EMERGENCE OF A NEW OTTOMAN MODEL: A NEW FOREIGN POLICY IN TURKEY

Stephanos Constantinides
Université du Québec à Montréal, Canada

INTRODUCTION

Modern Turkey, the nation-state republic, was born on the ruins of the Ottoman Empire after World War I in 1923. Established partly in Europe (area 23,623 km^2) but essentially in Asia (area 756, 953 $km^{2)}$, Turkey has a population of 60.8 million. European Turkey lies west of the Dardanelles, the Sea of Marmara, and the Bosphorus. The Black Sea is linked to the Mediterranean, giving Turkey control of important waterways. Asian Turkey, also known as Anatolia, constitutes the mainland of the country with fertile coastal plains.

The geostrategic importance of the country "at a multifold crossroads between East and West, North and South, Christendom and Islam," plus the fact that it was the main obstacle to Soviet expansion into the Mediterranean, "the southeast keystone of NATO during the Cold War,"[1] facilitated its integration to the Atlantic Alliance and its ties with Western Europe and the United States.

Turkey's economy still depends largely upon agriculture, although since 1980 more than half the population has lived in urban centers. Agriculture accounts for less than 20% of the GNP, and it employs almost half of the labor force.[2] Manufacturing provides about 30% of GNP but employs a relatively small percentage of the labor force. The per capita income remains lower than that of other industrialized countries (around US$5,000), but unemployment is under control because many Turks work abroad, especially in Germany. The inflation rate (approx. 20%) is very high in comparison with Western countries. Remittances from workers abroad, income from tourism and foreign aid provide the Turkish economy with the necessary foreign exchange. Despite these weaknesses, Turkey is on the road to industrialization. With its population of over sixty million, it constitutes an important market for Western countries.[3]

Although the foundation of the Republic in 1923 was seen as a new era based on pre-Islamic secular traditions, this situation has changed radically in recent years. From the vision of discontinuity of the Ottoman Empire and the Republic, one now observes an effort to create a kind of filiation between contemporary Turkey to the Empire. Kemal Atatürk's reforms are now challenged by Islamists and democrats, albeit from different points of view. The Islamists attack the secular State, while the democrats criticize the rigid form of

the national state, which refuses to accept the right of ethno-cultural minorities and entire peoples like the Kurds to exist.[4]

In foreign policy, Turkey is not guided by Kemalism any more. Contrary to Kemalist ideology, the country has renewed its Islamic and Ottoman imperial past and with ideologies that were formally rejected by Kemalism, participating in the Islamic conference and claiming influence to areas which were parts of the Ottoman Empire.[5]

I. "RE-ISLAMIZATION" OR "RE-OTTOMANIZATION"?

In focusing on Turkey's foreign policy, one has to raise the question of re-Islamization or re-Ottomanization. Most observers agree that Turkey is going on with re-Islamization. We will argue that Turkey's re-Islamization is going on accompanied with another process: "re-Ottomanization." Also, in the case of Turkey, Islamization is continuing according to the Ottoman tradition, that is to say that Turkey's situation is not comparable to Algeria's or Iran's.

Although many observers have noted that we are witnessing "re-Islamization" in recent years, especially since 1980, others argue that Turkey is living in the "twilight of Kemalism."[6] There is no doubt that Turkey has reached a significant point, even a crossroads, in its development as a nation State. For the first time since its creation from the ruins of the Ottoman Empire by Moustafa Kemal in 1923, Turkey is seriously threatened as a unitary state by the Kurdish revolt and other centrifugal movements. On the other hand, the reinforcement of Islamic radical movements challenge Turkey's secular orientation and European ambitions.

Kemalism—at least formally—gave up on any idea of an imperial pan-Islamism or pan-Turkism, renounced its former imperial territories and cut ties with the Ottoman past. Also contemporary Turkey is trying to play a major role in the area as a regional leader with ambitions that go beyond the Middle East to the ancient Soviet Republics of Caucasus and Central Asia to the Balkans and Europe. These ambitions are encouraged by the USA and some European countries, which see Turkey as a country of important strategic value and as a luxurious market for the West.

Even since the Soviet Union's collapse, Western analysts have considered Turkey as a "pivotal" state for American and Western interests, because of the country's:

- large population,
- important geographical location,
- economic potential ("emerging market").

What defines Turkey as a pivotal state, however, is, "its capacity to affect regional and international stability." It has also "the potential to influence countries thousands of miles from the Bosphorus."[7]

The revision of Kemalism began early in the 1930s but became more evident in the 1950s when "Islam re-entered the political domain as an important variable in the competition of power."[8] The government of Adnan Menderes liberalized the political, economic, and social life and gave Islam the opportunity to have a presence and influence in Turkish society.

This revisionism of Kemalist ideology encouraged a new Turkish foreign policy model, one of expansionism, the neo-Ottoman one, which led Turkey (with British blessing) to covet Cyprus and to participate in the Bagdad Pact. This participation in the Bagdad Pact provoked the Arab resentment because it was perceived as a revival of Turkish ambitions regarding the Arab world.

The coups d'état of 1960 and 1980 were a desperate effort to limit Islamic influence and support the eroded Kemalist ideology of secularism; however, the military embarrassed the Islamic-Ottoman tradition in foreign policy.

Even after these military interventions the renewal of Islam and Ottoman tradition continued. The Kemalist establishment tried to go ahead with a working arrangement with Islam, as re-Islamization was an inextricable reality of the Turkish society. Turgut Ozal, the dominant political figure of the 1980s, expressed this political compromise between the political Islam, the Ottoman Islamic tradition, and the Kemalist secularism.

This new balance, based on the compromise between Kemalist—especially the military—and Islam opened the door to a profound re-Ottomanization of Turkish foreign policy. Americans and Europeans encouraged this policy, first to use Turkey against Soviet penetration in the Middle East and later to counter the ambivalence of European States on Turkey's candidacy for becoming member of EU. Hence for the moment the European ambitions of Turkey are not incompatible with the country's neo-Ottoman foreign policy.

II. A NEW TURKISH POLICY: THE NEO-OTTOMAN IMPERIAL MODEL

The new Turkish model of foreign policy, the neo-Ottoman one, is verified in its application in various areas, especially in the Balkans, the Middle East and the Caucasus-Central Asian region. Turkey tried to develop special relations since the end of the Cold War and the collapse of the Soviet Union With these three regional entities. At the end of the Cold War, relations with the former Soviet Republics of the Caucasus and Central Asia were non-existent and they were limited with countries in the Middle East and the Balkans.

This was a new situation, a new international context, and Turkey managed to develop "new style" relations for which it was not well prepared, according to some analysts.[9] Furthermore, the country, according to these analysts, is hesitating over a choice among the three above-mentioned entities. Nevertheless it has become increasingly clear in recent years that the Balkans constitute a priority among those three areas.

On the other hand, the European option, as well as the American orientation, remains open. There certainly is, however, a link between the European and the Balkan orientation in terms of sphere of influence. Turkey can assume a complementary role to that of the Western countries in the Balkans mainly because of the significant Muslim population in the area. The Balkans also constitute a kind of entrance to Europe, if one takes into consideration Turkey's European ambitions.

Turkish elites are divided over all these options. The Western option is the preference of an important segment of the ruling elite—business, intelligentsia, and military. However, given the obstacles to becoming a full EU member, the temptation to develop an imperial neo-Ottoman external policy has gained ground, even within the traditional pro-Western elites. On the other hand, Islamists favorable to this neo-Ottoman imperial orientation have gained ground. In the elections of December 24, 1995, Necmettin Erbakan's Islamist party (Refah Partisi-Welfare Party) came first with 21% of the vote. Erbakan became Prime Minister by June, 1997, and made official visits to Iran and Libya. After a year in power Erbakan was toppled by the military in June 1997, and his party was outlawed. He himself lost his political rights. Nevertheless with Erbakan in power or without him, the Islamic movement has already established itself in Turkey. Because of the importance of the Islamist vote, Islamists are not confined to the Welfare Party or the Virtue Party created by Islamists after the first ban. On June 22, 2001, the Virtue Party was also banned but it has been replaced by two new parties after the Islamist movement split: the Saadet Party (SP) and the Justice and Development Party (AKP). Commenting on this ban the well known Turkish journalist Mehmet Ali Birand wrote that "Turkey fails in the democracy test" and Ilnur Cevik, editor of the *Turkish Daily News* noted that "the supreme court has become the first ever court in the world to ban the main opposition party. . . ."[10] In fact, the Islamist vote is divided among different parties, especially those of the right. Meanwhile the main political parties have incorporated a number of Islamic policies into their programs.

Associated with Ottoman tradition and controlled by the military, Turkish Islamism offers the basic ingredient for neo-Ottoman external policy. For the pro-European elite and the military, this policy compensates the little enthusiasm

of the European states to Turkey's full membership in the EU. For the West, the support of such a policy is the price to pay for the strategic importance of Turkey and for Western hesitations over the country's full acceptance in the European fold.

1. The Caucasian-Central Asia Turkish Policy

The Caucasian-Central Asia orientation of Turkish Policy has been a partial failure. The Americans wanted Turkey to play a major role in the area in order to counterbalance the Iranian influence; however, the lack of economic resources needed to play this pivotal role in the area coupled with Russian opposition forced Turkey to recognize its limits and to focus on limited bilateral ties. In fact, Russia had emerged in areas like the Caucasus as the dominant political force in Central Asia.

A Turkish journalist spoke of the "bankruptcy" of the Caucasian-Central Asia Turkish policy after Kazakhstan, Kyrgyzstan, Uzbekistan, and Tajikistan joined China and Russia to sign an agreement on June 15, 2001 creating a new economic and security bloc in Asia—the Shanghai Pact—from which Turkey has been excluded. The Shanghai Pact seems to be a serious setback for Turkey.[11]

The agreement, signed in Constantinople in November 1999 aims to build a 1,240-mile pipeline from Baku, capital of Azerbaidjan, through Georgia. This pipeline will reach Ceyhan, a Turkish port on the Mediterranean, and may seem a great success for Turkey and a defeat for Moscow. In fact, it is just a political agreement, and no assurance exists that the pipeline will be built because the oil companies find it very expensive and of little economic interest. On the other hand, one can only wait to see how Russia will react to a project which goes against its vital interests in the region.

On another front, however, Turkey—despite American apprehension—went ahead with an important $3 billion project to bring natural gas from Russia. The *New York Times* wrote that this project was "a setback in American efforts to curtail Moscow's influence in one of the world's most strategic regions." Furthermore the influential American newspaper noted: "The pipeline would increase Turkey's dependence on Russian natural gas from the current 66 percent to around 80 percent. From the outset, American diplomats have warned that it would give Russia too much leverage over Turkey, and that it would constrain gas development in neighboring countries."[12] What is clear here is that Turkey is trying to find a *modus vivendi* with its powerful neighbor and to develop a policy less dependent on the West. There is no doubt that the failure of Turkey's policy in the Caucasus and Central Asia forced the country to find

an accommodation with Russia in spite of the issues that separate them. Of course it should be mentioned that for economic and political reasons Turkey always managed to have good relations with Russia, from Kemal Atatürk's era on and even during the Cold War.

2. The Midde-East Option

The Midde-East option presents a series of obstacles, notably antagonism with certain countries and difficult relations with others (Syria and Iran), the Arab World's suspicions about Turkey as they have traditionally been dominated by the Ottoman Empire, and the suspicions of countries like Saudi Arabia, regarding a secular State and Turkey's good relations with Israel.

Nevertheless, Turkey has succeeded in normalizing its relations with many Middle-East countries and has exploited the booming market of oil producing countries. This normalization has included Turkish-Syrian relations, especially after Syria was forced to abandon support for Kurdish revolts and Turkish-Iranian relations as the two parties faced issues pragmatically, leaving aside ideological differences.

In 1995, under the auspices of the United States, Turkey concluded a military alliance with Israel. This agreement changed the whole balance of power in the area. Other agreements in fields such as business and trade were signed in 1996. The signed agreement, announced by Turkey on February 24, 1996, provided for joint air and naval exercises, access to port facilities and the opportunity for the Israeli air force to train over the Anatolian Plateau. This means a facility in case Israel needed to carry out an operation against Iran. The agreement also provided for cooperation in fighting against "terrorism" in order—according to some reports—to increase Turkey's capacity and effectiveness against the Kurdish revolt, aiding its war against the Kurdish Workers Party (PKK).

There is no doubt that the 1993 Oslo agreement between Israel and the Palestinians facilitated the new Turkish-Israeli alliance. On the other hand, the United States pushed the two countries to conclude this alliance hoping to enroll also the moderate Arab states as well. Turkey tried to persuade Egypt and Jordan that the pact with Israel was not aimed at "any other country in the region."[13] But on July 1998, *The Christian Science Monitor* reported that during the visit of the Turkish Minister of Foreign Affairs to Israel "Turkish sources say Ankara is building an air base in eastern Turkey exclusively for Israeli use."[14] Turkish officials denied the report, but the incident provoked more criticism of Israeli-Turkish alliance from Iran and Syria. Toward the end

of 1997, Turkey's chief of General Staff, Ismail Hakki Karadayi, visited Egypt to persuade the Egyptians not to be overly critical of the Israeli-Turkish military cooperation, repeating that it was not aimed at any third country in the region.

One of the major objectives of Turkey in concluding the alliance with Israel was obviously to put pressure on Syria to stop supporting the PKK and to stop sheltering Abdullah Ocalan. From this point of view we know that the Israeli-Turkish cooperation gave positive results.

The Israeli-Turkey alliance has led to another development: support of the American Jewish lobby to Turkey in order to oppose the Greek American lobby. The Jewish lobby in Washington helped end restrictions on weapons sales to Turkey; Turkish interests are now on the general agenda of groups such as the Jewish Institute For National Security Affairs (JINSA) and the American-Israel Public Affairs Committee (AIPAC).

Even if Israel did assure Greece and Cyprus that the alliance with Turkey was not directed against them, public opinion in the two countries remained very suspicious, particularly when two Israeli spies were arrested in Cyprus in November 1998. The Turkish press also published information that Turkish pilots were trained in Israel in order to attack Russian S-300 missiles bought by the Cyprus Government. It was reported that during his visit to Israel on September 7, 1998, Turkish Prime Minister Mesut Yilmaz asked for Israel's support in the event that Turkey went to war with Greece over Cyprus. It was also reported that Israel would continue to train Turkish pilots for an attack on the Paphos airbase if the S-300 missiles were deployed.[15]

Also the Israeli Air Force "has violated Cypriot airspace and has flown repeatedly over the newly constructed Paphos airbase on reconnaissance missions. There is evidence also that similar information has been gathered by Israeli spy satellite imagery." Even the Government of Cyprus spokesman recognized that violation of Cypriot space continued into 2001.[16]

It is true that Greece and Cyprus tried to improve their relations with Israel. Yiannos Kranidiotis, the late Greek alternate minister of Foreign Affairs, visited Israel in September 1999; the Government of Cyprus released from prison the two Israeli spies; Israeli President Weizman visited Cyprus and Cypriot President Glafkos Clerides visited Israel. Nevertheless there is still suspicions that in one way or in another the Israeli-Turkey alliance targets Cyprus and Greece.

For some observers, Turkey faces a tough situation as tension rises and conflict escalates in the present Middle East crisis. They note that "after 1998 Turkey started to pursue a more balanced policy between Arabs and Israelis . . . The hyperactivity in the bilateral relations of Turkey and Israel between 1995-1998 gave its place to a more balanced approach."[17] Furthermore, the military

agreement with Syria, an item that was on agenda, will be difficult to achieve under the present circumstances.

Nevertheless, Turkey is negotiating to supply water to Israel, another ingredient of tension with Syria and Iraq as the dams constructed on the Tigris and Euphrates which gave Turkey control of the headwaters of these rivers are of critical importance for these two Arab countries. In this sense, Syria and Iraq depend upon Turkey for their water supply and agricultural development.

3. The Balkan Turkish Policy

Turkey's choice of the Balkans as a priority area in which to develop its new imperial policy may work in concert with the country's European ambitions, but it may also be a response to awareness of the fate of Turkish and Muslim minorities of the area, but mainly this choice constitutes a challenge to Greece. Difficult relations with Greece over the Cypriot question and Aegean dispute may explain the efforts of Turkey to oppose the Greeks in their own yard.

On the other hand, the presence of Turkey in the Balkans as a defender of Islam facilitates its relations with some Middle Eastern countries. This presence enables the country to appear sensitive to the misfortunes of Bosnia's Islamic population. It may also assure Western countries, which prefer Turkish over Iranian influence in the Balkans. In a way, the Turkish Balkan policy is closely linked to its Middle-East policy. This link becomes especially apparent when we consider Turkey's policy in Eastern Mediterranean, notably the invasion and occupation of the northern part of Cyprus since 1974. Furthermore, this occupation is an example of the application of what one may call a neo-Ottoman imperial policy.

In analyzing current Turkish involvement in the Balkans, one must refer to the nineteenth century, and even earlier periods, when this area was part of the Ottoman Empire. The trends seen in Turkish involvement are both conflicting and controversial. From one point of view, people in the Balkans are very suspicious of every Turkish initiative in the region because of past occupation under Ottoman rule. From another point of view, the Bosnian issue, episodic tension between Greece and the FYROM (Former Yugoslav Republic of Macedonia), and difficulties in Greek-Albanian relations, have facilitated Turkey's return to the area.

The Turkish Balkan policy is part of a reorientation of the country's entire foreign policy, from the Kemalist model to a new one connected to the Ottoman imperial past. As a matter of fact, after the unsuccessful Turkish attempt to play

a major role in the Caucasus and Central Asia and the return of Russia in this area, Turkey became more aggressive in the Balkans.

Turkey has played the Bosnian and Bulgarian card in the Balkans, thus exploiting the presence of a Turkish minority in the area and maximizing the Kosovo crisis. One has also to remember Turkish support for the FYROM and accusations against Greece for mistreating the Muslim minority in Thrace.

III. THE TURKISH POLICY ON CYPRUS

The Turkish policy on Cyprus has been consistent since the Cyprus question was raised in the 1950s. It is not the purpose of this article to present a detailed historical analysis of this issue. Nevertheless, the invasion of the island by Turkey in 1974 changed the balance of power on Cyprus and even in the whole region radically. By invading in 1974, Turkey obtained area of strategic importance, almost 40% of the Republic of Cyprus, which can be used to neutralize any attempt to strike southern Turkey. The strategic interest for Turkey is the main element that explains the invasion and occupation of northern Cyprus. Turkish officials have recognized that even without the pretext of defending Turkish Cypriots, Cyprus remains a key strategic goal for the foreign policy of the country. From this strategic point of view, the ideal for Turkey would be occupation of the whole island. However, in this case, the political and even military cost would be very high. Therefore, Turkish policy since 1974 has been oriented towards a solution that would give Turkey indirect control of the entire island. This is a solution that would make Turkey a partner in the whole island and would transform Cyprus into a Turkish protectorate.

In 1974, Turkey imposed a forcible population exchange, or ethnic cleansing, by expulsing all Greek Cypriots from the occupied areas. In this way, the idea of establishing a federal Cyprus appeared as a viable constitutional option. Prior to 1974, the idea of federation had been rejected not only by the Greek-Cypriot side but also by constitutional authorities such as Lord Radcliffe in 1956 and by the UN mediator, Galo Plaza, in 1965. Nevertheless, Turkey went even further by proposing two independent states and a loose confederation, thus moving in complete contrast to the framework for federation accepted by the Government of Cyprus.

Even now, with a new perception of Greek-Turkish relations "earthquake diplomacy," the Turkish position on Cyprus remains unchanged. In his September 16, 2000 statement before the General Assembly of the United Nations, Turkish Foreign Minister Ismail Cem was very clear:

> There are two separate peoples, two separate states in Cyprus, told the Assembly, and a just and lasting compromise in Cyprus has to take in consideration these realities.[18]

As Turkish Prime Minister Bullet Ecevit put it, the Cyprus problem was solved in 1974. What remains now is the legitimization of the island's partition in order to avoid a political irritant affecting its relations with the United States and Europe. In fact, for Cyprus, the present *status quo* is preferable to a solution that will lead in reality not only to the partition of the island but to its transformation as a kind of Turkish protectorate.

Even after the Helsinki European summit that accepted its status as a candidate for membership in the European Union, Turkey refuses firmly to make any concessions in Cyprus. In a number of declarations, Turkish foreign minister Ismail Cem, Prime Minister Bulent Ecevit, and other Turkish officials have made it clear that Turkey will not sacrifice its strong position in Cyprus to favor its European option.[19] This position is also clear in the National Program of Action adopted in March 2001 in order to respond to EU Accession Partnership Document.[20]

It is worth noting that a few days after Papandreou's visit to Ankara, in April 2001, Ismail Cem made an "official three-day visit" to the occupied zone of Cyprus. This move gave a clear message that Turkey will integrate the occupied area of Cyprus if the Republic of Cyprus becomes an EU member.[21] The Turkish threats to react in the case that Cyprus becomes EU member are more and more frequent these days and Rauf Denktash spoke even of a possibility of a Greek-Turkish war.[22] Yet since its genesis, the Cyprus problem has been affected by the politico-strategic considerations and interests in the region of not only Turkey but also a number of other countries such as the United States and Great Britain. In the end, these politico-strategic considerations have reinforced Turkey and its expansionist neo-Ottoman policy. Cyprus is a typical example of the application of what one may call a neo-Ottoman imperial policy.

Nevertheless, voices were raised in Turkey after the Helsinki summit to ask for a new policy on Cyprus insisting that "if Turkey wants to become a full member in the EU, it should solve the Cyprus-Aegean questions (by considering national interests). It should inherit harmonious policies rather than maximalist policies. Without solving these two problems, Turkey should not even dream of becoming a full member."[23]

In another article, entitled "Cyprus Warnings Rising," Mechmet Ali Birand, argued that "there is a timetable" regarding the Cyprus problem and that

"Cyprus may attain the right to become a full member of the EU in 2002 and may complete accession in 2004." Noting that all messages sent to Ankara seek to persuade the Turkish Cypriot leader Rauf Denktash to return to the negotiating table, Birand wonders if "is there anyone who hears the bells of alarm in Ankara."[24] Nevertheless, the situation changed radically after the tragic events of New York and Washington on September 11, 2001. The Cyprus problem has been relegated to the second plan of international issues and Turkey's position has been enhanced. But again as Cyprus is included among the countries of the next European enlargement around the year 2002-2003, these dynamics forced Rauf Denktash to return to the table and to continue intensive negociations in 2002.

IV. THE EUROPEAN OPTION

Since the Kemalist reforms, Turkey has always been oriented towards Europe by its elites.[25] Soon after the creation of the European Common market by the Treaty of Rome in 1957, Turkey presented its application for associate status (1959). An Association Agreement was signed in Ankara in September 1963 and took effect in December 1964. Turkey is thus the oldest "associate" of the European Union.

Because of internal troubles in the late 1970s and the military coup of 1980, relations with Europe have moved slowly. The Ozal years in the 1980s marked a new era for the European orientation of Turkey. The Ozal government had formulated its economic policies with the goal of meeting certain EC criteria. In 1987, the Ozal government formally applied for full membership. However, once again Turkey's poor human-rights record, the occupation of northern Cyprus, tension with Greece and, in particular, the country's economic underdevelopment, dominated by agriculture, remained obstacles to Turkish European aspirations. Although some observers noted that these years marked "a second industrial revolution for Turkey,"[26] it was more like a superficial revolution.

Another important issue is Turkey's high rate of population growth. For Europeans this issue is undoubtedly the more serious one because of free labor movement among EU members. The figures frighten some given that Turkey's already large population is expected to surpass that of Germany, the most populous EU member, by 2010.

Despite these difficulties, a Customs Union was signed in 1995 under American pressure. Yet Turkey's ambitions to be a candidate for full membership were turned down in Luxembourg by the European Council on

December 13, 1997. The Council felt that Turkey did not fulfill the criteria to undertake negotiations for full membership.

V. THE HELSINKI ERA

At the Helsinki Summit (December 10-11, 1999), the Europe of Fifteen bowed to Washington's pressure by reversing the Luxembourg decision of 1997 and accepting Turkey's candidacy for EU membership. Before Helsinki, no candidacy had ever generated the number of problems and debates that Turkey's did. In fact never before had a country with a democratic deficit and a human rights record as poor as Turkey's knocked upon Europe's door. In the past, all states with a history of an authoritarian political régime had to adopt democratic political institutions before applying for EU membership, as did Greece when it drafted its membership application on June 12, 1975, after the fall of the dictatorship in July 1974. All this took place three days after the new Greek republic had passed a constitution comparable to the basic laws of the other EU-member states.

In Turkey's case, one year after Helsinki, the Commission in Brussels was obliged to submit to the candidate a "partnership for membership" outlining the need for constitutional reform, various obligations, e.g. resolving the Kurdish problem and terminating the occupation of northern Cyprus.

Given history and these circumstances, one can understand why the Americans felt obliged to pressure the Europeans into accepting the principle of Turkey's candidacy. Of course, Turkey's EU membership is strategically important to the United States. Washington wants to anchor Ankara to Europe so as to avoid any European defensive that is not "exactly coextensive and subordinated to NATO."[27] The United States considers NATO of capital importance as a means of defending its interests not only in Europe but even in Central Asia. The American concern that Turkey be accepted was understood by US allies who believe that this country provides a key market, an outlet for their economies.[28]

However, from the European vantage point, enlarging the Union implies high stakes. How far can enlargement go without major problems in terms of Europe's institutions and even its "soul"? After all, the goal of the "founding fathers" was not to create a new international structure or military alliance. They sought rather to establish a unique entity with its own identity.

Turkey, from a European perspective, poses many problems. For example, if Europe opens up to Turkey, what can be done with countries like Russia and states in Caucasia, Central Asia, or the Middle East? How can these culturally different nations and peoples be integrated? Obviously under the American

influence, the risk becomes one of heading too far in a universalist enlargement "to the detriment of the shared references and culture that shaped the initial vision of Europe."[29] Furthermore, rather than make Europe a strong political entity, this universalist direction would lead to a free trade zone with a UN-type structure. Obviously such a situation would meet the American need for an Atlantic Europe, scarcely differentiated from NATO, and, of course, well within the American fold.

In addition, the reaction to Turkey's European vocation hides Western prejudices as well as fears of Islam and the possible inundation of Turks immigrating to Europe. Most European leaders, regardless of their political stripe, secretly hope that Turkey will be unable to meet the criteria set in Copenhagen and that, in the long run, Turkey will participate in "reinforced cooperation" with the European "club." This line of thinking corresponds to an eventual Europe of concentric circles, a Europe surrounded by buffer states.[30] Perhaps Turkey's participation as a buffer within one of these peripherals of the European Union might just do the trick. In other words, a two- or multi-tiered Europe would solve the dilemma of the Turkish presence within the European Union.

However, one must go beyond European reservations and also consider Turkish apprehensions. Eric Rouleau pointed out that Turkish political parties have not mentioned that Turkish membership had ever been rejected for political or economic reasons. Instead, certain parties told the Turkish people that the EU simply did not want Muslims. As Rouleau said, "Turkish politicians have hidden the real reasons behind EU opposition to Turkey because they knew that the conditions imposed by Brussels would completely upset the Turkish political system."[31]

On the other hand, the Turkish army remains the best ally of Europeans who do not want Turkey to become a member of the EU family. The common rhetorical device among Turkish military leaders is to raise the issue of Turkish "particularity." This idea only fuels the fire of Europeans who prefer to see Turkey placed in the periphery of a two-tiered Europe. In sum, the issue of Turkey's specificity serves the Turkish military establishment, the Europeans against Turkish membership, and even Americans in that their Turkish ally would participate in a European security structure. It will be interesting to see if the pro-European forces in Turkey and the Turkish people will be satisfied with half-solutions in terms of democratization. There is no doubt that, after the Helsinki summit, Turkey is standing at the crossroads and experiencing a critical period in its history.

The question is to know if this imperial neo-ottoman policy, described above, is compatible with Turkey's alliance with the West. As Europe is not

prepared to accept Turkey as a full member of the Union, it may encourage the imperial orientation. Especially if the West succeeds to have this kind of policy under its control, it will be a compensating solution for Turkey for denying its access to the European Union.

Contrary to the conclusion drawn from some superficial analyses, the main obstacle to the European orientation of Turkey is not Greece. The fear of Europeans—especially the Germans and French—is the free circulation of Turks within the community. The presence of Turkish workers in Germany still constitutes a social problem for that country. Meanwhile, France has to cope with its population of North African origin. The fear of free circulation in Europe of thousands, if not millions of Muslim Turks, will not allow Turkey to become a full member of the European Union at this time.

Concerning Greek-Turkish relations, earthquake diplomacy does not affect the core of the dispute between the two countries. What is important to mention is that in its effort to obtain stability in the area Washington accepted or even encouraged the neo-Ottoman policy of Turkey in its relations with Greece and its policy on Cyprus: Furthermore, the USA encouraged the same Turkish policy in areas like the Balkans, Caucasus, and Central Asia. However, these Turkish policies do not lead to the regional stability that Washington was supposedly seeking.

The United States has also become Turkey's official sponsor in Europe. Washington has exercised pressure on the European Union to accept a country where politicians are forced to obey the military, human rights are not respected, and foreign policy is not conducted in a peaceful way.

V. ESSAY OF A THEORETICAL SCHEME FOR TURKISH FOREIGN POLICY: THE NEO-OTTOMANIST ORIENTATION

The concept of Neo-Ottomanism refers to the imperial Ottoman past which for some analysts "is a much more politically potent force in Turkey than Islam."[32] Some analysts suggest that Turkey has adapted this direction in its foreign policy since the collapse of the Soviet Union and end of the Cold War. But one can go as far back as the thirties, the beginning of the Republic, to find elements of this neo-Ottomanism. Indeed, events like the invasion of Cyprus in 1974, well before the end of the Cold War, already indicated that Turkey was reviving with its Ottoman past.

We consider that this direction in the Turkish foreign policy is compatible with the European direction. For the reasons mentioned above, the European Union cannot offer full membership to Turkey at this moment. The best Turkey can expect from Europe is economic integration and a privileged political

relationship. In fact Europe and the United States in a kind of compensation are supporting Turkey in its efforts to play the role of regional leader. The unsuccessful attempt to play a major role in the Caucasus and Central Asia has obliged Turkey to turn its attention in more traditional directions related to its Ottoman past; in other words, the Middle East and the Balkans.

Such a policy, however, supposes the end of the Kemalist ideology which has prevailed since the founding of the Republic in 1923. The Kemalist ideology has been an effort to cut with the Ottoman past and create a modern, secular state. As one analyst noted "in many respects Kemalist ideology of the Turkish State contributed to [the] political marginalization" of Turkey. "Atatürk set great store on the cohesion of the Turkish people, and on their differences from the peoples of adjacent states. This philosophy was reflected in Turkish diplomacy. Turkey was stoically isolated in the 1920s."[33]

Although this affirmation goes too far, there is no doubt that Kemalism as an ideology limited Turkey's diplomacy in the country's aspirations to cut with the Ottoman tradition. However, the Ottoman legacy left the Turkish elites with bitterness against the Arabs, a people who had "stabbed the Turkish nation in the back."[34] The same Ottoman legacy has guided the relations of Turkey with Iran, a relationship characterized by competition and tension.

From another point of view, contrary to Kemalist assumptions, Turkey is now assuming its Ottoman past and heritage. But one has to wonder if there really has been a cut with this Ottoman heritage (exception made perhaps for the first years of the Republic). For some observers, the erosion of Kemalist ideology began "as soon as President Imset Inonü decided in 1945 to dispense with one-party rule. . . ." From that time, "Islam re-entered the political domain as an important variable in the competition of power."[35] Since then, there is a steady re-Islamization of Turkish state in its internal affairs and a steady re-Islamization in its international affairs. The military intervention in favor of Kemalist secular ideology in the 1960s and 1980s only delayed the progress of this phenomenon.

Yet as pointed out above, re-Islamization in Turkey is inseparable from re-Ottomanization, especially in the area of foreign policy. By joining the Islamic Conference Organization in 1976, Turkey opened its doors to the Saudis, who financed Islamist activities. Indeed, the rigorous Kemalist secularism is now over and association with the Ottoman past is the new reality of Turkish foreign policy. Others have noted that Turkey engaged in a revision of the Kemalist ideology during the 1970s and 1980s, when it "became the champion of the Turkish minorities of Bulgaria, Cyprus and Greece."[36] The invasion of Cyprus in 1974 marked the beginning of an effective neo-Ottoman orientation of Turkish foreign policy.

Kemal Attatürk distanced Turkey "from Turkish-speaking populations, abroad, arguing that Ankara should not meddle in the internal affairs of foreign states, just as he had dissociated the young republic from the Islamic world."[37] With Necmettin Erbakan, the Islamist leader as Prime Minister, we see a confirmation of what some observers indicated in recent years: "the twilight of Kemalism" and the beginning of a new era. Even if the military forced Erbakan to leave power in 1997, it does not seem to be the end of Islamism as a political force in Turkey. Of course, Turkish fundamentalism does not resemble the Iranian or Algerian version. What indeed makes Turkish Islamism more moderate and open is the Ottoman tradition, one of a multilingual, multicultural, and multiconfessional Empire.

Europe and the USA support Turkey's direction without major problems. In this sense, Erbakan, the "Islamist" Turkish Prime Minister once declared: "everybody should know that it is in the interest of the West if the Welfare Party comes to power. Turkey will be a powerful country, ensuring peace and stability in the most sensitive region of the world. Turkey will be a strong economic power and as such will constitute a stronger partner for the West. Investments made by the West will be protected by the Welfare Party. The resulting stability will provide a state of comfort for the West."[38] Eric Rouleau, former French ambassador in Ankara, adds: "In spite of ambiguous language, its demagogic criticism of Western orientated policies and its radical rhetoric, Refah remains by and large a conservative, mainstream party. This explains, at least in part, why Washington greeted Refah's recent victory at the polls with a certain serenity."[39]

In domestic affairs, the Islamist Party of Erbakan is moderate in accepting a secularist-based state with "neutrality in religions matters, as is the case in the United States and France." Noting that Turkey is neither Algeria nor Iran, Erbakan declared before the elections of December 1995, that his party "will always submit to the popular will" and that in the case he will succeed in forming a coalition government—as was the case in 1997—his "two main objectives will be to defend democracy and human rights."[40]

One can understand why Washington and Brussels reacted cautiously and very moderately to Erbakan's visits to Iran and Libya. In reality, the present situation in Turkey is a working arrangement between the Kemalist establishment and the Islamists which permits a moderate re-Islamization accompanied by re-Ottomanization. It seems that the Kemalist establishment, which in recent years encouraged re-Ottomanization of Turkey's foreign policy, is reassured by this compromise between Islamism and Ottomanism.

Furthermore, perhaps the Islamists will be better able than the other parties to find a compromise solution in the Kurdish question, recognizing the Kurdish

identity inside the Ottoman tradition of a multinational and a multicultural society and State. It is therefore possible to suggest that a neo-Ottomanist direction of Turkey would rather facilitate its relations with the West and result in a stabilized regional power serving Western interests in this strategic area better.

One may assume that the concept of a neo-Ottoman policy refers to a compromise in the Kemalist movement and Islamic current that has developed in Turkey over the years. This concept does not correspond to the real or apparent conflicts perceived outside the country. The proof, as we have seen it for years now, is a revitalization of Islam in Turkish society. The Kemalist forces, with the army in front, accept this reality while trying to temper it with the repeated interventions and consolidating the compromise with the political Islam. With the Ottoman model being more open according to the Ottoman multicultural tradition, it would enable an expansionist foreign policy and a peripheral hegemonic role. This would also correspond to American interests and, naturally, those of the Turkish military establishment. This model would also allow the Europeans to justify refusing Turkey's access to the select club of a "multi-tiered Europe." Within this context, the socio-political pro-European movements would have no other choice than to agree to the compromise. In fact, this is how they behaved in the past alongside Kemalists in order to counterbalance the influence of Islamic fundamentalists.

Again, the question is to know whether the pro-European forces in Turkey and the Turkish people will be satisfied with half-solutions in terms of democratization or whether they will react positively to such a policy.

CONCLUSION

Although it is difficult and even hazardous to consider the future direction of Turkish politics, it seems that re-Islamization and re-Ottomanization are an inexorable process.

The main question is how gradual it will be in order to avoid the Kemalist establishment's reaction. There is always a risk of confrontation if this process goes too far or too fast. Such a confrontation would jeopardize the present relative stability of the country and force the West to reexamine its entire regional strategy.

The other unknown factor for the future direction of Turkish policymaking lies in "how" and "how much" politics will be affected by the European dynamics. Even if Turkey obtains full EU membership in the long term, that does not guarantee that the country will abandon its neo-Ottoman direction of the Turkish foreign policy. After all, Germany has not abandoned its hegemonic

visions in spite of its past and the European reality. Nevertheless in this case neo-Ottomanism will necessarily be adapted to the reality of the time, just as German hegemonic visions have been adapted to the new European context.

ENDNOTES

[1] Chase S. Robert, Hill B. Emily, and Kennedy Paul, "Pivotal States and U. S. Strategy," *Foreign Affairs*, January-February 1996, p. 47.

[2] Recent statistics reveal that agriculture produces only 16 percent of the GNP but provides work for around 50 percent of the population. It seems that the Turkish agricultural sector, controlled essentially by big land owners, is very strong politically as they finance political parties. But as one observer noted, these big land owners—only 5 percent of the agricultural population—receive $7 billion out of the $11.5 billion subsidies! It is with these subsidies that they finance politicians and they have no reason to increase their productivity; "they command the voting patterns" of the poor villagers "to ensure that the right men win the elections." Cuneyt Ulsever, "Structure of Turkish Agriculture," *The Turkish Daily News*, 3 April 2001.

[3] *L'Etat du Monde* 1994, 1995, 1996,1999, 2000, Paris : Editions La Découverte, Turquie. In 2001, the Turkish economy entered a severe crisis and only the massive injection of billions of dollars by the IMF succeeded in holding it in check.

[4] Robins Philip, *Turkey and the Middle-East*, London, The Royal Institute of International Affairs, Pinter Publishers, pp. 22-23.

[5] Some observers challenge even the principle according to which Kemal Atatürk's foreign policy—or at least the foreign policy of his successors in the thirties—was one of discontinuity with Ottoman imperial model. See, for example, Thanos Veremis, *Greek-Turkish Relations*, Athens, Ed. Ant. N. Sakkoulas, 1968 (in Greek).

[6] Péroncel-Hugoz, J. P., "Crépuscule du Kemalism" *Le Monde*, 27 mai 1986, Ozal Turgut, *Turkey in Europe*, French Edition (first published), Paris, Ed. Plon, 1988, p. 282.

[7] Chase R. S., Hill E. B, Kennedy P., op. cit., p. 37.

[8] Robins Philip, op. cit., p. 39. The annexation of Alexandretta-Hatay by the Turks, in 1939, is the best example of this revisionism. On the Kemalist

ideology see Speros Vryonis, Jr., *The Turkish State and History, Clio Meets the Grey Wolf*, Aristide D. Caratzas, Publisher, New Rochelle, New York, 1993.

[9] Robins Philip, "La Turquie à l'heure des révisions stratégiques," in Kodmani-Darwish Bassma and Chartouni-Dubarry May, *Perceptions de sécurité et stratégies nationales au Moyen-Orient*, Paris, Masson, 1994, pp. 199-134.

[10] *Turkish Daily News*, June 23, 2001.

[11] Ilnur Cevic, "Shanghai Pact, blow to Turkey in Central Asia," in *Turkish Daily News*, June 16, 2001.

[12] *New York Times*, June 8, 2001.

[13] *Hurriyet,* (a daily Turkish newspaper), July 1, 1998.

[14] *The Christian Science Monitor*, July 10, 1998. On the Turkish-Israel alliance see also Daniel Pipes, "The Real New Middle East," *Commentary*, November 1998, Amikam Nachmani, "The Remarkable Turkish-Israeli Tie" *Middle East Quarterly*, June, 1998.

[15] TRKNWS-L, September 8, 1998 On-line organization providing news of Turkey.

[16] Van Coufoudakis, U. S. *Perspectives of Security and Regional Cooperation in the Eastern Mediterranean*, paper presented in the 3rd International Conference of the Hellenic Institutes of Research, Montreal, May, 1999 published in *Hellenism in the 21st Century* (in greek), Athens, Editions Papazisis, 2000. For the violation of Cypriot airspace in the joint Turkish-Israel-USA military exercise on June 2001 see declaration of the Cyprus Government spokesman Michalis Papapetrou, cited by the Cypriot News Agency on June 9, 2001.

[17] *Turkish Daily News*, April 18, 2001.

[18] Anadolu Agency, September 17, 2000.

[19] See the views expressed by Ismail Gem during the visit in Ankara of his Greek counterpart George Papandreou in April 5-6, 2001. *The Turkish Daily*

News, April 5, 6, 7, 2001. See also the special issue of *Etudes helléniques/Hellenic Studies*, vol. 8, no. 2 (2000) and vol. 9, no 1 (2001). *The European Union and Eastern Mediterranean after Helsinki, Cyprus-Greece-Turkey*.

[20] On the National Program of Action see an analysis in *Etudes helléniques/Hellenic Studies*, vol. 9, n.1.

[21] *Turkish Daily News*, April 19, 2001.

[22] *Turkish Daily News*, June 6, 2001. Anadolu Agency, June 6, 2001 (Denktash addresse Deputies in Ankara).

[23] Mechmet Ali Birand, "We have to solve these problems," *Turkish Daily News*, March 21, 2001. The same journalist wrote widely on Cyprus throughout the year 2001 supporting a compromise on the Cyprus question in order to facilitate Turkey's European ambitions.

[24] *Turkish Daily News*, February 13, 2001.

[25] One can assume that this European orientation is present even before, in the last years of Ottoman Empire; especially with the Neo-Turk movement at the beginning of the twentieth century.

[26] James Pettier, *The Turkish Labyrinth-Atatürk and the New Islam*, London, Penguin Books, 1998, p. 160. Republic of Turkey, Foreign Ministry, Diplomatic Archives. See also Turkey's President Suleyman Demirel's statement on the Cyprus question Anatoli Agency, October 4, 1999.

[27] Georges-Henri Soutou, "Civilisation, histoire et géopolitique: La problématique de l'entrée de la Turquie dans l'Union européenne," in *Geopolitique*, no 69, avril 2000, p. 30.

[28] For more on this topic, see Henry Kissinger, *Diplomacy*, New York, Simon Schuster, 1994, p. 813 and Zbigniew Brzenzinski, *Le grand échiquier*, Paris, Boyard, 1997, p. 24.

[29] Interview with president Valéry Giscard D'Estaing, in *Geopolitique*, op. cit., p. 7.

[30] Jean-Paul Picaper, "L'Allemagne, tête de pont de la Turquie en Europe," in *Geopolitique*, op. cit., p. 47.

[31] Eric Rouleau, interview published in *Etudes helléniques/Hellenic Studies*, vol.8, no.2 (2000)—Turkey has been given its chance to enter the European Union—p.45.

[32] Barchard David, *Turkey and the West*, The Royal Institute of International Affairs, London, Routledge & Kegan Paul, 1985, p. 91. I acknowledge gratefully the concept of Neo-Ottomanism which was used for the first time by David Barchard of the Royal Institute of International Affairs in his paper *Turkey and the West*, op. cit., p. 91.

[33] Robins Philip, *Turkey and the Middle-East*, op. cit., p. 10.

[34] *Ibid*., p. 38.

[35] *Ibid*., p. 39.

[36] Eric Rouleau, "Turkey: Beyond Atatürk," *Foreign Policy*, Summer 1996, p. 71.

[37] *Ibid*., p. 39.

[38] *Ibid*., p. 79.

[39] *Ibid*., p. 79.

[40] *Ibid*., p. 79.

CHAPTER 16
AN ASSESSMENT OF AMERICAN STRATEGY IN THE SOUTH BALKANS SINCE THE DISSOLUTION OF YUGOSLAVIA*

Alexandros K. Kyrou
Salem State College

PROLOGUE

Five years have passed since the publication of my article, "Castle-Building in the Balkans: American Aspirations in Southeastern Europe Since the Dissolution of Yugoslavia," in the *Journal of Political and Military Sociology*. The analysis and tentative projections that I made in that article are revisited and assessed in this chapter. This five-year benchmark is coincident with the beginning of a new American administration, and precisely since my original article was focused on an assessment of American involvement in the Balkans, it is fair to consider the fact that the nature of American policy may indeed change with a new administration, moving from Democratic to Republican, especially if one contemplates the election campaign statements of Condelisa Rice, now President George W. Bush's national security advisor, concerning what will likely be a significant change in United States policy towards the Balkans, both in terms of the nature and level of American involvement in the region. Again, half a decade later we are starting a new administration, after two Clinton administrations with presumably strong policy continuity *vis-a-vis* the Balkans in the form of the strategy outlined in my original article, and Washington is taking stock of whether those strategic assessments and the policy may continue. In fact, if we look at the three linchpins of American policy in the Balkans—the Dayton Accords and the consequent creation of a multiethnic federation in Bosnia; preventive action through peacekeepers committed to the territorial integrity of the Former Yugoslav Republic of Macedonia, or FYROM; and related to the latter, the containment of Albanian expansionism/nationalism, or the so-called Albanian problem (the containment of the Albanian problem,

---

* I would like to express particular gratitude to Professor Elizabeth H. Prodromou, of the Department of International Relations and the Institute on Religion and World Affairs at Boston University, for her invaluable analytic comments and support that contributed immeasurably to this study. I alone am responsible for any deficiencies in this work.

specifically, over the last five years has occurred through various American actions, but the most important of which are the war against Yugoslavia in 1999, the expansion of the international, now NATO, military presence in FYROM, and the establishment of what amounts to a United States protectorate over Albania)—United States regional goals are more illusive at present than they were five years ago.

Increasingly, the two linchpins anchoring United States policy in the South Balkans—namely, containment of the Albanian problem and the sustainability of FYROM—and the policy cornerstone in the North Balkans are being exposed as highly unsuccessful. Instead, what we see five years later in the South Balkans is the spread of the Albanian problem in Kosovo to FYROM and increased fears of a collapse of FYROM, while in the North Balkans, Bosnia is beginning to fracture under escalating tensions between the government in Sarajevo and the Bosnian Croat portion of the federation. Through either preventive engagement or post-conflict terms, the linchpins of American foreign policy dedicated to the two strategic goals of supporting the territorial integrity and preservation of FYROM and containing the Albanian problem, are being revealed as failures. Indeed, my claim at the end of the original article that Washington is moving into a region where it does not understand the historical trajectory or the contemporary reality and therefore its actions will lead to the destabilization of the security environment in Southeastern Europe is a fact precisely being born out by what is currently happening in the South Balkans. In order to revisit and assess the validity of my original analysis of American intervention and its implications for instability, against current regional conditions, the following four sections of this chapter are drawn from the original article, while a new epilogue serves as an updated contextual conclusion.

GREAT POWER RIVALRY AS INTERVENTIONIST IMPERATIVE

The end of the Cold War and the disintegration of Yugoslavia have created not only problems but also opportunities for American foreign policy in the Balkans. The wars of succession in the former Yugoslavia have produced a regional power vacuum in Southeastern Europe. On the heels of the Eastern bloc's demise and the Soviet Union's subsequent collapse, Moscow, contrary to previously held Western expectations, has been rendered powerless to intervene in the Yugoslav void. Freed from the constraints of Soviet competition, the United States, after some initial reluctance, has adopted an uncharacteristically assertive policy in the region.[1]

The decision of the United States government, or more precisely the Clinton administration, to pursue an activist role in the Balkans underscores

Washington's new perception of regional conflicts as potential challenges to American prestige and to international order.[2] Although Washington's policymakers realize that the United States is incapable of filling the Yugoslav vacuum, they are reluctant to defer that task entirely to others.[3] Consequently, the United States finds itself competing with other states for influence over the former Yugoslavia and, by extension, the central Balkans. Underscoring the importance the Clinton administration attached to the projection of American influence in Southeastern Europe, then Secretary of Defense designate Les Aspin announced in 1993 that the Balkan conflict poses a threat to vital American interests and suggested that "the United States might be wise to become militarily involved even without the prospect of sure success."[4] Washington's activist policy of attempting to contribute to regional stability is driven at least in part by what it perceives to be a strategic imperative to maintain a balance of power between two historically rival centers of dominance—Germany and Russia.[5]

Washington views the Balkans in general, and the former Yugoslavia in particular, as an area ripe once more for Great Power conflict. Theorists and policymakers reason that, in order to reduce the potential for a dangerous collision of interests between an ascendant Germany and a reassertive Russia over the former Yugoslavia, the United States is obliged to perform a balancing act.[6] This task ostensibly requires Washington to establish its own sphere of influence in the region as a counterweight to Berlin and Moscow.[7] According to this thinking, it is generally expected that Russia's sphere of influence will extend, as in the past, over the Serbian lands of the former Yugoslavia, while Croatia and Slovenia will be drawn further into Berlin's orbit as German client states. German-Russian rivalry over the former Yugoslavia is, in part, illustrated through the military competition of proxies. Although Germany and Russia did not officially sanction the export of weapons to the former Yugoslavia, which would have been in open violation of the United Nations embargo, both states have been involved in a veritable arms race to supply their respective clients, Croatia and Serbia. Between April 1992 and April 1994 Berlin transferred 320 million dollars in arms to Zagreb, while Moscow sent 360 million dollars in munitions to Belgrade.[8] Putting aside the Bosnian quagmire, this new alignment presumably leaves the Former Yugoslav Republic of Macedonia and the central Balkans open to American penetration, and it is here precisely that Washington is anchoring its long-term regional ambitions.

The success of such a policy remains dependent on the United States' ability to respond to the area's current problems in a way that will promote regional stability, and so Washington has sought to mask its influence-building by linking proposals for expanded American involvement in the Yugoslav conflict with that

goal. Toward this end, Washington has benefitted indirectly from various political luminaries and journalists who have argued that the United States has vital national interests and moral obligations that demand an American presence in the Balkans.[9] In this sense stability is paradoxically both the objective of and the requirement for a successful regional level policy. An area conflict would inevitably create chaotic conditions that could forestall the establishment of a firm American sphere of influence, so local order is viewed as the necessary prerequisite for building such influence. Thus, in order that the United States' ultimate ambitions might be realized, Washington's immediate priority has become the preservation of the region's territorial *de facto status quo*.

SAFEGUARDING THE RECAST *STATUS QUO*

In order to safeguard the *status quo,* Washington has committed to two chief aims: first, to contain Albanian expansionism, and second, to sustain the Former Yugoslav Republic of Macedonia's political survival. Washington fears that the increasing nationalism of the large Albanian populations living outside of but bordering Albania poses a serious threat to the existing state of affairs.[10] Specifically, Washington worries that an explosion of the long repressed Albanian separatist movement in Serbian-controlled Kosovo has the potential to unleash a regional crisis involving several Balkan states.[11] Since 1992, Tirana has actively supported the efforts of Kosovo's approximately two million ethnic Albanians to achieve independence from Yugoslavia.[12] The Albanian government backs the separatist movement because it expects the final result to be the union of Kosovo with Albania.[13] Washington, however, is intensely opposed to any such plans for a Greater Albania, because their realization would disrupt the *status quo*. Consequently, American policy towards Kosovo has arrived at a peculiar compromise: the United States has officially pledged to safeguard indefinitely, with military force if necessary, the human rights of Kosovo's Albanian population against Serbian violations. In a letter delivered in late December 1992 to Serbian President Slobodan Milosevic and the Yugoslav army's commander, General Zivota Panic, President Bush declared that "in the event of conflict in Kosovo caused by Serbian action, the United States will be prepared to employ military force against the Serbs in Kosovo and in Serbia proper."[14] Weighed against this guarantee is Washington's warning to Tirana that it is unwilling to recognize any change in Kosovo's political status.[15] American and other "Western diplomats have, in fact, been at pains to tell Albanian leaders, both in Kosovo and in Albania proper, that the province cannot secede from Serbia."[16] In short, by this policy Kosovo's Albanians

should be allowed to live in peace but will be denied the freedom to determine their political destiny. The American-directed war against Yugoslavia and the subsequent occupation of Kosovo by KFOR, the NATO-led international peace enforcement force that entered Kosovo in June 1999 under a UN mandate, as well as the province's transformation into an international protectorate, have not led to any official policy changes on the issue of Kosovo's political status.

Anxieties over a Greater Albania also relate to Washington's policy towards the Former Yugoslav Republic of Macedonia, FYROM. If there is an overarching linchpin in the Department of State's Balkan strategy, it is the survival and territorial integrity of this *mélange* republic. Much has been written about the recent dispute and ongoing problems between Greece and FYROM and how they supposedly imperil, or imperilled, the prospects for peace in the region.[17] We are routinely reminded that countless struggles over the larger geographic area known as Macedonia have repeatedly led to war in this century and that once again the region could easily become the flashpoint for a conflict engulfing all the countries of the central and southern Balkans.[18] In an effort presumably to prevent such a crisis from occurring, the United States would in essence compel Greece to compromise its national security interests *vis-a-vis* Skopje for the hope of some illusory regional stability.[19] In short, Greece's critics, in government and elsewhere, contend that Athens' unwillingness to grant unconditional recognition and its attendant benefits to Skopje threatens, or threatened, to invite the destruction of that fledgling state.[20]

This simplistic view of the Macedonian problem, however, falls far short of the reality. The fact remains that grave domestic problems, and not external pressures, have brought FYROM's viability into question.[21] Greece drew sharp criticism for its February 1993 decision to impose a nominal trade embargo against FYROM as a counterweight to Skopje's policy of intransigence. Subsequent to this step, pundits rushed to assign the onus of responsibility to Athens for Skopje's serious economic problems. In fact, however, Greece's trade measures had only a marginal effect on FYROM's economy when measured against the impact of United Nations sanctions and Skopje's own regressive economic planning. The American-led United Nations sanctions against Serbia cut off FYROM's economy, once heavily integrated with the rest of the former Yugoslavia, from its major suppliers and markets. Furthermore, the government of FYROM has in effect destabilized its own domestic economy through acute fiscal mismanagement and the general continuation of socialist subsidization policies. To underscore these facts, by December 1994, whereas FYROM's losses incurred from the Greek sanctions were estimated at 300 million dollars, damages from the United Nations embargo and from Skopje's

support of lossmaking state-owned firms exceeded 7.5 billion dollars.[22] To quote from the noted British observer of the Balkan crisis, Misha Glenny: "The Greek decision is not the central difficulty affecting FYROM. It has merely exacerbated the increasingly visible tension between the Albanians of FYROM, who make up between 25 percent and 40 percent of the population depending on whose statistics you believe, and the Slav Macedonians. . . . The basis of consensus inside FYROM is breaking apart, and the Albanian community and the government in Skopje now appear to be moving toward a conflict."[23]

Glenny goes on to describe the Department of State's nightmare scenario, how an internal conflict between FYROM's major ethnic groups could rapidly escalate into a wider Balkan conflagration: "Its potential dangers can hardly be exaggerated. Should small-scale fighting between the Albanians and the Macedonian police break out, observers in Skopje believe that it will be exceptionally difficult to prevent the Albanian, Serb, and even the Bulgarian armies from going to war. If Macedonia were destabilized, Albania would protect its minority, the Serbs would move in defense of the small Serb minority in the north and the Bulgarians would have to consider whether to defend the Slav Macedonians (whom Bulgarians believe to be western Bulgarians)."[24] Furthermore, fears exist that Greece and Turkey would become directly involved in such a regional war.[25] Clearly, such a course of events would be disastrous for all the Balkan peoples and it would also spell the undoing of American ambitions in the region.

Attaching paramount value to FYROM's survival, the Clinton administration adopted an interventionist position.[26] American ground forces were sent to FYROM in the context of the United Nations, and later NATO, presence in the former Yugoslavia, to monitor its border with Serbia.[27] In addition, Washington has warned the Albanian government not to give open support to the growing secessionist movement within FYROM's Albanian community.[28] These measures are aimed at sustaining FYROM's territorial integrity and underscored the Clinton administration's apparent resolve in that area. However, Washington's approach to this and other regional issues is essentially limited to an unimaginative, perhaps even outdated, one-dimensional method: specifically, a preoccupation with military clout as a means to secure foreign policy objectives.

THE FLAWS OF DEPENDENCY THEORY

In order to establish institutional foundations for an American sphere of influence in the central Balkans, Washington hopes to make both Albania and FYROM dependent on the United States for their respective military

development and security.[29] The American military presence in FYROM is in large part intended to demonstrate the United States' interest in Skopje's national defense. At the same time, the Clinton administration launched efforts to forge a military alliance with Tirana. The first step toward this goal was taken in October 1993, when Albania and the United States signed an agreement providing for military cooperation between the two countries.[30] Moving closer to a formal alliance, in July 1994 United States Defense Secretary William Perry, while visiting Tirana, pledged to strengthen military ties with Albania and to study the possibility of its acceptance into NATO.[31] Indeed, subsequent developments seem to indicate that Albania will become the first former East Bloc Balkan state to join NATO.[32] Furthermore, Washington has offered to help reorganize Albania's armed forces. In November 1994, the United States signed a defense accord with Skopje providing for the American supplying and training of FYROM military personnel, balancing the equation.[33] Focusing on Tirana, since January 1995 the United States military has conducted more joint-training exercises with Albania than with any other member of NATO's Partnership for Peace. Underscoring the unique relationship between Washington and Tirana, Albania is slated to become the first state in the former Eastern Bloc to buy weapons from the United States. The planned purchase of American antitank and antiaircraft systems will be subsidized by the Pentagon which earmarked 2 million dollars in its 1996 budget to help Albania's weapons procurement program. United States military aid to Albania has run the gamut from more than 150 used vehicles to a 500-bed field hospital and shipments of army clothing. The Department of Defense's plans for 1997 included several training jets and two patrol boats to be given to Albania on a *gratis* basis. In short, the burgeoning relationship—which in 1995 alone included 9 major operational exercises and approximately 250 other events, such as seminars and trips for Albanian officers to the United States—has, according to the reporters John Pomfret and David B. Ottaway, "all the trappings of a military love affair."[34] These initiatives are, of course, driven by a higher purpose. The Clinton administration apparently reasoned that, if it could secure structural inroads into these two states' most powerful institutions—their military and police establishments—and in the process also make them dependent on the United States for their nation-building programs, Washington would be in a position to control their political conduct in the region. This stratagem would enable the United States to promote regional stability by exercising the direct leverage over Tirana and Skopje necessary to restrain their respective expansionist agendas.[35]

Despite the seemingly logical appeal of this diplomatic hypothesis, Washington's Balkan policy is predisposed to failure. The reasons for this negative assessment stem from what should be recognized as obvious policy flaws and contradictions. First, this approach does not enjoy uniform government understanding or support. Second, rather than easing tensions the present strategy actually contributes to uncertainty and instability in the region. And third, the entire policy is based on a fundamentally false premise and hence is unworkable. Regarding the first point, there seems to exist considerable confusion within the American government over what the United States' objectives are in the region. For instance, recently when Department of Defense and White House officials were asked separately by reporters how the American forces along FYROM's northern border would react in the event of a Serbian attack, two conflicting views emerged.[36] White House officials responded that American forces would act to protect FYROM's security, while the Department of Defense stated that American military personnel were in FYROM merely as monitors and would withdraw to safety in the face of hostilities.[37] Clearly, any new activist foreign policy has to first be made known and understood in Washington before it can be effectively implemented in the Balkans. Furthermore, Washington, by all accounts, has no policy or operational contingency in place to address or respond to the most likely threat to FYROM's existence—domestic interethnic violence.[38]

With respect to the second problem, American involvement in the Balkans has actually been counterproductive to the goal of future stability. To cite the most obvious example, Washington, by guaranteeing to protect the Albanian population of Kosovo against Serbian abuses, created conditions that contributed to a violent nationalist uprising that did ultimately lead to war, a crisis the policy was intended to prevent.[39] After all, separatist Albanians revolted against Serbian rule, confident that, should their insurrection not have succeeded, the world's only superpower would have intervened to shield them from retaliation.[40]

Last, the central defect in Washington's Balkan policy is its patently erroneous premise. The United States government apparently presumes that through practical incentives and clever inducements, it can manipulate the political will of the two countries around which it seeks to build a sphere of influence. Washington expects to win the cooperation of these states by bringing them into a dependent relationship with the United States, one in which they would conceivably need American aid for their respective military and national development. This plan, however, ignores a number of serious pitfalls. Even assuming that such a policy were plausible, any such influence undoubtedly would be fragile and short-lived. Obviously, once these governments become

more secure and stable, and thus less reliant on American support for their survival, they will feel less compelled to act in accord with Washington's wishes, especially if those wishes conflict with their own aspirations.

Furthermore, both Albania and FYROM are natural adversaries and unpredictable states whose behaviors cannot be made to conform to the theoretical expectations of the Department of State[41] Washington has little knowledge of, and even less experience with, these two polities. The United States shares no historical ties, no economic bonds, and no political or cultural affinities with either Albania or FYROM. Moreover, the political leadership in Albania and FYROM make their countries' actions as regional players impossible to forecast. Prior to Albania's slide into anarchy in 1997—the last year that the government in Tirana exercised genuine authority throughout Albania—the country's then president, Sali Berisha, headed an intolerant and authoritarian regime whose principal source of nationalist legitimation was its repression of Albania's large Greek minority.[42] Kiro Gligorov, the long-serving former president of FYROM, led a coalition made-up of recycled Communists and ultranationalists with a long record of terrorism and unabashed calls for aggression against Skopje's neighbors.[43] For these and other reasons, establishing and, more importantly, maintaining the kind of stable and collaborative relationship with these governments and their successors that the United States desires is simply unrealistic.

All other considerations aside, Washington's policy would be doomed in any event because of one overriding contradiction. The central goal of preserving the regional *status quo* is incompatible with active support for the governments of Albania and FYROM. Both these states are committed to territorial revisionist agendas and not to the preservation of the existing order. In short, current American policy is at cross-purposes with its own objectives. Left unaltered, it can serve only to contribute to the empowerment of the two Balkan regimes that most threaten long-term regional stability.

MISGUIDED DIRECTION AS MEDIATOR

An American role in the Balkans need not be predisposed toward failure. In place of neocolonialist adventurism, Washington can, if it chooses to exercise sound judgment, engage in a practical and constructive policy in Southeastern Europe. However, heretofore that has not been the case. Moreover, despite what have generally been characterized as recent American success at mediation in the

Balkans, a good deal of evidence shows that such American involvement has actually made the resolution of problems more difficult for the long-term. This fact is made abundantly clear when assessing the implications of Washington's policy of accommodation toward Skopje.

The Clinton administration was not reluctant to congratulate itself for the decisive role it played in the apparent easing of tensions between Greece and FYROM.[44] As a result of months of intense pressure by United States Assistant Secretary of State Richard Holbrooke, then Greek Foreign Minister Carolos Papoulias and his FYROM counterpart, Stevo Crvenkovski, signed an agreement on September 13, 1995, which provided for the lifting of Athens' economic sanctions against Skopje.[45] In exchange, FYROM is expected to amend its constitution to stress that it has no claim on Greek territory. Both sides will establish liaison offices within one another's capitals, and FYROM will remove a Greek symbol (the Star of Vergina) from its flag. This so-called "small package" of compromises has been criticized by many Greek opposition politicians for leaving the main issue in the dispute—the name of FYROM—unresolved.[46] Indeed, despite the progress toward the normalization of relations between Athens and Skopje, the continued refusal of FYROM's government to give complete assurances that it has abandoned expansionist designs against Greece has obliged Athens to still withhold full conventional diplomatic relations with the new state.

It is important to note that the Greek position is not based merely upon cultural sensitivity or a politicized preoccupation with historical verity. There are, in fact, major parties in FYROM that openly advocate the creation of a "Greater Macedonia" extending to the Aegean and including all of Greek Macedonia.[47] While FYROM hardly poses a military threat to Greece, that fact should not require Athens to accommodate a hostile neighbor engaged in an unrelenting propaganda war against it, anymore than Washington would be compelled to placate Havana in deference to the latter's military inferiority. Regardless, it would be a mistake to underestimate FYROM's aggressive abilities.[48] Such is the case, if for no other reason than Turkey's willingness to provide military assistance to Skopje points to FYROM's potential threat to Greek security as part of a multilateral coalition.[49] In addition, it is not unreasonable, given the historical record, that ultranationalist Slav Macedonians could engage in terrorist activities against Greece or other states.[50]

As a nation that has seen its own territorial boundaries redrawn during living memory, Greece views the shifting Balkan frontiers, and the prospect of irredentism and aggression on its borders, with justifiable alarm. Indeed, the

overarching theme of Greek foreign policy, and especially of Athens' approach to the turbulent dissolution of Yugoslavia, has been to emphasize the principle of preserving existing international borders.[51] When taking into account the unity of Athens' and Washington's primary goal of safeguarding the region's territorial *status quo*, in contrast to FYROM's official and unofficial revisionism, conventional logic, as opposed to the Department of State's present operational framework, would demand increased American support for the Greek position *vis-a-vis* FYROM.[52] Such backing, however, has not been forthcoming. Instead, Washington has increasingly tilted more and more in favor of Skopje and lavished its government with praise, while Athens was forced to endure public lampooning at the hands of senior members of the Clinton administration.

Clearly this brief essay is not the place to debate who, or what is, or is not, Macedonian. Suffice it to suggest, however, that in any coherent sense of cultural or historical affinities, Skopje is as close to ancient Macedonia as it is to modern Ireland. That the ancient Macedonians were Greeks and that Skopje has appropriated and intentionally distorted the former's history in order to help legitimize its present statehood is obvious.[53] Clearly ethnicity is not a matter to be decided by administrative fiat, but derives from a complex of history, social relations, and cultural symbols, including language, religion, and tradition. On this critical basis, the Slavs of FYROM are unquestionably ethnic Bulgarians and not "Macedonians" as the Skopje administration has decreed.[54] Therefore, despite the collective self-delusion of FYROM's Slavs, Greeks are unwilling to regard the assertion of a "Macedonian nationality" as anything other than a politically-inspired artifice founded on a usurpation of the Hellenic past—this fact explains Athens' reluctance in principle to recognize a "Macedonian" state.[55]

Yet, regardless of the validity of Athens' view of Skopjean constructionist identity, and its original political motives, the fact remains that the ethnological composition of the larger region of Macedonia is different today than in antiquity. Although Greek Macedonia is one of the most ethnically homogeneous areas in Europe, let alone the Balkans, the former Yugoslav Macedonia is predominantly Slavic in population. Thus, the logical compromise on FYROM's eventual name depends on both Athens and Skopje accepting the proposition that neither state can monopolize the name and geographic region of contemporary Macedonia. Therefore, FYROM and Greece should settle on a hyphenated name (Slav-Macedonia or Nova-Macedonia, for example) that will clearly and

judiciously differentiate Skopje's state from Greek Macedonia. Once all the involved parties begin to view Macedonia as a composite geographic region with distinct cultural and political components (Greek and Slav Macedonian), there will be stability and cooperation in the region.[56] Conversely, as long as Athens insists on the Greek monopolization of the name Macedonia, and as long as Skopje persists in its propaganda that the Greeks are foreign interlopers in Macedonia, that Greek Macedonia is unliberated irredenta, and that Skopje has exclusive historic rights to the name Macedonia, there will be insecurity and uncertainty.

What is problematic in this equation is that the United States, albeit in a position to exercise decisive leverage over FYROM, has apparently concluded that a reasonable compromise with Greece is not necessary for stability, let alone a requirement for American aid and protection. This sort of unconditional support sends a negative message to FYROM's policymakers—specifically, it sends the message that diplomatic intransigence on major issues carries no liabilities or risks. Such a situation, of course, negates any motivation for FYROM to negotiate in good faith with Greece or any other state. Consequently, if United States policy remains in place, FYROM will have no reason to move toward a real and lasting solution with Greece, which naturally requires mutual substantive compromise. In short, in its policy toward FYROM, the United States is actually contributing to the pressures of long-term instability in the Balkans. Summarily, Washington's inability or unwillingness to appreciate this and other critical facts underscores its misguided involvement in Southeastern Europe.

EPILOGUE

The two goals essential to a successful American strategy in the South Balkans—containment of Albanian nationalism and sustaining FYROM, indeed, both of which are inexorably linked—have failed. The deployment of KFOR and the establishment of an international protectorate in Kosovo has not diminished Albanian Kosovar demands or plans for a rupture of the territorial *status quo*—it has had the opposite effect. Most analytic sources now agree that the American-led war against Yugoslavia catalyzed ethnic cleansing by Milosevic and emboldened and gave capacity to the ultranationalism of the Kosovo Liberation Army, or KLA, both developments which have committed all Albanians to a final status for Kosovo that is separate from Yugoslavia.

Washington's contribution, either deliberate or unwitting, to the radicalization of the Albanian Kosovars directly relates to what seems to be a failed experiment in nation-building and state formation in FYROM. The KFOR occupation of Kosovo and the porousness of the Kosovo-FYROM-Albanian border has allowed the Albanians of FYROM to become part of an economic triangle built on the KLA's immensely lucrative international traffic in narcotics, arms, and human beings. By the same token, the current limited Albanian participation in Skopje's coalition government is superficial evidence of any commitment to FYROM's unity and preservation, while current reports show the Albanian population supporting the local KLA, calling itself the National Liberation Army. Meanwhile, Slav Macedonians remain committed to a notion of nation that is ethnically based and, moreover, based on an ethnic group that will, given Albanian and Slav Macedonian demographic trends and corresponding population projections, become a minority within the next two decades. The weakness, or altogether absence, of a multiethnic national identity has made the state vulnerable to domestic, as well as external, threats of a kind now posed by the KLA in western FYROM and beyond. In the final analysis, Washington's dependency strategy has failed largely because of the failure to understand Albanian nationalist ambitions.

ENDNOTES

[1] For a discussion of international involvement in the dissolution of Yugoslavia and the United States' escalating role in the crisis, see Lenard J. Cohen, *Broken Bonds: The Disintegration of Yugoslavia* (Boulder, Colorado: Westview Press, 1993), 215-219, 252-253, 261-263 (n 71). A concise examination of Yugoslavia's collapse is also found in Susan L. Woodward, *Balkan Tragedy: Chaos and Dissolution After the Cold War* (Washington, D.C.: The Brookings Institution, 1995).

[2] Daniel Williams, "Clinton's Policy in the Balkans Puts U.S. Prestige, Power on the Line," *Washington Post*, 11 February 1993. For a discussion of one of the analytical frameworks underlying direct United States involvement in Eastern Europe, see Thomas S. Szayna, *Ethnic Conflict in Central Europe and the Balkans: A Framework and U.S. Policy Options* (Santa Monica, California: Rand, 1994).

[3] For a discussion of the global policy source of this position, see Steven A. Holmes, "Christopher Reaffirms Leading U.S. Role in World," *New York Times*, 28 May 1993. See, for an example of the regional application of this view, Barton Gellman, "Allies Preview Emerging U.S. Plan for Balkans," *Washington Post*, 7 February 1993. An interpretation of the broader theoretical foundations of selective interventionism is found in Robert S. Chase, Emily B. Hill and Paul Kennedy, "Pivotal States and U.S. Strategy," *Foreign Affairs*, 75 (January-February 1996): 33-51.

[4] From Mark Matthews, "Balkan Strife Could Threaten Vital U.S. Interests, Aspin Says," *Baltimore Sun*, 8 January 1993.

[5] On the history of Great Power, in particular Russian, influence in the Balkans, see M.A. Anderson, *The Eastern Question, 1774-1923* (New York: St. Martin's Press, 1966); Charles Jelavich, *Tsarist Russia and Balkan Nationalism: Russian Influence in the Internal Affairs of Bulgaria and Serbia, 1876-1886* (Berkeley, California: University of California Press, 1958); Andrew Rossos, *Russia and the Balkans: Inter-Balkan Rivalries and Russian Foreign Policy, 1908-1914* (Toronto: University of Toronto Press, 1981); and M.D. Stojanovic, *The Great Powers and the Balkans, 1875-1878* (Cambridge: Cambridge University Press, 1968). The most prolific and authoritative scholar on the subject of Russian involvement in Southeastern Europe is Barbara Jelavich--her extensive publications in this area include five books: *A Century of Russian Foreign Policy, 1814-1914* (Philadelphia: J. B. Lippincott, 1964); *The Ottoman Empire, the Great Powers, and the Straits Question, 1870-1887* (Bloomington, Indiana: Indiana University Press, 1973); *Russia and the Formation of the Romanian National State, 1821-1878* (Cambridge: Cambridge University Press, 1984); *Russia's Balkan Entanglements, 1806-1914* (Cambridge: Cambridge University Press, 1991); and *St. Petersburg and Moscow: Tsarist and Soviet Foreign Policy, 1814-1974* (Bloomington, Indiana: Indiana University Press, 1974).

[6] See Nicholas S. Balamaci, "Havoc in the Balkans and Germany's Re-entry into the International Arena," *The Greek American* (New York), 12 February 1994. Germany's increasingly independent and assertive role in the Balkans is addressed in Cohen, 232-235. For a fuller discussion of Berlin's defiant foreign policy in the region, see Beverly Crawford, "Explaining Defection from International Cooperation: Germany's Unilateral Recognition of Croatia," *World Politics*, 48 (July 1996): 482-521. A scenario involving a collision between

Russia and the Western European powers over the former Yugoslavia is described in Ted Galen Carpenter, "The Balkan Crisis and the Faulty 1930s Analogy," *Mediterranean Quarterly*, 5 (fall 1994): 29.

[7] For analyses of Great Power influences and competition in the Balkans, see Marie-Janine Calic, "German Perspectives," in Alex Danchev and Thomas Halverson, eds., *International Perspectives on the Yugoslav Conflict* (New York: St. Martin's Press, Inc., 1996), 52-86; Andrei Edemskii, "Russian Perspectives," in Danchev and Halverson, 29-51; Paul A. Goble, "Dangerous Liaisons: Moscow, the Former Yugoslavia and the West," in Richard H. Ullman, ed., *The World and Yugoslavia's Wars* (New York: Council on Foreign Relations, 1996), 182-197; David C. Gombert, "The United States and Yugoslavia's Wars," in Ullman, 122-144; Thomas Halverson, "American Perspectives," in Danchev and Halverson, 1-28; Nicolai Kovalski, "Russia and the Balkans," in Theodore A. Couloumbis, Thanos M. Veremis and Thanos P. Dokos, eds., *The Southeast European Yearbook 1994-1995* (Athens: Hellenic Foundation for European and Foreign Policy [ELIAMEP], 1995), 609-617; and F. Stephen Larrabee, "Washington, Moscow, and the Balkans: Strategic Retreat or Reengagement?" in F. Stephen Larrabee, ed., *The Volatile Powder Keg: Balkan Security after the Cold War* (Washington, D.C.: The American University Press, 1994), 201-218.

[8] For more detailed information, see Paul Beaver, "Busting the U.N. Sanctions," *Washington Times*, 2 August 1994.

[9] For a critical analysis and response to this approach to the Yugoslav problem, see Carpenter, 17-29.

[10] For comparative discussions that trace the growth of the Albanian nationalist movement in the former Yugoslavia, see the chapters entitled "The Albanians in Yugoslavia," in Elez Biberaj, *Albania: A Socialist Maverick* (Boulder, Colorado: Westview Press, 1990), 107-132; and "The Albanians - Yugoslavia's Most Explosive Problem," in Stevan K. Pavlowitch, *The Improbable Survivor: Yugoslavia and its Problems, 1918-1988* (Columbus, Ohio: Ohio State University Press, 1988), 78-93. For reports on the more recent dimensions of the conflict between Belgrade and the Albanian Kosovars, see Yigal Chazan, "Radical Albanian Nationalists Gain Ground in Serbian Province," *Christian Science Monitor*, 29 September 1994; and Christine Spolar,

"Albanians in Kosovo Assert Nationalism, Serb Leaders Vow to Retain Control," *Washington Post*, 29 December 1992.

[11] See Henry Kamm, "Albanian Chief Urges West to Send Troops to Kosovo to Prevent War," *New York Times*, 31 May 1993; Mariana Katzarova, "Kosovo Waits," *The Nation* (25 January 1993): 77; Robert Marquand, "Kosovo Province: Balkans' Next Flash Point?" *Christian Science Monitor*, 28 December 1992; and Daniel Williams, "Kosovo Leader Asks U.S. for Troops," *Washington Post*, 17 February 1993.

[12] Alexandros K. Kyrou, "Albania," in Gregory C. Ference, ed., *Chronology of Twentieth Century East European History* (Detroit: Gale Research Inc., 1994), 57.

[13] For an excellent review of political developments in Albania, see Elez Biberaj, "Albania and the Albanians in the Post-Communist Period," in Larrabee, 27-50.

[14] As cited in John M. Goshko, "Bush Threatens 'Military Force' if Serbs Attack Kosovo Province," *Washington Post*, 29 December 1992; and Don Oberdorfer, "A Bloody Failure in the Balkans," *Washington Post*, 8 February 1993. Bush's policy has been reaffirmed by the Clinton administration. See "Clinton Warns Serbian Leaders on Military Action in Kosovo," *Washington Post*, 2 March 1993.

[15] See Misha Glenny, "Hope for Bosnia?" *New York Review*, 7 April 1994.

[16] From "Kosovo: Welcome to Balkania," *The Economist* (7 September 1996): 48-49.

[17] For a discussion of the nature and prevalence of distorted reporting on the Athens-Skopje dispute in the American press, see Phillip Spyropoulos, "The New York Times and the Kaplanesque," *The Greek American* (New York), 7 May 1994. A representative example of such press partisanship is found in "Mr. Clinton's Risk in Macedonia," *New York Times*, 30 April 1994.

[18] Invaluable examinations of the historical background are found in Elisabeth Barker, *Macedonia: Its Place in Balkan Power Politics* (London: Royal Institute of International Affairs, 1950); Evangelos Kofos, *Nationalism and Communism*

in Macedonia: Civil Conflict, Politics of Mutation, National Identity (New Rochelle, New York: Aristide D. Caratzas, Publisher, 1993); and Stephen G. Palmer, Jr., and Robert R. King, *Yugoslav Communism and the Macedonian Question* (Hamden, Connecticut: Archon Books, 1971). For briefer yet excellent historical reviews of this issue, see Barbara Jelavich, *History of the Balkans: Twentieth Century*, Volume 2 (Cambridge: Cambridge University Press, 1983), 89-95; and Charles and Barbara Jelavich, *The Establishment of the Balkan National States, 1804-1920* (Seattle, Washington: University of Washington Press, 1977), 207-213. For a recent and very succinct survey of the Macedonian issue, see David Fromkin, "Dimitrios Returns: Macedonia and the Balkan Question in the Shadow of History," *World Policy Journal*, 10 (summer 1993): 67-71. On the issue of a possible expansion of hostilities in the Balkans beginning in FYROM, see Eric Bourne, "Balkan States Worry Over Prospects of Widening War," *Christian Science Monitor*, 2 February 1993; Misha Glenny, "Is Macedonia Next?" *New York Times*, 30 July 1993; George Leopold, "Officials Warn of Balkan Escalation," *Defence News*, 22 March 1993; Cord Meyer, "Threats Beyond Bosnia," *Washington Times*, 12 February 1993; and David B. Ottaway, "The West Watches for the Ripple Effect," *Washington Post*, 26 December 1993.

[19] See "Greek Prime Minister Stresses Importance of National Security on Skopje," *The Greek American* (New York), 30 April 1994; "U.S. Recognition of Skopje as 'FYROM' Threatens Greece," *The Greek American* (New York), 12 February 1994; and Roger Fontaine and Dennis Mullin, "What will Papandreou tell Clinton?" *Washington Times*, 21 April 1994.

[20] For examples of this viewpoint, see Jim Hoagland, "Another Brink in the Balkans," *Washington Post*, 31 March 1994; and Trudy Rubin, "U.S. Needs More than Troops to Head off Trouble in Macedonia," *Philadelphia Inquirer*, 19 August 1994. A useful synthesis of the basic features of this problem is found in Van Coufoudakis, *The Macedonian Question and its Importance to Greece* (Toronto: The Legacy of Macedonia Semi-Annual Lecture Series, Pan-Macedonian Association, 1993). Much of the ill-informed derision levelled against Athens for its position *vis-a-vis* Skopje has as its intellectual referent the growing work of a small group of anthropologists actively reconstructing history in accord with changing political conditions in the Balkans. For a representative example of such writing, see Loring M. Danforth, *The Macedonian Conflict: Ethnic Nationalism in a Transnational World* (Princeton, New Jersey: Princeton University Press, 1995).

[21] See Glenny, "Hope for Bosnia?" and Henry Kamm, "Macedonia Sees its Albanians as its 'Biggest Problem,'" *New York Times*, 5 May 1994.

[22] Elisaveta Konstantinova, "Macedonia Limps Ahead With Reforms," *Illyria* (New York), 15-17 December 1994. According to officials in Skopje, whose statistics conflict with foreign estimates, the Greek and United Nations sanctions, while in place, cost FYROM approximately 40 million and 160 million dollars, respectively, per month. For more information, see Duncan M. Perry, "Macedonia: Balkan Miracle or Balkan Disaster?" *Current History*, 95 (March 1996): 113-117.

[23] Glenny, "Hope for Bosnia?"

[24] *Ibid*. For more on Bulgaria's position and its interests in the central Balkans, see Ivanka Nedeva, "Balkan Troubles, Bulgarian Hopes," *World Policy Journal*, 11 (fall 1994): 132-138; and Duncan M. Perry, "Bulgaria: Security Concerns and Foreign Policy Considerations," in Larrabee, 51-64.

[25] For a contrarian analysis that challenges the worst-case musings on the Balkan crisis, see Nicholas X. Rizopoulos, "A Third Balkan War?" *World Policy Journal*, 10 (summer 1993): 1-5.

[26] For a critical assessment of American interventionism in FYROM, see Ted Galen Carpenter, "A Back Door to War?" *Washington Times*, 2 September 1993.

[27] Since early July 1993 the United States has sent approximately 500 American troops to join a United Nations peace-keeping force in FYROM. For information on the composition, operations, and mission of the American contingent, see "U.S. Force for Macedonia Comes From Berlin Brigade," *Washington Post*, 25 June 1993; "U.S. Peace-Keeping Troops Begin Patrols on Macedonia Border," *Washington Post*, 21 August 1993; "U.S. Troops Arrive in Macedonia," *Christian Science Monitor*, 6 July 1993; "U.S. Troops Arrive in Macedonia: Goal is to Contain Balkan Conflict," *Baltimore Sun*, 6 July 1993; "U.S. Troops Begin Macedonia Patrols," *Washington Times*, 21 August 1993; Henry Kamm, "Kriva Palanka Journal: The Well-Equipped G.I.'s (But An Exercise Bike?)," *New York Times*, 11 May 1994; and Steve Vogel, "U.S. Troops Face Training in Macedonia: U.N. Commander Sets Rules of Engagement," *Washington Post*, 10 July 1993.

[28] Glenny, "Hope for Bosnia?"

[29] See John Pomfret, "U.S. Builds Arc of Alliances to Contain Serbia's Power," *Washington Post*, 19 December 1995. For a report on the expanding American influence over Tirana, see George Jahn, "Albania Inches Ahead With U.S. as Suitor," *Washington Times*, 10 May 1994. In reaction to the apparent emergence of American institutions in FYROM, the opposition press in Skopje has alleged that the United Nations peace-keeping mission was used as a pretext for establishing a United States military presence in the new state. See Grey Lusitana, "U.S.-Albanian Pact May Create Buffer," *Washington Times*, 15 February 1994.

[30] David Binder, "U.S. and Albania Sign a Military Agreement," *New York Times*, 21 October 1993. The formal "Memorandum of Understanding on Defense and Military Relations Between the Department of Defense of the United States of America and the Ministry of Defense of the Republic of Albania" is reprinted in Couloumbis, Veremis and Dokos, 623-625.

[31] Susanne M. Schafer, "Perry Promises U.S. Military Cooperation With Albania," Associated Press Wire Report, Tirana, Albania, 20 July 1994.

[32] *"He Albania Phlertarei me to NATO"* (*"Albania Flirts with NATO"*), *Bema* (Athens), 5 May 1996; "U.S.-Albania Military Ties," *Diaspora Newsletter* (San Jose, California), 2 (3 November 1995): 1-2.

[33] "Macedonia, U.S. Sign Pact," *Fort Wayne Journal Gazette*, 13 November 1994; "U.S. Agrees to Work With Albanian Military," *Baltimore Sun*, 21 October 1993; "U.S. Backs Macedonia," *Fort Wayne Journal Gazette*, 9 January 1995.

[34] John Pomfret and David B. Ottaway, "U.S., Albania Form 'the Weirdest Relationship,'" *Washington Post*, 20 November 1995. In addition to Pomfret and Ottaway, for detailed data on American military aid to Albania, see Marianne Sullivan, "Shalikashvili Cites Progress in Albanian Military," *Illyria* (New York), 19 October 1995.

[35] See Pomfret, "U.S. Builds Arc of Alliances to Contain Serbia's Power." For a frank discussion of FYROM's expansionist dogma and hostility towards Greece, see Robert D. Kaplan, *Balkan Ghosts: A Journey Through History* (New

York: St. Martin's Press, 1993), 66-68. Skopje's official irredentist position is presented in a volume entitled *Naselenite Mesta vo Egeiska Makedonija: Geografski, Etnicki, Istopanski Karakteristike* (*The Inhabited Places in Aegean Macedonia: Geographical, Ethnic, Agricultural Characteristics*; Skopje: Institute of National History, 1978). A scholarly analysis of recent state-sponsored expansionist propaganda is found in Evangelos Kofos, *The Vision of "Greater Macedonia:" Remarks on FYROM's New Schoolbooks* (Thessaloniki: Museum of the Macedonian Struggle, 1994). For documentary evidence related to FYROM's territorial design's against Greece, see Basil Kondis, Kyriakos Kentrotis, Spyridon Sfetas and Yiannis D. Stefanidis, eds., *Resurgent Irredentism: Documents on Skopje 'Macedonian' Nationalist Aspirations* (Thessaloniki: Institute for Balkan Studies, 1993).

[36] "White House, Pentagon at Odds Over Role in FYROM," *The Greek American* (New York), 3-9 September 1994.

[37] *Ibid.*; Rubin. The Department of Defense has repeatedly expressed serious misgivings about the mission it has been ordered to carry out in FYROM. Moreover, Pentagon analysts have warned that FYROM is "probably not 'economically or politically viable,' and that a major crisis is 'inevitable.'" From Fontaine and Mullin.

[38] For a discussion of interethnic tensions in FYROM and their potential to destroy the state, see Gilles Bertrand, "L'ex-Republique Yougoslave de Macedoine: Entre Apaisement et Destabilisation," *Etudes Helleniques/Hellenic Studies*, 3 (autumn 1995): 91-102.

[39] For an early prediction of the potential consequences of this policy, see Nicholas Gage, "Kosovo Powder Keg," *Washington Post*, 11 April 1993.

[40] *Ibid.*

[41] On the state of worsening relations between Skopje and Tirana, as well as those between the government of FYROM and the country's Albanian population, see Gilles Bertrand, "Les Meilleures Intentions L'ex-Republique Yougoslave de Macedoine Face a la Guerre dans les Balkans," *Etudes Helleniques/Hellenic Studies*, 3 (spring 1994): 81-96; "Ethnic Albanians Arrested as Plotters," *Washington Times*, 16 November 1993; "Macedonia Blocks Albanian University," *Washington Times*, 20 December 1994;

"Macedonia Demolishes University Building," *Illyria* (New York), 19-21 December 1994; "Macedonian Authorities Slap Down Bid to Establish Albanian University," *Baltimore Sun*, 15 December 1994; Misha Glenny, "Is Another Balkan War Inevitable?" *Odyssey: The World of Greece*, 1 (April-May 1994): 24-29; Christopher Hitchens, "Minority Report: Skopje/Tetovo, 'Macedonia,'" *The Nation* (18 April 1994): 511; Slobodan Lekic, "Averting Showdown Gains Macedonia Leverage," *Washington Times*, 7 December 1993; Cord Meyer, "Pressure on a Balkan 'Miracle,'" *Washington Times*, 15 October 1993; Duncan M. Perry, "Macedonia," *RFE/RL Research Report: The Politics of Intolerance*, 3 (22 April 1994): 83-86; and Helen Smith, "Albanians, Macedonia on a Collision Course," *Washington Times*, 23 December 1994.

[42] Since 1991 a considerable number of scholarly studies of the Greek population in Albania have been published in Greece. One of the most important works in this expanding bibliography is found in Thanos Veremis, Theodore Couloumbis and Elias Nikolakopoulos, eds., *Ho Hellenismos tes Albanias* (*Hellenism in Albania*) (Athens: Hellenic Foundation for European and Foreign Policy [ELIAMEP], I. Sideres: 1995). For a recent historical survey of the position of Albania's ethnic Greek population, see Nicholas Gage, "The Forgotten Minority in the Balkans: The Greeks of Northern Epirus," *Mediterranean Quarterly*, 4 (summer 1993): 10-29. See also "Albania Charges American, Others With Death Penalty Offenses: Tirana Actions Part of Systematic Abuse of Large Ethnic Greek Minority," AHEPA Press Release, Washington, D.C., 4 August 1994; "Albania Continues Persecution of Greek Minority," *The Greek American* (New York), 4 December 1993; "Albania's Greeks Fear Genocide," *Washington Times*, 5 July 1993; Elias Betzios, "Human Rights for Ethnic Greeks in Albania Needs Full Guarantee," paper presented before the 46th Session of the Sub-Commission on Prevention of Discrimination and Protection of Minorities held in Geneva, Switzerland, 12 August 1994, published in *The Greek Star* (Chicago), 8 September 1994; "Human Rights Abuses in Albania," letter dated 8 September 1994 from Jeri Laber, Executive Director, Human Rights Watch/Helsinki, to Albanian President Sali Berisha, published in *The Greek American* (New York), 17-23 September 1994; and Helena Smith, "Tension Grows as a Greek Tragedy is Played out in Albania," *Guardian*, 8 June 1994. For detailed accounts of state violence against Greeks in Albania, see "Albanian Ethnic Greeks Attacked," *The Greek American* (New York), 11 September 1993; and Tina Mavrikos, "69 Year-Old Greek Woman Killed by Albanian Police," *The Greek American* (New York), 30 September 1993. Although the Department of State has often acknowledged Tirana's

regular violations of the rights of its Greek minority, it has demonstrated an unwillingness to hold the Berisha regime accountable for either individual breaches of civil rights or for the general pattern of ethnic repression against Albania's Greek communities. See, for example, the comments of Joseph Lake in Committee on Foreign Relations, United States Senate, "ACDA and Ambassadorial Nominations: Hearings for Joseph Lake, United States Ambassador Nominate to Albania, 24 June 1994" (Washington, D.C.: Stenographic Transcript of Hearings by Alderson Reporting Company, 1994). Ultranationalist chauvinism outside the Albanian government is discussed in Robert Austin, "Albania," *REF/RL Research Report: The Politics of Intolerance*, 3 (22 April 1994): 72-74. On Berisha's growing authoritarianism, see "Albania Bars Ex-Communists From Office," *New York Times*, 24 September 1995; "Albania: Berisha Beacons," *The Economist* (18 May 1996): 52, 55; "Albania: You're Out," *The Economist* (7 October 1995): 58, 60; "Democracy Denied in Albania," *New York Times*, 30 May 1996; Merita Dhimagjoka, "Albania bars former Communists from government posts until 2002," *Washington Times*, 24 September 1995; and Jane Perlez, "2 Monitoring Groups Call Albania Vote Marred," *New York Times*, 30 May 1996. For a fuller discussion of this subject, see Anastas Angjel, "Problems of Albanian Democracy," *Mediterranean Quarterly*, 6 (fall 1995): 35-47.

[43] See Cohen, 148; Theodore A. Couloumbis, "The Macedonian Question: Achilles' Heel or Odyssean Wiles?" *Odyssey: The World of Greece*, 1 (August-September 1993): 9-10; and Hitchens. For a study of the origins and political objectives of the terrorist tradition, see Duncan M. Perry, *The Politics of Terror: The Macedonian Revolutionary Movements*, 1893-1903 (Durham, North Carolina: Duke University Press, 1988).

[44] The Clinton administration's self-eulogizing activism in the Balkans in general, and FYROM and Kosovo in particular, has benefited considerably from influential non-governmental organizations which have aggressively advocated United States leadership in the region through international intervention in the Yugoslav crisis. See, for example, "Center for Preventive Action Releases Report on South Balkans: Report Proposes Ways to Prevent Conflict in Kosovo," Council on Foreign Relations News Release, New York, 14 May 1996.

[45] For a complete accounting of the agreement's component provisions, see "The Full Text of the Interim Accord Between Greece and FYROM," Embassy

of Greece, Press and Information Office (Washington, D.C.), 15 September 1996.

[46] Jacquelyn K. Davis and Charles M. Perry, *European Issues and Developments: Progress Report for Considerations Affecting Global Nuclear Initiatives* (Cambridge, Massachusetts and Washington, D.C.: National Security Planning Associates, December 1995): 123-124.

[47] *Ibid.*, 124. See also Hugh Poulton, *Who are the Macedonians?* (Bloomington, Indiana: Indiana University Press, 1995): 206-207. For the historical background to this problem, consult Palmer and King, 117-130. An overview of the Macedonian issue which places the controversy within the context of current regional security concerns is found in Symeon A. Giannakos, "The Macedonian Question Reexamined: Implications for Balkan Security," *Mediterranean Quarterly*, 3 (summer 1992)): 26-47.

[48] For an excellent assessment and analysis of Skopje's potential as a security threat to Athens, see Nikolaos Zahariadis, "Is the Former Yugoslav Republic of Macedonia a Security Threat to Greece?" *Mediterranean Quarterly*, 5 (winter 1994): 84-105.

[49] "Albania, Turkey Start Joint Military Exercises," *The Greek American* (New York), 11 November 1995.

[50] Davis and Perry, 124.

[51] *Ibid.* For a discussion of Greece's foreign policy responses to the Yugoslav crisis, especially as they relate to FYROM, see Virginia Tsouderos, "Greek Policy and the Yugoslav Turmoil," *Mediterranean Quarterly*, 4 (spring 1993): 1-9. A peerless critical and detailed evaluation of the latter is found in Nikolaos Zahariadis, "Greek Policy toward the Former Yugoslav Republic of Macedonia, 1991-1995," *Journal of Modern Greek Studies*, 14 (October 1996): 303-327.

[52] An original and excellent analysis of the problems related to the external perceptions of Greek security within the current reconceptualization of the Western alliance system is found in Elizabeth Prodromou, "The Perception Paradox for Greece's Post-Cold War Security," in Graham Allison and Calypso Nicolaides, eds., *The Greek Paradox: Promise vs. Performance* (Cambridge, Massachusetts: The MIT Press, 1996), 123-132. For informative overviews of

Greece's strategic position in Southeastern Europe, its relationship with the United States, and its role as a stabilizing factor in the region, see Jean Catsiapis, "La Grece et Les Balkans, *Etudes Helleniques/Hellenic Studies*, 3 (spring 1994): 69-80; and Thanos Veremis, "Greece: The Dilemmas of Change," in Larrabee, 119-133.

[53] For a thorough discussion of ancient Macedonia, see R. Malcolm Errington, *A History of Macedonia* (Berkeley, California: University of California Press, 1990). On pages 3-4 of his authoritative study Errington makes the following observation concerning Macedonian identity: "That the Macedonians and their kings did in fact speak a dialect of Greek may be regarded nowadays as certain. . . . Ancient allegations that the Macedonians were non-Greeks all had their origin in Athens with the struggle of Philip II. Then as now, a political struggle created the prejudice."

[54] See the relevant sections in Palmer and King, especially pages 153-174, and 199-203.

[55] A detailed account of the official Greek position and attendant policy relating to the knotty controversy over Skopje's state appellation is found in Thodoros Skulakakis, *Sto Onoma tes Makedonias* (*In the Name of Macedonia*) (Athens: Greek Euro-publishers, 1995).

[56] This proposal, as explained within the context of competing Greek foreign policy schools of thought, is discussed in Couloumbis, 10.

REFERENCES

n.a. 1978, *Naselenite Mesta vo Egeiska Makedonija: Geografski, Etnicki, Istopanski Karakteristike* (*The Inhabited Places in Aegean Macedonia: Geographical, Ethnic, Agricultural Chracteristics*). Skopje: Institute of National History.

_________. 1993a. "Albania Continues Persecution of Greek Minority." *The Greek American* (December 4).

_________. 1993. "Albanian Ethnic Greeks Attacked." *The Greek American* (September 11).

_________. 1993c. "Albania's Greeks Fear Genocide." *Washington Times* (July 5).

_________. 1993d. "Clinton Warns Serbian Leaders on Military Action in Kosovo." *Washington Post* (March 2).

_________. 1993e. "Ethnic Albanians Arrested as Plotters." *Washington Times* (November 16).

_________. 1993f. "U.S. Agress to Work With Albanian Military." *Baltimore Sun* (October 21).

_________. 1993g. "U.S. Force for Macedonia Comes From Berlin Brigade." *Washington Post* (June 25).

_________. 1993h. "U.S. Peace-Keeping Troops Begin Patrols on Macedonian Border." *Washington Post* (August 21).

_________. 1993i. "U.S. Troops Arrive in Macedonia." *Christian Science Monitor* (July 6).

_________. 1993j. "U.S. Troops Arrive in Macedonia: Goal is to Contain Balkan Conflict." *Baltimore Sun* (July 6).

_________. 1993k. "U.S. Troops Begin Macedonia Patrols." *Washington times* (August 21).

_________. 1994a. "Albania Charges American, Others With Death Penalty Offenses: Tirana Actions Part of Systematic Abuse of Large Ethnic Greek Minority." AHEPAPress Release, Washington, D.C. (August 4).

_________. 1994b. "Greek Prime Minister Stresses Importance of National Security on Skopje." *The Greek American* (April 30).

_________. 1994c. "Human Rights Abuses in Albania." Letter dated 8 September 1994 from Jeri Laber, Executive Director, Human Rights Watch/Helskinki, to Albanian President Sali Berisha. *The Greek American* (17-23 September).

_________. 1994d. "Macedonia, U.S. Sign Pact." *Fort Wayne Journal Gazette* (November 15).

_________. 1994e. "Macedonia Blocks Albanian University." *Washington Times* (December 20).

_________. 1994f. "Macedonia Demolishes University Building." *Illyria* (December 19-21).

_________. 1994g. "Macedonian Authorities Slap Down Bid to Establish Albanian University." *Baltimore Sun* (December 15).

_________. 1994h. "U.S. Recognition of Skopje as 'FYROM' Threatens Greece." *The Greek American* (February 12).

_________. 1994i. "White House, Pentagon at Odds Over Role in FYROM." *The Greek American* (September 3-9).

_________. 1995a. "Albania Bars Ex-Communists From Office." *New York Times* (September 24).

__________. 1995b. "Albania, Turkey Start Joint Military Exercises." *The Greek American* (November 11).

__________. 1995c. "Albania: You're Out." *The Economist* (October 7).

__________. 1995d. "Memorandum of Understanding on Defense and Military Relations Between the Department of Defense of the United States of America and the Ministry of Defense of the Republic of Armenia." Pp. 623-625 in Theodore A. Couloumbis, Thanos M. Veremis and Thanos P. Dokos (eds.), *The Southeast European Yearbook 1994-1995*. Athens: Hellenic Foundation for European and Foreign Policy (ELIAMEP).

__________. 1995e. "U.S.-Albania Military Ties." *Diaspora Newsletter* 2 (November 3): 1-2.

__________. 1995f. "U.S. Backs Macedonia." *Fort Wayne Journal Gazette* (January 9).

__________. 1996a. "Albania: Berisha Beacons." *The Economist* (May 18): 52-55.

__________. 1996b. *"He Albania Phlertarei me to NATO"* ("Albania Flirts with NATO"). *Bema* (May 5).

__________. 1996c. "Center for Preventive Action Releases Report on South Balkans: Report Proposes Ways to Prevent Conflict in Kosovo." Council on Foreign Relations News Release, New York (May 14).

__________. 1996d. "Democracy Denied in Albania." *New York Times* (May 30).

__________. 1996e. "The Full Text of the Interim Accord Between Greece and FYROM." Washington, D.C.: Embasssy of Greece, Press and Information Office (September 15).

__________. 1996f. "Kosovo: Welcome to Balkania." *The Economist* (September 7): 48-49.

Anderson, M. A. 1966.*The Eastern Question, 1774-1923*. Cambridge: Cambridge University Press.

Angjeli, Anastas. 1995. "Problems of Albanian Democracy." *Mediterranean Quarterly* 6 (fall): 35-47.

Balamaci, Nicholas S. 1994. "Havoc in the Balkans and Germany's Re-entry into the International Arena. "*The Greek American* (February 12).

Barker, Elisabeth. 1950. *Macedonia: Its Place in Balkan Power Politics*. London: Royal Institute of International Affairs.

Beaver, Paul. 1994. "Busting the U.N. Sanctions." *Washington Times* (August 2).

Bertrand, Gilles. 1994. "Les Meilleures Intentions L'ex-Republique Yougoslave de Macedoine Face a la Guerre dans les Balkans." *Etudes Hellenique/Hellenic Studies* 3 (spring): 81-96.

__________. 1995. "L'ex-Republique Yougoslave de Macedoine: Entre Apaisement et D'estabilisation." *Etudes Hellenique/Hellenic Studies* 3 (autumn): 91-102.

Betzios, Elias. 1994. "Human Rights for Ethnic Greeks in Albania Needs Full Guarantee." Paper presented before the 46th Session of the Sub-Commission on Prevention of Discrimination and Protection of Minorities held in Geneva, Switzerland. *The Greek Star* (September 8).

Biberaj, Elez. 1990. *Albania: A Socialist Maverick*. Boulder, Colorado: Westview Press.

__________. 1994. "Albania and the Albanians in the Post-Communist Period." Pp. 27-50 in Stephen F. Larrabee (ed.), *The Volatile Powder Keg: Balkan Security After the Cold War*. Washington, D.C.: The American University Press.

Binder, David. 1993. "U.S. and Albania Sign a Military Agreement." *New York Times* (October 21).

Bourne, Eric. 1993. "Balkan States Worry Over Prospects of Widening War." *Christian Science Monitor* (February 2).

Calic, Marie-Janine. 1996. "German Perspectives." Pp. 52-86 in Alex Danchev and Thomas Halverson (eds.), *International Perspectives on the Yugoslav Conflict*. New York: St. Martin's Press, Inc.

Carpenter, Ted Galen. 1993. "A Back Door to War?" *Washington Times* (September 2).

__________. 1994. "The Balkan Crisis and the Faulty 1930s Analogy." *Mediterranean Quarterly* 5 (fall): 17-29.

Catsiapis, Jean. 1994. "La Grece et Le Balkans." *Etudes Helleniques/Hellenic Studies* 3 (spring): 69-80.

Chase, Robert S., Emily B. Hill and Paul Kennedy. 1996. "Pivotal States and U.S. Strategy." *Foreign Affairs* 75 (January-February): 33-51.

Chazan, Yigal. 1994. "Radical Albanian Nationalists Gain Ground in Serbian Province." *Christian Science Monitor* (September 29).

Cohen, Lenard J. 1993. *Broken Bonds: The Disintegration of Yugoslavia*. Boulder, Colorado: Westview Press.

Coufoudakis, Van. 1993. *The Macedonian Question and its Importance to Greece*. Toronto: The Legacy of Macedonia Semi-Annual Lecture Series, Pan-Macedonian Asssociation.

Couloumbis, Theodore A. 1993. "The Macedonian Question: Achilles' Heel or Odyssean Wiles?" *Odyssey: The World of Greece* 1 (August-September): 9-10.

Crawford, Beverly. 1996. "Explaining Defection from International Cooperation: Germany's Unilateral Recognition of Croatia." *World Politics* 48 (July): 482-521.

Danforth, Loring M. 1995. *The Macedonian Conflict: Ethnic Nationalism in a Transnational World*. Princeton, New Jersey: Princeton University Press.

Davis, Jacqelyn K., and Charles M. Perry. 1995. *European Issues Affecting Global Nuclear Initiatives*. Cambridge, Massachusetts and Washington, D.C.: National Security Planning Associates (December).

Dhimagjoka, Merita. 1995. "Albania bars former Communists from government posts until 2002." *Washington Times* (September 24).

Edemski, Andrei. 1996. "Russian Perspectives." Pp. 29-51 in Alex Danchev and Thomas Halversosn (eds.), *International Perspectives on the Yugoslav Conflict*. New York: St. Martin's Press, Inc.

Errington, Malcom R. 1990. *A History of Macedonia*. Berkeley, California: University of California Press.

Fontaine, Roger, and Dennis Mullin. 1994. "What will Papandreou tell Clinton?" *Washington Times* (21 April).

Fromkin, David. 1993. "Dimitrios Returns: Macedonia and the Balkan Question in the Shadow of History." *World Policy Journal* 10 (summer): 67-71.

Gage, Nicholas. 1993a. "The Forgotten Minority in the Balkans: The Greeks of Northern Epirus." *Mediterranean Quarterly* 4 (summer): 10-29.

__________. 1993b. "Kosovo Powder Keg." *Washington Post* (April 11).

Gellman, Barton. 1993. "Allies Preview Emerging U.S. Plan for Balkans." *Washington Post* (February 7).

Giannakos, Symeon A. 1992. "The Macedonian Question Reexamined: Implications for Balkan Security." *Mediterranean Quarterly* 3 (summer): 26-47.

Glenny, Misha. 1993a. "Is Macedonia Next?" *New York Times* (July 30).

__________. 1994b. "Is Another Balkan War Inevitable?" *Odyssey: The World of Greece* 1 (April-May): 24-29.

__________. 1994c. "Hope for Bosnia?" *New York Review* (April 7).

Goble, Paul A. 1996. "Dangerous Liaisons: Moscow, the Former Yugoslavia and the West." Pp. 182-197 in Richard H. Ullman (ed.), *The World and Yugoslavia's Wars*. New York: Council on Foreign Relations.

Gombert, David C. 1996. "The United States and Yugoslavia's Wars." Pp. 1-28 in Alex Danchev and Thomas Halverson (eds.), *International Perspectives on the Yugoslav Conflict*. New York: St. Martin's Press, Inc.

Goshko, John M. 1992. "Bush Threatens 'Military Force' if Serbs Attack Kosovo Province." *Washington Post* (December 29).

Hitchens, Christopher. 1994. "Minority Report: Skopje/Tetovo, 'Macedonia.'" *The Nation* (April 18): 511.

Hoagland, Jim. 1994. "Another Brink in the Balkans." *Washington Post* (March 31).

Holmes, Steven A. 1993. "Christopher Reaffirms Leading U.S. Role in World." *New York Times* (May 28).

Jahn, George. 1994. "Albania Inches Ahead With U.S. as Suitor." *Washington Times* (May 10).

Jelavich, Barbara. 1964. *A Century of Russian Foreign Policy, 1814-1914*. Philadelphia: J. B. Lippincott.

__________. 1973. *The Ottoman Empire, the Great Powers, and the Straits Question, 1870-1887*. Bloomington, Indiana: Indiana University Press.

__________. 1974. *St. Petersburg and Moscow: Tsarist and Soviet Foreign Policy, 1814-1974*. Bloomington, Indiana: Indiana University Press.

__________. 1983. *History of the Balkans: Twentieth Century*, Volume 2. Cambridge: Cambridge University Press.

__________. 1984. *Russia and the Formation of the Romanian National State, 1821-1878*. Cambridge: Cambridge University Press.

__________. 1991. *Russsia's Balkan Entanglements, 1806-1914*. Cambridge: Cambridge University Press.

Jelavich, Charles. 1958. *Tsarist Russia and Balkan Nationalism: Russian Influence in the Internal Affairs of Bulgaria and Serbia, 1876-1886*. Berkeley, California: University of California Press.

Jelavich, Charles, and Barbara Jelavich. 1977. *The Establishment of the Balkan National States, 1804-1920*. Seattle, Washington: University of Washington Press.

Kamm, Henry. 1993. "Albanian Chief Urges West to Send Troops to Prevent War." *New York Times* (May 31).

__________. 1994a. "Kriva Palanka Journal: The Well-Equipped G.I.'s (But an Exercise Bike?)." *New York Times* (May 11).

__________. 1994b. "Macedonia Sees its Albanians as its 'Biggest Problem'" *New York Times* (May 5).

Kaplan, Robert D. 1993. *Balkan Ghosts: A Journey Through History*. New York: St. Martin's Press.

Katzarova, Mariana. 1993. "Kosovo Waits." *The Nation* (25 January): 77.

Kofos, Evangelos. 1993. *Nationalism and Communism in Macedonia: Civil Conflict, Politics of Mutation, National Identity*. New Rochelle, New York: Aristide D. Caratzas, Publisher.

__________. 1994. *The Visison of "Greater Macedonia:" Remarks on FYROM's New Schoolbooks*. Thessaloniki: Museum of the Macedonian Struggle.

Kondis, Basil, Kyriakos Kentrotis, Spyridon Sfetas and Yiannis D. Stefanidis (eds.). 1995. *Resurgent Irredentism: Documents on Skopje 'Macedonian' Nationalist Aspirations*. Thessaloniki: Institute for Balkan Studies.

Konstantinova, Elisaveta. 1994. "Macedonia Limps Ahead With Reforms." *Illyria* (December 15-17).

Kovalski, Nicolai. 1995. "Russia and the Balkans." Pp. 609-617 in Theodore A. Couloumbis, Thanos M. Veremis and Thomas P. Dokos (eds.), *The Southeast European Yearbook 1994-95*. Athens: Hellenic Foundation for European and Foreign Policy (ELIAMEP).

Kyrou, Alexandros K. 1994. "Albania." Pp. 1-60 in Gregory C. Ference (ed.), *Chronology of Twentieth Century East European History*. Detroit: Gale Research Inc.

Larrabee, Stephen F. 1994. "Washington, Moscow, and the Balkans: Strategic Retreat or Reengagement?" Pp. 201-218 in Stephen F. Larrabee (ed.), *The Volatile Powder Keg: Balkan Security After the Cold War*. Washington, D.C.: The American University Press.

Lekic, Slobodan. 1993. "Averting Showdown Gains Macedonia Leverage." *Washington Times* (December 7).

Leopold, Geoerge. 1993. "Officials Warn of Balkan Escalation." *Defence News* (March 22).

Lusitana, Grey. 1994. "U.S.-Albanian Pact May Create Buffer." *Washington Times* (February 15).

Marquand, Robert. 1992. "Kosovo Province: Balkans' Next Flash Point?" *Christian Science Monitor* (December 28).

Matthews, Mark. 1993. "Balkan Strife Could Threaten Vital U.S. Interests, Aspin Says." *Baltimore Sun* (January 8).

Meyer, Cord. 1993a. "Pressure on a Balkan 'Miracle.'" *Washington Times* (October 15).

__________. 1993b. "Threats Beyond Bosnia." *Washington Times* (February 12).

Nedeva, Ivanka. 1994. "Balkan Troubles, Bulgarian Hopes." *World Policy Journal* 11 (fall): 132-138.

Oberdorfer, Don. 1993. "A Bloody Failure in the Balkans." *Washington Post* (February 8).

Ottaway, David B. 1993. "The West Watches for the Ripple Effect." *Washington Post* (December 26).

Palmer, Stephen G., and Robert R. King. 1971. *Yugoslav Communism and the Macedonian Question*. Hamden, Connecticut: Archon Books.

Pavlowitch, Stevan K. 1988. *The Improbable Survivor: Yugoslavia and its Problems, 1918-1988*. Columbus, Ohio: Ohio State University Press.

Perlez, Jane. 1996. "2 Monitoring Groups Call Albania Vote Marred." *New York Times* (May 30).

Perry, Duncan M. 1988. *The Politics of Terror: The Macedonian Revolutionary Movements, 1893-1903*. Durham, North Carolina: Duke University Press.

__________. 1994a. "Bulgaria: Security Concerns and Foreign Policy Considerations." Pp. 51-64 in Stephen F. Larrabee (ed.), *The Volatile Powder Keg: Balkan Security after the Cold War*. Washington, D.C.: The American University Press.

_________. 1994b. "Macedonia." *Radio Free Europe/Radio Liberty (RFE/RL) Research Report: The Politics of Intolerance* 3 (April): 83-86.

_________. 1996. "Macedonia: Balkan Miracle or Balkan Disaster?" *Current History* 95 (March): 113-117.

Pomfret, John. 1995. "U.S. Builds Arc of Alliances to Contain Serbia's Power." *Washington Post* (December 19).

Pomfret, John, and David B. Ottaway. 1995. "U.S., Albania Form 'the Weirdest Relationship.'" *Washington Post* (November 20).

Poulton, Hugh. 1995. *Who are the Macedonians?* Bloomington, Indiana: Indiana University Press.

Prodromou, Elizabeth. 1996. "The Perception Paradox for Greece's Post-Cold War Security." Pp. 123-132 in Graham Allison and Calypso Nicolaides (eds.), *The Greek Paradox: Promise vs. Performace*. Cambridge, Massachusetts: The MIT Press.

Rizopoulos, Nicholas X. 1993. "A Third Balkan War?" *World Policy Journal* 10 (summer): 1-5.

Rossos, Andrew. 1981. *Russia and the Balkans: Inter-Balkan Rivalries and Russian Foreign Policy, 1908-1914*. Toronto: University of Toronto Press.

Rubin, Trudy. 1994. "U.S. Needs More than Troops to Head off Trouble in Macedonia." *Philadelphia Inquirer* (August 19).

Schafer, Susanne M. 1994. "Perry Promises U.S. Military Cooperation With Albania." Asssociated Press Wire Report, Tirana, Albania (July 20).

Skulakakis, Thodoros. 1995. *Sto Onoma tes Makedonias* (*In the Name of Macedonia*). Athens: Greek Euro-publishers.

Smith, Helen. 1994. "Albanians, Macedonia on a Collision Course." *Washington Times* (December 23).

Smith, Helena. 1994. "Tension Grows as a Greek Tragedy is Played out in Albania." *Guardian* (June 8).

Spolar, Christine. 1992. "Albanians in Kosovo Assert Nationalism, Serb Leaders Vow to Retain Control." *Washington Post* (December 29).

Spyropoulos, Phillip. 1994. "The New York Times and the Kaplanesque." *The Greek American* (May 7).

Stojanovic, M. D. 1968. *The Great Powers and the Balkans, 1875-1878*. Cambridge: Cambridge University Press.

Sullivan, Marianne. 1995. "Shalikasshvili Cites Progress in Albanian Military." *Illyria* (October 19).

Szayna, Thomas S. 1994. *Ethnic Conflict in Central Europe and the Balkans: A Framework and U.S. Policy Options*. Santa Monica, California: RAND.

Tsouderos, Virginia. 1993. "Greek Policy and the Yugoslav Turmoil." *Mediterranean Quarterly* 4 (spring): 1-9.

United States Senate, Committee on Foreign Relations. 1994. "ACDA and Ambassadorial Nominations: Hearings for Joseph Lake, United States Ambassador Nominate to Albania, 24 June 1994." Washington, D.C.: Stenographic Transcript of Hearings by Alderson Reporting Company.

Veremis, Thanos. 1994. "Greece: The Dilemmas of Change." Pp. 119-133 in Stephen F. Larrabee (ed.), *The Volatile Powder Keg: Balkan Security after the Cold War*. Washington, D.C.: The American University Press.

Veremis, Thanos, Theodore Couloumbis and Elias Nikolakopoulos (eds.). 1995. *Ho Hellenismos tes Albanias* (*Hellenism in Albania*). Athens: Hellenic Foundation for European and Foreign Policy (ELIAMEP), I. Sideres.

Vogel, Steve. 1993. "U.S. Troops Face Training in Macedonia: U.N. Commander Sets Rules of Engagement." *Washington Post* (July 10).

Williams, Daniel. 1993a. "Clinton's Policy in Balkans Puts U.S. Prestige, Power on the Line." *Washington Post* (February 11).

__________. 1993b. "Kosovo Leader Asks U.S. for Troops." *Washington Post* (February 17).

Woodward, Susan L. 1995. *Balkan Tragedy: Chaos and Dissolution After the Cold War*. Washington, D.C.: The Brookings Institution.

Zahariadis, Nikolaos. 1994. "Is the Former Yugoslav Republic of Macedonia a Security Threat to Greece?" *Mediterranean Quarterly* 5 (winter): 84-105.

__________. 1996. "Greek Policy toward the Former Yugoslav Republic of Macedonia, 1991-1995." *Journal of Modern Greek Studies* 14 (October): 303-327.

A SELECTIVE ANNOTATED BIBLIOGRAPHY BY THE CONTRIBUTORS THEMSELVES*

George A. Kourvetaris and Andrew G. Kourvetaris

Sekel J. Laslo, Yugoslavia: The Process of Disintegration (translated from the Serbo-Croat by Vera Vucalic) Boulder, Colorado: Atlantic Research Publications.

This is a good book tracing the roots and determinants of disintegration in former Yugoslavia. This is attributed mostly in the failure of the Sovietization of Yugoslav society and state, the inability of former Yugoslavia toward modernization, and the resurgence of ethnonationalism.

Vujacic, Velijko and Victor Zaslavsky, 1991. "The Causes of Disintegration in the USSR and Yugoslavia: in *Telos: A Quarterly Journal of Critical Thought*. No. 88.

The authors argue that the Soviet and Yugoslav Crises were a result of the failure of traditional nationality policies and the collapse of communism. The unprecedented level of ethnic mobilization can be explained by the lack of alternative models of collective action. The linkage between territory, language, administration and ethnicity, and the overlap between regional economic and ethnic interests created the preconditions for ethnic mobilization. Finally, inter-ethnic strife itself was a factor of ethnic homogenization in the republics, since it leads to ethnic population transfer. The costs of disintegration were high. The new national governments were unable to guarantee minority rights, since the first goal of the new governments was ethnic homogenization and state consolidation.

Dusko Sekulic, Garth Massey, Randy Hodson "Who Were the Yugoslavs? Failed Sources of a Common Identity in the Former Yugoslavia" *American Sociological Review*, Volume 59, Issue 1 (Feb., 1994): 83-97.

The authors argue that Yugoslavia's leaders believed that a policy of equality among the many nationalities in Yugoslavia, under Communist Party hegemony,

---

*Each contributor was asked to submit a number of publications which in his/her judgement were important in the area the author wrote his/her chapter.

would permit nationalism within former Yugoslavia to exist. However, the identification of people with their nationality neglected Yugoslavia the identification associated with the state as a whole. Added to this was the failure of shared political power and modernization among the various nationalities, which contributed to the resurgence of ethnonationalism and subnationalism. These factors led to the disintegration of the federal Yugoslav state.

Premdas, Ralph R. S.W.R de A Samarasinghe and Alan B. Anderson, 1990. *Secessionist Movements in Comparative Perspective*. New York: St. Martin's Press.

This is an edited comparative book on a number of secessionist movements in the third world. It covers secessionist movements in many parts of the globe including Africa, Asia, and the Middle East. It is an excellent reader for those who want to understand the sociological, cultural, ethnic, economic, and political dynamics of these subnationalist movements.

Edward A. Tiryakian

Ash, Timothy Carton. "Kosovo: Was it Worth It?" *New York Review of Books*. September 21,2000:50-60. A balanced review essay of six recent works on the Kosovo War by one of the best informed Western observer of post-communist Europe.

Hodson, Randy, Dusko Sekulic, and Garth Massey. "National Tolerance in the Former Yugoslavia," *American Journal of Sociology*, 99 (May 1994): 1534-58. Data analyzed are based on 1989-1990 survey data, on the eve of the breakup of Yugoslavia, and therefore before the violent conflicts in Bosnia in 1994-95 and Kosovo in 1998-99. Authors tested two major models of ethnic relations: modernization theory and ethnic competition: each received partial confirmation. Ethnic heterogeneity leads to *both* tolerance and conflict. Disturbing factors are that young people and those who read the news more frequently are less tolerant toward other nationalities, and that religiosity has a powerful negative effect on tolerance. Though the materials need to be updated, they furnish an important base line for conflict in Kosovo and Macedonia.

Ignatieff, Michael. *Virtual War. Kosovo and Beyond. New York: Metropolitan* Books/Henry Holt 2000. Though not a social scientist, Ignatieff has followed with insights various aspects of nationalism and ethnic conflict in Europe. In this study he perceives the 1999 Kosovo War as a new kind of warfare, a virtual spectacle for external audiences spared the hazards of combat, while for the targets of the war, high technology used all means of destruction. When war becomes a spectator sport, proposes Ignatieff, the media become the decisive theater of operations. There are strong moral implications raised here.

Judah, Tim. *Kosovo: War and Revenge*. New Haven: Yale University Press, 2000. One of the best accounts of the war presenting fairly the Serb and the Albanian sides by a leading investigative reporter, who has long followed the affairs of Yugoslavia and its break-up in the 1990s.

Sherman, Arnold. *Perfidy in the Balkans. The Rape of Yugoslavia*. Athens: Psichogios Publications, 1993. An Israeli journalist living in Greece provides an unusual perspective on modern Balkan history, including factors involved in the break-up of Yugoslavia and the role of external powers. It provides an important background for the Kosovo War.

Tiryakian, E. A. "Party Involvement in Ethnic Conflict: The Case of the Kosovo War).

Kostas A. Lavdas

Bonvicini, G. 1998. "Making European Foreign Policy Work."In M. Westlake, ed. *The European Union after Amsterdam*. London: Routledge.

A useful summary of the prospects and limitations of the EU foreign policy structures and operations after the Treaty of Amsterdam. Informative and concise.

Hoffmann, Stanley. 2000. "Towards a Common European Foreign and Security Policy."*Journal of Common Market Studies*, 38. 2: 189-198.

An examination of the prospects and the significant shortcomings of the EU in international relations by an eminent US scholar. Includes Hoffman's reflections

on the role of the Yugoslav conflict in the development of EU foreign and security policy.

Lavdas, Kostas. 2001. "Republican Europe and Multicultural Citizenship." *Politics*, 21: 1-11.

An attempt to construct a neo-republican theoretical approach to the design of EU institutions which combines minimal political values and commitments and the recognition of multicultural pluralism cutting across national boundaries. It argues that tomorrow's EU can only be inclusive if it combines policy relevance at EU level and recognition of the politics of belonging at multicultural group level.

Pavkovic, Aleksandar, 2000a. *The Fragmentation of Yugoslavia: Nationalism and War in the Balkans*. Second edition. London: Macmillan.

This is becoming one of the standard accounts of the Balkan conflicts. Wide in its coverage and generally successful in maintaining high academic standards. Very informative and knowledgeable.

__________. 2000b. "Recursive Secessions in Former Yugoslavia: Too Hard a Case for Theories of Secession?" *Political Studies*, 48: 485-502.

An important attempt to use the experience of the Yugoslav conflict as a test case for appraising theories of secession. After examining the series of secessions in the context of the breakdown of Yugoslavia, the article focuses on "recursive secessions" (counter secessions by minorities within the new republics) as a complicating factor in the Yugoslav case.

Veremis, Thanos & Kofos, Evangelos, eds. 1998. *Kosovo: Avoiding Another Balkan War*. Athens: Hellenic Foundation for European and Foreign Policy.

This is a very useful overview of the Kosovo crisis. The volume includes contributions from various academic, political, and national standpoints and generally manages to maintain throughout consistently high academic standards.

Eleftherios Botsas

Because of the Kosovo war and the dissolution of Yugoslavia, most of the recent literature on the Balkans is devoted to the causes of ethnic strife and the two dictators who personified that ethnic strife: the late Croatian dictator Franjo Tudjman and the former Yugoslav leader Slobodan Milosevic. However, here there is a short list of relevant works.

1. Bass, Gary Jonathan. *Stay the Hand of Vengeance: the Politics of War Crimes Tribunals*. Princeton and Oxford: Princeton University Press, 2000. This is the best work on the legal issues and the national-interest politics of tribunals from the Napoleonic wars to the current disputes on Yugoslavia. It is a scholarly work on why some trials and judgments, like the Nuremberg trials, are well known while others, like the Constantinople trials of 1918 and the Smyrna catastrophe of 1923, are not. From the official records, Bass sheds light to the issue of whether there were British, French, or American, not Armenian, lives at risk for the trials of Turkish war criminals. Bass investigates both legalism and lofty principles of international justice. The sluggish pace of justice in The Hague is preferable to Kosovar vengeance. Do war-crimes tribunals work? Bass looks at the possible alternatives. "The five standard liberal arguments in favor of war crimes tribunals are far from weak, but they are not totally convincing either. But what alternative is there to legalism?" (p.304). Croatia has tried many Serbs on war crimes, but it refuses to let The Hague see the cases.

2. Chomsky, Noam. *The New Military Humanism: Lessons from Kosovo*. Monroe, ME: Common Courage Press, 1999. This is a small book (199 pages), but a powerful critique of the use of power by the then Secretary of State, the Pentagon, and NATO officials to justify the bombardments of Serbia in 1999. In reference after reference, Chomsky shows the deliberate use of lies to justify the destruction of an independent state. He considers the substitution of raw power for international order as being both immoral and dangerous for humanity. The fact that NATO was displacing the United Nations was leaving the weak states at the mercy of powerful countries.

3. Judah, Tim. *The Serbs: History, Myth & the Destruction of Yugoslavia*. New Haven and London: Yale University Press, 1997. This is a

readable, although many Serbs may not like it, account of Serbian history from medieval times to the atrocities of the wars that followed the break up of Yugoslavia. As a reporter for the London *Times* and *The Economist* he witnessed many of the war excesses in the early 1990s and tried to find out the historical roots of those excesses. Judah's book has a select bibliography and cross references, but, by comparison, it lacks the scholarship of Gary Bass' work.

4. Moore, John H. *Growth With Self-Management: Yugoslav Industrialization, 1952-1975*. Stanford, CA.: The Hoover Institution Press, 1980. Unlike the recent publications on the former Yugoslavia that deal with historical interpretations, Moore's book is an economic analysis of the then claimed superiority of "market socialism" as applied by Yugoslavia. Moore collected massive data to construct indexes of regional and sector production. He found that "economies of scale in industry were one reason for the rapid rate of industrial growth" (p. 114). the author was critical of the regional policies of transferring investment funds from the efficient and advanced regions to less efficient and backward regions of Kosovo and Bosnia. It is interesting that the regions which were gaining the most under Tito are the regions that revolted to overthrow centralism. By comparison, the new economies of Kosovo, Bosnia-Herzegovina, and the Former Yugoslav Republic of Macedonia are too small to achieve economic independence.

5. Tanner, Marcus. *Croatia: A Nation Forged in War*. New Haven and London: Yale University Press, 1997. Had I not received this book for a review, I would never know that a university press would publish something like this. It is a paean to Croatian nationalism. The Croats are the angels of Europe. It seems that as Balkan a correspondent of the London Independent never met a fascist Croat or a Croat he did not like. The book lacks even elementary scholarship.

6. World Bank. *The Road to Stability and Prosperity in South Eastern Europe: A Regional Strategy Paper*. Washington, B.C.: 2000. This is a collaborative strategy of the World Bank and the European Commission on ways to improve the living standards and cooperation in the region. It focuses on integration of the region with the European Union, creating transparency, fostering social inclusion, and investing

in infrastructure. It is the best survey of the needs of the region and the ways to achieve peaceful solution of the region's problems, with assistance from the international community.

7. Zimmermann, Warren. *The Origins of a Catastrophe: Yugoslavia and its Destroyers*. New York: Time Books/Random House, 1996. Zimmermann was the last US Ambassador to the former Yugoslavia. Therefore, the reader can assume that he has great analysis of the events and policies that lead to the dissolution of a polyethnic society. Zimmermann met all the main actors of this tragic drama. However, like most authors on this subject of Balkan conflicts, he tends to blame nationalism and, especially, two leaders who personified the worst elements of nationalism, Franjo Tudjman of Croatia and Slobodan Milosevic of Serbia. In his eyes, the Serbs are product of history. Another version of the always present simplistic pronouncements that the Balkan people are slaves of their historical background. Zimmermann's book, like David Owen's *Balkan Odyssey* (Harvest Book 1997), is more a diplomatic oversight of the role of the West in the Balkan conflict. His arguments are as good or bad as those of his superior, Madeleine Albright. Looking at superficialities rather than substance of US policies in the region.

Victor Roudemetof

Gordy, Eric D. 1999. *The Culture of Power in Serbia: Nationalism and the Destruction of Alternatives*. University Park, PA: Pennsylvania State University Press. A rich and detailed analysis of the political culture of Serbia during the 1990s. The author argues that the reasons that kept Milosevic in power were twofold. One the one hand, his regime benefited greatly by the passive nature of the rural voters. On the other hand, the regime sought to systematically destroy political, cultural, and institutional alternatives.

Larrabee, F. Stephen (ed.). 1994. *The Volatile Powder keg: Balkan security after the Cold War*. Washington, D.C.: American University Press. The essays provide a first rate introduction to the security concerns in contemporary Balkans. They also describe the close connection between

security considerations and the broader cultural, institutional, and political context in the region.

Ramet Pedro. 1992. *Nationalism and Federalism in Yugoslavia 1962-1991*. Bloomington: Indiana University Press. This is a detailed narrative of the evolution of the Yugoslav political system over three decades. By far, one of the best books of its kind, it is highly recommended as an excellent secondary source on post-World War II Yugoslavia.

Ramet, Sabrina P. 1999. *Balkan Babel: The Disintegration of Yugoslavia from the Death of Tito to the War for Kosovo*. Boulder, Co: Westview Press. This is a collection of essays that is discussing the cultural, political, and institutional context of the Yugoslav republics during the last two decades.

Roudometof, Victor (ed.). 2000. *The Macedonian Question: Culture, Historiography, Politics*. Boulder, Co: East European Monographs, distributed by Columbia University Press. Contributions are addressing the issue of Albanian and Macedonian minorities in the southern Balkans (Bulgaria, Albania, Greece, and the Republic of Macedonia).

Roudometof, Victor. 2001. *Nationalism, Globalization, and Orthodoxy: The Social Origins of Ethnic Conflict in the Balkans*. Westport, CT: Greenwood. Adopting a world-historical perspective, the author analyses the historical evolution of nationalism in Southeastern Europe over the last centuries. The basic thesis relates the recurrent phenomenon of ethnic conflict in the Balkans to the model of nationalism adopted by the Balkan nation-states during the last two centuries.

Stein, Jonathan P. (ed.). 2000. *The Politics of National Minority Participation in Post-Communist Europe: State-Building, Democracy, and Ethnic Mobilization*. Armonk, NY: M. E. Sharpe. The essays on Serbia, Bulgaria, and Albania are amongst the most informative summaries of the recent events in the 1990s.

Woodward, S. 1995. *Balkan Tragedy. Chaos and Dissolution After the Cold War*. Washington DC: Brookings Institution. An excellent discussion of the relationship between economic decline and the collapse of the second Yugoslavia. The author argues that the origins of the Yugoslav crisis were, to a considerable extent, economic rather than cultural or ideological.

Anna Triandafyllidou

Strath, Bo. 2000. Ed. Europe and the Other and Europe as the Other. Brussels: Berg.

The studies included in this volume explore the interconnections between European nations and nation-states and the idea of Europe. Attention is paid to the (in)compatibility of national and European identity as well as to the fact that identities are formed in interaction and hence are in a continuous process of negotiation. The role of Europe as a mediating image or identity that brings European nations together is also highlighted.

Tsoukalas, Constantinos. 1993. "Greek National Identity in an Integrated Europe and a Changing World Order." From H. Psomiades and S. Thomadakis. Eds. *Greece, the New Europe and the Changing International Order*. New York: Pella.

This study highlights the evolution of modern Greek identity in recent times. Emphasis is put in the role played by the international context and comparisons with other countries in promoting an ethnic, transcendental view of Greekness. The ambivalent position of Greeks towards Europe and the West is explored.

Triandafyllidou, Anna. 2001. *National Identity Reconsidered: Images of Self and Other in a United Europe*. Lampeter, U.K.: Edwin Mellen Press, forthcoming.

This book concentrates on the process of national identity re-definition that EU countries go through as a result of recent international developments, in particular the European integration process, on the one hand, and the increase in immigration flows towards member-states, on the other hand. The book examines the intertwining of each country's national identity with images of the European Union, fellow member-states, Eastern and Central European countries, ethnic minorities and immigrant communities. Images of the Other and the meaning of 'We, the nation' are studied through the analysis of the press discourse in four countries: Germany, Greece, Italy and the U.K. The

emergence of new notions of nationhood in contemporary European societies is also discussed.

Tziovas, D. 1994. "Η *δυτική φαντασίωση του ελληνικού και η αναζήτηση του υπερεθνικού*" (The western imaginary of Hellenism and the search for transnationality). From *Επιστημονικό Συνέδριο Εθνος-Κράτος-Εθνικισμός (Scientific Congress on Nation-State-Nationalism)*, V.A. Athens: Εταιρεία Σπουδών Νεοελληνικού Πολιτισμού και Γενικής Παιδείας.

This article highlights the Janus-faced character of modern Greek identity, caught in a trap between the European vision of what modern Greece should be—deeply influenced by the classical Greek heritage—and the reality of modern Greece characterized by its fundamentally "Eastern" socio-political experience in the past centuries.

Alexandros K. Kyrou

The collapse of Yugoslavia has produced a veritable flood of publications claiming to analyze the federation's failure and its consequent international ramifications. Unfortunately, heretofore the overwhelming majority of these books have been either journalistic accounts or highly partisan works whose authors have been motivated by opportunism and commercial gain or political interests, respectively. Nonetheless, the Yugoslav crisis has also been the subject of some exceedingly rigorous scholarly studies. Within this category the two most systematic and informative macro- and micro-level investigations are found in Lenard J. Cohen, *Broken Bonds: The Disintegration of Yugoslavia* (Boulder, Colorado: Westview Press, 1993 [published in 1995 under the title, *Broken Bonds: Yugoslavia's Disintegration and Balkan Politics in Transition*]), and Susan L. Woodward, *Balkan Tragedy: Chaos and Dissolution After the Cold War* (Washington, D.C.: The Brookings Institution 1995).

In the beginning of his expert work, Cohen explores the original conception and motives underlying the historical development of the Yugoslav state. In a thorough review of Yugoslavia's history, he examines the state's major problems, achievements, and ultimate failure. Thematically and organizationally, the book addresses the crisis of post-Tito socialism, the emergence of party pluralism, the fragmentation of the state's authority, nationalist ideology, the delegitimation of the federal system and the outbreak of civil war, and the subsequent international response. Through this discussion, Cohen effectively

answers a broad range of questions relating to the abandonment of reform socialism, the elimination of the Communist party's monopoly of political power, the dynamics of rivalry attendant to ethnically and regionally segmented elites, and the efforts and viability of the international community to effect an outcome of the crisis.

Woodward's approach to the Yugoslav conflict is quite similar to Cohen's but remains remarkably original and important for its ability to link and explain the problem in the context of international transformation. The author writes that the "conventional wisdom, which emerged rapidly after the war broke out in 1991, is that the war resulted from peculiarly Balkan hatreds or Serbian aggression. In fact, however, the Yugoslav conflict is inseparable from international change and interdependence, and it is not confined to the Balkans but is part of a more widespread phenomenon of political disintegration" (p. 3). Utilizing this construct, the study analyzes, among other things, how the Western response to the Yugoslav crisis not only failed to prevent the expansion of the violence, but how it actually contributed to and exacerbated the conflict.

Two excellent publications devoted specifically to the international dimensions of the Yugoslav crisis are found in Alex Danchev and Thomas Halverson, eds., *International Perspectives on the Yugoslav Conflict* (New York: St. Martin's Press, Inc. 1996), and Richard H. Ullman, ed., *The World and Yugoslavia's Wars* (New York: Council on Foreign Relations 1996). The compilation by Danchev and Halverson is composed of eleven contributions by as many field experts, and includes essays on the American, British, French, and Russian views and responses to the Yugoslav crisis. The book by Ullman consists of a solid introduction and eight essays by individual authors, each employing rigorous theoretical, as well as descriptive, standards in addressing Great Power politics and the international system in the Yugoslav imbroglio.

Finally, albeit not specific to the recent state of affairs in the former Yugoslavia, an invaluable work germane to the historical background is Barbara Jelavich, *History of the Balkans: Twentieth Century*, Volume 2 (Cambridge: Cambridge University Press 1984). Since its first publication and many subsequent reprintings, this work remains the definitive comprehensive history of the modern Balkans. Hence, it serves not only as a useful source for a review of the Yugoslav experiment, but as the central primer for understanding Yugoslavia within the broader regional context of Southeastern Europe.

George C. Thomas

Buchanan, Allen. *Secession: The Morality of Political Divorce from Fort Sumter to Lithuania and Quebec*, Boulder, Colorado: Westview Press, 1991.

This book written before the break up of Yugoslavia, examines the conditions under which secession from an existing state may be morally justified and when it is not.

Burg, Steven L., and Paul S. Shoup. *The War in Bosnia-Herzegovina: Ethnic Conflict and International Intervention*. Armonk, NY: M. E. Sharpe, 1999.

Winner of an American Political Science Association book award, this lengthy and comprehensive book written by two long-standing academic experts on the former Yugoslavia, rejects many of the standard claims and myths about the one-sided reports and analyses that prevailed about Bosnia wherein the Serbs were seen as evil and Muslims and Croats as good.

Hannum, Hurst. *Autonomy, Sovereignty and Self-Determination: The Accommodation of Conflicting Rights*, Philadelphia: University of Pennsylvania Press, 1990.

This book deals the opposing principles of state sovereignty and national self-determination, especially focusing on key cases in India, Canada, Nigeria and elsewhere.

Woodward, Susan. *Balkan Tragedy. Chaos and Dissolution After the Cold War*. Washington DC: Brookings Institution. 1995.

Written by a former Yale Professor and Brookings fellow, and one of the leading experts on Yugoslavia, this author in a voluminous and comprehensive study, looks at the roots of the problem and the various contemporary issues underlying the disintegration of the former Yugoslavia.

Tina Mavrikos-Adamou

Valerie Bunce in "The Historical Origins of the East-West Divide: Civil Society, Political Society, and Democracy in Europe," *in Civil Society Before Democracy: Lessons From Nineteenth Century Europe,* edited by Nancy Bermeo

and Philip Nord, focuses on how the state, economy, and society were integral for the development of civil society, which she distinguishes from "political" society. She compares and contrasts these in eastern versus western Europe in an attempt to establish what historical differences lay behind the ways in which democracy were established and maintained.

Civil Society, edited by John Hall, contains a collection of essays which attempt to unravel the meaning that civil society has taken on in the post-cold war era by focusing in particular societies stretching from Latin America, eastern Europe, the Islamic world and China. By analyzing particular societies this collection of essays expresses current debates surrounding the question of civil society and its usefulness as a sociological concept.

The chapter entitled "Civil Society" in Larry Diamond's *Developing Democracy Towards Consolidation*, clears up the confusion which has arisen as to what "civil society is and is not" in a descriptive analysis of the organizations which make up civil society at present. Furthermore, Diamond relates how civil society has been integral for the development and consolidation of democracy by alluding to several examples and particular cases. The volume as a whole takes up the issue of democracy at the end of the twentieth century, and what may lay ahead for the concept in the future.

Adam B. Seligman provides an important contribution to the civil society debate with his *The Idea of Civil Society.* The book begins with an historical look at the evolution of the concept which is followed by an analysis of the concept presently. Perhaps his most important contribution comes in chapter 4 where he compares the idea of civil society in the West with East-Central Europe, and then he further makes a contrast by examining briefly the case of Israel.

S. Victor Papacosma

Burg, Steven L., and Paul S. Shoup. *The War in Bosnia-Herzegovina: Ethnic Conflict and International Intervention*. Armonk, NY: M. E. Sharpe, 1999.

This study covers the dissolution of Yugoslavia and the Bosnia conflict in a comprehensive and authoritative fashion.

Clark, Wesley K. *Waging Modern War: Bosnia, Kosovo, and the Future of Combat*. New York: Perseus Book Group, 2001.

Having served as NATO's Supreme Allied Commander, Europe, General Clark offers a detailed account of the Kosovo campaign and critical commentary of the political constraints imposed on it.

Daalder, Ivo H., and Michael E. O'Hanlon. *Winning Ugly: NATO's War to Save Kosovo*. Washington, D.C.: Brookings Institution, 2000.

The authors provide important insights into the diplomatic prelude of the Kosovo campaign and the subsequent policy debates and decisions associated with NATO's controversial bombing mission.

Holbrooke, Richard. *To End a War*. New York: Random House, 1998.

A driving force in bringing about the Dayton Peace Accords, Richard Holbrooke details his version of the complex developments, including coverage of NATO's role.

Papacosma, S. Victor, Sean Kay, and Mark R. Rubin, eds. *NATO after Fifty Years*. Wilmington, DE: Scholarly Resources, Inc., 2001.

Individual articles in this volume cover aspects of NATO's post-Cold War adaptation during the 1990s.

Bob Donnorummo

Since this volume contains a number of annotated works focusing exclusively on Southeastern Europe, the works selected in this chapter deal with the global economy and regionalism.

1. Thomas Priedman (1999), "The Lexus and the Olive Tree," New York: Fairar,
Straus and Giroux.
Very readable analysis of the impact of advanced technology and increasingly open economic boarders on both developed and developing countries. Freidman does an excellent job of including cultural , political

and economic variables. Its weakness lies with its **lack** of depth on some issues, but this is more than compensated by it integrative approach and thoughtful analysis.

2. Alan Smith (2000), "Return to Europe: Reintegration of Eastern Europe into the European Economy," London: Macmillan Ldt.
Comprehensive, multi-dimensional analysis of the economic ramifications associated with the accession into the EU for both the existing members and the countries. He is stronger on economic than political issues. Assessments are clearly reasoned and based on excellent empirical data. A greater emphasis is placed on northern eastern Europe.

3. Klaus Meyer (1998), "Direct Foreign Investment in Economies in Transition," Cheltenham. UK: Edward Elgar.
Analysis is balanced in its presentation of the benefits and obstacles of FDI for transitional economies. The author scope's is broad and yet relies on excellent original research in putting forth numerous thoughtful positions on FDI and how its relates to regionalism and globalization. A greater emphasis is placed on transitional economies in northern eastern than southeastern Europe.

4. Nicholas Gianaris (1996), "Geopolitical and Economic Change in the Balkan Countries," Newport, Ct.: Praeger
Focus of the coverage is Greece and Turkey. The author offers a comprehensive view of the historical background, existing economic conditions and thoughtful projections on future developments. However, data base is sometimes hurriedly composed and lacks depth.

5. There are several reliable sources for data on foreign trade. Foreign Direct Investment, and economic conditions. One such source is the United Nation's Economic Commission on Europe publication of the "Economic Survey of Europe." Other sources include the reports of the World Bank and related institutions, OECD, and the European Bank of Reconstruction and Development.

Dimitrios Koukourdinos

Croatian post-communist transition has been largely ignored by English bibliography. There are very few books that address the issue of Croatian politics in the 1990s as such. More often Croatia is included in analyses that refer to the general events in former Yugoslavia, or as a case in general studies of Eastern European democratization. Even in those publications, most studies cover the issue of disintegration of the Yugoslav federation and the role of nationalism, rather than the question of internal democratic development and domestic politics. On the other hand, there are a number of more specialized articles that refer to specific issues of the Croatian transition since 1990.

Starting with the books, there are two general historical studies on Croatia, namely Ivo Goldstein's *Croatia: A History:* London: Hurst & Co., 1999, and Mark Tanner's *Croatia: A Nation Forged in War* New Haven, CT: Yale University Press, 1997. These two books, and especially the first one, are clearly historical rather than political science studies.

There is a third book, that could be helpful to students interested in Croatian post-communist transition, Brendan O' Shea' s *Crisis at Bihac* (Stroud, Gloucestershire: Sutton, 1998). O' Shea' s book is not a political science analysis but a journalistic account of the war in Croatia and in Bosnia, particularly the case of the Bihac region.

Zlatko Isakovic's book *Identity and Security in Former Yugoslavia* Aldershot: Ashgate Pbs, 2000 represents an attempt of assessing the security problem in former Yugoslavia, under the light of new theoretical models that link security with identity politics.

A first attempt to assess political developments in Croatia since 1990 was made by Lenard Cohen in Dawisha's and Parrot's book *Politics, Power and the Struggle for Democracy in South-East Europe* Cambridge: Cambridge University Press, 1997. In his chapter under the title "*Embattled democracy: postcommunist Croatia in transition*" Cohen gives a balanced analysis of the events before and after the declaration of Croatian independence.

Another account of postcommunist Croatian politics is Jill Irvine's article *Ultranationalist Ideology and State-Building in Croatia, 1990-1996*, published in the *Problems of Post-Communism* journal, vol 44, no 4, July/August 1997, pp. 30-43. Irvine is interested mainly in the ideological aspects of the Croatian transition, and the nationalistic character of HDZ government.

A second article is Vesna Pusić's "Croatia at the Crossroads" *Journal of Democracy*, vol 9, no 1, January 1998, pp. 111-124. Dr Pusić, academic and politician, was a strong critic of the HDZ politics. Her article is useful, as it

demonstrates the main objections of the Croatian opposition towards Tudjman's policies in the domestic arena, but also as regards to Bosnia.

As regards to Croatia's war policy, there is Norman Cigar's "Croatia's War of Independence: The Parameters of War Termination," *The Journal of Slavic Military Studies*, Vol 10, 1997, no 2, pp. 34-70. Cigar is strongly critical of Tudjman's policy, and argues that the war could have terminated succesfully for Croatia already from 1992, had the late President not tried to allegedly strike a deal with Milošević.

Finally, a good source for Croatian politics is the journal *Politièka Misao,* published by the Political Science Faculty of the University of Zagreb. The journal is accessible to non-Croatian readers, as some of the issues appear in English. In one of the issues there is an article by Dr Siniša Tatalović under the title "Military and Political Aspects of the Croato-Serbian Conflict," *Politièka Misao*, vol. 33, no. 5, 1996, pp. 166-190. The article gives a rather official version of events that took place during the war.

Pantelis Sklias

Ziegenhagen A. E. and Koutsoukis S. K., *Political Conflict in Southern Europe: Regulation, Regression and Morphogenesis,* New York, Praeger, 1992.

The crisis of the nation state system , the breakup of blocks and of empires , and the resurgence of ethnic nationalism and tribalism are changing all the dynamics of state systems. It is exactly this that makes this book intensely relevant. In this work, the emphasis is on the internal. This encompasses aspects of internal conflict in Southern European states including protests, riots, demonstrations, terrorism, assassinations and coups, and all forms of state-testing conflicts common and extraordinary, futile and revolutionary. Particularly relevant becomes the case of Balkan states with significant emphasis given on the issues of conflict, e.g. religious, ethnolinguistic and separatist disputes. General systems theory, multivariative techniques and stochastic models allow for exploration of significant policy issues. It becomes possible to draw some conclusions about complex relations and the direction of these relations.

Andreas Maheridis (ed.), *Balkans Observatory* ,Andreas Papandreou Institute of Strategic and Development Studies, 1999, Athens (Reports concerning nine Balkan countries).

Current decade has been shaping a *de facto* frame of new political and economic balances in Balkans. The continuous political, economic, legal and administrative changes in the neighboring countries led the Andreas Papandreou Institute of Strategic and Development Studies, to publish a series of reports for the following countries: Albania, Bosnia-Herzegovina, Bulgaria, Croatia, FYROM, FRY, Romania, Slovenia and Turkey. The reports aim at the better understanding of the social, economic and political situation of the above mentioned countries. The following issues are discussed in depth: the economic situation, defense and general army issues, international relations and foreign policy with emphasis on the relations with the neighboring countries, minorities, internal security, human rights, the political conditions. In the longer term, such reports may serve as a suitable background for the development of the relations between Greece and the above mentioned countries. In any case they serve as a stimuli for dialogue, discussion and exchange of useful ideas and experiences.

Papasotiriou X., *The Balkans After the End of the End of Cold War*, in Greek, Athens, Papazisis Publications, 1994.

The aim of the book is the development of an objective and systematic analysis of the effects that the end of the Cold War era has brought to the Balkan countries. The first two chapters refer to changes in the global system as a whole. The remaining six chapters deal with the main aspects of the above-mentioned changes in the Balkan Peninsula itself. The author makes an effort to analyze the Balkan political scene in the frame of the international one. The book is not a mere description of the historical sequence of different events during the latest decade, in the states concerned. Only one chapter reflects such a historical perception, while the rest tend to analyze the importance and the meaning of the major changes that the period 1989-1991 has brought in Balkans.

Sklias P., *International Political Economy: Balkans, Central and Eastern Europe, the ex-Soviet Union countries and their relations with the European Union*, Papazisis Publications, Athens, 2001.

In this book, International Political Economy is considered to be a serious alternative perspective to what concerns the ways we can anticipate a given network of social, economic and political parameters in the countries of reference. Adopting International Political Economy as a way to assess and analyze the things, the objective of the book is to evaluate the current political, economic and social situation in the countries of Central and Eastern Europe, the

ex-Soviet Union and their relations with the EU. In other words the author attempts an overall analysis of the development level as a result of the transition process, which started in 1990, as well as the role of the EU towards the accomplishment of this process. The main question this book tends to answer is to what extent the transition process equally integrates all segments of society or, on the contrary, less privileged groups are excluded. In order to reach the objective the author undertook a case study analysis for specific countries (Albania, FYROM, Bulgaria, Poland, Lithuania, Russian Federation). The issues examined are the following: the historical background, the political consequences of transition, the economic consequences of transition, the social consequences of transition, the role of NGOs, the external relations and the external environment.

Stephanos Constantinides

Speros Vryonis, Jr., *The Turkish State and History, Clio Meets the Grey Wolf*, The Institute of Balkan Studies-Thessaloniki and Aristide D. Caratzas, Publisher, 1993, New Rochelle, New York.

Professor Speros Vryonis, Jr., an authority on Greek, Byzantine and Ottoman-Turkish history, presents a critical view of the official history of Turkey as it has been produced under the auspices of the Turkish State. First the author reviews the book of Turgut Özal *La Turquie en Europe* (Paris, Plon, 1988) translated in English as *Turkey in Europe* and *Europe in Turkey* (Nicosia, K. Rustem & Brother Publisher, 1991). He continues on the Turkish historical thesis as it was developed under the guidance of Kemal Atatürk himself in the 1930s and lastly he refers to the efforts of the Turkish State and government to enforce their official versions of history in the United States.

Dr. Vryonis's essay is divided into three parts: *Part I*, The Turkish State and Turkish History: The Book of Mr. Turgut Özal, Clio Goes to Turkey, *Part II*, The Turkish Historical Thesis and the Sun Theory of Language, Clio Visits Central Asia with Atatürk, *Part III*, The Turkish Government and History in the United States, Clio Visits the Turkish Ambassador in Washington D. C.

Dr. Vryonis's essay focuses on the continuing efforts of the Turkish State created by Mustafa Kemal in 1923 to produce a particular version of history based on the new doctrines of Turkish nationalism that emerged in the post-

World War I era. The author is critical of the use of history and its interpretation as a tool of Kemalist ideology as seen in state policy during the years that followed the establishment of the Republic in writing an official particular version of history in order to form the idea of the Turkish nation. The result is what Clio, the muse of history, reproaches to Turkish officials the appropriation of the contributions of cultures that have succeeded one another in Anatolia, especially the Ionian Greek civilization, coopting even the famous Greek Poet, Homer. According to the author the political purpose of this enterprise is to suggest that European civilization is originated in Anatolia, thus that Turks are culturally not only connected to Europe but in some cases are the ancestors of this civilization.

James Pettier, *The Turkish Labyrinth Atatürk and the New Islam*. London, Penguin Books, 1998

This book focuses primarily on Turkey's nation-building process by Atatürk. The author refers to Kemalist efforts to create a new state in the ruins of the Ottoman Empire but he continues his investigation into Turkish political, economic and social life from the establishment of the Republic up to today. Important questions like Turkish foreign policy (Central Asia, Balkans, Middle East, Greek-Turkish relations, the Cyprus question, Turkey and European Union), the Armenian genocide, the Kurdish crisis, the Islamic renaissance, the Turkish Diaspora are all treated in this volume. The importance and the antagonism of the two main Turkish cities Ankara, the capital of the Republic, and Istanbul (Constantinople), the old capital of the Byzantine and Ottoman Empires, is also raised in the first part of the book.

The state of Turkish politics under the military's supervision and the presence of Islam in the Centre of Turkish life as well as major political, social and even economic issues are treated in this volume.

Issues related to Turkish identity in the process of nation-building process and later in the present situation of rapid social change, democratization and respect for human rights underscore how difficult it is for Turkey to choose between its authoritarian political system and its European ambitions.

The Turkish Labyrinth is completed by a chronology and a selected bibliography.

Études Helleniques-hellenic Studies. Vol. 4, No. 2, Autumn, 1996. "The Agean Dispute Le Differend Greco-Turc En Mer Egee"

This is a special issue of the bilingual academic journal of the Centre for Hellenic Studies and Research-Canada that presents the Agean Dispute. It brings together a wide range of views from Greek and Turkish academics who approach the problem from the point of view of history, law and strategy, treating such issues as the delimitation of territorial waters, continental shelf, international legal status of Athens FIR, and the stand of the European Union versus the United States on the Imia crisis.

Cristodoulos Yiallourides, Panayiotis Tsakonas. *Greece and Turkey After the End of the Cold War*. New York & Athens, Aristide D. Karatzas Publishers, 2001

This book, the first volume of the series "Ancient Regions, Modern Geopolitics," is a collective work, bringing together a wide range of views on Greek-Turkish relations. Twenty-one specialists provide an extensive survey of these relations for the critical period of the last decade of the twentieth century, after the end of the cold war. The work uses four themes: Political Culture and Foreign Affairs, Strategy and Foreign Policy, Specific Issues (The Aegean and Cyprus), and Systemic Factors, e.g. the United States, Russia, energy politics.

What makes this collective work interesting is the fact that it brings together a wide range of views on the present status of Greek-Turkish relations as well as for the future.

Etienne Copeaux, Espaces Et Temps De La Nation Turque. Analyse D'une Historiographie Nationaliste, 1931-1993, Paris, CNRS Editions, 1997

For French speaking people this is a very interesting book treating the birth of the Turkish national imaginary and its development between 1931-1993. The author considers that there has been a diversion of history by nationalism, an official operation in order to legitimate the Turkish identity and a kind of continuity between contemporary Turkey and the ancient civilizations of Anatolia. This ideology of nationalism is transmitted via the education system particularly the primary and secondary education.

Demetrius Andreas Floudas

Danforth, L. 1995. *The Macedonian Conflict: Ethnic Nationalism in a Transnational World*, Princeton: Princeton University Press, 1995.

Loring M. Danforth's *The Macedonian Conflict* examines the formation of the national identity of the people of Macedonia. His treatment of the diaspora community and its role in the development of a separate Macedonian national identity is one of the major foci of his book. His basic premise is that national identity is constructed, not primordial: One, who speaks Slav, is "a Greek first . . . a Greek from Macedonia" (p. 233). Others claim varying degrees of Greekness or Macedonianness. "From a Macedonian and even a Greek nationalist perspective, such people may seem incongruous, their nationality suspect, but from an anthropological perspective, the claims to Greek national identity of people who were born in Greece but speak Macedonian and not Greek are just as legitimate as the claims to Macedonian national identity of people who earlier in their lives identified themselves as Greeks" (p.225).

Karakasidou. Á. 1997. *Fields of Wheat, Çills of Âlood.* Passages to Íationhood in Greek Macedonia 1870–1990, Chicago: The University of Chicago Press.

This book has to be included in any annotated bibliography of the Macedonian Question, as it became a world-wide *cause celebre*. The author of this book has been vilified by Greek nationalists and praised by western journalists for having championed the cause of "ethnic Macedonians" in Greece. She explores how people in a village formerly known as Guvezna "twenty some kilometres from Thessaloniki," now named Assiros came to see themselves as belonging to this group rather than the other. She soon realises that in Macedonia ethnic identity, is "a fluid, historically rooted construct . . . subject to change," with people shown to choose (sometimes under pressure) who they want to belong to.

Sfetas, S. & Kentrotis, K. 1994. "Skopje: In Search of an Identity and International Recognition. A Critique of the Recent Publication by the Skopje Academy of Sciences and Arts: Macedonia and its relations with Greece (Skopje, 1993)," *Balkan Studies* 35, 337.

This is a meticulously documented and dispassionate point by point refutation of Skopje's Academy of Sciences and Arts 1993 publication *Macedonia and its relations with Greece.* It is very useful for the analyst as a comprehensive presentation of the official Greek point of view on every single point of contention. The authors attempt to prove beyond reasonable doubt that the ancient Macedonians were indeed Greeks; that no "Macedono-Slavonic nation" distinct from the Bulgars and the Serbs has ever existed and that the "Macedonian nation" is a construct of the Comintern in order to boost Tito's bid for supremacy in the Balkans at the expense of Bulgaria and Greece. Very appropriately, they point out that even if a *modus vivendi* is ever reached between Athens and Skopje "it will be very difficult for Balkan historians to reach any sort of agreement about the historical aspects of the Macedonian question."

Valinakis, G. 1992. *Greece's Balkan policy and the "Macedonian Issue,"* Entenhausen: Stiftung Wissenschaft und Politik, 1992.

Valinakis' work is a concise and thorough exposé of the entanglement between FYROM and Greece during the period 1990-92. The author deals with a period during which Greece could still depend on European political cooperation to extract a compromise on the issue of the recognition of the Former Yugoslav Republic of Macedonia. He foresees that subsequent developments could undermine the principle of cooperation and turn members of the EU into critics of the Greek position. It is quite interesting for the analysis of the internal constraints on the foreign policy of Athens.

Zahariadis, N. 1994. "Is the Former Yugoslav Republic of Macedonia a security threat to Greece?", 5 *Mediterranean Quarterly*, 84.

Zahariadis analyses the impact of Yugoslav Macedonian nationalism on Greek foreign policy and emphasises the importance of symbols and ideas as sources of interstate disputes. Although this thesis is rejected by most foreign analysts, he claims that recognition of FYROM under the name Macedonia, would pose a security threat to Greek sovereignty. The author argues that such a recognition poses two threats for Greece (that contradict one another) low-intensity conflict and collapse of the Former Yugoslav Republic of Macedonia, the latter being

the more dangerous of the two (thus echoing the hitherto focal point of Athens' policy on the matter)

Valinakis, G. & Ntalis, S. (*eds.*). 1994. *To Zitima ton Skopion: Episima Keimena 1990-1994* [The issue of Skopje: Official Sources 1990-1994], Athens: Sideris.

An excellent collection of a wealth of official documents on the FYROM-Greece dispute over the years 1990-1994. An invaluable acquisition for anyone who wants to systematically approach the subject. Its major drawback is that it is unfortunately only accessible to Greek-speakers.

PROFILES OF CONTRIBUTORS

ELEFTHERIOS N. BOTSAS Eleftherios N. Botsas is an Emeritus Professor of Economics at Oakland University, where he served as Professor of economics and management. He has been at Oakland University since 1966. His teaching and research specialties are: comparative economic systems, international trade and finance, multinational enterprises, the European economies, and the structure of the Balkan trade. He has published extensively on the Balkan economies, East Europe and the Greek economy including research articles on trade, the economic structure of the EU, and the economics of US-Cypress-Turkey and Greece.

BOB DONNORUMMO Ph.D. Bob Donnorummo is the Associate Director of the University of Pittsburgh's Center for Russian and Eastern European Studies. His publications include "The Peasants of Central Russia: Reactions to Emancipation and Market" (1987), co-editor and contributor to "The Emerging Markets and Higher Education" (2001) and articles on the political economy of the transformation in Eastern Europe.

STEPHANOS CONSTANTINIDES was born in Cyprus. He received his B.A. degree from Athens' university and his M.A. and Ph.D. degrees from Paris University-Sorbonne. He teaches political science at the Université du Québec à Montréal. He is the author of several books and articles on ethnic relations. He also completed research on Cyprus, Greece and the Balkans in various fields and has published widely in academic journals and collective works. He is now engaged in research on the Balkans, Turkey and Greek-Turkish relations. Dr. Constantinides is the editor of the academic journal Études Helleniques-Hellenic Studies and also director of the Centre for Hellenic Studies and Research-Canada.

DEMETRIUS ANDREAS FLOUDAS is a Senior Associate at Hughes Hall College, University of Cambridge and Associate Fellow of the Hellenic Institute of International and Foreign Law, Athens. He was an ARISTOTELES Visiting Fellow at the Université de Paris I (*Panthéon-Sorbonne*) in 1998 and has presented papers internationally on issues of the Yugoslavian crisis and Greek foreign policy. He is an Academic Member of the British Academy of Experts and also practices as a qualified Attorney-at-Law.

DIMITRIOS KOUKOURDINOS is a Ph.D. candidate at the Government Department, the London School of Economics and Political Science, and a

holder of a scholarship from the Greek State Scholarships' Foundation. His research focuses on the creation of military structures, as an integral part of state-building and democratization in former Yugoslav Republics. He has contributed articles to the monthly Greek magazine, *Epikentra*. He is currently a research fellow of the "Institute for Democracy-Constantine Karamanlis."

ANDREW G. KOURVETARIS is a Ph.D. candidate in Sociology at Columbia University. He is currently working on his dissertation "Local Races and Ethnic Political Emergence in New York." He received his M.A. in social sciences from the University of Chicago and his M.Phil. in sociology from Columbia University. His publications include "Natural Disasters and Community Health: A Case Study of the Mississippi River Flood of 1993 in the Quad-Cities" (1996), "Attitudes Toward European Integration Ethnic and Cultural Dimensions" (co-authored) (1996), and "Ethnicity and Identity: Language and Culture Among Greek-American Youths" (1998). His academic and research interests are research methods, intergroup relations, internationalal migration, and comparative politics.

GEORGE A. KOURVETARIS was educated both in Greece and the United States, where he received his Ph.D. from Northwestern University in 1969. He is currently a Professor of Sociology at Northern Illinois University. His major academic and research interests include political sociology, social theory, intergroup relations, and civil-military relations. He has authored, co-authored, or co-edited 14 books. His most recent books include *Social Thought* (1994, 1997, 1999), *Political Sociology*, (1997), *Studies on Greek Americans* (1997), and *Studies on Modern Greek Society and Politics* (1999). His forthcoming book will be *Studies in Social Organization: Ethnicity, Politics, Class, and Power*. He has also authored and co-authored 68 articles on a range of topics including political clientelism, electoral politics, class identification, political power, political participation, civil-military relations, intergroup relations, ethnonationalism, ethnicity, and multiculturalism. He is also the editor of the *Journal of Political and Military Sociology* which he founded in 1973.

KLEOMENIS KOUTSOUKIS, Former Lawyer, Professor of Comparative Politics, Panteion University of Social and Political Sciences and Director of the Hellenic Center of Political Research, Athens, Greece. His research interests include: Political development and conflict theory in the case of Greece, comparative political leadership and political corruption with emphasis on the Balkans, European and less developing countries. Among his recent publications

are *Facets of Civil War in Greece 1946-1949* (2001), *Pathology of Politics: Facets of Political Corruption in the Modern Hellenic State* (1997), *Sleaze in Contemporary Greek Politics* (1995), *Political Conflict in S. Europe*, in collaboration with E. Ziengenhagen (New York: Praeger, 1992).

ALEXANDROS K. KYROU is an Assistant Professor of History and Director of the Program in East European and Russian Studies at Salem State College in Salem, Massachusetts. He received his Ph.D. in East European History from Indiana University in 1993. Professor Kyrou is a former Post-Doctoral Research Fellow in the Program in Hellenic Studies at Princeton University. Prior to his appointment at Salem State College, he was Visiting Lecturer and Visiting Assistant Professor in the Departments of History and Political Science, respectively, at Indiana University-Purdue University at Fort Wayne, where he taught Byzantine, Ottoman, Balkan, and East European history, as well as Yugoslav and East European politics. His research has focused on humanitarian relief in Axis-occupied Greece, as well as Balkan, in particular Greek and Bulgarian, diaspora politics. His publications include several articles on Greek American history, Albania, and American foreign policy in Southeastern Europe.

KOSTAS A. LAVDAS lectures in Political Science at the University of Crete, Greece. He holds degrees in Political Science, Political Sociology, and Public Policy from the London School of Economics, the University of Manchester and the Massachusetts Institute of Technology and has published extensively in scholarly journals, including the *European Journal of Political Research* and the *Journal of Political and Military Sociology*. He is the author of *The Europeanization of Greece: Interest Politics and the Crises of Integration* (London/New York: Macmillan: St. Martin's Press, 1997) and co-author of *Politics, Subsidies and Competition: the New Politics of State Intervention in the European Union* (Cheltenham: Edward Elgar, 1999).

TINA MAVRIKOS-ADAMOU holds a B.A. in Politics from New York University, an M.A. in Political Science from the New School for Social Research, and a Ph.D. in Political Sociology from the University of Edinburgh, Scotland. She currently is an Assistant Professor of Political Science at the American College of Thessaloniki, Greece. Her research interests include the question of legitimacy in the Post-Cold war era, civil society, and Southeastern European politics.

S. VICTOR PAPACOSMA is Professor of History and Director of the Lemnitzer Center for NATO and European Union Studies at Kent State University. His Ph.D. is from Indiana University, and he has published extensively on Balkan issues, particularly on twentieth-century Greek politics and security topics. He has co-edited five volumes of Lemnitzer Center conference proceedings, including *NATO in the Post-Cold War Era: Does It Have a Future?* (1995), *NATO and the European Union: Confronting the Challenges of European Security and Enlargement* (1999), and *NATO after Fifty Years* (2001).

HARRY PAPASOTIRIOU is an Assistant Professor of Strategic Studies at Panteion University, Athens, Greece. He graduated from Oxford with a First Class BA in Philosophy, Politics and Economics. During his graduate studies for a Ph.D. at Stanford's Political Science Department he was awarded a two-year New Directions Mellon Fellowship. He has published books in Greek on the Balkans since the end of the Cold War, the War of Greek Independence, Byzantine grand strategy, and the role of the diaspora in Greek grand strategy.

VICTOR ROUDOMETOF is an Assistant Professor with the Department of Sociology, Gerontology and Anthropology at Miami University, Oxford Ohio. His research interests include the study of nationalism, globalization, and transnationalism. He is the author of *Nationalism, Globalization, and Orthodoxy: The Social Origins of Ethnic Conflict in the Balkans* (Westport: CT: Greenwood, 2001) and editor of *The Macedonian Question: Culture, Historiography, Politics* (Boulder, Colo.: East European Monographs, 2000); and co-editor and co-author of *American Culture in Europe* (Westport, CT: Praeger, 1998) and *Communities Across Borders: New Immigrants and Transnational Cultures* (London: Routledge, forthcoming). His latest book is *Collective Memory, National Identity, and Ethnic Conflict: Greece, Bulgaria & the Macedonia Question* (Westport, CT: Praeger, forthcoming).

PANTELIS SKLIAS, Ph.D., Associate Professor, Democritus University of Thrace, Department of International Economic Relations and Development, Komotini, Thrace, Greece, Post Doctoral Scholar at the Hellenic Center of Political Research, Panteion University of Social and Political Science, Athens, Greece (with the support of the State Foundation for Scholarships—I.KY.). His research interests include the broader field of International Political Economy with emphasis on the social, economic and political development in the Balkans, and the Third World countries. Among his recent publications are: *The Political*

Economy of Balkans, the Ex-Soviet Union and the Countries of Central and Eastern Europe (2001), *the Political Economy and the Consequences of the War in Kosovo in the Former Yugoslav Republic of Macedonia* (2001), the *New International Economic Relations and Trade Regime* (2000).

RAJU GEORGE C. THOMAS is the Allis Chalmers Professor of International Affairs at Marquette University in Milwaukee, Wisconsin. He was a Visiting Fellow at Harvard (1980-81 and 1988-89), U.C.L.A. (1982-83), M.I.T. (1988-89), the International Institute for Strategic Studies-London (1991-92), and the University of Wisconsin-Madison (1994). Between 1992 and 1997, he was the Co-Director of the University of Wisconsin-Milwaukee and Marquette University Joint Center for International Studies. Professor Thomas' dozen books and edited/co-edited books include *The Defence of India: A Budgetary Perspective* (Macmillan-India, 1978); *Indian Security Policy* (Princeton University Press, 1986); *South Asian Security in the 1990s* (IISS-London/Oxford University Press, 1993); *Democracy, Security and Development in India* (St. Martins Press/Macmillan, 1996); *The Great Power Triangle and Asian Security* (Lexington Books, 1982); *Energy and Security in the Non-Proliferation Regime* (Macmillan & St. Martin's Press, 1998); and *India's Nuclear Security* (Lynne Rienner/Sage, 2000). He is co-editor of the forthcoming *Nuclear India in the 21st Century* (Palgrave forthcoming 2002); and *Yugoslavia Unraveled: Sovereignty, Self-Determination, Intervention* (Frank Cass, forthcoming 2002). Between 1997 and 2001, he wrote most of the sections on India for Jane's Sentinel/Jane's Information (UK). Thomas has published over 35 book chapters and 30 articles in academic journals. Professor Thomas was educated at Bombay University, the London School of Economics, the University of Southern California, and U.C.L.A. from where he received his Ph.D. in Political Science.

E. A. TIRYAKIAN, (Harvard) Professor of Sociology at Duke University. He does research on comparative aspects of modernity, cultural change, national development, and ethnic nationalism. Recent publications include "The Wild Cards of Modernity," *Daedalus*. 126 (1997):147-81; "Secession, Modernity and Autonomy," *Society*. 35 (July/August 1998): 49-58; "War: the Covered Side of Modernity," *International Sociology*. 14 , no. 4 (1999): 473-89; and guest editor, "Rethinking Civilizational Analysis," special issue. *International Sociology*. 16, no. 4 (2001).

ANNA TRIANDAFYLLIDOU received her Ph.D. in Social Sciences from the European University Institute in Florence, Italy. She held teaching and research positions in Belgium, Britain, Italy, and the U.S. She currently works at the EUI in Florence, where she co-ordinates two research projects funded by the European Commission. She is the author of *The Social Psychology of Party Behavior* (1997 and 1998, Greek edition), *Immigrants and National Identity in Europe* (2001, in press), *National Identity Reconsidered: Images of Self and Others in a "United" Europe* (2001, forthcoming) and numerous articles on nationalism, immigration and communication.